systems and theories in psychology

McGRAW-HILL SERIES IN PSYCHOLOGY

HARRY F. HARLOW, *Consulting Editor*

BEACH, HEBB, MORGAN, AND NISSEN · The Neuropsychology of Lashley

VON BÉKÉSY · Experiments in Hearing

BERKOWITZ · Aggression: A Social Psychological Analysis

BERLYNE · Conflict, Arousal, and Curiosity

BLUM · Psychoanalytic Theories of Personality

BROWN · The Motivation of Behavior

BROWN · The Psychodynamics of Abnormal Behavior

BROWN AND GHISELLI · Scientific Method in Psychology

BUCKNER AND McGRATH · Vigilance: A Symposium

COFER · Verbal Learning and Verbal Behavior

COFER AND MUSGRAVE · Verbal Behavior and Learning: Problems and Processes

CRAFTS, SCHNEIRLA, ROBINSON, AND GILBERT · Recent Experiments in Psychology

DAVITZ · The Communication of Emotional Meaning

DEESE · The Psychology of Learning

DOLLARD AND MILLER · Personality and Psychotherapy

DORCUS AND JONES · Handbook of Employee Selection

ELLIS · Handbook of Mental Deficiency

FERGUSON · Personality Measurement

FERGUSON · Statistical Analysis in Psychology and Education

GHISELLI · Theory of Psychological Measurement

GHISELLI AND BROWN · Personnel and Industrial Psychology

GILMER · Industrial Psychology

GRAY · Psychology Applied to Human Affairs

GUILFORD · Fundamental Statistics in Psychology and Education

GUILFORD · Personality

GUILFORD · Psychometric Methods

GUION · Personnel Testing

HAIRE · Psychology in Management

HIRSH · The Measurement of Hearing

HURLOCK · Adolescent Development

John F. Dashiell was Consulting Editor of this series from its inception in 1931 until January 1, 1950. Clifford T. Morgan was Consulting Editor of this series from January 1, 1950 until January 1, 1959.

Systems and
Theories in Psychology

by MELVIN H. MARX
Professor of Psychology · University of Missouri

and WILLIAM A. HILLIX
Senior Scientist, Navy Electronics Laboratory · Assistant
Professor of Psychology · San Diego State College

McGRAW-HILL BOOK COMPANY
New York · San Francisco · Toronto · London

Systems and Theories in Psychology

Library of Congress Catalog Card Number 62-21803.

12 13 14 15 16 - MAMM - 7 5 4 3 2 1 0

40670

preface

Our primary purpose in writing this book has been to provide a single source containing the basic information about systematic and theoretical psychology which we think any student of psychology should have. The book is directed mainly at the senior undergraduate major and the beginning graduate student. We hope that it will serve a coordinating function in that it will help the advanced student to integrate some of the diverse materials and approaches to which he has been exposed in his various courses.

In accordance with this general objective, our treatment is extensive rather than intensive. The book gives surveys rather than exhaustive accounts of any one topic. No text of this scope can practicably do more, since each of the three sections in the present book deals with topics which could be the subject of several volumes. The student who goes on in scientific psychology can further his knowledge of systematic and theoretical problems through more specialized courses in history, experimental and theoretical methodology, and theory within particular subject-matter areas. If he does not go on, or does not touch further on the scientific concerns of psychology, the book should give him a broad overview and general understanding of fundamental systematic and theoretical problems.

Part I of the book is designed to give the student a basis for a critical analysis of the systems and theories that follow. Our experience in teaching this kind of material indicates that this is a necessary task, even at the senior and beginning graduate levels. It is true that much of the material is contained in some introductory courses, in courses in philosophy of science, or in some other course that the student may have had. It is also true that students often state frequently and strongly that they already know this material. The fact is, however, that we have found the typical senior student who takes the first course in systematic psychology badly in need of further exposure to these concepts. Part I, therefore, endeavors to fill in gaps in students' experience and lay the groundwork for their understanding of the relationship of basic scientific and systematic matters to psychology.

In presenting this elementary philosophy of science, we do not intend to give the impression that formal study of how science is made is necessary for the making of science. In fact, we talk more about the criticism of "finished" science as it may exist at a given time than about the construction of science. But we do feel that a little philosophy of science helps the student to avoid some of the more obvious errors that might be made by the scientifically unsophisticated and, further, that it is essential to the critical evaluation of systems and theories.

Part II of the book deals in abbreviated form with standard material usually covered in a textbook for systematic psychology. Although historical material is presented, we have tried to emphasize the portions of each system that have some present significance. Our choice of six systems was based on our estimate of the relative importance of the several systems usually treated. Structuralism, functionalism, and associationism were chosen because of their importance in the historical development of modern psychology. Behaviorism, gestalt psychology, and psychoanalysis were chosen because of their historical importance and their continuing importance in contemporary developments in psychology.

Part III of the book deals with these contemporary developments, particularly as they relate to the historical systems of psychology. Our purpose has been to provide a broad view of the contemporary theoretical scene, such as would not easily be obtained from more specialized treatments. To this end, also, we have included an appendix consisting of summaries by experts of the vigorous trends in non-American systematic developments.

One underlying theme of this book is that interest in psychology has shifted from the orthodox general system of twenty or thirty years ago to the more limited theories described in Part III. The reader may view Part I of the book as a presentation of the reasons why it was necessary that the shift occur. A portrayal of the shift and the explanation for it has been a part of our motivation for writing the book. Another reason has been that we felt the need, in the process of teaching a course in systematic psychology, for a single text that would be adequate to the task of presenting a background and a foreground to the development of systems as well as the systems themselves.

Authors in writing a book present their own biases toward the subject matter. Our biases are experimental, and we accordingly have written an experimentally oriented book. We have been only incidentally concerned with psychology as a therapy, an art, or an applied science. Our biases within experimental psychology are those of methodological behaviorism, S-R variety (broadly conceived). We have tried to compensate for these biases sufficiently to enable us to present other points of view in a relatively fair manner.

This book has been a thoroughly collaborative venture, with each of the authors participating in considerable additions to and revisions of the writing of the other. Nevertheless, in so far as responsibility for each of the chapters can be assigned, the senior author is the primary author for Chapters 5, 6, 7, 10, 11, and the Epilogue, and is also responsible for the over-all planning and execution of the book; the junior author is the primary author for Chapters 1, 2, 3, 4, 8, 9, 12, and 13.

The brief reading suggestions at the end of each chapter are designed to provide an easy referral to selected sources for further examination of the systematic and theoretical issues examined in this book. No attempt has been made to be in any sense comprehensive or exhaustive. Rather, a limited sampling of relevant materials is given, with emphasis more on books, both older (classic) and recent, than on journal papers, although the latter are cited where they are especially valuable. Although certain of the sources are also cited, and in some cases discussed, in the text, they are supplemented by a number of additional annotated references.

We wish to express our appreciation to the many publishers who have given permission to reproduce excerpts from their work, as indicated specifically in the credits in the acknowledgment section. We should also like to express our general appreciation to our colleagues at the University of Missouri and elsewhere for their direct and indirect contributions to the book. More specific thanks are due Mrs. Helen Oldham and Mrs. Charity Flack for their skill and patience in handling the multitude of secretarial details that attended our revisions. Specific thanks are also due Jo and Tom Tombaugh for their assistance, especially in the preparation of the Glossary. Finally, we are deeply indebted to our many students whose detailed criticisms of the various drafts of the book were extremely valuable.

Melvin H. Marx
William A. Hillix

acknowledgments

The authors wish to thank the following copyright owners, authors, and publishers for permission to reprint excerpts from copyrighted material:

The American Association for the Advancement of Science

Tolman, E. C. A stimulus-expectancy need-cathexis psychology. *Science*, 1945, **101**, 160–166. (Pp. 288–289.)

The American Journal of Psychology

Murray, Elsie. Peripheral and central factors in memory. Images of visual form and color. *Amer. J. Psychol.*, 1906, **7**, 227–247. (Pp. 72–73.)

Titchener, E. B. The schema of introspection. *Amer. J. Psychol.*, 1912, **23**, 427–448, 485–508. (P. 70.)

The American Psychological Association

Bergmann, G. The contribution of John B. Watson. *Psychol. Rev.*, 1956, **63**, 265–276. (Pp. 166–167.)

Boring, E. G. A psychological function is the relation of successive differentiations of events in the organism. *Psychol. Rev.*, 1937, **44**, 445–461. (Pp. 81–82.)

Brunswik, E. Representative design and probabilistic theory in a functional psychology. *Psychol. Rev.*, 1955, **62**, 193–217. (Pp. 295, 296.)

Citation to B. F. Skinner. From *Amer. Psychologist.*, 1958, **13**, 735. (Pp. 261–262.)

Guthrie, E. R. Psychological facts and psychological theory. *Psychol Bull.*, 1946, **43**, 1–20. (P. 12.)

McGeoch, J. A. The formal criteria of a systematic psychology. *Psychol. Rev.*, 1933, **40**, 1–12. P. 47.)

Mowrer, O. H. Review of dynamics of behavior by R. S. Woodworth. *Contemp. Psychol.*, 1959, **4**, 129–133. (P. 100.)

Tolman, E. C. A behaviorist's definition of consciousness. *Psychol. Rev.*, 1927, **34**, 433–439. (P. 165.)
Tolman, E. C. The determiners of behavior at a choice point. *Psychol. Rev.*, 1938, **45**, 1–41. (P. 125.)
Watson, J. B. Psychology as the behaviorist views it. *Psychol. Rev.*, 1913, **20**, 158–177. (P. 142.)

American Scientist

Skinner, B. F. The experimental analysis of behavior. *Amer. Scientist*, 1957, **45**, 343–371. (Pp. 54–56.)

Appleton-Century-Crofts, Inc.

Boring, E. G. *A History of experimental psychology.* (2d ed.) New York: Appleton-Century-Crofts, 1950. (Pp. 156–157.)
Boring, E. G. *The physical dimensions of consciousness.* New York: Century, 1933. (P. 81.)
Estes, W. K., Koch, S., MacCorquodale, K., Meehl, P. E., Mueller, C. G., Jr., Schoenfeld, W. N., & Verplanck, W. S. *Modern learning theory.* New York: Appleton-Century-Crofts, 1954. (Pp. 53–54.)
Heidbreder, Edna E. *Seven psychologies.* New York: Century, 1933. (Pp. 47, 157–158, 161–162.)
Thorndike, E. L. *Selected writings from a connectionist's psychology.* New York: Appleton-Century-Crofts, 1949. (Pp. 118–119, 124.)
Tolman, E. C. *Purposive behavior in animals and men.* New York: Century, 1932. (P. 159.)

Basic Books, Inc., Publishers

Jones, E. *The life and work of Sigmund Freud.* Vol. 2. New York: Basic Books, Inc., Publishers, 1957. (Pp. 210, 211, 221.)

Bollingen Foundation, Inc.

Jung, C. G. *Symbols of transformation.* New York: Bollingen Series XX, Pantheon, 1956. (P. 221.)

Bureau of Publications,
Teachers College, Columbia University

Thorndike, E. L. *The psychology of learning* (*Educational psychology* II). New York: Teachers College, 1913. (P. 120.)

Clark University Press

Hunter, W. S. Psychology and anthroponomy. In C. Murchison (Ed.), *Psychologies of 1925.* Worcester, Mass.: Clark Univer. Press, 1927. (P. 143.)

Watson, J. B. *History of psychology in autobiography*, Vol. 3. Worcester, Mass.: Clark Univer. Press, 1936. (P. 137.)

Watson, J. B. Recent experiments on how we lose and change our emotional equipment. In C. Murchison (Ed.), *Psychologies of 1925*. Worcester, Mass: Clark Univer. Press, 1926. (Pp. 150, 151.)

Watson, J. B. What the nursery has to say about instincts. In C. Murchison (Ed.), *Psychologies of 1925*. Worcester, Mass.: Clark Univer. Press, 1926. (Pp. 146–147, 149.)

Harcourt, Brace & World, Inc.

Ellis, W. D. *A source book of gestalt psychology*. New York: Harcourt, Brace, 1938. (Pp. 178, 179–180, 184, 188.)

Harper & Row, Publishers, Incorporated

Murphy, G. *Personality: A biosocial approach to origins and structure*. New York: Harper & Row, 1947. (P. 342.)

Holt, Rinehart and Winston, Inc.

Attneave, F. *Applications of information theory to psychology: A summary of basic concepts, methods, and results*. New York: Holt, 1959. (P. 357.)

James, W. *The principles of psychology*. New York: Henry Holt and Company, Inc. 1890. (Pp. 88, 176.)

The Journal Press

Lashley, K. S. Cerebral control versus reflexology: A reply to Professor Hunter. *J. gen. Psychol.*, 1931, 5, 3–20. (P. 160.)

J. B. Lippincott Company

Watson, J. B. *Psychology from the standpoint of a behaviorist*. (3d ed.) Philadelphia: Lippincott, 1929. (P. 138.)

Longmans, Green & Co., Inc.

Carr, H. A. *Psychology, a study of mental activity*. New York: Longmans, 1925. (Pp. 96–97.)

The Macmillan Company

Bridgman, P. W. *The logic of modern physics*. New York: Macmillan, 1927. (P. 13.)

Titchener, E. B. *An outline of psychology*. New York: Macmillan, 1899. (Pp. 67, 77.)

Titchener, E. B. *Text-book of psychology.* New York: Macmillan, 1910. (Pp. 76, 77.)
Wundt, W. *Principles of physiological psychology.* New York: Macmillan, 1904. (P. 62.)

McGraw-Hill Book Company, Inc.

Estes, W. K. The statistical approach to learning theory. In S. Koch (Ed.) *Psychology: A study of a science.* Vol. 2. New York: McGraw-Hill, 1959. Pp. 380–486. (P. 369.)
Tolman, E. C. Principles of purposive behavior. In S. Koch (Ed.) *Psychology: A study of a science.* Vol. 2. New York: McGraw-Hill, 1959. Pp. 92–157. (Pp. 283–284.)

National Society for the Study of Education.

Gates, A. I. Connectionism: Present concepts and interpretations. In *The psychology of learning. Yearb. Nat. Soc. Stud. Educ.,* 1942, 41, Part II. (P. 196.)

W. W. Norton & Company, Inc.

Watson, J. B. *Behaviorism.* New York: Norton, 1925. (Pp. 139, 141, 151.)
Watson, J. B., & McDougall, W. *The battle of behaviorism.* New York: Norton, 1929. (P. 156.)

Philosophical Library, Inc.

Bridgman, P. W. *The nature of some of our physical concepts.* New York: Philosophical Library, 1952. (P. 17.)

The Philosophical Review

Titchener, E. B. The postulates of a structural psychology. *Phil. Rev.,* 1898, 7, 449–465. (Pp. 66–67.)

The Ronald Press Company

Woodworth, R. S. *Contemporary schools of psychology.* (Rev. ed.) New York: Ronald, 1948. (P. 156.)

Scientific Monthly

Boring, E. G. When is human behavior predetermined? *Sci. Monthly,* 1957, 84, 189–196. (P. 52.)

Simon and Schuster, Inc.

Russell, B. *The history of western philosophy.* New York: Simon and Schuster, 1945. (P. 110.)

Springer-Verlag OHG

Harrower, M. R. Organization in higher mental processes. *Psych. Forsch.*, 1932, 17, 56–120. (P. 195.)

State University of Iowa

Lewin, K. Formalization and progress in psychology. *Univer. Iowa Stud. Child Welf.*, 1940, 16, 9–42. (P. 277.)

John Wiley & Sons, Inc.

Hall, C. S., & Lindzey, G. *Theories of personality.* New York: Wiley, 1957. (P. 219.)

Yale University Press

Hull, C. L. *A behavior system.* New Haven: Yale, 1952. (P. 245.)
Hull, C. L. *Essentials of behavior.* New Haven, Conn.: Yale, 1951. (P. 251.)

The authors also wish to thank the following authors and publishers for permission to reproduce figures and quotations from their publications:

The American Journal of Psychology

Orbison, W. D. Shape as a function of the vector-field. *Amer. J. Psychol.*, 1939, 52, 31–45. (P. 179.)

The American Psychological Association

Brunswik, E. Representative design and probabilistic theory in a functional psychology. *Psychol. Rev.*, 1955, 62, 193–217. (P. 296.)

Institute of Electrical and Electronic Engineering

Peterson, W. W., Birdsall, T. G., & Fox, W. C. The theory of signal detectability. Transactions of Professional Group on Information Theory, *Institute of Radio Engineers*, PGIT-4, 171–212, 1954, (P. 363.)

McGraw-Hill Book Company, Inc.

Lewin, K. *Principles of topological psychology.* New York: McGraw-Hill, 1936. (P. 274.)

The New York Academy of Sciences

Tanner, W. P., Jr. Physiological implications of psychophysical data. *Ann. N. Y. Acad. Sci.*, 1961, 89, 752–765. (P. 360.)

Springer-Verlag

Kohler, W. Gestaltprobleme und Anfange einer Gestalttheorie. *Jahresbericht u. d. ges. Physiol.*, 1922, 3, 512–539. (P. 184.)

W. P. Van Stockum

Brunswik, E. The conceptual focus of some psychological systems. *J. unif. Sci.*, 1939, 8, 36–49. (P. 293.)

University of California Press

Tolman, E. C., and Honsik, C. H. *Insight in rats*. Berkeley: Univer. of Calif. Press, 1932. (P. 286.)

University of Chicago Press

Brunswik, E. The conceptual framework of psychology. *Int. Encyclo. unif. Sci.*, 1952, 1, 1–102. (P. 293.)

contents

contents

part one PSYCHOLOGY AS SCIENCE

The status of psychology and of systems of psychology cannot be evaluated without a clear understanding of what science itself involves. Accordingly, our first chapter examines the nature of science. The second chapter examines the position of psychology within the domain of science, partially from the point of view of the present subject matter dealt with by psychologists. The third chapter is concerned with the nature of psychological systems and theories and the criteria to be used in evaluating them. Although it is impossible to arrive at final conclusions concerning the nature of science, the status of psychology, or the desiderata for psychological systems and theories, the reader should be able to approach the study of systems and theories with more sophistication after this review of the problems involved.

the nature of science 1

Science is a many-sided social enterprise that has been defined in several ways. Some prefer to emphasize a way of thinking—the *scientific attitude*—as the major characteristic. For others, science is primarily a way of doing; the *scientific method* is seen as the most important feature. Still others prefer to emphasize the product of this method— the systematically ordered *body of knowledge* that scientists have produced. None of these emphases can be accepted to the exclusion of the others. The safest procedure is to accept them all and consider science as the total enterprise: men thinking with a certain attitude, using scientific methods to produce facts and theories that are ordered descriptions and explanations of the world.

SOME CRITERIA FOR DISTINGUISHING SCIENCE FROM NONSCIENCE

There are a variety of legitimate ways of attempting to know and understand the world. The scientific way is thus but one among many. What is it that distinguishes science from other, nonscientific, types of enterprises? Science has many characteristics, and each of these has been selected at one time as *unique* to science. One of these, the use of control in observation, is most nearly unique; however, the other features are usually descriptive of science and merit some consideration before we turn to a discussion of the principle of control. It is the combination of its characteristics that defines science, rather than any characteristic taken alone.

Purpose. The general purpose of science is to provide an objective, factual, empirical account of the world. It is thus contrasted with the artistic, literary, philosophical, and religious ways of thinking. However, many laymen who are not classified as scientists have a similar

3

purpose in their enterprises: the police detective, for example, may wish to render an equally objective, factual account. Pratt (1939) has pointed out the difficulty of making an objective-subjective distinction that would allow us to set off science from nonscience on this ground. The generality of the scientist's knowledge may be stressed in order to contrast it with these more limited and specific endeavors, but then it cannot on this ground alone be separated from an artistic or religious account.

Subject matter. It is commonly said that science deals with a different subject matter than nonscience. This is only partially true. Scientists tend to work with subject matter which is somewhere in the borderland between knowledge and ignorance. Therefore, at some stage in the development of knowledge in a given area, it may be that only scientists are working with that subject matter. For example, there was a time when only psychologists or physiologists were interested in the changes in breathing rate or blood pressure that accompany emotion. Today the same subject matter interests the police officer. Conversely, the so-called "psi phenomena" (extrasensory perception) at one time interested chiefly nonscientists; today, whatever we think about the existence of these phenomena, we must recognize that they have been made the object of considerable scientific investigation. Certainly we cannot say that the scientist always deals with a different subject matter than the nonscientist.

Conclusions. The conclusions of science have been said to be more final, more correct, or more accurate than the conclusions reached by other disciplines. Poets, among others, may sometimes be indignant about this (Newman, 1957), but the claim is seldom made by working scientists themselves. They recognize the tentative nature of their own statements and look upon scientific methods as simply the methods that they themselves prefer to use in the quest for knowledge. A study of early theories about heat, light, nerve impulses, or matter itself is calculated to make scientists humble rather than dogmatic. Heat is no longer thought of as a subtle fluid, nor is the nerve impulse thought to travel at the speed of light, although both these beliefs were once reputable scientific theories and held by some as "facts." The scientist can only look forward to a continual process of revision of present facts. Since the scientist's conclusions are not correct or accurate in any ultimate sense, one cannot claim that scientific conclusions are necessarily superior to conclusions reached by other means. However, any truly scientific conclusion is based on a careful evaluation of the available evidence. Any well-established scientific theory, even though subject to revision, will lead to correct predictions to some approximation.

Prediction and control. Science is sometimes said to be distinguished by its concern with prediction and control of events. However, many groups share an interest in prediction and control. The baseball pitcher is concerned with the control of the behavior of a spheroid of a certain standard size and density, and the batter is most interested in predicting the behavior of that same ball. These interests are shared with the physicist. The mother, as well as the psychologist, attempts to predict and control the behavior of young human beings. Thus this kind of control does not distinguish science from nonscience.

In the present context we mean by control, "influence"; we should be quite sure to distinguish this meaning from the more common scientific or technical meaning of control as a method of eliminating extraneous variation in observations.

Theory versus applications. Science is not distinguished from nonscience by a concern with theory and an ignoring of applications. A scientist may work with either or both. His goal may be a highly practical result or mere satisfaction of his curiosity. During World War II, a group of physicists was assigned to the Manhattan Project with the task of developing the atomic bomb; they did develop it, and it was a very important applied result. Yet their work was based on the previous work of many men whose curiosity about the universe led them to formulate theories for their own satisfaction; some of them might never have published their results if application to bombs had seemed imminent. Thus, scientists may work toward either theory or practice and may work because of many different kinds of personal motivations.

Terminology. The terminology of the scientist is not necessarily unique or more precise in meaning than the language of others. Scientific language may include new words or redefine old words to the point where it seems to be mere jargon to the layman, but science may at times use almost exclusively the language of any layman. The language of mathematics is exemplary for its precision and sometimes its uniqueness; yet mathematics is not an empirical science. Engineers also may use a language as unique and precise as that of their scientific counterparts, physicists and chemists. We cannot, therefore, distinguish science from nonscience on the basis of the words that are used, although we shall see that science does use special methods for clarifying the meanings of words.

Exactitude. Exactitude and precision, especially in measurement, are often said to distinguish the scientist. Again, exactitude and precision are not the property solely of scientists. Equally precise and quantified measurements may be used by the engineer or the inventor.

Although none of these characteristics necessarily distinguishes science from nonscience, the notions did not occur by chance; these features describe science, but do not distinguish it. Science strives for rigor in terminology, for the ability to predict and control, for more quantification, for better theory, and for an objective account of the world.

However, the most adequate *essential* distinction between science and nonscience must rest upon one major characteristic of scientific methodology. It is this feature—the *principle of control*—that is most nearly unique to science among all human enterprises.

THE PRINCIPLE OF CONTROL

Control is a method used by the scientist in an attempt to identify the "reasons" for or "causes" of what he observes or, to put it another way, to identify the sources of variation in his observations. In an experiment, which is an ideally controlled situation, there are one or more conditions whose influence the investigator wishes to determine. These conditions, or factors, are generally called *independent variables*. The conditions which are directly measured or otherwise observed are called *dependent variables* (in psychology, these are typically responses of one kind or another). Now, in order to obtain unambiguous results—that is, changes in the dependent variables that can be attributed with reasonable confidence to the independent variables—the scientist needs to eliminate—control—all other potentially effective conditions. These are called *controlled variables*.

Consider a simple nonscientific example. Say that an employer is periodically losing sums of money from the cash register, and there are five people who have regular access to it; he is quite certain that nothing else could be happening to the money. He then carefully arranges matters so that four of them cannot get to the cash register at a given time, without letting the fifth one know he has done so. He rotates the four eliminated employees until the money disappears. He then knows which employee is the culprit, for he has controlled for the possibility that one of the other four might be guilty.

In science, the potential culprits are variables rather than people. If nothing were known about the determinants of rate of running by rats in runways, the scientist would first have to find out which variables were related to running speed; he might suspect age, sex, weight, hours since eating, number of trials, kind and quantity of reward, distribution of practice, and so on. In order to find out which ones actually were functionally related to running speed, he would have to hold the others constant so that he could assess the effects of each variable, one at a time.

This exercise of control over observations is an essential process in science; the use of experimentation rather than naturalistic observation is preferred because it makes better control possible. If control is not used, the sources of variation cannot be discovered with certainty because the uncontrolled variables will always remain potential alternative explanations.

Much of the elaborate paraphernalia of the scientist is directed at this one objective of control of observations. This is true of statistical analysis as well as apparatus. The role of each is often to eliminate extraneous variations, to increase the confidence of the scientist that his results are attributable to the particular variable or set of variables he is studying.

The fact that elaborate equipment or experimental procedures are sometimes used leads some people to think of controls *only* in terms of such complexities. This is a faulty conception of the principle of control. The following discussion is intended to demonstrate that there is a fundamental continuity in the principle of control through a variety of observational techniques.

Let us start by distinguishing between *method* and *technique,* as these are used with reference to scientific methodology. By method we mean the fundamental process by which all science proceeds; the key aspect of scientific method is control. By technique we mean the particular manner in which the general method is implemented; there are many techniques, often differing from one subject-matter field to another. When it is sometimes asserted, then, that psychology requires different methods in its scientific progress, we should revise the wording to say that psychology requires different techniques in its application of the basic scientific method. The failure to make this distinction between method and technique accounts for much of the experimental-clinical schism that is sometimes observed within psychology. Clinical and counseling psychologists are prone to regard experimental psychologists as of a different breed on the grounds that they use a different kind of method; the clinician may justify his own techniques by insisting that science permits of many methods and psychology does not need to ape the older sciences, especially physics, in its methodology. Experimental psychologists, on the other hand, very often prefer to dissociate themselves from the clinicians and the counselors on the assumption that the latter do not use scientific methodology. The heart of this prejudice is the belief that controlled observations are not adequately utilized. It is easy to see, in view of the distinction made between method and technique, how these misunderstandings arise.

A brief review of some of the major steps in the scientific process will set the stage for a further discussion of control and analysis. The scientist starts with a problem which *ultimately* derived from some common-sense or prescientific considerations. In present-day sciences, especially the more advanced ones, the problem more often arises from purely scientific considerations, with the ultimate common-sense origins long since obscured. In any case, the solution to the problem must be approachable via some kind of empirical evidence. Ordinarily, the scientist is familiar enough with the details of his subject matter to entertain a number of hypotheses concerning the problem. The next step in the process is the making of observations. Here is where the principle of control needs to be employed.

The activity continuum in controlled observation. Control can be better understood if we refer to an important continuum: the amount of *active* control over the subject matter exercised by the observer. It is easy to see that the experiment is the ideal example of optimal control: relevant variables are actively held constant by direct elimination of variation in them, either actually or statistically. Thus, in the experiment we have control in the sense of manipulation as well as in the sense of elimination of extraneous sources of variation: the controlled variables are immediately eliminated as possible sources of variation in the dependent observations. Many of the refinements of apparatus in psychology are directed toward this objective of increased control. But even on the other end of the activity continuum, away from experimentation, a kind of control can be exercised. The astute counselor, for example, entertains hypotheses which he attempts to check during the course of an interview. These hypotheses may be with respect to the condition of a particular client (*idiographic*) or with respect to more general problems (*nomothetic*). In the latter case, a series of clients would need to be checked (Hunt, 1951). This is the case with which we are more immediately concerned, since nomothetic hypotheses are of more direct scientific importance.

Once the counselor or clinician attempts to check evidence *selectively* on various factors or conditions, he must begin to apply some degree of control. Suppose that he is looking for certain kinds of consequents (symptoms, say) as related to antecedent factors (such as infant experiences or home conditions). In checking these possible relationships, he will sooner or later have to take into account other conditions in which he is not now interested (e.g., sex, age, or educational level). Controls are needed at this point. He may be forced to eliminate certain clients from consideration because they are not sufficiently similar in educational level, for example. When he does this, he is attempting to eliminate the effects of some variables while checking the influence of others. He is doing so without benefit of formal experimental design or active manipulation of variables; even so, what he is doing is applying the essence of the principle of control in what may be the only way possible in his situation.

There are enormous difficulties facing the scientist who attempts to utilize the principle of control in this passive manner. For one thing, he is faced with the constant necessity of keeping his hunches and hypotheses separate from the data that are meant to test them; that is, the observations upon which the hypotheses were originally based cannot also serve as tests of the hypotheses. Such clear separation of the hypothesis and its test is not encouraged in the passive situation.

The passive situation, where no formal design is used, also encourages reliance on memory or subjectively selected observations rather than on objective measures formally determined in advance. But the fact remains that it is possible to use the kind of thinking which is characteristic of the use of the principle of control even in observations made in situations which make active control impractical. This passive control can increase the scientific usefulness of otherwise uncontrolled observations.

THE ROLE OF ANALYSIS

A considerable amount of confusion has developed about another basic function in the tool kit of science—analysis.

Let us illustrate its role in controlled observations by an example from the recent history of psychology. In 1938 Norman Maier won the annual award given by the American Association for the Advancement of Science. His contribution consisted of a paper (Maier, 1938) read at the annual meeting (and accompanied by an impressive motion picture) in which he described his research on "neurotic" behavior in the rat. Maier had been able to produce very striking abnormal symptoms in rats by presenting them with an insoluble discrimination problem. His achievement seemed to be the culmination of several years of strenuous effort by psychologists to develop a technique for producing neurosis in the rat so that neurosis could be experimentally investigated with this handy subject.

Maier interpreted the abnormal behavior observed as a reaction to conflict. As his experimental procedure was studied—analyzed—some psychologists became interested in the role of a factor whose importance in the situation Maier had not emphasized. This was the use of an air blast to force the animal off the testing platform in the jumping-stand apparatus. For Maier this factor had no significance beyond that of forcing the animal to jump; he had found it to be effective for this purpose and so used it instead of some other technique. Not very long after, however, the Morgans (1939) reported that they could duplicate Maier's results—that is, produce the same convulsive and comatose behavior that Maier had—merely by use of a high-frequency, high-intensity sound from which the animal could not escape. Apparently the elaborate discrimination training and the presumed conflict resulting from the insoluble situation were not necessary. The term *audio-genic seizure* then became popular as a label for the convulsive behavior in view of its apparently auditory basis.

Without entering into the ensuing controversy over whether some other kind of conflict is or is not an essential factor, we can point to the present example as an interesting and important illustration of the necessity for the combination of analytic thinking and control as a basis for interpretations. Many other examples will be apparent to the reader of the psychological literature.

It is impossible for us to see how science can proceed without some analysis. The process of control implies that some variables have been analyzed that *need* controlling; different potentially relevant factors are isolated, controlled, and studied in relation to selected effects. The complexity of most everyday life situations is so great that scientifically useful relationships can be determined only through the twin processes of conceptual analysis and controlled observation.

Our emphasis on analysis should not be construed as any rejection of synthesis. Once relevant variables have been isolated through analysis, there must be synthetic laws which tell us how the variables combine in producing the final effect. Synthetic processes have tended to be preferred by clinically oriented psychologists; the synthesis of a number of variables is necessary in multivariable situations if interpretation and explanation must be attempted. Analysis may be rejected because its critic is primarily concerned with the world "as is," rather than with the "irreality" that comes from scientific analysis, abstraction, and control. Although analysis may not afford complete and practical answers, we feel that a rejection of analysis is fundamentally antiscientific. Synthesis has nothing to proceed with until analysis has done its work. Antianalytic attitudes will probably tend to disappear as the nature of the whole scientific process becomes better understood.

The importance of analysis and control follows from the kinds of materials with which science works. We can understand science fully only if we understand these materials. We note that finished science, considered as a body of knowledge, consists of statements. These statements are regarded in a different way from other items in our experienced world. Control, analysis, and synthesis play their roles in setting up the relationships that exist between the empirical and symbolic worlds. The next section examines the importance of these two kinds of items in assessing the nature of science.

THE EMPIRICAL AND THE SYMBOLIC

In the world of experienced things there is a class of things whose predominant function is to serve as stimuli which direct the behavior of human beings. We usually call these things or events *symbols*, *language*, or the like. All normal human beings receive an intensive course of training in correct usage of, or responses to, these stimuli. They thus come to have a special "meaning" for people. We can, in view of this training, divide the world into two hazily differentiated classes according to whether or not the member of the class has participated in the formal or informal course of training which gives it membership in the class of symbols.

Some people, such as mathematicians, logicians, and linguists, work almost exclusively with symbols. They seldom concern themselves with whether the symbols refer to any aspect of experience beyond the symbolic. These people are not scientists in the sense in which we intend to use the word. They concern themselves with the forms of symbolic systems and are not interested in the "truth" of the statements made in the sense that the statements need be representative of nonsymbolic reality.

Other people work largely with that aspect of experience which is not symbolic. The bulldozer operator and the businessman are not scientists. Their primary interest is in the manipulation of empirical objects, including other people, with no intent to add to the store of human knowledge. They apply existing knowledge in order to mold the world into forms more suitable to themselves.

The scientist sets up new relationships beween the two aspects of experience. In doing so, he manipulates the empirical world in order to make observations, and he may manipulate the symbolic systems in which he is interested as well; but the unique part of his contribution is the "between" relationships he sets up. He may describe his results by using already existing symbols; he may invent new descriptions or explanations of already well-known events; or he may do both. The nature of science is such that only certain kinds of statements can be accepted according to the rules of the game of science. Let us look at the nature of fact and the precautions which have been suggested to check the incautious use of terms in the invention of new concepts in science.

THE NATURE OF FACT

Scientists generally agree that a statement must be public and capable of communication before it can be a part of science. Science must be codified as communicable symbols that have an agreed meaning for the speaker and the person to whom he wishes to communicate the scientific fact. Before the statement can be an accepted part of science, it must be agreed to by other scientists familiar with the field and with the meaning of the statement.

Statements that receive this agreement are called *facts*. It is clear, then, that we mean by facts simply verbal statements agreed to by a certain group. Facts are relative to the group to which the statement is presented; the statement, "World communism is desirable and inevitable," will not be accepted as a fact in some places but will be in others.

Guthrie has been concerned with the nature of facts. He has said (1946, p. 1):

Objects and events are not facts; they are merely objects and events. They are not facts until they are described by persons. And it is in the nature of that description that the quintessence of fact lies. Only when an event has been given a very specific kind of description does it become a fact.

When we say, "Let's get down to the facts," what we are saying is much more than that we should look at or listen to or smell or touch real objects, or that we should all observe an event. What we are really proposing is that we all try to find certain statements on which we can all agree. Facts are the basis of human cooperation.

This view of facts robs them of much of the solidity and immutability that they are often felt to have. Neither cows nor falling bodies are facts; only the statements made about them are facts. Since facts are verbal, the manner in which they are stated is arbitrary. The statements which we call facts we usually also call "true"; thus truth as we use the word will have the same element of arbitrariness and relativity that facts have. What is true for one set of people may not be true for some other set. Further, for any one set of people facts change and the truth changes as we rephrase our statements about the universe and as our knowledge increases. We cannot insist that scratches on paper or vocally produced pressure patterns in the air are true; the scratches and the pressure patterns are stimuli that either are or are not useful in directing the behavior of people and that either do or do not produce the response "true" under appropriate conditions in people listening to or reading the statement. If the patterns of stimulation play their complex roles well in the learning situations in which they acquire meaning and in the situations where they direct behavior, then the patterns tend to persevere as true; if they do not, they will eventually be replaced by other truths, other facts.

OPERATIONISM

The physicist Bridgman (1927) was apparently the first man to point clearly to a precaution that should be taken if scientific concepts are to be reduced in ambiguity and, presumably, increased in longevity. Bridgman analyzed the historical habits of thought and expression in physics preceding Einstein; he wondered why Einstein's theories, indicating a need for a drastic revision of the concepts of length, space, and time, had come as such a shock to physicists. He wished to avoid a repetition of this shock. In his analysis, he discovered that the Newtonian meanings of time, length, and space contained elements of meaning which were not justified by the results of physical experimentation. To Newton, time was a kind of absolute scale, independent of any process that might be required to find out what time it is; Bridgman said of Newton's definition (1927, p. 4): "Now there is no

assurance whatever that there exists in nature anything with properties
like those assumed in the definition." When Einstein examined some
of Newton's concepts, he was led to reformulate them completely.

Bridgman proposed to place more stringent requirements upon the
definition of physical concepts, so that no such revolution as the one
brought about by relativity theory need ever again take place in
physics (1927, p. 5):

> The new attitude toward a concept is entirely different. We may illus-
> trate by considering the concept of length: what do we mean by the
> length of an object? We evidently know what we mean by length if we
> can tell what the length of any and every object is, and for the physicist
> nothing more is required. To find the length of an object, we have to
> perform certain physical operations. The concept of length is therefore
> fixed when the operations by which length is measured are fixed: that is,
> the concept of length involves as much as and nothing more than a set of
> operations; *the concept is synonymous with the corresponding set of
> operations.*

The last sentence of this quotation should make it clear why Bridgman's point of view has been labeled *operationism* and Bridgman's
kind of definition, *operational definition.* His aim was to clarify the
meaning of all concepts and to remove all connotations of terms which
might not be meaningful. In other words, the aim is to make sure that
concepts have a clear reference, a meaning in terms of operations for
the listener or reader as well as for their inventor or user.

There is continuing discussion and criticism of the operational point
of view within science; a recent book (Benjamin, 1955) examined
operationism from the point of view of the philosopher of science.
Operationism was early taken into psychology, and its acceptance was
early opposed. Stevens (1939) pointed out that operationism is not
regarded as a religion or a panacea; it is simply a formal statement of
the methods that have always been used within science when it is
necessary to clarify the meanings of words or other symbols with
physical referents.

There was at first much disagreement on the ground that many concepts have proved to be highly useful despite the lack of directly
observable operations or events to which they correspond. Bridgman
has been clear that paper-and-pencil operations and verbal concepts
are admissible even though they do not *immediately* correspond to
physical operations, but he insists that they must be eventually reducible to operations that actually can be performed, else they can have
no meaning for science. He recently reaffirmed the usefulness of such
abstract concepts (1952). Most scientists would probably now agree
that operationism formulates the rules which science must follow at
some stage of the game if it is to provide communicable knowledge.

Experience has shown that when a term is being defined, disagreement usually stops when we point to what we have done in defining the word and say, "This is what I mean by ————." We *must* in some way ensure that our statements inspire others to a predictable kind of response, for that is part of the business of science; operational definition is a way of doing this.

We can now return to the discussion of control from another point of view. The operations performed in defining scientific concepts must always take place within a specified context. If the context changes drastically, then the operations may of necessity change; for example, when the physicist measures length on an astronomical scale, he must abandon the simple technique of placing standard measuring rods end to end. When the operations change, the corresponding concept may also have to change. Conversely, if we wish to be able to point out the meaning of a concept or statement beyond reasonable doubt, then we must specify precisely the situation within which the operations are to be performed. Only then can the operations be repeated in any precise sense. Part of the specification of the situation must involve careful control of the variables within the situation. Our operations may have to be repeated in order to demonstrate the meaning of our concept or the truth of our assertions; therefore, control is a necessary aspect of making our statements reliably repeatable.

The scientist wishes to make statements about the relationships between events. He may wish to make a statement in the form "A is related to C." In order to do so, he must be certain that some other factor is not responsible for the supposed relationship. In an example previously cited, Maier wished to assert that conflict was responsible for the behavior observed in his experimental animals. Morgan, however, showed that another factor—high-frequency sound—was related to the behavior in the absence of the original type of conflict. This threw Maier's original statement into question. In general, then, only if alternative assertions are eliminated through control of variables can positive scientific statements be made. It is clear that control is a most pervasive characteristic of the scientific process. Historically, the need for control of all variables within a situation was, of course, recognized before Bridgman stated his views of operationism; however, we see that one way of regarding control is as a prerequisite for adequate operational definition of more complex relational concepts.

SCIENTIFIC HYPOTHESES

The foregoing discussion may make science sound like a cut-and-dried body of statements. Finished science may indeed be highly formalized, and the interpretation of the statements of science at a given time may require more perseverance than imagination. Yet we know that the creation of science requires imagination and ingenuity of the highest order as well as hard work. The thrill of scientific discovery is as satisfying as anything coming from any vocation. The devotion of many scientists to their work is a testimonial to this statement. The use of operational definitions and the control of variables are prerequisites of good scientific workmanship, but the employment of these techniques does not guarantee that the scientist will make a great contribution.

The scientist must work on significant problems and formulate effective hypotheses if he is to do important work. He must formulate a problem so that it can be attacked by scientific techniques. This implies that any questions must be expressed so that they can be answered empirically. The questions formulated initially are not a part of science but arise from prescientific considerations. Later questions may be suggested by the outcomes of previous experiments or may arise from a study of some theoretical framework which is itself related to experimental results.

The first requirement for a scientific hypothesis is that it be testable, and the first requirement for a scientific question is that it be answerable. Perhaps this boils down to saying that the terms of the hypothesis or question must be operationally defined, the operations performed as required by the question, and the results observed. If an experiment is performed for the purpose of testing some hypothesis, the hypothesis must be sufficiently clear in implication so that the results of the experiment are predicted in advance; one outcome must be specified from among the various alternatives. We shall later see examples in psychology of theories about behavior which purport to explain behavior after it occurs, although they cannot predict in advance which behavior will occur. Upon closer examination, these so-called theories turn out to be capable of explaining whatever behavior occurs. In short, no conceivable outcome could *disconfirm* the theory. One requirement for scientific hypotheses is that they be stated with sufficient precision so that they *can be disconfirmed*. Hypotheses that cannot be disproved are too general to be scientifically useful; science strives for, among other things, the ability to predict events given the preceding set of circumstances. If a hypothesis is so general that it cannot be disconfirmed, it is also so general that it cannot effectively predict. If someone tells us that the reason events proceed as they do is because this is the best of all possible worlds, we are still in no better position to predict the events of tomorrow. The statement is not disconfirmable and is scientifically useless.

The requirement that a hypothesis be testable or disconfirmable directly does not hold for all hypotheses. There are hypotheses that are analogous to mathematical postulates. Their function is not to specify directly an empirical outcome but to serve as a starting point for the derivation of other statements that do specify an empirical outcome. Such statements have operational meaning only in terms of their derivations. Examples of these are less common in psychology than in some more advanced sciences, but some recent mathematical learning theories seem to contain postulational statements; Estes' (1950) statements about stimulus pools and the organism's sampling from them are of this type. Hull's (1952) statement about afferent stimulus interaction is also postulational. Some people regard Freud's statements about the unconscious as the same type of statement, although here the case is less clear. Such postulates are always subject to revision in the light of new experimental results, despite their lack of direct experimental reference, and they must be interpretable at some stage in empirical terms. They must lead to predictions.

One requirement for theories and hypotheses is that they be as simple as possible. The *principle of parsimony* (sometimes called Occam's razor) is the traditional statement that unnecessary complication should be avoided. Lloyd Morgan's canon is an adaptation of this principle to psychology; Morgan held that behavior should never be explained in terms of a faculty found higher in the phylogenetic scale if some faculty found lower in the scale was adequate. Morgan was originally objecting to a tendency to anthropomorphize when apparently intelligent behavior was observed in animals.

The desire for simplicity should not be construed to mean that a simpler hypothesis should be held to in the face of contrary evidence or when it is found to be inadequate. If this were the case, physicists would still be clinging tenaciously to a model of an atom as a single, unbreakable particle. They do not, because evidence has been amassed which shows that such a simple theory is inadequate. When complexity is required, simplicity is abandoned.

The foregoing discussion makes it clear that hypotheses and theories are never final. If evidence accords with them, confidence in their validity grows (even though it should not, from the point of view of strict logical argument). If confidence in a hypothesis is great, it may become part of a theory. By theory we shall mean what Bergmann means (1957, p. 31): "A theory is a group of laws deductively connected." In this sense, a scientific law is an honored hypothesis, one that has been widely accepted and whose implications have been observed to hold without fail. Our psychological theories, unfortunately, do not always consist of laws; in psychology, the hypotheses found in theories are often without much honor, and they may have a deductive connection only in the loosest sense.

Though hypotheses and even laws may finally be replaced, that does not mean that the old statement was useless; it was required to have predictive value within the range and era of its usefulness. There is no one who would argue that Newton's laws were useless, even though they have been replaced as complete physical accounts. Even now, Newton's statements are used for many applications because they are simpler. As another example, we could predict the passage of heat from one body to another if we conceived of heat as a subtle fluid, just as we do now that it is conceived of as related to molecular movement. Heat is no longer conceived of as a fluid, not because one could not predict temperature changes with this view, but because this view of heat does not fit well into the over-all theoretical account of the nature of the matter.

THE SCIENTIFIC ATTITUDE

Working within the general kind of framework outlined here seems to lead scientists in general to take a somewhat unique attitude toward the world and toward their work. In his quest for facts, the scientist tends to rely upon observations of the empirical world as the final arbiter of truth; in this way he has found that he can bulwark his statements and reach agreement with other scientists. The modern scientist tends to be suspicious even of the intuitively obvious because the obvious has so often been wrong; on the other hand, he may be a seeker after relationships which superficially do not seem possible. The scientist, although he is a user and sometimes creator of abstract systems of mathematics and logic, remains skeptical concerning derivations from them; he is always fearful that the statements generated within these systems may not turn out to be empirically true.

The modern scientist sees clearly the schism between the empirical and the formal, symbolic realms. On the one hand, he says (Bridgman, 1952, p. 28):

> It would appear that paper-and-pencil operations, or mental experiments in general, may have a useful role in suggesting programmes of investigation in the laboratory.

On the other hand, he also says (Bridgman, 1952, p. 14):

> There is never any question of proceeding to a limit in the mathematical sense, and logically the hiatus between the paper-and-pencil operations of the calculus and our instrumental operations cannot be closed. We do not regard this hiatus as particularly serious, however, and think of a law of nature when formulated in differential form as something of which it has meaning to say that it may be directly verified.

Certainly these statements imply a recognition both of the distinction between the two realms and of the relationship between the realms. They are related usefully if the symbolic statement (like the calculus) stimulates the user of the system to correct action, causes him to expect what actually occurs.

Since he recognizes the tentative nature of his statements, the scientist generally remains objective about them and refrains from dogmatism. He tries to be disinterested and unbiased even about the statements he himself originates; he knows that he will make errors and that others too will make errors. He is intellectually honest enough to admit any errors he discovers. In order to be comfortable, he must be tolerant of ambiguity, for it is inescapable.

Two important qualifications to this portrait of the scientist's attitude must be recognized. First, the attributes described are idealized ones and apply to scientists collectively rather than necessarily to any particular scientist. Progress in science is made largely because scientists as a group show these characteristics; an individual scientist may or may not be rated high on any given trait. Second, although scientists in their professional work may tend to behave more in accordance with these attributes than nonscientists, it does not follow that they do so in their private lives. For example, the scientist making a political statement may be as vehement and biased as anyone else, and he may have no more grounds for his statement; and when scientists do work in a field outside their training and special competence, they may show a marked lack of skill.

SUMMARY AND CONCLUSIONS

The aim of this chapter has been to outline the nature of science. Our discussion suggests a loose definition. Science may be considered a body of statements which have been gathered, or constructed, in a certain way and about which scientists familiar with the field agree. The "certain way" in which the statements have been gathered is via the scientific method, which involves operationism, analysis, and the principle of control. Scientific study always involves reference to empirical systems and their relationship to symbolic systems, in contrast with other disciplines, which may be exclusively concerned with either empirical or symbolic systems.

It is obvious that the scientist can be motivated to act only if he assumes that there is some kind of orderliness in nature which he can discover. It seems that scientists usually take their experience as unanalyzed, as a "given," and proceed with experience as the basic tool of science. As scientists, they are usually concerned very little with such philosophical questions as the ultimate reality of an external world.

With this background, it will be easier to discuss questions such as, "What is the status of psychoanalysis as a science?" We might rephrase the question as, "Has the body of statements which make up psychoanalysis been constructed by the methods of science?" In addition, we could ask whether the attitudes of the people making the statements conform to the attitudes generally held by scientists. It is always dangerous to bring up the idea of conformity in science, but the discussion might nevertheless be enlightening. These questions will be treated in the chapter on psychoanalysis as a school, and similar questions will be posed and discussed with regard to behaviorism, structuralism, functionalism, gestalt, and other schools of psychology.

further readings .

For abundant examples and discussion of the nature and importance of the principle of control in science, see Valentine and Wickens's *Experimental foundations of general psychology* (1949); Sidman's *Tactics of scientific research* (1960) is a down-to-earth, positivistic account of experimental practice which can be read with profit by interested persons regardless of their methodological biases. Garner, Hunt, and Taylor's paper, "Education for research in psychology" (1959), provides further stimulating material for discussion of fundamental methodological issues, especially as they relate to scientific training. Pratt's *The logic of modern psychology* (1939), while now somewhat dated, still offers a readable logical analysis of behavioral methodology. *An introduction to logic and scientific method,* by Cohen and Nagel (1934), also may still be recommended as a most useful introduction to general logical problems in science. Bridgman's *The logic of modern physics* (1927), which opened up the formal operationism movement, remains a classic; for recent developments, see Benjamin's *Operationism* (1955). An excellent historical treatment of the relations among behavior psychology, operationism, and the logical positivism movement in philosophy is available in Stevens's paper, "Psychology and the science of science" (1939). Skinner's *Verbal behavior* (1957b) is good for the present purpose because of its examination of the empirical-symbolic relationship and how it comes about. Heisenberg's *The physicist's conception of nature* (1958) is a concise survey of the history of science and several very basic problems in the philosophy of science. It does this in under 200 pages. That should be enough to qualify it as a dessert for the present topic. Interesting and informative accounts of some of the contemporary problems relating science and other aspects of society may be found in two issues of the journal *Daedalus,* recently edited by Holton: "Science and the modern world view" (1958) and "Science and technology in contemporary society" (1962).

psychology's place in science   2

The question whether psychology is a science is of historical interest
only. Psychology has its scientific side and its technological side just
as biology in general has these facets, and he who would maintain
today that psychology cannot be a science is trying to get another jump
out of a long-dead horse. Neither this chapter nor the preceding one
gives special attention to the defense of psychology as a science, for no
such defense is presently needed.

Rather, we turn our attention to a sketch of certain ideas that historically seem important in the development of science and the
emergence of psychology as an independent science. The schools of
psychology can be better understood with these ideas clearly in mind.
Accordingly, this chapter first sketches the emergence of science from
prescience and then turns to an examination of psychology's emergence; this background should help the reader to understand how
some of psychology's contemporary problems have arisen.

THE GROWTH OF SCIENTIFIC IDEAS

Table 1 presents, for ready reference, a summary of some of the men
who were the most important contributors to the development of scientific ideas. Many of their contributions are discussed in more detail
in the text to follow, but it will be helpful if the reader has an over-all
view of them before examining certain key concepts.

Internal explanation.   There was a time in the history of man when
events were typically explained in terms of forces outside the scope of
observable natural events. For example, Norse mythology explained
storms by saying that the warrior of the gods was angry, and Homer
explained victory in war in terms of the favoritism of the Greek gods.
From the scientific point of view, there are two very basic things

Table 1 Summary of major contributions
to the development of modern science

PHILOSOPHY

Man	Date	Contribution
Thales	6th century B.C.	Naturalistic explanation; universe composed of water
Democritus	5th century B.C.	Universe composed of atoms
Aristotle	4th century B.C.	Rationalistic and observational methods; classification systems for biology; laws of associative memory
Roger Bacon	13th century	Emphasis on free empirical observation
Francis Bacon	16th century	*Novum organum:* Gave philosophical support to empirical science
Descartes	17th century	Dualistic interactionism; action of body mechanistic
La Mettrie	18th century	Mechanistic explanation applied to man's behavior

ANCIENT BIOLOGY

Hippocrates	4th & 5th centuries B.C.	"Father of medicine"; an excellent observer
Herophilus and Erasistratus	3d century B.C.	First inference of distinction between sensory and motor nerves
Galen	2d century	Famous physician and anatomist; performed animal experiments

PHYSICS AND ASTRONOMY

Archimedes	3d century B.C.	First well-known experimental physicist
Ptolemy	2d century	Alexandrian astronomer; his view of earth as center of universe held for centuries
Copernicus	16th century	Polish astronomer who placed sun at center of solar system, changed man's view of his own importance
Galileo	17th century	Reestablished observation as final court of appeal; made astronomical and physical discoveries
Newton	17th century	Coinventor of calculus; set pattern of physics for 200 years
Bessel	19th century	Astronomer at Königsberg; worked out personal equations and thus posed a problem for psychology

Table 1   Summary of major contributions
to the development of modern science (Continued)

MODERN ORIGINS OF BIOLOGICAL SCIENCE

Vesalius	16th century	First thorough treatise on human anatomy
Harvey	17th century	Demonstrated the circulation of the blood
van Leeuwenhoek	18th century	First effective microscope; discovery or identification of protozoa, bacteria, human sperm
Linnaeus	18th century	Binomial system of biological classification
Darwin	19th century	*Origin of species:* Primary publication on organic evolution

EMERGENCE OF MODERN PHYSIOLOGY

Mueller	19th century	Comprehensive *Handbuch der Physiologie des Menchen;* doctrine of "specific energies of nerves"
Bernard	19th century	Concept of the internal environment
Helmholtz	19th century	Eminent physiologist; first experimental measurement of speed of nerve impulse; theories of hearing and seeing

EMERGENCE OF PSYCHOLOGY

Weber	19th century	Pioneer physiologist; formulated law: $dR/R = C$; really a psychological law
Fechner	19th century	*Elemente der Psychophysik:* Believed by some to mark beginnings of experimental psychology; modified Weber's law into Weber-Fechner form: $S = C \log R$
Galton	19th century	Work in eugenics, statistics, individual differences; set many problems for psychology
Wundt	19th century	Founder of first psychological laboratory, at University of Leipzig

wrong with these explanations: (1) they refer the explanation to unobservables, and (2) the events used as explanations do not fit within the same natural context as the events to be explained. Such explanations are therefore called external, as opposed to internal.

Although there are still people who explain disasters in terms of "the wrath of God," scientific explanation does not have recourse to such descriptions. Thales, a Greek philosopher of the sixth century B.C., is sometimes given credit for initiating attempts to explain natural events in terms of other natural events; he explained the nature of matter in terms of a single basic *natural* element, water. Democritus soon after explained matter in terms of basic particles called atoms, and modern man still holds to a similar conception. Whether these men really deserve credit for the swing toward internal explanation, however, is not important; the important thing is that science as we know it depends on the use of explanations which refer to observables within the same natural framework at some stage of the scientific game.

The Grecian culture that developed this idea eventually disappeared, and the ensuing Middle Ages showed little concern for internal types of explanations or for scientific problems; perhaps the attitude was that great interest in natural events was bad for the soul. An example of the external thinking that was predominant is the typical treatment of convulsions by flogging; such action was thought to drive out of the body the demons or evil spirits that were considered to be responsible for convulsive behavior. Today, of course, such treatment is not used because convulsive behavior is generally viewed as determined by organic conditions within the body (an internal explanation).

Such science as there was during the medieval period was largely in the East. It remained for the Renaissance, beginning with Galileo (1564–1642) and his contemporaries, to renew European interest in natural science.

Reliance on observation. Parallel with the use of internal explanation was an increasing reliance on observation. Most of the earlier Greek thinkers relied more on rationalistic methods than was the case later. For example, Euclid early developed a deductive geometry, and Pythagoras and his followers had a mystic belief in the efficacy of numbers. Certainly there is no clear-cut line between induction and deduction or between rationalistic and empirical types of thinking. Even the most rationalistic philosophers begin with certain plausible statements, which probably come from some kind of empirical observations. On the other hand, the most empirically minded, "hardheaded" scientists eventually make general statements based on their observations, and generalizations are closely related to deductions. Science has tended to emphasize the empirical more than the rational at its basis. The final arbiter of the truth of a statement for a scientist is not what rationally *ought to be* but what observationally *is*.

Aristotle was one early thinker who used observational as well as rational methods. He was an advocate of logic and reasonableness but not a respecter of authority. His authority, however, was accepted during the Middle Ages at the expense of observational methods. Galileo was important in renewing the scientific attitude toward observation and authority. He relied, for example, upon the *observation* of the time of fall of bodies of unequal weight rather than upon the authoritative statement that heavy bodies fall faster than light ones. Francis Bacon, in his *Novum organum* of 1620, made one of the most famous appeals for empiricism; he felt that science should work strictly by induction, piling observation upon observation until general facts emerged from specific facts. But even in discarding rationalism, Bacon was forced to use rationalistic methods in his arguments. He again illustrates the impossibility of using a pure approach.

Simplification. Thales and Democritus tried to simplify the apparent complexity of nature by appeal to simpler elements and to assumptions which allowed them to derive the observed complexity from the assumed simplicity. Their attempts were also *reductionistic,* since they reduced complexity by explanations depending on the existence of phenomena at a different, "lower" level; for example, Democritus supposed man to be built of particles much like those that composed other forms of matter. Physiological psychologists make similar reductionistic statements when behavioral data are explained in terms of physiological events, which again are at another level of observation. It may or may not be that a reductionistic account will also be a simple account or the simplest available. Science seeks and accepts, not only simple hypotheses, but the simplest over-all theory which adequately explains the observations made.

Placement of man in nature. The Greeks seem to have regarded man as having no special status apart from the rest of nature. Many of the Greek philosophers would probably have agreed that the behavior of man is lawful and predictable, just as is the behavior of inanimate nature. The Middle Ages, however, took a different view of man. He was regarded as a creature with a soul, possessed of a free will which set him apart from ordinary natural laws, subject only to his own willfulness and perhaps to the rule of God. Such a creature, being free-willed, could not be an object of scientific investigation. Even the body of man was regarded as sacrosanct, and dissection was dangerous for the dissector. These strictures against observation hindered the development of anatomy and medicine for centuries, and misconceptions that are today considered incredible persisted for over a thousand years. A science of man could not flourish in such an atmosphere.

Descartes's (1596–1650) views were part of a trend toward the view that the behavior of man is predictable. He regarded the body of man as a machine, which will move and behave in predictable ways if we know what the "inputs" are. He salvaged free will for man by possessing him of a soul which was free and which decided the actions of the body. Such a view made at least dead (soulless) bodies accessible to scientific investigation; animals, since they were regarded by Descartes as soulless, were also accessible.

The idea that man might be an object of scientific study was furthered by La Mettrie (1709–1751). He was convinced, apparently largely by the deterioration of his own thought processes during a fever, that man was altogether a machine, dependent in mind as in body upon physical events. He espoused this view, despite opposition, until his death. The important point about the views of Descartes and La Mettrie is not their analogy between man and machine, for man is obviously different from a machine. The important thing is that machines are lawful and that viewing man mechanically implies regarding man as a lawful being susceptible of scientific study.

There was still much resistance to viewing man within a deterministic, natural framework when Charles Darwin (1809–1882) advanced his theory of organic evolution. Evolution itself was not a new idea, but Darwin buttressed the evolutionary theory with so much evidence that it took the scientific community by storm. Evolution restored the continuity between man and other animals which Descartes had denied when he attributed a soul to man alone. It also contradicted the Biblical account of creation; the theologically based opposition aroused a heated controversy which persisted into the twentieth century. Today there is little question about the correctness of the general outlines of evolutionary theory; evolution is a fact for the scientific community if not for all the lay community. Its acceptance has made the science of psychology more acceptable; it has also made the study of animals an important part of that science, since it is now easier to assume that knowledge gained in the study of animals will have significance for the behavior of men.

Many historians have noted the late development of the science of psychology and the apparently stepwise progress of the sciences beginning with those farthest from man and moving toward those closest to him and his immediate affairs. Astronomy and physics were the first sciences to develop. Archimedes in the third century b.c. was in some ways a sophisticated physicist. The mathematical description by Kepler (1571–1630) of the motions of the planets around the sun was the culmination of a long line of astronomical discoveries. The body of man was investigated long before the mind of man: Harvey in 1628 described the circulation of the blood correctly; this was about 250 years before Ebbinghaus's pioneer work on memory. Two reasons have been suggested for neglecting the behavior of man until last. One is the sanctity of the human being as maintained by human institutions. The other is the complexity of the human being as proclaimed by those who have tried to study him.

The foregoing statements, of course, are selected to make the general point and do not imply that man was not concerned with himself; philosophers and laymen have long wrestled with explanations of the human being, but there was not a formal science of behavior as there were other sciences.

PSYCHOLOGY'S LEGACY OF PROBLEMS

Finally, then, the behavior of man came to be regarded as lawful, and a science of psychology was possible. But the basic scientific and philosophical assumptions prerequisite for the development of a science were not the sole legacy of psychology when it began as a formal science. Psychology also inherited certain problems that had developed within science and philosophy before psychology won its independence. Problems, as well as necessary assumptions, must exist before a new science is needed. Some of the problems passed on to psychology were phrased in such a way that their scientific resolution through experiment was impossible, but they nevertheless stimulated research in an attempt to get those elusive answers. We shall consider four problem areas: the mind-body problem, the physiology of perception, the reaction-time problem, and statistics and individual differences.

The mind-body problem. The ghostly apparitions of dreams may first have convinced man that there was more to him than met the physical eye. The writing of Plato (fourth century B.C.) shows that the thinking of his time divided man into two components. Descartes's dualistic views did not differ greatly from Plato's. Both systems fit into the Christian theology; some unobservable component is necessary if the immortality of man is logically to be maintained, since the observable portions of man are mortal. Even today, the thinking of the layman separates man into compartments.

If man has both a mind and a body, then the question arises, "What is the relationship between the two parts?" A long tradition of thought made the question inevitable. Before psychology ever had a formal beginning as a science, a German physicist, Theodor Fechner (1801–1887), started work on the problem. It was his intention to write equations that described the functional relationships between the psychic and physical realms. Boring (1950, p. 483) has questioned whether Fechner really intended a dualism, but certainly his problem was stated in dualistic terms. For example, in his *Elemente der Psychophysik* (1860), Fechner said he was concerned with "the exact science of the functional relations or relations of dependency between body and mind." In order to demonstrate these functional relations, it is necessary to measure mind and body separately. That is what Fechner thought he was doing: on the one side he had the stimulus, which acted on the body; on the other side he had the sensation, which he thought of as a mental event. Fechner wished to demonstrate the identity of the two kinds of events, but he wrestled with a difficult problem when he tried to unite the two aspects that had originally been separated by assumption.

The major mind-body solutions that have been offered by philosophers are classified and summarized in Table 2. The reader should

Table 2   Major philosophical solutions to the mind-body problem
        (early important exponent identified in parentheses
        with approximate date of contribution)

DUALISM*

Cartesian interactionism (Descartes, 1641)	Two separate and interacting processes assumed
Psychophysical parallelism (Spinoza, 1665)	Two separate, independent but perfectly correlated processes assumed
Occasionalism (Malebranche, 1675)	Two separate and independent processes assumed; correlated by intervention of God

MONISM†

Materialism (Democritus, 400 B.C.)	A single underlying physical reality assumed
Subjective idealism (Berkeley, 1710)	A single underlying mental or spiritual reality assumed
Phenomenalism (Hume, 1740)	There are neither minds nor bodies; as far as can be known only ideas resulting from sense impressions exist

COMPROMISES

Double-aspect view (Russell, 1915)	Two processes assumed to be a function of one underlying reality
Epiphenomenalism (Hobbes, 1658)	Mind assumed to be a noncausal by-product of body

* Any point of view implying a basic difference between mind and body and therefore a relationship to be explained.
† Any point of view ignoring either mind or body, or subsuming both under the same rubric.

familiarize himself with the general outline presented here, for the solutions proposed recur in the following chapters. There is no view which is generally accepted, and there is thus far no scientific method for deciding among them. Early psychologists, however, felt it necessary to take some stand on the mind-body problem.

The psychology of perception. Other scientists, notably physiologists, were interested in another relationship, that between physiological processes and perception. Hermann Ludwig Ferdinand von Helmholtz (1821-1894) is the most famous of those interested in this relationship; he modified Thomas Young's color theory and developed his own theory of hearing. Helmholtz, along with the English empiricists, believed that all knowledge depends upon sense experience. If this is our assumption, then the problem of sense physiology is also the problem of epistemology—the problem of the origins, nature, and limitations of knowledge. Physiological findings in this area of study have philosophical implications. Helmholtz tried to refute Kant's statement that there is innate knowledge. Kant had believed that the axioms of geometry are known independently from experience. Helmholtz asked whether we would have developed the same geometry if we had inhabited the inside surface of a hollow sphere. He discussed non-Euclidian geometries in a spirit which is surprisingly modern.

Sense physiology with its philosophical implications helped to give our young science its initial impetus. The problem, however, concealed the same dualistic thinking which was more explicit in the mind-body problem, for perception is no more solid, no more observable, no more physical than mind. Modern psychologists (e.g., Stevens, 1951) prefer a different formulation of what is being studied, but the experimental variables are much the same, and the early experimental work done within a more dualistic framework is still valid.

The reaction-time problem. This is another problem with epistemological implications that preceded formal psychology. F. W. Bessel (1784-1846) read an account of the firing of an assistant at Greenwich because the assistant's readings did not agree with the readings of the head astronomer. Bessel recognized the possibility that the error might be simply a difference in the time required for different observers to react rather than the result of carelessness. He checked his hunch by comparing his times with those of other astronomers and found discrepancies in nearly all cases. He then tried to write *personal equations,* or correction terms, which would reduce all the readings to a common basis. However, it was obvious that there could be no absolute standard of correctness. It was again shown how dependent our knowledge is upon observers and upon methods of observing and recording. If the determination of the time at which a star crosses a line is subject to error, then it seems logical that more complex judgments and observations must be even more subject to error.

Psychology took over the problem that Bessel had discovered. Wundt and many other early psychologists believed that by making the reaction required successively more difficult, the time for sensing, perceiving, apperceiving, discriminating, etc. could be found by subtracting the time for the next simpler reaction from that for the just more complicated reaction. Few psychologists would still hold this view; it is not clear that perceiving involves sensing plus perceiving. The whole nature of the process being timed may change as the task is progressively complicated. The subtractive assumption is invalid.

Statistics and individual differences. Two psychological fields of study that have remained extremely active to the present day are statistics and individual differences. Much of the credit for American acceptance of psychology has gone to the effectiveness of aptitude testing, which is part of the study of individual differences. Sir Francis Galton (1822–1911) pioneered in the development of both statistics and individual differences. He developed the technique of correlation in connection with his inheritance studies. He was led to it by the observation that children typically *regress* toward the mean relative to their parents in such characteristics as height and intelligence; that is, children of extremely tall or short, or bright or stupid, parents *tend* to be closer to the norm in these characteristics than their parents. Correlation is symbolized by *r*, for regression, and Galton is remembered for his early perception of the importance of statistics.

The major factor underlying the development of these interests was the Darwinian theory of evolution. Stress on the organism's adjustment to the environment, as a determining condition of survival or nonsurvival, became a primary concern of psychology. The intellectual ferment produced by this theory raised questions that led directly to Galton's interest in individual differences, mental testing, statistical evaluation of differences, and eventually, as we shall see, to the flourishing school of functionalism in the United States.

THE INITIAL SUBJECT MATTER
OF PSYCHOLOGY

We now turn from our discussion of prepsychological scientific developments to the discussion of psychology's beginnings. The prepsychological problems that we have discussed were all taken over as experimental problems, but the systematic framework imposed on psychology by Wilhelm Wundt (1832–1920) at the University of Leipzig in Germany was not exactly what one would expect.

It seems natural that psychology should be experimental, physiological, and interested in problems of sensation and perception. Since it came out of philosophy, one would also expect it to be interested in epistemological problems. Physiology actually played a very small direct role. Although Wundt called his psychology an experimental physiological psychology, there was really no physiological experimentation at all. This is doubly surprising because Wundt was himself a physiologist. However, psychology needed only the name of physiology. Physiology had prestige which the young science of psychology wanted. Accordingly, physiology was, and even today is, often invoked to illustrate the scientific respectability of psychology in general and of specific theories in particular. Physics and mathematics have served similar functions, and controversies have raged about whether the alleged dependence of psychology on older disciplines is good or bad. In the case of physiology, at least, much progress has been made. Psychologists today are much more prone to practice physiology and much less prone merely to invoke it.

Wundt was able to justify avoiding physiological experimentation because of his philosophical position on the mind-body problem. He believed that the mind and body ran parallel courses but that one could not say bodily events *caused* mental events; external events simply gave rise to certain bodily processes and, at the same time, to parallel mental processes (cf. Table 2). He thought the primary task of psychology was to discover the elements of conscious processes, the manner of their connection, and the laws determining their connection. Since mind and body were parallel, the simplest way to do this, in Wundt's opinion, was to make a *direct* study of the mental events through the method of introspection. Psychology might later turn to the question of just what bodily processes accompanied given mental processes, but this problem was secondary.

Wundt thus brought a kind of dualism to psychology. He also brought a strong belief in the necessity for psychology to use the experimental method. His research was laboratory introspection, not armchair introspection. He intended to rule metaphysical speculation out of psychology. He was constantly looking for experimental ways of attacking mental processes.

Wundt's experimentalism implied that he had accepted the necessary ideas which had developed within science and which had to be accepted before a *science* of psychology could become a reality: the necessity for internal explanation, the reliance on observation, and the placement of man within the realm of the scientifically knowable. His search for the elements of consciousness also showed his attempt at simplification, or his reductionism, if one prefers.

The Leipzig laboratory, officially founded in 1879, also took over many of the specific problems that were waiting for a psychology. The reaction-time problem has already been mentioned. Problems in sensation and perception were taken over from Helmholtz, Fechner, and others.

There was less at Leipzig to remind one of psychology's predecessors on the other side of the channel. Only through a brash American student, James McKeen Cattell, did the Leipzig laboratory turn out any work on Galton's problem of individual differences. Wundt, with prophetic accuracy, called Cattell's interest *ganz amerikanisch* (typically American); it has indeed turned out to be America's armies, schools, and industries that have placed great emphasis on the testing of individuals for most efficient placement.

It would be interesting to trace the beginnings of psychology further than this passing glance allows, but our present purpose is simply to place the field of psychology in some kind of perspective relative to its history and role in modern science. Therefore, we now turn to an examination of the subject matter of psychology as it appears from a modern viewpoint. This will give us a basis for comparing what we now know to be the subject matter of our field with the more limited views of the proper subject matter of psychology usually adhered to by the members of various of psychology's older schools. We shall also see later how the emergence of each new school tended to add breadth to the prior conceptions of the subject matter of psychology.

Modern psychology's subject matter. There is no way to define the subject matter of psychology so that the definition will please all psychologists. Any definition turns out either too exclusive to be useful or too general to be meaningful. Yet some approximate lines of demarcation may be sketched in.

First, there is practically universal agreement that psychology studies, in one way or another, the behavior of organisms. Many definitions of psychology further stipulate that the behavior be emitted by an intact organism or that the behavior be studied in terms of large, molar, units. With this latter restriction, the swinging of a bat would be considered an appropriate unit for psychological study, while the flexion of the left arm would not. Others might exclude the smaller, molecular, units on the ground that there was no purposefulness in such responses, although this criticism is now less frequently heard. In fact, neither the restriction to intact organisms nor the restriction to molar units seems justified in terms of what psychologists are now actually studying. Although it is true that most studies are concerned with large units of behavior, some theorists (e.g., Guthrie, 1952) believe that the most effective conceptualization and experimentation will be in terms of more elementary units of behavior, such as flexions of individual muscles. No one denies that these men are psychologists. Therefore it seems meaningless to deny that what they are studying is psychology; we should agree with Bergmann and Spence (1944) that the choice of units of study is a matter of convenience.

Similarly, we see no reason to stipulate that psychology, by definition, can study only intact organisms. That stipulation would exclude from psychology much interesting experimentation, for example, that on brain-damaged monkeys (Harlow et al., 1952). The line between intact and nonintact organisms would have to be carefully drawn; recent work on the effects of electrical and chemical stimulation of tiny areas of the brain (Olds, 1955; Miller, 1958) would have to be brought before the court for a ruling on whether the damage done was sufficient to disqualify the organism from intactness. There is no point in such quibbling. Let the man who calls himself a psychologist study whatever he pleases; we can best discover what psychology is by seeing what he studies.

Science, and psychology as a part of it, studies relationships. What, then, does psychology study in relation to responses? The answer seems to be: nearly everything that *can* be related. Stimulus-response (S-R) psychology has today become so popular that it almost obliterates the fact that many of the relationships studied by psychologists are relationships between responses made at two different times; for example, the responses made on an intelligence test, or rather the numbers assigned thereto, may be related to any of a number of other response-determined numbers assigned in a scholastic or industrial situation. This is an important part of psychology. The stimulus-response relationships are also important; historically, these became an object of study very early. Bessel became interested in the time relationships between stimulus and response and initiated the reaction-time experiments; Helmholtz, with his interest in the relationship between the stimulating situation and the contents of perception, was actually studying a functional relationship between stimulus and verbal response. Thus it hardly seems necessary to reiterate the importance of such laws relating stimulus and response.

There are, in addition, many experiments relating antecedents to behavior where the antecedents are neither stimuli nor responses. These antecedents may usually be characterized as *state variables* (see Skinner, 1938); for example, we may change the state of an organism by injecting certain drugs, by extirpating part of the brain, by administering electroshock, or by starving the organism. We might study individual differences in behavior; this would mean a study of the effects of different initial conditions of unknown nature and perhaps origin upon behavior. We might, of course, enlarge the conception of stimulus to include all these instances of antecedents, but this would simply make "stimulus" equivalent to "any antecedent condition that we do not call a response." We may as well preserve the orthodox general definition of a stimulus as a physical energy impinging upon a receptor and note that the above-mentioned state variables do not exclusively affect receptors.

A rough initial definition of psychology, then, might be: "Psychology is the science which studies the relationships between antecedent events or conditions and consequent behavior of organisms." This is admittedly a broad definition, but psychology has become a broad field. A narrower definition might more cleanly excise psychology from the rest of the body of science, but we feel that it should not be so excised. Just as the physiologists initially found themselves studying psychological problems, so the psychologist finds himself studying physiology in order to understand psychology better. Some of the first psychological studies were psychophysical; modern psychologists still find themselves making physical measurements in describing stimuli, so some overlap with physics remains. Certainly the overlaps on the other end of the scale, with sociology and anthropology, are equally striking and equally important. Psychologists do not seem to have restricted their interests to any clearly defined field, and it will hardly advance psychology (or any other science) to be prescriptive and say, "As a psychologist you shall study only ————." The early systems of psychology would have served their purpose better had they been less prescriptive of its subject matter.

Not much more can be said about the definition of psychology's subject matter. Instances of studies undertaken by psychologists could be multiplied indefinitely. Their scope is awesome, ranging from pure to applied, from physiological to sociological, from experimental to clinical, and from the five-hour to the fifty-year observation time. These activities include fitting simple mathematical models to learning curves for white rats, fitting space-suit requirements to astronauts, determining the effects of radiation on behavior, studying the response of single neurons to controlled stimulation, studying the cultural impact of racial integration, and specifying the roles to be played by men and by computers in very complex industrial and military systems. These are just a few of the diverse areas which fall within the boundary of psychology's subject matter. Today's psychology refuses to be bound by any systematic prescription to a narrow subject matter.

PSYCHOLOGY AND A HIERARCHY OF SCIENCE

A hierarchy of science is diagramed in Table 3. The major scientific fields are ordered in terms of their dependence upon those below them in the table: the things taken as elements at one level of the table may be themselves explained in terms of variables at a lower, that is, a more basic, level. For example, a biologist may take the behavior of single cells as the explanation of more molar phenomena, while the cell's internal function may be explained in chemical and physical terms by referring to the variables studied at the next lower level; the psychologist may stop his analysis with a reflex which is itself explained in terms of physiological variables.

The so-called "tool" sciences are placed at the base of the hierarchy. Mathematics and logic are shown separately, although the former may be subsumed under the latter, broadly conceived. Neither mathematics nor logic has any *empirical* content of its own, but each may serve all the empirical sciences. Each does, of course, have its own subject matter and problems, which are investigated intensively by mathematicians and logicians and often utilize content borrowed from the various empirical sciences.

The most fundamental natural sciences, physics and chemistry, are placed immediately above the tool sciences, since they deal with the basic structure of nature.

Table 3   A hierarchy of science and scientific occupations

SCIENTIFIC FIELD	PRACTITIONERS	TECHNICIANS
Social: Political science	City manager	
Economics	Certified public accountant	Bookkeeper
Sociology	Social worker	
	Probation officer	Police officer
Behavior: Social psychology Psychology	Clinical psychologist	Psychometrist
	Counselor	Interviewer
Biological: Physiology	Physician, surgeon	Nurse, medical technician
Embryology		
Genetics		
Zoology	Veterinarian	
Botany	Horticulturist	
Biophysics		
Biochemistry		Pharmacist
Physical: Astronomy	Navigator	Sailor
Geology		
Chemistry	Engineer	Draftsman
Physics		
Physical chemistry		
Tool: Mathematics	Statistician	Comptometer or calculator operator
Logic	Programmer (computer)	

Biological sciences are shown next, at a higher level of organization; they deal with the structure and function of a special kind of physical material—that composing plants and animals.

Behavior science, with psychology here included as the major example, is interpolated immediately between the biological sciences and the social sciences. These disciplines all deal with living organisms in varying degrees of relationship—and hence complexity. If psychology has its feet planted in biology, its upper regions clearly extend into the more complex realm of social science. The extent to which the various major social sciences are accepted as science varies, but they are shown here in increasing order of complexity. The best rule of thumb is to include them to the extent that they have demonstrated their ability to apply the fundamental method of science. Scientific techniques may change to some extent with the progress of science, and the latitude within which a study may remain a science is a matter for individual preference to decide.

The only adequate way in which a given field, or subject matter, of science can be differentiated is in terms of the kinds of variables that are treated. In this respect it is the dependent variables, the particular aspects of the phenomena which are measured, rather than the independent variables, that differentiate fields of study. This kind of distinction underlies the hierarchic arrangement shown in Table 3. Interdisciplinary fields, such as biochemistry, biophysics, and social psychology, are indicated in the hierarchy to call attention to the fact that the old boundaries of fields are quite arbitrary, often having been fixed by historical accident, and do not represent immutable lines of cleavage. Some of the most interesting and important research is being done in the interdisciplinary fields. As research progresses in any interdisciplinary field, the new field becomes established and is increasingly recognized as a subject matter, or discipline, in its own right (e.g., biochemistry, biophysics). This process of increased differentiation, or cleavage, is one mark of *maturity in science.*

As an adjunct to this arrangement of sciences, the most closely related fields of application of some of the sciences are shown at the right of the diagram. These are placed under the rubric "practice," and the personnel involved in their pursuit are called "practitioners" (a term which has most often been associated with the medical field). These persons are not, in any strict sense, scientists. They are *not* applied scientists, although that term might seem logically to apply to them. They are the *users* of scientific knowledge and technological developments. There is no reason why they cannot also be engaged in scientific work; to the extent that they are so engaged, they are scientists. That would imply that they are actively engaged in attempting to discover, through scientific methods, new knowledge, since this is the distinguishing characteristic of the scientist.

Generally at a somewhat lower level of training and competence are the various technicians. Theirs is a more circumscribed service. They do not, as technicians, make diagnoses or prescribe treatments but instead provide important technical information and service to the practitioner. The medical laboratory technician and the psychometrician are familiar representatives. Other examples listed are less clear-cut, since many of the jobs at the technician level may be filled by persons without real technical training and since it is difficult to classify certain occupations. For example, is a pharmacist a practitioner or a technician? This debatable point accounts for the gaps in the technician column of Table 3. There is no reason why such technicians cannot also be practitioners or even scientists. But they are handicapped in this regard by the specialized nature of their professional training as compared with the more extended training of scientists and practitioners. The heavy service requirements demanded by their conditions of employment limit the time they can devote to other pursuits. This is also an important factor often limiting clinical psychologists in their stated purpose of doing scientific research.

In considering the three types of professional activities outlined here, it is necessary for the reader to remember that the distinctions are often blurred in real life; that is, not only may a given individual serve in more than one role at the same time, as suggested above, but also he may shift from one role to another as his training progresses or his job changes.

Blurring of the distinction between scientist and practitioner has been most pronounced within recent years in the various engineering fields, as physicists and engineers have rubbed elbows in all sorts of enterprises in new areas, such as the development of nuclear energy.

Nevertheless, most individuals can be clearly placed in a single category, and in any case this occupational differentiation is meaningful in terms of an understanding of the various occupational roles involved in scientific work.

A fourth type of professional person, less closely connected with the academic world than the others, is the inventor. His main objective is the development of new kinds of gadgets and devices. In this respect, he may be considered a special kind of engineer. He may also have scientific interests and make important scientific discoveries, but these will be independent of, although perhaps sometimes encouraged by, his role as an inventor.

PURE AND APPLIED SCIENCE

In actual practice, a firm line cannot be drawn between *pure* and *applied* scientists. The only way they can be separated is in terms of their motivation, and this is a tricky problem, as students of psychology should know. Nevertheless, a rough but basic distinction can be made. Pure scientists are persons who are primarily concerned with the discovery of new facts and the development of theories without immediate regard for the utility of such knowledge. Applied scientists are persons who have the same primary objective but who are immediately concerned with the application of such knowledge. There does tend to be some difference in the kinds of problems with which each type of scientist works, but no hard and fast distinctions are possible. The applied scientist chooses for investigation variables and relationships that appear immediately relevant to some practical problem.

Many apparently applied scientists have made major contributions to basic knowledge. For example, Pasteur's primary interest was in the production of vaccines, but he was also instrumental in the development of the germ theory of disease. On the other hand, many apparently pure scientists have discovered facts and produced theories which have then been more or less directly applied to practical problems. The most recent and spectacular example of this is the contribution of the host of mathematical physicists whose work in one way or another was utilized in the development of atomic energy. This example of collaboration between the scientific and the engineering professions is characteristic of many less striking cases and illustrates the fact that the ultimate utility of new knowledge cannot be readily predicted in advance (Bronk, 1954).

SPECIAL PROBLEMS RELATED TO THE SUBJECT MATTER OF PSYCHOLOGY

Controls. We have emphasized the fact that control is essential to the development of science. Only through appropriate measures can we be sure of the relationships among variables that we hypothesize. Fundamentally, psychology is no different from any other science in its need for control. It *is* different in its ability to impose the necessary controls, especially when the object of our curiosity is human behavior. For example, we may wonder whether form perception in the human being is highly dependent on early experience with the visual world. In order to do this, we need a supply of human infants who can be deprived of all visual stimulation for varying periods of their early life. Where is our supply of such infants? Our value system does not condone treatment of this kind. We may wonder whether social isolation in childhood is really conducive to the development of schizophrenia; we have the same problem of unavailability of subjects. We may wish to study the effects of mating individuals with certain characteristics on the behavior patterns of the offspring; but who will engage in this carefully controlled mating? Examples could be multiplied indefinitely. There are limits to the manipulations we can perform with human subjects. It is true that if we wait long enough the events we desire may happen by chance, or we can piece together isolated cases that represent something of the kind of treatment we need; but the progress of science is slowed when it must wait for the desired events to occur. Psychology and astronomy are in similar positions in this regard; the astronomer must wait, for example, until Mars comes close to Earth before he can make the most useful observations.

It is largely this limitation which has turned many psychologists to the study of animals. The limitations of control with animals are much less severe, so the psychologist need not wait for the chance occurrence of the situation he wishes to observe.

Quantification. Mathematics is a specialized language. It is closely related to logic: both are abstract, both are somewhat remote from the language of everyday life, and the grammar of logic and mathematics is restricted and precise. These characteristics have made specialized symbolic systems useful for the well-established sciences, especially physics and chemistry. However, both are *only* symbolic systems, and no magic inheres in either. They are abstract systems which are empirically empty and are thus testable only when given some empirical content. The usefulness of such systems depends on the fact that empirical predictions are made on the basis of logical deductions; these predictions then hold within the empirical relationships to which the appropriate mathematics has been coordinated through precise definitions.

Different types of mathematics are useful for different problems even within physics; for example, the complex number system is useful for problems in electric circuitry, and non-Euclidian geometry is useful for relativity theory. An inappropriate type of mathematics would only lead to confusion in any given case. The only way one can discover whether a given mathematics or logic or geometry is useful for treating a given empirical system is to set up the appropriate definitions relating the symbolic system to the empirical system and see whether the predictions made on the basis of the permissible deductions within the symbolic system lead to empirical sense or empirical nonsense.

Psychology has not yet been so successful as the older sciences in its attempt to apply mathematical treatment to its problems. However, a recent book on mathematical developments in psychology (Luce, 1960) indicates the strong efforts being put forth and the progress being made in this direction.

Before we can use mathematics, we must establish the required relations between the empirical object of study and the mathematics we wish to use. We call this process *quantification* when we are using the ordinary mathematics of real numbers; a more general word for the establishment of the required relationship to the elements of any mathematical system is *scaling*. Stevens (1951), among others, has discussed the different types of scaling. Psychology, in nearly all cases, has had to be content with coordinating its subject matter with weaker kinds of systems than the mathematics of real numbers; but the bulk of our subject matter is treated only with the language of the everyday world, and probabilities are assessed with statistics that may or may not be appropriate.

The subject matter of psychology may not lend itself to traditional measurement and traditional mathematics. Some different symbolic systems may be necessary. It is too early in the history of our science to know the answers to these questions. Weitzenhoffer (1951) has suggested that psychologists persist in their attempts to measure in the traditional fashion; Reese (1943) has suggested that we go ahead and use mathematics as though we were justified in doing so, being always careful to remember just what our measurements mean, assigning them no meaning beyond the operations performed.

In view of this rather confused state of affairs, we cannot say for sure that quantification is unusually difficult for psychology or more difficult than for the other sciences; at the present stage, it *seems* more difficult. Certainly more psychologists need more sophistication in handling mathematics and logic so that they can use or develop appropriate systems, appropriate coordinations of existing systems to psychological problems, or both. Many psychologists must concern themselves with the development of deductive systems before psychology will be a finished science. We cannot say whether enough empirical data are available to make extensive attempts of this kind feasible at present.

Some have argued against the desirability of quantification. These critics say that quantification may interfere with the meaningfulness of the phenomenon in question. Others argue that the attempt to quantify is an instance of the tail wagging the dog, of the method unnecessarily restricting the problem. They argue that quantification can succeed only if the problem dealt with is so restricted as to lose all significance. None of these arguments can be positively refuted, but the usefulness of quantification in the other sciences argues against their premature acceptance.

Quantification has two advantages: mathematical statements are precise and clear, and the richness of deductive possibilities is greatly increased when dimensions are quantified. With regard to the first point, we know that the prediction of outcomes must be sufficiently clear and precise so that all outcomes are not predicted, and mathematical statement makes it clear which outcome must be predicted. On the second point, Hull et al. (1947) exemplify psychologists who feel that the advantages in richness compensate for the great deal of time and effort expended in quantifying. Consider the relative deductive possibilities that would come from two alternative kinds of statements, one quantified and the other not.

The first kind of statement that Hull and his coauthors could have made is just that reaction potential increases as habit strength and drive increase. In symbolic form, we might say that $_sE_R = f(_sH_R, D)$.

Here the nature of the function, f, is not specified except that it is an increasing function. With this type of statement, we cannot predict the amount of increase of $_sE_R$ with increases in $_sH_R$ and D. The direction of change of $_sE_R$ cannot be predicted if one of the independent variables increases and the other decreases.

The second type of statement is based on quantification of each of the three variables involved and exact specification of the type of relationship between the three variables. The resulting statement might be $_sE_R = {_sH_R} \times D$. Given this simple multiplicative relationship, we can make an infinite number of *exact* predictions of the value of $_sE_R$! This is what we mean by richness of deductive possibilities (see also Chapter 10).

Subjectivism.   Psychology involves the study of living organisms, often people. It seems to be more difficult to achieve the unbiased scientific attitude toward this subject matter than toward any other. The medical student studying anatomy doubtless has certain qualms when he pulls his first cadaver out of the formaldehyde, and part of the qualm doubtless comes from the realization that the object of his investigation and dissection bears a marked similarity to himself. Psychology has had some difficulties on the same score; as the analysts would say, there have been resistances to the acceptance of certain ideas, among them the basic one that man's behavior can be studied scientifically.

Beyond this, the psychologist himself has difficulty in achieving objectivity toward his field. Since psychologists are people, they have a tendency to anthropomorphize; the objects of psychological study seem especially receptive objects for the projection of our own ideas, even though sober evidence may be lacking. The call of common sense, too, is particularly strident when we feel that we understand humankind to some extent simply by virtue of being human. Yet the facts may be exactly otherwise; we might achieve undreamed-of insights were we but Martians studying man in the cool light of an Earth day.

Complexity.   There are certain senses in which the subject matter of psychology seems to be more complex than that of many sciences. From a reductionistic point of view, for example, one would have to understand much of chemistry in order to understand the nature of nerve transmission, which one would have to understand before one could completely understand behavior. However, the biologist might argue that his field is equally complex on this score, and the sociologist might argue that his field is even more complex, since an understanding of individuals would presumably be necessary for social behavior to be understood.

Another, and perhaps more fundamental, way in which complexity can be defined is in terms of the number of interacting variables that are effective in determination of some consequence. Certainly behavior appears to be influenced by a large number of such variables. But the same thing can be said of many other sciences, and how many important variables operate in behavior determination remains to be discovered.

Thus, the common argument that the subject matter of psychology is more complex than that of the other sciences does not rest on perfectly firm ground. Nonetheless, psychologists agree that the subject matter is sufficiently complex for them, in many instances downright confusing. Perhaps another hundred years of study will give a better indication of relative complexity; in our present state of ignorance, the argument that many of psychology's difficulties can be explained in this way is appealing.

Our general thesis throughout has been that the criteria that apply to science in general also apply to psychology. The discussion of problems that seem to be accentuated because of the nature of the subject matter is not to be construed as meaning that psychology is in any way apart from science. It follows that psychology shares the general problems and will find its special solutions as the other sciences have done. Perhaps the only problem which cannot be circumvented is that science can advance only through work, and work takes time. Psychology has not existed long enough to solve its problems. The weaknesses that we shall see in its systems exist partially for that reason.

SUMMARY AND CONCLUSIONS

This chapter has examined the emergence of psychology from science. Several scientific ideas had to develop within science before this emergence could occur. These were that explanation of events should be sought within the same system as the one within which the events occurred, that observation is the arbiter of scientific truth, that man is a part of the natural order, and hence that his behavior can be studied scientifically to determine the laws governing behavior.

Certain problems were willed to psychology because of the immediate prehistory within science and philosophy. There were the problems of relating the dual aspects of man, of explaining the physiology of perception and contents of perception, of determining the basis and description of the personal equation, and of studying individual differences and heredity. The effects of these problems upon experimental psychology as it was conceived by its founder, Wilhelm Wundt, have been examined summarily.

The subject matter of modern psychology has been defined broadly. The intensification of certain scientific problems because of the nature of the subject matter has been pointed out: the difficulty of controlling conditions is enhanced; the problem of quantification is rendered more difficult; the subject matter disposes the psychologist toward subjectivism; and the subject matter is complex. These problems are not unique to psychology but are exaggerated there.

further readings

For the general historical background of psychology, the student can consult Boring's A history of experimental psychology (1950) or Murphy's *Histori-cal introduction to modern psychology* (1949). The four volumes of auto-biographical material edited by Murchison (Volumes I to III: 1930, 1932, 1936) and by Boring et al. (Volume IV, 1952) are extremely valuable in providing insight into some of the personal factors, ordinarily out of sight or in the background, in the careers of many historically important men in the field. Dennis's *Readings in the history of psychology* (1948) provides selected classics ranging from Aristotle (ca. 330 B.C.) to Hull (A.D. 1930) for the student who likes his history at first hand. For a general orientation to the history of science, the following classic works may be recommended: Conant's *On understanding science: A historical approach* (1947) and *Harvard case histories in experimental science* (1957); Butterfield's *The origins of modern science: 1300–1800* (1957); and Sarton's A *guide to the history of science* (1952). A variety of works in the philosophy of science is available for the reader who wants to delve into this area. Particularly relevant to the mind-body issue is *Concepts, theories, and the mind-body problem,* edited by Feigl, Scriven, and Maxwell (1958) and published as Volume II in the *Minnesota studies in the philosophy of science.* Volume I in that series, edited by Feigl and Scriven (1956) and titled *The founda-tions of science and the concepts of psychology and psychoanalysis,* also contains many informative papers. Feigl and Maxwell's *Current issues in the philosophy of science* (1961) contains papers and rebuttals read at symposia in the 1959 meetings of the American Association for the Advance-ment of Science. Several books of readings in this field are available: for example, Danto and Morgenbesser's *Philosophy of science: A reader* (1960); Wiener's *Readings in philosophy of science* (1953); Feigl and Sellars's *Readings in philosophical analysis* (1949); and Feigl and Brodbeck's *Readings in the philosophy of science* (1953). For the student in a quandary about quantification, Reese's little-known article (1943) should be useful. And for a student who has sufficient nerve and desire, Koch's introduction to Volume I of *Psychology: A study of a science* (1959) may be recommended.

systems and theories ⟨3⟩

A sophisticated evaluation and criticism of psychological systems and theories depends upon some knowledge of the general nature of and requirements for system and theory. Several key terms must be understood if one is to talk intelligibly on these issues. The present chapter proceeds from the definition of these terms to a brief discussion of systematic and theoretical problems and requirements.

DEFINITIONS OF BASIC TERMS

Primitive term.   A primitive term is a term which is not defined by its relationship to any more basic term within a theory. Therefore, its definition must be external to the system of which it is a part. A primitive term may be defined by pointing to some observable operation, event, or object; it may be defined in words that are not part of the system; or it may simply be left undefined. In mathematics, words or symbols like "element" or "greater than" or "successor" are primitive. In Hull's (1952) system, a postulate gives a functional relationship between habit strength ($_sH_R$) and number of reinforced trials (N). The equation is $_sH_R = 1 - 10^{-a}N$. Since $_sH_R$ is the dependent variable in this equation, we may regard it as defined in terms of N. In this postulate, N would function as the primitive term. Extensive examination of the theory might reveal that N is defined by recourse to other theoretical terms (for example, reinforcement, stimulus, and response) and hence is not a primitive term after all.

The over-all point is that the determination of which terms of a theory are primitive requires a careful examination of the whole theory. Many theories are unclear in their structure, and it is therefore very difficult to determine which terms are primitive and which are not. Only when the structure of a theory is set forth clearly and completely is it possible to determine with ease the terms and relations involved in the theory. Psychoanalytic theory has been pointed out as a particularly important instance of a theory which is not sufficiently clear from a logical point of view for this kind of analysis.

The fact that an abstract system has primitive terms makes possible its coordination with an outside, empirical system. The abstract primitive terms are given an empirical interpretation and are then empirically meaningful. If the relations within the theory are appropriate, then manipulations within the abstract system will result in further empirically meaningful and accurate statements.

Construct.   A construct is a special kind of concept. It is not a simple concept, like "man" or "house" or "boat"; these concepts are applied on the basis of those common, point-at-able properties shared by the members of the class to which the concept is applied. Rather, a construct represents *relationships* among objects or events. Common psychological constructs such as "anxiety," "fear," and "habit" are in this respect similar to more generally used constructs like "patriotism," "school spirit," and "justice." All these refer not merely to objects or to events that are relatively straightforward actions of objects, but to some kind of relations among objects, that is, to a relatively complex kind of event. Thus, responses alone are insufficient to define the concept of fear or habit; some reference to the stimulus situation as well as to the response situation must be given. In defining habit, we must know the probability of a certain response to a given stimulus situation, not just that a response has occurred. Similarly, patriotism refers to a response to a specified class of stimuli, not just to the responses made, which may be common to many situations not necessarily involving patriotism.

Constructs are useful in summarizing relationships succinctly, and they may also be helpful in generalizing from some sets of observed relationships to other, as yet unobserved sets. However, many difficulties in psychology stem from a failure to define constructs unambiguously. The development of simpler and more empirically meaningful constructs is an important objective of contemporary psychology. This is the area in which the simple basic proposition of the operationist—that we make clear the empirical referents of our complex terms—has the most to offer.

Postulate.   This term has two major usages. First, it is used to refer to a fundamental assumption which is not to be directly or intentionally tested. The assumption may be essential to the pursuit of science. An example of this type is the assumption that the phenomena under investigation are consistently orderly and that the order is discoverable by man. The assumption may be of more restricted importance, as in the case of the early behavioristic assumption that all behavior can be analyzed into stimulus-response relationships. It is generally held that such assumptions, which are often on a philosophical level, should be as few, simple, and carefully set forth as possible.

In its second usage, a postulate is a theoretical proposition. A set of these propositions is used within a given logical framework to yield further propositions implied by the original set. The further propositions (theorems) derived will depend upon the rules for deduction as well as upon the original statements. Within mathematics or logic, theorems are true by definition, given the original statements and the rules for deduction. Within science, theorems must at some stage make statements about empirical observations if they are to have any scientific utility. The postulates are thus tested indirectly by observing the concurrence or lack of it between theorems and observations. The best example of an extensive and highly formalized set of postulates within psychology is afforded by the work of Hull (Hull et al., 1940; Hull, 1943, 1951, 1952), which is described in Chapter 10.

Hypothesis. The hypothesis is a guess about the explanation of some natural phenomenon. Its elaboration may take many forms. One important dimension along which hypotheses vary is their degree of specificity. The most specific hypotheses apply to a particular situation. The best example is the *experimental hypothesis,* which is the particular prediction that is made about the outcome of the experiment. Such particular hypotheses may come from more general theoretical frameworks or from sets of more general, but not well-established, hypotheses.

In one form or another, the hypothesis plays a central role in the advance of science. Two different types of hypotheses with quite different roles should be carefully distinguished. These are what we will call *public* and *private hypotheses.* Public hypotheses are those that have been formally explicated and publicly advanced, usually in published form. Private hypotheses are those that have been entertained by some investigator or thinker but have not been publicly expressed.

Although it is the public, or formally explicated, hypothesis that receives most of our attention, a little reflection quickly reveals the more pervasive nature of the private hypothesis. For every public hypothesis there are uncounted numbers of private hypotheses. In scientific thinking these undergo almost constant revision, and the point at which they are made public varies with the investigator and many situational factors. Charles Darwin, for example, was working on his private hypotheses about the theory of evolution for more than twenty years before the appearance of a competitive manuscript containing the same basic idea stimulated him to make the hypotheses public.

The source of hypotheses—and why some persons are so much better than others at producing them—is a fascinating problem. Little progress has been made to date toward its solution. About all we can say is that as a person becomes more and more thoroughly immersed in his subject matter, he tends to develop more and better ideas. More specific rules of thumb for developing effective scientific ideas await future investigations.

The public hypothesis also has a most important function. We may think of the mass of all scientific hypotheses as like an iceberg. It is only the top one-tenth (or much less) of the total thought that is open to the criticism and empirical attack of the scientific public. Publication of a hypothesis invites such attack, and it is only through such attack that effective scientific evaluation can be made. Unfortunately, the necessity for publicizing their hypotheses in this way is not always recognized by psychologists. Public formalization of a hypothesis for empirical attack does not require the investigator to stop thinking and revising his hypotheses, but it is a necessary step if the product of his thinking is to be tested by others.

Law. A scientific law is generally held to be a well-established empirical relationship; for example, water freezes at 32°F. Laws constitute the anchorage points for theories and sometimes the backbone of the theory itself. Laws are generalizations of an empirical sort that have the greatest degree of factualness. The science of physics has developed a large number of lawful relationships. Many observers believe that psychology must develop a larger number of such laws than it now has before it can develop effective theory.

The term law is also used to refer to an especially well-established theoretical proposition. The proposition becomes well established because it successfully plays its part in the derivation of predictions which are empirically tested. It is often hard to draw the line between the two kinds of usage of the word law. The step from the concrete observation to its verbal statement always involves some degree of abstraction. There is thus no purely empirical law in the strictest sense of the word. On the other hand, the most abstract proposition may rest on some kind of informal observation of nature by the proponent of the proposition. In spite of this difficulty of making the distinction, we should recognize the dimensions of abstractness and of generality when speaking of scientific laws.

THE NATURE OF SYSTEMS

Part II of this book consists of examples of psychological systems. The present section gives some of the general characteristics of systems. Psychological systems are closely related to those of philosophy. One important similarity is that both philosophers and psychological systematists tend to give great scope to their systems; a system is thus a set of very general statements. McGeoch's definition of a system affords a starting point for understanding what a system attempts to be (1933,

p. 2): "By the term 'psychological system' is implied a coherent and inclusive, yet flexible, organization and interpretation of the facts and special theories of the subject."

This definition makes it clear that a system is a large order. It is inclusive and organizes theories, which themselves possess generality. The definition leaves a good deal of room for ambiguity, for words like coherent, flexible, organization, and interpretation come from the lay language and are not clearly defined from a logical or mathematical point of view. These words seem rather to be an attempt to put a high value on systems, to make them seem desirable.

According to McGeoch, we cannot have systems until we have facts and theories, since systems are organizations of these prior elements. We have few real theories in psychology, in the strict sense of the terms; most psychological theories are better viewed as programs or at best as informal theories. One can thus question whether psychology has ever had a system in McGeoch's sense of that word. But certainly there have been plenty of systems of some kind.

Heidbreder said of the same problem, at about the same time McGeoch was writing (1933, p. 3): "Psychology, especially in the United States, has risked everything on being science; and science on principle refrains from speculation that is not permeated and stabilized by fact. Yet there is not enough fact in the whole science of psychology to make a single solid system."

Heidbreder's comments are still applicable today if we mean by system what McGeoch meant: some inclusive framework which serves as a general theory of the subject. In fact, most psychologists would agree that there is not yet enough fact to build one completely solid limited *theory*. Therefore, one cannot even yet have a psychological system which contains within itself the means for making accurate and general predictions about the interrelationships between the variables involved within the subject matter.

What, then, was the function of the systems that did exist? If they did not have the facts that Heidbreder said science requires or the predictive power implied by McGeoch's definition, what power did they have? Heidbreder (1933, p. 9) felt that they had a sort of comforting power: they served in place of knowledge in the absence of real knowledge. We should put it in a somewhat different way. A theory, or a *finished* system of the kind McGeoch described, would tell a scientist or a layman what to expect as a result of any given manipulation of the subject matter of psychology; it would provide for the prediction, and perhaps for the manipulation, of the events within the scope of the system. But there is a time in the development of any science when the information for such prediction and manipulation is simply not available. The chief problem then is to *direct the scientist in his study of the subject matter* so that his efforts will be most efficiently used to further knowledge. When this is the state of affairs, a system for directing his efforts tends to appear. Thus, one aspect of the philosophy of science is an attempt to describe the scientific process as it is and ought to be and thereby to direct scientists in general in what they should do; a system of psychology partially does the same thing, except that it is concerned with psychologists rather than with scientists in general. Such systems contain statements about what the subject matter in question is or ought to be. They tell the psychologist what problems ought to be studied, by providing a purpose for the scientist. They tell him how he ought to go about studying the suggested problems. These directive statements, however, are not couched in a form which makes their functions obvious. They are not directed to the scientist in the form of orders; yet his behavior is influenced by them.

We can make this last point by rephrasing some of the key contentions of some of psychology's systems in a form which makes their influence more obvious. *Structuralism:* You ought as psychologists to study the contents of consciousness through the method of introspection. *Behaviorism:* You ought to study stimulus-response connections through strictly objective methods. *Gestalt psychology:* You can arrive at useful formulations only through the consideration of large units of both stimulus and response; you should study configurations or fields. *Functionalism:* Prime concerns of psychology should be study of the function of behavior in adapting to the environment and formulation of mathematical functions relating behavior to antecedent variables.

Systems that direct the scientific behavior of their proponents are important. They help to determine what facts and theories will be discovered or invented. After some empirical work has been done under the banner of such a system, the empirical and theoretical findings in the problem area tend to become stirred into the system, so that the system as we find it at any given time is a mixture of a directing system for the scientist and the preliminary findings that have been made. A word which applies roughly to the directive or superordinate aspects of a system is *metatheory*. A metatheory in general is a set of methodological considerations used in constructing a theory; it is, so to speak, a theory about theory. A metatheory differs from a psychological system in being more frequently self-conscious about its function and more highly formalized.

CRITERIA FOR SYSTEMS

McGeoch (1933) presented six criteria which he felt should be met by a system of psychology. Table 4 is adapted from McGeoch's criteria.

The criteria are consistent with our contention that the systems of psychology served chiefly to direct the behavior of psychologists in their pursuit of scientific knowledge about psychology. Why should McGeoch require a system to provide a definition of the field? Because the definition functions to tell psychologists what to study. The postulates McGeoch is talking about also have at times a directive function. McGeoch's postulates are not the type from which theorems in the formal sense are derived; they are the underlying assumptions that direct or justify the behavior of the man who accepts them. The nature of the data to be studied must be specified sufficiently clearly to direct scientific investigation. Requirements IV to VI specify problems that McGeoch felt must be dealt with. To meet the last two requirements—principles of organization, connection, and selection—the system would have to consist of at least some empirical information, unless the principles were based completely on rational guesses.

Table 4   McGeoch's criteria for a system*

   I. The system must contain a definition of the field of psychology
  II. The system must make its postulates explicit
     A. Postulates should be as few as possible
     B. The postulates should be necessary
     C. The postulates should contain little of the finished system
 III. The nature of the data to be studied must be specified
     A. Objective-subjective
     B. Qualitative-quantitative
     C. Units of description
     D. Provide genetic starting point
 IV. A mind-body position must be taken
  V. The organization of the data, its principles of connection, must be accounted for
 VI. Principles of selection must be given

---

* Adapted from McGeoch (1933).

    The modern attitude toward several of these requirements differs from McGeoch's. Most modern psychologists would feel that a definition is not important. If a theory can be developed that makes adequate predictions about any area of behavior science, whether or not the theory is restricted to "psychology" as someone defines it is not too important. Modern psychologists like to feel free to attack any promising problem, free of the shackles of definition.

    McGeoch's requirements for postulates, if applied to *formal* postulates, are certainly reasonable. However, they may not be so important if intended to apply to the informal assumptions or hypotheses which were developed—and may be discarded—in connection with the development of the formal postulates.

    Psychology today uses all kinds of data. A given psychologist uses whatever data are helpful in attacking a problem. While we like to feel that our data are objective, the distinction between objective and subjective is difficult to make. We require that our data be of a kind that can be gathered again by any investigator who wishes to check the validity of our results. Beyond this, we can say little. Units of description are chosen for the sake of convenience, and if the data cannot be quantitative, qualitative data are used.

McGeoch himself said of the mind-body position (1933, p. 8): "The problem need not, of course, be stated in traditional metaphysical fashion. . . . The point is that the problem is there and must be treated (or avoided) somehow if an adequate system is to be constructed." He thus left open the alternative of avoiding the problem. Many psychologists today choose this alternative and would argue that the problem is *not* there until someone poses it and that it is not a useful problem to pose, at least at present. We shall discuss these issues at greater length when we consider the attack of the behaviorists on consciousness.

The last two requirements are still legitimate. They require for their fulfillment the statement of relevant variables and the statement of the functional relationships between them. Much of science is concerned with such statements.

These criteria provide a sample of what psychologists of three decades ago felt a system should be. The requirements are stated without great attention to detail. No attempt is made to apply them to a particular theory or system. The desired characteristics are generality and scope of attempted coverage rather than predictive power. We shall see later in the chapter a set of standards which contemporary psychologists seem to be more interested in; meanwhile, we must discuss the nature of theory, to which the newer standards apply.

THE NATURE OF THEORY

Often theory is used in contrast to practice or application. This popular usage is correct only in so far as it implies some involvement with the abstract. Some authors use theory to refer to a hypothesis that has received a considerable amount of empirical support. When theory is used in this sense, the term law is used for the most thoroughly tested and verified propositions (Warren, 1934, p. 128).

In its more general scientific usages, theory refers to some proposition from which a large number of empirical observations can be deduced. For example, Bergmann (1957, p. 31) defined a theory as a "group of laws deductively connected." If he limits the components of theory to laws, laws then refer to either of the two meanings discussed previously. Theories can certainly be built from postulates which are not well demonstrated empirically or which are incapable of empirical demonstration, or even from analogies whose parts are known not to correspond to the phenomena covered by the theory. An example of the latter would be the hydraulic analogy with electric currents. We are quite sure that there is no water in the wires, yet predictions can be made from such an analogy if the appropriate mathematics is used.

Bergmann's requirement for any theory, then, is that the key components be "deductively connected." This simply means that there must be a method of arriving at new statements from the original statements; there must be appropriate operations which result in deductive statements.

Let us construct a very limited abstract set of statements and give them deductive relationship. Consider: (1) *'* — " (2) "'" — +. These two statements will serve as the postulates in our theory. We will now have a rule which states that any symbols to the left of a — may be replaced, wherever they appear, by symbols to the right of the —; that is, we may replace *'*, where it appears, by "; we may replace "'" by +, and conversely in both cases. Now, if we begin with postulate (2), we can quickly arrive at *'*'*'* — +, a statement deduced from the two postulates and the one combination rule. So far, our statements seem appallingly meaningless and abstract; but if we let * stand for one apple, " for two apples, and + for four apples, the statements take on some empirical meaning. Let ' correspond to the usual operation "plus," and — to "equals." We now see that our theorem states that one apple plus one apple plus one apple plus one apple equals four apples, a statement derived from our postulates "one apple plus one apple equals two apples," as empirically interpreted, and "two apples plus two apples equals four apples."

If we can perform meaningful operations of substitution on the universe of empirical apples, and if the apples behave analogously with our symbols, it will turn out that the theorem is true of apples. Our little exercise, which started out as a rudimentary logic, would become a rudimentary scientific theory since it now said something about apples. If it were the best postulate set available on apples, it would no doubt be accepted as a theory about apple combinations (e.g., applesauce). It has all the necessary elements of a scientific theory; abstract formal statements, rules for manipulating these abstract statements, and definitions that relate the primitive terms of the abstract theory to the empirical world.

The abstract portions of a theory may be developed because the theorist has either of two motives: he may wish to deal with the empirical world more effectively and want an abstract system to help him do so, or he may just be playing a mathematical game and develop the system as a matter of curiosity. Euclid's geometry was probably based ultimately on problems of surveying. Most modern mathematicians deal with symbols at a very abstract level and do not much care about any possible correspondence between the mathematical system and any empirical system. There are, therefore, many extant mathematical systems available for new scientific applications if the scientist has the necessary sophistication to find them and to set up appropriate relationships between his subject matter and the mathematical system. Kurt Lewin (1936) took advantage of a relatively new mathematics (topology) in developing his psychological theory.

Scientific theories may differ in many ways. They yield deductions about different subject matters. They differ greatly in generality; Hull's theory (1952) dealt with all simple mammalian behavior, while Estes' theory (1950), as he originally proposed it, dealt only with the probability of a certain type of response. Theories differ in precision of statement: some make predictions that are at best qualitative, while at the other end of the scale are the very precise quantitative statements. Even within the same degree of quantitativeness of prediction, theories may differ as to the degree of rigor of the predictions: sometimes the argument, though involving quantitative statements, may be loose and relatively informal. In other cases, the processes of derivation and prediction may be better formalized and more rigorous logically. Theories differ in the origins of their component statements, or postulates: some theories are combinations of empirically based statements, which are verifiable or potentially verifiable; other theories are composed of statements arrived at rationally rather than empirically. No theory, whatever its qualities, is ever final, even though all the predictive statements made from it have been verified perfectly. There always remains the possibility that any given theory will be replaced by another theory which is simpler or is more general or is more consistent with other relevant theories.

On the other hand, theories are seldom discarded simply because they are too specific or even because some of the predictions made from them are wrong. Rather, they are discarded when they are replaced by something better. A theory will generally be modified and used so long as it is the only thing available within some problem area.

Model. A model is a particular subclass of theory as we have defined theory. Some authors separate them completely, but we prefer to make models a subclass of theories, since both function in the derivation of theorems and in making predictions. Boring summed up the difference between the two succinctly (1957, p. 191).

> Today we hear less about theories and more about models. What is the difference? The theory claims to be true, even though we all know that assurance about the validity of these claims varies greatly from theory to theory and from time to time for the same theory. The theory is an *as*, whereas the model is an *as-if*. The theory is indicative; the model, subjunctive. The model is a pattern to be abandoned easily at the demand of progress.

By an *as*, Boring means that the theorist expects to observe, or has observed, empirical referents for the terms of his theory. The postulates of the theory are, or can become, empirical laws. The postulates of a model are not expected to become laws. The model builder knows that his postulates are purely abstract and cannot be coordinated with the empirical observations at the postulate level. We might draw an example from psychoanalysis. Freud's thinking with regard to the id, ego, and superego was doubtless *as-if* thinking; these elements functioned in a model. Yet labeling the functions or aspects of personality in this way (drawing diagrams of them, etc.) led many to believe that these words represented actual, observable entities; that is, these people believed that Freud had a theory, not a model.

The model may be differentiated from the metatheory in terms of its closer relationship to the structure of the empirical measures and the observations. That is, the metatheory provides general guidelines for the kind of theory to be developed; the model provides more specific guidelines for the empirical research, and thereby the laws that are developed.

CRITERIA FOR THEORIES

Estes et al. (1954) presented an outline for the criticism of learning theories. In comparing this outline with McGeoch's criteria, several contrasts strike us. The questions asked in the outline are specific and logically sophisticated. They concern the ability of the theory to make predictions. There are no questions or requirements which *demand* any directive statements regarding the behavior of the investigator. There is one question about generality ("range of data for which interpretation or explanation in terms of the theory has been claimed"), but there is no implication that the range must be great. The authors' first concern seems to be with the *language* of the theory. This implies a growing recognition that much of science is verbal behavior. The outline deals with theories rather than with the more inclusive systems and thus would not be expected to parallel exactly McGeoch's discussion; however, this dealing with smaller problems is itself a significant trend in psychology. Initially, all sciences tend to present "big," general problems. These problems usually are not amenable to experimental attack until they are broken into smaller problems and perhaps rephrased completely.

Some attitudes of Estes et al. toward the evaluation of theory are given in a quotation from their discussion of the outline (1954, pp. xiv, xv):

> We believe wide agreement would obtain among current writers in the logic of science that an adequate review of any scientific theory must include essentially the same features. . . . Scientific theories are evaluated, not on some absolute scale of "theoryness," but with respect to what we expect them to do. Some of the functions of a useful theory are: (1) clarifying the description of the world possible in ordinary language, (2)

summarizing existing knowledge, (3) mediating applications of our knowledge to new situations, (4) leading to fruitful lines of experimental inquiry.

Table 5 presents the outline in full. The student should study every point very carefully, both because this table represents the kind of concern of leading contemporary psychologists and because it ties together nearly all the points made in this chapter.

TRENDS IN SYSTEMS

We can now look back on what has been said and see what has happened and is happening to systems. First, they are growing more limited and more explicit.

Theorists are no longer content with superficial statements without real predictive value; even the most sophisticated-appearing theory is subjected to careful examination and may at times be found lacking. For example, Cotton (1955) has recently shown that Hull's learning theory really is not adequate for making some predictions that it purports to be able to make. Psychologists are no longer content with comfortable generalities that allow labels to be tacked on to results after they occur; they want theories or systems to say what is *going to* happen and to say it clearly and exactly. They want theorists and systematists to be able to show exactly how they know and how they predict. It follows from these demands that any contemporary system that fulfills them must be a miniature system, covering only a very small range of behavior, perhaps only for a single kind of organism in a single simple situation. We still have too few facts to build full-scale systems.

The demand for precision leads to a growing concern for measurement and for mathematical statements. The same kinds of demands have lead increasingly to the laboratory and to carefully controlled experimentation. Many psychologists of the less tough-minded variety have objected to the increasing abstraction of the mathematical statement and the artificial environment, preferring to stick to the fuzziness of felt reality found in the statements of common sense. Skinner is one of many who have defended the position of the laboratory worker in psychology (1957a, p. 370):

> Have we been guilty of an undue simplification of conditions in order to obtain this level of rigor? Have we really "proved" that there is comparable order outside the laboratory? It is difficult to be sure of the answers to such questions. Suppose we are observing the rate at which a man sips his breakfast coffee. . . . It is unlikely that we shall record a smooth curve. . . . But although our behavioral curve will not be pretty, *neither will the cooling curve for the coffee in the cup.* In extra-

*Table 5   Outline for reviews of theories**

I. STRUCTURE OF THE THEORY

  A. Delineation of empirical area
    1. Data language
      Is the data language explicit and theoretically neutral?
      How does the theorist relate his empirical variables to the data language?
    2. Dependent and independent variables
      How does the selection of variables compare with those of other learning theories?
      What influence does the choice of variables exert upon the form of the theory?
  B. Theoretical concepts
    1. Primitive terms
      Are the primitive terms of the theory reducible to physical or object language?
      Is the usage of primitive terms fixed by implicit or explicit definitions?
    2. Principal constructs
      Do these serve only a summarizing function or are they related by definition or by hypothesis to terms of other disciplines (e.g., physiology)?
    3. Relations assumed among constructs
      How are the major theoretical variables interrelated in the foundation assumptions of the theory?
      How are such interrelations constructed from the observation base of the theory?
    4. Relations assumed or derived between constructs and experimentally defined variables

---

II. METHODOLOGIC CHARACTERISTICS

  A. Standing of the theory on principal methodologic "dimensions"
    1. Explicit axiomatization
    2. Quantitativeness
    3. Consistency and independence of principal theoretical assumptions
    4. Use of physical or mathematical models
  B. Techniques of derivation
    Are the empirical consequences of the theory developed by informal arguments or formal derivations?

---

*From Estes et al. (1954, pp. xiii, xiv).

Table 5 Outline for reviews of theories* (Continued)

III. EMPIRICAL CONTENT AND ADEQUACY

A. Range of data for which interpretation or explanation in terms of the theory has been claimed
B. Specificity of prediction demonstrated
C. Obvious failures to handle facts in the area III-A
D. Tours-de-force
Has it been possible to predict new experimental phenomena?
Have any predictions of this sort been confirmed?
Does the theory account for facts not predictable from competing theories in the same area?
E. Sensitivity to empirical evidence
F. Programmaticity
G. Special virtues or limitations: Techniques which may prove useful outside the context of the specific theory

* From Estes et al. (1954, pp. xiii, xiv).

polating our results to the world at large, we can do no more than the physical and biological sciences in general. Because of experiments performed under laboratory conditions, no one doubts that the cooling of the coffee in the cup is an orderly process, even though the actual curve would be difficult to explain. Similarly when we have investigated behavior under the advantageous conditions of the laboratory, we can accept its basic orderliness in the world at large even though we cannot there wholly demonstrate law.

There are two quite divergent contemporary tendencies, both of which are related in different ways to a demand for more rigor. On the one hand, there is a greater tendency to regard theoretical statements as "as-ifs," that is, a tendency to use models rather than theories. If the psychologist is ignorant of what physiological events correlate with his behavioral observations, rigor dictates that he should not couch his theory in physiological terms. Many psychologists simple ignore physiology on these grounds and point out that the predictive value of a model does not depend on any assumptions about the existence of components of the model. On the other hand, there are many psychologists today who feel that ignorance of physiology is deplorable. However, they generally *do not* "physiologize," that is, they do not talk about physiological explanations in the absence of physiological knowledge. Physiologizing in this sense is, we hope, disappearing from psychology.

Despite all the changes, parts of the old systems still persist in the "orientative attitudes" that we saw mentioned by some of our leading modern theorists (see Table 5). These orientative attitudes are still defended and attacked, and the struggle still generates friction, heat, and, we may hope, experimentation. Psychology's systems may be dead, but the remnants are still with us. It is a fascinating business to study their modern rearrangements and modifications. If systems are regarded chiefly as specializations of the general philosophy of science for application to a particular discipline, then some kind of system will always be found in every science.

SUMMARY AND CONCLUSIONS

A working idea of what a system is, and should be, is necessary for our later evaluation of systems. The origins of systems were largely philosophical. They may be loosely defined as organizations of facts and theories. Yet psychology's systems have not really been exemplifications of our definition; they have been less statements about the subject matter of psychology than statements about the way that subject matter ought to be approached. They have had some usefulness in motivating people to do experiments and to be cautious and critical; they have hindered by turning attention too much to big questions that at present are only answerable on the basis of rational guesses. There is a growing tendency to replace the traditional system with a more limited type of theory; to use models as well as theories; and to demand far more precision, logical development, and explicitness of the more limited statements. Yet the basic orientative attitudes of the old systems live on in modern psychology.

further readings

The two articles which were used to organize this chapter should be required reading: the introduction to Estes et al., *Modern learning theory* (1954), and McGeoch's paper, "The formal criteria of a systematic psychology" (1933). A further impression of how systematic issues have changed (or, sometimes, remained the same) can be gained from Heidbreder's old but very readable *Seven psychologies* (1933). Among the many recent contributions to the philosophy of science and the logic of scientific methodology, the following may be especially noted: Frank's *Modern science and its philosophy* (1949), Bergmann's *Philosophy of science* (1957), Popper's *The logic of scientific discovery* (1959), Braithwaite's *Scientific explanation* (1955). (See also the various compendiums cited in Chapter 2.) Also illuminating is *The language of psychology*, by Mandler and Kessen (1959). Marx's *Theories in contemporary psychology* (1963) treats a variety of issues in theory construction. Finally, the seven volumes in the series edited by Koch, *Psychology: A study of a science* (1959–   ), contain much of methodological as well as substantive interest in systematic and theoretical psychology.

Table 6 *Major figures in the formation and development of six psychological systems*

	1870	1880	1890	1900	1910	1920	1930	1940	1950	1960
STRUCTURALISM		Wundt	Titchener							
FUNCTIONALISM	James			Dewey	Angell	Carr Woodworth		McGeoch	Melton Underwood	
ASSOCIATIONISM		Ebbinghaus		Pavlov	Bekhterev	Thorndike	Guthrie		Estes	
BEHAVIORISM					Watson Meyer Weiss	Hunter Tolman	Skinner Hull	Miller Spence		
GESTALT THEORY					Wertheimer Koffka	Köhler				
		Mach	von Ehrenfels							
PSYCHOANALYSIS	Breuer	Freud		Adler Jung	Rank Jones Ferenczi	Horney	Sullivan	Fromm		

part two SYSTEMS OF PSYCHOLOGY

We turn now to consideration of the major systematic developments in the recent history of psychology. Our plan of procedure is to present a minimal account of the historical antecedents of each of the systems treated, in order to indicate their ties with the past. In each case the founding of the system, its major structural characteristics with regard to content and methodology, and its development and fate are treated. The six criteria listed by McGeoch (1933) are utilized as a framework for the exposition of each system in order to facilitate comparisons.

Table 6 shows the major figures associated with the origin and development of each of the six systems treated. These names are placed on a common time line to indicate temporal relationships.

structuralism 4

The highly developed introspective psychology that goes under the name of structuralism or existentialism is represented in its finished American form by the work of E. B. Titchener. He gave the system its name in 1898 when he pointed out its similarity to the study of structure in biology. Titchener's system was a refinement of the psychology of his mentor, Wilhelm Wundt, founder of the Leipzig laboratory. During the early years of psychology, in Germany, structural psychology was *the* psychology. Its purpose was the introspective analysis of the human mind; psychology was to be a kind of chemistry of consciousness. The primary task of the psychologist was to discover the nature of the elementary conscious experiences and, later, their relationships to each other. Introspection by a highly trained person was thought to be the necessary tool.

The major significance of structuralism has been threefold. First, it gave psychology a strong scientific impetus, getting the name psychology attached for the first time to a scientific type of endeavor with formal academic recognition and clearly separated from the two main parental fields, physiology and philosophy. Second, it provided a thorough test of the classic introspective method as the only method for a complete psychology. Third, it provided a strong orthodoxy against which the functional, behavioristic, and gestalt forces could organize their resistance. The newer schools arose from a progressive reformulation and final discarding of the basic structural problems. This fact alone makes the analytic introspective psychology of Wundt and Titchener a necessary subject for contemporary study.

ANTECEDENTS OF TITCHENER'S STRUCTURALISM

The psychology of Wundt. It is customary, at least in America, to cite Titchener as the founder of structural psychology. Certainly he

61

named it, developed it, and buttressed it against functional and behavioristic trends. However, Titchener's system was basically the same as that of Wilhelm Wundt (1832–1920), under whom Titchener had studied. Wundt himself was a self-conscious systematizer and the "father" of the new experimental psychology. He established the first formal laboratory for psychology at the University of Leipzig in 1879. We shall, however, follow American tradition and treat Wundt as a forerunner of the structuralist school, meanwhile recognizing that he was far more than a mere antecedent.

Wundt believed that psychology could and must be experimental. The subject matter was regarded as *immediate experience*, as con-- trasted with *mediate experience*. By mediate experience Wundt meant experience used as a means of knowledge about something other than the experience itself. This is the usual way in which we use experience in acquiring knowledge about the world. We say, "The *leaf* is green"; the quotation implies that our primary interest is in the leaf, not in the fact that we are experiencing green. Immediate experience for Wundt was experience per se, and the task of psychology was the study of this immediate experience in itself. If we attempt to describe the experience we have in connection with a toothache, we are concerned with im- mediate experience. The physicist studies experience only as mediate, but the psychologist, if he is a Wundtian, studies immediate experi- ence. The study of experience was to be accomplished by *introspec- tion*, by self-observation (*Selbstbeobachtung* was Wundt's word). Introspection was the *controlled* observation of the contents of con- sciousness under experimental conditions. Nonexperimental introspec- tion was useless for scientific purposes. Wundt clarified his position in the preface to his *Principles of physiological psychology* (1904, p. 45):

> All accurate observation implies that the object of observation (in this case the psychical process) can be held fast by the attention, and any changes that it undergoes attentively followed. And this fixation by the attention implies, in its turn, that the observed object is independent of the observer. Now it is obvious that the required independence does not obtain in any attempt at a direct self-observation, undertaken without the help of experiment. The endeavor to observe oneself must inevitably in- troduce changes into the course of mental events—changes which could not have occurred without it, and whose usual consequence is that the very process which was to have been observed disappears from conscious- ness. In the first place, it (the experimental method) creates external conditions that look towards the production of a determinate mental proc- ess at a given moment. In the second place, it makes the observer so far master of the general situation, that the state of consciousness accom- panying this process remains approximately unchanged.

Wundt thought that mind and body were parallel, but not directly interacting, systems. Thus the mind did not depend on the body and could be studied directly with profit. Psychology was formally called physiological psychology, but the explanation of the mind through the study of physiology could, at the very least, come later. Wundt did not think that introspection yielded the only psychological knowledge, however (1904, p. 5):

> We may add that, fortunately for the science, there are other sources of objective psychological knowledge, which become accessible at the very point where the experimental method fails us. . . . In this way, experimental psychology and ethnic psychology form the principal departments of scientific psychology at large. They are supplemented by child and animal psychology, which in conjunction with ethnic psychology attempt to resolve the problems of psychogenesis. Workers in both these fields may, of course, avail themselves within certain limits of the advantages of the experimental method. But the results of experiment are here matters of objective observation only, and the experimental method accordingly loses the peculiar significance which it possesses as an instrument of introspection.

Wundt at least formally recognized methods and areas of psychology other than the particular brand in which he was most interested. Moreover, he did not simply talk about such topics as ethnic psychology; he published ten volumes of his *Völkerpsychologie* (1900–1909) between 1900 and his death in 1920. He did largely "simply talk" about child and animal psychology. The translation of his work, *Human and animal psychology* (1894), devotes only 26 of its 454 pages to animal psychology. Wundt's publications and those of his students indicate that he felt these aspects of psychology were of much lesser importance.

Wundt conceived of the problem of experimental psychology as threefold: to analyze conscious processes into elements, to discover how these elements were connected, and to determine the laws of connection. Wundt's attitude toward the thing analyzed, toward consciousness, left some room for ambiguity. He explicitly talked about mental *process*, not mental *contents* (1894, p. 236): "As a matter of fact, ideas, like all other mental experiences, are not *objects*, but *processes, occurrences.*"

Yet the view of psychology as the science that searched for the elements of process was a difficult one. The result of the lack of clarity was that Wundt was accused of a static elementism—of regarding the contents of consciousness as though they were stationary, structural elements. The name existentialism was affixed to the school because it seemed that the elements of consciousness were regarded as existing just as physical objects existed. The experimental work at Leipzig sometimes seemed to justify the critics in their accusations, in spite of the systematic opposition of Wundt to such a view of his psychology.

Other European psychologists. Although Wundt was clearly the most important systematizer and organizer in the early formative days of psychology, he was by no means the only psychologist in the European tradition who influenced Titchener. Many followed Wundt's lead more or less closely, but others sprang from a different lineage. None of them, however, disagreed with Wundt about the central importance of introspection as *the* methodology to be used in psychology. As Boring (1953) has pointed out in his account of the history of introspection, none of these early psychologists thought of themselves especially as *introspectionists;* they were simply *psychologists,* regarding the importance of introspection as absolutely axiomatic. The only arguments were about the details of the method.

Franz Brentano (1838–1917) was perhaps the most influential of the non-Wundtians because of the diverse effects he had within psychology. He was originally trained for the priesthood, but took a doctoral degree in philosophy and taught this subject on university appointments first at Würzburg and later at Vienna. He resigned his priesthood because he could not accept the doctrine of infallibility of the Pope. He was known as a great Aristotelian, and he influenced gestalt psychology and psychoanalysis, in addition to providing a contemporary competitor to Wundt and Titchener.

Brentano's name is associated with *act psychology.* Its major tenet is that psychology should study mental acts or processes rather than mental contents. He believed that mental acts always referred to objects; for example, if we regard hearing as the mental act, it always refers to something heard. In this case, the truly mental event is the hearing, which is an act and not a content. If we see a color, again it is the seeing which is mental, not the thing seen. His *Psychologie* (1874) was the most important of his psychological publications. Brentano was basically a philosopher rather than a scientist and an empiricist rather than an experimentalist. He influenced structural psychology by his opposition rather than by any positive contributions.

Carl Stumpf (1848–1936) was Wundt's major direct competitor. In 1894, he was awarded the outstanding professorship in German psychology at the University of Berlin, when Wundt, as dean of German psychologists, had seemed the logical choice. It has been rumored that the opposition of Helmholtz prevented Wundt from getting the appointment.

Stumpf was strongly influenced by Brentano. This influence may have been the cause of his accepting a less rigorous type of introspection than that considered acceptable by Wundt. Their difference of opinion is illustrated by the fact that they carried on an acrimonious argument in a series of publications. The problem concerned tones, and the issue was whether one should accept the results of highly trained introspectors (Wundt) or of trained and expert musicians

(Stumpf). Stumpf, whose special field of research was audition and whose love was music, refused to accept the results obtained in Wundt's laboratory.

Stumpf's laboratory at Berlin never rivaled Wundt's in scope or intensity of research, but there were a number of research projects. Berlin turned out several men who were destined to be of great importance in the development of psychology—notably the three founders of gestalt psychology, Wertheimer, Köhler, and Koffka; Kurt Lewin, an important field theorist; and Max Meyer, who was an early behaviorist. Stumpf, like Brentano, was of greater significance for his differences from Titchener than for his similarities to him, although he accepted without question the use of introspection.

The most capable and productive experimental psychologist of the time was G. E. Müller (1850–1934). He spent some forty years directing the laboratory at Göttingen. His major work was in the fields of memory, psychophysical methodology, and vision. With Pilzecker, he developed the interference theory of forgetting, and they called the phenomenon wherein new learning interferes with old, *retroactive inhibition*. Müller also refined Fechner's techniques in psychophysics and extended Hering's theory of color vision.

More than Wundt or Stumpf, Müller succeeded in cutting free from philosophy and metaphysics, which had been his own early interests. In this respect he was similar to Titchener, who also struggled to free himself of the encumbrance of too much concern for philosophy.

Oswald Külpe (1862–1915) was trained in the Leipzig laboratory by Wundt and for a shorter time in the Göttingen laboratory by Müller. While at Leipzig, Külpe became a friend of Titchener, but the two men were later to have fundamental disagreements; Külpe was not to be a carrier of the Wundtian orthodoxy, and Titchener essentially was.

The first part of Külpe's psychological career was spent in more or less classic research efforts. He published a textbook (1895), which was quickly translated by Titchener, in which he attempted to report only the experimental facts obtained by careful experimental introspection. Very soon thereafter he went to Würzburg, where he directed a series of ingenious and provocative introspective experiments on thought. Classic introspection was found to be incomplete; the continuity in thinking appeared to elude the orthodox introspective analysis. The Würzburg interpretation of the results was that there were *impalpable awarenesses* which did not appear in consciousness as contents usually did and which should be regarded as functions. They were to be included, however, as genuine conscious data. The points of view of both Brentano and Wundt were accepted by Külpe when he accepted both contents and functions (acts) as conscious experience.

Külpe had a more direct relationship to Titchener in that he made the distinction between psychology and physics on a different basis than did Wundt; to Külpe and later to Titchener, psychology was distinguished by its concern with the dependence of experience upon the experiencing organism. Both men apparently borrowed this distinction from the philosophers Mach and Avenarius.

TITCHENER'S STRUCTURALISM

Edward Bradford Titchener (1867–1927) was exposed to Wundt's conception of psychology as a student at Leipzig. Although he was an Englishman by birth, he was a German by virtue of two years of training with Wundt, and he remained a German for the thirty-five years he lived in the United States, where he came in 1892 to take over the laboratory at Cornell. Titchener's continuing Germanness of personality has become a legend: his autocratic personality; the formality of his lectures in academic robes; and even his bearded, Germanic appearance. Every lecture was a dramatic production, with the staging carefully prepared by assistants. It was gravely discussed afterward by staff members and graduate assistants, who were expected to attend.

Titchener's intellectual Germanness is quite as remarkable as this legendary Germanness of personality, although it may not be as much emphasized. There were other non-German students whose exposure to Wundt was more protracted than Titchener's but whose deviations from the line of orthodoxy laid down by Wundt were marked; a number of these students came from America and returned to America. Perhaps the English culture from which Titchener came provided better nurture for a German psychology than did the practical-minded American spirit. Wundt did owe a great debt to the English empiricists, and no doubt Titchener in England had already been influenced by these predecessors of Wundt.

At any rate, psychology for Titchener was very much like psychology for Wundt. States of consciousness were the only proper objects of psychological study, and they were to be studied by introspection. Titchener named and launched structural psychology in the United States in a paper called "The postulates of a structural psychology" (1898, pp. 449–450; see also in Dennis, 1948, p. 366):

> Biology, defined in its widest sense as the science of life and of living things, falls into three parts, or may be approached from any one of three points of view. We may inquire into the structure of an organism, without regard to function—by analysis determining its component parts, and by synthesis exhibiting the mode of its formation from the parts. . . .
> We find a parallel to morphology in a very large portion of "experimental" psychology. The primary aim of the experimental psychologist has been

to analyze the structure of the mind; to ravel out the elemental processes from the tangle of consciousness, or (if we may change the metaphor) to isolate the constituents in the given conscious formation. His task is a vivisection, but a vivisection which shall yield structural, not functional results. He tries to discover, first of all, what is there and in what quantity, not what it is there for.

It is difficult to tell, from this quotation, just what Titchener thought about mind and consciousness. He changes metaphor, self-consciously, in midsentence. From the context it seems that the bulk of his writing and thinking fits the second metaphor, although he speaks of consciousness as composed of processes rather than elements in his most rigorous, self-conscious writing. Yet by analogy he lends reality status to consciousness, since the word "structure" and the biological attitude toward morphology lend such reality status.

Consciousness was defined by Titchener as the sum total of a person's experiences as they are at any given time. Mind was regarded as the sum total of a person's experiences considered as dependent on the person, summed from birth to death. Thus (1899, p. 12):

"Mind" is understood to mean simply the sum total of mental processes experienced by the individual during his lifetime. Ideas, feelings, impulses, etc., are mental processes; the whole number of ideas, feelings, impulses, etc., experienced by me during my life constitutes my "mind."

Titchener also listed three problems for psychology that were very similar to Wundt's (1899, p. 15):

The aim of the psychologist is three-fold. He seeks (1) to analyze concrete (actual) mental experience into its simplest components, (2) to discover how these elements combine, what are the laws which govern their combination, and (3) to bring them into connection with their physiological (bodily) conditions.

Titchener modified Wundt's distinction between psychology and physics much as Külpe did. He could not agree with Wundt that physics studied mediate experience and psychology immediate experience; he thought that all experience must be regarded as immediate. The distinction, rather, was in the *attitude* to be taken toward the study of the ever-immediate experience. The physicist studied the experience as independent of the experiencing person, while the psychologist studied the experience as it *depended* on the experiencing person.

One might object that the astronomers after Bessel were quite concerned with the dependence of experience upon the nature of the experiencing observer and that the physicists would also be prepared to evince concern. The reply to such an objection might be that the physicists' concern with the role of the observer was evinced only so that observations could again be made completely reliable and independent of the observer and thus illustrated their basic attitude rather than an exception to it.

Titchener's concept of *stimulus error* was related to the distinction between psychology and physics. By stimulus error, Titchener meant the error of paying attention to and reporting on the known properties of the stimulus rather than the sensory experience itself. This is probably the most important and the most obvious error made by untrained introspectors. Titchener pointed out that this tendency to describe the conscious state in terms of the stimulus rather than of the experience per se is beneficial and necessary in everyday life. All of us, therefore, grow up with strong habits of this kind, since responses to the objective character of the stimulus are ordinarily the effective ones. But such strong habits must be unlearned if one is to become an adequate psychological observer, and the only way to do this is through a new and intensive learning effort. Thus the trained introspector is one who learns to ignore the objects and events as such and to concentrate instead on the pure conscious experience.

The use of a reduction screen in visual research offers a good illustration of this situation. If the experimenter permits the subject to see the stimulus object and also the illumination impinging upon it, the subject reports that a piece of white paper is white even if it is very dimly illuminated—and is actually reflecting less light energy to the eye than, say, a piece of coal under bright illumination. The common judgment of untrained subjects is that the paper is brighter than the coal. This stimulus error can be eliminated by means of a reduction screen, which permits the subject to see only a small part of the stimulus object through a kind of peephole. Such a device prevents the subject from seeing either the nature of the object or the amount of illumination, and now his judgment follows the "true" character of the isolated sensory experience: a piece of white paper dimly illuminated is called dark gray, and a piece of black coal brightly illuminated is called light gray. These latter judgments are more in accord with the physical energies of the stimuli, although they are less-accurate descriptions of the reflectivities of the coal and the paper. Neither type of sensory description need be viewed as more true in any ultimate sense. The structuralists wanted the description that correlated most closely with the momentary stimulation. Titchener felt that a kind of functional reduction screen needed to be built into each psychological introspector through extensive practice. Physicists and all other scientists make the stimulus error as a matter of course. They wish to report on observations in such a way that their reports agree with the objective character of the stimulus, regardless of any momentary effects that may presently be determining their perception of the stimulus. Only the introspective psychologists want to know the pure character of the present experience.

Titchener thought psychology ought to study experience as it seems to exist when we try to detach it from learning; that is, we should refuse to attribute meaning to it and thus avoid committing the stimulus error. These meanings become attached to stimuli through learning, and our reactions to the stimuli so directly incorporate the related experiences that the "percept" is no longer a product of the stimulus only.

Titchener exorcised child psychology and animal psychology from the main body, which we saw that Wundt did not do. Titchener did not deny that the study of the behavior of children and animals would yield valuable information; he denied rather that the information would be *psychological* information.

Wundt's hardheaded experimentalism was expressed in perhaps more exaggerated form by Titchener. He not only held that psychology must be experimental; he held that it must also be *pure*. Applied science seemed to Titchener a contradiction. The scientist, as Titchener saw him, must keep himself free of considerations about the practical worth of what he is doing. He accordingly never accepted the work by Cattell and others on individual differences as making any important contribution to psychology. He decried the notion that the function of psychology was to find ways of ministering to sick minds. He was caustic about the possibility of becoming a psychologist through the process of untrained, morbid self-examination.

Titchener at first accepted Wundt's psychophysical parallelism as his practical solution to the mind-body problem, but philosophy really did not interest him. He accepted it because it allowed him to pursue the study of psychology with the methodology in which he believed. Titchener, like Wundt, boasted about the new freedom of psychology from philosophical speculation.

This new freedom was given by use of the experimental method. The psychological experiment should be a controlled introspection, with states of consciousness held constant by the external conditions and the factors within the situation varied one at a time in different experiments. The experimenter need only set up apparatus, devise and explain the problem, and record the trained introspector's comments.

THE METHODOLOGY OF STRUCTURALISM

The technique of investigation for Titchener, as for Wundt, was introspection; but, as indicated above, Titchener's introspection was an even more highly formalized and practiced procedure than Wundt's *Selbstbeobachtung* had been. Introspection, according to Titchener, could be carried on scientifically only by exceptionally well-trained observers.

One instance of his feelings about naïve observers is given in a discussion of phenomenology (1912b, p. 489):

> In the present connection, I mean, by a phenomenological account of mind, an account which purports to take mental phenomena at their face value, which records them as they are "given" in everyday experience; the account furnished by a naïve, common-sense, non-scientific observer, who has not yet adopted the special attitude of the psychologist. . . . It is more than doubtful whether, in strictness, such an account can be obtained.

It is clear that Titchener did not favor the use of untrained observers, nor did he at this time favor phenomenology as science.

It is difficult for untrained observers to say just what it is that the trained observers learned to do. Introspection changed to some extent as the years passed. Apparently Titchener thought introspection was becoming more refined and more generally applicable with the passage of time. He commented (1912a, p. 427): "Our graduate students—far better trained, it is true, than we were in our generation—sit down cheerfully to introspective tasks such as we had not dreamed of."

Still—although we are told that the graduate students were getting better at something—it is hard for an outsider to be sure what that something was. Introspection has been said to be the direct observation of consciousness, of mental processes. However, Titchener said (1912b, p. 485): "The course that an observer follows will vary in detail with the nature of the consciousness observed, with the purpose of the experiment, with the instruction given by the experimenter. Introspection is thus a generic term, and covers an indefinitely large group of specific methodological procedures."

Even Titchener seems not to have had an easy time finding a satisfactory definition of introspection and to have fallen back on a specification of the experimental conditions, a commendably operational procedure. But are there then no commonalities among the different applications of the term? Surely there is a self-consciousness about introspection, an awareness of observing? Not according to Titchener (1912a, p. 443): "*In his attention to the phenomena under observation,* the observer in psychology, no less than the observer in physics, *completely forgets to give subjective attention to the state of observing.*"

If this is truly the case, and if this is the whole truth about introspection, then we would seem to have little to question. There would be no difference between the psychologist's report that something is green and the physicist's report of the same thing. But Titchener was speaking of a trained introspector. What happens to the observer as he undergoes training? We note that he gives verbal reports from the beginning; we do not deny that we may get interesting results in physics by accepting the reports of other experimenters who describe the things they have seen, and other investigators do not question the fact that we have seen certain things. We accept the words of another's report with only the reservation that he must be able to tell us exactly what he means, by pointing to an instance if necessary.

The observer learning to introspect, however, is in a different kind of circumstance. Certain classes of words, which we may call "meaning words," are not accepted. A structural psychologist is not interested scientifically in the statement, "I see a table," for table is a meaning word, based on preknowledge about the aggregation of visual and tactual sensations by which we identify the table. The structural psychologist believes that he is interested in this aggregate as a meaningless aggregate; he does not want the aggregate summarized in a meaning word, for he is interested in the direct contents of experience, not in the inferences made on the basis of the contents. So when the observer says "table," he is cautioned against the stimulus error, and eventually he excludes this type of word from his professional vocabulary. What words are left then? Are only such words left as have no external referents, but referents only in experience? Again it is a difficult question. Wundt and Titchener alike emphasized that the external conditions must be carefully controlled so that the contents of consciousness can be precisely determined and so that more than one observer may experience the same thing and therefore cross-check the results of the experiment. We can then say that a workable vocabulary should be possible, based on the commonalities in experience under the carefully controlled conditions. After all, how else do we agree on a convention for the meaning of the word "table"? A reasonable inference is that we check that part of our experience which consistently occurs in conjunction with the use of the word "table" by others. Therefore, it seems possible to create a language, or language usage, of the type the structuralists required. However, it must be easier to correlate words with objects than with experiences, since we have more useful object languages within science than we have experience languages. It may be too difficult a task for the introspector to isolate that aspect of his manifold experience to which a particular word should apply. Certainly two introspectors cannot reach agreement on the relevant aspect by pointing to it, as one can do in the case of objects. The findings of introspection could not always be agreed upon, even with very careful control of conditions. Had it been possible to secure sufficient scientific agreement on introspective statements of findings, the structural school might still be a vital force today.

That it was not possible we shall see later. Meanwhile, we may attempt to delineate introspection by discussing those features of it that a nonintrospective psychologist of today can understand. Introspection may be more, but it involves at least this: a generic term for several types of observation carried out in psychology. Different investigators, for example at Cornell and Würzburg, tended to use somewhat different subvarieties. The Cornell variety of observation was carried out under laboratory conditions, with the stimulating situation, including instructions, carefully determined by the investigator. Only those subjects were used who had been carefully trained by the investigator or by another investigator who was versed in the method. The training included, among other things, at least the admonition to observe the contents of experience and report on them. It also included punishment when the observer used words that we may designate meaning words or thing words as we ordinarily conceive of these classes of words. The use of words that were considered descriptive of conscious states was no doubt rewarded.

In order to give the reader something of the flavor of the introspective method, as developed by Titchener, we reproduce below part of a representative account of an introspective experiment. In it the subjects, observers (*Os*) C. and P., were instructed to report their memory images; the stimuli used were geometric shapes of various colors. Murray's account (1906, pp. 230–231) follows:

1. *Introspections.* Manner of appearance of image. As a rule, the memory image appears spontaneously at the beginning of the recording period, or in the preceding after image period. Thereafter it returns at irregular intervals, which usually grow longer toward the end of the minute. On a few occasions, C. reports, the image was apparently evoked by chance twitches of the eyeball or eyelid, by inspiration, or, automatically, by rhythmic pressure of the key. Occasionally, also, the observer reports a faint anxiety at the momentary failure of the image, and a temptation to summon it by movement of the eyes (*O. C.*), by steady fixation, or by recall of detail after detail (*O. P.*)

2. *Localization of image.* The memory image usually appears in the same direction and at the same distance as did the original. P. distinguishes it from the sensory after image by its position outwards on the screen (the after image appearing "on the eyelids"), and remarks that "Its appearance is often accompanied by the feeling of turning toward it." Occasionally it seems to be situated "in the head," but in this case its distinctness is materially lessened.

That this localization is correlated with the presence of motor elements, actual or ideated, has abundant evidence. Thus C., noting that the memory image usually appears as an object with spacial relations, states that in this case "the feeling of accommodation" is present, with "tendency to move the eyes and locate the image directly in space." The less real this feeling (of accommodation and convergence), the less distinct the image. Thus, toward the end of the recording period (C. sometimes reports), the images become less vividly "visual," are accompanied by almost no tendency to fixation, and are localized, not in any definite portion of the visual field, but vaguely, "in the head,"—a type of image described by C. as "more subjective," or "more purely memorial."

It seems probable that P. also refers to the muscular sensations attending fixation in her less concretely phrased account of the semispontaneous recall of images. "I seem to turn my attention toward the place where I expect the image to appear. If I hold my attention on this place, several more images are likely to follow." And again, "my attention vacillates about the place on the board where the image is expected, then settles down, and below unfolds the image, sometimes indistinctly, but as the attention turns more decidedly toward it growing in vividness."

3. *Incompleteness of image.* Images are rarely complete. The lower right hand portion is most often missing, and the upper left hand portion the most distinct,—a condition possibly correlated with the characteristic grouping of matter on the printed or written page, and the acquired habit of attending primarily to the upper left hand word. In cases *where the outline is complete, it is often doubtful whether* there are not gaps in the main body of the figure. Whether complete or incomplete in relation to the original, the image is usually reported as flashing in and out as a whole, without growth or alteration.

EMPIRICAL PROPOSITIONS

In science, not only do observations determine theory; theory determines observations. The empirical propositions of structuralism seem today to be mixed with theoretical presuppositions, but to the structuralists their propositions seemed to be based directly on observation.

The three basic elements of consciousness that came down all the way from the English empiricist philosophers seemed to be verified by the introspective observations of Wundt and later of Titchener. These three elements were *sensations, images,* and *feelings.* The elements were thought to be basic and incapable of further analytic reduction.

Images were the elements of ideas, and sensations were the elements of perception. Images were supposed to differ from sensations by being less vivid, less clear, less intense, and sometimes less prolonged. Both images and sensations had four basic attributes: *quality, attensity, intensity,* and *protensity.* Quality had its usual meaning of a difference in kind; attensity was synonymous with clearness, except that it was understood to mean a type of clearness which varies with attention rather than with the objective characteristics of the stimuli; intensity had its usual meaning of strength; and protensity was a word for the duration in time of the sensation of image. Some sensory modalities produced sensations with the additional attribute of *extensity* in space.

Titchener saw that it was not easy to distinguish image from sensation but held that there was at least a difference of a quantitative sort; for example, there would be a point along the attensity dimension at which image turned into sensation. An experiment by Perky (1910) at

Cornell illustrated the difficulty of deciding what was image and what sensation: subjects told to "project" a banana on a blank screen did not report the appearance of a dim picture of a banana actually flashed on the screen, but attributed the sensation to unusually clear imagery on their part at that time; other subjects told to observe the actual banana failed to report when it was turned off, apparently maintaining a sort of equivalent of the dim sensation via their own imagery. We should note that Perky was distinguishing between image and sensation on the basis of the presence or absence of an objective stimulus; this is not a distinction on the basis of conscious contents and seems inconsistent from the point of view of a structuralist. However, Perky's experiment cast doubt on the sensation-image distinction, and as a result there was a tendency to speak more about the attributes of sensations and less about images.

The Würzburg school got into heated controversy with Titchener on the subject of "imageless thought," which they claimed to have "discovered." The admission of such an entity would have necessitated a revision of Titchener's view that images were the elements of thoughts. Accordingly he rejected the views of Külpe, Binet, and Woodworth on imageless thought and felt that their results might have been caused by faulty introspection. In any event, he did not find clear evidence for the existence in consciousness of this new upstart element, this imageless thought. His subjects, in fact, failed to confirm Woodworth's experimental findings. Titchener's verdict was that the so-called "thought" element was probably an unanalyzed complex of kinesthetic sensations and images, which were always difficult to find in consciousness. The "will" element was also excluded. An *act of will* was simply a complex of images forming ideas in advance of action.

Titchener was able to bring *attention* into his system in a simple way, by equating it with clearness of sensation. He found in some subjects only a two-part breakdown of clearness, into central and clear versus peripheral and unclear; in other subjects, there was a multistep progression from clear to unclear.

Titchener rejected Wundt's tridimensional theory of feeling. Of the three dimensions—pleasant-unpleasant, strained-relaxed, and excited-calm—he retained only the first. He reduced the other two to sensations and images, especially kinesthetic. They were therefore not to be regarded as special characteristics of feeling; in fact, they were not feeling at all.

Nafe (1927), one of Titchener's students, later reduced even the remaining attribute of feeling to sensations: pleasantness was regarded as a "bright pressure" localized in the trunk at a higher level than the "dull pressure" of unpleasantness. He suggested that vascular changes might be responsible for these sensations. If Nafe's point of view were accepted, even affect would be reduced to sensation.

So far, we have examined the empirical propositions which had direct systematic relevance for Titchener. In addition, there are more directly empirical propositions (statements of experimental results), which were generally accepted by the structuralists; some of these are asystematic and acceptable to any psychologist regardless of systematic beliefs. For example, Titchener's first "empirical" chapter in *An outline of psychology* (1899) is entitled "The quality of sensation." In it are examined the qualities of visual, auditory, olfactory, gustatory, and other sensations. Each examination of these qualities is based on a relevant experiment or demonstration. The data may be of interest in the modern area of "sensation and perception." An argument could be made that such directly experimental results constitute the basic contribution of every psychological system.

STRUCTURALISM AS A SYSTEM

Definition of psychology. McGeoch's criteria for a system (see Table 4) can be applied with profit to structuralism. The level of the criteria is neither too refined nor too crude for applicability to the kind of broad system constructed by Titchener. The structural definition of psychology was "the analytic study of the generalized adult normal human mind through introspection." This summarizes our previous discussion; "generalized" adds the feeling of Titchener and of Wundt before him that psychology is not basically concerned with individual differences; and "normal" excludes the mentally disturbed and defective.

Basic postulates. The postulates of structural psychology were not formal postulates, but statements designed to guide the behavior of the scientist. The underlying assumptions of structuralism are not explicated in easily available form, but must be combed out of the statements of the structuralists and sometimes must be garnered by inference from their proponents' behavior. It is impossible to make any adequate logical statement about the number, sufficiency, or adequacy of the structuralistic postulates.

The best that can be done is to make a few possibly defensible statements about the assumptions of the school. Certainly both Wundt and Titchener accepted the two basic methods of science: control and analysis. They put extreme emphasis on experimentation and excluded other methods as unscientific. Neither could affirm too strongly that psychology had won its fledgling wings and was independent of metaphysics. Knowledge was empirical, not a priori. Mind and consciousness were clearly assumed to be useful concepts and the proper province for psychological study. Introspection was assumed to be a valid method for that study, and introspection was assumed to be a method which required extended training for efficient performance.

Consistency and law were assumed to hold for the realm of consciousness, and mind and body were supposed to be parallel systems.

Nature of the data. To summarize the previous discussion: Titchener believed that the primary data of psychology must be obtained by means of introspection and under strict experimental conditions. Today we should call such data subjective, but Titchener no doubt believed that the data were as objective as any data could be.

Mind-Body position. Titchener's postulate regarding a mind-body position has already been discussed. However, lest we too easily accept the view that Titchener simply accepted Wundt's psychophysical parallelism, we should note another Titchenerian theme (1899, p. 366): "The metaphysics to which Science points us is rather a metaphysics in which both matter and spirit disappear, to make way for the unitary conception of *experience.*" Here, Titchener sounds as though he accepts a monism of experience, or the view that mind and body are two aspects of experience. His view is similar to that of Mach, of whom Titchener was fond, and who emphasized experience as the basis of all science. If Titchener accepted parallelism at all, it was probably just in order to save thought, since he avoided metaphysics and probably had no strong metaphysical position.

Principles of connection. The problem of connection was a secondary problem for Titchener; until the detailed nature of the elements to be connected was worked out, there was no point in trying to connect them. His view of connection was similar to his view of function; he recognized the necessity for working out functions eventually but felt that the study of structure must come first.

To the extent that he concerned himself with connections, he explained them by association. Titchener reworded the principle of association by contiguity as his main law (1910, pp. 378–379):

> Let us try, however, to get a descriptive formula for the facts which the doctrine of association aims to explain. We then find this: that, whenever a sensory or imaginal process occurs in consciousness, there are likely to appear with it (of course, in imaginal terms) all those sensory and imaginal processes which occurred together with it in any earlier conscious present. . . . Now the law of contiguity can, with a little forcing, be translated into our own general law of association.

His law of association furnished him with a principle of successive connection; that is, item A tends to elicit item B immediately afterward. There remained the problem of connection of the elements within the cross section which is consciousness. This was to be solved by the presentation of the laws of synthesis. This task seems never to have been completed. From his discussion, it is clear that Titchener recognized the difficulty of synthesis, that the elements did not simply sum to the unitary experience which was there in the first place (1899, p. 17):

If the conscious elements were "things," the task of reconstruction of an experience would not be difficult. We should put the simple bits of mind together, as the bits of wood are put together in a child's puzzle-map or kindergarten cube. But the conscious elements are "processes"; they do not fit together, side by side and angle to angle; they flow together, mix together, overlapping, reinforcing, modifying or arresting one another, in obedience to certain psychological laws.

Titchener was never able to give these laws, for his first task of analysis was never finished.

A further kind of connection for Titchener to explain was the problem of meaning: how does meaning become connected with sensation? He regarded the problem as outside psychology but developed an explanation, his famous *context theory*, anyway. The meaning of a sensation for Titchener's theory was simply the context in which it occurred in consciousness. A simple sensation does not have meaning; it only gets meaning from the other sensations or images accompanying it. The context of the sensation, and hence its meaning, is a result of past experience with the sensation; it is the result of associations between past sensations or images. What we call meaning is simply the totality of sensation accompanying the meaningful sensation (1910, pp. 367–369):

> No sensation means; a sensation simply goes on in various ways, intensively, clearly, spatially, and so forth. All perceptions mean. . . . For us, therefore, meaning may be mainly a matter of sensations of the special senses, or of images, or of kinesthetic or other organic sensations, as the nature of the situation demands. Of all its possible forms, however, two appear to be of especial importance: kinesthesis and verbal images. . . . But is meaning always conscious meaning? Surely not; meaning may be carried in purely physiological terms.

Principles of selection. The basic problem of explaining why certain stimuli were selected in consciousness was handled by the use of the concept of attention, which was reduced to sensory clearness. Titchener initially believed there were two degrees of clearness, but one of his students at Cornell, L. R. Geissler (1909), found that subjects could rate up to ten gradations along a numerical scale. Wirth at Leipzig produced similar findings (1906).

According to Titchener, there are three general stages of attention: (1) native, involuntary primary attention, where native factors like the intensity and quality of the sensory experience determine attention along with involuntary attentive set or perhaps novelty; (2) voluntary secondary attention after the novelty wears off—this stage is difficult to get through in terms of attempting to maintain attention at a high level of clarity; (3) derived primary, or habitual, attention, which is the ultimate objective; the attention is again involuntary, this time because of its history of learned development rather than because of native, unlearned factors.

As stages, these three conditions were obviously intended to be viewed as continuous and not as clearly separable. An example of this continuity in stages is the development of interest in reading a certain kind of subject matter, such as that in a psychology text. Originally, attention will be held by factors like novelty and certain expectations generated by presuppositions concerning the subject matter. As reading progresses, however, negative or inhibitory factors may develop as a result of the student's encountering new and unfamiliar terminology, difficult expositions, and the like, and also, perhaps, as a result of disappointment of some of the expectations. The second stage will thus appear, and the student will find it difficult to keep attending clearly, to reading assignments, for example. Fixation at this stage of attention is a serious problem in education and helps to account for much academic difficulty as well as for many students' complaints. If this troublesome stage can be survived, according to Titchener's account, the third stage will emerge. Then familiarity with the material will suffice to maintain a certain level of attention. Reaching this stage of derived involuntary attention in a variety of subject matters is an important objective of education.

CRITICISMS OF STRUCTURALISM

Such was the system called structuralism. It made many positive contributions to the science of psychology: it freed it from metaphysics, gave it a careful experimental method and a nucleus to organize around, and contributed experimental facts. Yet perhaps its greatest contribution to psychology was the criticism it elicited.

Introspection.   The severest attack on structuralism was on its very heart, the introspective method. Many of these criticisms were recognized as problems by Wundt and Titchener, and they took steps to make sure that the criticism would not remain valid. The following are key problems that were considered.

Introspection must really always be retrospection, since it takes time to report on a state of consciousness. Forgetting is rapid, especially immediately after having an experience, so that some of the experience will perhaps be inadvertently lost. It is also possible that the necessity for retrospection will lead to embellishment or error, especially if the introspector has a vested interest in a theory that will be affected by the experimental results.

This objection was answered partly by having only well-trained observers work with time intervals short enough to reduce forgetting and partly by postulating a *primary memory image,* a kind of mental echo which preserves the experience for the introspector until he can report it. If the report is made within the limits of this immediate memory, before conscious attention has changed, then little of value will be lost.

A second difficulty recognized by structuralists and critics alike is that the act of introspecting may change the experience drastically. The classic example is an introspection regarding anger; if the state is attended to, the state tends quickly to disintegrate and may even disappear completely. Thus the measuring technique interferes with experience, as it does with electrons for the physicist. A somewhat analogous situation concerns the role of the cultural anthropologist who wishes to observe in detail the habits and customs of some other culture. His very presence in the household serves to contaminate the behavior of his subjects. The undesirable effects of such an intrusion can be minimized if the observer comes to live in the household and is eventually accepted; the behavior of his subjects will become progressively more normal and unaffected by his intrusion. But this process, like that of training oneself to accept the act of introspecting into the mental household, can only be accomplished by long and arduous effort. In the case of the mental household, the state of affairs may be affected by the training process. Wundt postulated an independence of the thing observed with experience, but Titchener apparently did not claim as strong a position; he did feel that the experienced observer became unconscious of the act of observation with practice.

A third difficulty is that psychologists relying on the introspective method at different laboratories were not getting comparable results; rather, scientists in one laboratory asserted things that contradicted the results of scientists elsewhere (Boring, 1953). In our discussion previously, we said that it does not seem to be *in principle* impossible to agree on a language describing experience as it is observed by the introspector; this would be possible, however, only because of the control over external elicitors of sensation. It does seem to have been *empirically* impossible to devise a useful, agreed-on introspective language. Titchener continued to maintain that agreement could be reached eventually, but to no avail; the tide of criticism rose ever higher until structuralism was engulfed.

A fourth argument was perhaps the most decisive. There was growing concern for data that seemed properly to belong to psychology but that were not accessible to introspection. Titchener himself recognized unconscious meanings. The Würzburg school was pressing for the existence of imageless thoughts as elements; today we might say that the status of thought was not clear, that thought seemed to go on independently of the elements that introspective analysis had so far revealed. The animal psychologists were getting interesting results without using introspection; the psychonanalysts had clearly demonstrated the importance of *unconscious* influences in maladjustment. The rising tide that had been pitching over the wall of orthodoxy eventually tore it down, and introspection was no longer the exclusively accepted psychological method.

Other objections. There were other criticisms besides those that pertained to method. The narrowness of the definition of psychology given by structuralists was attacked. Titchener was an outstanding compartmentalizer; he seemed to prefer excluding an area of investigation from the sphere of psychology to including it in cases of doubt. To him, what we now regard as animal psychology and child psychology were not psychology at all. In practice, even physiological psychology as it is now conceived was a subsidiary problem to be attacked only much later. This conception of psychology was too narrow to withstand the explosive pressure of the empirical interests manifested by a growing band of psychologists.

Structuralism was castigated for its artificiality and its emphasis on analysis. These shortcomings were most vigorously attacked by the gestaltists, who deplored the loss they felt must be engendered by analysis. They pointed to the primacy of the whole as whole, a whole that they felt could never be recovered by any synthesis of elements. For them, the primary method was phenomenological observation, not the analytic introspection of Titchener.

A last criticism was based on the pragmatic American attitude, with its emphasis on the importance of overt behavior. What difference did the elements of experience make in initiating action? The functionalists perhaps were the first to ask this type of question. Beginning with James, the question was, "What is the function of consciousness in adjustment?" The behaviorists were more extreme, pointing to the fact that the law of conservation of energy must hold in physical systems and that consciousness must therefore be irrelevant to predicting and explaining the behavior of organisms considered as physical systems. These matters are examined at greater length in our discussion of behaviorism (Chapter 7).

THE FATE OF STRUCTURALISM

Structuralism, like any other system, was sensitive to criticism and empirical results. It started with an ambiguous view of its subject matter, consciousness, a view which at least failed to deny vehemently enough that consciousness could be thought of as an existent real. This led to an alternate name, existentialism, for the school. The search for the elements of this consciousness finally led to the conclusion that there was but one established element, sensation. In Titchener's posthumous publication, *Systematic psychology: Prolegomena* (1929), he concluded that introspective psychology deals exclusively with sensory materials. Its problem by this time was reconceived as an examination of the dimensions of sensation.

In this reformulation of its problem, structural psychology may be said at the same time to have solved its original problem and to have arrived exactly nowhere. The problem of searching for elements had been eliminated; there seemed to be no laws of combination of elements to look for, since there was but one element to work with.

Time was running out for structural psychology as it ran out for Titchener. E. G. Boring's book, *The physical dimensions of consciousness* (1933), was in effect the death throe of structuralism. As a prominent student of Titchener and in some ways his most likely successor, Boring in 1933 was actually concerned chiefly with correlating conscious and physiological processes; this was Titchener's third problem. Boring seems still to have been trying to salvage whatever he could of the structuralist systematic position (1933, p. vii):

> The doctrine of conscious dimensions, which I believe without proof to be essentially Titchener's way of meeting the challenge of Gestalt psychology and the anti-atomists, seems to me very important and the correct approach to the adequate description of mind. However, I am not willing to stress the doctrine as much as some of its friends would like, because I believe that categories of description, whether they be the psychological dimensions of quality and intensity or the physical dimensions of space, mass and time, are scientifically arbitrary and temporary, matters of the convenience or economy of description. One does not attempt to discover conscious elements, attributes, or dimensions; one makes them up and uses them as phenomenological exigencies require.

At this point, Boring was trying to wed structuralism and the increasing scientific and logical sophistication of his vantage point in time. He recognized the arbitrariness of scientific concepts and the importance of verbal convention even in the communication of introspective results. Yet the influence of Titchener was still strong, and Boring was fighting to salvage consciousness as a fit subject of scientific investigation.

Four years later, he had apparently given up the struggle. He examined the definition of consciousness and the role of private experience. He concluded that private experience could not be scientifically useful until it became public; therefore, it was defined out of science. After arriving at "an awareness of an awareness" as the closest approximation to a definition of consciousness, he had this to say about the word (1937, p. 458):

> Having understood, tough-minded rigorous thinkers will, I think, want to drop the term *consciousness* altogether. A scientific psychology is scarcely yet ready to give importance to so ill defined a physiological event as an awareness of an awareness. This concept might never have come to the fore had not people tried to interpret others in terms of their own

"private" minds—that egocentric Copernican distortion which properly leads to desolate solipsism.

Thus Boring furnished first the capstone, then the tombstone, of structuralism. Structuralism today is dead. Its positive contributions have been absorbed back into the body of its mother science. Other bits of it are still showing above ground in psychology, but these are few and insignificant indeed. It died of a narrow dogmatism, a disease which no school of psychology can long survive. Structuralism lacked the support of practical application and of connections to other areas of psychology; its demise was mourned by few.

The foregoing comments on the fate of the structural system must not be interpreted to mean that all use of introspection as a methodological tool is also past. It is not. If by introspection we mean the use of experience and the use of verbal reports based on this experience, then "introspection" is simply coextensive with science and will presumably always be used. However, the kind of introspection used is not the structuralistic kind, and reports are in the language of behavior rather than in the language of the structuralists. The various contemporary forms of introspection have been summarized by Boring (1953).

SUMMARY AND CONCLUSIONS

Structuralism was launched in 1898 by E. B. Titchener as *the* psychology. Its problems were the discovery of conscious elements, their mode and laws of combination, and their relation to the nervous system. Its method was introspection, conceived by Wundt as the study of immediate experience and by Titchener as the study of experience as dependent upon the experiencing organism. Both Titchener and his teacher, Wundt, emphasized the indispensability of the experimental method for psychology. The structural school succeeded in winning academic recognition for psychology as an independent science. Titchener tried to free psychology as a method from metaphysics and in general established it as an empirical science, although structuralism as a school was not completely free from some problems that today would be considered metaphysical.

Structuralism was criticized for its methodology and its narrowness in general. The critics prevailed, and today modern psychology tends to accept only the basic scientific attitude of structuralism and the empirical results that were obtained in such a way that they were independent of systematic preconceptions. Various forms of introspection are still in use, but the systematic formulations of structuralism are of historical interest only.

further readings

Wundt's *Principles of physiological psychology* (1904) gives a good picture of the general structuralist systematic position, as the student has already seen in the quotations in the present chapter. This book, supplemented by Titchener's "The postulates of a structural psychology" (1898) and Boring's "A history of introspection" (1953), is adequate to give a very good understanding of the tenor of the structuralist psychology early in the present century. The student might browse through issues of the *American Journal of Psychology* printed prior to Titchener's death in 1927. These issues give an insight into the everyday experimental implications of the structuralist metatheory which can be obtained today in no other way. Titchener's *Text-book of psychology* (1910); Boring's *The physical dimensions of consciousness* (1933); and Boring's short article with a long title, "A psychological function is the relation of successive differentiations of events in the organism" (1937) will then finish the picture, showing how structuralism developed and why it disappeared.

functionalism 5

Functionalism was the first American system of psychology. Its development began with William James, who is apparently still regarded as the greatest American psychologist by his profession (Becker, 1959), and led directly to Watsonian behaviorism. Part of the early strength of functionalism was drawn from its opposition to structuralism, just as later part of the strength of behaviorism came from its opposition to structuralism and the less extreme functionalism.

Functionalism has never been a highly differentiated systematic position. In fact, according to Woodworth (1948, p. 13): "A psychology that attempts to give an accurate and systematic answer to the question 'What do men do?' and 'Why do they do it?' is called a *functional psychology.*" In terms of such a weak specification, functionalism could not die until our linguistic habits of asking what, how, and why had been replaced by others. But this is probably an inadequate specification of functionalism. Though its definition must remain as loose as the system, we can at least add that a functionalist is characteristically concerned with the function of the organism's behavior and consciousness in its adaptation to its environment. The functionalist is also likely to be concerned with functional, or *dependency*, relationships between antecedents and consequents; here function is used in its mathematical sense. American psychology, influenced by evolutionary theory and a practical spirit, has been concerned with the utilities of consciousness and behavior. Thus it has tended to be functional.

As shown in Table 7, three groups of psychologists contributed to the development of functionalism. The *pioneers* are those early psychologists who laid the groundwork for the later growth of functionalism by opening up a wide variety of new fields of inquiry, such as child and animal behavior. The *founders*, John Dewey and James Angell, established functionalism as a system. And the *developers*, Harvey

Carr and Robert S. Woodworth, were responsible for the maturation and further elaboration of the system.

Three primary antecedent influences, all British in origin, are also shown at the left of Table 7. Charles Darwin (1872) engaged in the study of animal behavior as well as in the development of the modern theory of organic evolution. Galton was influenced by evolutionary theory and initiated the scientific study of human capacity. Romanes and Morgan gave additional impetus to the study of animal behavior. James, Hall, and Baldwin were directly influenced by evolutionary theory, and Hall was also interested in testing and individual differences. Carr was more interested in animal studies than his most direct predecessor, Angell. Baldwin, Ladd, and Scripture are included because they had a hand in setting the stage for the development of functional psychology; they are not considered important enough to the basic tenets of functionalism to require treatment in the text. Early in his career E. L. Thorndike had strong interests in animal research and was related closely to both James and Cattell. His connectionism might have been included in this chapter as a special kind of functionalism rather than in the next chapter on associationism.

Table 7 excludes two men who, although originally trained by functionalists, were subsequently involved in the development of other schools. John B. Watson was functionally trained and later turned behavioristic; he took his degree with Angell. Bergmann (1956) goes so far as to regard Watson as the last and greatest functionalist. Walter S. Hunter is another product of the Chicago school, although he also tended to regard himself as a behaviorist. Nevertheless, his development and guidance of a small but very active and productive laboratory at Brown University justifies at least mention in the present overview. The research produced for many years at Brown had a strong functionalist flavor and would certainly rate with that produced at Columbia and Chicago in general excellence if not in quantity or scope.

As its own leaders have pointed out, there was never a single functional psychology in the same sense as there was a single structuralism. There were only the many functional psychologies, each a little different from the others. Today there are not even these; functionalism as a *school* disappeared, when Carr retired from Chicago, at a time when there seemed little need for systematic emphasis. If functionalism is viewed simply as a system opposing existentialism (structuralism), then it died with existentialism. If it is considered as a methodology, independent of its subject matter, then it was superseded by the more forceful, extreme, and outspoken behaviorism. But functionalism conceived of as a fundamental set of values and procedures emphasizing adaptive acts and empirically demonstrated functional relationships has remained a strong influence in psychology and even today represents much of the main stream of American psychology.

Table 7 Important men in American functional psychology

BRITISH ANTECEDENT INFLUENCES	AMERICAN FUNCTIONALISTS		
	Pioneers	Founders	Developers
Individual differences, mental tests, statistics	George T. Ladd—Yale (1842–1921)		
Sir Francis Galton (1822–1911)	Edward W. Scripture—Yale (1864–1945)	John Dewey—Chicago (1859–1952) (Columbia)	Robert S. Woodworth—Columbia (1869–1962)
	James McKeen Cattell—Columbia (1860–1944)		
	G. Stanley Hall—Clark (1844–1924)		
Evolutionary theory	James Mark Baldwin—Princeton (1861–1934)	James R. Angell—Chicago (1869–1949)	Harvey Carr—Chicago (1873–1954)
Charles Darwin (1809–1882)	William James—Harvard (1842–1910)		
Animal behavior	Edward L. Thorndike—Columbia (1874–1949)		
George John Romanes (1848–1894)			
C. Lloyd Morgan (1852–1936)			

THE PSYCHOLOGY OF JAMES

William James (1842–1910) was the leading American antecedent of functionalism. He was a talented and extremely influential writer whose very famous two-volume work, *Principles of psychology* (1890), has been a classic since its appearance. James was not an experimentalist; he contributed to the growth and development of psychology through his ability to synthesize psychological principles and to make shrewd intuitive guesses that filled in many gaps in psychological knowledge.

Chronologically, James belongs between Wundt (who was ten years his senior) and Titchener (twenty-five years his junior). As has been pointed out (Heidbreder, 1933), he both precedes and succeeds Titchener—in the sense that his ideas reach further back into the past for metaphysical roots and at the same time have lost so little of their freshness that James is still not only readable but also surprisingly modern, although necessarily outmoded in most details. He had an unusual talent for being practical, readable, interesting, and popular— and at the same time commanding scientific respect. His writing was by no means mere popularization; a great deal of original thought and interpretation went into it.

James came from a well-known New England family. His brother, Henry James, was an eminent novelist. William James started out in medical training, but it was interrupted by a breakdown in health. At about the same time, he apparently experienced some serious conflicts between his religious and scientific beliefs. Nevertheless, he returned to his medical studies and received an M.D. degree at Harvard. He later became an instructor in anatomy there.

It was while he was teaching anatomy that he started to conduct informal psychological experiments, although he had no established laboratory. This venture into psychology occurred around 1875, a few years before the formal founding of the laboratory at Leipzig by Wundt. Shortly thereafter, James started to write the *Principles,* which he worked on for approximately twelve years before their publication.

As a result of this shift in interest from anatomy and physiology to psychology, James's title was changed first to professor of philosophy, later to professor of psychology (1889). Soon thereafter, however, strictly philosophical matters began to predominate, and the remainder of his career was spent in philosophy. The recognition of his basically philosophical rather than scientific bent apparently came early for James—in 1865, while he was in Brazil on a scientific expedition with the naturalist Agassiz. James is said to have expressed such feelings in a letter home (quoted in Kallen, 1925, p. 22): "If there is anything I hate, it is collecting. I don't think it is suited to my genius at all."

James as a critic. James rebelled against what he considered to be the narrowness, artificiality, and pointlessness of the German, or Wundtian, tradition in psychology, as exemplified in Titchener and the Cornell school. James was a most important factor in leading to the more general protest that the functionalists were later to make. It is best to let James speak for himself, as in the following two quotations from the *Principles,* to demonstrate the forcefulness of his criticism as well as the fluency and persuasiveness of his literary style. Of Fechner, for example, he said (1890, I, p. 549):

> But it would be terrible if even such a dear old man as this could saddle our Science forever with his patient whimsies, and, in a world so full of more nutritious objects of attention, compel all future students to plough through the difficulties, not only of his own works, but of the still drier ones written in his refutation.

And, speaking more generally of the subsequent Wundtian psychology (1890, I, pp. 192 ff.):

> Within a few years what one may call a microscopic psychology has arisen in Germany, carried on by experimental methods, asking of course every moment for introspective data, but eliminating their uncertainty by operating on a large scale and taking statistical means. This method taxes patience to the utmost, and could hardly have arisen in a country whose natives could be *bored.* Such Germans as Weber, Fechner, Vierordt, and Wundt obviously cannot; and their success has brought into the field an array of younger experimental psychologists, bent on studying the *elements* of the mental life, dissecting them out from the gross results in which they are embedded, and as far as possible reducing them to quantitative scales. The simple and open method of attack having done what it can, the method of patience, starving out, and harassing to death is tried, the Mind must submit to a regular *siege,* in which minute advantages gained night and day by the forces that hem her in must sum themselves up at last into her overthrow. There is little of the grand style about these new prism, pendulum, and chronograph-philosophers. They mean business, not chivalry. What generous divination, and that superiority in virtue which was thought by Cicero to give a man the best insight into nature, have failed to do, their spying and scraping, their deadly tenacity and almost diabolic cunning, will doubtless some day bring about.

The positive program. It would be a mistake to assume that James was merely a clever critic of elementarism and Wundtian introspectionism. On the contrary, he had an extensive positive program for psychology. While he himself preferred not to experiment, he recognized the value and the necessity of the experimental method, for psychology as well as for the older disciplines. More broadly, however, the keynote of his program is his emphasis on *pragmatism,* which implies that the validation of any knowledge must be in terms of its consequences, values, or utility. Useful knowledge for psychology, James felt, would come from a study of behavior as well as consciousness, of individual differences as well as generalized principles, of emotion and nonrational impulses as well as intellectual abilities.

Underlying all this kind of study was the general assumption that psychology must study *functions*—that psychology is a part of biological science and man must be considered in his adaptation and readaptation to the environment. In keeping with the newly influential evolutionary theory, James felt that man's behavior, and especially his mind, must have had some function to have survived. The effects of James's early medical training are also evident throughout his writings in his stress on the importance of the *conditions* of mind and behavior; conditions for him meant the nervous system. James retained an active interest, on a literary level at least, in neurophysiological theorizing. His most famous original theoretical contribution—his theory of emotion—is a nice illustration of this tendency, since James makes the sensory feedback from bodily actions the focal point of the emotional process.

James on consciousness. The breadth of James's views on consciousness, when contrasted with those of Titchener, is especially instructive as a cue to the difference between the structural and functional approaches to psychology. First, James pointed out the *characteristics* of consciousness, which are studied only by psychology: it is *personal*, individualistic—belongs only to a single person; it is *forever changing*—is essentially a process and should be studied first as such (his famous phrase "stream of consciousnesss" was coined to express this property); it is *sensibly continuous*—in spite of gaps, individual identity is always maintained; it is *selective*—it chooses, with attention providing the relevance and continuity for choice; and it occurs in *transitive* as well as *substantive* form.

This last point, the dichotomy between clear content and so-called fringe states of consciousness, is one of James's more noteworthy emphases. James held that transitive conscious processes are less easily noticed but are very important and that they had not been given sufficient credit or study. He thought that all ideas enter consciousness as transitive, marginal in attention, and often fleeting, and may or may not then proceed to substantive form, in which the idea has more stability, more "substance." In any case, transitive or fringe ideas (as of unfamiliarity, relation, and the like) account for much meaning and behavior.

Second, James emphasized the *purpose* of consciousness. Here, as suggested above, he was much influenced by the new evolutionary theory and felt that consciousness must have some biological use or it would not have survived. Its function is to make man a better-adapted animal—to enable him to choose. Conscious choice is to be contrasted with habit, which becomes involuntary and nonconscious. Consciousness tends to become involved when there is a *new* problem, the need for a *new* adjustment. Its survival value, as James reasoned, is in relationship to the nervous system (1890, p. 144): "The distribution of consciousness shows it to be exactly such as we might expect in an organ added for the sake of steering a nervous system grown too complex to regulate itself."

Third, James thought that psychology had to study the conditions of consciousness. In contrast to Titchener with his psychophysical parallelism, James felt that consciousness could not be considered apart from the body. In the *Principles* James examined in detail the mind-body solutions of his time and found that he had to reject them all. Later, as a full-fledged philosopher himself, he developed more fully a mind-body position of his own (James, 1909).

One product of his neurophysiological speculations was the notion of ideomotor action. James felt that the nervous system functioned in such a way that sensory processes tended to express themselves in motor processes unless something inhibited them; thus it is to be expected that any idea, unless inhibited by other ideas, will lead more or less directly to action. James's own example of the value of this hypothesis was that if one has trouble getting out of bed in the morning, one has simply to keep getting up in mind and clear out all conflicting ideas. According to the hypothesis, he will soon find himself standing up.

PIONEER AMERICAN FUNCTIONALISTS

G. Stanley Hall.   Granville Stanley Hall (1844–1924) had one of the most amazingly varied careers of any professional psychologist. Hall did things in spurts of great interest, leaving others to fill in the details. He is important in a systematic sense because he opened up new fields and new activities, mostly of a utilitarian or functional nature. Although he did not contribute formally to the founding of functionalism, his contributions had an obvious functional flavor before there was a functional school.

Born a farm boy in Massachusetts, Hall went to Williams College to study for the ministry. However, his ideas seemed too liberal for this calling, and he turned to philosophy. He spent three years studying philosophy and physiology in Europe. Upon returning to the United States, he finally took his divinity degree but preached for only ten weeks. After various minor academic jobs, Hall went to Harvard to study and took in 1878 under James the first American doctorate in psychology. The experimental work for his dissertation, which dealt with muscular cues in the perception of space, was performed in Bowditch's physiology laboratory. There were only two years' difference in age between Hall and James; however, there was a tremendous difference in temperament and in subsequent professional history.

After getting his doctorate, Hall returned to Europe to spend two more years in Germany, becoming Wundt's first American student at Leipzig in 1879. He sampled a variety of scholarly fields (studying physiology under Ludwig at Leipzig, for example, while living next door to Fechner). He then returned to the United States and proceeded to found a remarkable number of institutions. In 1883 he founded at Johns Hopkins University what has been called the first psychological laboratory in this country. In 1887 he founded the *American Journal of Psychology*. In 1888 he was called to the presidency of a new graduate school, Clark University, in Massachusetts. In 1891 he founded the *Pedagogical Seminary* (now the *Journal of Genetic Psychology*). In 1892 the American Psychological Association was planned in a conference in his study, and he became the first president.

Hall's development of psychology as a scientific academic discipline at Clark is of considerable interest; it resulted in the unusual situation of having the newest of the scientific disciplines assuming the most important part in this graduate school established primarily for scientific training. He brought in E. C. Sanford from Hopkins to head the laboratory and maintained an active personal interest in psychology. His wide range of interest is illustrated by his bringing Freud, Jung, and Ferenczi—leading psychoanalysts—to the Clark University celebration in 1909.

Hall continued to develop new areas in psychology, proceeding from child psychology—where he popularized the use of the questionnaire as a research tool—through adolescent psychology—where his two huge volumes, *Adolescence,* are probably his most influential publications—and on into the psychology of old age, publishing *Senescence* (appropriately, at the age of seventy-eight!). In addition, he worked in the fields of applied psychology; educational psychology; sex (after his discovery of Freud, in whom he took an early interest), religious psychology (his book, *Jesus, the Christ, in the light of psychology* representing a revival of his early theological interests); and even alimentary sensations!

Hall's influence was mostly felt indirectly, through the opening up of interest and activity in this great variety of fields. All these fields had a utilitarian or functional flavor, especially as contrasted with the strict introspectionism of Titchener. Although he turned out eighty-one Ph.D.s at Clark (to be contrasted with the fifty-four produced at Cornell by Titchener), only a few of these became prominent in psychology. Lewis Terman, long an American leader in the field of testing and individual differences, is perhaps the best known of them. It is suggestive of Hall's personal influence that fully a third of his doctoral candidates eventually went, like himself, into administrative positions. In any case, the career of this most remarkable man had much to do with the variegated development of early American psychology and particularly with the strong tide toward functionalism.

James McK. Cattell. James McKeen Cattell (1860–1944) had an active and varied career, similar to Hall's. He was particularly active in editing and publishing. While he avoided philosophy and psychological systematizing, he helped lay the groundwork for functionalism by his development of mental tests and his long-continued interest in individual differences.

Cattell in 1883 went to Leipzig to become Wundt's first (and self-appointed) assistant in the new laboratory. Himself a very aggressive, opinionated, and forceful individual, he never completely accepted Wundt's definition of psychology and persisted even at Leipzig in working with an unorthodox subject, that of reaction times. After three years he returned to the United States to establish the psychology laboratory at the University of Pennsylvania; then he went to Columbia University in 1891, where also he founded the psychology laboratory. He was discharged in 1917, on account of his outspoken pacificism, and returned on a full-time basis to his editing and to the Psychological Corporation, a leading center for applied psychological research which he had founded in New York City.

The most important of Cattell's editorial accomplishments were the founding of the *Psychological Review* (with Baldwin, in 1894); the editing of the periodical biographical volume, *American Men of Science;* and the editing of the journal, *Science,* official organ of the American Association for the Advancement of Science. The latter publication was sold to the association by the Cattell family the year after his death.

Of more direct importance to the development of functionalism was Cattell's promotion of mental tests. He was giving mental and physical tests, of a relatively simple sort, to Columbia University students in the 1890s, before the Binet-Simon Scale had been produced. However, the success of this more comprehensive battery eclipsed the earlier work at Columbia. Cattell continued his activity in the field of individual differences and capacity (for example, in perception and reading, in psychophysics, in free and controlled association), working in later years mostly through the Psychological Corporation.

THE FOUNDING OF FUNCTIONALISM

Functionalism as a formal school started at the University of Chicago with John Dewey and James Angell. Both of them came in 1894 to teach at the newly organized university.

John Dewey (1859–1952), a philosopher, educator, and psychologist, was one of the eminent Americans of recent times. He studied with Hall at Hopkins, taking his doctorate there, and taught at Michigan and Minnesota before going to Chicago. In 1886 he published *Psychology*, the first such text by an American author. It was popular at first but was soon overshadowed by the even more successful *Principles* of William James.

Ten years after his book appeared, Dewey made what was to be a more influential contribution to psychology in a short paper, "The reflex arc concept in psychology" (1896). The paper became a classic and is considered to be the most significant landmark in the beginning of the functionalist movement. Dewey objected to the reflex-arc analysis, which broke behavior down into the separate stimulus and response units and assumed that the sensory and motor nerves that participated in reflexes behaved thus separately. According to the reflex-arc schema, the behavior chain can be broken down into (1) an afferent, or sensory, component initiated by the stimulus and mediated by sensory nerves; (2) a control, or associative, component, mediated by the spinal cord and the brain; and (3) an efferent, or motor, component, mediated by motor nerves and culminating in a response.

Dewey took examples from James and from Baldwin to show the inadequacy of their formulations of behavior in terms of reflexes. He developed an organismic position, stressing behavior as a total coordination which adapts the organism to a situation. He followed the spirit of James when James urged the continuity of consciousness rather than when James talked about reflex action. Dewey regarded stimulus and response as convenient abstractions rather than realities and pointed out the necessity for having a response before we can meaningfully say we have a stimulus; the over-all reflex is not a composition made of successive stimulus and response, because there is no such successive relationship involved. The stimulus-response distinction is artificial; it is a result of the holding over of the old mind-body dualism. (Dewey said this in 1896!) The two main points Dewey made were that behavior should be considered as it functions and that molar units of analysis should be used in order to prevent too much elementaristic analysis. The first point marked the beginning of functional psychology, and the second was a gestalt point made twenty years before gestalt psychology existed.

Unfortunately, the reflex-arc paper was the last of Dewey's contributions to psychology proper. During his stay at Chicago, he worked mostly in education and philosophy. He laid out the program for the progressive education movement in an address, "Psychology and social practice" (1900), delivered upon his retirement as president of the American Psychological Association. Dewey remained the titular head of this movement until his death. He more than anyone else was responsible for the application of pragmatism to education—the notion that education is life, learning is doing, and teaching should be student-centered rather than subject-centered. We cannot hold Dewey responsible for the occasional excesses of his followers in the progressive education movement; we can be sure he would not have approved all the interpretations given his educational beliefs. In 1904, Dewey went to Columbia University Teachers College as professor of philosophy; he remained there for the rest of his career.

Dewey's importance in psychology follows primarily from his stimulation of others, and particularly from his laying down the philosophical groundwork for functionalism, rather than from any positive substantive contributions. His best-known contribution is the analysis of thinking in adaptive, problem-solving terms (Dewey, 1910); this is probably his only lasting achievement of a purely psychological nature. It stands also as a good example of the early functionalist point of view, emphasizing the continuity and integration of adaptive behavior.

James Angell.   James Rowland Angell (1869–1949) took his M.A. in psychology at Michigan and studied with James at Harvard and with Erdmann at Halle in Germany. After a year at Minnesota, he came to Chicago in 1894. His first paper (1896), published jointly with A. W. Moore in the same volume of the *Psychological Review* as Dewey's reflex-arc paper, was an experimental study of reaction times. It attempted to resolve the controversy between Titchener and Baldwin. Titchener had held that reaction times are faster when the subject concentrates on the response (*motor* condition); Baldwin had claimed that, on the contrary, they are faster when the subject concentrates on the stimulus (*sensory* condition). Angell and Moore reported that there were wide individual differences in reaction times among naïve subjects, with some giving faster sensory times (supporting Baldwin), but that with continued practice motor times generally were faster (supporting Titchener). This resolution pointed up the basic difference between the structuralist position, with its emphasis on the highly trained observer, and the developing functionalist position, with its acceptance of data from naïve as well as trained observers.

In his paper replying to criticism of his type of psychology, Titchener borrowed from James the term structural psychology as opposed to functional psychology. The terms structural and functional were used as the basis of the newly defined "isms" in psychology; Titchener was thus responsible for the naming of both systems.

As we have already observed, Titchener was fighting a losing battle. As the century ended, developments in educational psychology, animal psychology, mental testing, and related fields were helping to strengthen the basic functionalist position. It was James Angell who became the leading champion of the new trend. He published a paper on the relations between structural and functional psychology (1903), a textbook (1904), and finally the clearest expression of the functionalist position in his (1906) address as president of the American Psychological Association, "The province of functional psychology" (1907, pp. 61–94):

> Functional psychology is at the present moment little more than a point of view, a program, an ambition. It gains its vitality primarily perhaps as a protest against the exclusive excellence of another starting point for the study of the mind, and it enjoys for the time being at least the peculiar vigor which commonly attaches to Protestantism of any sort in its early stages before it has become respectable and orthodox. The time seems ripe to attempt a somewhat more precise characterization of the field of functional psychology than has as yet been offered.

Angell proceeded in his address to outline three separate conceptions of functional psychology. First, functionalism might be considered as a psychology of mental operations in contrast to a psychology of mental elements. This view presents a direct antithesis between the structuralist and the functionalist positions. From the functionalist point of view, Angell notes, the complete answer to the question "What?" with respect to the mind must include answers to the corollary questions "How?" and "Why?" Second, functionalism might be considered the psychology of the fundamental utilities of consciousness. Angell presents in this second connection a view very similar to James's, with the mind functioning to mediate between the organism and its environment and becoming active primarily in accommodating to the novel situation. Third, functionalism might be considered as the psychology of psychophysical relations. Here functionalism is the psychology of the total relationship of organism to environment, including all mind-body functions. This third view leaves open the study of nonconscious, habitual behavior.

Angell believed that the first and second views were too narrow: each of them restricted functionalism to the study of conscious experience, and the first put too much emphasis on opposition to structuralism. The third view was most satisfactory, although Angell felt that the three views of functionalism were interdependent.

At Chicago, Angell built up the department of psychology and made it a center for functional studies. Then, in 1921, he went to Yale University as president. He remained there until his retirement in 1937; during his Yale years he left his active role in psychology for administrative matters.

THE CHICAGO SCHOOL: HARVEY CARR

Harvey Carr (1873–1954) received his doctoral degree at the University of Chicago in 1905. He succeeded Angell as chairman of the department at Chicago, actually in 1919, officially in 1921. Since it was under Carr that Chicago functionalism flourished and took on as much definition as it ever had, we shall consider his system in some detail as the most comprehensive representative of functionalism.

The attitude at Chicago under Carr was not such that it encouraged much systematic fuss or bother. What was being done at Chicago was regarded as *the* psychology of the time, and there was apparently little need felt for formal systematizing. One consequence of this view was the feeling that pretensions of alternative systematic movements like behaviorism, gestalt psychology, and psychoanalysis, were over-emphasized. These movements were seen as exaggerated and over-dramatized developments of relatively limited aspects of psychology. Thus, the behaviorist, with his stress on and use of measurements of overt behavior, was merely taking up where the functionalist had already more quietly broken the ground. The gestalt psychologist was emphasizing points about the stimulus field which the functionalist had been investigating all the while. The psychoanalyst was pointing to the great importance of motivation, a concept that had been basic all along to functionalist stress on purposive and adaptive behavior. The functionalists felt that the new schools added little beyond what their own all-embracing psychology had always included in its scope.

Carr's functionalism as it appeared in his 1925 textbook, *Psychology*, will be considered according to the six systematic criteria of McGeoch. The stress throughout Carr's book is functional in the broadest sense; organismic adjustment is the central theme.

Definition of psychology. Psychology is the study of *mental activity*, which is the generic term for adaptive behavior. According to Carr (1925, pp. 72 ff.), the adaptive act is a key concept for psychology. It involves three essential phases: (1) a motivating stimulus, (2) a sensory situation, and (3) a response that alters the situation to satisfy the motivating conditions. The motive is a stimulus that dominates the behavior of the organism until the organism reacts in such a way that the stimulus is no longer effective. Motives, as thus defined, are not conceived of as necessary to behavior but as directive forces that in general determine what we do. There are three ways in which a motive may be resolved by an adaptive act. The act may remove the stimulus, disrupt it by introduction of a stronger stimulus, or resolve it through sensory adaptation to the stimulus.

Carr felt that adaptive behavior was the subject matter of both psychology and physiology. The two disciplines were to be distinguished, however, in terms of the kinds of variables studied. Carr made the following distinction (1925, p. 7):

Psychology is concerned with all those processes that are directly involved in the adjustment of the organism to its environment, while physiology is engaged in the study of vital activities such as circulation, digestion, and metabolism that are primarily concerned with the maintenance of the structural integrity of the organism.

On the role of a strictly introspective psychology, Carr took a definite stand. Consciousness, he held, is an artificial abstraction, an unfortunate and unnecessary reification; something is supposed to exist, whereas all that exists in reality is a set of processes. The concept of consciousness is similar to other abstract concepts like intelligence, will power, and crowd mind; none of these concepts exist apart from the acts and processes that give them meaning, and none of them can serve directly as the subject of empirical investigation.

Postulates. The postulates of functionalism, as in the case of all early psychological systems, were not explicitly stated. However, several assumptions stand out clearly. (1) Behavior is intrinsically adaptive and purposive. (2) All sensory stimuli affect behavior—not just motives, as defined above. For Carr, there was no absolute difference between a motive and any other stimulus; a motive might become an ordinary stimulus after it was resolved as a motive. (3) All activity is initiated by some sort of sensory stimulus: no response occurs without a stimulus. (4) Each response modifies the stimulus situation. Behavior, as earlier pointed out by Dewey, is essentially a continuous and coordinated process.

Mind-Body position. Here Carr followed Dewey, rather than James, and minimized the problem (see Table 2, for a summary of mind-body positions). He felt that there was no need for a detailed solution because there was no real problem. The psychophysical integrity, or integration, of the organism was simply assumed. Functionalism thus tends to adopt either a monistic or a double-aspect position but has no elaborate or strongly held position of any kind. The earlier functionalists, like Angell, might tend toward a parallelism or might even take a position that seemed to imply interactionism, like James; but Carr felt that psychology as an empirical and natural science did not need to concern itself with metaphysical problems. Carr did point out the inadequacy of psychophysical parallelism as adopted by Titchener, and the general functionalist position was in turn vigorously attacked by Watson as being in reality interactionist. Angell had earlier made the point that an epiphenomenal position must be rejected if one accepts the functionalist belief that consciousness has adaptive value, a belief that does seem to imply interactionism.

Nature of the data. Although in its stress on organismic adjustment to the environment, functionalism has a behavioristic flavor, functionalism does not eliminate introspection as a method of obtaining data. Its data are thus both objective and subjective, with increasingly more stress on the former kind as functionalism matured as a system.

There are ample studies of animals in the functionalist experimental literature to illustrate the use of objective data. On the other side, Carr's interests in perception and thinking illustrate his use of concepts that might not fit within a behavioristic framework. *Perception* as Carr used the word referred to the apprehension of the immediate environment through present spatial stimuli; *thinking* referred to apprehension of a situation that was not immediately present in the environment. Introspective data were acceptable in the study of either.

Principles of connection. The principles of connection are the principles of learning and as such were the heart of the functionalist research program. Learning, basically, was a process of establishing associative connections or of organizing elements of behavior through association into new and larger units. Most functionalists, like Carr, were willing to take over associationistic principles in their explanations of learning.

The functionalists usually preferred the *relative* approach to the interpretation of learning. They avoided what Carr called the quest for constants and emphasized instead a *dimensional* analysis through structuring a total learning situation into specific continua which could eventually be measured. As Underwood put it (1949, p. 7): "When any phenomenon can be demonstrated reliably (consistently) to vary in amount with respect to some specific characteristic, we have a *dimension.*" His two books on experimental psychology (1949, 1957) are generally illustrative of the functionalist approach. McGeoch's earlier work on human learning (1942; rev. as McGeoch & Irion, 1952) also provides an excellent example of the functionalist approach to the problems of learning. The position taken on the problem of the learning curve, which was a controversial and apparently exciting issue to the early generations of experimental psychologists, is representative. Until dimensional analyses could be completed, the functionalist was willing to accept gracefully the fact that there is no curve that can be called *the* learning curve; there is too much dependence of results upon the influence of the specific situation.

Functionalist research has dealt with factors influencing the rate and course of learning rather than with the basic nature of the learning process; it has also dealt with problems of retention and transfer. McGeoch's (1942) attitude typifies the usual atheoretical stand, accepting the empirical law of effect as an adequate explanatory principle and refusing to take a stand on the theoretical necessity of effect. A summary of recent functionalist learning theory and research is given by Hilgard (1956).

Principles of selection. The main agents of behavior selection for Carr were *attention, motives,* and *learning.* Attention is conceived of as a preliminary act or sensorimotor adjustment, whose major function is to facilitate perception. Motives, defined as persistent stimuli, direct action and so have a major role in determining which behavior occurs.

Learning operates in three main ways: (1) certain adaptive mechanisms must be acquired by necessity in living; (2) as adjustive mechanisms are thus acquired, other aspects of the stimulating situation come to be associated with the response (as in conditioning) and thus capable of eliciting it; and (3) certain associations are imposed by society (for example, fear of the dark or of thunderstorms, dislike of particular ethnic groups).

The experimental program. Laboratory experimentation, as we have suggested, was the keynote of functional psychology under Carr at Chicago. One example of Carr's own research interests stands as an important contribution in its own right and as an interesting indication of how the functional principles were actively implemented in the experimental program. Research on guidance, or tuition, was a persistent laboratory problem. The main problem here was under what conditions and at what time active guidance should be introduced. Research on the rat in the maze was utilized to develop important and far-reaching principles. For example, it was concluded that, as far as possible, the animal's own initiative should be utilized, with active guidance used sparingly, and that such guidance as is given should be administered early in training. Carr's attempt to apply such principles to human teaching and learning (1930) represents a good early example of how results on animals may, with caution, be generalized to human problems.

Besides Carr, the two most important figures in the experimental program at Chicago were K. S. Lashley, an early behaviorist whose best-known contribution was his program of brain extirpation related to learning efficiency (see Chapter 11), and L. L. Thurstone, best known for his contributions to factor analysis and the study of primary human abilities. In addition, prominent psychologists from all over the country were brought into Chicago for short periods, especially during the summer sessions, so that during the 1930s the university developed into one of the leading centers—if not the leading American center—of psychology.

THE COLUMBIA SCHOOL: R. S. WOODWORTH

Robert Sessions Woodworth (1869–1962) was one of psychology's most remarkable men. His career spanned the period from Thorndike's early work with cats in puzzle boxes to the present era. He received the first American Psychological Foundation Gold Medal Award in 1956, published *Dynamics of behavior* in 1958, and started revising his popular *Contemporary schools of psychology,* no doubt in the midst of a busy schedule of other activities. Woodworth got his Ph.D. at Columbia with Cattell in 1899. After four years, one spent with the neurophysiologist Sherrington at Liverpool, he returned to Columbia and stayed until he "retired" in 1942. The list of his publications is long and includes several textbooks.

Woodworth's systematic viewpoint was first expressed in his *Dynamic psychology* (1918). There are many close resemblances between Woodworth's position and that of the Chicago functionalists; however, to a great extent he developed his position independently, and dynamic psychology might be considered an independent school. We shall follow the example of Boring (1950) and Hilgard (1956) in including it as a branch of functionalism.

Woodworth shares common antecedents with Chicago's functionalists: James and Dewey, Hall and Cattell. His system, like theirs, is moderate and unassuming, with no pretensions to finality or completeness. Both views are experimentally oriented, with very restricted theoretical superstructure. Woodworth shows the functionalist eclecticism in extreme form, seeking to take the best features from each system. Mowrer tells a story about Woodworth which illustrates this attitude (1959, p. 129):

> There is a story, perhaps apocryphal, to the effect that a colleague once good-naturedly chided Professor Woodworth for having "sat on the fence" during much of his professional lifetime, instead of getting down and becoming involved in prevailing controversy. To which Woodworth, after a moment's reflection, is supposed to have replied: "I guess I have, as you say, sat on the fence a good deal. But you have to admit one gets a good view from up there—and besides, it's cooler!"

This point of view may not be true of his last book (1958) but is certainly true of Woodworth's earlier eclecticism; he tended to accept contributions irrespective of their origins.

Woodworth's dynamic psychology was less a protest against Titchenerian structuralism than was the Chicago functionalism. Woodworth accepted introspective techniques to a greater extent and was even at times a staunch defender of introspection. Nevertheless, he rejected structuralism as well as behaviorism as providing an adequate methodology for psychology. He was less influenced by associationism and a strict stimulus-response approach. The S-R theorists have often talked as though the stimulus led directly to a response, without mediation of the organism or dependence upon the organism to determine the response; this is the basis of the complaint that much psychology deals with "the empty organism." Woodworth emphasized the importance of considering the organism and insisted upon putting the organism into the basic formula which expressed the relationships psychology dealt with. Thus he wrote, not S-R, but *S-O-R*. As a partial corollary to his emphasis on the organism, Woodworth gave more emphasis to motivation than did the Chicago functionalists. Carr might define motivation as a persisting stimulus, but Woodworth insisted on considering the physiological events which underlie motivation. Woodworth generally wrote more extensively about the physiological substratum of behavior; the Chicago functionalists paid more lip service than laboratory service to physiology.

The heart of Woodworth's system is his concept of *mechanism*, which more or less has the same meaning as Carr's adaptive act. Mechanisms for Woodworth were purposive responses or sets of responses. He made the same distinction as Sherrington (1906) between preparatory and consummatory reactions; the former prepare for oncoming reactions, while the latter carry out the intention. Thus we open our mouths (preparatory reaction) before we can receive the food and swallow (consummatory reaction).

Drives for Woodworth were closely related to mechanisms. Although drives are generally defined as internal conditions that activate mechanisms, Woodworth preferred to think of internal drive processes as being themselves kinds of responses. The reverse was also true: mechanisms, the overt behavioral ways in which drives are satisfied, could become drives! Woodworth felt that practically all mechanisms could become drives and thus run under their own power, so to speak. Allport (1937) later advanced a similar notion in his theory of the "functional autonomy of motives."

A later contribution of Woodworth offers another illustration of this kind of thinking. This is his suggestion that the act of perceiving is intrinsically reinforcing, which was proposed in an unpretentious paper entitled "Reënforcement of perception" (1947). Perception is here interpreted as an adaptive behavior whose successful performance is reinforcing without the operation of either extrinsic drive conditions or extrinsic reward conditions. This paper and his latest book seem to put him more in the cognitive camp than in the S-R-reinforcement camp, since he does not see any necessity for external reinforcing operations in order that behavior be maintained.

CRITICISMS OF FUNCTIONALISM

Definition. For Titchener, the functionalist was not dealing with psychology at all, as he had defined it. Later, a Titchener-trained psychologist, C. A. Ruckmick (1913), objected to what he claimed was the vague and vacillating use of the term function. He found it used in two senses: first, as an activity or a use, and second, in the mathematical sense, indicating a dependence of one variable on another (a functional relationship). Although it may be true that there was some vagueness in the functionalist's usage of the word function, there is nothing wrong with using a word in two different ways, as long as the two usages are generally acceptable and are not illegitimately interchanged. The two separate usages are quite closely related; both refer to the same process. The functionalist was interested in the process for its own sake (first usage) and for its relationships to other conditions (second usage). Carr said that the mathematical meaning could also be shown to include the others.

Applied science. The fact that the functionalist, with his multiple interests in utilitarian activities, did not distinguish carefully between pure and applied science was disturbing to some of the early critics. Contemporary psychologists take a position much like that of the functionalists. It is now generally accepted that the essential scientific procedures are identical and that pure and applied science can be distinguished only with respect to the intent of the investigator (i.e., the degree to which he has an application in mind). Many important basic relationships have been discovered as a result of strictly applied efforts, and it is perhaps more significant that some of the *most* important applied findings have been incidental results of the carrying out of pure research. Thus the contemporary position would be that the pure-applied distinction is not absolute or even very important and that the functionalist should be congratulated rather than criticized for de-emphasizing the distinction.

Teleology. The functionalist, with his interest in utility and purpose, was accused of using the ultimate consequences of behavior to explain behavior; in the absence of relevant evidence, such an explanation is generally referred to as *teleological*. This criticism may apply to some functionalists, but not to Woodworth or Carr; Carr was particularly careful to disclaim teleology and to postulate only proximate stimuli as causal. He recognized that an explanation in terms of the effects of behavior was incomplete at best, tending to stop investigation before the detailed nature of the relationship between the stimulating situation, the physiology of the organism, and the behavior was worked out. The tree-climbing behavior of certain larvae may be taken as an example. Their climbing has the effect of taking them up to a place where they feed on leaves. Thus the behavior may be an important factor in the evolutionary survival of the species; but if we say that they climb up the trees in order to eat leaves, we are giving a teleological explanation that really tells us nothing about the why of the behavior of the individual organism. As Carr said (1925, p. 81): "Each act must be explained in terms of the immediate situation and the animal's organization in reference to it." Thus, if we can point out that the larvae always make a positive response to light and that there is a gradient of brightness which leads them up the tree, we have escaped from the illusory finality of the teleological explanation and are on the way to an explanation of the behavior in terms of proximate factors.

Eclecticism. Because functionalists have generally been willing to accept so many different kinds of problems and techniques of investigation, they have often been accused of being vapid and nondescript eclectics. Henle (1957) has recently criticized the eclectic position, directing her attention mostly to Woodworth. She maintains that an eclectic tends to accept the good features of contradictory positions at the expense of blurring the differences between them. However, she does not distinguish clearly between different possible types of eclecticism.

Henle is speaking of eclecticism at a theoretical level. She maintains that when there are alternative deductive systems for deducing empirical statements we cannot afford to fall between them, lest we lose deductive capacity. Thus, the eclectic must choose a theory or devise one of his own. But there are other *levels* of eclecticism and other eclectic positions regarding theories even at this level.

First, one may be an eclectic at the level of rules for theory building as well as at the level of theory itself. That is, one may accept both gestalt and behavioristic methodological pronouncements and do work typical of both schools. Data of subjective and objective nature may be accepted. An eclecticism of methodology we shall call a *metatheoretical eclecticism*. In the present state of uncertainty about the specifics of methodology, especially in psychology, a certain degree of tolerant but skeptical metatheoretical eclecticism is a necessity, not a handicap. We have already seen how too narrow a metatheory contributed to the downfall of structuralism. Failure to attack problems because they do not fit into a fixed methodological framework is always dangerous in science. Only the most basic and general premises of science, as discussed in our first three chapters, are sufficiently well established to accept even tentatively, and these are accepted within all systems.

Even at a theoretical level, eclecticism may be safe; that is, the eclectic may admire many theories for their successes and be sorry for their failures, ideally while trying to improve on them. The eclectic may accept *no* theory rather than all; since he belongs to no system, he is freer to reject than he might otherwise be. The eclectic misses some of the stimulation, as well as the acrimony, of controversy; his temperament will determine whether or not this is good.

Functionalists have tended to take a more inductive viewpoint than have exponents of other systems. They have, therefore, tended to ignore theory construction, paying greater relative attention to empirical findings. Thus, if one does not like eclecticism, a criticism of functionalism on the grounds that it is too eclectic is justified. Henle is such a critic. However, eclecticism may be made the grounds for a compliment rather than a criticism. Certainly, the eclecticism of the Chicago and the Columbia functionalists must not be considered as evidence of soft-mindedness or weakness. On the contrary, these functionalists generally tended to be very astute and tough-minded critics, particularly with regard to empirical problems.

THE CONTRIBUTION OF FUNCTIONALISM

Because of the moderation and lack of presumption with which functionalism has gone about its business, it is easy to overlook the importance of its contribution to psychology. True, it has erected no fancy theories; it has not even been much of a school or system, in a formal sense. But its early opposition to the stifling restrictions of structuralism provided a real service to American psychology at a time when the embryonic outlines of the new discipline were just emerging.

Nor should the obvious fact that functionalism has been pushed from the systematic spotlight by livelier schools and systems be taken to mean that its service to psychology is over. As a matter of fact, functionalists have continued actively to stimulate and perform experimental research in all the fields where the early functionalists pioneered; learning, animal as well as human; psychopathology; mental testing; and genetic and educational psychology.

Two research products may be cited as good illustrations of the functionalist program. Woodworth's scholarly manual, *Experimental psychology* (1938; Woodworth & Schlosberg, 1954), is a classic of its kind. It is a scientific handbook in the old style, dealing intensively and comprehensively with the data and theories of a large variety of experimental problems. The other example is Underwood's series of experiments on the interrelationships of the phenomena of distributed practice in human learning; the series of published reports reached number 22 in 1962. Underwood illustrates the functionalist tendency to deal intensively with interdependencies of empirical variables.

Among the functionalists actively conducting research were some of the Chicago graduates who worked under Carr: John McGeoch, with his extensive set of human verbal learning and retention studies (and his own protégés and students, A. W. Melton, B. J. Underwood, and A. L. Irion); M. E. Bunch, with his long-time program of human and animal research on transfer and retention; Fred McKinney, who shifted his interests from learning to mental health and counseling, and subsequently to television instruction and the problem of values in teaching; and Henry N. Peters, who similarly shifted from early research on a judgmental theory of emotion to the application of basic learning techniques to the motivating of chronic schizophrenics. None of these men have produced anything like the elaborate theoretical superstructure characteristic of Hull and some others, but they have pursued empirical problems carefully and intensively. Such work must provide the basis for scientific advance, and empirical work, even without fanfare, will always have important theoretical implications.

SUMMARY AND CONCLUSIONS

We have been concerned in this chapter with the diverse origins and manifestations of functionalism in psychology. Functionalism has been described as a loose and informal systematic development, but one that represented more than any other the main stream of American psychology. Its major antecedents and pioneers were William James, G. Stanley Hall, and James McK. Cattell; its founders were John Dewey and James Angell; its mature representatives were Harvey Carr at the University of Chicago, where the more formal development occurred, and Robert S. Woodworth at Columbia University, where a collateral branch flourished as dynamic psychology. Functionalism as a systematic movement arose in opposition to Titchener's structural psychology. It emphasized learning, mental testing, and other utilitarian subject matters. Functionalism declined in systematic importance as the need to oppose structuralism disappeared. However, its characteristics fit many psychologists, and functionalism has therefore continued to go its unpretentious way even after its systematic decline.

Functionalism, especially as represented in the psychologies of Carr and Woodworth, has been identified as basically experimental; concerned more with functional interrelationships of variables than with theoretical superstructures; accepting both introspective and behavioral data but utilizing mainly the latter; stressing adaptive behavior and purposive, motivated activity within either an S-R (Carr) or an S-O-R (Woodworth) framework; and revealing always an active systematic eclecticism in combination with a tough-minded approach to experimental problems. It has made and will continue to make a most important contribution to the advance of psychology as a science, but will do so largely in the absence of systematic pretensions.

further readings

The antecedents to functionalism are best represented by James's two-volume *Principles of psychology* (1890), which is perhaps the best known of all psychological writing and as such should be at least somewhat familiar to all students, and Dewey's highly influential paper on the reflex-arc concept (1896). For the Chicago development, Carr's *Psychology* (1925) is a good historical source. For the Columbia development, Woodworth's early *Dynamic psychology* (1918) and his more recent *Dynamics of behavior* (1958) are excellent sources. In addition, Woodworth's systematic textbook, *Contemporary schools of psychology* (1948), expresses the functionalist, or middle-of-the-road, point of view very well. Woodworth's *Experimental psychology* (1938), revised by Woodworth and Schlosberg (1954), should also be mentioned; this book stands as a classic experimental approach to the older problems of psychology. For the more recent developments, Underwood's two books, *Experimental psychology* (1949) and *Psychological research* (1957), offer prime examples of a thoroughly functionalistic approach to experimental problems and methodological issues. McGeoch's *Psychology of human learning* (1942), revised by McGeoch and Irion (1952), summarizes much of the early type of functionalist research utilizing verbal human materials and subjects. Chapter 10 in Hilgard's *Theories of learning* (1956) treats the functionalist approach to research and contains a number of examples from the learning literature.

associationism 6

Associationism is more a principle than a school of psychology. The principle of association derives from epistemological questions within philosophy. The epistemological question, "How do we know?" is answered by empiricist philosophers, "Through the senses." Immediately the next question arises, "Then where do the complex ideas come from, since they are not directly sensed?" The answer to this second question gives us the first principle of association: "Complex ideas come from the association of simpler ones."

Since associationism thus has its roots in philosophy, its history extends back into antiquity. Its influence extends into the present, since it is still an active force underlying much of psychology. In one form or another associationistic ideas have been taken over by all the schools. Historically, associationistic concepts have served as substitutes for more detailed learning theories.

The British empiricists probably constitute the closest approach to a "school" of associationism. It was their attempt to explain mental activity which led to the development of the several factors important in forming associations. In our description of the development of British empiricism, we shall attempt to show the continuity of thinking in which empiricism and associationism were fused. Although these philosophers were concerned more with epistemological than with psychological problems, they definitely anticipated later psychological developments in their attempt to apply something more than purely philosophical efforts to these problems.

Three men stand out as contributors to the associationistic movement. Hermann Ebbinghaus caused a profound shift in the associationistic way of working. Prior to his studies on the learning of nonsense syllables, the tendency had been to begin with the associa-

107

tions already formed and attempt to infer backward to the process of formation of the associations. Ebbinghaus began at the other end, with the study of the formation of the associations; it was thus possible for him to control the conditions under which the associations were formed and to make the study of learning scientific. I. P. Pavlov, the great Russian physiologist, has primary responsibility for shifting the kind of association studied to S-R connections rather than ideas. His prior research on the conditioned reflex thus helped to objectify psychology. E. L. Thorndike developed the most complete account yet rendered of psychological phenomena along associationistic lines; we shall therefore treat his system as the most appropriate representative of associationism.

It is difficult to single out modern associationistic systematists, since they do not belong to any cohesive school. A man is considered an associationist to the extent that he uses associationistic principles; but associationistic principles pervade recent and contemporary psychology, so we must select "associationists" according to their tendency to use *only* or *primarily* associationistic principles.

BRITISH EMPIRICISM

The British empiricists used the same principles of association that had been suggested centuries ago by Aristotle. He had suggested that items which were similar or opposite or contiguous tended to be associated with one another. The last principle, contiguity, comes closest to winning universal acceptance: if two things are experienced near to one another in time, they are likely to be associated. Similarity and contrast are accepted by some and rejected by others. The only principle of association added to Aristotle's list by the British empiricists was the principle of causality suggested by Berkeley. Its importance was severely curtailed by Hume, who reduced it to contiguity; he thereby questioned causality not only as a principle of association but also as a meaningful concept in general. Our experience gives only temporal contiguity—succession—not necessity. Thus causality is a habit of mind, not a natural phenomenon, according to Hume.

Table 8 summarizes the principles of association accepted by the most important figures within the associationistic movement.

Thomas Hobbes (1588–1679) was a political philosopher who helped to found British empiricism. He saw reason as the dominant guiding factor in man's behavior; however, he took a strongly deterministic, mechanical view. Mental content was accounted for by recourse to sensual data only, eliminating the need for innate ideas. The lawful succession of ideas was held to be responsible for all thought and action. Hobbes accounted for this succession in terms of association by contiguity: if an idea had been followed by another previously, it would again tend to lead to the contiguous idea.

John Locke (1632–1704) is usually regarded as the originator of British empiricism, although Hobbes preceded him. Locke's early life was mainly concerned with political activities, as Hobbes's had been, and he was relatively late in maturing as a philosopher. Only the last fourteen years of his life were spent in philosophy.

Table 8   Principles of associationism

Author	Date	Principles			
		Contiguity	Similarity	Contrast	Causality
Aristotle ca.	330 B.C.	X	X	X	
Thomas Hobbes	1651	X			
John Locke	1700	X	X		
George Berkeley	1733	X	X		
David Hume	1739	X	X		(X)*
David Hartley	1749	X			
James Mill	1829	X			
John Stuart Mill	1843	X	X		
Alexander Bain	1855	X	X		
Herbert Spencer	1855	X	X		

* Subsequently reduced to contiguity.

After twenty years of thinking on the problem, Locke published his famous work, *Essay concerning human understanding,* in 1690 at the age of fifty-seven. In this work his main concern was the problem of the validity of knowledge. Locke said that all knowledge comes from experience, either through the senses or through reflection on sensory data. This extreme empiricism with no innate knowledge allowed represented a return to the Aristotelian notion of the *tabula rasa* (blank tablet, symbolic of the infant "mind," on which sensory experience is presumed to write) and an attack on Descartes's belief in innate ideas.

Locke returned to Aristotle's ideas in his emphasis on association. He added a chapter entitled "Of the association of ideas" to the fourth edition of the *Essay.* Although he did not otherwise emphasize the word association itself, he did point out that ideas were combined in experience according to principles very much like those of similarity and contiguity.

Locke also developed a special theory of *primary* and *secondary qualities,* which were said to be the basis for sensory "ideas." According to this dichotomy, primary properties are those that inhere in bodies. They offer the main avenue between the mind and the external world. Properties such as solidity, figure, motion, and number are representative of this category. Secondary properties, such as colors, sounds, and tastes, do not belong to objects but are instead functions of the mind itself. Locke's primary and secondary qualities are reminiscent of Titchener's distinction, two centuries later, between independent and dependent experience. In both cases, the first class is not considered to depend on the organism, the second is.

George Berkeley (1685–1753) was Locke's immediate intellectual successor. A one-time bishop of Cloyne, he was also a philosopher and educationalist. In contrast to Locke's late publication, Berkeley published his two important works at about the age of twenty-five: *New theory of vision* (1709) and *Principles of human knowledge* (1710).

Philosophically, Berkeley was a subjective idealist. For him mind was the ultimate reality. This position is represented by the famous Latin phrase *esse est percipi* (to be is to be perceived). For Berkeley the main problem was not the relation of mind to matter (Descartes) or how matter generates mind (Locke), but how mind generates matter. This kind of position leads, to follow it to its logical conclusion, to a solipsism (belief that there is only one mind, one's own, in which all else, including other minds, exists only as ideas).

In spite of this basic philosophical position, Berkeley was an active and ingenious psychological thinker. He used tactual and kinesthetic sensations to break down the distinction Locke had made between primary and secondary qualities. Berkeley pointed out that the alleged primary qualities are really also functions of perception. This argument is congruent with his philosophical idealism. He believed that visual depth perception depended upon experience. He stressed tactual and kinesthetic sensations and their association with ocular movements in looking at near and far objects; the complex association then became "depth." This contribution represents one of the first attempts to utilize the principle of association in an important psychological problem.

In line with his theological background, Berkeley attempted to explain the stability, independence, and order of external objects by bringing in the all-perceiving mind of God. His metaphysical position is humorously presented in the following limerick (quoted in Russell, 1945, p. 648, and attributed to Ronald Knox):

> There was a young man who said, God
> Must think it exceedingly odd
> If he finds that this tree
> Continues to be
> When there's no one about in the Quad.

Reply:

Dear Sir:
    Your astonishment's odd:
    I am always about in the Quad.
And that's why the tree
Will continue to be,
Since observed by
        Yours faithfully,
            God.

ASSOCIATIONISM AS A SYSTEMATIC DOCTRINE

Associationism as a system growing out of empiricism was founded during the eighteenth century. David Hartley (1705–1757) was a scholarly physician who, more than anyone else, established associationism as a systematic doctrine. He took Locke's chapter title, "The association of ideas," and made it his thesis. Hartley developed his psychology around associations, thus making associationism a formal doctrine with a name.

In contrast with the earlier politically active philosophers, Hartley led a relatively unexciting, orderly, and leisurely life. His single major publication was *Observations on man* (1749). He was much influenced by Newton and Locke. His theorizing was somewhat similar to earlier, less elaborated speculation by Hobbes on motion as an explanatory concept in brain activity; Hartley postulated vibratory actions within the nervous system which corresponded to ideas and images. More intense vibrations were sensations, and less intense vibrations ideas. He thus gave a physiological interpretation to Hume's distinction between impression and idea. Since vibrations take a little while to die out, sensations persist after removal of the stimulus; this was offered against the then-current view of flow of animal spirits in tubular nerves. Contiguity was stressed as the principle of association, and associationistic principles were used to explain visual depth perception, following Berkeley. Such principles also were said to explain divers other phenomena, such as pleasure and pain in emotions, and the meaning of words.

Following Hartley, the next important development in associationism occurred in Scotland. Thomas Brown (1778–1820) rephrased Hartley's principles as principles of suggestion in order to get around the orthodox Scottish school's objection to associationism and its analytic tendencies; however, there was no real difference in the substance of what Brown was saying and what the British empiricists had been saying about the basic principles of mental activity.

Brown is notable because of his emphasis on secondary principles of association. He was concerned with the problem of selection, in a train of associations, of the single association that actually occurred when there were several that might occur. In this sense, he was interested in the problem of improving prediction. He presented several factors that might account for the selection of the particular association: the number of times it had been associated with the preceding mental content, how recently the association had previously occurred, the vividness of the original association, its duration, and the number of ideas now present which had connections with the following idea and thus added to its associative strength. Several of these factors are still to be found in contemporary learning theories; the number of associations is especially common as a parameter of associative strength.

James Mill (1773–1836) presented one of the most extreme associationist positions. His *Analysis of the phenomena of the human mind* (1829), published after seven years of summer-vacation writing, presents Mill's "mental mechanics." He held that the law of association could account for the most complex mental experience. The idea of "every thing," for example, presumably contains all lesser ideas and is simply their sum. Simple ideas were supposed to coalesce to form more complex ones, which might through long usage become so consolidated that they appeared as a single idea. Once the complex idea appeared thus, it might in turn coalesce with other ideas to form even more complex ideas. Mill's position was the ultimate in simplicity, if not in accuracy, because of his use of simple addition and a single principle of association—contiguity.

John Stuart Mill (1806–1873) transformed the mental mechanics of his father into a kind of "mental chemistry." According to his more sophisticated notion, ideas lose their original identity in fusion into more complex ideas by association. He accepted his father's notion of coalescence of ideas in association, but believed that very rapid combinations result in a loss of some parts. As Mill put it (1843; 1956, p. 558):

The laws of the phenomena of the mind are sometimes analogous to mechanical, but sometimes also to chemical laws. When many impressions or ideas are operating in the mind together, there sometimes takes place a process of a similar kind to chemical combination. When impressions have been so often experienced in conjunction, that each of them calls up readily and instantaneously the ideas of the whole group, those ideas sometimes melt and coalesce into one another, and appear not several ideas but one; in the same manner as when the seven prismatic colors are presented to the eye in rapid succession, the sensation produced is that of white. But in this last case it is correct to say that the seven colors when they rapidly follow one another *generate* white; so it appears to me that the Complex Idea, formed by the blending together of several simpler ones, should, when it really appears simple, (that is, when the separate elements are not consciously distinguishable in it) be said to *result from,* or be *generated by,* the simple ideas, not to *consist* of them. . . . These are cases of mental chemistry: in which it is possible to say that the simple ideas generate, rather than that they compose, the complex ones.

Alexander Bain (1818–1903) was nominally a logician (at Aberdeen, Scotland), but represents the closest approach we have met to a formal psychologist. Bain was largely a self-made college student and had difficulty in securing Scottish university professorships, finally moving into London circles with John Stuart Mill. He published a comprehensive and systematic two-volume psychology with a strong associationistic basis, *The senses and the intellect* (1855) and *The emotions and the will* (1859). Although at first slow to sell, these books were ultimately very successful, requiring several revisions and remaining the standard psychological text in Britain for almost fifty years. They may be considered a kind of physiological psychology, since they emphasized sensory phenomena. In 1876 Bain founded the first psychological journal, *Mind.* He supported it financially until 1892.

Bain had a well-developed set of laws of association. There were two principles of the formation of associations: contiguity and similarity. In addition, there was a kind of summation effect, whereby "associations that are individually too weak to operate the revival of a past idea, may succeed by acting together" (1886, p. 544). And there was a principle of creativity, whereby "by means of Association, the mind has the power to form *new* combinations or aggregates, *different* from any that have been presented to it in the course of experience" (1886, p. 570). Bain thus accepted Brown's secondary principle that associative strength is increased by several ideas working together and J. S. Mill's notion of the generation of complex ideas.

Herbert Spencer (1820–1903) applied associationism in a new area. He was a biologist and social philosopher who related associationism to Lamarckian evolutionary theory. He speculated that hereditary tendencies, such as instincts, might have been produced in the evolution of the phyla by countless repetitions of reflex behaviors which became associated through contiguity. The inheritance of such associations acquired during the lifetime of the individual was assumed to occur cumulatively, over many generations, in accordance with Lamarck's theory of the inheritance of acquired characteristics.

The failure to obtain satisfactory experimental evidence for Lamarckism doomed this view to relative obscurity. Spencer's contributions, however, were by no means limited to his theory of evolutionary associations. In his *Principles of psychology* (1855), for example, he preceded James in suggesting *relations* between feelings as an important mental component. Nevertheless, while his writings were widely read around the turn of the century, his influence did not persist into contemporary psychology.

British associationism left a legacy of the utmost significance to the newly developing experimental science of psychology. A major part of this significance lay in the methodological point of view which associationism developed and refined. The stimulus-response type of thinking and experimenting grow more or less directly out of it. This is so much part and parcel of our own basic mode of thinking—even for those of us who are most critical of some aspects of modern associationism— that we tend to take it for granted, along with the rest of our cultural heritage.

A somewhat less important part of the heritage of associationism was the content of associationistic theorizing. By and large this contribution consisted of the various laws concerning the formation of associations. Much of the historical content of associationism was more or less directly absorbed into the assumptions and biases of the early psychologists; for example, we have noted the resemblance between one aspect of Titchener's systematic formulation and the earlier notions of Locke and Hume.

We now turn to the kind of associationism that emerged during the last decades of the nineteenth century. Association of ideas was gradually replaced, in psychology, by association of stimuli and responses. The shift was related to the transition of psychology, so long a part of philosophy, into an empirical and natural science in its own right.

THE ASSOCIATION OF STIMULUS AND RESPONSE

Ebbinghaus's invention of the nonsense syllable. Hermann Ebbinghaus (1850–1909) was an extremely capable German experimentalist who published (1885) the first systematic laboratory investigation of memory. He is to be credited as the first psychologist to make a thoroughly empirical study of association, or learning, although his major interest was in memory. He was concerned with controlling the kind of learning whose retention he wanted to investigate and so devised the nonsense syllable in an effort to minimize prior associations (prior, that is, to his laboratory study). The nonsense syllable simply consisted of two consonants separated by a vowel (e.g., WOY, XAM, CIR). Ebbinghaus thought he would be able to obtain more reliable memory curves if his learned materials were more homogeneous than ordinary words, whose associations with other words from prior learning would vary widely. The measure of Ebbinghaus's success is the fact that the negatively accelerated recall curve which he reported for the human subject, with number of syllables retained plotted as a function of time, has not been radically revised over the succeeding decades. Seldom do empirical curves retain their form despite the onslaught of new apparatus and more refined methods.

Ebbinghaus's contribution was particularly important since he was able to show that orderly results could be obtained by means of carefully controlled objective data even in so complex and variable a function as human learning and memory. This first laboratory application of strict associationistic principles was a milestone in the history of scientific psychology.

Pavlov's discovery of the conditioned reflex. Ivan P. Pavlov (1849–1936) was a distinguished Russian physiologist, from 1890 to his death in 1936 director of the physiological laboratory at the Institute for Experimental Medicine. In 1904, he was awarded a Nobel prize for his investigations of glandular and neural factors in digestion. Somewhat earlier, however, he had made an accidental discovery which was destined to change entirely the direction of his scientific career and to have a profound and lasting effect upon the development of psychological science.

Pavlov had developed an apparatus which made it possible to hold and measure the amount of saliva secreted by a dog under various conditions of feeding. In essence, this consisted of a calibrated glass tube inserted through a fistula in the animal's cheek. Pavlov went to some lengths to ensure a very high degree of control over environmental stimuli in the laboratory situation; the animal was harnessed in the apparatus within a relatively isolated experimental chamber, with recording devices outside. Pavlov's discovery consisted of his noting the persistent occurrence of *anticipatory* salivary flow. That is, the stimuli previously associated with the feeding of the animal (e.g., the approach of the attendant or the sight of the food dish) came to initiate salivation in animals as their training proceeded.

Extended thinking about the implications of such signals in the adaptive behavior of the animal eventually led Pavlov to a program of active research primarily designed to lead to new insights concerning the physiology of the brain. The term *conditioned reflex* was used, taking account of the acquired nature of the stimulus-response relationship. Pavlov's continuing interest in cortical functions is indicated in his choice of other terms to refer to processes he investigated; for example, *irradiation,* implying a presumed excitatory brain function, for the phenomena that are more commonly now called *generalization.* His entire research program was devoted to an exhaustive analysis of the factors involved in conditioning, on the assumption that by investigation of this relatively simple kind of reflexive learning he would be able to penetrate some of the mysteries of the so-called "higher mental processes."

It is somewhat ironic that Pavlov's great influence has been in psychology, a discipline toward which he never seemed to feel too kindly (cf. 1932), rather than in the area of brain physiology, with which he was primarily concerned. The details of his work are beyond the scope of our present endeavor (see Pavlov, 1927, 1928, 1941, 1955 for some of his own reports, in translation), but should be familiar, at least in skeleton form, to every student of psychology. His research represents completion of the shift of the concept of association from its historical application to ideas, to the relations among entirely objective and highly quantifiable glandular secretions and muscular movements with which the behaviorist was soon to become concerned. Once discovered by Watson, Pavlov's research provided a most useful grist for the behaviorist mill, as we shall see in the next chapter. However, the significance of his work for psychology is indicated by the fact that it has outlived the early period of Watsonian behaviorism and continues to stimulate the much more sophisticated theories of the neobehaviorists.

Bekhterev and motor conditioning. The third major figure in the shift of associationism away from ideas and toward overt behavior is Vladimir M. Bekhterev (1857–1927). His most significant contribution was the motor conditioned response. Pavlov's research had been almost entirely with glandular secretions, whose direct influence on overt behavior seemed somewhat restricted. Bekhterev, a Russian contemporary and rival of Pavlov, extended the conditioning principle to involve the striped musculature. His major research paradigm involved the application of shock to the paw of a dog or the hand of a man following the presentation of a conditioned stimulus, such as a buzzer (1913).

Bekhterev had studied psychology under Wundt and was much more concerned than Pavlov with developing a kind of behavior system and relating his research to other behavior problems. His *reflexology* became the dominant theme in Russian psychology. Although American psychologists have preferred his motor conditioning technique to the salivary conditioning of Pavlov, they have found the latter's comprehensive experimentation and conceptualization more stimulating. Consequently, Bekhterev played a less important role than Pavlov in the further development of associationism as a laboratory technique.

THORNDIKE'S CONNECTIONISM

The systematic stimulus-response psychology of Edward Lee Thorndike (1874–1949) represents the closest approach to a purely associationistic system since James Mill. Thorndike began his psychological career with the laboratory study of learning in various animal species but soon shifted his interests to human learning and many aspects of educational and social psychology. Although he did not initiate a school in the same sense as Titchener or Watson did, his mode of thinking was thoroughly associationistic throughout all his investigations in many diverse fields. Thorndike's connectionism offers, therefore, a wide-ranging application of associationism to psychological problems.

Thorndike studied under James at Harvard and under Cattell at Columbia. He began his investigations of animal learning at Harvard, where he trained chicks to run through improvised mazes (formed by placing books on end). He carried on this kind of research at Columbia, then working with cats and dogs in the puzzle box, which he devised, and took his doctorate there in 1898. His dissertation was entitled *Animal intelligence: An experimental study of the associative processes in animals.* It was subsequently republished (1898) together with new material on associative learning in chicks, fish, and monkeys. Thorndike was appointed an instructor in psychology at Teachers College, Columbia University, in 1899. He stayed there for the remainder of his career. He retired in 1939 after four decades but continued his activities for another decade until his death. Shortly after his original appointment he shifted his interests, at the suggestion of Cattell, to problems of human learning and education. It was in these areas that he spent most of his succeeding years.

Thorndike's fully developed system of connectionism is nowhere presented in a single, comprehensive account. This is understandable: Thorndike did not think of himself as a systematist or of his thinking and writing as contributing to a school. However, some of his later papers and chapters from books are collected in *Selected writings from a connectionist's psychology* (1949), which probably offers the best single source of his work. Our analysis of his system in terms of McGeoch's criteria (Chapter 3) is based primarily on this collection.

Definition of psychology. Thorndike's opinion on definitions is suggested by his statement that "excellent work can surely be done by men with widely different notions of what psychology is and should be, the best work of all perhaps being done by men such as Galton, who gave little or no thought to what it is or should be" (1949, p. 9). His own definition of psychology is implicit in his writing. Thorndike was a functionalist in his emphasis on utilitarian aspects of psychology. More particularly, however, psychology was for him first and foremost the study of stimulus-response connections, or bonds. But Thorndike's conception of such associations went far beyond the simple connections between discrete, molecular, and highly localized events sometimes assumed to be characteristic of his thinking by his critics. The following excerpt indicates the scope of his interpretation of connections and indirectly gives us a picture of what Thorndike considered to be the subject matter of psychology (1949, p. 81):

> Connections lead from states of affairs within the brain as well as from external situations. They often occur in long series wherein the response to one situation becomes the situation producing the next response and so on. They may be from parts or elements or features of a situation as well as from the situation as a whole. They may be largely determined by events preceding their immediate stimuli or by more or less of the accompanying attitude, even conceivably by his entire makeup and equipment. They lead to responses of readiness and unreadiness, awareness, attention, interest, welcoming and rejecting, emphasizing and restraining, differentiating and relating, directing and coordinating. The things connected may be subtle relations or elusive attitudes and intentions.

Postulates. Although explicit statements of postulates are not available in Thorndike's writing, some implicit assumptions are clearly made. The most fundamental one is probably that behavior can be analyzed into associations of the kind described by him in the quotation given above. Another is that behavioral processes are quantifiable. He is responsible for the much-cited proposition to the effect that if something exists, it must exist in some amount, and that if it exists in some amount, then it can be measured. An interesting incidental indication of the extent to which Thorndike was prone to practice his preaching on this topic is his estimate, given in his autobiographical sketch, that he had "probably spent well over 20,000 hours in reading and studying scientific books and journals" (1949, p. 7).

Mind-Body position. In accord with his functionalist sympathies, Thorndike was not concerned with this problem and adopted no formal mind-body position. He stated (1949, p. 2): "Under no circumstances, probably, could I have been able or willing to make philosophy my business." His common use of the words mind and mental has therefore no implication for a mind-body view but is indicative merely of his acceptance of a functionalist terminology.

Nature of the data. Thorndike's data are predominantly objective and very often, as has been noted, quantified. One incidental example of his use of quantified estimates has been mentioned. His research on the "goodness" of cities offers an illustration of the way in which he used quantification and objective data professionally. His own succinct summary of this research follows (1949, pp. 10, 11):

> It seemed to me probable that sociology would profit by studying the differences of communities in the same way that psychology studies the differences of individuals. Therefore I collected nearly 300 items of fact concerning each of 310 cities, studied their variations and intercorrelations, computed for each city three scores for the general goodness of life

for good people for each city (G), for the personal qualities of its residents (P), and for their per capita income (I), and studied the causes of the differences among cities in G.

Principles of connection. Thorndike's best known and most controversial contribution to psychological theory is his *law of effect.* In his early research with animals in puzzle boxes, he had been impressed with the gradual learning of the correct response and gradual elimination of the incorrect one. Although this kind of learning has come to be called *trial and error,* actually Thorndike recognized the primary role of *accidental success* in the fixation of responses. *Exercise,* or frequency of occurrence, was accorded some strengthening powers, but not as much as occurred with the addition of success. He published the following formal statement (1905, p. 203):

> Any act which in a given situation produces satisfaction becomes associated with that situation, so that when the situation recurs the act is more likely than before to recur also. Conversely, any act which in a given situation produces discomfort becomes disassociated from the situation, so that when the situation recurs the act is less likely than before to recur.

After extensive research on human learning (1931, 1932), Thorndike later decided that the role of punishment or dissatisfaction was not at all comparable, on the negative side, to the positive action of reward. He therefore revised his law of effect to give the predominant role to reward; punishment served mainly to make the organism try something else rather than directly to dissociate the response from the situation.

Thorndike suggested a cerebral function, the so-called "confirming reaction" (1933b), as the physiological basis of reinforcement, but this suggestion was not closely connected with his strictly behavioral research program.

In 1933, Thorndike reported an extension of his theory of reinforcement. He had discovered what he called "an independent experimental proof of the strengthening after-effect" (1933a, p. 2). This was the so-called *spread of effect,* according to which nonrewarded stimulus-response connections close to the rewarded connection also acquire, in a gradient manner depending upon their proximity to the reward, a certain amount of reinforcement beyond that occurring from exercise alone. Although the empirical data in support of this phenomenon have been amply verified, Thorndike's interpretation has not been generally accepted (cf. Marx, 1956). If something like his interpretation can be verified, as some recent research has suggested (Marx, 1957a, b; Postman, 1961), his general reinforcement theory will be greatly strengthened.

Principles of selection. Stimulus-response associations account for the selection of behavior as well as for its acquisition. Thorndike's recognition of the problem of selection in behavior is clearly given in the following excerpt from his *The psychology of learning* (1913, pp. 111–112):

> All man's learning, and indeed all his behavior, *is selective*. Man does not, in any useful sense of the words, ever absorb, or re-present, or mirror, or copy, a situation uniformly. He never acts like a *tabula rasa* on which external situations write each its entire contribution, or a sensitive plate which duplicates indiscriminately whatever it is exposed to, or a galvanometer which is deflected equally by each and every item of electrical force. Even when he seems most subservient to the external situation—most compelled to take all that it offers and to do all that it suggests—it appears that his sense organs have shut off important features of the situation from influencing him in any way comparable to that open to certain others, and that his original or acquired tendencies to neglect and attend have allotted only trivial power to some and greatly magnified that of others.

He interpreted problems of selective behavior, such as creativity in thinking (*learning by influence*), in terms of the same set of principles as he applied to all learning, as indicated in this statement from the same source (1913, pp. 112–113):

> A closer examination of selective thinking will show that no principles beyond the laws of readiness, exercise, and effect are needed to explain it; that it is only an extreme case of what goes on in associative learning as described under the "piecemeal" activity of situations; and that attributing certain features of learning to mysterious faculties of abstraction or reasoning gives no real help toward understanding or controlling them.
>
> It is true that man's behavior in meeting novel problems goes beyond, or even against, the habits represented by bonds leading from gross total situations and customarily abstracted elements thereof. One of the two reasons therefor, however, is simply that the finer, subtle, preferential bonds with subtler and less often abstracted elements go beyond, and at times against, the grosser and more usual ones. One set is as much due to exercise and effect as the other. The other reason is that in meeting novel problems the mental set or attitude is likely to be one which rejects one after another response as their unfitness to satisfy a certain desideratum appears. What remains as the apparent course of thought includes only a few of the many bonds which did operate, but which, for the most part, were unsatisfying to the ruling attitude or adjustment.

CRITICISMS OF CONNECTIONISM

Elementarism. The essence of an associationistic position is that it is elementaristic. It was through their empiricism, elementalism, and analytic attitude that the British empiricists furthered psychology's progress as a science. It was through his acceptance of these attitudes, as manifested in his specificity, matter-of-factness, and attention to detail, that Thorndike made his most important contributions. Yet such views are open to attack, especially by those who want psychology to concern itself immediately with "the big picture."

Thorndike's theory of transfer of training (Thorndike & Woodworth, 1901) is the epitome of his elementarism. The theory was that improved efficiency at one task, acquired as a result of training, would transfer to another task only in so far as the two tasks had "identical elements." The more identical elements, the greater the transfer of efficiency from one task to another. This is a simple and specific view, one that is open to experimental attack through the manipulation of the number of elements that are similar. It has, therefore, certainly been of some value. However, in some situations it has appeared that some principle was learned which transferred perfectly to other tasks whose individual elements were quite different; therefore, the theory requires at least some qualifications before it can be accepted as a complete theory of transfer. Gates (1942), in his carefully documented defense of connectionism, has pointed out that Thorndike's elements were never intended to mean only the narrowest S-R connections; rather, they meant such things as factors, features, aspects, or relations, and thus could mean such things as principles. "Identical," too, might be modified slightly to allow for degrees of similarity and to allow the theory more flexibility.

Trial and error. Thorndike has been attacked for his emphasis on the randomness of learning, as implied in his characterization of learning as a trial-and-error process. Köhler (1947) and other gestaltists have been especially active critics of all aspects of Thorndike's connectionism. The gestaltists have suggested that learning in puzzle boxes and mazes necessarily appears to be random, stupid, and undirected because the animal cannot get an overview of the whole situation. The animal appears stupid because he is in a stupid situation, not because he is really lacking in insight.

Thorndike's supporters might offer several defenses to such criticism. First, the behavior of the animal in the puzzle box is by no means altogether random or stupid; much of the early behavior is directed at the exit, rather than at the device arbitrarily selected by the experimenter to release the animal. Such behavior is not stupid; it is intelligent in terms of the animal's past experience. Second, there may be a considerable amount of trial-and-error behavior which is not observed or recorded in the more open, less controlled situations which allow the animal an overview of the problem. It may be that Thorndike's situation was designed to reveal more clearly the nature of the basic learning process. Third, and last, there is plenty of evidence from outside the puzzle box to show that learning can be slow, random, blind, and continuous rather than fast, intelligent, and sudden. The psychological clinic or the counseling situation provides many cases which seem to exemplify connectionistic rather than gestalt learning processes; criticisms of Thorndike's description should be tempered by this consideration.

Exercise. The sufficiency of frequency of occurrence, or the exercise principle per se, was seriously and tellingly questioned by the gestalt critics. Here so strong a case was made that Thorndike revised his learning theory to add a new principle, *belongingness* (1935). The evidence against exercise came partly from experiments which showed that contiguous terms were not necessarily associated in ordinary learning situations. For example, suppose that a subject has learned a set of paired associates such as A-1, B-2, C-3, D-4. These have been presented in the order indicated. He responds perfectly with response terms 1, 2, etc. to stimulus terms A, B, etc. Now, however, if he is given one of the response terms—such as 1 or 2—as a stimulus, he does not readily respond with the learned stimulus term that actually followed—in this case B and C. But B followed 1 and C followed 2 just as closely in time as 1 followed A and 2 followed B. A similar situation holds for successive sentences, such as "John is tired; Jim is hurt." Here the connections John-tired and Jim-hurt are more readily formed and remembered than the connection tired-Jim, even though the purely physical relationship of these two terms is more nearly contiguous. Obviously something beyond mere contiguity in these cases is required for an effective association, and belongingness is the concept Thorndike used. He held that it is an important modifying condition of the strength of associations but is not essential to the formation of associations.

Thorndike's own research (1932, p. 184) gave further evidence against the sufficiency of the old law of exercise. Subjects attempting to draw lines of a certain specified length while blindfolded did not show improvement even with many repeated trials. Thorndike's general conclusion was that exercise is a framework within which other conditions, such as effect, can operate.

Law of effect. This oldest of Thorndike's contributions has been attacked by behaviorists as well as by gestalt critics. First, some behaviorists objected to what they felt was a mentalistic and subjective concept; they interpreted effect to mean pleasurable sensations or something similar. However, Thorndike met this challenge (1913, p. 2) by pointing out that by a satisfying state of affairs he meant simply a state of affairs which the animal did nothing to avoid, often doing things which maintained or renewed it; by an annoying state of affairs he meant one which the animal often did something to end. Thorndike was not proposing a hedonism; he meant effect, not affect.

Once it became clear that Thorndike was defining terms in a behavioral manner, he was subjected to the accusation that his law was circular. Critics said that acquisition of response would have to be measured in order to determine whether or not the state of affairs was satisfying, and acquisition was just what the law of effect was intended to explain. If justified, this charge would show that Thorndike was saying, "If an animal will learn when his behavior is followed by a given state of affairs, he will learn when his behavior is followed by this state of affairs." This criticism is not fully justified, for the operations that Thorndike specified for satisfaction and annoyance may be different operations from those which constitute a test of new learning. Once satisfiers and annoyers have been determined in some standard situation, they can be used in other situations to test their efficacy as reinforcers. Such tests will be tests of the law of effect. The question, then, becomes one of how generally a given effect will reinforce behavior. Meehl (1950), among others, has directed considerable attention to this point.

Another criticism has been that Thorndike assumed that the satisfier or annoyer had to act backward upon a connection which had already occurred in order to strengthen it. However, it is just as easy to assume that the action is upon the persisting traces that are still active from the occurrence of the stimulus and response that preceded the satisfaction or annoyance. Neobehavioristic Hullian theory (1952) has a specific postulate about stimulus traces which assumes that the action of a reinforcer depends upon its temporal relationship to the stimulus traces. This is simply a more sophisticated statement of Thorndike's position. There is no necessary retroaction implied by Thorndike's law of effect.

A last criticism has been of the automaticity of the strengthening which was supposed to occur. Thorndike believed that learning could occur independently of any consciousness about what was being learned or why it was being learned. He was particularly gratified by the discovery of the spread-of-effect phenomenon (1933a), since even the most ardent of his critics would not attempt to explain the strengthening of errors as an intelligent or purposive process. The extent to which Thorndike was correct in his emphasis on automaticity cannot yet be determined, so we cannot say whether or not the criticisms of his position were justified; there is currently a considerable body of empirical evidence for both sides. It is interesting, however, that something very much like Thorndike's hypothesized "O.K.," or confirmatory, reaction is suggested by the intracranial self-stimulation technique (Olds, 1955; Miller, 1958); electrical stimulation of certain brain areas apparently has an automatic reinforcing effect on preceding responses.

Mechanistic determinism. Our final example is related to the last criticism. It concerns the widespread feeling that mechanistic science, such as that represented by Thorndikian connectionism, destroys human values. Thorndike had a characteristic answer to this kind of objection. Here is the way that he posed the problem (1949, pp. 346–347):

> We must consider one final objection to using the methods of science *in* the world of values. Science, according to a very popular view, deals with a fatalistic world in which men, their wants and ideals, are all parts of a reel which unwinds year by year, minor whirls in a fixed dance of atoms. Values can have no place in such a world, and efforts to attain them by science must fail.
>
> The truth of the matter, which is rather subtle, may best be realized by considering what I have elsewhere called the paradox of science, which is that scientists discover "causal" sequences and describe the world as one where the same cause will always produce the same effect, in order to change that world into a form nearer their heart's desire. Man makes the world a better home for man and himself a more successful dweller in it by discovering its regular unchangeable modes of action. He can determine the fate of the world and his own best, not by prayers or threats, but by treating it and himself by the method of science as phenomena, determined, as far as he can see, by their past history.

And here, in a nutshell, is his solution (1949, p. 362):

> Thus, at last, man may become ruler of himself as well as of the rest of nature. For strange as it may sound man is free only in a world whose every event he can understand and foresee. Only so can he guide it. We are captains of our own souls only in so far as they act in perfect law so that we can understand and foresee every response which we will make to every situation. Only so can we control our own selves. It is only because our intellects and morals—the mind and spirit of man—are a part of nature, that we can be in any significant sense responsible for them, proud of their progress, or trustful of their future.

THE CONTRIBUTIONS OF THORNDIKE

Thorndike's fifty years of professional activity at Teachers College were among the most productive that have ever been recorded for a single man. Quantitatively, he accumulated a bibliography which at his death in 1949 had reached the amazing total of 507 items (Lorge, 1949). Many of these were long books and monographs, and many of them were stuffed full of quantitative data. Thorndike worked and published in a remarkably wide range of fields: he initiated the systematic laboratory investigation of animal learning; produced the first formalized associationistic learning theory; proceeded to an exhaustive analysis of human learning, as a result of which he revised his learning theory; became an active leader in the area of mental testing and educational practices; pioneered in the application of quantitative measures to certain sociopsychological problems; and contributed to the development of new techniques in the field of lexicography. All this within the span of a single lifetime!

Thorndike brought to all these fields the same direct and factual kind of approach that was so generally characteristic of his thinking. He was able to cut through to what he saw as the heart of a problem with a minimum of the verbiage and double talk found in many writers. Whatever one may think of some of his ideas and whatever their eventual fate, we cannot fail to admire the freshness and perseverance of attack that he brought to the discipline.

Systematically, Thorndike's influence has declined, first as the more brash behaviorism took over in the 1920s, and more recently as the more sophisticated versions of neobehaviorism have emerged. But his work remains a bulwark of associationism, especially in the fields of animal and human learning and of educational psychology. Hilgard (1956) has given over his first chapter to Thorndikian connectionism, while recognizing the decline within psychology of interest in the system. He quotes Tolman on the importance of Thorndike as a standard; Tolman's judgment was (1938, p. 11):

> The psychology of animal learning—not to mention that of child learning—has been and still is primarily a matter of agreeing or disagreeing with Thorndike, or trying in minor ways to improve upon him. Gestalt psychologists, conditioned-reflex psychologists, sign-gestalt psychologists —all of us here in America seem to have taken Thorndike, overtly or covertly, as a starting point.

Two decades later the picture has changed, as new kinds of learning theories and models have appeared. But Thorndike's systematic significance remains secure. If James Mill represented the culmination of a crude associationism of ideas, Thorndike represented the climax of a gross associationism of S-R relations. If Titchener gave introspectionism a thorough trial, Thorndike gave simple S-R associationism an equally thorough trial. His work is a major and lasting contribution.

CONTEMPORARY ROLE OF ASSOCIATIONISM

Interpreted most broadly, associationism is practically synonymous with an orthodox interpretation of science: it is a belief that the primary job of science is to relate phenomena, to look for functional relationships. This is a methodological characteristic it shares with functionalism. The two systematic movements have been closely connected in this country, as we have suggested throughout the discussion. Thorndike could well have been considered, along with Hall and Cattell, as a pioneer functionalist. But there is a justification for considering associationism separately. For one thing, it is a special kind of functionalism. And certainly one can be a systematic functionalist without being an associationist (James and Dewey are examples); contrariwise, one can be a systematic associationist without accepting anything but the shared methodological characteristic from functionalism (as is true of many neobehaviorists). Moreover, most associationists have a more restricted view than the functionalists, attempting to explain behavior with a more limited set of variables. Older associationists attempted to explain complex thought and behavior as *nothing but* the association of ideas. Thorndike was also a "nothing butter": behavior was explicable on the basis of nothing but stimulus-response connections, inherited or acquired. Present-day association theorists tend to be more cautious in their objectives and accept a more restricted domain—a miniature system—for their theory.

Today associationism as a methodological tool, if not as a systematic position, has been fairly well incorporated into the body of psychology; association of variables is generally recognized as a fundamental task of science. However, exactly what is to be associated remains one of the critical problems for psychology. Thorndike's answer emphasized the wide range of possible stimulus and response factors, although his own work was not a convincing demonstration, important as it was in a limited way. Whether S-R associationism can be effectively applied to a broad range of behavioral problems will need to be determined by the more refined varieties of associationism currently being developed.

There are four interrelated lines of such development. First, systematic research on the conditioned reflex as a primary learning phenomenon continues. Most of this is occurring in Russia, where the reflexology emphasis stimulated by Pavlov and Bekhterev has remained a strong force (see Appendix B and Razran, 1961), but at least one modification of this interest has occurred in the United States. This is the research of Gregory Razran (1949), who made an interesting adaptation of Pavlov's salivary conditioning procedure to human subjects. Razran used cotton dental plugs, inserted into the subject's mouth, to gather the saliva; he has been concerned with problems of verbal conditioning.

Second, the neobehavioristic stimulus-response theory of Hull and his many followers and collaborators represents a very important continuing influence. Here again the interest has been mainly in the field of learning, animal as well as human, where in addition to Hull himself, Kenneth Spence (1956, 1960) has been one of the foremost users of strict associationism (see Chapter 10). A more flexible kind of S-R associationism is evident in the work of Neal Miller and John Dollard (e.g., Miller & Dollard, 1941; Dollard & Miller, 1950), where the basic S-R concepts have been extended into the fields of social and abnormal behavior (see Chapter 11).

A third line is represented by the early associationistic theory of Guthrie (1935, 1952) and the more recent mathematizing of this kind of thinking in Estes' statistical association theory of learning (Estes, 1950). Here associationism is presented in perhaps its boldest form, since the single principle of contiguity between stimulus and response is utilized as the fundamental law of learning. Within learning theory, Guthrie has long been, almost singlehanded, an articulate supporter of a single contiguity position wherein learning is seen as fundamentally a matter of associations and nothing else; Estes' mathematical theorizing has given rigorous quantitative expression to this basic associationistic principle. In later writing (1959, pp. 402–405), Estes has indicated some acceptance of reinforcement as a descriptive concept if not an explanatory principle. These issues are elaborated in Chapters 10 and 13.

Finally, there are some versions of associationism that are somewhat less orthodox than the preceding but have enjoyed vigorous success. Two important examples are the learning theories of Tolman and Skinner. Tolman's purposive behaviorism (1932) is a cognitive type of learning theory that postulates association between stimuli—a sign-gestalt or sign-significate theory (see Chapter 11). Skinner (1938) has been concerned with the stimulus as well as the response aspects of the relationship that he called generically the *reflex*, but most of his interest has centered on *operant*, or emitted, behavior, and he has been content to assume internal eliciting forces for such behavior without speculating on or investigating them. The important association for him is between the response and the reinforcement (see Chapter 10).

SUMMARY AND CONCLUSIONS

In this chapter we have traced associationism from its origins and development in British empiricism, where the important tradition of association of ideas was elaborated, through its modification more recently to an association of behavior, and to its emergence in the work of Thorndike as a full-fledged association of stimulus and response. We have treated Thorndike's connectionism as the best representative of associationism, although it was not developed by him as a comprehensive system. We have tried to indicate the kinds of answers that can be given to some of the major criticisms of Thorndikian connectionism and have presented our evaluation of the significance of Thorndike's work. We have indicated the role of associationism in contemporary psychology, pointing out that in a broad methodological sense association of variables is the primary task of all science. Finally, we have sketched the major lines of current development of the basic associationistic principle.

It is clear that the associationistic principle must be accorded a key role in psychology, whatever the ultimate fate of the various systems and theories which build upon it as a necessary and sufficient principle. Some kind of associationism is certainly necessary, in a methodological if not a systematic or theoretical sense; whether it is also sufficient as a learning theory is much more doubtful but still remains to be seen. In any case, it is remarkable that so ancient and simple a notion should persist so long, let alone be accorded an increasingly significant role in contemporary behavior theory. Its long viability attests to its vitality, especially when one considers that empirical tests have been applied since the work of Ebbinghaus and Pavlov. It will be most interesting to observe the fate of associationism under the increased empirical and theoretical attack which it is now sustaining, as in the rapidly expanding research utilizing mathematical models.

further readings

Historical treatments of the important British empiricists and associationists are found in Boring's *History of experimental psychology* (1950) and Murphy's *Historical introduction to modern psychology* (1949). Pavlov's *Conditioned reflexes* (1927) is still perhaps the best introduction to the classic Russian contribution, although a number of more recent presentations of his work have appeared. Recent surveys of the Russian post-Pavlovian developments are available in Razran (1961), Mintz (1958, 1959), and Brozek (1962), as well as in the latter's chapter in the appendix to the present volume. Kimble's revision of Hilgard and Marquis's *Conditioning and learning* (1961) offers an up-to-date American treatment of the vast conditioning literature. Thorndike's connectionism is most readily available in the single volume, *Selected writings from a connectionist's psychology* (1949). The modern associationism long promulgated by Guthrie is summarized in his *The psychology of learning* (1952). Estes' development on statistical association theory is documented in Chapter 13.

behaviorism 7

The system of objective psychology called behaviorism by its founder, John B. Watson, is by far the most influential and most controversial of all the American schools. Behaviorism came to play a prominent role not only in psychology but also in general cultural affairs, where its influence has rivaled that of the European import, psychoanalysis. The methodological point made by Watson is so well accepted today that it is no longer controversial, although isolated persons still ride out to joust against other aspects of the old Watsonian behaviorism.

Watson had one main positive and one main negative interest. He proposed a completely objective psychology. He wished to apply the techniques and principles of animal psychology, in which he had been working, to human beings. This positive aspect of behaviorism has been called *methodological* or *empirical* behaviorism, and it is widely accepted. Watson's negative emphasis was his inveighing against mentalistic concepts in psychology. He protested against both the introspective psychology of Titchener and what he considered the inadequacies of Angell's functionalism; Watson alleged that Angell had retained an interactionistic bias and still accepted introspective data. Though Watson deplored the prominence of metaphysical problems in psychology, he took a definite metaphysical position by denying, by implication at least, the existence of mind. This denial constituted his *metaphysical,* or *radical,* behaviorism, which has been less widely accepted. Radical behaviorism has been the center of much of the controversy that has raged around Watson and his ideas.

The present treatment begins with a consideration of the three major trends out of which Watsonian behaviorism developed: the philosophical traditions of psychological objectivism (whose direct influence on Watson is questionable), animal psychology, and functionalism. We then describe the founding of behaviorism; outline Watson's system, with special emphasis on the mind-body issue; consider some of the secondary characteristics of Watson's thinking; and discuss some of the more important of the early behaviorists other than Watson. We conclude with a treatment of the various criticisms offered against Watsonian behaviorism, an analysis of the factors responsible for the acceptance of behaviorism, and finally an evaluation of Watson's contribution.

EARLY TRENDS TOWARD PSYCHOLOGICAL OBJECTIVISM

Watson was by no means the first to stress the need for objectivity in psychology. There is a long history of such efforts, mostly involving philosophers (see Chapter 2 for a related trend). Our treatment of this history is indebted to the classic review by Diserens, who defines psychological objectivism as including "any system in which the effort is made to substitute objective data and the universal method of science, direct observation, for subjective data and the special method of introspection" (1925, p. 121).

We have already seen how Descartes and La Mettrie took some of the first steps toward the use of objective data in psychology by extending mechanistic explanations to the body, and finally the mind, of man. Cabanis (1757–1808) then attempted to define mind in terms of objective factors, especially physiological functions. According to him (1824), "mental" events were functions of the total organism and not simply of the mind.

The most important name in this series is that of another Frenchman, Auguste Comte (1798–1857), who founded a movement called positivism. All varieties of positivism emphasize positive (i.e., not debatable) knowledge; there is sometimes disagreement about what kind of procedure gives such knowledge. Comte believed that only social, objectively observable knowledge could be valid; introspection, which depended upon a private consciousness, could not provide valid knowledge. He denied the importance of the individual mind and vigorously criticized mentalism and subjective methodology. He believed that human critical thinking advanced through three stages, from the theological through the metaphysical to the positivistic, or scientific, mode of thought. Comte referred to traditional psychology as the last phase of theology. He stated that "in order to observe, your intellect must pause from activity, and yet it is this very activity you want to observe. If you cannot effect the pause, you cannot observe; if you do effect it, there is nothing to observe. The results of such a method are in proportion to its absurdity" (1896, p. 11). More constructively, Comte emphasized two types of study of affective and intellectual functions: (1) determination with precision of the organic conditions on which they depend and (2) observation of the behavioral sequence. These two types of study certainly should provide data acceptable to Watsonian behaviorists.

Subsequent French and British materialists, followers of Comte, carried on in this tradition. The most important of these were Antoine Cournot, G. H. Lewes, and Henry Maudsley. Maudsley stated the following behavioristic program for psychology (1899, p. 28):

> He only is the true psychologist who, occupied with the observation of the whole of human nature, avails himself not only of every means which science affords for the investigation of the bodily conditions which assuredly underlie every display of function, conscious and unconscious, but also of every help which is furnished by the mental manifestations of animal and man, whether undeveloped, degenerate, or cultivated.

ANIMAL PSYCHOLOGY

We have already seen how important Darwinian evolutionary theory has been in the development of psychology as a science and particularly as a background factor determining the form of functional psychology. The theory also gave great impetus to the study of animal psychology, which in turn was perhaps the most important single factor which led Watson to formulate his behavior psychology.

Animal psychology grew more or less directly out of evolutionary theory. Darwin's theory had a great influence among British intellectuals, but strong opposition to the theory arose, particularly among the clergy and theologians. A primary objection was to Darwin's assumption of mental continuity between man and the lower animals. The most effective answer to the objection was to demonstrate such mental continuity in somewhat the same way as Darwin's evidence had already demonstrated the physical continuity. This demonstration necessitated an animal psychology. One way to defend Darwin's theory was therefore to show the presence of mind in infrahuman organisms (contrary to Cartesian tradition) and to exhibit its continuity with the human mind.

Charles Darwin himself began the defense. His main theme in *Expression of emotions in man and animals* (1872) was that emotional behavior in man is the result of the inheritance of behavior once useful to animals but now useless to man. Darwin's great wealth of observation on animals was drawn upon for many examples. One of the most famous is man's curling of his lips in sneering; this was held to be a remnant of the baring of the canine teeth in rage by carnivorous animals. The tendency found in the dog to turn in a circle several times before sitting down was likewise held to be an evolutionary remnant of behavior once useful in the more primitive stage of his ancestors, presumably as a precautionary measure against snakes and the like and to flatten out a bed.

One of Darwin's personal friends, George John Romanes (1848–1894), later undertook the defense. Romanes culled the literature for all sorts of stories, both scientific and popular, on animal behavior. He accumulated a great mass of material from which he wrote the first comparative psychology, *Animal intelligence* (1886). Romanes's method of gathering data is now called the *anecdotal method.* In spite of the fact that he had explicitly laid down rules for using the stories, Romanes was unable to avoid using some inadequately controlled observations, since he had no way of checking on the original sources. The tendency to anthropomorphize—to read human motives and abilities into animal behavior—played into Romanes's hands, since he wished to demonstrate a continuity between man and animal. Anthropomorphizing, like the anecdotal method, is today thoroughly disapproved of in psychology. In spite of the limitations of his methodology, Romanes deserves credit for stimulating the initial development of comparative psychology and preparing the way for the experimental methodology that followed.

C. Lloyd Morgan (1852–1936) used a semiexperimental methodology and partly controlled observations in the field in his studies on lower animal forms. He is better known today for his methodological contributions than for his substantive findings. Morgan adapted the law of parsimony (also called, more picturesquely, William of Occam's razor) to comparative psychology. In what came to be known as Lloyd Morgan's canon, he expressed this position (1899, p. 59): "In no case may we interpret an action as the outcome of the exercise of a higher psychical faculty, if it can be interpreted as the outcome of the exercise of one which stands lower in the psychological scale." This dictum was intended to counteract the tendency to anthropomorphize, and the point was well received. (See Newbury, 1954, for an extended discussion of Lloyd Morgan's canon in its various interpretations.)

If one does not anthropomorphize, how does one demonstrate the desired continuity? For one thing, Lloyd Morgan's canon applied not just to animals but also to man; in the latter case it implied that we have a tendency to "anthropomorphize" when interpreting the behavior of other men, in the sense that we may give them too much credit for higher mental functions. Romanes was demonstrating continuity by finding mind everywhere; Morgan also wished to demonstrate continuity but suggested that it might be done as well if we could find mind nowhere. Morgan relied upon habits, rather than intelligence, as the main explanatory factor, and trial-and-error learning was stressed. He assumed that human and subhuman learning processes were continuous. Thorndike's later laboratory experimentation is closely related to Morgan's work in both content and outlook; Watson also was stimulated in his animal research by reading Morgan's reports. It is interesting that all three men tended to explain all learning in terms of a few simple principles which apply to man as well as to animals low on the phyletic scale. Others, like the gestaltists, are more like Romanes in their tendency to see insight, characteristic of human learning, even in animals lower on the scale.

Lloyd Morgan's canon has been attacked by some psychologists who recognize, correctly we believe, that in many cases the more complex of two alternative interpretations is the appropriate one. However, this does not invalidate Morgan's canon or the principle of parsimony; these rules apply only to cases in which all the alternatives are *equally* supported by the available data. Naturally, if there is a flaw in the simpler explanation, it is not acceptable, and there is no issue at all. But it is incumbent upon the proponent of the more complex account to show why his account must be accepted over the simpler one; if he cannot, the simpler account is preferable.

Jacques Loeb (1859–1924) is the next important man in the development of animal psychology. Loeb, a German biologist, came to the United States in 1891 and spent the greater part of his professional career here. Loeb is responsible for the wide acceptance of the concept of the *tropism*, or forced movement, as an explanatory factor in animal behavior. In a tropism, the response is a direct function of the stimulus and is in this sense forced. Loeb felt that all the behavior of the lowest of animal forms was tropistic and that a considerable proportion of the behavior of higher forms was also. One familiar example of a tropism is the apparently mechanical and irresistible movement of certain moths into light (positive phototropism), even though flight directly into a flame results in their destruction. Naturally, not all tropisms are so maladaptive.

Loeb was not reacting against Darwinism but against the anthropomorphic tendency which we have seen represented by Romanes. Despite the fact that Loeb felt tropistic factors could account for a great deal of the behavior of higher forms, he did not attempt to deal with human problems. He did, however, contribute to a problem arising from the human being—the problem of consciousness. He suggested an objective way to determine whether a given organism was conscious. His criterion was whether the organism manifested associative memory. Certainly this criterion is not very exclusive; protozoa, for example, seem to show evidence of associative learning. The question of what organisms are conscious can be given only an arbitrary answer; our operational criterion of consciousness in animals can be chosen at will, and we should be quite clear that various answers to the problem are possible. Any other attempt at solution would have to fall back on our tendency to anthropomorphize.

By this time the study of animal behavior within the biological sciences was becoming widespread. In support of Loeb's position, the biologists Thomas Beer, Albrecht Bethe, and Jacob J. von Uexküll came out strongly for the elimination of psychological terms and the substitution of objective ones. The biologist H. S. Jennings, on the other hand, obtained evidence for the modifiability of behavior in the protozoan, *Paramecium*, and opposed Loeb's mechanistic interpretations of animal behavior. Hans Driesch also opposed Loeb and maintained a vitalistic position (i.e., there is something qualitatively different about living organisms and they are not reducible to physicochemical reactions). Sir John Lubbock was studying ants, wasps, and bees, and the Frenchmen Fabre and Forel were also studying insects. Albrecht Bethe published a mechanistic interpretation of the social life of ants and bees. Certainly animal psychology was a going concern. The pressure of these various researches was beginning to push objective psychology to the fore long before behavioristic psychology was founded as a school in America.

In America, we have already seen how systematically E. L. Thorndike was working with animals. In this he was not alone. Robert M. Yerkes (1876–1956) began his animal investigations in 1900. Yerkes studied crabs, turtles, frogs, dancing mice, rats, worms, crows, doves, pigs, monkeys, apes, and finally man. His research on the apes is the most significant; it is comprehensively summarized in *Chimpanzees: A laboratory colony* (1943). Yerkes at one time collaborated with Watson in the development of visual testing techniques for animals. However, Yerkes was not a behaviorist by persuasion, despite the fact that he did work in comparative psychology that was typically behavioristic in method. Yerkes was an admirer of Titchener and felt that the investigation of experience was one of the most interesting of psychology's problems. Yerkes's contribution to behaviorism was simply in strengthening the position of comparative psychology, especially through his establishment of the chimpanzee experimental station at Orange Park, Florida; the station was named the Yerkes Laboratories of Primate Biology when he retired from active administration in 1941. Yerkes made a great contribution to the advancement of the application of psychology during World War I when he was a leader in developing the program of testing of Army recruits.

W. S. Small at Clark devised the first rat maze in the same year that Yerkes began his animal investigations—1900. The albino rat was so well adapted to being studied in the maze that it has ever since been the outstanding laboratory animal in psychology, and the rat-in-the maze has been a standard situation for the study of learning. Growth of the study of animals was so rapid between 1900 and 1911 that the *Journal of Animal Behavior* was founded then. Finally, Titchener's first doctoral student, Margaret Floy Washburn, published a compendium of animal psychology (1908). The book was essentially an analogical study of human and animal mental processes, but it contained a great deal of factual information and became a classic in the field. Thus, some of the impetus for a behavior psychology came from the camp of the structuralists.

AMERICAN FUNCTIONALISM: 1910

American functionalism was the third trend that led toward behavior-ism. A number of psychologists anticipated Watson in the first decade of the century by pointing, in one way or another, to behavior and objectivity as important for psychology. William McDougall (1871–1938), for example, defined psychology as the positive science of conduct. He made experimental observations on color discrimination in infants in 1901, and his books (1905, 1912) contain objective data; the latter book was even named *Psychology, the study of behavior*. However, McDougall was an outspoken purposivist. He also accepted consciousness and used introspective data and thus cannot be considered a rival to Watson in the formulation of an exclusively objective psychology.

Max Meyer (1873–   ) would be a more serious candidate. He published *The fundamental laws of human behavior* in 1911, a book which reflected his thoroughgoing objectivism. By 1921, he had indicated his behavioristic inclinations more overtly by titling another book *The psychology of the other one*. But Meyer was more an avoider than a seeker of publicity and never became known as Watson did. Meyer was content to pursue his research and writing without systematic aspirations.

A number of other psychologists, some only peripherally related to American functionalism, were talking about behavior. Cattell and Thorndike, we have already noted, were engaged in strictly objective research. We have also mentioned the Russian reflexology school, initiated by I. M. Sechenov and developed by Pavlov and Bekhterev; the latter entitled one of his major books *Objective psychology* (1913); the book was apparently published in Russian about 1910.

The most prophetic of the lot in America, however, was James Angell, whom we have seen as a founder of functionalism. He seemed to recognize that psychology, already largely functional in character, was about ready for a further step in the direction of objectivity. Two expressions of his changing point of view preceded Watson's first published behavioristic pronouncements. In 1910, at the Minneapolis meetings of the American Psychological Association, Angell had this to say (1913, p. 255):

But it is quite within the range of possibility, in my judgment, to see consciousness as a term fall into as marked disuse for everyday purposes in psychology as has the term soul. This will not mean the disappearance of the phenomena we call conscious, but simply the shift of psychological interest toward those phases of them for which some term like behavior affords a more useful clue.

Two years later, at the Cleveland meetings of the association, he presented a paper on this topic which was written just before Watson's first systematic paper. He now spoke at more length (1913, pp. 256 ff.):

> The comparative psychologists have from the first been vexed by the difficulty of ascribing to animals conscious processes of any specific kind in connection with intelligent behavior. . . . Obviously, for scientists engaged in this field of investigation, it would from many points of view be a material gain, in convenience at least, if the possible existence of consciousness might be forgotten and all animal behavior be described objectively. Nor has there been, so far as I am aware, any general objection to this proposal. . . . It is furthermore not unnatural that finding it practicable and convenient, as undoubtedly it is, to waive reference to consciousness in matters relating to animal behavior, the tendency should manifest itself to pursue a similar line of procedure in dealing with human conduct. This tendency does not so much represent any formally recognized program like that of our world-reforming realists, as it does a general drift occasioned by several different sources. Its informal and unselfconscious character is probably indicative of a more substantial and enduring basis than belongs to movements more carefully and more purposely nurtured.

Boring has summarized the situation in American psychology just prior to Watson's founding of behaviorism (1950, p. 642): "America had reacted against its German parentage and gone functional. . . . Behaviorism simply took from functionalism part but not all of the parental tradition . . . the times were ripe for more objectivity in psychology, and Watson was the agent of the times."

THE FOUNDING: JOHN B. WATSON

John Broadus Watson (1878–1958) was born in South Carolina and took his M.A. at Furman University after five years of study. He was attracted to the University of Chicago by an interest in John Dewey, but was "steered into" experimental psychology as a major field by Angell. He also received training at Chicago in physiology and neurology under H. H. Donaldson and Jacques Loeb. After three academic years and three summers he took his Ph.D. in 1903.

Although he had developed an undergraduate interest in philosophy and had taken graduate work in it, apparently this kind of thinking "wouldn't take hold." Watson explained briefly (1936, p. 274):

I got something out of the British School of philosophers—mainly out of Hume, a little out of Locke, a bit out of Hartley, nothing out of Kant, and strange to say, least of all out of John Dewey. I never knew what he was talking about them, and, unfortunately for me, I still don't know.

While at Chicago, Watson worked mainly with animal subjects. Some three decades later, he put his feelings this way (1936, p. 276):

> I never wanted to use human subjects. I hated to serve as a subject. I didn't like the stuffy, artificial instructions given to subjects. I always was uncomfortable and acted unnaturally. With animals I was at home. I felt that, in studying them, I was keeping close to biology with my feet on the ground. More and more the thought presented itself: Can't I find out by watching their behavior everything that the other students are finding out by using *O*'s [observers].

Watson's doctoral dissertation was accordingly done with animal subjects. Directed jointly by Donaldson and Angell, it involved the correlation between the increasing complexity of behavior in the young albino rat and the growth of medullation in the central nervous system. A somewhat better-known piece of research completed at Chicago was his analysis of the sensory cues used in maze learning by the rat. Here Watson followed the techniques of Small, Morgan, and Thorndike and concluded, after systematic elimination of the various senses, that kinesthesis (which he could not completely eliminate) was the most basic to maze learning.

In 1908, Watson accepted a professorship in psychology at Johns Hopkins University. There he continued his experimental laboratory research on animals, collaborating with Yerkes (who was for a short time at Hopkins in the medical school) on an apparatus for testing animals' visual abilities, taking course work and laboratory work with Jennings, and apparently making satisfactory professional progress.

According to his own statement, Watson had early begun to think in more thoroughly objective terms. His animal researches at Chicago stimulated him to his first conversational formulation in 1903; this formulation was not encouraged. Apparently the chief objection at that time was that the formulation applied to animals but not to human beings. His first public expression came in a lecture given at Yale University in 1908, when he was again discouraged, this time on the ground that his formulation was descriptive and not explanatory. Finally, in 1912, he gave a more definitive expression in the course of some public lectures delivered at Columbia University. The first published polemic, a paper entitled "Psychology as the behaviorist views it," appeared the following year in the *Psychological Review* and marked the official launching of the behavioristic school.

Here is the keynote of Watson's original position (1913b, p. 158):

Psychology as the behaviorist views it is a purely objective experimental branch of natural science. Its theoretical goal is the prediction and control of behavior. Introspection forms no essential part of its methods, nor is the scientific value of its data dependent upon the readiness with which they lend themselves to interpretation in terms of consciousness. The behaviorist, in his efforts to get a unitary scheme of animal response, recognizes no dividing line between man and brute. The behavior of man, with all its refinement and complexity, forms only a part of the behaviorist's total scheme of investigation. . . . The time seems to have come when psychology must discard all reference to consciousness; when it need no longer delude itself into thinking that it is making mental states the object of observation.

This first paper on behaviorism was followed shortly by a second one on the concepts of image and affect (1913a). He reduced images to implicit language responses and affect to slight vascular changes in the genitalia. These two early papers were combined into the introductory chapter of his first book, *Behavior: An introduction to comparative psychology*, which appeared in 1914.

In 1919 Watson published another book, *Psychology from the standpoint of a behaviorist*. This volume completed the program outlined in his earlier papers. Objective methods were definitely extended into human behavioral problems. Introspection was accepted as a kind of "verbal behavior." The stress was on genetic factors, and the 1924 revision gave detailed results of Watson's work at the Johns Hopkins Hospital on infantile emotions and emotional conditioning.

Watson felt that psychology as a scientific discipline needed to make a complete break from the past. He declared (1929, p. 3):

[Psychology] made a false start under Wundt . . . because it would not bury its past. It tried to hang on to tradition with one hand and push forward as a science with the other. Before progress could be made in astronomy, it had to bury astrology; neurology had to bury phrenology; and chemistry had to bury alchemy. But the social sciences, psychology, sociology, political science, and economics, will not bury their "medicine men."

In 1920 Watson obtained a divorce. He was asked to resign his professorship at Hopkins; he did, and never returned to academic life. He was displeased with the way the academicians had let their opinions of his personal life influence his career. He went into the field of advertising, where he stayed until his retirement from active life. For several years, however, he continued to lecture in New York City and to publish on psychological topics. In 1925 his *Behavior-*

ism appeared, as a series of lectures, with a strong environmentalist position and a positive program for the improvement of human beings. This was the book that provoked the most attention from the non-psychological public, both favorable and unfavorable. Watson continued to publish occasionally, producing one book on child care and a number of popular articles. However, he was careful to point out the scientific inadequacy of these in his autobiographical statement (1936). Nothing new or significant was produced by him following the mid-20s; this man, whose systematic pronouncements did so much to influence the course of psychology, dropped completely out of professional activity. Whatever our systematic position, we must regret the untimely loss of a figure whose vitality and clarity of expression commanded so much attention and (depending on one's bias) admiration or amazement.

WATSONIAN BEHAVIORISM: SYSTEMATIC CRITERIA

Definition of psychology. Psychology for Watson was "that division of natural science which takes human behavior—the doings and sayings, both learned and unlearned, of people as its subject matter" (1929, p. 4). No mention need be made of the psychic life or consciousness—these are "pure assumptions." Watson clearly included verbalization as a kind of behavior (1925, p. 6): "*Saying* is doing —that is, *behaving*. Speaking overtly or to ourselves (thinking) is just as objective a type of behavior as baseball."

Watson's behaviorism had two specific objectives: to predict the response, knowing the stimulus, and to predict (really *postdict*) the stimulus, knowing the response. The terms stimulus and response represented for Watson broader concepts than their usual definitions allow. Thus (1925, pp. 6, 7):

> The rule, or measuring rod, which the behaviorist puts in front of him always is: Can I describe this bit of behavior I see in terms of "stimulus and response"? By stimulus we mean any object in the general environment or any change in the tissues themselves due to the physiological condition of the animal, such as the change we get when we keep an animal from sex activity, when we keep it from feeding, when we keep it from building a nest. By response we mean anything the animal does —such as turning toward or away from a light, jumping at a sound, and more highly organized activities such as building a skyscraper, drawing plans, having babies, writing books, and the like.

Postulates. Watson's assumptions were stated directly and carefully, although not necessarily in the form of postulates. The major ones may be summarized as follows:

(*1*) Behavior is composed of response *elements* and can be successfully *analyzed* by objective natural scientific methods.

(*2*) Behavior is composed *entirely* of glandular *secretions* and muscular *movements;* as such it is reducible ultimately to physiochemical processes.

(*3*) There is an immediate response of some sort to every effective stimulus; every response has some kind of stimulus. There is thus a strict cause and effect *determinism* in behavior.

(*4*) Conscious processes, if indeed they exist at all, cannot be *scientifically* studied; allegations concerning consciousness represent supernatural tendencies, and as hangovers from earlier prescientific theological phases of psychology must be ignored.

A number of secondary assumptions, having to do with the nature of thinking, the role of the environment, and the like, are discussed in a later section because they are not essential to the central behaviorist argument.

Nature of the data. The character of the data for behaviorism has already been fairly well indicated in the material included under the two preceding criteria. Briefly, they are always objective reports—of muscular movements or glandular secretions in time and space; these must be, at least in principle, quantitatively analyzed; and stimulus-response relationships are the units of description (although they may be rather large-scale units, such as "building a skyscraper," and not merely "muscle twitches").

Principles of connection. Here Watson adopted, at first, merely an older version of associationism—the laws of frequency and recency minus the "effect" aspect that Thorndike had added. Apparently he saw in effect too much of the old mentalistic attitudes, although, as we have noted, a strictly objective and operational interpretation is possible. Watson emphasized that the successful response must always occur and terminate the behavior; Thorndike's retort was that very often certain errors, such as entrances into the more popular blind alleys in a maze, were much more frequently made than the corresponding correct response. Watson subsequently shifted his emphasis to classical conditioning as demonstrated in the laboratory by Pavlov and Bekhterev (see Chapter 6). This he came to recognize as the basis for all learning; the most complex habits could be most appropriately conceived of as combinations and chainings of simpler reflexes. It is interesting, as Woodworth notes (1948, p. 88), that in spite of his enthusiasm for classical conditioning Watson apparently never recognized the very great similarity between Pavlovian reinforcement and

Thorndikian effect; he continued to hold to an exercise law (frequency and recency factors) while accepting classical conditioning principles and even using them himself in his experiments on emotional conditioning in infants.

Principles of selection. Watson assumed a large number of inherited reaction tendencies to stimulation and the "almost immediate" modification of these through conditioning into more and more complicated and individually differentiated tendencies. Thus he wrote (1925, p. 13):

> One of the problems of behaviorism is what might be called the ever increasing range of stimuli to which an individual responds. Indeed so marked is this that you might be tempted at first sight to doubt the formulation we gave above, namely that response can be predicted. If you will watch the growth and development of behavior in the human being, you will find that while a great many stimuli will produce a response in the new-born, many other stimuli will not. At any rate they do not call out the same response they later call out. For example, you don't get very far by showing a new-born infant a crayon, a piece of paper, or the printed score of a Beethoven symphony. . . . It is due to conditioning from earliest childhood on that the problem of the behaviorist in predicting what a given response will be is so difficult.

Thus Watson maintained that selectivity of response and of the sufficient stimulus depends only on innate and acquired S-R connections. Selection does not constitute a unique problem. The older mentalistic concepts of purpose and value are eliminated as explanations.

THE MIND-BODY PROBLEM

The mind-body solution proposed by Watson is at the heart of what has been called radical or metaphysical behaviorism. Historically, the mind-body issue has been of considerable importance, especially with respect to the controversy about behaviorism. We therefore treat the issue at some length; however, we do not feel that the issue has the contemporary importance that might be inferred from the length of the treatment. We wish to express our own bias on this problem quite plainly. We agree with the belief, to which Watson himself sometimes subscribed, that the mind-body issue is not presently a problem for psychology as a science. It is unfortunate that Watson's emphasis upon the mind-body issue tended to preserve it as a problem for psychology. Centuries of philosophical endeavor have netted little of scientific value concerning this philosophical problem. No one has formulated a concept of mind in such a way that it demands the attention of the scientist; its only legitimate meaning for scientific purposes is as a construct or intervening variable, which means that mind has no *unique* status as an object of study. Scientific issues fundamentally are questions of fact; this means that there must be some empirical basis for accepting or rejecting the statements made, with the result that the statements either gain scientific acceptance or can be discarded. There are not yet any factual statements on the mind-body issue. If eventually sufficient empirical data that demand a concept like mind for their examination and explanation become available, mind will become the concern of psychology. Today we are not in a position even to formulate scientifically useful questions regarding mind, let alone give their solutions. And without a science of this thing called mind, there cannot be a science concerned with its relationship to another thing called body. Until there is, the psychologist will continue to study whatever he can study, without concern for its classification or relation to the mind-body problem.

Avowed behaviorists, however, felt a need to accept some more positive position. They did not wish to study consciousness or mind and therefore wished to deny its importance; this they could do only if they accepted some appropriate mind-body position. Of the available positions (see Table 2), two were best fitted to their purposes. First, an epiphenomenal view would imply that consciousness had no causal efficacy and therefore little interest for science; it might or might not attend bodily events and would be of little importance. According to this position, mind would have a role comparable to that of a shadow; it would often, but not always, accompany and more or less follow the outline of the physical object (body) to which it related but would itself have no substance and accomplish no causal effects upon the physical objects producing it (i.e., would not interact). This analogy, like all analogies, is not perfect but is useful in clarifying the general nature of the epiphenomenal view.

Second, a completely physical monism would deny the very existence of mind and would from this point of view serve the purposes of behaviorism admirably.

Watson's early pronouncements were of a less extreme sort. For example (1913b, p. 174):

Will there be left over in psychology a world of pure psychics, to use Yerkes' term? I confess I do not know. The plans that I most favor for psychology lead practically to the ignoring of consciousness in the sense that that term is used by psychologists today. I have virtually denied that this realm of psychics is open to experimental investigation. I don't wish to go further into the problem at present because it leads inevitably over into metaphysics. If you will grant the behaviorist the right to use consciousness in the same way as other natural scientists employ it—that is, without making consciousness a special object of observation—you have granted all that my thesis requires.

Other expressions of this point of view may be found in papers by Walter Hunter and A. P. Weiss. Hunter, for example, said (1926, p. 89):

A brief inspection of the writings of any behaviorist will convince you that he is neither blind, deaf, anosmic, ageusic, or anaesthetic. He lives, and admits quite frankly that he lives, in the same world of objects and events which the pyschologist and the layman alike acknowledge. Let us, therefore, hear no more from the psychologist that his opponent denies the existence of these things.

Weiss also accepted conscious processes as real, even if no more than epiphenomenal. He held that "consciousness (the totality of our sensations, images, and affections) is a purely personal experience and has no scientific value or validity unless it is *expressed* in some form of behavior, such as speech or other form of representation" (1917, p. 307). The general position here clearly stated is that the physical facts of behavior are sufficient; the "mental" correlates to these facts are unreliable and superfluous.

Acceptance of this methodological behaviorism put the behaviorist into the somewhat embarrassing position of admitting that experience exists, even if in a most shadowy manner, and yet cannot be attacked by scientific tools. Thus, faced with the dilemma of either admitting that there are some psychological facts which he cannot explain by natural scientific techniques or denying the existence of such alleged facts, the radical behaviorist, following Watson, chose the latter course: the explicit denial of the existence of any conscious correlates to introspective reports.

By 1924 Watson seems to have come to this alternative. For example, in his debate with McDougall, he said that consciousness "has never been seen, touched, smelled, tasted, or moved. It is a plain assumption just as unprovable as the old concept of the soul" (Watson & McDougall, 1929, p. 14). And, more at length (p. 26):

He then who would introduce consciousness, either as an epiphenomenon or as an active force interjecting itself into the physical and chemical happenings of the body, does so because of spiritualistic and vitalistic leanings. The Behavorist cannot find consciousness in the test tube of his science. He finds no evidence anywhere for a stream of consciousness, not even for one so convincing as that described by William James. He does, however, find convincing proof of an ever-widening stream of behavior.

Another early behaviorist, K. S. Lashley, likewise supported an extreme position. In his single excursion into such polemic, he wrote (1923, pp. 351–352):

There can be no valid objection by the behaviorist to the introspective method so long as no claim is made that the method reveals something besides body activity. . . . The attributes of mind, as definable on introspective evidence, are precisely the attributes of the complex physiological organization of the human body and a statement of the latter will constitute as complete and adequate an account of consciousness as seems possible from any type of introspective analysis.

This view reduces mind entirely to physiological functions and thus represents a radical behavioristic position.

There were several common behavioristic arguments against the existence of consciousness. Though we present them, we do not vouch for their validity. First, the critics asked how the so-called gaps in consciousness, such as allegedly occur during sleep, can be explained? What is lost? What returns? There appears to be no measurable, physical loss. But there are behavior differences. The behaviorists answered that unconsciousness (as in sleep or anesthesia) simply means that certain neural pathways are blocked off so that the person is unable to report stimulation.

Second, the behaviorists maintained that the stimulus is really the important thing in introspection, not the alleged conscious correlates. Introspection is simply a way of reporting what has been learned by language training. Situations in which the "wrong" terms are learned are instructive: for example, the calling of a "red" stimulus "gray" by a color-blind person is wrong only because it is not consistent with most other language reports on the stimulus.

Third, and most important, the behaviorists argued that the assumption of nonphysical events interacting with physical clearly violates the conservation-of-energy principle. Physics tells us that energy is neither created nor destroyed in physical systems; it is only transformed. All the energy within physical systems can be accounted for physically; none is gained from or lost to any nonphysical system. If conscious events affected the body or its physiological processes, they would have to do so by adding or subtracting energy or mass. But this is impossible, according to the conservation-of-energy principle, which is scarcely to be overthrown on the basis of old theological and philosophical dogma. Thus the fact of experiencing, the allegedly mental process, cannot influence even the muscular efforts necessary to speech. And if ideas *can* influence muscles, then they must themselves be physical events occurring in the nervous system—and therefore nonmental.

To follow up the implications of this argument, the radical behaviorist next disposed of both major dualistic positions in the following manner. If mind is granted, for the sake of argument, then it must either (1) affect behavior (interactionism) or (2) not affect behavior (parallelism). But if (1) is true, then the law of the conservation of energy, otherwise inviolate in physics, is violated. If (2) is true, how can one say that one has an "idea," unless so saying is induced by the "idea" itself, as according to (2) it cannot be. Belief in such a well-coordinated set of coincidences overstrains credulity, and the assumption of some outside coordinating force—such as God (occasionalism)—is scientifically unacceptable. Thus ideas cannot be proved unless they affect the nervous system, but to do this they must be within the physical system, and this is quite satisfactory to the behaviorist because it means that ideas are no longer "mental."

Finally, the behaviorists insisted, the conservation-of-energy principle can be applied to the epiphenomenal view. If conscious correlates are accepted as strictly noncausal events, they must nevertheless be produced by physical events. But this means that energy is used to produce them; how else could the physical events operate? Such expenditure of energy without demonstrable physical loss of energy or mass is likewise incompatible with generally accepted physical principles.

The radical behaviorist therefore turned to a strict physical monism, according to which mental is merely a description of the way the physical events function, and consciousness has no independent or unique existence.

WATSON'S EXPERIMENTAL PROGRAM

Although Watson's early work was with animal problems, as indicated above, the best example of his experimental behavioristic program is probably the research he conducted on conditioning and reconditioning of emotional responses in infants. This work also represents the best example of the application of the conditioning technique by any of the early classical behaviorists. The early research is most comprehensively described by Watson in three papers in the volume, *Psychologies of 1925*, from which the following exposition is mainly derived.

Starting from the vantage point provided by the extensive studies of behavior during the fetal and early postnatal periods in animals, Watson began the comparable study of very young human infants in an effort to determine the kind and variety of congenital behavior that could be reliably identified and that was presumably inherited. He states that "almost daily observation" was made of several hundred children through the first thirty days of postnatal life and of a smaller number for longer periods ranging into early childhood. The result of these observations was a catalog of the "birth equipment of the human young," as Watson called it. A long list of behaviors was developed, with objective descriptions for each, but the only experimental, or semiexperimental, observations at this time involved some interesting work with twenty babies on the causal factors in handedness.

Watson's conclusion was that "there is no fixed differentiation of response in either hand until social usage begins to establish handedness" (1926a, p. 29).

Watson was also concerned with the genetic (longitudinal) study of the emotional life of the infant and child. Again the fully objective technique of behavior description was applied, this time intensively to a sample of three-year-olds. Watson found, not too surprisingly, that most three-year-old children are shot through with useless and actually harmful emotional reactions. Not content with what he described as the historically orthodox interpretation of such emotional behavior as inherited, Watson saw the need for new experimental techniques. He early discovered that children taken from typical homes did not make good subjects for the study of the origin of emotions. The obvious need for controlled emotional backgrounds in such subjects was met by use of "strong healthy children belonging to wet nurses in hospitals, and other children brought up in the home under the eye of the experimenters" (1926a, p. 42). With these subjects he instituted a prolonged series of simple tests, primarily made by the introduction of various kinds of animals, at the zoological park as well as in the laboratory. He was unable to find evidence of fear and concluded that accounts of the inheritance of emotional responses to such stimuli were false.

One of the best known contributions of this phase of the research program was Watson's description, as a result of further semiexperimental observations, of the basic conditions that could be reliably depended upon to produce fear, rage, and love in infants. As most students of elementary general psychology have been told, Watson found fear produced by loud sounds and sudden loss of support; rage by hampering of bodily movement; and love by tickling, rocking, patting, and stroking of the skin.

This pioneer research of Watson's constituted an advance and a stimulation to further research. Bridges (1932) questioned the ability to discriminate different emotions in the infant, and her results showed that the only sure distinction was between a general excited state and a quiescent one. It is now generally conceded that adults cannot make reliable judgments of the emotion being shown by an infant unless they have knowledge of the stimulating situation (i.e., pinprick versus stroking). Despite the modification of Watson's conclusions suggested by later research, his basic point that infants show very few varieties of innate emotional behavior has not been contradicted.

From 1918 on, Watson reported, he conducted experimentation designed to determine some of the factors underlying the acquisition and loss of emotional responses in children. "We were rather loath at first to conduct such experiments," he said, "but the need of this kind of study was so great that we finally decided to experiment upon the possibility of building up fears in the infant and then later to study practical methods for removing them" (1926b, p. 51). Watson found it relatively easy to establish fear in a subject through a simple conditioning procedure. This aspect of the research was completed by the demonstration of spread, or generalization, of the conditioned fear response to similar but previously neutral stimuli, in a manner comparable to that found for other kinds of conditioned responses without emotional components.

Finally, Watson turned to the problem of eliminating conditioned fears. A variety of commonly used techniques was first tried experimentally on subjects in whom conditioned fears had been produced: disuse, verbal appeal, frequent application of the fear stimulus, and use of a social (unafraid) model. None of these was effective. Then, in experimentation performed by Mary Cover Jones under Watson's direction, clear evidence for the effectiveness of the unconditioning, or reconditioning, technique was obtained from one subject with whom intensive work was done. This was achieved by bringing in the conditioned fear stimulus at some distance, so as not to elicit the fear response, while the child was eating. After daily introductions of the stimulus (a rabbit) at progressively closer points on the long lunchroom table, the child was finally able to handle it without fear while continuing to eat. Generalized fear responses to similar objects were also found to be eliminated by this procedure.

Watson concluded from the preliminary results of this research that emotional organization was subject to the same laws as other habits; he congratulated himself upon putting the study of emotion upon a natural scientific basis. No doubt he was correct in asserting that his formulation would lead to more research than had James's earlier formulation of the problem of emotion.

SECONDARY CHARACTERISTICS OF WATSONIAN BEHAVIORISM

Today, the methodological characteristics of the behavioristic position are felt to be the most basic because of the wide acceptance of the methodological point and the rejection of, or controversy about, the other points. The secondary aspects of Watson's thinking are not implied by the word behavioristic. However, much of the attack on behaviorism has been directed at these secondary points, and they are many times confused or mixed indiscriminately with the primary characteristics (see Koch, 1954, pp. 5–6).

It is safer to distinguish the critical and secondary propositions. For example, although it is natural for the behaviorist to view thinking as a peripheral process that is easily accessible to behavioral observation, it is not necessary that one accept Watson's peripheralism in order to remain a "good" methodological behaviorist. Characteristics like this one are treated as secondary. We shall discuss language development and thinking, the role of environmental factors in behavior, and determinism and personal responsibility as examples of the secondary characteristics.

Language development and thinking. Because of its use as an example of a behavioristic interpretation of a mentalistic concept, the theory of language development plays a key role in behavioristic thinking. It goes as follows. First, many separate syllables are naturally produced by the normal vocimotor apparatus of any human child. The normal instigation for the first of such mouthings—for example, the common sound "da"—is probably some obscure physiological stimulus. A *circular conditioned response* eventually becomes established as a result of the concurrence of the sound "da" with the saying of it. That is, the infant hears "da" as he says it, and the sound itself becomes a conditioned stimulus to the saying—circular because it is obviously self-perpetuating. The kind of babbling that is characteristic of early vocalization thus develops, with the infant stopping the sequence of repeated syllabizing only when distracted by some other stronger stimulus or when fatigued. Second, the mother or some other adult hears this kind of babbling and repeats the sound, thus producing the conditioned stimulus and causing the child to repeat it. In this manner the child soon learns to imitate many of the sounds the mother makes—or at least to approximate them. Finally, the mother shows the child an object, such as a doll, while repeating the appropriate syllable. In this way new connections between visual stimuli and established sounds are developed. The further process of language development is a long-continued elaboration and refinement of this basic process.

Evidence for the soundness of this general interpretation was adduced from the case histories of deaf mutes—babies born deaf whose initial babblings are not continued and who do not learn to speak, presumably because of the absence of normal auditory conditioned stimuli. Also, with normal children, the behaviorist can point to the common occurrence of parents using so-called "baby talk" in communicating with their infants.

In all this, the behaviorist takes pains to point out, there is nothing save brain connections and reconnections; no mental events are necessary. The child learns to say blue or red or green, or loud or shrill or bass, because of the conditioning of brain events and not because of sensory experience such as sensations. Watson himself preferred to avoid the old terminology as contaminated with mentalistic connotations, but Weiss and some of the less radical behaviorists were willing to use the old terms with new behavioristic meanings.

Watson extended this interpretation into the field of thinking, considered as implicit, or covert, behavior. Such behavior consists of tendencies toward muscular movements or glandular secretions that are not directly observable by the usual techniques of observation but may nonetheless play an important role in activating or mediating other, more overt behavior (e.g., *action currents* detectable in musculature by electronic devices in the absence of any overtly observable movements). As language functions develop in the young child, from two years or so on, much of his motor activity tends to be accompanied by a more or less complete language description. For example, the child will tend to say "Johnny eats"—or some approximation thereto—as he eats. Under parental and other adult pressures, however, he is gradually forced to reduce this overt speech, which is generally regarded with disfavor. It then tends to turn into silent speech —or thinking—in adulthood.

Past training in the form of conditioning accounts for both overt body behavior and language responses, overt and implicit. If the overt behavior aspects are inhibited, the implicit language responses may still be kept; the person is then said to be thinking. Thinking is thus primarily trial-and-error behavior of the laryngeal mechanism (or, as a humorist epigrammatically put it, Watson made up his windpipe that he had no mind). Watson further pointed out, however, that under certain conditions language behavior of this sort might also be suppressed, and then thinking could continue in the form of either overt body activity or visceral reactions. A later Watsonian position was thus that we think with our whole bodies. Because of the poor connections between the visceral and the laryngeal series of muscle changes, visceral thinking responses are largely unverbalized. They are therefore fundamentally important in thinking of an unverbalized sort (determining tendencies, hunches and intuitions, and feelings of unfamiliarity, familiarity, approaching familiarity, certainty, and the like). Although thinking occurs primarily in verbal terms, it may go on in other forms.

Watson's position on the developmental control of unverbalized thinking is well summarized in the following statement (1926b, p. 56):

I want to develop the thesis sometime that society has never been able to get hold of these implicit concealed visceral and glandular reactions of ours, or else it would have schooled them in us, for, as you know, society has a great propensity for regularizing all of our reactions. Hence most of our adult overt reactions—our speech, and movements of our arms, legs, and trunk—are schooled and habitized. Owing to their concealed nature, however, society cannot get hold of visceral behavior to lay down rules and regulations for its integration. It follows as a corollary from this that we have no names, no words with which to describe these reactions. They remain unverbalized.

Although Watson held an essentially peripheral theory of thinking, with stress on muscular reactions and tendencies toward them as the basis of thinking, other behaviorists carried the assumption of progressive suppression of muscular actions on to its logical conclusion. This means a central theory of thinking, with only brain states involved. However this problem is eventually decided, it will not affect the methodological tenets of behaviorism, but only Watson's elaboration of them. B. F. Skinner's treatment of verbal behavior (1957b) shows that Watson's basic behavioristic position regarding language and thinking is very much alive today.

Emphasis on the environment. Although in his earlier writing Watson accepted the importance of inherited behavioral tendencies, in his later work he placed the major emphasis on the role of the environment in the molding of adult human behavior. He declared that the concept of instinct was no longer needed in psychology but took pains to make it clear that he did not doubt the important role of inherited *structures.* Performance then was dependent upon the way in which the environment acted on such structures. The following example attempts to clarify his position (1926a, p. 2):

> The behaviorist would *not* say: "He inherits his father's capacity or talent for being a fine swordsman." He would say: "This child certainly has his father's slender build of body, the same type of eyes. . . . He, too, has the build of a swordsman." And he would go on to say: ". . . and his father is very fond of him. He put a tiny sword into his hand when he was a year of age, and in all their walks he talks sword play, attack and defense, the code of duelling and the like." A certain type of structure plus early training—*slanting*—accounts for adult performance.

In his emphasis on the importance of the environmental factors, Watson pointed to the very great variety of human traits and habits associated with different climates and different cultures. Although recognizing the limitations of available data, he felt that every normal human baby had within it essentially similar potentialities. This presumption led him to make predictions for which he has been strongly attacked. For example, he stated (1926a, p. 9): "I would feel perfectly confident in the ultimately favorable outcome of careful upbringing of a *healthy, well-formed* baby born of a long line of crooks, murderers, thieves and prostitutes. Who has any evidence to the contrary?" Then, admittedly going beyond the facts, Watson went on to state a challenge for which he is famous (1926a, p. 10):

> I should like to go one step further tonight and say, "Give me a dozen healthy infants, well-formed, and my own specified world to bring them up in, and I'll guarantee to take any one at random and train him to

become any type of specialist I might select—a doctor, lawyer, artist, merchant-chief and, yes, even into a beggar-man and thief, regardless of his talents, penchants, tendencies, abilities, vocations and race of his ancestors." . . . Please note that when this experiment is made I am to be allowed to specify the way they are to be brought up and the type of world they have to live in.

Determinism and personal responsibility. In the long-standing disagreement between science, with its acceptance of a strictly determined natural world, and theology and various types of philosophy, in which freedom of the will is generally accepted, there is no question at all about where Watsonian behaviorism stands. Since all behavior, including that called voluntary and involving choices, is interpreted in physical terms, all acts are physically determined in advance.

Watson's own interest was less in the theoretical problem of determinism per se than in the consequent or corollary question of personal responsibility. Along with many other behavioristically inclined psychologists and sociologists, he argued strongly against the assumption that individuals are personally responsible for their actions in the free-will sense. The implications of this belief are especially important in relation to such social problems as crime. The behaviorist would accept punishment of criminals as a part of a general system of social control but not on the basis of a theory of retribution. Instead of retributive treatment by which an errant individual is made to pay for his violations, Watson argued for treatment on the basis of the individual's need for reeducation. He conceded that if criminals could not be salvaged for society—that is, if satisfactory reconditioning could not be achieved—then they should be kept under restraint or destroyed.

Watson himself developed quite a visionary program for social improvement—a so-called "experimental ethics" to be based on behaviorism. His early training in functionalism (if we may apply a behavioristic dictum to Watson's own career) thus shows through particularly at the very end of his *Behaviorism*, where he states (1925, p. 248):

I think behaviorism does lay a foundation for saner living. It ought to be a science that prepares men and women for understanding the first principles of their own behavior. It ought to make men and women eager to rearrange their own lives, and especially eager to prepare themselves to bring up their own children in a healthy way. I wish I had time more fully to describe this, to picture to you the kind of rich and wonderful individual we should make of every healthy child; if only we could let it shape itself properly and then provide for it a universe in which it could exercise that organization—a universe unshackled by legendary folk lore of happenings thousands of years ago; unhampered by disgraceful political history; free of foolish customs and conventions which have no significance in themselves, yet which hem the individual in like taut steel bands.

OTHER PROMINENT EARLY BEHAVIORISTS

Although Watson was without question the first and foremost systematic behaviorist, he had a number of important and sometimes vociferous supporters. One, Albert P. Weiss (1879–1931), was born in Germany but came to the United States at an early age. He was appointed an assistant to Max Meyer, who himself had come from the University of Berlin in Germany to establish the psychology laboratory at the University of Missouri in 1900. Meyer has already been mentioned as an early objectivist whose "psychology of the other one" antedated Watson's behaviorism. Weiss took his Ph.D. with Meyer at Missouri in 1916 and pursued an active career at Ohio State University. Weiss' *A theoretical basis of human behavior* was first published in 1925. Weiss saw behavior as ultimately reducible to physicochemical terms. Psychology was thus a branch of physics. The first chapter of his book, for example, is entitled "The ultimate elements" and consists of a discussion of the structure of matter, the nature of energy, the concept of force, and the like.

The reader should not be misled into assuming that Weiss was merely a farfetched and unrealistic theorist. On the contrary, he was among the most careful and ingenious of the early behaviorists, certainly far more careful than Watson in the matter of defining terms and developing concepts. A single example will suffice to indicate this quality of his theoretical thinking: his attempt to explain voluntary activity (a problem whose resolution Watson did not bother to attempt). The problem for Weiss was to determine what kind of behavior is conditioned to the word "voluntary." Whereas the mentalist says that the mind does the choosing, the behaviorist says that physiological brain states operate and that the term "voluntary" is applied when there is some conflict, or at least potential conflict, between the tendencies to action associated with different sets of stimuli. One set of stimuli eventually achieves a clear physiological channel, and the individual makes a "choice." This is of course determined by past experience as it has shaped the brain connections. "Will power," which is allegedly exercised on difficult choices, was for Weiss merely the spilling over of brain excitations into motor tensions which build up because they are not allowed immediate outlet. The effort of the "will" is assumed from the muscular contractions that are themselves by-products of brain action. Voluntary behavior is thus basically no different from other types but does have this apparently additional characteristic of muscular tension.

Weiss regarded psychology as a biosocial discipline because of the nature of the variables with which it was concerned. He set up an experimental program of research on child behavior, but his early death prevented its consummation.

Edwin B. Holt (1873–1946) was influential mainly through his books, in which he gave strong philosophical support to the behavioristic movement. As Boring (1950) has noted, Holt's greatest specific influence in contemporary psychology has probably come through his role in stimulating E. C. Tolman to a behavioristic combination of purposivism and cognitive theory. *The Freudian wish and its place in ethics* was published in 1915, and *Animal drive and the learning process* appeared in 1931. Holt was a philosophical neorealist who attempted to integrate the essential parts of the behavioristic and the psychoanalytic ("dynamic") movements. He took his Ph.D. at Harvard in 1901 and subsequently taught both there and at Princeton.

Walter S. Hunter (1889–1953) made some of the most important methodological contributions to the field of animal learning. Like Watson, Hunter was trained in functionalism at Chicago, taking his Ph.D. there in 1912 with Angell and Carr. After teaching at Texas, Kansas, and Clark universities, he was at Brown University from 1936 until his death. At Brown, he developed and maintained a small but active department of experimentalists. His methodological innovations included the delayed-response and double-alternation tasks, which were devised for the investigation of higher symbolic abilities in animals. Hunter was primarily interested in laboratory research rather than in theory, but he did attempt to push his new name for the science of behavior, *anthroponomy* (1926). Like most terminological innovations, this one did not stick.

Karl S. Lashley (1890–1958) was a student of Watson's and received his Ph.D. at Hopkins in 1915. He was later at the universities of Minnesota and Chicago, then at Harvard, and finally at the Yerkes Laboratory of Primate Biology. Lashley was a leading physiological psychologist and ventured only occasionally into systematic problems. He is best known for his work on brain extirpation in the rat, which demonstrated the limits of localization.

Lashley's two famous principles of equipotentiality and mass action are generalizations based on this extirpation work. The first principle states that one part of the cortex is essentially equal to another with respect to its contribution to tasks like maze learning. The second states that the efficiency of learning depends upon the total mass of cortex left functioning.

Lashley moved away from a stimulus-response toward a field-theory frame of reference (see Chapter 11), partly as a consequence of the theoretical import of his own findings on brain functions. This shift should not be construed as implying that Lashley's attitude toward a basic behavioristic psychology changed; rather, he changed his position with respect to some of Watson's secondary points. He no longer believed that the most fruitful analysis was to be made in terms of discrete S-R connections which were strengthened via some kind of conditioning process.

Floyd H. Allport (1890–   ) took his Ph.D. in 1919 at Harvard and went on to popularize behavioristic concepts (for example, the circular conditioned reflex theory of language development, described above) in his social psychology text (1924). Allport has continued, at Syracuse University, to apply behavioristic principles to social psychology. More recently, he has turned to the psychology of sensory processes (Allport, 1955). He is perhaps best known because of his description of the J curve, which describes the distribution of responding when some social institution exerts pressure toward some prescribed mode of responding. In such cases, most people behave according to prescription, and the number responding in this way are responsible for the high part of the J. Others, however, scatter away from the modal response, as represented by the lower part of the J. A commonly cited example is the behavior of people at a stop sign: most conform to social pressure and come to a complete stop; others nearly stop; while a few extreme cases continue onward without abating speed.

Z. Y. Kuo (1898–   ) is a Chinese psychologist who was trained in this country (Columbia University). He adopted an extremely environmentalistic position (1922, 1924), far more radical even than Watson's. All alleged instincts were to be explained on the basis of inherited structure and environmental influences. Kuo was far from an armchair speculator on the problem. He watched the development of behavior in the embryo chick by replacing part of the shell with a small transparent window (1932a–e). He found that much chick behavior which may appear to be instinctive is really learned during the embryonic period as a function of conditions within the egg. For example, the alternate stepping behavior of the normal newly hatched chick was shown to be dependent upon certain mechanically induced alternative hind-limb movements inside the shell. Cramping from the yolk sac often acted as a stimulus to the movements. Kuo differed from Watson in that he preferred to think of continuities in behavior rather than conditioning as a basic explanation of behavior changes.

In other research Kuo showed that the cat's reactions to rats are not strictly determined by heredity but can be easily altered from the normal predatory form by appropriate experiences (1930, 1938).

These results all fit well into his environmentalism. Kuo concluded that inherited structures are important but that even these can be molded via environmental influences. He did not believe in any direct native behavior tendencies beyond those that are strictly the result of structural factors.

CONTEMPORARY BEHAVIORISTS

A list of contemporary psychologists who accept the behaviorist methodological point would be a large list indeed. There are four men, however, who have bridged the gap between Watson and the present; they were important during Watson's lifetime and are still important. These four men are E. C. Tolman, E. R. Guthrie, C. L. Hull, and B. F. Skinner. Their contemporary importance is such that their systems are discussed in the third part of the present book. Their past role has been winnowing Watson's behaviorism for the good that was in it and adding their own personal contributions. In addition, we note the important role of such men as C. H. Graham (1951, 1958) and W. R. Garner (Garner et al., 1956) in applying the basic behavioristic notions to the experimental psychology of visual perception, and of D. O. Hebb (1949) and R. C. Davis (1953) in applying these notions to physiological psychology. The psychology that has emerged because of the creative efforts of all these men is far more sophisticated than anything Watson himself produced.

WATSONIAN BEHAVIORISM:
CRITICISMS AND REPLIES

The critical attacks made upon Watson and his brand of behaviorism hit all aspects of the system. Since we cannot consider them all, we shall select those that refer to the methodological and metaphysical points that are most crucial. In addition, the criticisms of Watson's experimental ethics are presented as representative of the attacks upon the more peculiarly Watsonian aspects of behaviorism.

Methodological behaviorism. Although psychology was reasonably well prepared for the stress on objectivity, not all psychologists were satisfied with Watson's pronouncements. An immediate objection was that Watson's extreme formulation left out important components of psychology. This point was made even by those who in general supported much of the objective program. Woodworth, for example, has complained that the early behavioristic emphasis upon strict objectivity hindered the development of research into sensory and perceptual processes by turning the attention of younger men away from this problem area. Acceptance by Watson of the "verbal report" was not satisfactory. For example, Woodworth criticized Watson for attempting to deal, within the strictly objective framework, with the phenomena of afterimages. He stated (1948, p. 84):

> The "phenomena" which Watson finds so interesting and valuable in the after-image experiment are the after-images themselves, not the subject's speech movements. We may conclude that verbal report is not a behavioristic method and that Watson's use of it is practically a confession of defeat for methodological behaviorism.

A broader and more vigorous attack was made by McDougall, who presented himself, as we have noted, as an earlier proponent and user of the strictly behavioristic experiment. McDougall's strictures of this methodological incompleteness of Watson's position may be summarized in the statement that a completely objective approach cannot obtain an adequate account of (1) the functional relations of conscious experiences (e.g., their dependence on external or bodily conditions), (2) the accuracy of verbal report (e.g., whether or not a subject is malingering, as in military service), and (3) the meaningfulness of the verbal report (e.g., in regard to the analysis of dreams). He was particularly eloquent in regard to the incompleteness of the behavioristic account of the finer things in life, specifically music (Watson & McDougall, 1929, p. 63):

> I come into this hall and see a man on this platform scraping the guts of a cat with hairs from the tail of a horse; and, sitting silently in attitudes of rapt attention, are a thousand persons who presently break out into wild applause. How will the Behaviorist explain these strange incidents: How explain the fact that the vibrations emitted by the cat-gut stimulate all the thousand into absolute silence and quiescence; and the further fact that the cessation of the stimulus seems to be a stimulus to the most frantic activity? Commonsense and psychology agree in accepting the explanation that the audience heard the music with keen pleasure, and vented their gratitude and admiration for the artist in shouts and handclappings. But the Behaviorist knows nothing of pleasure and pain, of admiration and gratitude. He has relegated all such "metaphysical entities" to the dust heap, and must seek some other explanation. Let us leave him seeking it. The search will keep him harmlessly occupied for some centuries to come.

On a somewhat different level of argument, Boring has also criticized Watson for his acceptance of verbal report (1950, p. 645):

> [Watson] wished to let in discriminatory verbal report when it was accurate and verifiable, as it is, for instance, in the observation of difference tones, and to rule it out when it was unverifiable, as it is when it consists of statements about the nature of feeling or about the impalpable contents of imageless thinking. . . . The admission of verbal report

was a damaging concession, for it made it appear that behaviorism was asking only for verbal changes and not for a reform in scientific procedures.

The modern behaviorist's answer to Boring's objection is simply agreement. The point basic to the whole behaviorist revolution was to use only verifiable, accurate data in psychology. The thing that furnishes such data is behavior and only behavior. Verbal behavior is behavior and constitutes valuable data if it is verifiable and repeatable. Not all behavior, and hence not all verbal behavior, furnishes useful data; the behaviorist is not obliged to accept data indiscriminately.

McDougall and Woodworth, despite their objections, must use behavior as their datum. Whenever their metaphysics makes them try to use something else, they get into trouble; and we find those who try to use consciousness as the basic datum involved in useless squabbles about what they find there. Consciousness is a tool for the scientist, not an object of study.

As an example of the behavioristic attitude, consider a blind man who is interested in studying visual afterimages. Given someone to set up the equipment, he could successfully conduct research by writing down the verbal responses emitted by his assistant and by his subjects. He would ask no questions about the contents of either his own consciousness or the consciousness of his subjects. He would be unable to use his own experience directly to give him data; he would use the behavior of others. If he could himself respond to light, he might use his own responses as data, but he would not use his own experience directly. Since he cannot use his own responses, the blind man would be truly objective in collecting data, although handicapped as to apparatus. If he were skeptical, he might doubt that his subjects were conscious. As Washburn (1908) early pointed out, the situation is exactly the same for animals as for people other than ourselves; we can only *infer* that others are conscious, and the inference is of no scientific use.

Watson's initial attempts to translate some of the older mentalistic concepts of psychology into behavioristic language have been criticized from two points of view. On the one hand, some have contended that the acceptance of any mentalistic terms weakened his strictly objective system. On the other hand, Heidbreder has taken Watson to task for (1933, p. 275):

. . . a tendency to indulge in feats of translation, and apparently at times to regard translation as an explanation. It is difficult, when reading some of the behavioristic accounts, to escape the impression that the writers regard it as an explanation to say that a wish is an organic set, that a meaning is a bodily attitude, that thoughts are language mechanisms. Yet little is added to the knowledge of wishes, meanings, and thoughts by these statements, which after all consist largely in taking over what is known about these happenings from common sense and the older psychology and devising, often not on the basis of known facts, some possible physiological explanation of them.

Although we agree with Heidbreder that Watson actually did little with such translations, we think they can be regarded as starting points in the objectification of psychological problems. While Watson was guilty as charged of premature enthusiasm, final evaluations of the success of the fully objective program need to await more extensive applications of detailed research like that which Watson himself initiated on emotional conditioning in infants and children. No behaviorist would today rest content with such a purely verbal translation, and probably that is not what Watson really intended either. The point is that the mentalistic terms as they were used had no behavioral meaning, and the translation was really a definition. The concept was then not explained but defined and made workable. Wishes and thoughts did not need translating; they needed *some* meaning that would be useful in a natural scientific framework. Skinner's book, *Verbal behavior* (1957b), makes its chief contribution through such a reformulation rather than through the presentation of new empirical results. This book presents many independent variables, all observable, which seem likely to be useful in the explanation of verbal behavior. It does not, as one example, translate ideas into other terms; ideas are simply not part of the formulation. Watson himself was often content simply to let mentalistic terms disappear rather than translate them into some other language. This elimination of fruitless concepts and the hardheaded attitude toward all concepts were behaviorism's outstanding contributions.

Another line of methodological criticism involves the charge that Watson was backtracking on his own restriction of psychology to observables by including implicit behavior tendencies, which were not directly observed, albeit in theory observable. Woodworth, for example, has complained that Watson, even while postulating such implicit behavior, restricted his own research on emotion to the directly observable overt aspects of behavior and made no effort to investigate the presumably important visceral components.

The answer to this objection is similar to that given to the previous one. Certainly Watson, in his impatient enthusiasm to get to a new and thoroughly objective psychology, went beyond the available data in drawing conclusions and did not himself begin all the necessary research to back up his assumptions. Nevertheless, there is no necessary inconsistency in the assumption of implicit behavior tendencies and the holding to a strictly objective systematic and experimental framework. No one can do everything. Attempts were made to observe the implicit responses, for example, tongue, mouth, and larynx movements in implicit speech, and much later even muscle potentials in deaf mutes. Watson's own research utilized observable responses for its data. It was only natural to make the explanatory system of behaviorism consistent with the data system, and the responses were not expected to *remain* unobservable.

A related criticism has been developed strongly by another avowed behaviorist, E. C. Tolman, who finds in overt behavior a purposiveness that Watson did not admit. Tolman early criticized Watson's research on emotions and stated his position most succinctly as follows (1932, pp. 6–7):

> In short, our conclusion must be that Watson has in reality dallied with two different notions of behavior, though he himself has not clearly seen how different they are. On the one hand, he has defined behavior in terms of its strict underlying physical and physiological details. . . . We shall designate this as the *molecular* definition of behavior. And, on the other hand, he has come to recognize . . . that behavior, as such, is more than and different from the sum of its physiological parts. Behavior, as such, is an "emergent" phenomenon that has descriptive and defining properties of its own. And we shall designate this latter as the *molar* definition of behavior.

Tolman's psychology is proof that he prefers the molar definition of behavior, that he thinks purposiveness must be introduced in order to have a useful psychology. Purpose generally alludes, in Tolman's usage, to some influence of the animal's behavior on the environment; for instance, we may speak of the purpose of an animal's behavior as being the release of a food pellet or the depression of a bar. Usually, the bending of a limb would not be considered a purpose, although this would be a purposeful description compared to the flexion of a muscle. Tolman contends that it is more useful to define responses in molar behavioral than in molecular physiological terms. Watson, like most psychologists before and after him, agreed in practice with this point. He wished to make the additional point that purposive behavior is in principle reducible to the physiological level, although he did not actually work on this level. Other behaviorists, like Guthrie (1952), have attempted to work on a more molecular level. If the problem of psychology is to explain the behavior of an animal in his environment, and if we define purpose in terms of the influence of the animal on the environment, then it seems that a complete psychology must consider purpose as so defined. Watson would no doubt be a purposivist when purpose is so defined. Tolman's quoted statement suggests that he believes Watson recognized this kind of purposivism, since he rightfully accuses Watson of using behavior in both senses.

However, Watson would not agree, nor would most contemporary behaviorists, that purpose as an explanatory concept in the McDougallian sense is legitimate.

The gestalt psychologists have been vociferous in their complaints against the allegedly molecular brand of S-R psychology, as we shall see in the following chapter. But, again, a particularly telling argument came from within the behavioristic camp itself. As suggested above, K. S. Lashley began his professional career as an avowed and enthusiastic behaviorist. His own research, however, convinced him that some of the behavioristic assumptions were in error. As he himself has told the story (1931, p. 14):

> I began life as an ardent advocate of muscle-twitch psychology. I became glib in formulating all problems of psychology in terms of stimulus-response and in explaining all things as conditioned reflexes. . . . I embarked enthusiastically upon a program of experiments to prove the adequacy of the motor-chain theory of integration. And the result is as though I had maliciously planned an attack upon the whole system. . . . The conditioned reflex turned out not to be a reflex, not the simple basic key to the learning problem. . . . In order that the concept of stimulus-response should have any scientific value it must convey a notion of how a particular stimulus elicits a particular response and no other. . . . When viewed in relation to the problems of neurology, the nature of the stimulus and of the response is intrinsically such as to preclude the theory of simple point-to-point connection in reflexes.

Watson's own research efforts were certainly not of the muscle-twitch variety with which he is so often identified; much of the debate over behaviorism has resulted from the discrepancy between the actual behavioristic experimental program and the theoretical framework. According to the theoretical framework of men like Watson and Weiss, all complex behavior is ultimately reducible to combinations and chainings of simple reflexes and even to the terms of physics and chemistry. It is this kind of aspiration that is responsible for much of the opposition. But it would be a mistake to assume that behaviorism is tied to a muscle-twitch view of psychology. It would even be a mistake to assume that Lashley became less a behaviorist because of his findings. In the methodological sense, one can be a field theorist and a behaviorist at the same time; a good example is Tolman himself. The issue between the orthodox S-R behaviorists on the one side and the S-S (Tolman) behaviorists and the field theorists on the other side is still a source of systematic controversy, but its outcome will have nothing to do with the acceptance of behaviorism.

Metaphysical behaviorism. Criticisms of Watson's rejection of the introspective technique were blunted by his acceptance of the verbal report as behavior, as indicated above. The argument that he was neglecting useful data was therefore not valid. The brunt of the critical attack upon his system was transferred to the essentially metaphysical argument against interactionism and against his denial of the existence, and not merely the scientific usefulness, of mind. As we have already stated, we do not regard this issue as a legitimate problem for psychology. Watson's defense of his position, therefore, is of no greater scientific value than the critical attacks of his detractors. Nevertheless, the arguments advanced are of something more than merely historical interest in that they are related to more strictly scientific methodological problems, as we shall attempt to show.

Early attacks upon the extreme behavioristic position on mind were made by behaviorists and nonbehaviorists alike. Angell, for example, cautioned (1913, p. 267):

> After all is said and done, something corresponding to consciousness in its vague common meaning does exist and it is within its compass that the problems of science arise. We must be cautious therefore that in seeking for bettered means of knowing human nature in its entirety we do not in effect commit the crowning absurdity of seeming to deny any practical significance to that which is its chief distinction—the presence of something corresponding to the term mind—the one thing of which the fool may be as sure as the wise man.

And the behaviorist Hunter likewise expressed doubt about the radical position in his conclusion that "no more denial of the existence of 'consciousness' can permanently win a wide following among psychologists" (1924, p. 4). In this prediction Hunter would seem to have been fairly well borne out, since the radical behavioristic position has never been generally accepted.

Some of the attacks upon methodological behaviorism may be more or less directly traced to the underlying assumption of the monistic metaphysical position. A good example is the criticism by Heidbreder. She pointed out that if the behaviorist makes an outright denial of consciousness (1933, p. 281):

> . . . he finds it extremely difficult to explain what he means by some of his terms. When he says that thinking is merely a matter of language mechanisms, or emotion an affair of visceral and glandular responses, he is at a loss to tell where he gets the terms "thinking" and "emotion." He cannot get them from his own awareness of his own inner speech or disturbed heart-beat, for, by hypothesis, such awareness is impossible. The heart and the larynx, to be sure, belong to the physical world, but one's immediate awareness of their action can be based only on one's personal and private sensations. Does the behaviorist mean, then, that a person cannot be aware of his own anger except by means of kymograph tracings, or blood-analysis, or some other evidence of his bodily reactions

that is accessible to others as well as himself—by catching sight of his flushed face, in a mirror, for example, or by seeing directly his own clenched fist?

Heidbreder also pointed out that "in actual practice, behaviorism rejects awareness that arises through the interoceptors and proprioceptors; awareness which arises through the exteroceptors it accepts without question. In this fact lies the clue to the acceptances and rejections that characterize behaviorism" (1933, p. 218).

The behaviorist's reply would probably be to point out that it is difficult for anyone to say how he attributes meaning to words like thinking and emotion. Actually, the behaviorist would urge, they are not learned by some kind of connection to internal events; we learn to say "pain" in certain situations, such as when we observe blood on others or ourselves, or "thinking" when a problem has been presented and the person is oriented toward the problem but otherwise quiescent. We do not actually learn these things on the basis of the contents of our own consciousness alone, otherwise our language would be private. It is not surprising that the awareness which arises through the interoceptors is rejected, while that which arises through the exteroceptors is accepted. For the language of exteroceptors is based on public events, observable at the same time by anyone. The language of interoceptors is based on private events, observable only by one individual. Science is a public enterprise, and only a public language, only public events, are appropriate for its subject matter.

The more recent criticism of Watson's extreme metaphysical position is represented by Bergmann's professional philosophical evaluation (1956, p. 266): "Watson's particular mistake was that in order to establish that there are no interacting minds, which is true, he thought it necessary to assert that *there are no minds*, which is not only false but silly." Bergmann suggests that Watson failed to keep out of trouble because he saw himself as a champion of the revolt not only against structuralism but also against functionalism; for this reason, presumably, he was not willing to stay with the more moderate metaphysical positions of the earlier systematists.

Bergmann's view is probably fairly representative of the modern attitude toward Watson's metaphysics. Watson seems to have felt it necessary to do more than divorce psychology from metaphysics; others within the school that he opposed had already tried to do that. He felt it necessary to destroy the very existence of mind in order that psychologists be freed from the methodological error of attempting to study this presumed entity. Part of Watson's contribution, then, is that he was wrong on a metaphysical point—wrong so courageously and forcefully that he was able to lead psychologists out of the wilderness on a false premise. (The above, of course, is not to be taken as a literal description of Watson's motivation.)

Watson's experimental ethics. There has been a plethora of attacks upon the more specific positions that Watson himself took upon psychological problems. One particular issue is of sufficient generality and interest to justify a detailed account as representative of such arguments. This is Watson's stand on determinism and personal responsibility as it relates to his espousal of experimental ethics.

To begin with, it was pointed out that there is a paradox in the situation where a strict determinist talks as though he is trying to tell people what they should do—as though they could choose for themselves! A related argument is directed against the assumption by the behaviorist of a strict S-R interpretation of behavior, which is seen as mechanistic and therefore of dubious explanatory value in practical problems. McDougall, for example, said (Watson & McDougall, 1929, pp. 71–72): "If all men believed the teachings of the mechanical psychology (and only beliefs that govern action are real beliefs) no man would raise a finger in the effort to prevent war, to achieve peace or to realize any other ideal. So I say that the mechanical psychology is useless and far worse than useless: it is paralyzing to human effort."

Before describing the behaviorist answer to such attacks, we should like to clarify one confusion that is well represented by the excerpt from McDougall. This is the confounding of determinism and mechanism. Now, the defense of mechanism aside, there is no good reason why a basically determinist position should be any more mechanistic than nonmechanistic. It is true that men like Watson, who hold what appears to be a mechanistic view, are also determinists; but so are most field theorists, at least ones like Köhler and Lewin. There is simply no necessary connection between determinism, as a fundamental scientific view, and mechanism. Determinism implies only the belief that events occur according to some kind of natural law, while mechanism implies that the events occur in a machinelike fashion.

The behaviorist would also note that the existence of practical difficulties such as McDougall mentioned does not break down determinism or establish free will. It might be true that man cannot work for his own betterment, undesirable as this may seem. The behaviorist would argue further that the claim of many opponents of determinism that they are for freedom is an illusory one; what they are actually for is not a true freedom but a determinism of another sort than the scientist endorses. Generally, at least in the case of most of those opponents who have a fundamentalistic theological background, this is a determination by some divine force: the individual is free only in order that he can accept the fully determined rule of God.

Finally, the behaviorist would take note of one mistaken claim of those who hope to establish the existence of free will. The Heisenberg principle of uncertainty, or limited measurability, has often been invoked as a proof that free will must exist for the human being, since it presumably does so for the electron. But the Heisenberg principle involves no such assertion for the electron. It is simply a mathematical demonstration that the simultaneous measurement of the position and the momentum of an electron is impossible. There is disagreement within physics about the philosophical implications of this demonstration; Einstein, for example, would not forsake a strictly deterministic picture of even the behavior of the electron on the basis of this principle. Even if the behaviorist accepted his own positivistic medicine regarding the meaningfulness of determinacy in electrons under these circumstances, he would still have a way out. Before the principle could be applied to behavior problems, it would need to be shown that behavioral variables are influenced by the indeterminacy of electron behavior. It may be that the indeterminacy at the atomic level disappears in going to the far more molar level of behavior; certainly indeterminacy has only minute and utterly insignificant effects on molar physical events, such as the flight of golf balls. The behaviorist's conclusion would be that there is thus no really sound scientific basis at the present time for attempting to utilize the Heisenberg principle in relation to psychological problems.

We should like to add some final comments to this discussion. Determinism amounts mostly to a kind of faith, since at best our knowledge can be only partially complete. A test of complete determinism cannot be obtained. This does not constitute any support for the opposite contention that there is some kind of free will. Our own position on this problem is similar to that earlier stated in connection with the ancient mind-body issue: it will take a great deal more relevant data than we presently have or can even envisage before a sound scientific position can be taken on the problem.

To return to the problem originally posed by the paradox of the determinist attempting to influence people, we must concede that there is really no completely logical and satisfactory answer to it. The determinist will most probably agree with Thorndike's point of view as earlier presented (Chapter 6). Essentially, we are free only if determined; we can determine the behavior of other people and build a better world only if the world is lawful. Yet if everything is determined, including our efforts to make changes in nature, as we assume, the behaviorist can only hope that it is favorably determined and that the world will get better. Certainly McDougall's statement that mechanists (he really means determinists) will not raise a finger to prevent war, etc. is false. People who hold this view strongly, like

Watson and Thorndike, *do* attempt to make the world better. This is simply a matter of observation.

THE APPEAL OF BEHAVIORISM

The response to Watson's plea for complete objectivity in the methods and facts of psychology was far from predominantly negative. Both within psychology and without, he was greeted with acclaim of the kind accorded outspoken men of great vision.

The primary reason for the appeal of Watsonian behaviorism is that American psychologists were ready and willing to leave the cramping confines of introspective study. Watson's call for an explicit extension of natural scientific methodology into the field of behavior was bound to be welcomed enthusiastically by many of the younger men. An indication of the extent to which this enthusiasm went is given by E. C. Tolman, who said (1927, p. 433):

> This paper should have been called "The frantic attempt of a behaviorist to define consciousness." In fact, the doctrine I shall present seems to me quite unprovable and to you it will no doubt seem something far worse. And yet so great is my faith that behaviorism must ultimately triumph that I should rather present even the following quite doubtful hypothesis than hold my mouth and say nothing.

Strong supplementary support for the behavioristic doctrine came from the operational movement in physics, which was very quickly welcomed and adapted to psychology, and from the new positivism in philosophy as represented by the Vienna Circle. The relationships of these movements to behaviorism are well discussed by Stevens (1939). The relationship is roughly one of equivalence to methodological behaviorism. All result in an insistence upon the use of the same kind of data and the same attitude toward the data.

There are a number of secondary reasons for the striking success of Watson's call to arms. These have been well summarized by McDougall in his polemic directed against Watson. First, behaviorism was so simple as to be easily understood and undertaken, in contrast to gestalt psychology and structuralism particularly; McDougall's further comment was that Watson's views (Watson & McDougall, 1929, pp. 41–42):

> . . . abolish at one stroke many tough problems with which the greatest intellects have struggled with only very partial success . . . by the bold and simple expedient of inviting the student to shut his eyes to them, to turn resolutely away from them, and to forget that they exist. This naturally inspires in the breast of many young people, especially perhaps

those who still have examinations to pass, a feeling of profound gratitude.

Second, in addition to its natural simplicity, Watsonian behaviorism had the advantage of being a peculiarly American product and so being readily comprehended in this country. Third, Watson's own forceful personality was a factor in the spreading of his gospel.

Two additional factors were suggested by McDougall. First of all, behaviorism was said to be attractive because some people are attracted by anything which is bizarre and preposterous. Second, some were attached to behaviorism out of pity for what they saw as Watson's misguided efforts, especially if they themselves were well informed. These explanations of behaviorism's appeal are more entertaining than serious; McDougall, although he seems to have regarded behaviorism as bizarre enough, certainly showed it little pity. In this he was typical of behaviorism's opponents; there was little relenting on either side.

The response to Watson's appeal was in some ways even more striking outside psychology and the academic-scientific sphere. Woodworth (1948, pp. 93–94) gave some interesting specimen comments from newspaper and magazine reviews of Watson's *Behaviorism*, which called for social reforms. Most instructive are the brief quotations from the *New York Times* ("It marks an epoch in the intellectual history of man") and the *New York Herald Tribune* ("Perhaps this is the most important book ever written. One stands for an instant blinded with a great hope"). Woodworth concluded that Watson's behaviorism was "a religion to take the place of religion." There is no question but that in its fervor and faith it had some of the aspects of religion and that these were partly responsible for its great appeal.

THE CONTRIBUTION OF WATSONIAN
BEHAVIORISM TO PSYCHOLOGY

By now we have probably made clear our opinion that, in spite of his shortcomings, Watson made a very great contribution to the development of a scientific psychology. The primary contribution is the one that we cited as responsible for the welcome reception with which many psychologists greeted behaviorism: it called out plainly and forcefully for a strictly objective study of behavior. The influence of Watsonian behaviorism in objectifying psychology, as to both methodology and terminology, has been enormous. Methodological behaviorism has been so well absorbed into American psychology that it no longer need be argued. As Bergmann said, "Methodological behaviorism, like Functionalism, has conquered itself to death. It, too, has become a truism. Virtually every American psychologist, whether he knows it or not, is nowadays a methodological behaviorist" (1956, p. 270).

An appreciably smaller number would care to be listed as Watsonian behaviorists. Woodworth's 1924 comment is still relevant and applicable to many psychologists (1924, p. 264):

> In short, if I am asked whether I am a behaviorist, I have to reply that I do not know, and do not much care. If I am, it is because I believe in the several projects put forward by behaviorists. If I am not, it is partly because I also believe in other projects which behaviorists seem to avoid, and partly because I cannot see any one big thing, to be called "behaviorism"—any one great inclusive enterprise binding together the various projects of the behaviorist into any more intimate union than they enjoy from being, each and severally, promising lines of work in psychology.

Even Watson's extreme metaphysical position, which we believe was unnecessary, made a kind of contribution. Just as Titchener's strenuous effort to develop Wundtian structuralism gave a thorough trial to that brand of psychology, so Watson's insistent laboring of the mind-body issue has helped to point up the scientific fruitlessness of the problem. There is no necessary relation between one's mind-body position and his experimental or theoretical research. Even Titchener apparently was little concerned with the problem and behaved as though he wished the issue would go away and leave him to his research on more strictly psychological problems. Watson helped to eliminate the problem for today's experimenters. A mind-body position seems to have little influence on research even in fields like psychosomatic medicine, where there is a superficial plausibility to such a relationship. Examination of the actual operations of the researcher, however, will soon indicate that the relationship is an illusory one.

Watson's own personal contribution was primarily, as Boring put it, "as a dramatic polemicist and enthusiastic leader" (1950, p. 645). In addition, we have described several pieces of important research, both with animals and with human young. Nevertheless it is true that he himself contributed little of importance in the way of new technique or new substantive theory; even his loosely formulated notions of thinking and the like were mostly revisions of older ideas. Bergmann went so far as to say of Watson (1956, pp. 267–268): "As I see him, Watson is above all a completer and a consummator—the greatest, though not chronologically the last, of the Functionalists." It is difficult ever to say that a man is really an originator. But if he states issues for the first time clearly and unequivocally, as Watson did, he is at least in this much an innovator. Seldom has a man had such an impact upon the general method and formulation of a science.

Watson's emphasis on the noninteraction of the mind and body within an individual has been emphasized by Bergmann as the major point in his behavioristic program; but in our opinion, Watson's most important contribution rests on the scientifically more significant contention that there is no interaction *among minds*. Washburn believed that consciousness was a useful concept and introspection a useful method. Yet she recognized that the existence of consciousness in any other organism must rest upon an analogy. It must remain an inference based upon behavioral observations. The great import of the Watsonian revolution in psychology was to clarify and elaborate this point: the only interaction among minds is through physical events (words or other forms of overt behavioral cues). Since Watson wished to relegate the mystical minds to the dust heap, we should do him more justice to say that organisms interact only through physical processes. Since science is made by human organisms, and since they have defined it as *public* knowledge, the subject matter of science must be observable by more than one member of the species. It must be *objective*. This is the methodological contribution, a far more important point than the philosophical rejection of mind-body interaction.

In conclusion, Watson's own comments on his contributions are interesting. We quote both from his first polemic statement and from what is probably his last professional word (1913, p. 175):

> In concluding, I suppose I must confess to a deep bias on these questions. I have devoted nearly twelve years to experimentation on animals. It is natural that such a one should drift into a theoretical position which is in harmony with his experimental work. Possibly I have put up a straw man and have been fighting that. There may be no absolute lack of harmony between the position outlined here and that of functional psychology. I am inclined to think, however, that the two positions cannot be easily harmonized. Certainly the position I advocate is weak enough at present and can be attacked from many standpoints. Yet when all this is admitted I still feel that the considerations which I have urged should have a wide influence upon the type of psychology which is to be developed in the future.

And, in his brief autobiographical statement, he concluded (1936, p. 281):

> I still believe as firmly as ever in the general behavioristic position I took overtly in 1912. I think it has influenced psychology. Strangely enough, I think it has temporarily slowed down psychology because the older instructors would not accept it wholeheartedly, and consequently they failed to present it convincingly to their classes. The youngsters did not get a fair presentation, hence they are not embarking wholeheartedly

upon a behavioristic career, and yet they will no longer accept the teachings of James, Titchener, and Angell. I honestly think that psychology has been sterile for several years. We need younger instructors who will teach objective psychology with no reference to the mythology most of us present-day psychologists have been ·brought up upon. When this day comes, psychology will have a renaissance greater than that which occurred in science in the Middle Ages. I believe as firmly as ever in the future of behaviorism—behaviorism as a companion of zoology, physiology, psychiatry, and physical chemistry.

SUMMARY AND CONCLUSIONS

Behaviorism, like all other schools, has a long past. It goes back directly to Descartes, who viewed the body of man as a complex machine. Watson's real contribution was the consistency and extremity of his basic viewpoint; he simplified and made objective the study of psychology by denying the scientific usefulness of mind and consciousness. He espoused a metaphysics to go with his methodology and felt it necessary to deny the existence as well as the utility of consciousness, or at most to regard it as an epiphenomenon with no causal effects on behavior. His methodological point today is accepted, either wittingly or unwittingly, by nearly all experimental psychologists. Most other psychologists also are methodological behaviorists, and the indication at present is that unanimity is increasing rather than decreasing.

His metaphysical point, like most metaphysical points within science, is neither accepted nor rejected for scientific purposes but simply called irrelevant. There seems to be no evidence that a mind-body position has a marked influence on the work done by a psychologist. Rather, the scientist seems more likely to accept a mind-body position which harmonizes with his work.

Watson's secondary positions on issues like environmentalism and peripheralism have served to encourage research. However, they are today regarded as preliminary formulations and no longer useful or meaningful as originally phrased.

The reasons for the acceptance of Watsonian behaviorism are related to the clarity and force of Watson himself. The close relationship of his psychology to the American tradition also made his credo more desirable. Contemporaneous and somewhat later developments in physics (operationism) and philosophy (positivism) accorded so well with behaviorism that the conjunction of the three movements added power to all. The confining influence of structuralism also added impetus to any movement that was away from it.

Criticisms of behaviorism have been and continue to be vociferous. They have swept away most of the excesses of behaviorism and changed its form markedly. Metaphysical behaviorism, many of Watson's secondary tenets, and any mechanistic views that may have been associated with too rigid an S-R reflex formulation have disappeared in the storm of protest. The foundation stone, behavioristic methodology, has stubbornly resisted and must today be regarded as a solid and apparently enduring contribution of John B. Watson. However, a stone is not a house, and a methodological restriction not a system; so today, as there is no structuralism, there is no complete system called behaviorism.

further readings

Diserens's (1925) paper on psychological objectivism is a classic historical treatment of behavioristic antecedents. The most useful primary publications of a behavioristic sort are Watson's *Behaviorism* (1930), Meyer's *The psychology of the other one* (1921), and Weiss' *A theoretical basis of human behavior* (1925). Tolman's *Purposive behavior in animals and men* (1932) represents an important broadening of the basic behavioristic doctrine. For the flavor of the early polemics, the student will do well to consult the interesting little volume reporting the debate between Watson and McDougall, *The battle of behaviorism* (1929). A recent comprehensive volume on the various facets of the mind-body problem is edited by Feigl, Scriven, and Maxwell (1958). Secondary sources, mostly from a critical point of view, are to be found in Woodworth's *Contemporary schools of psychology* (1948), Heidbreder's *Seven psychologies* (1933), Murphy's *Historical introduction to modern psychology* (1949), and Roback's *A history of American psychology* (1952). Stevens's classic (1939) paper, "Psychology and the science of science," relates the behavioristic trend to logical positivism and operationism and is a most useful historical treatment. Finally, a recent treatment of behaviorism from a highly sympathetic point of view is found in Spence's (1948) paper. Other recent treatments are cited in Chapter 10.

gestalt psychology 8

Gestalt psychology was born with Max Wertheimer's (1880–1943) paper (1912) on apparent movement. The paper was a report of work by Wertheimer, Wolfgang Köhler (1887–   ), and Kurt Koffka (1886–1941), the cofounders of the new school. Like most new schools, gestalt psychology cleared away some of the old problems in psychology and pointed the way to new ones. Its rejection of the artificiality of much of the psychological analysis of the day led to a collateral concern for problems closer to everyday-life experiences. The problem of the organization of elements into wholes and the laws of such organization were emphasized. The gestalt type of examination and explanation of perceptual phenomena, such as afterimages and apparent movement, was begun. Learning theorists were forced to consider gestalt principles, such as organization and insight, in the formulation of their theories. We have already seen Thorndike's belongingness as an example of such a concession to gestalt principles.

Gestalt psychology was and is especially prone to be misunderstood. It was the product of European culture, with its credo originally published in a foreign tongue. Fortunately, gestalt psychology had founders who remained active in psychology. The sojourns of the three founders in the United States after they fled Nazism helped to clarify the gestalt position and to make its principles available in English. The early misunderstandings are beginning to dissipate. Köhler's book (1947) has been especially helpful. For example, he has pointed out (p. 168) that gestalt psychology does not reject analysis in general. Many American psychologists had felt that the gestalt derogation of artificial introspective analysis implied a rejection of all analysis. Köhler has also pointed out that the gestalt opposition to quantitative statements was a prescription for psychology because of

171

its youth, not an objection to the ultimate desirability of such formulations.

This improved understanding of the gestalt position and the interaction of gestalt psychology with the more Americanized brands have resulted in the general acceptance of several fundamental gestalt ideas even in the relatively unfriendly climate of American psychology. An acceptance of the gestalt point that there are wholes which lose much of their identity and importance by an analysis into parts has helped make the study of relatively unanalyzed, global variables more respectable in experimental psychology. The size of the unit of analysis is now seen as arbitrary and a matter of convenience. This position is quite different from the Watsonian theoretical tendency to reduce every molar act to chained reflexes, using only relatively molecular units of analysis. An "atomistic reductionism" is no longer the exclusive concern of psychology. If the psychologist does analyze situations into a number of simpler variables, he recognizes the need for what may be called *combination laws.* These combination laws specify the relationships between the several simple variables and tell how they combine in the production of the final behavior. It is no longer considered sufficient to specify the relationships between single independent variables and the dependent variable, "other things equal." Situations can be completely understood only when we know how the several relevant variables interact. The gestalt point that new phenomena are created (*emerge*) in complex situations is accepted.

The gestalt emphasis on phenomenology makes it difficult for present-day users of introspection to ignore the phenomenological contents of experience, that is, the direct, naïve reports of untrained observers. Since the phenomenological report contains meanings directly, it is no longer necessary to quibble about stimulus errors, which presumably arise from prior knowledge about the stimuli. The report, with its meaning, can be accepted as such. Since the wholes given in phenomenological experience are assumed to be legitimate phenomena in their own right, there is less concern with an attempt to break every experienced whole into its constituent elements. The concept of constancy in perception has been rethought. The old concept, which was based on constancy in response when local stimulation varied (as when you move away from a man and the retinal image changes, yet he continues to appear to be the same height) was no longer meaningful. The gestaltists insisted that *local* stimulation should not be expected to coincide with *local* response, for both were parts of a total field whose influence would be expected to change the nature of the response to every local stimulation present. Thus the man should be *expected* to remain the same perceptual height, for the field of which he is a part retains many of its relationships through the shift in distance.

THE ANTECEDENTS OF THE GESTALT MOVEMENT

When one speaks of antecedents of modern psychological systems, Wundt comes readily to mind. He was the villain against whom the systematists rebelled, and his role was necessary. His elementaristic position was a target for gestalt psychology just as it was for functionalism and behaviorism. However, he was an antecedent in a more direct sense; his principle of creative synthesis was an early concept that implied some recognition of the difference between wholes and the sum of their parts. This concept was much like John Stuart Mill's mental chemistry. Both ideas recognized that new characteristics might emerge from the combination of elements into wholes. Neither man, however, did enough about his notion to satisfy the founders of gestalt psychology.

Franz Brentano, whom we have discussed in relation to Wundtian psychology (Chapter 4), believed that psychology should concentrate upon the process or act of sensing rather than upon the sensation as an element. He used introspection, but his introspection tended toward the naïve phenomenological variety. He considered Wundt's introspection artificial and strained. Thus he anticipated the gestalt method of introspection and made the direct, naïve expression of experience respectable. However, he did not recognize the emergence of new phenomena with increasing complexity.

Carl Stumpf (1848–1936) was another antecedent of gestalt psychology, but in a strange sense. Köhler dedicated a book (1920) to Stumpf, his teacher; Wertheimer and Koffka were also students of Stumpf's. One would expect that the man who taught all the founders of gestalt psychology must have given them many of their ideas for the new movement. Yet, according to Hartmann (1935, p. 32), Stumpf himself denied any direct systematic influence on the new movement. The three founders do not mention any such direct influence either. Stumpf's psychology did, however, represent some concession to phenomenology. Boring (1950, p. 595) reports that Husserl and Brentano won Stumpf over to phenomenology.

Most of the other antecedents had a more direct systematic influence. Ernst Mach (1838–1916) was a physicist who came into the history of psychology by the back door. He was interested, it is true, in the new psychology and contributed to it both in theory and in experiment. He insisted that sensations form the basis of all science. This was a point that a physicist could make as well as a psychologist, for it relates to the general question of epistemology. Yet in his specification of the nature of sensations, he was led to postulate the existence of two entirely new types of sensation: sensation of space form, as in a circle or any other type of geometrical form, and sensation of time form, as in a melody. These sensations of space form and time form Mach correctly (according to the gestalt psychologists) stated to be independent of their elements. For example, circles can be red, blue, large, or small and lose nothing of their circularity. Similarly, the notes of the melody can be played in another key without any alteration of their time form.

Christian von Ehrenfels (1859–1932) shared with Mach an interest in the new psychology. Although he was a philosopher for the most part, he elaborated Mach's psychological notions of the new elements into a theory and called it *Gestaltqualität*. He is generally recognized as the immediate intellectual precursor of the gestalt movement, although the gestalt theorists have denied any direct influence. In his analysis of the new sensational elements, he was faced with the problem of whether they were really new. Could the new qualities be reduced to combinations of the other qualities? He decided that although the qualities depended upon the elements arranged in a certain pattern, they are nevertheless immediately experienced and do not inhere in any of the component elements. They are present in the mind and not in the physical events.

These men postulated new elements, but they were not gestalt psychologists. We miss the point of the gestalt revolution unless we see that its precursors, like Mach and von Ehrenfels, were in reality merely carrying on in the old atomistic tradition. They simply discovered new elements, rather than eschewing elementarism as the gestaltists did. They pointed out the problem but gave an entirely wrong solution. They complicated rather than simplified. Primarily for this reason, the gestaltists have disclaimed any direct relationship.

Alexius Meinong (1853–1920) gave the same wrong answer as von Ehrenfels had. He was a pupil of Brentano's and the leader of the Graz school of psychology. He elaborated the ideas of von Ehrenfels and changed his terminology, but added nothing essentially new. His methodology tended toward the phenomenological, again anticipating gestalt. The break of act psychology and the psychology of the Graz school with the academic tradition was not clean enough. These schools did not flourish and gain adherents as did gestalt psychology later. And, although we can see them now as antecedents in the intellectual, systematic sense, there was no real continuity of the personnel of these schools and the originators of gestalt psychology. The origin of gestalt psychology can therefore be thought of as occurring by the very process that gestalt psychology later was to advocate as the basis of learning—an insight!

Several psychologists at Göttingen were important precursors and supporters of gestalt psychology. G. E. Müller (Chapter 4) directed the laboratory there and supported a program of introspective research that savored of the gestalt phenomenological approach. He was later to claim (Müller, 1923) that there was really nothing new in the gestalt approach to perceptual theory. The research of three other men in his laboratory lent strong support to his contention. Had events taken a different turn so that these men had had the inspiration to make their results the ground for a school, the names of gestalt psychology's founders might have been Erich R. Jaensch (1883–1940), David Katz (1884–1957), and Edgar Rubin (1886–1951). All three men were working on and publishing phenomenological investigations in 1911 or 1912, which was the year Wertheimer published his results and launched gestalt psychology.

Jaensch was working with visual acuity, and he showed that large interacting systems had to be considered in the discussion of acuity; the elementary atomistic approach would not do. Katz had already published an investigation of color in 1907, and in 1911 he published an extensive monograph on color. It contained a careful phenomenological description of the different kinds of colors: surface colors, volumic colors, and film colors. He described the conditions under which each type of color could be observed and did *not* try to explain the different types of colors by recourse to the combination of sensations of color with some other elements, as the Wundtians would have. Rubin did not begin his work until 1912, the year the gestalt school was founded. He developed the distinction between figure and ground in his phenomenological investigation. He noted that commonly part of the total stimulus configuration stands out, while part of it recedes and is more amorphous. He produced several demonstrations in which the figure and ground can be reversed. He did not publish until 1915; the gestaltists pounced on his work immediately and appropriated it to their system, since it was another instance of evidence which required the consideration of the totality of stimulation for its explanation.

Meanwhile, others were being beckoned by problems similar to the one so ingeniously solved by the gestalt triumvirate. In England, G. F. Stout (1860–1944) in 1896 raised questions about the whole-part relationship. He was chiefly concerned with form and concluded that "an element which is apprehended first as part of one whole, and then as part of another, is presented in two different points of view, and so far suffers transformation" (1902, p. 71). He had stated clearly the gestalt point that there exist wholes which influence the mode of existence of the parts.

Even earlier, William James in the United States had challenged psychological atomism. He said (1890, I, p. 255): "The traditional psychologist talks like one who would say a river consists of nothing but pailsful, spoonsful, quartpotsful, barrelsful, and other moulded forms of water. Even were the pails and the pots all actually standing in the same stream, still between them the free water would continue to flow." Like the water, the stream of consciousness for James had a reality independent of its atomistic analysis.

Curiously, James also used an analogy that was almost exactly like one used by Köhler many years later (1890, I, p. 279, footnote):

> In a sense a soap bubble has parts; it is a sum of juxtaposed spherical triangles. But these triangles are not separate realities. Touch the bubble and the triangles are no more. Dismiss the thought and out go its parts. You can no more make a new thought out of ideas that have once served you than you can make a new bubble out of old triangles. Each bubble, each thought, is a fresh organic unity, sui generis.

Had James seen fit to elaborate his point sufficiently, gestalt psychology might have had an earlier founding.

We have already met another American who was surprisingly close to gestalt principles, although his point was made relative to quite another empirical area. John Dewey in his reflex-arc paper (1896) was advocating a field approach, a study of the whole situation in itself, a discarding of the artificial analysis into stimulus and response. The reflex arc was seen to be an organic unity, losing its meaning and reality in the analysis (cf. Chapter 5).

The very atmosphere of thought just prior to the founding of gestalt psychology seemed to be permeated with the notion of fields, the notion of organic wholes. And thought of this sort was not limited to psychologists and philosophers. For example, E. B. Wilson, a leading biologist, said that the cell must not be regarded as an independent unit, the only real unity being that of the organism.

THE FOUNDING OF THE GESTALT SCHOOL

In 1910, Max Wertheimer arrived at the Psychological Institute in Frankfurt am Main. Köhler and Koffka helped him to do research on apparent movement, serving as subjects, and the three of them had long discussions of the results of their research. The apparent-movement phenomenon, whose best-known everyday-life application is probably the motion picture, had long been a difficult problem for psychological interpretation. In essence, the problem was how to explain the perception of movement resulting from a series of still stimuli.

Wertheimer worked with two slits, one vertical and the other inclined 20 or 30 degrees from the vertical. When light was thrown first through one slit, then the other, the slit of light appeared to move from one position to the other if the time between presentations of the two lights was within the proper range. Wertheimer worked out the range within which movement was perceived. The interval of around 60 milliseconds was optimal. If the interval between presentations was longer than about 200 milliseconds, the light was seen successively first at one, then at the other position. If the interval was too short, 30 milliseconds or less, both lights seemed to be on continuously. Wertheimer gave one type of movement that occurred the name *phi;* he wished to give it a name that would emphasize its independent character as a phenomenon in its own right. It was a phenomenon which could not result from the summation of individual stimulations, for certainly an elementarist could not argue that the addition of a second stationary stimulation to a first stationary stimulation could yield, by summation, a sensation of movement. The founders of gestalt psychology were perhaps fortunate in working with an experimental paradigm which made it so crystal clear that the over-all situation was critical in determining what was perceived.

Wertheimer's monograph (1912) describing the research contained an explanation of apparent movement so simple, yet so ingenious, that it served as the basis of the new school of psychology. The explanation was essentially that apparent movement did not need explaining! It simply existed as a real phenomenon in its own right, a phenomenon irreducible to simpler sensations of any kind. An attempt to analyze it into simpler sensations, in the orthodox Wundtian manner, would destroy the reality of the phenomenon as such. Apparent movement would not be found to exist except in situations where prescribed *relationships* between elements held.

This apparently simple beginning of gestalt psychology was really not so simple as it might now seem. Its principles were completely counter to most of the academic tradition of German psychology. To regard a complex experience as having an existence of its own amounted to revolution. To maintain, as Wertheimer did, that the *primary* data of perception are typically structures (*Gestalten*) was heresy to the German introspectionistic tradition and to its American counterpart which was flourishing under Titchener. Structures, for these psychologists, were things to be broken down into the elements, which were primary.

In addition, Wertheimer maintained that it was legitimate for introspection to use simple, naïve, descriptive words. He maintained that local sensations should not be expected to concur with local stimulation because both were part of a field, a whole, which influenced the individual parts in a way depending on the structure of the whole.

Not only did Wertheimer advocate these things, Köhler and Koffka advocated them vociferously. As Köhler said in his obituary for Koffka (1942, p. 97):

Those were years of cheerful revolt in German psychology. We all had great respect for the exact methods by which certain sensory data and facts of memory were being investigated, but we also felt quite strongly that work of so little scope could never give us an adequate psychology of real human beings. Some believed that the founding fathers of experimental psychology had done grave injustice to every higher form of mental life. Others suspected that at the very bottom of the new science there were some premises which tended to make its work sterile.

With such cheerful revolutionists, the movement gained momentum. There were many in Germany, as in America, who were dissatisfied with the artificiality and paucity of results of the older psychology. Gestalt psychology quickly gained support from them. Many psychologists were happy to find a way to avoid the proliferation of elements needed to explain each new complex experience. They did not believe that the legitimacy of the phenomenal approach, or of the emergent real phenomena, could any longer be denied. This was the primary assumption of the developing school. Let us look further at the set of tenets developed by the new psychology.

THE TENETS OF GESTALT PSYCHOLOGY

The whole-part attitude.   The attitude of gestaltists toward wholes has sometimes been difficult for others to grasp. Certainly it is not a new distinction that they make between a whole and the sum of its parts; the Chinese sage, Lao-Tse, is said (Hartmann, 1935, p. 9) to have expressed in 600 B.C. the notion that the sum of the parts is different from the whole. Skinner (1938, p. 29) said that the question whether the whole is different from the sum of its parts is a pseudo problem. Yet many have been concerned with it, and it may justify as much investigation as that other long-lived puzzle, the mind-body problem, in order to find out whether or not it is a profitable question to ask.

Max Wertheimer had this to say about the whole-part problem as it occurs with respect to the given in experience (Wertheimer, 1922, as translated in Ellis, 1938, p. 14): "*The given is itself in varying degrees structured* (Gestaltet), *it consists of more or less definitely structured wholes and whole-processes with their whole-properties and laws, characteristic whole-tendencies and whole-determinations of parts. Pieces almost always appear as parts in whole processes.*"

Wertheimer was here emphasizing the fact that the structure of experience, like the structure of a house, is important. The nature of the human being is such that our perception, though it may be based on unstructured aggregates of items, is itself to some extent structured. And experience as structured has a structure character that is unique to a particular structure; if it is structured in some other way, it will be quite different. Visualize, for example, six dots in a line versus the same dots in a circle. Here the different structures are given in the stimulus, but certainly there is a vast difference between the experiences. Orbison (1939) gave a demonstration which can be used as a clear and dramatic proof that the mode of appearance of a part is affected by the structure of which it is a part. The objectively identical squares in Figure 1 appear quite different because they are parts of different wholes, or patterns.

Analogies from other fields which demonstrate the importance of structure and the difference between wholes and the sums of parts are common. One of the oldest and most familiar is water, which is quite

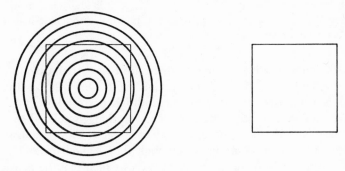

FIGURE 1. An illustration of the dependence of perception of a part upon the pattern of the whole. (*Adapted from Orbison*, 1939, *p.* 42.)

different from a simple mixture of its elements, hydrogen and oxygen. Water has emergent qualities, that is, qualities that emerge only in the combination of its elements. We can know about the characteristics of the compound, water, only by studying water directly; the characteristics could not, at least until very recently, be predicted by a knowledge of the characteristics of the elements alone. Although new advances in theories and techniques of wave mechanics have made it possible to make such predictions, the extent to which these recent developments in methodology will invalidate the gestalt argument remains to be seen.

Köhler's Die physischen Gestalten (1920) is a relatively clear statement of the gestalt view of the whole-part relationship, although such a complex problem with so many facets is never really simple. Here Köhler said in part (1920, as translated in Ellis, 1938, pp. 18–19):

Let us consider under what conditions a physical system attains a state which is independent of time (i.e., a state of equilibrium or a so-called stationary state). In general we can say that such a state is reached when a certain condition is satisfied for the system *as a whole*. The potential energy must have reached a minimum, the entropy a maximum, or the like. The solution of the problem demands not that forces or potentials assume particular values in individual regions, but that their total arrangements relative to one another in the whole system must be of a certain definite type. The state of process at any place therefore depends in principle on the conditions obtaining in all other parts of the system. If the laws of equilibrium or stationary state for the individual parts can be formulated separately, then these parts do not together constitute a *single* physical system, but each part is a system in itself.

Thus an electric circuit is a physical system precisely because the conditions prevailing at any given point are determined by those obtaining in all the other parts. Contrariwise, a group of electrical circuits completely insulated from each other constitutes a complex of independent, single systems. This complex is a "whole" *only* in the mind of one who chances to think of it as such; from the physical standpoint it is a summation of independent entities.

Hartmann has pointed out that there are two extreme views of the physical world and the role of systems in it. One view is that the world is composed of independent additive parts whose total constitutes reality. The other view is that everything is related to everything else, and there are no independent systems. The gestaltists held neither of these extreme views, although they leaned toward the latter. They recognized that there are systems which may be considered independent for practical (including practical scientific) purposes. Hartmann has concluded (1935, p. 42): "Both evils are avoided as soon as one recognizes that *the laws of science are the laws of systems,* i.e., structures of finite extent—a generalization applicable to both physics and psychology."

The gestaltists, then, wished to extend these ideas about physical systems to psychology. They maintained that, in biology and psychology as in physics, there are phenomena whose character depends on the character of the whole field. In visual perception, for example, the thing seen was thought to be a function of the total, over-all retinal stimulation rather than of the stimulation of any specific local point. Unfortunately, the nature of the psychological field is not always clear.

In 1955, at the American Psychological Association meeting in San Francisco, the physicist Robert Oppenheimer (1956) said he had no idea what a "psychological field" could mean. The statement drew laughter and applause from the audience of American psychologists. Apparently many of them did not know either and felt either that there is no such thing or that it is a concept overworked and ill defined. Yet Köhler's analogy, quoted above, seems simple and reasonable enough. The real question is whether or not the application can meaningfully be made to psychology. Let us examine this question. What meaning can wholes, systems whose parts depend on the whole, or fields, have in psychology?

One of the key issues is the determination of what constitutes an isolated system. The gestalt contention has been that the fields or systems are widespread in psychology and that the elementaristic analysis of structuralism or behaviorism destroys the meaningful relationships these fields might have in psychological laws. At the same time, the gestaltists have not denied that the proper use of analysis is necessary. How can we determine whether or not a particular field can be further analyzed without destruction of the very relationships we intend to study? It seems that the only way to do so is by attempting both analysis and the use of the unanalyzed field in the construction of psychological laws. The decision about which should be used will eventually be made on a pragmatic basis. If the molar, gestalt approach leads to more useful laws, and if no further analysis is necessary, then this approach will be adopted for the particular purpose. On the other hand, if this approach does not succeed, further analysis must be carried out.

The gestalt psychologist proceeds on the assumption that the unit of description should be chosen by the organism being studied; that is, the organism's responses determine what constitutes a meaningful whole. For example, if in a study of perception an observer reports that he sees a tree, then "tree" will become a unit of description, rather than some combination of greens, browns, textures, and the like. For this particular analysis, the tree as perceived will be assumed to be a reasonably isolated system and a meaningful unit of analysis. The acceptance of phenomenological description implies an acceptance of the units decided upon by the phenomenological describer.

Many times, the unit is chosen that seems most natural to the scientist; he makes a phenomenological decision himself. For example, he may decide to choose as a response unit any depression of a bar by a rat. This is the unit of response that seems most useful to the scientist. Since people make science, some such method seems inevitable. The gestaltist in his willing acceptance of phenomenological description has recognized that knowledge will always depend in part on the nature of the perceiving organism and at the same time has decided to live graciously with that limitation.

GESTALT PSYCHOLOGY AND PHYSIOLOGY

Gestalt psychology has frequently used the concept of field, and most of its examples of fields have been borrowed from physics. From Oppenheimer's remarks, we may infer that field does not always mean the same thing in psychology as in physics, since he understands one kind and not the other. In physics, the field is an inference made directly from the movements of particles within a portion of space. The field is then given a mathematical description so that all such movements can be predicted from the description. The field has only these mathematical properties; it has no existential properties.

In psychology, a similar situation *may* obtain. By "perceptual field," the careful psychologist may mean nothing more than certain antecedent-consequent relations and the verbal or mathematical description of a state of affairs which would allow the derivation of the observations. The concept of field is most likely to be used where the consequent (verbal report or other behavior) does not depend in a point-to-point fashion upon the local characteristics of the stimulus. If field is used in this strict sense, as a mathematical device for describing relationships, there is a considerable kinship between psychological and physical fields. Of course, if the psychological field does not allow predictions, it is essentially meaningless. A psychological field, used thus strictly, is many times more "physical" than a physiological field, which is quite likely to be a pure assumption, especially when used by psychologists. That is, there will often have been no observations of any kind at the physiological level. If the physiological field is recognized as a model which helps in making predictions, there is nothing wrong even with this usage, for it makes no difference to its predictive power whether the field is thought of as physiologically localized or not. The unfortunate thing is that the reader may be misled into thinking that the physiological field is based on some physiological evidence.

As yet, the picture of cerebral action is quite incomplete. The early ablation work of Franz and Lashley, referred to in Chapter 7, demonstrated that the mode of action of the brain must be extremely complex, a conclusion that has never been brought into question. There is a good possibility that some type of field action is involved. On the other hand, Hebb's *The organization of behavior* (1949) shows that the attempt to explain brain action without the invocation of a field concept has not been abandoned. And, whatever the final explanation, there is certainly no detailed field explanation which is accepted at the present time. The description of brain fields given by the gestalt psychologists depends largely upon data from perceptual, not physiological, experiments. Prentice (1959, p. 451) cites recent physiological research which provides some exceptions to the above statement, but the physiological results thus far are not overwhelmingly impressive.

We must conclude that the gestaltists' physiological statements should be regarded as models which presumably make possible the predictions of results on the psychological (behavioral) level, although it is not clear that these predictions would actually be possible in all cases.

An instructive instance is the theory of cohesive and restraining forces. Cohesive forces are tendencies of excitations in the cortex to attract each other if nothing restrains them. Restraining forces prevent such movement and are generally the result of present stimulation. When stimulation is presented and then removed, cohesive forces are free to manifest themselves. Brown and Voth (1937) demonstrated cohesive effects in an experiment on apparent movement. Four lights are arranged in a square pattern and flashed on, one at a time, successively around the square. As the rate of succession increases, apparent movement is perceived from one position to the succeeding position. As the rate increases further, the path of the movement becomes curved until the path followed finally becomes circular. The perceived path of movement has a diameter too small for the path to intercept the actual positions of the lights! A circle, in order to pass through the lights, would have to have a considerably larger diameter than the path of the perceived movement.

This phenomenon was explained by invoking cohesive forces. The excitations begun by the flashes of light attract each other, thus constricting the path of the perceived movement. The locus of the attraction is presumably the brain. However, it is clear that the inference about cohesive forces is made from observation of a stimulus-response relationship, and the cohesive forces would be equally useful as an explanatory concept if they were presumed to occur in the stimulus field, or a psychological field.

Isomorphism. Gestalt theorists have tended to make easy inferences from stimulus-response observations to physiological events because they accept the principle of isomorphism. An isomorphism is a 1:1 relationship, assumed in this case to hold between brain fields and experience. The structural properties of brain fields and experience are assumed to be topographically identical; that is, we may think of the relationship between the two as being identical as to order. The so-called constancy hypothesis of the traditional associationist (e.g., Wundt, Titchener) was attacked by the early gestaltists for holding to a 1:1 fixed relationship (or isomorphism) between the external stimulus and the perception.

Köhler stated an isomorphism with respect to experienced space as follows (1947, p. 61): *"Experienced order in space is always structurally identical with a functional order in the distribution of underlying brain processes."* Woodworth (1948, p. 135) used an analogy to the relationship between a map and the country it represents to clarify what the gestaltists mean by isomorphism. The map and the country are not the same, but their structure is identical in the sense that we can read off the characteristics of the country from the map, and vice versa. The identity is a very restricted identity. All that the gestaltist seems to demand is that the physiological and experiential fields have *some* identity, perhaps not one as strong as that between a map and country. To extend Woodworth's analogy, the "scale of miles" involved in going from physiology to experience and back may not be the same for all parts of the map or country. In addition, the map may, of course, be folded or wadded up without destroying the isomorphism. Nevertheless, the gestaltist assumes that we will eventually be able to read off information about physiology from what we know of experience, and vice versa; we just need more directions for reading and need to open the physiological events to easier view.

Nativism-empiricism and the contemporaneity principle. Both the components of the gestaltists' isomorphism are components that presently exist. Both the physiology and the correlated experience are available for present study. Thus present experience is explicable solely on the basis of its relationship to the present state of the physiological field. It is only natural that this relatively ahistorical point of view led the gestaltists to show less interest in past experience than did the members of the other schools. They did not deny that past experience might play a role in perception and behavior, but they tended to deemphasize its role. They emphasized that the past experience must have modified the present condition of the organism before it could have any effect. Thus a complete knowledge of the present would leave nothing out of the immediate causal account, while a study of the past would be handicapped by the distortions worked upon earlier events by later ones as well as by the complexities introduced by the participation of the historical effect in the present field.

Köhler stated part of the case against past experience as an exclusive explanatory principle as follows (1925, as translated in Ellis, 1938, p. 58):

> It would be extremely unfortunate if the problem were thrust aside at this point as being after all only another case of the influence of past experience. No one doubts that past experience is an important factor in *some* cases, but the attempt to explain all perception in such terms is absolutely sure to fail, for it is easy to demonstrate instances where perception is not at all influenced by past experience. Fig. 1 is an example. We see a group of rectangles; but the figure may also be seen as two H's with certain intervening lines. Despite our extensive past experience with the letter H, it is, nevertheless, the articulation of *the presented object* which determines what we shall see.

Here is Köhler's Figure 1:

Köhler was not insisting that past experience is irrelevant to present perception, nor was he insisting that perceptual behavior is innate. There are three types of variables that may influence perception:

genetic, historical, and present. Nativism is commonly understood to be the position that genetic variables completely determine present perceptual responding. The gestalt position is not nativistic in this sense. The gestaltists have simply insisted that the historical variables do not completely determine perceptual responding and concomitantly have emphasized the two other classes of variables.

Egon Brunswik was a psychologist with gestaltlike leanings (see Chapter 11). Yet he apparently did not see anything contradictory in the position that the gestalt laws of organization, which were concerned with features of the presented stimulus, might be learned. Brunswik and Kamiya (1953) did a preliminary study of the stimuli furnished in photographs of natural objects to see whether or not it was conceivable that elements in proximity might be seen as parts of the same object because people had *learned* that elements in proximity belonged to the same object. If elements in proximity within the stimulus tended to belong to the same object, then people could learn to organize proximate objects into the same whole because other experiences had shown that they (the perceptual elements) probably arose from the same object. Brunswik and Kamiya found that there is a tendency, relatively weak, for proximate elements to belong to the same object. Their conclusion was that the principle of proximity could be learned by the individual, although to show that it is would require further investigation. The possibility that the visual system had "learned" the principle through the process of evolution would have to be eliminated.

The attitude toward analysis. Gestalt psychology began partly as a revolt against the allegedly artificial analysis of the introspectionist. Still, the gestalt psychologists recognized that analysis is at the very heart of science. The objection was not to analysis as such but to a particular kind of analysis. Köhler (1947) said that if we analyze as the orthodox introspectionists do, then those experiences that are most important will be neglected completely. Common experience, the experience of everyday life, is not to be found in the introspectionist's psychology. Köhler did not argue that the introspectionist's findings are unreal, just that the reality is contrived and artificial. Gestalt psychologists have objected, not to the artificiality of the laboratory as such, but to the artificiality of a stilted type of method and a sterile conception. Gestalt psychology is not an applied psychology, but the gestaltists have tried to make it a psychology whose results apply to real experience.

Gestaltists have also been interpreted as rejecting quantification within psychology. Their feeling was not that quantification is illegitimate or unnecessary, but that it is often premature. They have held that psychology should first concern itself with important qualitative discoveries. The attitude toward quantification *as such* was not negative, but the attitude toward quantification *for its own sake* was quite negative. The feeling is summed up in Köhler's statement that "one can hardly exaggerate the value of qualitative information as a necessary supplement to quantitative work" (1947, p. 49). He went on to say, of his own work on learning (p. 50): "Everything that is valuable in these observations would disappear if 'results' were handled in an abstract statistical fashion."

Koffka (1935, pp. 13–15) gave a more thorough and sophisticated treatment of quantification, making essentially the same points. He destroyed the antithesis felt by some to exist between quantity and quality, concluding that "the quantitative, mathematical description of physical science, far from being opposed to quality, is but a particularly accurate way of representing quality" (p. 14). Koffka would therefore agree that psychology must eventually express its laws in quantitative form in order to reach maximum precision.

EMPIRICAL STATEMENTS

Principles of organization. The best-known empirical statements made by the gestalt psychologists are the principles of perceptual organization put forth by Wertheimer (1923). These principles are typically given a demonstrational type of proof, and that precedent is followed here. Hochberg and McAlister have commented on the status of the laws of organization (1953, p. 361): "Empirical study of the Gestalt principles of perceptual organization is, despite their great heuristic value, frequently made difficult by their subjective and qualitative formulation." Thus, if the reader sometimes has difficulty in understanding the following laws, he need not feel that the inadequacies are all his; even the more emphasized perceptual factors, outlined below, are lacking in precision of statement.

(*a*) *Proximity:* Elements close together in time or space tend to be perceived together. For example, the lines in Figure 2*a* tend to be seen as three pairs of lines rather than in some other way.

(*b*) *Similarity:* Like elements tend to be seen together in the same structure, other things equal, as in Figure 2*b*.

(*c*) *Direction:* We tend to see figures in such a way that the direction continues smoothly. This factor is illustrated in Figure 2*c*.

(*d*) *Objective set:* If one sees a certain type of organization, one continues to do so even though the stimulus factors that led to the original perception are now absent. Consider the series shown in Figure 2*d*. As the dots are looked at progressively from left to right, one tends to continue to see the pairs of dots as on the left, even though on the right the proximity factor no longer favors this organization.

(*e*) *Common fate:* Elements shifted in a similar manner from a larger group tend themselves to be grouped, as in Figure 2*e*.

(*f*) *Prägnanz:* Figures are seen in as "good" a way as is possible under the stimulus conditions. The good figure is a stable one. For example, as shown in Figure 2*f*, gaps in a figure are frequently closed

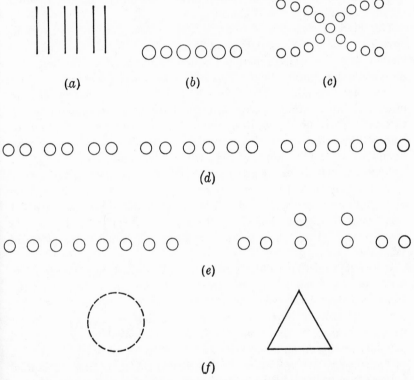

Figure 2. Examples of perceptual factors in gestalt psychology.

because the resulting figure is more "pregnant" (subprinciple of closure). A good figure is one which cannot be made simpler or more orderly by a perceptual shift.

Wertheimer recognized the influence of past experience or habit. If we have frequently seen a given figure, it is more likely to be seen again. However, the gestaltists have generally deemphasized the influence of learning on perception (Köhler, 1947).

Wertheimer recognized that the laws of organization were far from final or even completely stated. He suggested by implication some of the work that needed to be done to improve them (1923, as translated in Ellis, 1938, pp. 76–77): "What will happen when *two* such factors appear in the same constellation? They may be made to cooperate; or, they can be set in opposition. . . . In this way, it is possible to test the strength of these factors."

Koffka, writing twelve years later, could say (1935, p. 166): "A measurement of the relative strength of these factors would be possible, as Wertheimer has already suggested, by varying these relative distances." Now, more than a quarter of a century after Koffka's statement, there is still no quantitative formulation of the relative strengths of the factors in organization.

This kind of situation is, unfortunately, a common one in psychology. The effective variables, or at least some effective variables, are known, but the exact functional relationships relating the effective independent variables to the dependent variables concerned are not known. The gestaltists proceeded in just the way they criticize in others. Demonstrations were constructed wherein the individual factors can clearly be shown to operate, *other things equal*. The laws of combination of the factors, their relative strengths, and even precise definitions of the meanings of the variables were and are missing.

Learning principles. Gestalt psychologists have not worked nearly so extensively in learning as in perception. However, they have done some highly suggestive studies. Köhler's *The mentality of apes* (1925) was based largely on his study at the anthropoid station at Tenerife in the Canary Islands, where he had been marooned during World War I.

It was natural that Köhler saw the problem-solving process in quite a different way from the behaviorists and associationists or even the functionalists. Gestalt psychology is based on the premise that perception is determined by the character of the field as a whole. What is more natural than that the gestaltists should explain learning and problem solving in an analogous fashion? That is just what Köhler did. Problem solution for him became a *restructuring* of the perceptual field. When the problem is presented, something necessary for an adequate solution is missing. The solution occurs when the missing ingredient is supplied so that the field becomes meaningful in relation to the problem presented. For example, one of the chimpanzees in Köhler's experiment was given two sticks which could be joined in order to reach a banana that could be reached in no other way. After many futile attempts to reach the banana with one stick by itself, the chimp gave up and continued to play with the sticks. When he accidentally (or at least idly) joined the two sticks, he immediately reached out and got the banana. The missing perceptual ingredient for the solution had been supplied. The perceptual field had been restructured.

Much gestalt work has concerned problem solving rather than learning. The two areas are distinguished roughly. Problem solving involves the combination of already learned elementary elements in such a way that a solution is achieved. Learning usually is concerned with the acquisition of relatively simpler, more discrete responses. The distinction is to some extent arbitrary, as is certainly clear from Köhler's experiments with apes, which could be considered either learning or problem solving.

Wertheimer's *Productive thinking* (1945) suggested effective methods for problem solving. He applied the gestalt principles of learning to human creative thinking. He said that thinking should be in terms of wholes. One should take a broad overview of the situation and not become lost in details. Errors, if inevitable, should at least be good errors, errors with a possibility of success, not blind errors made without regard to the limitations of the situation as a whole upon acceptable solutions. As a learner should *regard* the situation as a whole, so a teacher should *present* the situation as a whole. He should not, like Thorndike, hide the true solution or the true path and require errors. One should not be required or even allowed to take a single blind step but should rather always be required to keep the goal and the requirements for success in view.

Duncker (1945) performed an extensive gestaltist analysis of the problem-solving process. He analyzed the factors in the situation and in the problem-solving procedure which determine difficulty of solution. Like Wertheimer, he believed that the tendency of the subject to narrow the possible solutions is one of the most serious obstacles to successful performance. He devoted a great deal of attention to discussion of fixedness of response. Errors were regarded as helpful in the sense that thinking does not regress to the original ideas about possible solutions when leads are found to be false. Thus errors direct further responses, serving a positive function as well as simply being eliminated. The requirements of the problem situation "ask for" a solution with the required attributes; that is, responses are determined by the total situation, the problem field. Duncker's classic monograph contains many ingenious ideas and examples but has the usual gestalt characteristic of being largely nonexperimental and programmatic.

The gestaltists have generally emphasized the *directed* character of behavior in problem-solving situations. Thorndike emphasized trial-and-error learning, as though the behavior of the animal in the situation were blind and random. Köhler and Wertheimer pointed out the blindness of Thorndike's situation. They believed that the random nature of the activity inhered, not in the animal, but in the situation. A good solution is possible only if the whole situation is available to the animal. In Thorndike's puzzle-box situation, only the experimenter can see the over-all situation. The animal is *reduced* to trial and error by the situation, but to say that learning in general is by trial and error is itself an error.

Thorndike, a favorite gestalt target (see Chapter 6), had stated that learning is a gradual process of elimination of errors with the accompanying fixation of the correct response. The gestaltists said that more frequently learning is not gradual at all but a process involving insight. We might think of insight as a sudden shift in the perceptual field. There seems to be no basic theoretical reason why the gestaltists should say that the perceptual shift should be sudden rather than gradual, but Köhler's empirical observations indicated to him that sudden learning did occur. Four behavioral indices of insight learning are usually cited: the sudden transition from helplessness to mastery, the quick and smooth performance once the correct principle is grasped, the good retention, and the immediacy with which the solution can be transferred to other similar situations involving the same principle. Once the sticks had been joined to reach the banana, they would be joined in other situations for reaching other objects if insight were truly involved.

The disagreement about whether learning is continuous, as Thorndike thought, or sudden, as the gestaltists stated is typically the case, gave rise to the continuity-noncontinuity controversy in learning. According to the continuity position, each trial or reinforcement contributes some increment of response strength. This assumption is denied by the noncontinuity position, which emphasizes sudden discontinuous increments, such as are associated with insights, rather than a slow building up of strength.

This controversy, like many such controversies, is no longer regarded as answerable in a simple yes-or-no fashion. Both continuous and discontinuous improvements in performance occur. A complete learning theory will define all the variables affecting learning and give their functional relations to performance. Both continuous and discontinuous learning curves will be possible, depending upon the values of each of the effective variables over successive trials.

Spence (1940) has shown that Hull's theory, which is a strict continuity theory, can predict sudden increments of performance if the constants in his equations are chosen properly. Then, if there is a sudden shift in a parameter like hours of deprivation from a trial to its successor, there will be a sudden increment in performance. The gestalt assertion is just that such sudden changes can occur. The gestalt learning theorist is now faced with the task of writing the equations needed to make a gestalt learning theory as sophisticated as its competitors, which can now predict the same phenomena. The occurrence of insight, however, is not critical to the basic tenets of gestalt theory.

Insight involves structuring, or restructuring, the situation as a whole. Thus it is predicted, from gestalt theory, that there will be occasions when an animal will respond, not absolutely to the local stimulus, but to a relationship between stimuli. This is exactly the situation that is said to hold for perception, where the perception accords with the whole field rather than with the local, elementary stimulation. So behavior should depend on the situation as a whole.

The transposition experiment is an example of this principle. An animal is trained to respond to the darker of two gray cards; he always finds food behind it. The traditional associative explanation of what has happened in training is that the dark card is now associated with reward, so that the animal approaches it. The lighter card has no association, and the animal does not approach it. However, when the dark card is put with a still darker card, the animal under some conditions chooses the new darker card, even though responding to it has never been reinforced. Koffka (1935) said that, in looking at the two cards, a *step* is perceived from lower to higher brightness, and the animal responds to the lower step. Thus, the whole field must be considered in making predictions.

Spence (1937b) has derived the observed relational responding by introducing gradients of generalization of reinforcement from the reinforced card to other values of gray and of inhibition from the lighter card to other values. If the generalization curves are given appropriate shapes, the animal should respond to the new card according to associative principles. Even so, the general gestalt point is again made—that the combination of simple elements gives a complexity requiring new laws for its description (in this case, new equations describing generalization). Perhaps the gestaltists would themselves insist that any associative approach is inherently mistaken and wasteful, but it seems that they need not so insist.

Krechevsky (1932) noted that animals tended to persevere over a number of trials with systematic responses. For example, the animal might respond in terms of a position habit, then suddenly shift to a choice of the brighter of two stimuli. These consistent tendencies he called "hypotheses," by analogy with a situation in which a human being tries out various alternative solutions until the correct one is found. This finding lent some support to the gestalt contention that animals were not responding blindly or randomly in their solution of problems. Spence (1936) observed that hypothesis is just a name for a persistent response tendency whose history of reinforcement we do not know. Harlow (1951) pointed out that the typical paradigm for insight learning is one in which we do not know the past experience of the animal with the component parts of the problem. Insight did not occur in some experiments in which the subjects were animals without such previous experience. Gestalt psychology has pointed to a number of interesting phenomena in the field of learning, but it has not worked out many detailed answers, and the experimentation carried out has often lacked any control of critical background factors that might influence the outcomes. Gestaltists' theorizing has been highly general, and their explanations usually *ad hoc.*

Lewin is a case in point. He is a field theorist, and his is the most sophisticated of the field theories of learning. Even so, examination of the theory (Estes, 1954b) has revealed that its usefulness is severely curtailed because of its failure to make specific predictions capable of verification or disproof. If the most sophisticated of the gestalt learning theories suffers from this evaluation, the less sophisticated ones suffer still more from a lack of any predictive power. Lewin's theory will be treated in greater detail in Chapter 11 because it is of contemporary, as well as of historical, interest.

GESTALT PSYCHOLOGY AS A SYSTEM

Definition of psychology. The gestaltists tended to define psychology as the study of the immediate experience of the whole organism. They intended to include all the areas of psychology within their scope, but they began with perception and have thus far emphasized perception more than the other areas. Thus the gestaltists and those following them have tended to pay more attention to the relationships between antecedents and perception than to those between perception and behavior. They contrast markedly with the behaviorists, who skipped the way station of perception to study the relationships between antecedents and behavior directly.

Postulates. We present here only the few postulates that we feel are most basic, and even these are divided into a primary and a secondary set. The reader can find a more complete list in Helson (1933) or in the original sources.

Gestalt psychology, like behaviorism, seems to have only one really primary postulate which relates to its name and which has finally commanded wide acceptance. This is the postulate related to the whole-part attitude. Any shorter discussion than the one given earlier in this chapter must fail to do it justice, but the following sentences indicate this attitude. The whole dominates the parts and constitutes the primary reality, the primary datum for psychology, the unit most profitable to use in analysis. The whole is not the sum, or the product, or any simple function of its parts, but a field whose character depends upon all of itself.

The secondary postulates, like those of behaviorism, are not necessary to a gestalt psychology, although the founders made them a part of *the* gestalt psychology that has developed. The most important of these is the isomorphism principle. A related principle, or perhaps a corollary, is the contemporaneity principle. More specific principles related to the whole-part attitude are the laws of organization. The noncontinuity postulate regarding learning has been discussed as secondary.

None of the gestalt postulates was entirely new. Even the basic postulate had been anticipated. The thing that made gestalt psychology new was itself a gestalt. It was the organization, pattern, or structure of things that gestaltists said about the whole-part attitude that distinguished gestalt psychology from its philosophical forerunners which had made a case for emergence and from its psychological forerunners which had made a case for phenomenology.

Mind-body problem. The gestaltists, like most psychologists, tried to evade this issue by pointing to the unity of the organism and maintaining that there was no real problem. However, their recognition of experience and their use of the principle of isomorphism implied some kind of dualism, for isomorphism must be a relation between two different sets of events. Isomorphism itself says nothing about the particular subvariety of dualism that should be chosen. Since the gestaltists attempted to make light of the problem, and since their whole-part attitude emphasized the emergence of new levels of description, new *aspects* of complex phenomena, the mind-body position that seems most consistent with their general position is a dual-aspect view (see Prentice, 1959, p. 435). This view gives two aspects that can be isomorphic, yet it allows the statement that there is somehow really only one basic reality seen in two views, that the organism is really unitary and integrated.

Nature of the data. Immediate, unanalyzed experience obtained by naïve introspection furnished the bulk of the data for gestalt psychology. The given, as they called such experience, was used as data. Behavioral data were also used, notably in the fields of learning and problem solving, but behavioral data were less important because of the larger number of perceptual studies.

Because the behaviorists were making a different point and because they deemphasized experience, it is easy to miss the fact that both schools tended to accept the same types of data and that both schools were making a point that converged on the same criterion for acceptability of data. The behaviorists, although they rejected consciousness, accepted verbal behavior as data when there were consistency and agreement within the given experimental condition. The gestaltists, although accepting experience and consciousness, rejected a certain kind of analysis of that experience. They retained the given in consciousness. Now, that given was generally very nearly coterminous with the class of verbal behavior which was acceptable to a behaviorist. Wertheimer, when he talked about the given, talked about trees and windows. Watson, when he wished to make the point that consciousness was not part of science, contrasted it with things that were

—contents of test tubes, things that he could see and feel and lift. Both men were using primarily an object language, a language that a long history of verbal usage has endowed with a great amount of agreement about meaning. Thus, although the two schools started from quite different points, they tended to accept about the same kinds of data as being of interest in their kind of psychology. The gestaltists were more tolerant; they could afford to accord a kind of reality to the results of the old introspection, while the behaviorists, whose whole existence was based on a methodological point, could not.

Principles of selection. Gestalt psychology in one sense eliminated the need for principles of selection. The given was not selected or rejected. It was simply structured. The problem for the gestaltist was not to explain why something was selected, since every part of the field played some role in the perceptual structuring, but to explain why the actual structure, among possible alternative structures, emerged. One principle was that in a given perceptual whole, part of the perception will be figure, part ground. Rubin's laws governing the selection of the figure are detailed statements of laws governing this kind of selection. Wertheimer's laws of organization are also laws of selection in the same sense; they explain the particular form taken by the figure out of alternative possible organizations. Neither Rubin nor Wertheimer was giving laws which governed selection on the stimulus side. The selection took place on the perceptual, or, if we prefer, the response side.

Principles of connection. The form of the problem of connection was also different for a gestaltist. Since elementarism was rejected, one form of the question of connection could also be ignored. It is not meaningful to try to reconstruct wholes by connecting elements which are supposed to be the parts of the whole. The gestaltists believed that the *bundle hypothesis* was completely fallacious. The bundle hypothesis treated complex perceptions as though they were a bundle of simple perceptions and treated meaning as though it arose from such a bundling. Thus one of the gestalt principles was negative; it was that the bundle hypothesis is invalid, and therefore one of the problems of connection is an artificial problem arising from an artificial analysis. The laws of organization are not principles of connection, for organizations are not elements connected. The laws state what structures will arise, not what elements will be connected.

Another form of the problem of connection cannot be avoided by any system. This is the problem of the connection or relationship between antecedents and consequents in laws. The gestaltists have stated that the relationships are dynamic and that the significant relationships are between fields. Their experiments have illustrated a few of these relationships, and their principle of isomorphism states another relationship in advance. But the gestaltists have not specified these principles, as indeed no system can at the present time.

CRITICISMS OF GESTALT PSYCHOLOGY

Gestalt psychology has been criticized chiefly for its nebulous character. Many hardheaded scientists have maintained that it does not really assert anything. This criticism seems to be at least partially justified. Harrower, one of Koffka's students, may be typical of the gestalt school in her attitude toward the problem of definition of terms in psychology (1932, p. 57):

> Much criticism has accrued to Gestalt theory for its use of the term "organization," which has not yet been sufficiently rigorously defined to meet the demands of many psychologists. And if, in the realm of perception, where as yet it has been predominantly employed, one meets with the criticism of its vagueness and ambiguity, how much more open to attack will be its preliminary appearance in investigations concerning the higher mental processes.
> And yet we deliberately give no precise definition of our use of the term, for with Dewey we believe that "Definitions are not ends in themselves, but instrumentalities for facilitating the development of a concept into forms where its applicability to given facts may best be tested." And since we believe that the concept is already in such form as to make it applicable to our facts, we leave more precise definition until experimental results can contribute towards it.

Harrower shows a tendency to bow coolly in the direction of definition and afterward to ignore the problem. This does not solve the problem or furnish any help in bringing experimental facts to bear. The psychologist needs to have some way of distinguishing a situation that is an organization from one that is not if he is to carry out empirical investigations on the subject. We have seen nearly the same criticism raised in reference to the principles of organization, and the fields selected for criticism on this point are fairly typical of gestalt psychology as a whole. However, the gestaltist can certainly defend himself by pointing his finger at other psychologists, who are also often obscure or incomplete in their definitions, although presumably much concerned with problems of definition. The often conflicting usages of the basic words *stimulus* and *response* are examples; Koch (1954) gives a specific treatment of conflicting usage by a single author, which could easily be applied to many others. The gestaltist, perhaps, has been more cautious, preferring to await more results before rigidifying meanings of words.

Gestalt psychology has been criticized for having too high a ratio of theory and criticism to experiment and positive empirical statements. Gestalt psychology has certainly been experimental, but the devastation wrought by its criticism has not always been repaired quickly by its positive statements. A closely related criticism is that gestalt psychology has not often furnished a system with predictive power. Gates, in defending Thorndike's identical-elements theory of transfer of training, has presented a criticism which, if justified, invalidates the gestalt theory of transfer (1942, p. 153):

> The Gestaltists somewhat similarly insist that transfer depends upon "insight." The objection to these views is not that they are wrong, but merely that they are too vague and restricted. To say that one transfers his learning when he generalizes is not saying much more than "You generalize when you generalize." "You get transfer when you get it." We must go deeper than that. In a scientific sense, no theory of transfer is a full or final explanation, but the Thorndike formulations at least point to a number of factors, observation and study of which enable us to improve learning.

Gates's criticism can probably be generalized to other areas but is especially true of learning, where the associationists, functionalists, and behaviorists have been able to present some fairly specific theories. The gestaltist has said, in effect: "Your theory is necessarily inadequate for the following reasons, and an adequate theory must take the following form." But the gestaltist has not often said what the specific statements of this programmatic theory shall be. Thus, the proponent of the theory attacked can often say that the gestaltist may be correct in his criticism but has done no better or has in fact presented *nothing but* criticism. But this is true of most critics. They do not have time to present correct theories in detail, especially where such theories must wait upon empirical spadework.

These first two criticisms picture gestalt psychology as more nebulous and programmatic than most systems. Even if there is at least a grain of truth in these criticisms, the third criticism, that gestalt psychology has been metaphysical and mystical, is certainly not justified. The feeling that it is mystical probably comes largely from the difficulty of presenting its central points clearly. This difficulty was initially compounded in the United States by problems of translation and by the fact that gestalt psychology arose from a cultural background somewhat foreign to Americans. When gestalt psychology is properly understood, it seems to be as much a natural science as behaviorism and often is more sophisticated. Gestaltists universally reject vitalism, which is often a mark of some degree of mysticism. Sometimes certain behaviorists who cannot think in other than mechanistic terms accuse those who reject mechanistic explanations as vitalists, and certainly a part of gestalt psychology's paradigm is a rejection of a simple view of mechanism.

One of the specific objections to the speculation found in the gestalt system has been to its physiological assumptions. As we have previously pointed out, the principle of isomorphism has made these speculations easy. However, speculation is a part, and a useful part, of every system. The gestaltists have frankly admitted, in most cases, that their physiologizing is speculative. It has no effect on the validity of their experimental results and has in fact stimulated or suggested experimentation. (See Prentice, 1959, for a vivid account of the relation between theory and experiment.) Besides, orthodox physiologizing, like Thorndike's assumptions about synaptic changes with learning, is just as speculative and no more likely to be correct.

The criticism that gestalt psychology is antianalytic has already been countered in the discussion of the gestalt attitude toward analysis.

The experimentation of gestalt psychologists has been criticized for being poorly controlled, nonquantitative, and nonstatistical. Experimenters have been accused of giving the subjects cues which affected learning in unknown ways and of ignoring possible effects of past experience. It is true that the gestaltists' level of sophistication in experiments has not been up to their level of criticism and metatheory construction. However, they consciously feel that qualitative results must come first. Thus the experiments have purposely been nonquantitative and nonstatistical. Since new areas have been explored, or old areas explored from an entirely new point of view, it is natural that the experiments performed have often been of a preliminary, tentative sort. Anyway, such a criticism of experimentation, if valid in some individual cases, is not a criticism of gestalt psychology but of particular gestalt psychologists. Gestalt psychology certainly does not advocate poorly designed experiments. Poor experiments have been done under the aegis of every school but with the sanction of none.

Other criticisms can be treated very lightly. One is that gestalt psychology is not new. This can always be said, but (1) gestalt psychology is as new as any school ever is, a point almost too obvious to discuss, and (2) the criticism is not even relevant to the merits of the system as it stands. The criticism that gestalt psychology sets up straw men to attack in each of the older systems is also irrelevant; it applies to gestalt psychology as an objection to other systems but not to its positive program.

THE CONTRIBUTIONS AND PRESENT STATUS OF GESTALT PSYCHOLOGY

The experiments done by gestaltists are an unquestioned contribution to psychology. This is the statement that is safest about any system. Gestalt psychologists have often done experiments which challenged the cherished beliefs of others. For example, latent learning and Zeigarnik effects (see Chapter 11), experimentally demonstrated, contributed to the difficulties of associationistic learning theorists and stimulated much research. Sometimes gestalt psychology itself could not have predicted the results, but a fresh-thinking upstart can afford to create difficulties for himself as well as for others.

There is no sign that gestalt psychology has stopped in the experimental creation of difficulties. Hochberg (1957) reviewed recent experimental results in a symposium on the gestalt revolution and concluded that the perceptions of space, depth, and distance are largely unsolved problems. The discussion of experiments by Ivo Kohler (1951) is of particular interest. Kohler experimented with several types of disturbances to normal stimulation and observed perceptual and behavioral adaptations to the disturbances. In one rather representative experiment, the left half of each of a pair of spectacles was made blue, and the right half yellow. Then, when the spectacles were worn, white objects to the left of center were seen as blue, and white objects to the right as yellow. After long adaptation, objects remained constant in color despite eye movement. Then, when the glasses were taken off, the world appeared yellow with eyes left and blue with eyes right!

Other experiments by Johansson (1950) have shown that perceived motion depends in complex ways upon the totality of stimulation, with common motion of parts often "partialled out" and seen as motion of the whole, and with the motion of individual parts contributing only the residual motion. Thus the seen motion of a part depends, as to the gestaltists it should, upon the properties of the whole.

These experiments and others provide abundant illustration that local stimulation may not be well correlated with local sensation. Though Kohler's observations emphasize the importance of perceptual learning, this direction of emphasis is by no means diametrically opposed to gestalt precepts. The gestalt position tended toward nativism because an antidote was needed. The structuralists had tended too often to hide behind the skirts of past associations whenever empirical facts belied what their elementaristic analysis led them to expect. Now that structuralism is gone, and the nebulous past associations are passé as a refuge, the gestalt position on nativism-empiricism can relax to a more natural neutral position.

Recent evidence gathered by Land (1959), apparently independently of any systematic preconceptions, gives powerful support to the gestalt antimosaic hypothesis. Color perception, according to Land, is to a large extent independent of the nature of the stimulation of the individual retinal receptors; the perception of color depends, rather, upon relationships over the whole retina. Land's findings could not give better support to gestalt psychology if they had been specifically made up to support the theory. This does *not* mean support in detail, for Land, at least initially, believed that his results demanded a reformulation of color theory, including theories held by members of the gestalt school. Walls (1960) disagreed with Land, holding that traditional explanations in terms of principles like contrast and induction are adequate to explain the phenomena. Regardless of which explanations turn out to be most economical, Land's redirection of attention to these color phenomena again vindicates the general gestalt methodological emphasis on field phenomena.

Gestalt psychology, then, is not a useful failure like structuralism. It is a going concern. It is more actively a school today than any of the systems we have discussed so far. One of its founders, Wolfgang Köhler, in 1956 received a Distinguished Contribution Award from the American Psychological Association; in 1959 he served as president of the American Psychological Association. One of the reasons that gestalt psychology still has some of its school character is probably that its main points are not quite as well assimilated into psychology as the main points of the older schools and the more native (to America) behaviorism. Then, too, it still has a founder to organize around.

This founder, Köhler, has lived to see the gestalt whole-part attitude accepted as at least theoretically correct. Psychology has also accepted the theoretical correctness of the contemporaneity principle, although many psychologists still study historical variables because of their easier availability. The primacy of perception and the methodological dependency of sensation on perception are also accepted.

Lastly, gestalt psychology has contributed to psychology even where its tenets were rejected. Its sharp criticism has required some reexamination and revamping on the part of every system which wished to stand in opposition to it. It has pointed to phenomena which existing systems could not incorporate, and these systems were energized by an order of criticism and competition that they might not otherwise have had.

SUMMARY AND CONCLUSIONS

Gestalt psychology originated in Frankfurt am Main, Germany, between 1910 and 1912. Wertheimer, Köhler, and Koffka arrived at their basic position after an examination of the experience of apparent movement (phi phenomenon). Their psychology was more phenomenological than that of Wundt; they accepted introspection but changed its character. One of their basic objections to the old psychology was to its artificiality of analysis. They disliked the quest for the elements of experience and noted that the simple combination of elements was inadequate to produce the features of the whole. The *whole* in psychology, as in physics, required laws of its own, and psychology should try to find these laws.

For the gestaltists, the laws of science were the laws of systems. They set out to apply their points of view to the fields of perception and learning. In perception, they put forth the laws of organization. In learning, they found the same kinds of principles. They objected to the overuse of past experience as an explanatory concept both in perception and in learning. Learning and problem solving were seen in relationship to restructuring of the perceptual field. Only influences on this field that were presently active could be used in the explanation of perception and behavior. Gestalt psychology has been accepted in part in America. Many of its criticisms of structuralistic and behavioristic psychology have been accepted as cogent, and these criticisms have forced the reformulation of those theoretical positions. Gestalt psychology is still itself an active force.

further readings

Hartmann's *Gestalt psychology* (1935) is a fine source for the student who seeks information and appraisal of gestalt psychology in the same book. It gives excellent historical background and a good explanation of the basic position. Köhler's *Gestalt psychology* (1947) is the most readable of the primary sources by the three founders; Koffka's *Principles of gestalt psychology* (1935), while less readable, is more thorough. Koffka's book is the most comprehensive treatment in English by one of the founders. Wertheimer is represented in English by the posthumous *Productive thinking* (1945), which is brief and incomplete. For translations of early papers, Ellis's *A source book of gestalt psychology* (1938) is, as the title suggests, a classic source for some of the most important of the basic gestalt writings. Henle's *Documents of gestalt psychology* (1961) also provides a useful source for many of the basic gestalt writings. Prentice's article entitled "The systematic psychology of Wolfgang Köhler" (1959) is an easily available summary of what one of the founders has been doing recently. Hochberg's summary of the Cornell symposium (1957) is a succinct appetizer for those who are curious about the kind of perceptual work which is now being done with a methodology which is gestalt in orientation.

psychoanalysis 9

Psychoanalysis is the most widely publicized psychological system, especially to the nonpsychologist. Although it has long been rejected by some academic psychologists, it has been more popular in other scientific and technical areas (for example, social work), in literary circles, and with the lay public. More recently, it has become a growing concern within some of the previously recalcitrant groups of academic psychologists.

The body of psychoanalytic writing is enormous. Freud's collected works alone, in their English translation, run to twenty-four volumes. No chapter of the scope of the present one can attempt to give a comprehensive picture of even one psychoanalytic theory; we therefore present a synoptic treatment, with emphasis upon certain of the more critical problems associated with the system.

The fact that a discussion of psychoanalysis has a critical tone cannot today be taken as a denial that Freud and his followers made an enormous contribution to psychology; the importance of that contribution is generally well accepted. The reader should bear this in mind when reading the critical parts of the present chapter, which, in themselves, might be taken as such a denial. These criticisms should be regarded, rather, as a pointing out of important flaws which need to be eliminated.

HISTORICAL ANTECEDENTS OF PSYCHOANALYSIS

Psychoanalysis fell upon the world like a bomb. The shock of some of its concepts and principles was so great that most people regarded it as entirely new. Yet it, too, had many antecedents—so many that they again resign us to the fact that there is rarely anything entirely new in the world of ideas.

In the development of psychoanalysis, there are two kinds of influences. There is an intellectual tradition in which Freud can be placed, as Bakan (1958) has suggested, and there is another set of more direct personal influences on Freud. Let us consider the former first.

Early in the eighteenth century, Leibniz developed a theory about the elements of reality that differed in kind from most of the previous theories. His elements were called monads, and they were extremely unlike the mechanistic atoms of Democritus. They were not even material in the usual sense but could better be described as centers of energy. Each such center was independent of the others, with a source of striving within itself; a monad might even be regarded as a center of motivation, a self-moved entity. Activity was the basic condition for being. Freud took a decisive step in his career when he turned away from the mechanistic tradition, in which he had been nurtured scholastically, to the more dynamic tradition represented by Leibniz.

Leibniz also pointed to the unconscious and to degrees of consciousness. A century later, Herbart took over some of Leibniz' ideas and worked out a mathematics of the conflict of ideas as they strive to become conscious. Freud, then, was not the first to "discover" the unconscious; his unique contribution was his detailed characterization of the unconscious and its mode of operation. Freud (1938, p. 939) yielded precedence to Schopenhauer for the idea of repression into the unconscious and resistance to recognizing repressed material; however, he said that he developed the same ideas without having read Schopenhauer.

Freud attended the lectures of Franz Brentano, who was at the time a very popular lecturer in Vienna. No doubt Brentano introduced him to the Leibnizian mode of thought, for Brentano based his own psychological ideas on *activity* rather than on elements.

The German romantic scientific tradition played a somewhat more direct role for Freud. Schelling and Goethe were two of the most important men in this tradition. Freud apparently chose a scientific career after reading one of Goethe's essays on nature. Jones (1953) has suggested that Freud saw his way to power through a really deep understanding of nature.

However, Freud's formal training put him in quite another tradition, the more mechanistic school of Helmholtz. For Freud, its direct representative was Ernst Brücke, with whom he was closely associated for years at the Vienna Physiological Institute. Brücke and du Bois-Reymond had formed an antivitalistic pact with Helmholtz when both were in their student years. They intended to force acceptance of the notion that there are no forces within living bodies that are not to be found in nonliving bodies. Part of the motivation for Helmholtz's earlier paper on the conservation-of-energy principle was to show that there is no unique energy unaccounted for within the organism considered as a physical system. Perhaps contact with this tradition later helped Freud to view the dreams and fantasies, wit and errors, of man as determinate and to formulate his own version of the determinacy of man's behavior, which he called psychic determinism.

Freud was no doubt reinforced in his determinism by his reading and discussion of Charles Darwin's evolutionary thesis with others in the institute and in the hospital where he studied during the course of obtaining his medical degree. He tended to take a biological view of man in accord with Darwin's biological view, and many of his ideas drew directly upon evolutionary theory; an example is the death instinct, which depended upon speculation about the origins of life.

Two somewhat conflicting traditions, which we may call the romantic and the mechanistic, thus had some influence on Freud. The romantic and mystical side was strengthened by Freud's Jewish religious background, which contained strong mystical components. The Jewish writings also attributed a mystical significance to sex. Bakan (1958) has documented this influence.

One man, Gustav Fechner, seems to have shared the mechanistic-romantic conflict with Freud and finally to have solved it by being rigorously scientific about an essentially mystical, romantic problem— the mind-body issue. Ellenberger (1956), among others, has shown in some detail that there was a direct relationship between the two men. Freud confessed to an admiration for Fechner and was familiar with his writings. Freud's concern with the intensity of stimulation, with mental energy, and with the topographical concept of mind were related to Fechner's prior work.

THE LIFE OF SIGMUND FREUD

Sigmund Freud (1856–1939) is almost universally considered a giant among psychologists, even by those who think he was a misguided giant. The details of the life of such a man deserve more attention than do those of the lives of less important psychologists. Furthermore, the kind of system which Freud evolved is more intimately related to his life than are more academic systems to their founders, and some understanding of his life is therefore of more than ordinary importance in evaluating his system.

Freud was born in what is now Pribor, Czechoslovakia, on May 6, 1856. The town was then Freiberg, Austria. His father, Jakob Freud, was a wool merchant and relatively poor. Jakob Freud had a total of eight children; Sigmund was the eldest son by the young second wife. He early showed great academic aptitude and finally decided to become a physician, that apparently being a profession more open to Jewish boys than were many others.

Although he had decided upon medicine as a career, he did not like the practice of medicine; nor did he ever identify himself with the profession. He postponed the taking of the medical examinations while he spent his time working under Brücke in the institute on problems that were purely scientific and thus more friendly to his temper. He hoped eventually to become a professor of anatomy, rather than a physician. He finally gave up hope of academic advancement and decided to take his medical examinations and training at the hospital in order that he might enter private practice as a physician. Brücke had apparently helped him to this decision. Freud's Jewishness may have impeded his advancement, but another factor was apparently the great length of time that might elapse before a position became available.

Even prior to his taking the examinations for the M.D. degree, Freud felt an interest primarily in neurology or psychiatry among the medical specialties. In the hospital, his feelings were reinforced. During the years from 1880 on, he wavered between study of the anatomy of the nervous system and study of psychiatry. He published many papers on anatomy, among them a new method of staining nervous tissue and a paper containing the germ of the neuron theory. At one time he became interested in cocaine and suggested its efficacy to one of his colleagues, who discovered its anesthetic properties; Freud seemed more interested in its potency as a tranquilizer and recommended its use to friends. At least one of his friends substituted a cocaine addiction for a prior addiction, and Freud's somewhat incautious attitude earned reprimands from colleagues who suspected the dangers of cocaine.

From the 1870s to the early 1890s, Freud was befriended by Josef Breuer, a practicing physician. Breuer gave his impoverished younger colleague money as well as advice and friendship. The two later were estranged at about the time Freud became closely attached to another physician, Wilhelm Fliess. The Fliess association led to an unusually close relationship during the years when Freud was first formulating his notions on psychoanalysis.

In 1885, Freud obtained a grant to study in Paris. He spent about half a year studying under Charcot, a famous Parisian hypnotist, teacher, and authority on hysteria. Freud already had some interest in hypnosis as a method of treatment, and the interest was strengthened by Charcot. Back in Vienna, he reported to his colleagues what he had seen and learned about hysteria and hypnosis. His report was poorly received, and the young pioneer was embittered. He continued, however, to use hypnosis in his practice to supplement massage, baths, and the mild kind of electrotherapy then in vogue. He later discontinued the latter, commenting that the only reason he disagreed with those who attributed the effects of electrotherapy to suggestion was that he did not observe any results to explain.

By 1895, Freud had lost interest in anatomy. He and Breuer had published together the work which marked the beginning of the psychoanalytic school. He wrote no more articles or books on neurology, with the exception of one encyclopedia article in 1897.

It was about this time, too, that Freud became estranged from Breuer and established Fliess as his mentor—this in spite of the fact that Fliess was two years Freud's junior and intellectually his inferior. Freud was highly dependent upon Fliess during this most neurotic period of his life. He was at this time overdependent, jealous, sometimes domineering, overly concerned with death, and hypochondriacal; he never overcame some tendencies to the latter.

In 1897, Freud began a full-scale self-analysis. One of its results was the growth of his ability to stand on his own feet. Fliess and Freud had a disagreement in 1900, perhaps over some of Fliess' highly speculative ideas about the periodicity of behavior. Freud later attributed their alienation to an analysis he had made of Fliess' choice of occupation. The final separation followed several years later; Freud had indirectly been responsible for the plagiarism by one of his own patients of Fliess' ideas on bisexuality and had refused first to acknowledge any responsibility and then later to apologize.

Perhaps the greatest milestone in Freud's career was the publication of his *The interpretation of dreams* in 1900, two years after the death of his father. According to Jones (1953, p. 324) and to Freud's own interpretation, the necessary freeing of the unconscious could occur only after the father was gone. Not long after this he began to gain recognition and soon had gathered around him a group of collaborators. His role became that of the father rather than of the son. Jung, Adler, Rank, and Ferenczi were first disciples and then rebels. Various difficulties in personal interaction usually started the rebellion, and the young group of psychoanalysts was intolerant of disagreement within its ranks. At one time a committee of the faithful was formed composed of Abraham, Eitingon, Ferenczi, Rank, Jones, and Sachs. The committee was to further analytic work. Freud gave each member a setting for a seal ring like the one he wore.

Through the committee and an ever-growing body of publications, Freud became successful and widely known. One of the first marks of his international recognition was G. Stanley Hall's invitation to speak at Clark University's twentieth anniversary celebration in 1909. Freud spoke, as did Jung; Ferenczi, Jones, and Brill were present. James Putnam, a professor of neurology at Harvard University, became a steadfast friend of analysis at this time.

Jung later returned to the United States for further lectures and reported that he had little trouble in getting analytic doctrine accepted if he ceased to emphasize sex so heavily. This widened an already existing breach between Jung and Freud.

Despite growing recognition and success, Freud's personal difficulties were by no means over. There were the dissensions and defections within analytic ranks, and finances were always a matter of concern for Freud and his large immediate family, including six children and a sister-in-law. World War I brought anxiety and hardship, but he continued to work through it all, and his fame grew. He attracted an increasing number of English and American students who helped to keep him going in the years after the war when Austrian money was of little value. He continued to expand and modify his theories and to regulate the rapid expansion of psychoanalysis. One of his devices for control was his voluminous correspondence, wherein he admonished and praised his followers.

In the fateful year 1923, a cancer was discovered in Freud's mouth; it seems highly probable that Freud's cancer was connected with the fact that he characteristically smoked twenty cigars a day. Parts of the palate and upper jaw had to be removed, necessitating the wearing of a prosthesis to separate the mouth from the nasal cavity and to make eating and talking possible. Freud accepted the series of operations and almost continuous pain that attended the last sixteen years of his life with his characteristic blend of realism, pessimism, and fatalism.

Finally, the year 1938 brought the long-dreaded invasion of Austria by the Nazis. Ernest Jones, fearful that Freud might be persecuted, arranged for him to leave for England. That it is well he did is indicated by the fact that four of Freud's sisters were later killed.

Freud was well received in England but was unable to enjoy the last year of his life there very much because of his cancer. He never really recovered from the last operation of a series of more than thirty and died on September 23, 1939.

THE FOUNDING OF PSYCHOANALYSIS

The germ of psychoanalysis appeared in a paper, *Studies in hysteria*, published by Breuer and Freud in 1895. Freud had met the older Breuer in the late 1870s, and they shared a strong scientific interest. Both were interested in hypnotism as a therapeutic device. Breuer had an interesting case, Fraulein Anna O., whom he treated until 1882; that fall he told Freud about it. The highly intelligent girl came to Breuer with multiple symptoms, including paralysis of three limbs, contractures, and a tendency to dual personality. In the course of treatment, it was found that if she related the origin of a symptom to Breuer while in a kind of transition state between the two personalities, the symptom would disappear. Breuer then began to hypnotize her daily so that she could rid herself of the symptoms faster. She christened the method they had discovered the "talking cure," or "chimney sweeping" (now commonly called *catharsis*). Breuer devoted an hour a day for over a year to her and in the course of this time developed a strong affection for her. When he recognized the situation that was developing, he became concerned and terminated her treatment.

Freud was greatly interested in the case and urged Breuer to publish it. However, the full-scale *Studies* followed the case by thirteen years, and even a preliminary report was eleven years in the making.

Meanwhile, in 1885, Freud spent his half-year with Charcot. Charcot was famous for his treatment of hysteria and other functional nervous diseases by hypnosis. After several months, Freud returned to Vienna and resumed private practice. It was at about this time that he abandoned electrotherapy. He also observed that not all his patients could be hypnotized, and, perhaps feeling that his technique was deficient, he went to study at Nancy with Bernheim for a few weeks. He took along a patient in whom he had been unable to induce a deep trance, but Bernheim also failed. However, Freud was impressed by his observation that posthypnotic suggestions could be carried out, and the suggestion forgotten; he was probably equally impressed with the demonstration that the patient would remember the suggestion after sufficient insistence on remembering by the hypnotist.

Freud now began to modify his technique in cases where it was not possible to induce hypnosis. He was determined to save the talking cure; he insisted that the patient remember the origin of symptoms even though not hypnotized, and supplemented his insistence with suggestions that the patient would remember when Freud pressed upon his forehead. At this stage, Freud was exerting a great deal of guidance on the patient's processes of association. One patient told him that he was interrupting too much and that he should keep quiet. This suggestion was the final impetus that converted Freud from the hypnotic trance to free association as a method of treatment.

By the time the *Studies* appeared, Breuer and Freud were in possession of many of the ideas that were to provide the basis for psychoanalysis; several of the ideas had come from Breuer's observations of Anna O., others from Freud's observations of hysterical patients. The first of these ideas was a conviction of the importance of unconscious processes in the etiology of the neuroses. This conviction came partly from the observation that symptoms often seemed to be expressions of events which the patient could not remember or of impulses of which he was unaware. The influence of posthypnotic suggestions, which the subject did not at the moment remember, may have contributed to the belief in the strength of unconscious processes.

Freud was himself convinced by this time that sex played a predominant role in the psychic aberrations of the neurotic. Breuer did not share Freud's certainty on this point, and their disagreement seems to have resulted in some underplaying of the theme—according to Freud's tastes—in their publication. Charcot had apparently remarked at one time that a certain type of case always had a sexual basis. Freud also claimed that Breuer and a gynecologist named Chrobak had made similar remarks about nervous disorders. Freud himself observed that most of his hysterical patients reported traumatic sexual experiences, often with members of their own families, in their childhood. He concluded that no neurosis was possible in a normal sex life.

The importance of symbolism was also recognized by Freud at this time. Symptoms seemed to be distorted, but symbolic, representations of repressed events or conflicts. In the case of Anna O., the symbolic relation between the origin of the symptom and the symptom itself was clear to the patient and to Breuer when the patient was able to recall the origin of a particular symptom. The symptoms were thus not arbitrary.

In every case, the situation at the time the symptom originated had involved strong impulses to do something, which had been opposed by forces preventing its occurrence. For example, the girl might wish to cry in the presence of her father because of her grief over his illness and yet be unable to cry for fear it would upset him over his condition. The repressed impulse might later manifest itself, in symbolic form, as an inability to see. The existence of contradictory tendencies was evidence for the importance of conflict in the creation of symptoms and in the production of neuroses in general.

As the preceding discussion implies, an acceptance of the unconscious is intertwined with the notion of repression into the unconscious; undesirable impulses and memories are pushed into the unconscious and are forgotten and unavailable as conscious material under ordinary circumstances. Only through their recovery and working out (*abreaction*) can the patient be cured.

In the quest for the origins of symptoms, for the repressed material represented by the symptoms, Freud was forced further and further back into childhood; his belief in the importance of childhood experiences in the production of neuroses was growing. Many of these childhood experiences were sexual; in hysteria particularly, Freud found reports of early sexual experiences. However, he believed that these experiences gained their traumatic force only after the patient had reached puberty. He had not yet been driven to his later opinions about the early genesis of sexuality in childhood.

The last, and possibly most important, discovery was the transference relation. We have already seen how Breuer became fond of his patient (countertransference); it was also true that she became fond of him. It seemed that the patient transferred to her therapist the feelings that she earlier had for other people, especially her parents.

At some stages of the therapeutic relationship, these feelings might be strongly positive, even sexual, in nature; later, the feelings might become as strongly negative. In either case, the patient was able to live through, to work out, the impulses that had earlier been incapable of expression. The transference could thus become one of the most useful tools of the therapist.

Transference, however, might evoke fear in the timid, as we have seen in the case of Breuer. It was probably his anxiety about the transference relations he found himself in that led to his leaving the field that the two were beginning to open up. There was also the storm that was breaking over the two men about the importance attributed to sexuality; Breuer, since he could not decide whether sexuality was really so important or not, chose the easier course and left psychoanalysis to Freud.

FREUD'S SYSTEM

We turn now to a presentation of Freud's system in its final form. A clear distinction should be made between this theoretical superstructure of constructs that Freud built, with which we are most directly concerned, and psychoanalytic techniques as (1) therapy and (2) producers of empirical data. These three facets of psychoanalysis need to be separately evaluated; much of the confusion in regard to criticism of psychoanalysis results from a failure to keep them separate. For example, methodological criticisms of the system need not apply to the therapy; and conversely, positive results of the therapy do not necessarily provide support for the system.

It should be understood that Freud did not suddenly develop the ideas to be presented; nor did he always continue to adhere to an idea if it seemed to contradict evidence that he himself gathered in his work. For example, a pronounced modification of his position on hysteria came about after he discovered that in many cases the traumatic sexual incidents reported by the patients had not occurred at all; yet he had resisted all attempts by others to get him to change his position. For a scientific investigator, he was extremely insensitive to criticism from the outside, especially from those unsympathetic to psychoanalysis; however, he was sensitive to self-criticism, and his system was accordingly flexible. Seldom did he present his theories as certainties; they were, rather, usually presented as tentative conclusions that seemed to be supported by his clinical data. It is largely his resistance to external criticism and his feeling that experimental support for his notions was not necessary that has given him the reputation of being cocksure and dogmatic about his conclusions.

Freud had a surprising attitude toward the reality of his conceptions. He might, when being self-consciously correct about methodology, admit that they were convenient fictions invented for explanatory purposes, but his usual attitude was that he was dealing with real things. For example, he once used Janet's statement that the unconscious was a manner of speaking as an example of Janet's low level of understanding (Jones, 1957, p. 214). It seems that Freud really regarded the unconscious as a country which he was exploring rather than as a system which he was constructing.

The psychic apparatus. As we have already seen, Freud believed that he found two "states" within the country, the conscious and the unconscious. Different kinds of laws determine what happens in these two states: the unconscious operates according to a set which Freud called the *primary process,* the conscious according to the *secondary process.* Ordinary logic applies to the latter but not to the former; the mechanisms that can be observed in dreams characterize the action of the primary process. Some of the things that can occur are the *condensation* of several thoughts into a single symbol, the *displacement* of an impulse or affect from one symbol to another, the *timelessness* characteristic of dreams, the *conversion* of an impulse into its opposite, and so on. The illogicality of the dream is characteristic of the primary process as a whole.

Part of the energy for the mental apparatus is called *libido;* its source is in biological tensions, and certainly the most important of these to the mental economy is sexual. Most of the sexual energy derives from the erogenous zones, bodily areas especially sensitive to stimulation. The *id* is the primordial reservoir of this energy and, being unconscious, operates according to the primary process. Various instincts which reside in the id press toward the discharge of their libidinal energy. Each instinct, therefore, has a *source* in biological tensions, an *aim* of discharge in some particular activity, and an *object* which will serve to facilitate the discharge.

The id operates according to the *pleasure principle.* In general, the elimination of tension is what defines pleasurableness, although it is not always clear whether it is the elimination of all tension or the maintenance of a constant level of tension which is pleasurable. Departure from a low level of tension or any heightening of tension is unpleasurable. One should remember that the id operates *only* according to the pleasure principle; it does not, for example, distinguish between the hallucinatory fulfilling of a hunger need and the actual fulfilling of the need. However, the tension does not remain reduced except through contact with objects which are in reality appropriate.

Accordingly, another psychic structure develops and complements the id. It is called the *ego.* It operates according to the laws of the secondary process and, being in contact with reality, operates according to the *reality principle;* that is, it is an evaluative agency which intelligently selects that line of behavior which minimizes pain while maximizing pleasure. The ego is still in the service of the pleasure principle through the reality principle but sometimes temporarily turns aside the direct gratification of needs in order that their over-all gratification be greater.

As a result of contact with the cultural realities, especially as embodied in the parents, a third mental agency develops. It functions as a suppressor of pleasurable activity in the same way that external agencies did at one time. It has two subsystems, a conscience which punishes and an ego ideal which rewards behavior. The conscience brings about feelings of guilt, and the ego ideal feelings of pride. The *superego* is unlike the ego (which serves the pleasure principle and only postpones gratification) in its attempt to halt completely certain pleasurable activities. The operation of the superego is largely unconscious; that is, a large part of its operation follows the laws of the primary process.

Freud himself came to the conclusion that the instincts active throughout the psychic apparatus could be divided into two groups: the life instincts and the destructive instincts. The latter were more commonly called the death instincts, since their aim is the death of the individual. Freud viewed the instincts as conservative; that is, they aim for a return to a previous state and thus explain the *repetition compulsion* which manifests itself in some behavior. Since living matter arises from dead matter, the ultimate previous state must be a state of complete quiescence, of death. The death instincts work for a disintegration of the individual, while the life instincts work for the continued integration of the individual. The death instinct is the part of Freud's theory least frequently accepted by other analysts; many articles written in analytic publications have been unfavorable to this Freudian conception (Jones, 1957, p. 276). The life and death instincts had the advantage for Freud of giving him a polarity, a pair of opposite elements in conflict. Jones (1957, p. 422) points out how fond Freud was of the dualistic mode of thought in preference to monistic or pluralistic conceptions.

The energy in the service of the life instincts was called by Freud the libido; no name was given especially to the energy that activates the death instincts. As the individual develops his ego, more and more of the available psychic energy comes under the dominion of the ego rather than of the id, which originally directs it. The ego attaches the energy to psychic representations of external objects; such an attachment is called a *cathexis*. The kind of object cathected depends upon the instinct which has energy available; the distribution of energy over the instincts is flexible. In the original version of the analytic theory, the distribution was assumed to change gradually so that more and more energy was available for the self-preservative instincts of the ego and less and less for the sexual instincts of the id.

This version made the basis of conflict the self-preservation versus the sexual instincts rather than life versus death.

In the course of an individual's development, there is a stage in which much of the libidinal energy is cathected onto the parent of opposite sex; in the case of the boy, this leads to the development of the Oedipal conflict. Like the mythical Oedipus, the boy loves his mother. He is also jealous and resentful toward his rival, the father. His sexual feelings are directed to the mother, but the child is blocked from direct expression of the instinctual urges toward incest. Because of his impulses, which are repressed, the boy has a fear of castration by the father. It is at this time that the urges toward the mother are repressed into the unconscious, so strongly repressed that all sexual urges enter the latency period. They emerge again at puberty, when the increase in sexual tensions is sufficient to upset the psychic economy and allow the impulses to overcome the repressive forces. The Oedipal conflict was felt by Freud to be a major contribution of psychoanalysis; one of the presuppositions necessary for its acceptance is that sexuality is really developed very early in life.

Treatment of neurosis. Let us now consider the implications of the psychoanalytic position for the treatment of neurotics. In doing so, we should keep in mind that we are reversing the process from what actually occurred; in reality, the theory grew out of the therapy and the observations that attended it, rather than vice versa, as our treatment might erroneously suggest.

In the first place, ordinary methods of gathering information about the genesis of the symptoms will not do. We have seen how unwelcome memories and impulses are repressed by the ego at the behest of reality or the superego. They are not conscious. They are not even in the in-between zone that Freud called the *preconscious,* where the simple application of sufficient effort may make them conscious. Any attempt at recollecting them will be met by *resistance;* accordingly a special method, such as hypnosis or free association, is required. Dreams, since they are governed to a considerable extent by the primary process, provide an avenue to knowledge about the unconscious if they are interpreted correctly. Correct interpretation depends upon the knowledge that the function of dreams is to fulfill wishes; since the id does not recognize the difference between hallucinatory and actual satisfaction of wishes, the existing psychic tensions may press toward discharge in dreams. In order to determine the precise meaning of the dream—that is, in order to uncover the hidden (latent) impulses expressed—the patient is instructed to give his associations to the elements of the dream. In this way, the symbols in the dream can be related to their meanings and the repressed material brought to consciousness.

The analysis of resistance to recall of repressed materials is then one of the most difficult and most important tasks of the analyst. If the resistance is too strong, the patient continues to refuse to recognize the existence of the repressed material even when the analyst can present it verbally to the patient. It is only when the patient can overcome his inner resistance and accept the analysis that he can improve. By overcoming the resistance, he brings the impulses under the control of the ego, where they obey the laws of the secondary process. As the dominion of the ego is enlarged, the ego is strength-- ened, and the patient obtains rational control over his impulses. He cannot be freed from the rule of the pleasure principle, but he can obtain more over-all gratification when the impulses must also conform to the reality principle.

The overcoming of the resistance is made possible, at least in some cases, by the transference to the therapist of a considerable portion of the libidinal energy. This energy is therefore available to the therapist for application of counterforce to the resistance. In turn, the transference itself becomes an object of analysis, and it must be overcome before the patient is independent and can be said to be cured.

In overcoming the resistance and tracing the significant repressed materials, the patient must be forced to recall material that goes further and further back into childhood. The childhood years are critical in the development of every individual; if he becomes fixated at some early stage of sexual development or returns (regresses) to an earlier stage in the face of later trauma, the scene is set for the development of neurosis. The early experiences that are most likely to be punished, and hence repressed, involve sex. Therefore, the significant material that will be recovered will concern sex. Even more specifically, we can say that the Oedipal conflict and its resolution will be central to the analysis, and insight into it by the patient central to his recovery.

In the discussion of the cure of neurosis, we see Freud's rather peculiar position on determinism at work. He believed in psychic determinism and is famous for his work on the determination of errors in speech and writing, on forgetting, and on losing objects. He showed that the apparently chance nature of these events conceals the fact that the error reveals the unconscious motivation of the person who has erred or forgotten. A published example (Freud, 1938, p. 75) concerns a member of the United Daughters of the Confederacy, who, in concluding her eulogy of Jefferson Davis, said "the great and only President of the Confederate States of America—Abraham Lincoln!" It would seem that she should have belonged to another organization.

The peculiarity in Freud's position arises from the fact that he seems to have felt that determinism can be abrogated if only the impulses can be brought under the sway of the secondary process. In this way the patient achieves *self*, rather than *impulse*, control. He was relatively little concerned with the operation of determinism within the secondary process, although his followers (including his daughter Anna) have spent more time in the study of ego processes. For Freud, man's hope of improvement lay in becoming rational in the true sense. Although neither Freud nor his followers believed that the achievement of insight is a sufficient condition for affecting a cure, it is for them at least a necessary condition. Furthermore, the insight has to be "deep"; that is, there has to be a real emotional acceptance of the analysis, not just an intellectual parroting of the words of the analyst.

THE REBELS

Four important early members of Freud's group first occupied a favored position and then disagreed with the Freudian beliefs and established rival analytic factions. They were, in order, Adler, Jung, Rank, and Ferenczi. Their defections have been used by opponents of psychoanalysis to demonstrate either that analysts do not all agree among themselves or that Freud was a kind of despotic tyrant who brooked no opposition. As we might expect, the charges were neither wholly true nor wholly false. There were both fundamental agreements and fundamental disagreements among the five men presently being considered. As to the personality factors, these are difficult to assess; in every case, some of the blame can probably be laid at each doorstep. We shall say a few words on the subject as we discuss each individual. Perhaps it would be fair to apply Freud's own dictum to himself; he said (Freud, 1943) that when an individual is repeatedly "victimized" by the same kind of external circumstance, we may be fairly sure that his own psychological makeup is such that he is repeatedly putting himself into situations where he can be so victimized. With this foreword, we now turn to a brief exposition of the four men and the modifications they proposed.

ALFRED ADLER

Alfred Adler (1870–1937) was a Viennese physician who early attached himself to the Wednesday-night group that started meeting with Freud in 1902 to discuss psychoanalysis. Adler and Stekel were Freud's two oldest followers; they withdrew from the society in successive years (1911–1912). Stekel had contributed to the field of symbolism but, according to Jones (1955, p. 135), had no scientific conscience and formed no school of his own after he left the fold of psychoanalysis.

Adler's case was quite different; he made a greater contribution to psychoanalysis, formulated a partially independent theory of behavior, and set up a rival school.

The difficulties between Freud and Adler became intense after Freud insisted that Jung be made president of the international association; the Viennese were jealous of their positions, since they had been the first followers. Then, the year after the international meetings in 1910, it was decided to hold discussions and debates about Adler's theories. After the discussions, the disagreements about theory seemed obvious, and Adler and his faction resigned from the Wednesday Society before the end of 1911. Adler formed a rival school which he finally named *individual psychology*.

Adler's contributions had at first been tolerated or even welcomed by Freud. Adler initially stressed organ inferiority in the backgrounds of neurotics. At first blush, this seems a more biological view even than Freud's. However, appearances are deceptive in this case, for Adler emphasized the psychological reaction to either real or *imagined* organ inferiority rather than the biological facts themselves. *Compensation* for this inferiority accounts for the nature of many neurotic symptoms and helps to determine the individual's *life style*, the way in which he deals with problems in general. The analysis of the compensatory mechanisms was seen by Adler as the major task of both the theory and practice of analysis.

Although Adler emphasized the conflict between masculinity and femininity as very important, his views on sexuality were very different from Freud's. He saw the overcoming of femininity by both males and females ("masculine protest"), rather than sexuality in itself, as the important thing. The will to power was thought to be the most important motivating force in the lives of men, and sex at times was a symptom of this will, the sex act representing the domination of the female rather than the running off of truly sexual impulses.

The will to power and the need to overcome inferiority arise, according to Adler, because of the conditions of life that universally obtain for human infants. The infant is not a small sexual animal whose incestuous desires must be repressed, but a small and helpless organism whose every need must be ministered to by relatively powerful adults. Necessarily, then, the infant develops feelings of inferiority relative to these adults and must strive to overcome his inferiority and rise above his dependent status. The Oedipal conflict, if it exists at all, should be understood as a conquering of the mother rather than a direct expression of any infantile sexuality.

Adler thus shifted the emphasis away from inborn biological instincts and energies toward the social relationships within the family as the children grow up; he concluded that the position within the family (as eldest son, second son, youngest child) is extremely important in determining how an individual deals with reality (i.e., his life style). Sibling rivalry is bound to occur and affect the personality. In Adler's theory, we see that the important conflicts often occur between the individual and his environment, rather than within the individual, as Freud had held.

Adler presented a more hopeful view of man than the orthodox analysts. He saw man, not so much as a group of segments at war with themselves, but more as an integrated, striving individual. He laid much less emphasis on the uncovering of the unconscious and its dark forces. He perceived man as largely conscious and creative, living partly by adherence to a "fictional future," which consisted of precepts presently believed in. Such precepts, although not necessarily true, might nevertheless direct behavior, for example, the precept "your reward will be in Heaven."

Adler and his school made therapy a shorter process and, at least sometimes, dispensed with the Freudian couch. Practical applications of the Adlerian theory to educational and social problems helped to popularize the theory, as did the ease with which such terms as inferiority complex and sibling rivalry were assimilated in the lay language. Adler's theory is generally closer to common sense than Freud's and probably shares the strengths and weaknesses common to such theories.

CARL JUNG

Relationship to Freud. Carl Gustav Jung (1875–1961) was a Swiss psychiatrist who became interested in Freud's theories after reading his *Interpretation of dreams,* which appeared in 1900. Jung visited Freud and his Wednesday Society in Vienna in 1907, and the two men were immediately strongly attached to each other. Freud soon viewed Jung as the crown prince of the psychoanalytic movement. In 1909, Jung accompanied Freud to America for the Clark University lectures and later returned to America alone to give additional lectures. At the first meeting of the new International Psychoanalytic Association, Freud insisted over the Viennese opposition that Jung be elected president. He wanted a younger man who was not a Jew to head the new movement, for he felt that the resistance to Jews would impede the progress of the analytic movement were a Jew to lead the association. On these grounds, Jung seemed the logical choice. The Viennese, who were nearly all Jews, were jealous of their own priority in the movement and were also resentful because of Jung's own known anti-Semitism. But Freud overcame their objections, and Jung was elected.

Soon after, the relationship between Jung and Freud began to weaken. Jung was not performing his presidential duties as well as Freud had expected; he deemphasized sex in his lectures and in his therapeutic analyses; he changed the concept of libido. Personal frictions were straining the relations between the two men. By the end of 1912, they had agreed to discontinue their personal correspondence. By 1914, Jung had withdrawn completely from the movement; he never resumed his former friendship with Freud. He soon founded a new school which he called *analytical psychology*.

Basic attitudes and methodology. Jung had early assumed that there must be some physical changes which accounted for the development of schizophrenia. In this he was emphasizing a contemporaneous factor rather than a historical factor, as Freud was in the habit of doing. Although Freud at that time agreed with Jung about this particular point, he would not have agreed in general with Jung's emphasis on the present rather than on the past in the study of neuroses. Jung was more like the gestaltists, Freud more like the behaviorists, on this issue. Not only did Jung emphasize the *present* as important, he believed that one must understand the future, the potentialities, of man in order to make sense when talking about him. The goals and intentions of men were to Jung as important in directing man's behavior as his history. He deplored Freud's study of causality exclusively in terms of the past and thought Freud's theorizing too reductive and mechanistic. Jung recently suggested (Jung & Pauli, 1955) a principle called *synchronicity* for those events which occur together in time but do not cause one another; his archetypes, which are primordial images that entail inherited response tendencies, are supposed to fulfill themselves psychically and physically within the real world at the same time without the two manifestations being causally related. This view sounds like Hume's reduction of causality to contemporaneity, or the doctrine of psychophysical parallelism.

Jung changed his position on scientific methodology as time went on. At first, he was interested in bridging the gap between academic psychology and psychoanalysis via the association experiment. In this way he hoped to make psychoanalysis more scientific. Later, Jung lost interest in "proving" analysis through traditionally conceived experiments. He and his followers turned more to the study of mythology and art as more useful methods of revealing the form of the unconscious. Jung became the most negative of the leading analysts toward the traditional methods of empirical science.

Jung's therapy, in accordance with these basic views, put less stress upon the past of the individual and more upon his present situation and desires for the future. Jung saw man as more creative and less a passive recipient of environmental influence than Freud; Jung was accordingly more optimistic in his psychology. Freud saw Jung's therapy as something that might be expected from a priest, with moral exhortation, appeals to will power, and an attempt to develop man's yearnings after the divine (Freud, 1938, p. 975). Jung believed that man's primitive urges might be channeled into a quest for self-actualization or for the divine; if the energy were not recognized and used properly by the ego, it might so warp man's functioning that he would become neurotic or psychotic.

Basic energies and instincts. Jung's views about the basic energy of man were closer to a common-sense conception than Freud's. He regarded the libido as a general biological life energy, not necessarily predominantly sexual. Where Freud saw sexual energy concentrated on different body zones at different stages (oral, anal, phallic, latency, genital), Jung saw the life energy simply manifesting itself in the form which was at the moment most important for the organism; for example, in relation to eating, elimination, and sex. The early concentration of gratification upon the oral zone was accounted for by the relation of the oral zone to eating rather than to the pleasurable sensations (conceived of by Freud as sexual in the broad sense) which arise from oral stimulation. Jung did not like Freud's lumping together of all pleasurable sensations as sexual.

Since he did not conceive of the basic energy as altogether sexual, he was free to reinterpret analytic observations that had previously been assumed to represent sexual strivings. The Oedipal conflict was reinterpreted, as it had been by Adler. This time the nutritive functions, as we might expect, become important in the child's attitude toward the mother. These become overlaid and combined with sexual feelings as the child develops in his sexual functioning. Combined with these feelings are certain primitive unconscious predispositions to react toward the mother. The Oedipal relationship is then not based, as Freud thought, almost exclusively on sexuality.

Jung transferred concepts from physics almost directly into dicta about psychic energy. He did not believe that psychic energy can be destroyed any more than can physical energy. If the energy is used in some psychic function, the amount available for that function will decrease but will reappear in the form of increased energy available for some other function. If the energy disappears from some psychic system, it will reappear in some other. This view is not very unlike Freud's; he, too, talked of the reappearance of unused psychic energy in other forms, as when sexual energy is sublimated and used for artistic creativity. Jung did not believe that the sum of the available psychic energy remains constant, for energy can be exchanged with the external world through such things as muscular work and the ingestion of food. Energy, since it can flow from one psychic system to another, tends to move from the points of higher energy toward the points of lower energy. The system, in short, tends to reach a state of balance, although the tendency is never fully realized. Even were a balance to be reached, it would soon be upset by exchanges between some psychic system and the external world. For example, if most of the available energy were concentrated in the personal unconscious, it would tend to share energy with other systems, such as the ego.

Then an exchange with the external world might occur. The ego would further increase the energy supply, and the direction would now be reversed.

Views on psychic structures.   Hall and Lindzey (1957, p. 79) have given an excellent thumbnail summary of Jung's position:

> The total personality or psyche, as it is called by Jung, consists of a number of separate but interacting systems. The principal ones are the *ego*, the *personal unconscious* and its *complexes*, the *collective unconscious* and its *archetypes*, the *persona*, the *anima*, or *animus*, and the *shadow*. In addition to these interdependent systems there are the *attitudes* of introversion and extraversion, and the *functions* of thinking, feeling, sensing, and intuiting. Finally, there is the *self* which is the fully developed and fully unified personality.

Jung's ego is something like the layman's conception of himself; it is the conscious mind in contact with reality, and it contains the conscious memories. It is felt to be the center of identity and personality. Jung's ego is not dissimilar from the conscious component of Freud's ego.

The personal unconscious is the region just "interior" to the ego. Since it is in contact with the ego, materials may be repressed into it from the ego. The personal unconscious is not unlike a blend of Freud's unconscious and preconscious; the contents of the personal unconscious are available to consciousness and contain only materials which have come into the unconscious as a result of the personal experiences of the individual and the collective unconscious.

Deeper still than the personal unconscious is the collective unconscious. In this dark and misty region are those things which man has inherited phylogenetically. The things that are inherited are called archetypes; they are something between symbols and predispositions to perceive or act in a certain way. Archetypes are formed as a result of the universal experiences of man in his evolution; Jung thus was forced to accept the doctrine of inheritance of acquired characteristics. Since the presumed experiences are universals, the archetypes too are universals. Jung discovered their existence as a result of his study of the myths and art productions of different ages and different cultures; he found certain symbols that were common to all, despite the fact that no direct exchange between the cultures could ever have occurred. Examples of archetypes are birth, death, the hero, the child, and God.

Four archetypes are better developed than any of the others: the persona, the anima, the animus, and the shadow. These are so well developed that they have become separate personality systems. The persona is the mask presented by an individual to his society. It is that part of himself which he wishes to publicize and may or may not serve the function of concealing the real personality.

The anima and the animus are Jung's recognition of man's bisexuality. The anima represents the feminine part of man; the animus, the masculine part of woman. These archetypes evolve, like any other, as a result of experiences: the anima, as a result of man's experiences with woman, and the animus, as a result of woman's experiences with man.

The shadow consists of that part of the unconscious which was inherited from man's prehuman ancestors; it is the animal instincts. Immoral and passionate impulses emanate largely from the shadow. When these impulses appear in consciousness, they may be expressed or repressed, with the result in the latter case that some of the materials of the personal unconscious originate in the shadow.

A fifth well-developed archetype is the most important one of all. It is the self. Jung found this archetype represented in various cultures by a symbol which was called the mandala or magic circle. It represented man's striving for unity, for wholeness, for integration of the personality. Jung made the self, accordingly, a separate system, changing from his earlier conception of the self as equivalent to the whole psyche. The self holds all the other systems together. It apparently strives for oneness of the individual with the world through religious experiences as well as oneness of the psychic systems within an individual. The self can appear only as the other psychic systems become separate enough to require integration, which does not occur until middle age. Some of Jung's disagreements with Freud were based on this "breaking point" in middle age; Jung thought Freud might be essentially correct about the importance of sexual motivation before middle age, but he believed that Freud had simply ignored what happened after this point had been passed, when the self had developed and when sex had become a subsidiary consideration.

The two attitudes toward the world distinguished by Jung, extraversion and introversion, are better known than any other part of his system. In extraversion, most of the individual's attention is directed to the external world; in introversion, the opposite is the case. Usually, the ego and the personal unconscious have opposite attitudes, since both attitudes are always present to some extent somewhere in the personality; the nondominant attitude, then, tends to be repressed. The stronger the conscious expression of one attitude, the stronger the unconscious development of the other. Sometimes an upset allows the libido attached to the unconscious attitude to overwhelm the repression, and the dominant attitude is overcome.

Finally, there are the functions, any one of which may be dominant. Jung's definitions of thinking, feeling, sensing, or intuiting do not differ from their common meanings. He did not think there was anything arbitrary about the statement that there are exactly four functions; it was a statement of fact as far as he was concerned. Generally, two of the functions predominate at the expense of the other two; the latter are then developed unconsciously, just as in the case of the repressed attitude. If an individual is described in terms of function and attitude, we have a sort of typology; thus a feeling-intuiting-introvert might be a prophet or a monk. All functions and both attitudes are necessary for successful living; accordingly, there are no pure types. The whole individual has all these factors in harmony. As pure types are approached, the pathological is approached.

Contribution and evaluation. Jung is especially difficult to evaluate. When Freud was alive, Jung and all other analysts were in his shadow. In addition, it has frequently been pointed out that Jung is difficult to comprehend; as Jones has said (1957, p. 32): "Then his mentality had the serious flaw of lacking lucidity. I remember once meeting someone who had been in school with him and being struck by the answer he gave to my question of what Jung had been like as a boy: 'He had a confused mind.' I was not the only person to make the same observation."

Although Jones may have been somewhat biased in his estimate because of his friendship with Freud, there does seem to be some justification for his attitude. Recently, a reviewer of the English translation of Jung's published works said that Jung's statement about one of his works seems applicable to many; that statement is (Jung, 1956, p. xxiii): "It was written at top speed, amid the rush and press of my medical practice, without regard to time or method. I had to fling my material hastily together, just as I found it. There was no opportunity to let my thoughts mature. The whole thing came upon me like a landslide that cannot be stopped." A book so written could hardly be easy for the reader. In addition to the style problem there is the problem of translation for most English-speaking readers; only seven of a total of at least eighteen volumes have thus far appeared in English.

Even when the difficult problem of reading and understanding Jung is passed, many others remain. Jung's dislike for traditional scientific methodology makes his type of persuasion foreign to psychologists who like statistical or laboratory proof. If these are demanded, Jung can be dismissed at once.

It is even difficult to find any logical system to evaluate, for Jung was not a systematist. Whatever system there is must be distilled from his writing and then fitted together; Jung has presented no postulates or derivations. In this, he is in the company of the other analysts.

Yet Jung has seemed to grow in importance within recent years. He outlived Freud by twenty-two years, and his works are appearing in English. His ideas are novel and provocative. His view of man furnishes a refreshing antidote to Freud's; it is optimistic and consistent with the religious point of view. Jung is himself erudite and enthusiastic. His followers, once they understand him, are typically loyal and greatly impressed. A man with the qualities of Jung, despite his scientific shortcomings or anomalies, cannot be lightly dismissed.

RANK AND FERENCZI

These two men can be treated together because they published together and because their defections from Freud were somewhat related to each other. Rank's schism from Freud was earlier, more severe, and more complete than Ferenczi's. Neither man has yet assumed the stature of Freud, Adler, or Jung, although both have made significant contributions to the theory or practice of psychoanalysis.

In 1922, Otto Rank (1884–1939) began to present his ideas on birth trauma. In addition, he and Ferenczi were collaborating on a book entitled *The development of psychoanalysis* (1925). The book advocated the possibility of shorter therapy and stirred considerable dissension among analysts later. Even more disturbing was the book Rank wrote alone, *The trauma of birth* (1929). Freud himself reacted quite positively to the book at first, but he was later ambivalent about it. Complicating the picture was Rank's aversion to Jones; Freud apparently did not know whose side to take in these disagreements. A series of declarations of independence by Rank, followed by declarations of friendship, finally resulted in Rank's complete separation from Freud and the orthodox analytic movement.

Initially, Ferenczi showed some hostility to the members of the committee and was disappointed at his treatment at party congresses; he was never elected president by a full congress. However, his final separation from Freud was neither so early nor so dramatic as that of Rank. He simply drifted away from the other analysts, partially because of his therapeutic beliefs. There was little or no real bitterness between him and Freud, at least until very near the end of Ferenczi's life in 1933; by this time Ferenczi's physical illness may have affected his mind (Jones, 1957, p. 176).

Rank's background contributed a professional issue to psychoanalysis. He had come from a technical school to the Wednesday Society and had been encouraged to attend the university. His application of psychoanalysis to cultural developments endeared him to Freud. Rank thereby swayed Freud in favor of lay analysts. Freud had never identified with the medical profession himself and did not see any absolute necessity to study medicine in order to practice analysis.

Rank's more direct contribution was largely connected with the birth trauma. In a sense, Rank was pushing Freud's concern with the early years to its logical conclusion. He saw the neuroses as originating in the trauma of birth, where the child experiences a forcible and painful expulsion from the comfort of the womb into the terrors of the world. This trauma, he believed, is never forgotten. The "separation anxiety" that results from the birth trauma is basic to neurotic symptoms. The clash of will between child and parent that later attends the growing-up process is also important. The job of the therapist, then, is to alleviate both the guilt of the patient over this clash and his anxiety over separation. In order to get the patient to really work during therapy and to ensure that he does not become overdependent on the therapist, a definite date is set for the separation of therapist and patient. The therapy is then terminated at the agreed time, and the patient develops in therapy the ability to function alone after this time.

There is one interesting side light on Rank's theory. Freud was ordinarily quite opposed to statistical treatment. The only known exception was made when Freud was in a critical mood toward Rank's theory; he suggested (Jones, 1957, p. 68) that he would never have proposed the theory without prior statistical evaluation of the mentalities of those who were first-born, had difficult births, or were delivered by Caesarean section.

Sandor Ferenczi (1873–1933) made no theoretical modifications as sweeping as Rank's. His chief defections were in therapeutic technique. He shared with Rank the belief that it is not always necessary to exhume the historical origins of neurotic symptoms; thus a briefer therapy should be possible. Ferenczi thought that the warm relationship with the mother was missing in the lives of most of his neurotic patients and that the therapist should supply this missing element. Accordingly, he coddled patients, holding them in his lap and kissing them at times (Jones, 1957, pp. 163–164). Freud saw this as opening the door to therapeutic techniques which could discredit psychoanalysis completely, and Ferenczi was hurt by Freud's doubts. However, he would not be dissuaded from his belief that *acting out* the unconscious problems is the way to mental health and continued to use his unique therapy until his health became so poor that he could no longer work.

This concludes the purely expository portion of the present chapter. It is in no sense a complete history of psychoanalysis even up to the time of Freud's death in 1939; it is a sample of high lights only. More recent developments will be presented later, but they too must be incomplete. Psychoanalysis is an organic movement that is forever growing and replacing parts of itself, so that no cross section can give a realistic or at all a complete picture. However, we now turn to some evaluation of the cross section we have presented here.

PSYCHOANALYSIS AS A SYSTEM

In view of the differences between those systems usually called psychoanalytic, psychoanalysis cannot be discussed as a single system. However, there are important commonalities even among the widely divergent systems, and we shall try to keep these commonalities in the focus of the discussion. Wherever we discuss a point which is not common to all systems, Freud's system will be used rather than any of the others. Even with these restrictions, it requires some forcing to fit Freud's system into the boundaries of criteria set up by an academic psychologist. Nevertheless, the questions raised by McGeoch's criteria are important ones for psychoanalysis.

Definition of psychology. Although Freud was not within the tradition of psychology as such, psychoanalysis was to him perhaps the only psychology worthy of the name. He was interested in developing a systematic framework but not in stating definitions. His followers did not differ from him on this point. Freud *distinguished* psychoanalysis at one time by its concern with resistance and transference; at another time he said that the distinguishing mark of an analyst was his concern with sexual factors. But these were not definitions. We may attempt a definition "from the outside" based on what psychoanalysis seems to us to be. Psychoanalysis is that discipline which began in the study of neurosis through the techniques of hypnosis, dream analysis, and free association. It has emphasized unconscious motivational conditions. It has since broadened its fields and methods of study to include anthropological investigation; laboratory experiments; testing techniques; and the study of normal persons, cultures, and cultural records. Several basic assumptions are made by analysts, and these assumptions must be included as a part of the definition of the school; only those who accept some minimum number of them are accepted analysts. These assumptions are next examined.

Basic postulates. According to Munroe (1955), nearly all varieties of analysts accept four basic assumptions. First, the psychic life is *determined.* Second, the *unconscious* plays a predominant role in determining the behavior of man, which previously had been thought to follow rational patterns of determination. Third, the most important explanatory concepts are *motivational* (i.e., "dynamic"). Many different behavioral manifestations can be explained by recourse to a single underlying motivational concept; the emphasis is on the purposiveness of action rather than on more mechanical S-R connections. Fourth, the *history* of the organism is of extreme importance in the determination of contemporary behavior.

In addition to these four primary postulates, more orthodox analysts usually accept several others which may be summarized as follows.

The basic drive is sexual and has its foundation in the biology of the organism. The manifestation of this primal biological energy is seen in the various instincts. There is a basic conflict of life and death instincts (we have already seen that this is one of the least popular postulates). A structural, topographical model is needed to explain unconscious activity; Freud's id, ego, and superego are the usually accepted structures. Parental relationships to the young child account for the neuroses. The individual goes through various stages of libidinal development—oral, anal, phallic, latency, and genital. The individual is defended from psychological harm through the use of the defense mechanisms under the control of the ego. Finally, dreams, slips of the tongue, wit, and various errors have symbolic meaning related to repressed sexual content.

Although we have included the above assumptions under the name postulates, this name should not be taken literally. Freud was an inductive thinker, at least as he conceived the process. He did not see himself as postulating at all but merely as reporting or summarizing the results of his observations. His reaction to Janet's saying the unconscious was a manner of speaking shows that Freud did not like to have his concepts put on a postulational level. The behavior of many of his followers indicates that they tend to think the same way. This is not necessarily a telling criticism, for it does not matter how concepts are viewed as long as they play a useful part in theory.

Nature of the data. The basic data of psychoanalysis have been gathered in the therapeutic setting. They are the data of verbal report, or of introspection. The type of introspection is markedly different from the classic type, but the difficulties of the classic type are still present, often in aggravated form. If psychoanalytic introspection is supposed to give information about past events, then the original stimuli for the verbal report occurred months or years previously. Many of the hypotheses of psychoanalysis are about relationships between events in the history of the patient and his present behavior. In fact, some critics have felt (e.g., Skinner, 1954a) that one of the main contributions of psychoanalysis has been its emphasis on the causal importance of events in the life of the individual. Yet these events have been little studied in any direct way. The data are the *present* verbal productions of the patient. Freud was himself puzzled when he found by checking the reports of his patients against the reports of other family members that many of the reported events could not possibly have occurred. He decided that it made no difference whether the event had occurred; the fact that the event had been fantasied made it important for therapy. Ezriel (1951) has argued on the basis of such reasoning that analysis is *not* a historical method. It seems that he is right. The analyst really works on the assumption that *reports* about the past are important; operationally speaking, the analyst has nothing to do with the past of the patient. He studies the personality of the individual through an observation of his interaction with another person (the analyst), not through the reconstruction of the past. Psychoanalysis is a dynamic, not a genetic, method, working with contemporary rather than genetic data.

The relationship between the data and the theory of psychoanalysis is thus far from clear. If the theory is about genetic factors, then most of the data are highly questionable. The past events must be *inferred* from the kind of data collected. We remember from the criticisms of structural psychology that psychologists have generally not been content to trust the human memory for more than a few seconds, even under strictly controlled conditions. If the data are recognized for what they are—appropriate to statements about the present only— then the form of Freudian theory would seem to require modification. This kind of criticism is, of course, less appropriate to Jung or even to Adler, since they recognized more explicitly the importance of the present in their theoretical presentations. Even in their cases, however, many of the hypotheses are about the past—in Jung's case even the phylogenetic past, where no direct data at all are available.

A second difficulty arises necessarily from the nature of the therapeutic relationship. Many of the statements made by the patient must be kept in strictest confidence. The analyst must play the role of therapist during an analytic session and can take the detached role of scientist only after the session is over. He may forget or select only confirmatory data. What the patient says may be influenced by previous statements of the analyst. Freud himself taught his patients some analytic theory in the therapeutic process, although he did not do so to as great an extent in later years; suggestions may thus have inclined the patient toward those statements that would be confirmatory as far as the theory was concerned. The net result is that the data are not generally available even to the scientific public. Scientists generally, then, cannot evaluate their quality. The confirmation by a patient that an analysis of some of his productions (for example, a dream) is correct is of little scientific value. The patient himself participates to some extent in the interpretation, and his agreement or verification may be a result of unintentional suggestion by the analyst that the interpretation is correct. There is no outside source which can confirm or deny the correctness of the analysis.

One might wish to ignore the need for such data and demand only data on the success of therapy. Even data on therapeutic success are seldom available in any quantity. There are, of course, plenty of reports of patients who got better, but there are few studies with control groups, equal in other respects, which are given some other type of therapy or no therapy at all. Each analyst sees so few patients, even over a lifetime of therapy, that it is difficult to get a large sample. Even if one could get such control groups and such samples, it would be extremely hard to show that the individual analyst's application of the theory had been correct or that extraneous factors had not contributed to the outcome. Altogether, it is very difficult to demonstrate a tight logical relationship between the theory and the outcome of therapy. A therapeutic situation does not seem to be the place to prove a scientific theory.

Observational data have come in from other situations. Kardiner (1939), Mead (1950), and Malinowski (1950) have gleaned relevant data from primitive societies. These data have sometimes bolstered the system and sometimes necessitated its modification; for example, the data have not supported the supposed universality of the Oedipal complex (Toulmin, 1948).

Hilgard (1952), among others, has reported some recent data from human subjects in laboratory or classroom situations. These data are necessarily fragmentary. They are concerned with isolated portions of psychoanalytic theory, as nearly any closely controlled study must be at this stage. Still absent is the painstakingly detailed longitudinal study which would be needed to give sound underpinning to psychoanalytic genetic assumptions. Pumpian-Mindlin (1952) is typical of those who feel the need for a psychoanalytic institute to carry on such research.

Sears (1943) has reviewed the objective research prior to 1942 which attempts to verify psychoanalytic concepts. Many of these studies have been with animals, and a disproportionately large number have been tests of fixation or regression. There is some question about the significance of such research, but certainly the experiments are relatively well controlled and indicate a salutary concern with the scientific acceptability of the concepts tested. The overconcern with limited concepts probably indicates a weakness in the theory; most of the analytic statements are too general or too ambiguous to allow easy testing. It is in most cases not possible to test predictions based on derivations from several postulates because there is never any quantitative statement and seldom even any statement of the relative qualitative importance of the several possible factors which might bear on a behavioral outcome. Thus the kinds of data and their relevance to analytic theory are partially limited by the condition of the theory.

Mind-body position. Freud was a modern in this respect; he did not much concern himself with the question. Jones (1953, p. 367) has said that passages could be quoted from Freud which would place him in any one of several philosophical mind-body positions; Freud self-consciously declared himself a psychophysical parallelist. He held that psychical processes cannot occur in the absence of physiological processes and that the latter must precede the former. He thus assigned some priority to the material, a priority that may have been held over from his student days when he espoused a radical materialism,

Principles of connection. Since psychoanalysts are outside academic psychology, it is unnecessary for them to begin with the problem of connection as such. However, their basic method is the free-association method, and one can ask how it happens that the associations are connected in such a way that they provide, as Freud said of the dream, a "royal road to the unconscious." The principles of connection are of several kinds.

First, there are the classic principles of contiguity, similarity, and opposition. The elements that have been contiguous to each other in an individual's experiences tend later to be connected in an associative train. Also, elements that are similar for an individual, or that are opposites, may evoke or substitute for each other.

More importantly, associations run along the strands of motives or feelings. The similarity or opposition may be one of motive or feeling rather than of the objective stimuli. A recognition of this fact enables the analyst to recognize connections which are not apparent to the academic psychologist. The determination of associations by these factors also explains why the "free" associations of the patient involve material relevant to his basic problems; these problems beget motives which in turn control the associations.

Still other and more complex principles are needed to explain completely why certain symptoms arise from their problems and why certain manifest content arises from its latent content in the dream. These are the special principles of symbolism which have been mentioned earlier: distortion, displacement, and condensation are such principles. Finally, there are the defense mechanisms of the ego— rationalization, projection, etc.—which explain the connections between certain overt behaviors and their motivational bases. The complexity of these principles of symbolism and defense is such that they have long been the objects of extended analytic investigation.

Principles of selection. Motivation provides the key to selection as well as to connection; it seems that in most systems the principles tend to be simply the obverse of one another. Analysts have emphasized the selectivity exercised in the movement of material into consciousness from the preconscious or unconscious more than the selection of stimuli in the environment. The selection of an idea or memory is dependent upon the dynamic balance between repressive forces and those instinctual forces which strive for the expression of the repressed material. Repression acts selectively to remove material from consciousness, and resistances act to keep the emotionally toned material out. The job of the analyst is to redistribute the libidinal energy available so that the repressive forces of the ego or superego are lessened relative to the expressive forces. Often the libido attached to the repressed material is so strong that it forces its own selection for acting out in disguised form; for example, repressed hostility may be expressed through its projection onto other persons, who are then reported to be hostile. The ego is continually selecting appropriate repressed materials for such symbolic expression. The principles of connection are also involved in selection; the ego must *select*, according to the principles of *connection*, the symbols that are needed to give vent to repressed impulses.

We see from such examples that a considerable part of Freud's contribution was the detailed development of principles of connection and selection in cases where they had previously been regarded as arbitrary and lawless. He extended the principles to the unconscious, where different laws were required, and this extension is at the heart of his system.

Recently, research involving the so-called "new look" in perception has been concerned with the effects of motivation on the perception of objective stimuli. Such selective perception has been demonstrated in the laboratory and represents an extension of the kind of thinking typical of the analysts. Although the interpretation given the experiments is in doubt (e.g., Goldiamond, 1958), there can be no doubt that variables which were earlier thought inappropriate are now being studied in the perceptual context. An example of the observed results is the finding that more time is required for the perception of a guilt-arousing than a neutral word. The analytic interpretation would be that an ego-defensive mechanism is at work and tends to repress its perception.

CRITICISMS OF PSYCHOANALYSIS

Immorality. The lay and religious publics have been vindictive toward Freud and psychoanalysis because of its alleged irreligiosity, amorality, and emphasis on sex. It has been said that Freud reviled and desecrated religion and childhood. Freud was not personally religious, and he attempted to explain religiosity in natural scientific terms. It is also true that Freud extended the concept of sexuality into childhood and that he advocated somewhat less repressive attitudes toward sex; he was, for example, in favor of sex education of a realistic sort.

Regardless of what Freud's personal feelings were or of what he said on these subjects, the arguments are altogether irrelevant to the truth or falsity of any scientific hypothesis. If one regards Freud's pronouncements on these subjects as philosophical rather than scientific, then their rejection can be on the ground of value rather than truth. Thus if a reader does not like the pessimism of Freud as a philosophy of life, he can reject it for a more optimistic view. His acceptance or rejection will have nothing to do with science.

Origins. Several critics have pointed out relationships between Freud's personality or background and the theory that he evolved. For example, some might read Bakan's book (1958) as a denunciation of psychoanalysis, since it points out in a clear and scholarly way the relationship between Jewish mysticism and psychoanalysis, with side excursions into Freud's messianic feelings and their implications for theory. It is no rarity to see the Oedipal part of analysis explained by recourse to Freud's own relationship with his young mother or to see his tendency to oppose traditional views reduced to a reaction to his membership in the Jewish minority.

These criticisms, too, are fundamentally irrelevant. Nevertheless, psychoanalysis has been more often subjected to such criticisms than better-established disciplines. We have already seen that its data do not have the quality of conviction typical of most scientific data. Therefore, if a critic explains a part of analysis by recourse to mysticism, it is incumbent upon the defender of analysis to show that that part of analysis rests also upon some firmer foundation of scientifically acceptable data.

Theory. No system thus far discussed in this book has provided anything close to an adequate theory in Bergmann's sense (see Chapter 3), which is essentially the sense in which we have been using the word. Psychoanalysis is no exception. Only in an extremely broad sense of the word is there a psychoanalytic theory. There are a large number of empirical generalizations, and there are some parts which constitute a rudimentary model. Walker (1957) has recently outlined very clearly the nature of the unconscious as a scientific model. Freud regarded himself as a beginner only, his system as a beginning only. Perhaps the analogy between psychoanalysis and phrenology (see Dallenbach, 1955) is not so unfair as it would at first appear; both disciplines made important beginnings toward sciences, although the beginning made by analysis will no doubt eventuate in a far more comprehensive science.

In view of these considerations, it is not surprising that there is really no such thing as a psychoanalytic theory. If one wished to test psychoanalytic theory, he would not know where to go to find the theory. Presumably the theory exists in the collected works of Freud or perhaps in interpreters like Fenichel (1945), but nowhere is there a clear statement of what are postulates, what are theorems, what their relations are, what quantitative values are to be assigned; in short, one misses all the paraphernalia usually associated with a scientific theory. The data so far brought forward concern themselves with empirical generalization, not with deductions from any theory.

There are several reasons why the casual observer may be misled into thinking some theory exists. In the first place, there have been a great many statements made about matters of fact by analysts. The outsider may believe that these statements, some of which may be correct, are derived from some theory. The fact is that they are generally derived from observation; they are descriptive statements, or generalizations thereof. A second reason is that analysts have been willing to explain all sorts of behavior—dreams, forgetting, symptoms, and the genesis of given neuroses. Since there is a language and a set of statements available for explaining such otherwise inexplicable occurrences, the observer may believe that a scientific theory must be available. The unfortunate truth is that the *analysts' statements are so general that they can explain whatever behavior occurs.* A genuine scientific explanation cannot do this; it must predict one behavior to the exclusion of all other behaviors. Otherwise the theory is empirically empty and says, in effect, "Anything may happen."

No over-all criticism of psychoanalytic theory can be meaningful until an over-all theory exists. It will be a very long while before a rigorous theory can exist, for the area of behavior which such a theory must cover is indeed broad and complex. Meanwhile, psychoanalysis will fill the need for a model which will "go anywhere, do anything, and be good at dealing with people" (Walker, 1957, p. 122).

As is usual with systems like psychoanalysis, empirical confirmation must apply itself to the limited, confirmable statements rather than to the theory itself. Farrell (1951) has given a list of propositions which at that time seemed confirmed: that infants obtain pleasure from oral stimulation or genital stimulation, that manual masturbation is more frequent among preschool boys than girls, and that small children exhibit extensive pregenital play. Other propositions he regarded as disconfirmed: that all small girls have penis envy and wish to be boys and that all children exhibit sexual attraction and attachment for the parent of the opposite sex and sexual jealousy of the parent of the same sex. A third class of propositions is regarded as untested or untestable, such as the hypothesis about substitutability of erogenous zones.

Whether or not one agrees with Farrell's classification of these few propositions, his procedure at least illustrates the necessarily piecemeal nature of the confirmation process. It is unrealistic to hope for any real confirmation or disconfirmation of the theory at the present time. We must agree with Farrell that "psychoanalytic theory is, qua theory, unbelievably bad." Although this is true of most psychological theory, analysts seem less concerned with this undesirable state of affairs than do most academic psychologists. We have said earlier that theories are discarded, not because they are wrong, but only because they are improved upon or replaced by superior theories. It is not likely that psychoanalytic theory, being flexible, will ever suddenly be replaced; it will serve as a framework into which new findings are fitted, until eventually the past and present elements and form of the theory are so changed that they are no longer recognizable.

Criticisms of therapeutic outcomes. Toulmin (1948) said that "if a fully-fledged analytic explanation is not part of a successful cure, we do not regard it as a 'correct' explanation; therapeutic failure is as fatal to an explanation in psychoanalysis as a predictive failure is to an explanation in physics." We must disagree with Toulmin on this point. A psychoanalytic explanation may be correct, but the course of the illness may nevertheless be irreversible because the independent variables which, if manipulated, would result in cure may not be under the control of the analyst. A somewhat analogous challenge might be to ask a physicist to change the orbit of Mars and refuse to accept his explanation of the laws of moving bodies if he were unable to do so. The lack of favorable therapeutic outcomes, therefore, may be a basis for criticizing the practicality or usefulness of the therapy but in itself cannot be a criticism of the theory. The theory could be criticized on the basis of therapeutic outcome only if it could be shown, first, that the theory were applicable and perfectly applied to the case and, second, that the therapist were able to manipulate all circumstances just as he pleased. We have already pointed out that there are few controlled data on therapeutic outcome; we may add here merely that a difficulty in getting such data is that there are no adequate and acceptable scientific criteria for improvement. The subjective judgment of the patient, analyst, or relatives may be used, but all are open to serious question. Despite the lack of data, the therapy as well as the theory will continue to be used until replaced by something demonstrably better.

Lack of control. This criticism, to some extent, has already been met in all the other criticisms. It is the focal point of all the others. As discussed earlier (see Chapter 1), the control we are speaking of here is not the control the physicist might lack if he wished to change the orbit of Mars; it is the control of variables which would enable him to say what factors were at work in any given observation. The analyst lacks this control. He cannot isolate possible influences on a patient one by one but must attempt to disentangle relationships from the complex matrix of life as the patient happened to live it. He cannot be sure that descriptions of the past, or even of the present, are adequate or, for that matter, accurate. He cannot back up and see what would have happened if events had been changed in some way; he cannot try out the effect of some single manipulation on the patient's future behavior, for there is no way of isolating people from a multitude of other influences. No wonder it has been said the situation is uncontrolled!

A common answer to this criticism is that the analysts have proceeded through *clinical validation*. This seems to mean that successive confirmations of a theoretical prediction within the clinical setting constitute acceptable demonstrations of the accuracy of the principles involved. Such argument is basically unsound. We have to know what alternative explanations are possible, and these alternatives must be eliminated by means of appropriate controlled changes in the situation. Otherwise, despite an infinite number of clinical validations, it is possible that the same artifacts continue to give the same outcomes which happen to be consistent with the theoretical predictions. In reality, it is extremely improbable that clinical validation would ever be as systematic and careful even as we have pictured it; it is difficult to imagine a clinician finding enough cases appropriate to some prediction to permit him to repeat test after test of some good, operationally defined, clear hypothesis.

It is not easy to suggest improved methods for testing psychoanalytic propositions. This is clearly due to the state of the theory. A necessary step involving a huge amount of labor and ingenuity is the improved definition of terms and the formalization of the theory. It is not likely that the components of the theory have themselves been well enough tested to make the attempt profitable as yet. A prior step, then, would be to try to define operationally the terms that occur in the isolated propositions so that these will be more experimentally testable. Mullahy (1948, pp. 316 ff.) has given several examples of the need for clarification and elimination of contradiction.

There are several levels of behavioral observations and corollary realms of discourse involved in analytic theory and its testing. Most of the orthodox observations have been of verbal materials. Investigations at this level of observation might be improved by the use of more objective measures of the verbal behavior of the subject, as with psychological tests of various kinds. Stephenson (1953) has developed a technique, the Q sort, which is a compromise between the usual completely free analytic situation and the more strictly objective type of personality test, and has shown how the technique can be used to test analytic propositions. This technique has the advantage of dealing in a quantitative way with some of the attitudinal dimensions that are related to psychoanalytic theory.

A second level at which psychoanalytic propositions can be investigated is that of everyday-life behavior. Social caseworkers can make observations on the real-life characteristics of the individual and relate these observations to the events in therapy. These data would go beyond what is usually available to the analyst. We have already suggested that behavioral observations unrelated to therapy are also needed; although Freud felt that the best way to get information about the psychic apparatus was to study cases in which it was malfunctioning, we also need more information about the genetic events in the lives of normal people.

A third level at which the propositions need further study is the fully experimental one in which full scientific abstraction and control are reached. Although many analytically inclined people doubt the possibility of testing the propositions in this way, we shall never know unless we try. We might even wonder whether the objectors question the possibility or fear the outcome. Furthermore, such investigations would be valuable in their own right, regardless of their bearing on psychoanalytic propositions. It would be surprising if *any* investigation produced results which were perfectly in keeping with the original speculations that instigated them. If they generally did so, experimentation would become unnecessary.

Dogmatism and cultishness.   We have already had some discussion of this point in other connections; for example, we saw the sense in which Freud was dogmatic and the sense in which he was not. We have met "the committee," composed of men who might almost be called disciples; Eitingon, for example, always made a pilgrimage to see Freud on his birthday. There are other points which suggest cultishness. Only the analyzed can analyze, as though one had to be personally initiated in a trial by fire before one could carry the word.

A given psychoanalytic interpretation of a particular case is often accepted without question by its proponent; alternative views are simply not entertained. Finally, the adherence to a single systematic view is frequently combined with an emotional fervor such as is seldom seen in scientific circles.

These characteristics indicate why psychoanalysis from the outside has seemed almost as much a religion as a science. Again, this argument has nothing to do logically with the value of the theory or the therapy, but it has had something to do with the acceptance of the theory by scientists, who feel that science is not a cult. Agreement with a gospel or subjective evaluations of persons should have nothing to do with evaluations of scientific propositions, and psychoanalysts have sometimes seemed to use these criteria.

An interesting form of dogmatism is the criticism by analysts of the detractors from psychoanalysis. If a critic refuses to accept some aspect of psychoanalysis, he is said to be manifesting resistance. We can find such inherent dogmatism in Freud himself. When he wished to show why Adler was wrong, he said (Freud, 1938, p. 964); "I shall, therefore, use analysis only to make clear how these deviations from analysis could take place among analysts." No doubt Adler analyzed Freud in return in order to show why Freud had resisted the new ideas.

CONTRIBUTIONS OF PSYCHOANALYSIS

Psychoanalysis is in the paradoxical position of being often rejected as a scientific system yet accepted as an outstanding contributor to science. Freud is more often regarded as a pioneer, as a prescientist, than as a scientist; he called himself a conquistador. Whatever he is called, he is recognized even by his enemies as a great man and perhaps the greatest genius within psychology. He made contributions to many fields. Let us look at some of his contributions to psychology.

He stimulated thinking and observation of many neglected areas of psychology: the significance of unconscious factors in determining behavior, the widespread importance of sex in normal and abnormal behavior, the importance of conflict, of childhood, of the irrational, and of the emotional. He personally made acute observations throughout a long life of daily work and contributed hypotheses or facts—we cannot yet tell which are which—about broad areas of human behavior.

He developed highly provocative explanations of kinds of behavior previously considered outside the realm of scientific explanation, such as errors and dreams. The fact that such areas were examined and such explanations developed by a serious worker would have been an important contribution regardless of the eventual correctness or even usefulness of the explanations. A field of study was opened up that was virgin for all practical purposes when Freud touched it.

Even in technique and methodology, where psychoanalysis so often falls short of traditional scientific criteria, Freud either made contributions or reinforced points made by others. His development of the techniques of free association and dream analysis for the study of unconscious processes has been compared to the invention of the microscope for studying cellular processes. Equally important, his emphasis on the study of unconscious processes preceded and reinforced the behaviorist and gestaltist point that the traditional methods of introspection were altogether inadequate for the development of a complete science of man. One could argue that Freud made incidentally a point that became a central thesis of behaviorism. In this sense, psychoanalysis has been the source of a great optimism; psychology is now viewed as a discipline that will certainly become a full-fledged science and develop whatever techniques are necessary. Without Freud, the conviction might have been slower in growing.

Psychoanalysis has contributed much empirical observation. Intensive studies of individual cases are available in the psychoanalytic literature as in no other place. Freud himself published only four case histories of his own patients, but other analysts have contributed, and the distillation of such observations presumably appears indirectly in analytic propositions. Hall and Lindzey (1957) believe that Freud's use of internal consistency as a method of testing hypotheses was one of his most important contributions to research strategy. As applied within psychoanalysis, internal consistency refers to the checking and cross-checking of a particular hypothesis by means of a large variety of different indicators; homogeneity of results is interpreted as supporting the hypothesis, much as a test is evaluated in terms of the extent to which the separate items can be shown to be positively correlated. Internal consistency becomes important as a research strategy only when there is a great deal of data on a single case. It makes possible a kind of reliability not otherwise easily obtained.

Another contribution is not easily weighed in a scientific scale: psychoanalysis has contributed to the popularity of psychology and psychiatry with the lay public. The average man has analytic words and notions from all schools in his repertoire and uses some analytic modes of thinking about the behavior of others—and perhaps occasionally his own. Psychoanalysis has thus revealed the importance of psychology to the lay public in a way that other systems have not. It may be that money and talent are easier to recruit to the science of psychology because of the analytic contribution.

Psychoanalysis presents explanations of normal and neurotic behavior in a language and at a level that people are prone to believe they understand. For better or for worse, it deals with practical situations in an exciting and challenging manner. Its method and theory contrast markedly with the slow, tiresome, painstaking program characteristic of most scientific research and theory construction. Therein lie both its appeal and its weakness.

SUMMARY AND CONCLUSIONS

Psychoanalysis deals with the interesting and mysterious, yet practical and important, regions of man's existence. Its adherents have hung together in a kind of cult; psychoanalysis is apparently thoroughly understood by few persons who are not analysts. Still, enough of its theory and practice has filtered out to others so that its terms enrich the lay vocabulary more than the terms from any other psychological system.

Psychoanalysis is more an art, a philosophy, and a practice than a science. The theory is loose and nebulous, sometimes even self-contradictory. The therapy has not demonstrated a greater effectiveness than other kinds of therapy, which in turn have seldom presented conclusive evidence that they are better than no therapy at all. The data and methodology which gave rise to analytic theory are markedly inadequate. Analysts have typically shown too little desire to improve the form of, or evidence for, the theory; this is not to imply that the theory does not show frequent changes as a result of new observations in therapy or, occasionally, in better controlled studies, although examples of the latter would be hard to demonstrate.

Many of the modern variations on Freud's theory have followed

Adler down the path of increased emphasis upon cultural factors, with some compensatory deemphasis upon biological factors. Much analytic effort has gone into increased specification of the nature and genesis of ego functioning; it is this area of study which probably gives the most promise of a *rapprochement* with academic psychology. Jung is typical of those who have placed increasing emphasis upon the unity and the creative potential of the self. The common rejection of the death instinct is typical of the less pessimistic outlook on human nature shown by modern analysts.

Despite its glaring systematic and scientific defects, psychoanalysis is the most vital psychological school which has retained a clearly recognizable identity; it has been a powerful force since 1900 and is gaining ever wider acceptance of some of its basic ideas. Among these ideas are the unconscious model and the importance of sexuality. There are currently several training institutes for analysts within the United States. Each teaches analysis with some idiosyncratic modifications, but there is a strong core of Freudian doctrine common even to those who would prefer to deny it.

Among the solid contributions to psychology are the opening up of new areas of investigation such as the unconscious, sex, the impetus to motivational research, and the stress on childhood and genetic factors in personality; most of the empirical observations; and defense mechanisms, which are often accepted by otherwise unfriendly psychologists. A significant task of future behavior scientists will be to convert the brilliant insights of Freud into scientifically acceptable propositions. In this process, it may well be that the peculiar flavor of psychoanalysis will be lost.

further readings

So much has been written on psychoanalysis that a reading list must be presented with great temerity. The books that follow are good, but are only a tiny fraction of the total number of good books. Jones's three volumes, *The life and work of Sigmund Freud* (1953–1957), are in many ways the best single source on psychoanalysis. These books can be read as absorbing biography and will infuse large quantities of knowledge painlessly into the unwary brain. A fine little book which is just what it claims to be is Hall's *A primer of Freudian psychology* (1954). This book provides a solid basic introduction to Freud's system. Hall and Lindzey in their *Theories of personality* (1957) do the same thing for all the important psychoanalytic theorists. Munroe's *Schools of psychoanalytic thought* (1955) is a friendly psychologist's look at psychoanalysis. If the student has taken a dislike to psychoanalysis and wants to find out how vitriolic critics can be, Ludwig's *Doctor Freud* (1947) will provide this extreme. On the other hand, Bakan's *Sigmund Freud and the Jewish mystical tradition* (1958) shows relationships which would otherwise be unsuspected by all except the most devout scholars and is worth reading just as an example of how the fine line between scholarship and readability can be navigated by a skillful writer. Freud's *A general introduction to psychoanalysis* (1943) is probably the most readable effort by Freud himself. The translations by Brill of Freud's *The basic writings of Sigmund Freud* (1938) are easily available and provide a good sampling of Freud's work. A classic exposition of psychoanalytic theory is Fenichel's *The psychoanalytic theory of neurosis* (1945). Useful methodological criticisms, including some of a friendly sort, are to be found in a symposium on psychoanalysis in the November 1954 issue of *Scientific monthly;* Skinner's (1954a) and Frenkel-Brunswik's (1954) papers are especially valuable.

part three CONTEMPORARY THEORIES

This final part of the present volume is concerned with some theoretical developments in contemporary psychology. Although our primary purpose is to present the theories, we have also attempted to show the relationship of contemporary theories to older systems.

We have selected those theories which have been most generally influential within American psychology and which relate to general systematic considerations rather than those which concern specific subject matter. Therefore, some very important but more specialized theories (such as those in the field of color vision) have been omitted.

Contemporary theories have been treated in three groups, which can be more or less identified within the functional schema of stimulus-organism-response (S-O-R). Thus, the stimulus-response theories have been primarily response-centered; so-called field theories have developed largely from gestalt psychology and have been primarily stimulus-centered (or perception-centered); and personality theories concentrate upon the organism and its characteristics. This simple schema cannot be pushed too far, since few theories deal exclusively with any one of these categories, but it indicates primary emphasis.

The final chapter deals with a new and exciting development—the influences upon psychological theory of mathematical and engineering concepts and procedures. It can be predicted with some assurance that these influences will have an increasing effect on a wide range of psychological research and theory construction.

varieties of S-R theory   10

Contemporary S-R theory can be divided into two broad classes, which differ in the role accorded the *reinforcement*, or response-strengthening, process.

The first of these classes may be called S-R reinforcement theory. Both of the two major subtypes of this theory afford reinforcement a central role, but they interpret the nature of this role differently. Many psychologists, like Hull, have interested themselves in the mechanism of the reinforcement process; some form of "need-reduction" has been most often identified as the necessary and sufficient condition for reinforcement. Others, like Skinner, have stressed the importance of reinforcement without commitment to the underlying nature of the process. This view may be classed as descriptive S-R theory, since the fact of reinforcement is accepted in a descriptive or theoretically neutral sense.

The second class of modern S-R theory is generally called contiguity theory. Following Guthrie, contiguity theorists hold that all that is essential to learning is contiguity of stimulus and response. Reinforcement, in the sense of presentation of a so-called "reinforcing stimulus" such as food or money, is important only because it changes the stimulus situation and so preserves associations already established. From a historical point of view, modern contiguity theory is a highly refined associationism (see Chapter 5).

Several writers have suggested combinations of these two major views. These two-factor theories are treated briefly. With the exception of Mowrer's latest (1960a) version, they present few new theoretical positions but rearrange the basic points already present in the two major positions.

All the different S-R theories have a great deal in common, probably more than theories of perception or personality. For one thing, they

241

are all primarily *learning* theories. Because of the central role that learning has played in these theories, it is often very difficult to distinguish between learning theory and general behavior theory. Hull, for example, considered himself a general behavior theorist and thought of learning constructs as central but not exclusive determiners of performance. To most psychologists, however, Hull has been a learning theorist because he has been primarily concerned with behavior *modification*. Similar statements could be made about most of the other theorists discussed in this chapter.

A second characteristic common to all S-R theorists is their neobehaviorism. The most marked difference between modern *neo*behaviorism and Watsonian behaviorism is the greatly increased theoretical sophistication of the former. Watson, Weiss, and Holt had to be content with making gross generalizations based on very limited empirical evidence. Today, however, detailed logical justification as well as empirical evidence is demanded by and of neobehaviorists.

S-R REINFORCEMENT THEORY: THE HULL-SPENCE SCHOOL

The main lines of modern S-R reinforcement theory were laid down by Clark L. Hull. In the development of this systematic effort he had the assistance of many psychologists, notably Kenneth Spence and Neal Miller. Both were associated with him for many years at Yale University, and both helped to determine the way in which Hull's theory developed. Spence especially has been consistently interested in the form of the theory and has trained and sent forth a large number of theoretical devotees. For these reasons our heading is "the Hull-Spence school." Miller not only worked directly with the theory but also extended it to the explanation of personality. This gives him a place in Chapter 12.

Hull's career

Clark Hull (1884–1952) was born in New York and reared in Michigan. Throughout his childhood and early adult years, he was beset by illnesses. Throughout his life, he suffered from very poor vision. He persevered in his schooling in spite of these physical handicaps and attended the University of Michigan as a special student. He taught in rural schools before returning for graduate work at the University of Wisconsin. His doctoral research there was performed on the problem of concept formation (Hull, 1920).

Hull stayed on at Wisconsin as a member of the psychology staff. One of his early research efforts concerned the effects of tobacco smoking on efficiency of behavior. These much-cited experiments (Hull, 1924) were marked for their especially good control of the sensory factors involved in smoking (such as the warmth of the air produced by a pipe). The control of suggestibility by concealing whether tobacco was actually present presaged Hull's later concern with the general problem of suggestion.

As a result of being assigned a course in tests and measures, Hull surveyed the literature in that field and eventually published an important early text, *Aptitude testing* (1928). He did not continue these activities, however, because of what he has called his "pessimistic view as to the future of tests in this field" (1952, p. 151).

Hull's next persistent research interest was in suggestibility, hypnotic and otherwise. He became involved because he had to present academic lectures and laboratory work to medical students. He spent ten productive years in research on suggestion, supervising a large number of senior theses. By his own count, some twenty persons engaged in the research, which was reported in thirty-two papers. He has stated that his interest in hypnotic research was not encouraged after he moved to Yale because of medical opposition, which had not been encountered in the Midwest (1952). His publication of the book summarizing the research, *Hypnosis and suggestibility* (1933), marked the end of this phase of his research career. The book remains a classic in the field of hypnosis.

Hull's third and final major research interest was learning theory. He studied Anrep's translation of Pavlov's *Conditioned reflexes* (1927) and became progressively more interested in learning and general behavior theory. In 1929 he became a research professor in Yale's Institute of Psychology (which was shortly to become the Institute of Human Relations). Thenceforth he turned to the development of behavior theory on a full-scale basis.

development of Hull's system

The focal point of Hull's theoretical thinking was the conditioned reflex, as conceptualized by Pavlov. Hull regarded it as a kind of simplified learning function which was admirably suited for experimental analyses. The findings could then be extended to other more complex phenomena. Hull made the extension by basing the axioms of his system on experimental findings from conditioning experiments. For example, Hull's postulate 2 in his final system (1952) states what happens to the "molar stimulus trace" as a function of time since stimulation. This axiom arose very directly out of the empirical relationships observed in conditioning experiments. Such use of conditioning as a source of axioms is a distinct change from previous behavioristic practice; Watson, for example, used the conditioned reflex grossly, as an element from which complex behavior could be directly constructed.

In justifying this position, Hull published a series of brilliantly conceived theoretical papers on conditioning during the 1930s. Perhaps the best known of these was his presidential address before the American Psychological Association, entitled "Mind, mechanism, and adaptive behavior" (1937). The general purpose of these papers, exemplified in the title cited, was to show how basic conditioning principles might be extended to complex behavioral processes. As a methodological, rather than a metaphysical, behaviorist (see Chapter 7), Hull was concerned with behaviorally redefining mental phenomena.

A brief excursion into the field of verbal rote learning followed this early theoretical work. Here Hull enlisted the aid of a set of mathematicians and logicians, as well as psychologists, and attempted a rigorous quantitative analysis of the kind of rote verbal learning first studied by Ebbinghaus (see Chapter 6). Although the book that emerged from this effort has been hailed as a landmark in the development of scientific psychology, it has been seldom read, less often understood, and unproductive of research. *Mathematico-deductive theory of rote learning* (Hull et al., 1940) thus remains an idealized but relatively fruitless model of psychological theory construction.

Hull's next major publication, *Principles of behavior* (1943), had quite the opposite effect. Its appearance marked the beginning of an era of psychological research in which Hull became the unquestioned leader of learning research in this country and one of the most controversial figures in the field. In the *Principles* Hull attempted to lay down the framework for a comprehensive theory of all mammalian behavior. He outlined a set of postulates and corollaries, logically interlaced in the hypothetico-deductive style that he had come to consider a model of scientific theorizing.

Although many psychologists did not think the book fulfilled the great promise of Hull's early theoretical papers, *Principles of behavior* nevertheless had an enormous influence on research in the learning area. Hull became by far the most cited writer in the field. Untold numbers of master's theses and doctoral dissertations were performed to test various of the implications of Hull's theoretical system. Up to the time of his death in 1952, Hull remained the dominant figure in the field of learning theory.

A major factor in the success of the *Principles of behavior* in stimulating research was its detailed spelling out of the postulate-corollary set. Hull deliberately laid the system out in as explicit a manner as possible in order to expedite continuous and persistent empirical checking. This characteristic was probably the most important feature of his systematic endeavor.

In terms of content, perhaps the most important aspect of Hull's theorizing was its attempt to reconcile the basic Thorndikian notion of effect with the conditioning paradigm and methodology of Pavlov (see Chapter 6). In essence, what Hull attempted to do was to incorporate the effect principle—now called reinforcement—into a conditioning type of framework. Unlike Watson, he did not think that frequency and recency of response were sufficient principles to account for learning. The emphasis on effect was evident in the last organization of his postulate set. Hull began with introductory postulates that dealt with "unlearned stimulus-response connections" (postulate I) and "stimulus reception" (postulate II). He then stated the key principle of reinforcement, first described as the *law of primary reinforcement* (1943, p. 80), as follows (1952, p. 5–6):

Postulate III. Primary Reinforcement
Whenever an effector activity (R) is closely associated with a stimulus afferent impulse or trace (s) and the conjunction is closely associated with a rapid diminution in the motivational stimulus (S_D or S_G), there will result an increment (Δ) to a tendency for that stimulus to evoke that response.

Immediately following were corollaries that dealt with secondary motivation and secondary reinforcement and postulate IV, which stated the law of habit formation, utilizing the variable of number of reinforcements.

Hull's last books were *Essentials of behavior* (1951) and *A behavior system* (1952). The latter work attempted to extend the application of quantitative methods within the system and to extend the system to problems of individual behavior. A final contemplated work on social behavior was never begun. As a matter of fact, Hull, who was very ill during his last years, did not live to read the galley proofs of *A behavior system.*

Most of the modifications of the original (1943) system in Hull's final works were relatively minor, mainly consisting of rearrangements of postulates and corollaries and changes in details. The most important modification was the shift in the relationships of antecedent stimulus determinants to the constructs $_sH_R$ and $_sE_R$. This shift left the habit construct, $_sH_R$, a function only of number of reinforcements and gave the reaction-evocation construct, $_sE_R$, increased importance in that it was directly determined by the stimulus factors formerly held to affect $_sH_R$ (see Figure 3). After the shift, a relatively simple derivation of latent learning was possible (see Hilgard, 1956; Koch, 1954). Latent learning had been the most important of the experimental results produced by cognitive non-S-R theorists and advanced as especially embarrassing for Hullian S-R theory (cf. Chapter 11).

Hullian methodology

Objectivity. Hull was first and foremost a behaviorist. He rejected metaphysical behaviorism, with its denial of consciousness (cf. Chapter 7), but fully and enthusiastically endorsed methodological behaviorism. Hull was considered the archobjectivist of the 1940s by both his followers, who reveled in this identification, and his opponents, who chose it as a point of attack. Hull's definition of both stimulus and response tended toward physicalism, at least in theory. Like most objectivists, Hull did not always manage to stick to a perfectly physicalistic data language in his actual experimental practice, but even his critics have usually found his data language adequately objective.

Hull's more sophisticated behaviorism was also intensely concerned with many methodological problems not considered by Watson. His theory contained a number of intervening variables. These variables functioned in the theory as quantities that were functions of antecedent stimulus conditions. The same intervening quantities then entered further equations that determined what the properties of the observed response should be (cf. Figure 3). It is often tempting in a psychological system to postulate intraorganismic variables whose quantity is appropriate to predict the response properties needed in the system. Hull was very careful to avoid this kind of trap; he insisted that every intervening variable be anchored in both stimulus and response conditions. His intervening variables were thus assured of being meaningful. At the very least, they were terms summarizing observable stimulus-response relationships.

Hypothetico-deductive form. Hull was greatly impressed by the elegance of the formal mathematical and physical systems, such as those developed by Euclid and Newton. As his interest in developing a general behavior system grew, he determined to model it upon these examples. The result was that he attempted to build a highly formalized and comprehensive behavior theory in a hypothetico-deductive framework. Formal postulates and corollaries were advanced, together with theorems laid down as deductive consequences. Such a system is hypothetico-deductive because it begins with *hypotheses* which are sufficiently well connected in a logical system so that their consequences can be *deduced*. The deductions (theorems) are related by the theorist to statements of empirical observations which should be made under the conditions specified by the theorem. The validity of the empirical statements is then checked by the experiment. If the statements are true, the hypotheses are retained; if false, the hypotheses require modification or rejection.

In *Principles of behavior* (1943) Hull laid down sixteen primary principles, as postulates, and a large number of corollaries; in the

(1951) revision of the system a total of eighteen postulates and twelve corollaries was produced. In accordance with the hypothetico-deductive procedure that Hull intended to follow, these primary principles were to be used deductively to predict secondary principles, such as the goal gradient and latent learning.

A single relatively simple example will serve to illustrate the way in which Hull used some prior empirical knowledge, one or more primary principles (postulates or corollaries), and some deductive derivation combined with a little quantification to produce theorems that could be tested empirically. Consider the problem of the order of elimination of blind alleys in maze learning, as by a rat. It had long been known that the blind alleys closest to the goal are eliminated first, a principle called the "goal-gradient hypothesis" by Hull (1932). Hull incorporated this empirical fact into a logical postulate by assuming that the response potential of any response is a function of its distance, in time, from the reinforcing event (in this case, the reaching of the food incentive in the goal box). Thus his corollary iii, delay in reinforcement (J), read (1952, p. 126): "A. *The greater the delay in reinforcement of a link within a given behavior chain, the weaker will be the resulting reaction potential of the link in question to the stimulus traces present at the time.*"

This principle, the logical derivation of which was given (1952, Chap. 5), led to a number of empirical predictions, stated as theorems, for multidirectional maze learning (1952, Chap. 9). Among these, for example, were the propositions that a long blind alley, since it entails a greater temporal delay of reinforcement, will be eliminated more quickly than a short blind alley (theorem 104, p. 282) and that the rate of locomotion through the maze will become progressively faster for the later, compared with the early, parts (theorem 110, p. 286). Now it is important to note that neither of these two predictions could be generated directly from the first empirical result itself, the observation of a gradient of error elimination, but could be logically derived from the general principle concerning temporal delay of reinforcement which was developed from the empirical data. Such logical deduction of many new and different empirical predictions from a small number of key principles is considered to be a major contribution of a hypothetico-deductive system. Hull's *A behavior system* is full of such derivations, with quantitative calculations, and so represents a much closer approximation to hypothetico-deductive methodology than does the more programmatic *Principles of behavior*.

To Hull's credit, it must be said that he did not attempt to hold to a static or fixed system; indeed, his thinking was extremely fluid, and his formal theory went through an almost continuous series of revisions. He thus used the hypothetico-deductive system in the way it was intended. An indication of the extent to which he practiced the methodology he preached may be seen in the fact that beginning in 1915 he kept written notes on his various research plans and notions; according to his own count (Hull, 1951, p. 120), there were twenty-five volumes of such handwritten notebooks. In addition, periodic mimeographed memoranda were distributed, informally and on a small scale, among interested persons. Copies of certain of these were deposited in the libraries of a small number of universities. Extensive critical discussion of these ideas occurred in Hull's seminars at Yale.

Quantitative character. Hull felt very strongly that theoretical progress in psychology would come as a consequence of the successful extension of quantification. His own theory was supposed to be a primarily quantitative one. Quantification was achieved in two main ways. First, and most generally, throughout his career as a theorist Hull did not hesitate to assign numerical values to constants and variables within the system. This he did largely on the basis of empirical curve fitting. For example, Hull's final formalization of the basic law of habit-strength formation held that it is a positive growth function of number of trials reinforced, with some increment occurring on every reinforced trial. His formulation of this law is:

$$_sH_R = 1 - 10^{-a\dot{N}}$$

where $\dot{N}$ is the number of evenly spaced reinforced trials and a is an empirical constant with an approximate value of .03 (Hull, 1951, p. 32). In addition, Hull used a centigrade scale for the strength of the habit construct, with the *hab* as the basic unit (equal to .01 of the maximal value). However, this scale was not used in his final work (1952).

A second and more specific type of quantification employed by Hull was his major research effort to quantify the performance construct, $_sE_R$, by means of the careful scaling of latency data in a simple runway situation with rat subjects (e.g., Yamaguchi et al., 1948; Felsinger et al., 1947). This research serves as a useful model of concentrated effort in a difficult and relatively uncharted field.

summary of system

Essentially, as an S-R system, Hullian theory deals with three types of variables: the stimulus (antecedent or input), the intervening (intra-organismic), and the response (consequent or output). The following highly abbreviated account is intended to give something of the general nature and flavor of the system. The basic system is represented diagrammatically in Figure 3. For a more detailed exposition the reader is referred to one of the original sources (e.g., Hull, 1943, 1951,

1952) or to a secondary explanatory source (e.g., Hilgard, 1956; Spence, 1951a, b).

The input, or stimulus, variables are such objective factors as number of reinforced trials, deprivation of incentive, intensity of the conditioned stimulus, and amount of reward. These various factors are directly associated with resulting processes hypothesized to function within the organism: intervening variables of the first order. Examples are habit strength $(_sH_R)$ as a function of number of trials

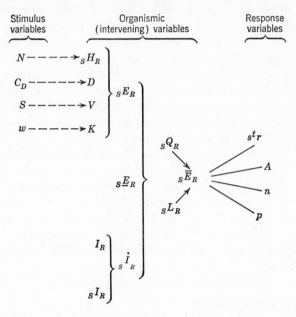

FIGURE 3. Simplified diagrammatic representation of the Hullian system. See text for explanation of symbols and relationships.

(N), drive (D) as a function of drive condition such as deprivation of incentive (C_D), stimulus-intensity dynamism (V) as a function of stimulus intensity (S), and incentive reinforcement (K) as a function of amount of reward (w).

Certain of these direct, or first-order, constructs are assumed now to coalesce into a smaller number of second-order intervening variables. The major construct is reaction potential or response evocation $(_sE_R)$, which is a joint function of $_sH_R$, D, V, and K. Also to be considered at this level are generalized reaction potential $(_s\underline{E}_R)$, which is a function of the amount of similarity of the present conditioned stimulus to ones previously experienced for which habit strengths have been established, and the aggregate of the negative reaction tendencies, $(_s\underline{I}_R)$. The latter construct is a function of reactive inhibition (I_R)

and conditioned or learned inhibition $(_sI_R)$, both of which are the direct consequence of work performed in the response.

At the final level, the higher-order intervening constructs then are net reaction potention $(_s\bar{E}_R)$, a function of the two excitatory factors and the one inhibitory factor just mentioned, and two more speculative and less well-specified constructs which modify its action. These are the oscillation $(_sO_R)$ and threshold $(_sL_R)$ of reaction potential. Finally, on the output side, there are four major measures of the effectiveness of response: latency $(_st_R)$, amplitude (A), number of responses to extinction (n), and probability of response (p).

Supplementary to the above descriptive account are a number of stimulus-trace concepts, such as the drive stimulus (S_D) and the fractional goal response (S_G), which are of primary importance in the system and also in more recent modifications of it, especially that of Spence (1956); these were omitted from the summarizing description so that the essential system could be presented in as simple a manner as is consistent with its character.

Also of great importance, but not included in the above summary, are a number of secondary or derived principles which Hull developed in an effort to bridge the gap between the normal complexities of molar behavior and the abstracted simplicity of his postulate set. Most important among these are the *habit family hierarchy*, the total set of habits which may occur in a given stimulus situation ordered in a hierarchy of strength, and the *goal gradient*, which has already been described.

criticisms of Hullian system

Few psychologists have met such a searching and often vehement criticism as has Hull. As a leading neobehaviorist, he inherited the kind of criticism that had earlier been accorded Watson. Much of this criticism has been polemic, or based on fundamental methodological or theoretical differences of opinion, and much seems to have been trivial or even personal in nature. Nevertheless, the solid critical points persistently lodged against Hull merit our attention.

Synthetic approach. As we have seen, Hull attempted to work out a complete and comprehensive theoretical account of mammalian behavior almost at a single stroke. His systematic venture was essentially a synthetic one. He endeavored to fashion and put together the pieces of his puzzle in advance of much research. In Hull's defense, however, it must be said that he started with such empirical evidence as he could find and persistently tried to build up additional evidence. Although he has also been criticized for ignoring certain contradictory evidence, it may be maintained in answer that not all of this is considered relevant to the kind of system involved.

Hull attempted to emulate the formal elegance of the systems of Euclid and Newton within a much shorter time than these beautifully integrated formal systems required for their development. The neatness and elegance of the final product in the case of such formal theory hide the fitfulness of actual development; it may be that theoretical progress is expedited by less ambitious efforts at the start. It is now generally conceded, even by many of those sympathetic to the Hullian brand of psychology, that his efforts represented an overly optimistic approach to an exceedingly complex set of problems.

Particularistic approach. Perhaps the most persistent criticism from sympathetic sources has been that Hull relied too much upon certain particular values of critical variables within special experimental circumstances. If his system was to apply to all mammalian behavior, as he indicated, surely a wide variety of representative organisms and experimental situations would need to be explored. The problem of generality, always a knotty one in behavior theory, was noted early by Koch (1944, p. 283) in his review of *Principles of behavior;* the point has more recently been made by Hilgard (1956, p. 181), who has cited the dependence of Hull's system upon particular constants from rat bar-pressing and human eyelid experimentation.

An indication of the extreme particularism of certain aspects of Hull's theorizing, in the sense of dependence upon particular experimental setups, may be seen in his provisional definition of the *wat* (honoring *Watson*) as the unit of reaction potential (1951, p. 100):

> *The wat is the mean standard deviation of the momentary reaction potential* (sE_R) *of standard albino rats, 90 days of age, learning a simple manipulative act requiring a 10-gram pressure by 24-hour distributed trials under 23 hours' hunger, water available, with reward in the form of a 2.5-gram pellet of the usual dry dog food, the mean being taken from all the reinforcement trials producing the habit strength from .75 to .85 habs inclusive.*

The impracticability of generalizing from such particular values of food weight and manipulandum pressure to other variables in animal behavior itself, let alone more complex behavioral functions of higher mammalian forms such as humans, should be quite evident. Thus while Hull's specificity is in some respects admirable, the aspirations of his theorizing seem rather far removed from the actual achievements. Reservations concerning the generality of his theory were made increasingly by Hull in his later writings (cf. Koch, 1954, pp. 167 ff.) and are especially evident in the more restricted tone of his final work (Hull, 1952).

The only reasonable answer to these criticisms is simply that the results will determine the efficacy of the approach. More important, this is also the only answer to the more general criticism made against

S-R theorists that they oversimplify complex behavioral problems. Until we try we cannot really be sure whether an approach such as Hull's will be adequate to account for the complexities of mammalian behavior; and the only scientific way to be sure is to try.

Logical weakness. Probably the most telling critical attack upon Hull's theory involves the demonstration that his system was not at all the tight-knit, logical one that he intended it to be and that many for a while after its publication believed it to be. Hull sometimes failed to build in logically necessary connections among his constructs. A number of careful critical attacks have recently appeared. Koch's (1954) critique is particularly devastating because of its extremely detailed documentation and logical sophistication (in spite of his unsympathetic and sometimes unfair attitude). The easy testability of construct relationships that Hull envisioned is now seen to be largely illusory.

Two reactions to the growing realization of the logical inadequacy of Hull's theorizing are typical: first, a marked swing to a purely descriptive kind of positivism, such as that provided by Skinner; and second, an intensification of the attention paid to so-called miniature systems, whereby more limited problem areas are more thoroughly attacked (cf. Chapter 3). Hull himself showed signs of limiting his approach in *A behavior system* (1952), where he systematically explored problem areas and emphasized the over-all system less than previously.

Hull's contributions

Objective terminology and methodology. Hull's provision of a widely accepted objective terminology was a major advance. More than terminology itself is involved: terms like habit strength, reaction potential, and inhibition represent new ways of dealing with the data of psychology rather than simply the renaming of old concepts. The fruitfulness of the methodology implied by these terms assures them a continued place in psychology irrespective of the fate of the over-all theory in which Hull embedded them.

Hull's most important contribution to psychology was his demonstration of the possibility of setting one's sights upon the ultimate goal of a thoroughly scientific and systematic behavior theory. He lived his own scientific life in pursuit of that goal and thereby influenced even those who disagreed most vehemently with the substantive and methodological details of his work. No other psychologist has had so extensive an effect on the professional motivation of so many researchers. He popularized the strictly objective behavioristic approach as it had never been popularized previously.

Problem areas. Hull opened new problem areas in a rather peculiar sense. He did not develop important new pieces of apparatus or initiate research in previously untouched general areas. Rather, he reconceived ways of viewing problems and suggested new relationships to be studied. When he formulated a postulate or derived a theorem from his postulate set, other investigators were prone to perform experiments to test the stated relationships; for example, after Hull stated his belief about the shape of the generalization gradient, research focused on the empirical determination of the gradient. The very attempt to formalize a theory of behavior forced Hull and his followers to see what must be known before the formalization could be completed. Key concepts, such as stimulus, and processes, such as reinforcement, had to undergo intensive examination.

Although Hull was most strongly attacked by cognitive theorists and field theorists (cf. Chapter 11), in one respect his system was more fieldlike than the typical field theory. Hull specified as many of the relevant variables as he could reasonably conceive and also stated their hypothesized mode of interaction (cf. Figure 3). Not only is this high degree of theoretical specificity a far cry from the largely speculative utilization of conditioning by the early behaviorists, such as Watson, it is also a good deal more concrete than anything offered by Hull's critics, who were more prone to counter the Watsonian speculation with their own speculation than to provide specification of the composition of the psychological field (cf. Estes, 1954b).

Finally, Hull has been criticized by some psychologists of other persuasions for giving too much direction to research effort. He and his system concentrated effort on the solution of those theoretical problems which he believed had to be solved before behavior theory could make significant advances. However, some have felt that we cannot, at the present time, afford to decide the direction of research on formal theoretical grounds. Rather, those empirical areas should be studied which are producing results that are interesting in themselves. We believe that there is value in both views and that it is fortunate there are large numbers of psychologists available to take both paths; Hull made a great contribution in providing one kind of guidance.

Hull's place in history

Clark Hull's place in psychological history seems to be assured. He may have been one of those rare men who actively influence their times to such an extent that they can redirect a science. On the other hand, one may prefer the alternative view that this apparent influence is an illusion resulting from a man's merely moving within the historical stream of events and so actually moving *with* the times. The latter point of view is one that Boring (1950) has particularly emphasized (as stressed in the concept of *Zeitgeist*, or spirit of the times), in contrast to Carlyle's "great man" interpretation of history.

Whatever the causation, it is true that Clark Hull found psychology still wrestling hard with broad systematic issues, and he left large segments of it wrestling with criticisms of his postulates and theorems. In a sense both kinds of wrestling are misspent. The systematic issues were elusive foes for the psychologist, and Hull's system revealed gaps to the serious student that made criticism almost superfluous. Yet Hull taught psychology a new type of game, one so enthralling that now all but the strictest of positivists want to play.

It is paradoxical that Hull changed metatheory by being concerned with theory. His predecessors, the earlier behaviorists, had done their utmost to turn psychology away from verbal issues and toward more empirically meaningful problems. But this never quite came off. Hull brought it off with a positive effect. Hull was certainly deeply and intelligently concerned with metatheory, and his system is the grandest ever attempted in the behavioristic tradition. His distinction and his influence are based on the fact that he did not stop there. His attempt to push on into the tangled unknown where specific issues are resolved was largely unsuccessful. That was inevitable at the time. He did not come back with maps that were likely to be serviceable, but none before Hull had even given psychological explorers much of a feel for what a psychological theory should be.

Another paradox is Hull's lack of rigor. His system had the appearance but not the reality. He never had time to smooth out wrinkles. In this he is in the company of all psychology's greatest men. If there is in psychology a man excessively afraid of being wrong, that man has published no extensive theory. Hull, even while striving for a rigorous statement, had to stand with those who had no such fear. In this rather peculiar way, he carved his niche in history between the systematists and those following him who will construct more lasting behavior theories.

Spence's theory

Kenneth W. Spence (1907–   ) is currently the most important successor to Hull as a systematic S-R reinforcement theorist. He took his doctoral training at Yale, where he was strongly influenced by association with Hull, and since 1942 has been actively engaged in research on learning and motivation at the State University of Iowa. A long series of experimental and theoretical reports has culminated in his *Behavior theory and conditioning* (1956) and *Behavior theory and learning: Selected papers* (1960).

Spence's first important research and theorizing dealt with the problem of discrimination learning (Spence, 1936; 1937a, b). He produced a classic demonstration of how a conditioning theory involving positive and negative reaction tendencies, which interact algebraically as a function of stimulus similarity, can account for the primary data of discrimination. His theorizing here has served as a model of simplicity and clarity and has helped to stimulate similar conceptual attacks upon more complex problems. In this respect his early work is similar to Hull's early theoretical papers on conditioning and complex behavior.

While recognizing his debt to basic Hullian theory, Spence has been careful to point out the differences between his own theoretical efforts and those of Hull (cf. especially his 1956 book). He has been less concerned with the comprehensive formality with which Hull endowed his work and more concerned with the quantification of variables. He has not shared Hull's enthusiasm for physiological suggestions and speculations, feeling that until physiology has more to offer psychology it can most profitably be kept out of behavior theory. He has said (1956, p. 57) that he has not accepted the Hullian emphasis on need-reduction as the essential component of the reinforcement process; no specific physiological assumption is made about the nature of the action of a reinforcer. Finally, he has been much more cautious than Hull in regard to "hazarding a set of theoretical postulates on the basis of a minimum of empirical data" (1956, p. 58). Spence also has pointed out that, on the related question of generality, he intends his own work to be restricted to the particular experimental situations from which his data have come.

One substantial difference between the Hullian and Spencian theories is particularly important. This involves the treatment of the key motivation variables. Hull assumes a multiplicative relationship between the consummatory drive factor (D) and incentive motivation (K). Spence assumes an additive relationship. The practical difference between these two views is that at least some minimal value is required for each variable, in the multiplicative relation, for a response to occur. The additive relation permits the occurrence of a response even in the absence of one or the other of the motivational variables. No definitive conclusion can be reached on the basis of existing data as to which of these contrasting views is correct.

Following his early development of theory applicable to simple discrimination learning, Spence directed extensive research projects on eyelid conditioning, latent learning, transposition, secondary reinforcement, and "anxiety" as measured by a questionnaire technique (see Spence, 1960). One important extension of an original Hullian suggestion is Spence's elaboration of the fractional anticipatory goal response and its stimulus component, together designated $r_g - s_g$. The ingenuity with which he and his students and adherents have utilized this concept to explain complex behavioral phenomena is impressive. It will be an especially great achievement if matched in the future by direct experimental demonstrations of the ability of this construct to predict new behavioral consequences not readily predictable on other grounds.

In the 1956 version of Spence's theory, he has pointed out the possibility of a two-factor learning theory which is precisely reversed from the usual one. Usually, contiguity factors are assumed to account for classical conditioning, reinforcement for instrumental conditioning. The contiguity explanation for instrumental learning leaves habit independent of the incentive-motivation factor, K (based on the presumed r_g —s_g mechanism). In this respect Spence has shifted to a theoretical position basically similar to Tolman's long-standing position (see Chapter 11). It will be interesting to observe the development of these originally Hullian, but already radically modified, theoretical notions as the current experimental attack upon motivation-learning relations proceeds.

Another potentially fruitful offshoot of Hull-Spence systematizing is Frank A. Logan's development of a so-called *micromolar* approach (1956). The fundamental micromolar assumption is that when some measure of response, such as running speed, varies, different responses are indicated. The more traditional view has demanded a qualitative difference for responses to be considered different. Logan's work on correlated reinforcement, where reward values are varied in accordance with response differences (1960), is intended to provide quantitative data to show whether a micromolar approach is necessary.

REINFORCEMENT THEORY: SKINNERIAN POSITIVISM

Skinner's career

B. F. Skinner (1904–   ) has had a most remarkable career. It is similar to that of Sir Francis Galton in its demonstration of great breadth of interest and exceptional ingenuity of empirical operations. Skinner's contributions have been kaleidoscopic. His lively intellectual curiosity has refused to be contained within the narrow confines of a specialized area. He has concerned himself with an analysis of verbal learning, with missile-guiding pigeons, with teaching machines, and with the control of behavior by scheduled reinforcement. The ingenious apparatus to his credit includes an automatized baby-tending device, used with one of his own children and later marketed commercially. In his leisure time, Skinner has even managed to write a novel on a utopian theme, *Walden two* (1948b).

Skinner received his doctoral degree from Harvard in 1931. Following several years of postdoctoral fellowships he taught at the University of Minnesota (1936–1945) and Indiana University (1945–1947), where he was chairman. He returned to Harvard in 1947.

Skinner's impact upon young contemporary psychologists has been second only to that of Hull and as a matter of fact has been increasing markedly in recent years even as that of Hull has declined. Methodologically, Hull and Skinner represent opposite poles. Where Hull has stressed formal theoretical efforts of a hypothetico-deductive sort, Skinner has tended to eschew theory and to practice a strict positivism.

methodological emphasis

Skinner is best known for his insistence upon a strictly descriptive, atheoretical approach to behavior research. He has long felt that the state of knowledge in psychology is inadequate to justify elaborate formal theorizing. Skinnerians often state that when theories are developed and espoused, personal satisfactions from confirmations and disconfirmations, rather than acquisition of facts, tend to become the issue. Skinner believes that more effective progress toward the prediction and control of behavior can be obtained through a careful collection of data. The "functional analysis of behavior" has been his objective. In this, experimental techniques are to be utilized, and the relationships among variables are to be established. Eventually, Skinner holds, sufficient empirical relationships will be established to justify the formation of some limited theories or more comprehensive generalizations, but these must be prepared with caution. Such integrative principles should be allowed to develop, not forced prematurely.

A second important methodological emphasis of Skinner has been his insistence upon a thorough analysis of the behavior of a single organism and his disinclination to use large groups of subjects. Large numbers of subjects have too often been used, he contends, to cover up lack of experimental controls; with adequate controls, a single subject, or a very small number of subjects, should be sufficient. Related to this contention is his general neglect of statistics; he believes that statistics also too often cover up the lack of experimental controls. When large amounts of data from a single animal are collected under stringent controls, the results will be clearly replicable, and no statistical techniques are necessary.

Thirdly, Skinner has objected particularly to physiological speculation in the guise of theory. He has been against what he has considered excessive and futile physiologizing; when physiological data have more concrete points on which behavioral observations can turn, then they should be permitted to influence psychology, but not before. This generally aphysiological attitude has been shared by Spence, and together they have contributed to the prominence of the so-called "empty-organism" era in recent psychological thinking.

A fourth major methodological characteristic of Skinner has been his emphasis on operant, as compared with respondent, behavior. Skinner early distinguished between responses made in direct response to stimulation (such as classical conditioned responses of a Pavlovian sort) and those emitted by the organism in the absence of any apparent external stimulation (the operant). The eliciting stimuli for the operant are unknown and assumed to be irrelevant to understanding operant responding. The free operant is an operant whose emission does not directly preclude successive emissions of the same response; its study has been especially favored by Skinnerians. The free operant is best exemplified by the bar pressing of rats and by the key pecking of pigeons. Both animals usually respond in the Skinner box. These boxes are insulated against noise; temperature and lighting are closely controlled. Data gathered under such controlled conditions tend to be more uniform than the data that are usually available. Skinner has typically used the rate of emission of a response as his dependent variable; the response is a simple one, and the measure, therefore, is relatively uncomplicated. A cumulative recorder which directly produces a cumulative frequency curve of responses, rather than the typical learning curve, has been used to record the data.

major contributions

Perhaps the most significant feature of Skinner's research and thinking has been his continuing work on the problem of reinforcement scheduling in operant conditioning. His early emphasis on intermittent reinforcement (1938) culminated recently in the exhaustive volume, *Schedules of reinforcement* (Ferster & Skinner, 1957). He worked first with the rat in the Skinner box, subsequently with the pigeon in a comparable chamber, and ultimately with human subjects. Use of children as subjects in operant-conditioning studies involving various reinforcement schedules has recently mushroomed and promises now to become a very important feature of behavioral research, involving psychologists of varying degrees of adherence to Skinnerian principles.

A number of examples may be cited from everyday-life situations to illustrate the effectiveness of intermittent reinforcement in controlling behavior. One of the most apt is the control of behavior exercised by the occasional payoff of the slot machine or by other gambling devices. Examination of other situations indicates that reinforcement is characteristically scheduled intermittently, rather than continuously, as it has more typically been scheduled in learning experiments. Thus the child's behavior produces approbation in the parent, but not invariably; the student succeeds on examinations, but also fails or misses particular items; and the typical fisherman returns home empty-handed from a very large proportion of his trips.

In laboratory investigations of the effects of different schedules of reinforcement, four major types have been used. These are *fixed interval* (FI), in which the first response made after some fixed period of time is reinforced; *variable interval* (VI), in which the first response made after some variable period of time is reinforced; *fixed ratio* (FR), in which the first response made after some fixed number of responses is reinforced; and *variable ratio* (VR), in which the first response made after some variable number of responses is reinforced. The two variable schedules (VI and VR) and the fixed-ratio schedule (FR) characteristically produce a remarkably regular rate of performance; more irregular cumulative performance curves, featuring bursts of responses just preceding the usual reinforcement time (the so-called "scallops"), are given by the fixed-interval schedule.

Skinner's research with control of animal behavior is another long-standing contribution. He developed the method of *shaping*. Shaping is accomplished by giving an animal a reward if his response approximates the desired response. For example, if a rat is to be taught to climb a ladder, he would first be given food if he simply approached the ladder; then he might be required to reach up the ladder, then to get on it, and finally to climb it in order to receive his food reward. Skinner's method has been taken over by a large number of animal trainers. One of his early students, Keller Breland, left the academic field to become an animal trainer and has been very successful (Breland & Breland, 1951, 1961).

During World War II Skinner conducted applied research on animals under the auspices of General Mills in Minneapolis. Apparently he was well along in the development of a training program whereby pigeons could be used in the guiding device in a bomb when the development of atomic weapons ended the war and removed the immediate urgency from this research. The project has only recently been declassified, and a fascinating account given by Skinner (1960).

One of the most striking of Skinner's demonstrations of the potency of shaping in control of animal behavior is his research on "superstitious behavior" in pigeons (Skinner, 1948a). He demonstrated that clear-cut and uniquely individual responses could be quickly developed in hungry pigeons when they are put on a fixed-interval schedule of reinforcement; reinforcements (pieces of grain) are supplied to the animal after so many seconds or minutes regardless of what he does. In such a situation some operant response, which just happens to precede a reinforcement early in the session, will generally be fixated and will predominate in the behavioral repertoire of the animal during the experimental period. This occurs because one or two early reinforcements increase the rate at which the particular response is emitted, thus making more and more likely its occurrence just prior to subsequent reinforcements. The particular response reinforced, such as wing flapping, neck craning, leg raising, etc., varies from one animal to the next, apparently as an accidental effect of the early reinforcements.

Another of Skinner's interests has been research and systematic thinking about verbal behavior. His conceptualization of the important human behavioral problems of language has been influential in the field. This interest has recently culminated in publication of a major work, *Verbal behavior* (1957b). According to Skinner's interpretation, language as verbal behavior is basically similar to other behavior and can be best understood when viewed in this general conceptual framework. This view stands as a challenge to those who hold to more complex interpretations.

criticisms of Skinner

The most persistent attacks have been concentrated on Skinner's positivism. Critics have maintained that Skinner is deluding himself if he believes theory has no value. Theory is inevitable. Every experiment and observation is in some way planned, based on hunches or ideas; therefore, say the critics, it is better to bring the presuppositions into the open and formalize them. Then they can be recognized and critically evaluated rather than hidden. In addition, formal theory in the older sciences has afforded a generality which Skinner's fact gathering alone can never achieve.

The Skinnerian's reply to such criticism would at least hold that presuppositions should be kept to a minimum; thus experimentation will be freed from the necessity of being suggested by a particular theory. He would maintain that he is not against theory in psychology; he is just against it for now. He might reiterate the prevalence of personal involvement in theory and let the matter rest.

Skinner has also been criticized for his peripheralism. This kind of argument has two major facets. One involves his aphysiological bias; this is largely a matter of taste. If one prefers not to think in physiological terms, surely this is his privilege. The other involves his refusal to posit intervening processes of a psychological sort (such as Hull's habit strength or inhibition, Spence's incentive motivation, and the like). Here too the issue is one of personal preference, but difficulties arise when one side attempts to force its views on the other. This is particularly evident in regard to the attempt by many Skinnerians to purify psychological language by eliminating terms like emotion, motivation, and perception. Certainly these terms are much abused and highly variable in meaning. However, there may be some core of useful meaning in them, and the terms may be useful in posing problems. It would be a serious disservice if such problems were neglected because certain terms relating to them were eliminated. Furthermore, the mere discarding of old language gives no guarantee of effective research.

Skinner has been criticized for extrapolating well beyond his data (cf. his proposals about complex human problems in *Science and human behavior*, 1953a). Here he is certainly vulnerable to criticism. He is at least inconsistent, for his proposals are certainly derived from his conceptual framework, or system, and this clearly violates the facts-first keynote of his experimental methodology. But if these are accepted as merely suggestions stemming from his conceptual framework, they may serve at least as a kind of intellectual stimulant; and the extent to which simple principles can ultimately be applied to apparently complex situations and processes is still an empirical problem and one that cannot be safely prejudged.

Finally, Skinner has been criticized on many technical points (cf. especially Verplanck, 1954). Probably he is open to criticism for ignoring the stimulus factors involved in operant behavior. His reliance on visual interpretation of cumulative curves, in the absence of quantitative criteria, has also been questioned; many critics feel that statistical evaluations should be applied. We should add that cumulative curves tend to average out much behavioral variation that is apparent in other types of curves. Though we should not wish to imply that Skinner's experimental controls are less than excellent, more behavioral variation occurs even in the Skinner box than meets the naked eye looking at a cumulative curve. Finally, the efficiency of his general procedure has been questioned; for example, *Schedules of reinforcement* (Ferster & Skinner, 1957) summarizes about 70,000 hours of continuously recorded behavior of individual pigeons consisting of approximately one-quarter of a billion responses! (Skinner, 1958). These data are presented in a total of 921 separate figures with almost no interpretive, or even summarizing, comment.

Skinner's role in contemporary systematic psychology

The extent of Skinner's systematic contributions to modern experimental psychology is nicely summarized in the formal citation accompanying the American Psychological Association's Distinguished Scientific Contribution Award granted him in 1958. This citation is as follows (*Amer. Psychol.*, 1958, 13, 735):

An imaginative and creative scientist, characterized by great objectivity in scientific matters and by warmth and enthusiasm in personal contacts. Choosing simple operant behavior as subject matter, he has challenged alternative analyses of behavior, insisting that description take precedence over hypotheses. By careful control of experimental conditions, he has produced data which are relatively free from fortuitous variation. Despite his antitheoretical position, he is considered an important systematist and has developed a self-consistent description of behavior which has greatly increased our ability to predict and control the behavior of organisms from rat to man. Few American psychologists have had so profound an impact on the development of psychology and on promising younger psychologists.

Whereas in 1945–1950 there was no more enthusiastic band of psychologists than those working actively within the Hull-Spence systematic framework, today the same thing can be said of the Skinnerians, as they are often called. In addition to the group with Skinner at Harvard, there has been for years a tightly knit group trained under Fred Keller and William Schoenfeld at Columbia University. Skinnerian psychologists, resenting the orthodox restrictions of the American Psychological Association's journals (particularly the unwritten regulations concerning sample size and statistical tests), have recently established their own journal, *Journal for the Experimental Analysis of Behavior*. Skinnerian techniques are widely accepted by a growing number of psychologists. In some respects he represents a renewal of the old-time behaviorism and like Watson has attracted to him many young psychologists eager to make behavior study an exact science. As one reviewer recently said (MacLeod, 1959, p. 34): "Watson's spirit is indestructible. Cleaned and purified, it breathes through the writings of B. F. Skinner."

CONTIGUITY THEORY: GUTHRIAN ASSOCIATIONISM

Guthrie's career

Edwin Guthrie (1886–1959) was for several decades the leading exponent of a simple contiguity principle of learning. Throughout a long period, while first one, then another, opposing school developed, Guthrie held steadfast to a small number of strict associationistic principles. This patience has finally paid off in the modern appearance of statistical models of learning largely based upon the Guthrian pattern. However, Guthrie's own contribution has remained that of a prophet and overseer more than that of an active experimentalist or detailed theorist.

Guthrie remained at one school, the University of Washington, throughout his entire academic career (1914–1956). He had less than the usual formal training in psychology, having been trained instead in philosophy and mathematics. He took his doctor's degree in 1912 at the University of Pennsylvania after earlier degrees at the University of Nebraska. With one major exception (Guthrie & Horton, 1946), he preferred writing and argumentation to experimentation. His several books, especially *The psychology of learning* (1935, rev. 1952) and *The psychology of human conflict* (1938), are full of persuasive anecdotal supports for his general associationistic principles but contain little controlled evidence.

Watson's doctrines so influenced Guthrie that he became a thoroughgoing behaviorist, although he differed from Watson on many points of theory. Guthrie's interest in psychology was apparently kindled during his graduate training by the philosopher E. A. Singer. He has stated that his year's collaboration on a textbook with the psychologist Stevenson Smith (Smith & Guthrie, 1921) gave him "invaluable training" in psychology. He retained his early interest in problems of philosophy of science throughout his career; his final major work (Guthrie, 1959) treats many methodological matters.

Guthrie's basic principles

Guthrie believed that a small number of primary principles was sufficient to account for the fundamental facts of behavior modification. His most famous principle is popularly referred to as *one-trial learning*. Guthrie held that S-R associations, as the basis of learning, are established by contiguity per se in a single pairing of stimulus and response. He early stated this principle as follows (1935, p. 26): "A combination of stimuli which has accompanied a movement will on its recurrence tend to be followed by that movement." A related principle is (1942, p. 30): "A stimulus pattern gains its full associative strength on the occasion of its first pairing with a response." Guthrie offered a final simplified version (1959, p. 186): "What is being noticed becomes a signal for what is being done." This statement reflects his concern with the active role of the organism (the old problem of attention). In his final paper he also placed increased emphasis on the problem of patterning in stimulus complexes (cf. Guthrie, 1959, pp. 186 ff.).

His early distinction between *acts* and *movements* enabled Guthrie to hold to his basic principle and still account for the fact that behavior modification typically requires repeated pairings of cue and response to achieve adequate predictability. Although acts, such as hitting a basket with a ball, are ordinarily *measured*, particular movements are actually *conditioned* as responses. While observable in principle, in practice the latter are not easily noticed and are generally overlooked in theorizing. Also, on the stimulus side, the total situation is composed of a great many components, some of which are not present on every trial. The net result of this complexity of stimulus and response components is that it requires a large number of presentations of the gross stimulus and occurrences of the gross response (the act) before satisfactory regularity can be found in the behavior being measured. This is so because large numbers of the stimulus and response components need to be involved in the conditioning process. If exact replications of stimuli and responses could be achieved, single presentations would be sufficient to produce perfect conditioning.

An additional complication to the above picture is the fact that the movements themselves, which are the responses actually conditioned, also produce stimuli which serve to modify the stimulus complex (so-called *movement-produced stimuli,* or mps) and so increase the difficulty of demonstrating one-trial learning.

evaluation of Guthrie

Guthrie's theory has been directly supported in the laboratory mainly by his own investigation of stereotypy in the cat's behavior in the puzzle box (Guthrie & Horton, 1946) and by two investigations of Voeks (1948, 1954). Voeks (1950) has also published a useful formalization of the theory in terms of postulates and theorems. For example, her postulate of postremity, or recency, states that only the last response made to a stimulus remains conditioned. Earlier tests by Seward (1942) and by Seward, Dill, and Holland (1944) found Guthrie's views inadequate.

The most searching criticism of Guthrie's theory has been offered by Mueller and Schoenfeld (1954). They have indicated that the simplicity of Guthrian notions is more apparent than real and has been achieved only at the expense of failure to be explicit about key problems. They have also suggested that Guthrie has developed no real system at all, in clear contrast to many of the leading alternative theorists. He has been satisfied merely with repeating, over the years, certain of the key assumptions with which he started. Finally, they have raised some serious questions concerning the interpretation of the Guthrie and Horton (1946) data on stereotypy of behavior. Their treatment should be consulted, along with Guthrie's final authoritative paper (1959), by anyone interested in evaluation of Guthrian theory.

Guthrie's success in maintaining his position as a leading learning theorist is surprising in view of the relative paucity of experimental support his theory received. This success has probably been due to a combination of several factors. Foremost among these is the apparent simplicity of his theory compared with the leading alternatives, such as Hull's. There is no difficulty in grasping at least the basis of Guthrie's views; and this simplicity appeals to many psychologists.

A second factor has been the difficulty experienced by opposing theorists in presenting evidence which clearly contradicts the Guthrian theory. Finally, there is the fact that Guthrie and some of his adherents, notably Sheffield, have been consistently able to point to weaknesses and contradictions in the alternative accounts. Hull's need-reduction principle has been a special target (e.g., Sheffield, 1948; Sheffield, 1949; Sheffield & Roby, 1950; Sheffield, Wulff, & Backer, 1951). The fact that these successful attacks depend upon the greater predictive specificity of the alternative accounts does not seem to have reduced the effectiveness of the Guthrian attack. A consequence of this success in criticism has been that Guthrie's theory has remained a formidable alternative account, even though its laurels may have been won on largely negative grounds.

Despite these limitations, Guthrie has been more than merely an astute critic and propounder of simple generalizations supported by fluent ancedotal stories. He is one theorist who has stood by his theoretical guns, consistently espousing a contiguity principle as the basis of all learning. He has supported his emphasis on movements as the theoretical response elements by experimental studies of sterotypy and has shown how well stereotypy observed by other experimenters can be subsumed by his theoretical analyses. Guthrie has demonstrated the theoretical roles that can be played by mediating mechanisms like movement-produced stimuli. This ingenious mechanism is much like Hull's fractional anticipatory goal response in that both serve as the forgers of links in the chain of behavior. Guthrie received the American Psychological Foundation Gold Medal Award in 1958 as recognition for his contributions.

CONTIGUITY THEORY:
STATISTICAL ASSOCIATION THEORY

The rise of mathematical learning models has been a most interesting development in postwar learning theory. Although for many years there had been sporadic efforts at producing rational learning theories, these had not caught on with learning psychologists. (See Hilgard, 1956, pp. 386–388, for a brief review.) Usually they did not lead to empirical tests but were content to show how a small segment of old data might be mathematically explained. Estes (1950) and Bush and Mosteller (1951a,b) presented two new and more promising mathematical models within a period of about one year. We shall describe only the former theory; it has been more popular, and Estes and others have produced much related experimentation. A more extended account is given in Chapter 13, but it is appropriate at this point to place the mathematical theories in their general systematic context.

Estes' model

William K. Estes (1919–   ) took his doctor's degree with Skinner in 1943 and went with him from Minnesota to Indiana in 1945. When Skinner moved on to Harvard, Estes stayed at Indiana and became the leading figure in the development of mathematical learning models.

In a most comprehensive account of the background and early development of these models, Estes (1959b) has emphasized that the failure of the older learning systems to lead to adequate predictability even for simpler learning phenomena helped open the door for mathematical models. These he has characterized as *probabilistic* rather than *deterministic*. In this he follows the pattern of thinking earlier initiated by Brunswik (see Chapter 11) rather than that of the earlier S-R theorists, as exemplified by Hull. Estes' distinction emphasizes the willingness of probabilistic theory to accept raw data pretty much as they appear, without theoretical preconceptions or interpretations; deterministic theories are held to begin with at least some postulation of the important determining factors in learning.

The older learning model that Estes used as the basis for his first attempts at developing a quantitative model was Guthrie's contiguity theory. It was admirably suited for this purpose, particularly since it emphasized the variable nature of stimulus and response as a primary characteristic of the associative process. These assumptions, relatively undeveloped over the years by Guthrie, were elaborated by Estes into a definitive model using stimulus and response populations. Connections between stimulus and response elements are assumed to reach maximum strength through their association on a single trial. The gradual increase in response probability actually observed occurs, according to the model, because only a *sample* of the stimulus population appears on a given trial, and successive samples from the population may not always contain enough elements that are conditioned to the response to make the response occur.

One of the most impressive features of Estes' theory thus far has been its rapid extension into new areas (e.g., Estes 1953, 1954a, 1959a; Estes & Burke, 1953) and its ability to stimulate a large amount of empirical research. Also, Estes has not hesitated to change certain of his guiding assumptions. For example, although he began with a clear-cut Guthrian set of assumptions, he has recently seemed to accept the reinforcement function (1959b, p. 405) as well as the fundamental contiguity principle.

Estes' theory has the basic advantages shared by the other statistical theories of learning. It has the precision of statement and rigor of derivation which usually go with such theories. In addition, the assumptions that are necessary to relate theoretical dependent variables to their empirical counterparts are simply generally acceptable mathematical assumptions. Thus less arbitrariness is involved than in the Hullian system. For example, Hull had to select equations to connect his theoretical dependent variable, $_sE_R$, with empirically observable variables like $_st_R$ (latency) or trials to extinction. Estes, on the other hand, can derive what the latency must be without making other than mathematical assumptions, once he has taken probability of response as his basic datum.

Estes has also circumvented another really severe problem which Hull did not solve. Hull based his theory on group data and largely begged the question of the shapes of individual curves. Estes began with a look at individual performance and developed a system wherein the shapes of the group-performance curves can be derived by combining the individual results. Thus Estes' theory, unlike Hull's, does not have so many degrees of freedom through *post hoc* explanations based either on assumptions about the functions relating theoretical variables to empirical variables or on assumptions about individual differences.

Estes has hesitated to attempt a systematic evaluation of his efforts, largely on the ground that he began with few presuppositions about what a system *should* be like and so cannot easily say exactly where he is in regard to any definite a priori objective (Estes, 1959b). Furthermore, the system has been in almost constant flux and is not likely to stand still enough for a clear-cut picture within the immediate future. However, his paper (1959b) does contain a detailed exposition of his statistical association theory and compares it with certain other competing stochastic models (especially Bush & Mosteller, 1955).

TWO-FACTOR THEORIES

There have been a number of attempts to combine the reinforcement and the contiguity principles into a duplex theory. Early versions were produced by Schlosberg (1937) and by Skinner (1938). Skinner's suggestion involves the type-S and type-R conditioning dichotomy which he proposed. Type-S conditioning, presumably mediated through autonomic musculature, results from the contiguity of the unconditioned and conditioned *stimuli* (much as in classical conditioning of the Pavlovian sort). Type-R conditioning, presumably mediated through the skeletal musculature, results from the relationship of the *response* to the reinforcement. Such operant conditioning, Skinner felt, is far more important than the type-S variety, the evidence for which he held to be rather questionable.

A more direct two-factor theory was proposed by Mowrer (1947, 1951, 1954). He contrasted conditioning and solution learning. The acquisition of emotions, meaning, attitudes, and the like is mediated through simple contiguity of stimuli—conditioning. Overt instrumental learning—solution learning—occurs through reinforcement, or law-of-

effect learning. Since Mowrer was originally a strong Hullian reinforcement theorist, his shift was an important one. His interpretation
was criticized by his earlier collaborator, Neal Miller (1951), among
others.

A suggestion for a different kind of two-factor theory has been
made by Spence in his Silliman Lectures (1956). As he pointed out,
one might develop his suggestions into a two-factor theory "exactly
the opposite of the well known two-factor theory espoused by Schlosberg, Mowrer, and others" (p. 151). Reinforcement would thus be
accorded a determining role in the case of classically conditioned responses, which are emphasized in Spence's systematic theorizing,
rather than in that of instrumental behavior.

The most recent and by far the most ambitious effort at a two-factor
theory has been provided by Mowrer (1956, 1960a,b) in a drastic revision of his earlier two-factor theory. Actually, this new theory is no
longer "two factor" in the original sense; Mowrer has come to accept
now only conditioning or sign learning as the single basic learning
process; solution learning is regarded as a special, derived case of
conditioning. It is still a two-factor theory, however, in the sense that
it stresses two *types of reinforcement. Decremental reinforcement* refers to the need-reducing type of process stressed by Thorndike and
Hull in their theories; *incremental reinforcement* refers to the growth
of "fear" with consequent avoidance behavior from excessive stimulation.

The present theory was developed mainly by means of an extension
of the secondary-reinforcement principle. Mowrer assumes that when
a hungry animal obtains food, response-produced stimuli become conditioned as secondary reinforcers—as "promising" stimuli which arouse
"hope." In this "feedback theory of habit," as Mowrer calls it, hope is
thus conditioned in fundamentally the same manner as fear is conditioned in aversive learning. The parallelism is stated by Mowrer
(1960b, p. 8): "A conditioned stimulus not only makes the subject
salivate: it also makes him *hopeful,* just as surely as a stimulus which
has been associated with the onset of pain makes a subject *fearful."*

It remains to be seen how effective this interesting revision of
earlier theory will be in stimulating research. Research directed at
specifying the nature of the hypothesized promising stimuli and their
relationship to performance measures will be needed, and care must
be taken to ensure against a relapse into vernacular thinking occa-
sioned by the vernacular terminology used.

SUMMARY AND CONCLUSIONS

In this chapter we have surveyed some theoretical positions loosely
called S-R. In the main, these are neobehavioristic and concentrate on

t.e proble... of learning. They are distinguished on the basis of their treatment of the problem of reinforcement.

The reinforcement theory of Clark L. Hull represents a combination of the Thorndikian law of effect and the Pavlovian conditioning paradigm. This hypothetico-deductive system is highly formalized. It is by far the most ambitious theoretical and systematic effort of its kind. Compared with Watson, Hull was a sophisticated theorist, much concerned with logical as well as experimental specifications and empirical tests; he was a methodological, rather than a metaphysical, behaviorist. In spite of, or even perhaps partly because of, his high aspirations, Hull's direct systematic influence has declined markedly in recent years. This decline has been a function both of the fundamental faults found in his system and of the increasing popularity of a strictly positivistic psychology of the kind advanced by B. F. Skinner. Today Hullian psychology is represented mainly in the theoretical efforts of Kenneth W. Spence and his associates and, in much more modified form, in the work of Neal E. Miller.

Skinnerian positivism differs from Hullian psychology both in its methodology (radically positivistic as compared with hypothetico-deductive) and in its position on reinforcement. Skinner has not been concerned with theory except in an inductive, summary sense: when sufficient empirical results, or facts, are available, theory can be used as a set of summarizing statements which cover the facts. This procedure is obviously at the opposite methodological pole from that of Hull.

In keeping with his metatheoretical beliefs, Skinner has emphasized the process of reinforcement in a strictly atheoretical, descriptive manner. His research has been among the most provocative and stimulating to be found in psychology. His interests have been wide and free-ranging. He is best known perhaps for his emphasis on operant, as contrasted with respondent, conditioning and for the pioneering research on schedules of reinforcement.

The major opposition within the S-R camp to the various reinforcement theories has been provided by the contiguity theorists, who hold to some kind of associationistic principle. They argue that reinforcement operates mainly to protect S-R connections formed through contiguity per se. E. R. Guthrie has been the most influential contiguity theorist over several decades. Within the past decade, however, the basic Guthrian contiguity principle has been cast in mathematical form by W. K. Estes and his associates. Their use of mathematical models has given a strong impetus to empirical research as well as to theoretical development.

A number of two-factor theories have also been developed. These have historically attempted to combine the reinforcement and contiguity positions. The most recent of these, by O. H. Mowrer, does offer something of a novel approach. It involves two kinds of reinforcement, both based upon the conditioning or contiguity principle.

An important conclusion to be drawn from the wide variety of theoretical approaches outlined is that no one procedure can be guaranteed in advance to be more productive than any other. Rather, all kinds of empirical and theoretical endeavors are to be encouraged, as long as the fundamental requirements of scientific procedure are met. Each approach that is given a thorough trial will help to motivate and organize research. Which kind of research will eventually be seen to be most significant must await the verdict of history.

further readings

For an understanding of Hull's system, the most useful of his books are probably *Principles of behavior* (1943) and *A behavior system* (1952). His 1937 paper on conditioning theory, cited in the text, indicates the fundamental development of his thinking, and his autobiographical statement (1952) is unusually frank in detailing personal factors in his career. Spence's adaptation of Hullian theory is presented in his *Behavior theory and conditioning* (1956) and in the volume of collected writings, *Behavior theory and learning* (1960). Of Skinner's many papers and books, the most important sources are his beginning text, *Science and human behavior* (1953a), and his collected writings, *Cumulative record* (1959). Two particularly influential books by psychologists writing in the Skinnerian framework are Keller and Schoenfeld's *Principles of psychology* (1950), which presents an integrated set of principles based on operant conditioning, and Sidman's *Tactics of scientific research* (1960), which is a persuasive elaboration of the positivistic approach to experimentation. Guthrie is represented by his two basic books, *The psychology of learning* (1935, rev. 1952) and *The psychology of human conflict* (1938). The simplest introduction to Estes' mathematical model is possibly his paper, "Growth and function of mathematical models for learning" (1961). Two books are particularly valuable for material of special relevance to most of the S-R theories here considered: *Modern learning theory*, by Estes et al. (1954), which includes highly critical reviews of Hull (by Koch), of Skinner (by Verplanck), and of Guthrie (by Mueller and Schoenfeld); and Koch's Volume II of *Psychology: A study of a science* (1959), which contains two papers on the Hullian system and its derivatives (by Logan and Miller), Guthrie's final systematic effort, Skinner's "A case history in scientific method," and an excellent detailed account of statistical theories by Estes. Hilgard's *Theories of learning* (1956) describes many of the S-R theories as well as certain of the field theories.

varieties of field theory   11

The term *field theory*, as used within psychology, arose as an analogy with the notion of fields of force in physics (cf. Chapter 8). Although the analogy has not been a very strict one, the term has persisted in the psychological literature because it serves to identify a variety of theories that share certain major metatheoretical characteristics. Most of these characteristics relate to the general propositions that patterns of organization are primary factors in behavior and that the analysis of single or isolated conditions cannot give an adequate picture of such patterns. Here the field theorist seems to differ most radically from the typical S-R theorist, whose emphasis has been upon an analytic association of stimulus and response elements. This apparent dichotomy has been questioned on the ground that the contemporary S-R theorist not only takes account of interacting factors in his experimental situation but also handles them, in practice, more adequately than the field theorist (e.g., Estes, 1954b). It is certainly true that methodological differences between S-R and field theory are today much slighter than previously; we use the dichotomy merely as a convenient means of arranging our discussion. In any case, there is little question that the emphasis in field theory is upon the organized totality of events that is the determining condition in behavior. The various field theories differ in their detailed implementation of this general principle, as is indicated in the following pages.

Apart from these metatheoretical considerations, there has been a high degree of commonality of theoretical content among field theories. Most important here are the widely shared interest in problems of perception and cognition and the correlated tendency to utilize perceptual and cognitive processes as explanatory factors. This is hardly surprising in view of the close relationship between modern field theories and classic gestalt psychology, which was primarily concerned with similar emphases.

Principally, but by no means exclusively, field theory as used in psychology has come to refer to the metatheory of Kurt Lewin; his system is therefore the first of the several versions described in the present chapter. The unique combination of behaviorism and gestalt psychology achieved in the purposivism of E. C. Tolman is included as the second important specimen of field theory. The theoretically more circumscribed but increasingly influential thinking of Egon Brunswik is next described. Finally, other systematists (K. S. Lashley, J. R. Kantor, and R. H. Wheeler), whose work may be classified as falling within some kind of field-theoretical classification, are more briefly described.

VECTOR FIELD THEORY: LEWIN'S LIFE SPACE

The contributions to psychological theory made by Kurt Lewin (1890–1947) have been among the most significant of recent decades. On the one hand, Lewin was a brilliant researcher. Even his severest critics recognize him as a most ingenious experimenter; the series of experimental studies which he directed while at the University of Berlin in the 1920s is a model of theoretical creativity and imagination combined with sound experimental methodology. On the other hand, throughout his career he remained a strong advocate of the primacy of directive theory in research, and he is best known for his development of the motivational, or vector, system of psychology, most commonly referred to as field theory.

Although Lewin was associated with an active center of gestalt psychology at Berlin, he retained little identification with the orthodox group, and his systematizing went well beyond the usual confines of the school. As a matter of fact, there was no formal relationship between his theories and those of the gestaltists. Lewin's early efforts were largely concerned with motivational problems of the individual subject, which led to an interest in problems of personality organization; his later efforts were mainly concerned with a wide variety of problems in social psychology, including his initiation of the group-dynamics movement and his assistance in the development of *action research* (i.e., research directed at producing social changes). In between, he was peripherally concerned with problems such as the nature of learning, cultural factors in personality structure, and child development. But in all these diverse areas Lewin brought to bear on critical issues the same fundamental approach: an emphasis always upon the psychological, rather than the simple environmental, factors in the situation (or field). This emphasis is comparable to the earlier gestalt distinction, most explicitly made by Koffka, between the "behavioral" and the "geographical" environment. The crux of the distinction is that the effective meaning of the environmental conditions depends upon more than merely physical attributes; that is, a description in terms of such factors alone is inadequate.

Lewin's career

Kurt Lewin was born in Prussia and received his higher education at the universities of Freiburg, Munich, and Berlin (Ph.D., 1914). He was thus present during the early, formative years of the gestalt movement. After a five-year interlude of military service, he returned to Berlin and remained in various academic capacities until 1932, when he came to the United States. He spent that year as visiting professor at Stanford and the following two years at Cornell. The decision to establish permanent residence in this country was made as a consequence of the rise of Nazi power in Germany, where his Jewish ancestry became a handicap. Lewin went to the Child Welfare Station of the State University of Iowa as professor of child psychology in 1935 and finally to Massachusetts Institute of Technology in 1944. In this last appointment he was director of the Research Center for Group Dynamics, a movement which he had only fairly well started at the time of his death in 1947.

Lewin's major publications were in the form of journal reports and contributions to various collections of papers. His own papers have been collected in four small volumes. The first two of these, *A dynamic theory of personality* (1935) and *Principles of topological psychology* (1936), represent the earlier European phase of his career; the last two collections, *Resolving social conflicts* (1948) and *Field theory in social science* (1951), relate to the later American phase.

topology and hodological space

Lewin selected topology, a relatively new geometry, as providing a mathematical model upon which he could base his conceptual representation of psychological processes. In brief, topology is a geometry where spatial relationships are represented in a strictly nonmetrical manner. Positional relationships among areas or regions are maintained in spite of various kinds of changes in size and shape. The primary concern is with the connections among bounded regions and with their spatial relationships; for example, one area will remain inside another throughout a wide variety of stretchings and distortions. (See Brown, 1936, for a relatively simplified introduction to Lewin's use of the topological geometry.) Lewin felt that such positional relationships were the best way to conceptualize the structure of psychological relationships. There was, however, one serious limitation to topology: its lack of directive concepts. To represent the

psychological concept of direction Lewin then invented a new qualitative geometry (Lewin, 1938), which he named *hodological space*
(from the Greek *hodos,* translated as "path"). He developed the
characteristics of such a space that he felt were necessary for an adequate representation of the dynamic factors, usually called vectors, in
psychological relationships. More recent research, following up some
of Lewin's original ideas, has utilized a new mathematical tool, the
linear graph, which is said to have important methodological advantages over the planar map (cf. Cartwright, 1959, pp. 61–65).

life space

Lewin's objective in adapting and even inventing such geometries
was to clarify his conceptualization of the psychological field, or *life*

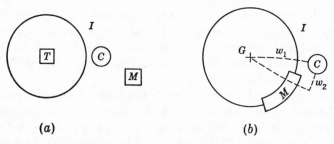

(a)   (b)

Figure 4. Situation in which a young child wishes to reach a toy which lies
inside a circular barrier. (*a*) Physical situation; (*b*) psychological situation. C,
child; T, toy; I, barrier; M, mother; G, goal; w_1, w_2, paths. (*From Lewin*, 1936,
p. 147.)

space. The life space is most simply defined as the totality of effective
psychological factors for a given person at some particular time. It
consists of a number of differentiated *regions,* which represent significant conditions in the person's life. Although the totality of factors
is emphasized in definitions such as the above, in actual practice only
the most relevant ones are ordinarily included in diagrammatic presentations of the life-space concept.

Let us illustrate Lewin's distinction between physical and psychological representations by a relatively simple example from his writing. Figure 4 shows both the physical situation, in (*a*), and the psychological representation, in (*b*), where a goal object (toy) is placed
out of reach within a circular area. Direct physical approach to the
goal via path w_1 is not possible, but psychological locomotion, via
path w_2, is effective if mother can be persuaded to obtain the toy. Although the example pictured involves a physical barrier, the same
psychological situation might obtain with a barrier produced by verbal restriction involving the toy, especially for an older child. Or, in

somewhat similar situations, the barrier might consist of more strictly personal or intraorganismic factors such as politeness in a child trained not to take things without asking or timidity or even fear in some other child. In these cases the physical picture would show no barrier, but the psychological representation, for this slice of the life space, might look very much like that shown in the figure.

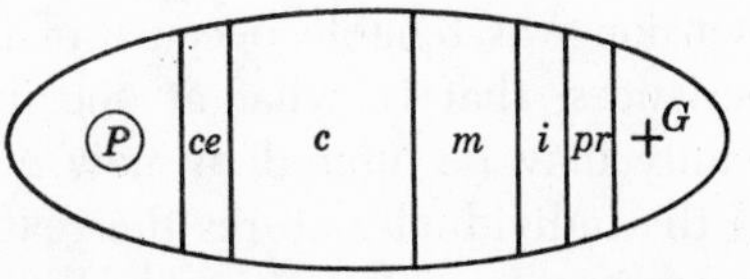

FIGURE 5. Situation of a boy who wants to become a physician. P, person; G, goal; ce, college entrance examinations; c, college; m, medical school; i, internship; pr, establishing a practice. (*From Lewin*, 1936, *p.* 48.)

A somewhat more comprehensive example of a typical life space is shown in Figure 5. Here Lewin depicted a series of locomotions involving a particular occupational choice for a young man. Lewin pointed out that the passing of the college entrance examinations, while not a physical locomotion, represents a "real change of position in the quasi-social . . . life space. . . . Many things are now within his reach which were not before" (1936, p. 48). It is this kind of crossing from one region to another that is emphasized in the life-space schema.

Important dimensions of the life space, as Lewin conceptualized it, are its temporal and reality characteristics. As the child grows older, not only does his life space become increasingly differentiated into regions as a function of his maturity and expanding personal problems, but it also develops temporal and reality-irreality dimensions. For example, the child begins to plan for the future as well as to respond more effectively in longer time units. Further, he begins to use imagery and fantasy and thus to live, in some degree, on an irreality level; there he is less restricted in his behavior by the usual barriers of the real world.

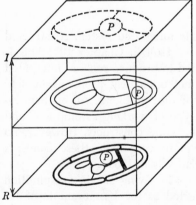

FIGURE 6. Representation of different degrees of reality by an additional dimension of the life space. R, more real level; I, more irreal level; P, person. In a level of greater reality the barriers are stronger and the person P is more clearly separated from his environment. (*From Lewin*, 1936, *p.* 200.)

The reality dimension is illustrated in Figure 6, in which Lewin showed three levels of this variable in the life space.

This dimension Lewin considered of prime significance in a psychological analysis, and so it was given considerable attention in his work. Lewin did not believe that an absolute reality or irreality dimension was tenable because of the continually changing field of experiences; that is, what at one instance may be considered absolute reality may be altered by new events and experiences. Furthermore, as the individual matures the reality-irreality dimension broadens and becomes more differentiated (1936, p. 204).

Perhaps the most widely known Lewinian contribution within the life-space framework is his conceptualization of conflict. He stated that there are three basic types of conflicts producing frustration: approach-approach, approach-avoidance, and avoidance-avoidance. Approach-approach conflict occurs when an individual desires to achieve two goals, only one of which is obtainable (e.g., one has two invitations for the same evening). Approach-avoidance conflict is characterized by a goal which is both desired and undesired (e.g., one desires the money but not the effort entailed in a proffered job). An avoidance-avoidance conflict is present when anticipated consequences are both undesirable (e.g., one must accept an unwanted invitation or offend an esteemed friend). This type of conflict is characterized by a vacillation between the alternatives or by an attempt to escape the situation ("leave the field").

Lewin's system

It is impossible to describe any single integrated system constructed by Lewin (such as that described for Hull in Chapter 10). This is mainly because Lewin never attempted to produce such an integrated system; when not concerned with methodological problems in field theory, he worked on a variety of different problems. All of them involved somewhat the same general type of working assumptions and procedures and to a great extent the same constructs. However, no serious attempt was made by Lewin to coordinate these concepts into one systematic framework (cf. Cartwright, 1959).

The coordinated series of researches involving Lewin's assumption of the *tension system* has been selected as the best example of his work; in some respects it comes close to being an integrated system. A continuing series of experimental studies, some of them described below, were all based upon implications of this central concept. Lewin himself has provided a theoretical account of these researches, emphasizing the formal assumptions and derivations (Lewin, 1940, pp. 13–28; 1944, pp. 4–20). Our treatment follows this account as well as the more informal description given by Deutsch (1954, pp. 199 ff.).

The background for Lewin's development of the construct of the tension system goes back to his first psychological research (1917). He was interested in refining some of Ach's (1910) earlier research on the strength of the will. The general procedure here was to establish associations of nonsense syllables through repeated pairings and then to evaluate the strength of the voluntary factor, manipulated by instructions, by opposing it to the habitual tendency. (See Hilgard, 1956, pp. 258 ff., for a description of this research and the theoretical rationales.) Lewin finally rejected Ach's attempt to supplement the association factor with such new constructs as set and determining tendency, in the tradition of the Würzburg school to which Ach belonged (see Chapter 4). He felt that Ach had not gone far enough in his interpretation. Rather than accept *both* association and voluntary factors, Lewin concluded that the best conceptualization was to assume that there were simply two voluntary factors. He pointed out that association per se provided no motive power. As he later put it (1940, p. 14):

> Dynamically, an "association" is something like a link in a chain, i.e., a pattern of restraining forces without intrinsic tendency to create a change. This property of a need or quasi-need can be represented by coordinating it to a "system in tension." By taking this construct seriously and using certain operational definitions, particularly by correlating the "release of tension" to a "satisfaction of the need" (or "reaching of the goal") and the "setting up of tension" to an "intention" or to a "need in a state of hunger," a great many testable conclusions were made possible.

The first formal effort to test the tension-system proposition thus developed by Lewin was the doctoral-dissertation research done by Zeigarnik (1927) under his supervision. Her experiments were based on the assumptions that (1) tension systems would be established in a subject when he was given simple tasks to perform and (2) if such tension systems were not dissipated, as would normally occur with the completion of the tasks, their persistence would result in a greater likelihood of subsequent recall by the subject of the names of the tasks. Her results in a variety of experiments substantially confirmed this prediction, since interrupted tasks were generally better recalled by subjects than completed tasks. There has been an extensive experimental literature (cf. Alper, 1948; Deutsch, 1954) concerning this interesting phenomenon, the so-called *Zeigarnik effect*.

The next experimental test of the tension-system construct was performed by Ovsiankina (1928). She showed that subjects would voluntarily resume interrupted activities more often than they would return to activities that had been completed.

Following the confirmatory results of these first two studies, a large number of further experimental tests were performed. Among the better known of these are the studies of Lissner (1933) and Mahler (1933) on the role of substitute activities as effective dischargers of tension; of Hoppe (1930) and Frank (1935) on success and failure, especially as these are related to the "level of aspiration" expressed by the subject; and of Karsten (1928) on "psychical satiation," which concerns the problem of the reduction in performance of an activity as a function of the continued repetition of the activity. A summary of these and other related studies is provided by Lewin (1935, pp. 239 ff.). Although we do not have space here to present a further development of Lewin's contributions to research and theory via the tension-system construct, its fruitfulness is well attested by the manner in which these concepts and problems have been utilized in personality theory (cf. Deutsch, 1954).

Lewin's later concern with systematic problems of social psychology may be illustrated by his interesting, and somewhat unusual, wartime research on food habits of people (Lewin, 1943b; see also Lewin, 1951, Chap. 8). Here Lewin raised first the question of why people eat what they do. Interaction of psychological factors (e.g., cultural tradition, individual preference) and nonpsychological factors (e.g., food availability, cost) was investigated in the framework of a so-called "channel" theory. According to this viewpoint, most of the food that appears on the table is eventually eaten by someone or other in the family group, so that the primary question reduces to one that concerns the particular channels by which food is obtained for family use. The two major sources of food in this country during World War II were store purchases and gardening (minor channels were country buying, home baking and canning, and the like). Lewin emphasized the role of the "gatekeeper"—ordinarily the housewife—as the individual who determines for each channel how much of each foodstuff shall be procured and taken through the various stages of preparation for consumption (in the case of home gardening, of course, a larger number of steps are necessary before the final usable products are available for the table).

The psychology of the gatekeeper, as Lewin phrased it, thus became a focal point of this research. Although a large number of interesting questions were asked in the pursuit of the problem, we shall outline only one that received considerable empirical attention. That is the question of the most effective procedure to change opinions. Here attention centered on individual versus group procedures. Lewin pointed out (1951, Chap. 10) that an a priori expectation might well be that single individuals, being "more pliable" than groups of like-minded persons should be easier to convince. An opposite conclusion, however, is supported by the preponderance of much research (on a variety of social problems, such as alcoholism and prejudices, as well as food habits). Once the group standards themselves are changed, as by group rather than individual discussions, individual opinions are much more readily altered.

One illustrative study concerned increased consumption of fresh milk. No pressure was used in the individual or group discussions, and equal time was spent in each case. The results showed clearly that compliance by housewives with the requested change was greater following the group procedure. Similar results were found for other types of foodstuffs (such as evaporated milk and orange juice) and for quite different social problems (such as increased productivity in factory workers).

This research is a good example of the way in which Lewin's work combined theoretically important questions with practically significant problems and procedures (the role of food acceptability assuming larger-than-usual proportions during wartime as a result of shortages of normally preferred foods).

Criticisms of Lewin. Most of the critical objections to Lewin have been methodological ones, centering around his development and use of the field-theoretical approach.

One persistent criticism has involved Lewin's alleged misuse or misappropriation of topological concepts (London, 1944). The charge here is that Lewin has merely borrowed the terminology and certain of the gross conceptualizations from this geometry and has failed to utilize anything like the full set of fundamental topological relationships. In answer to this objection, Lewin has argued that all that can legitimately be required of a psychologist who attempts to apply a mathematical model is that he coordinate some of the conceptual relations with empirical processes (1951, p. 22): "There can be no other meaning and no other proof of the applicability of these geometries to psychology than the fruitfulness of predictions based on such coordination." If one accepts this modest objective as legitimate and sufficient, one can hardly argue with Lewin's appropriation and invention of geometries, at least as far as this aspect of his methodology is concerned.

Another criticism, voiced by some strongly sympathetic with Lewin (Deutsch, 1954) as well as by less friendly critics, has been that he has failed to specify which of several possible interpretations he intended for key terms, such as "person," or key relationships, such as "person" to "life space." A related but much more fundamental criticism (Estes, 1954b) has been that Lewin has generally failed to indicate the empirical basis of his psychological concepts, such as life space, in spite of his admirable emphasis upon the necessity of strict operational coordinating definitions among concepts.

A corollary to the above stricture is the objection that Lewin in his emphasis upon the central cognitive aspects of behavior has tended to ignore the motor aspects. Field theorists generally, with their perceptual or cognitive orientation, have tended to undervalue the response side of the S-O-R formulation.

A much-cited criticism by Brunswik has gone even further, holding that Lewin's "encapsulation into the central layer" means that his life space "is post-perceptual and pre-behavioral" (Brunswik, 1943). Lewin's reply to this particular comment has been that he does not think that psychology needs to study the objective physical and sociological factors which do not have implications for behavior. However, he is willing to include the study of such objective factors as are potential determiners of the life space; this kind of study he called "psychological ecology" (Lewin, 1943a). Cartwright's recent paper contains a carefully detailed formulation of this problem of the "boundary zone" of the life space (1959, pp. 69 ff.).

Other critical evaluations of the more technical aspects of Lewinian field theory may be found in Leeper (1943) and Cartwright (1959). Comprehensive reviews by Deutsch (1954) and Escalona (1954) cover the contributions of his work to social psychology and child psychology, respectively.

Finally, a serious objection to Lewin has been that he failed to make his general conceptual system sufficiently precise and specific so that it can be disconfirmed by experimental test. To quote Estes (1954b, p. 332):

> This informal development of coordinating definitions in use enables the theorist to give plausible accounts of concrete situations, but with no possibility of having the theory refuted by the outcome of the behavioral situation, since the correspondence between theoretical and empirical terms is adjusted in accordance with the empirical findings and is never formally incorporated into the system. Flexibility is obtained at the cost of testability.

It is necessary to recognize the important distinction between Lewin's effective experimental-theoretical research on specific problems, emphasized in the following section, and his theoretical efforts of a systematic sort, criticized in the preceding paragraph for their lack of adequate empirical specification. Although there may have been some general stimulating effects from his over-all systematic position, Lewin's experimentation was not tightly tied to his formal theorizing, at least not to that represented by the life-space schemas. These diagrammatic representations seem to have been useful mainly as pedagogic devices and are of quite limited value in setting up experiments.

Lewin's contributions

On the positive side, Lewin made important contributions to the development of psychology as a behavior science. First, Lewin has few peers in psychology as a creative conceptualizer *and* an ingenious experimenter. It was this ability to implement his theoretical insights with concrete empirical situations that largely accounts for his pre-eminence. This ability was apparently based, at least in part, upon insightful observations of the everyday-life scene. For example, his conceptualization of the tension system in relation to memory (cf. the Zeigarnik phenomenon, described above) is said to have been suggested by his observation that waiters in Berlin restaurants had a remarkably accurate memory for the detailed amount of each bill—until after it was paid (Hartmann, 1935, p. 221). Similarly, in his later career, his interest in problems of social interaction, such as the role of a social minority, was at least partially stimulated by his own keen awareness of the tragedies which he observed in the real world (Deutsch, 1954).

Second, Lewin's specific contributions to psychological theory were of great scope and depth. He developed concepts and experimental techniques, such as level of aspiration, that have enjoyed widespread acceptance in the fields of personality and motivation. These contributions to personality theory have had a strong, continuing influence.

Finally, Lewin's pioneering efforts in the field of social psychology would be sufficient to guarantee him a lasting and prominent place in the history of psychology. His early research in social psychology in this country is exemplified by the pioneer studies (Lewin, 1939; Lippitt & White, 1943; Lippitt, 1940) on behavior in social climates that were experimentally manipulated. For example, leadership techniques were experimentally varied in boys' clubs (laissez-faire, democratic, autocratic), and various behaviors, such as aggression, were correlated with different social climates that resulted (Lippitt & White, 1943). These studies not only opened up an important new area of social research but also had some influence upon educational and social practices (Cartwright, 1958).

The final phase of Lewin's research, concerned mainly with group dynamics, found him taking more of an administrative and supervisory role and leaving to others the detailed working out of hypotheses and collection of data. In *Resolving social conflicts* (1948), Lewin reported on various experimental efforts to change social behavior in real, everyday-life situations (such as interracial factory workshops). It is unfortunate that his relatively early death prevented further contributions to this kind of research program.

COGNITIVE FIELD THEORY: TOLMAN'S PURPOSIVE BEHAVIORISM

The most important contribution of Edward C. Tolman (1886–1959) to the development of behaviorism has already been noted (Chapter

7). The emphasis which he early placed on a *molar* interpretation of behavior as *purposive* (1932) persisted throughout his long and illustrious career. Although Tolman cannot be said to have developed a definitive theory, his system of psychology, with its primarily cognitive, or S-S, position on learning, has been extremely influential. He has been the most acceptable of the major avowed behaviorists to nonbehavioristically oriented psychologists. His system represents the seemingly paradoxical combination of important elements of behaviorism and gestalt psychology. His primary orientation has been stimulus-centered, or cognitive, rather than S-R; in his later papers especially (e.g., 1949a) he has not only professed a deep-seated admiration for the field-theoretical views of Kurt Lewin but in addition has adopted an essentially Lewinian position with regard to fundamental theoretical problems. For these reasons Tolman is treated here as a kind of field theorist.

Tolman's career

Edward Tolman was born in Massachusetts and took an engineering degree at the Massachusetts Institute of Technology. He switched to psychology and received his M.A. in 1912 and his Ph.D. in 1915 from Harvard. He served as an instructor in psychology at Northwestern University from 1915 to 1918. Tolman then moved to the University of California, where he established a rat laboratory. From that time he remained on the Berkeley campus, except for an appointment in the Office of Strategic Services during the war (1944–1945) and a period of almost three years (1950–1953) during which he was a leader in a faculty fight against the state loyalty oath. Appointments at the University of Chicago and at Harvard were held during this time.

Tolman's system

The foundation of Tolman's purposive behaviorism was present in his first and major book, *Purposive behavior in animals and men* (1932), in a loosely formulated manner. Until recently, little effort was expended to organize the major ideas into anything like an integrated system. Predictions about experimental outcomes were not related to each other in any logically rigorous manner. In a word, Tolman has long been considered a programmatic theorist. A detailed attempt at a more definitive formalization of his major principles was made by MacCorquodale and Meehl (1954), and in a final work Tolman himself (1959) has endeavored to present a somewhat more organized picture of his system. We shall present here a summary of certain of his most salient principles.

The primary principle in Tolman's systematic thinking about behavior is that in its purposive or adaptive activities the organism utilizes environmental objects and develops *means-end readinesses* with regard to them and their role in relation to his behavior. This phrase is but one of many awkwardly compounded terms which Tolman coined early in his career and has consistently utilized in his writing; this one is particularly emphasized in his recent work (1959). The term is roughly synonymous with cognitions, or expectancies. It refers to the kind of learning which Tolman felt was central to behavior—sign learning. Briefly put, the organism learns "what leads to what." Like the gestalt theorists, Tolman felt that the actual behavior is relatively unimportant; the primary determiners of action are central, not peripheral, as the typical S-R theorist would hold.

A more formal structure in Tolman's system was developed in his final comprehensive statement (1959). There he presented a systematic schema for five representative situations: simple approach to food, simple escape from electric shock, simple avoidance of electric shock, choice-point learning, and latent learning.

Without going into a detailed explication of these paradigms and the notation system used by Tolman, we may note several salient considerations suggested by the scheme. First, a somewhat superficial similarity to the Hullian system is evident. To some extent this logical interrelating of concepts was induced by the form of presentation requested by the editor of the book for which this particular paper was prepared; to some extent, perhaps, this kind of formalization was encouraged by the earlier effort of MacCorquodale and Meehl to put Tolman's thinking into Hullian form. In any case, it should also be mentioned, in fairness, that a somewhat comparable, though much simpler, tabular arrangement was early used by Tolman (e.g., 1936, 1938).

Second, and more important, Tolman's final formulation illustrates the central role played in his theory by the cognitive constructs. Here a little explanatory detail is in order. Two major cognitive constructs are involved. The means-end readiness is a relatively pure acquired cognitive disposition—pure in the sense that it endures independently of the present motivational state of the organism; that is, he may know where food is whether or not he is hungry. The expectation, on the other hand, is the concrete product of the means-end readiness— a cognitive event that applies directly and specifically to the present situation. Tolman summed up the two concepts (1959, pp. 113–114):

A means-end readiness, as I conceive it, is a condition in the organism, which is equivalent to what in ordinary parlance we call a "belief" (a readiness or disposition) to the effect that an instance of this *sort* of stimulus situation, if reacted to by an instance of this *sort* of response, will lead to an instance of that *sort* of further stimulus situation, or else, that an instance of this *sort* of stimulus situation will simply by itself be accompanied, or followed, by an instance of that *sort* of stimulus situation. Further, I assume that the different readinesses or beliefs (dispositions) are stored up together (in the nervous system). When they are concretely activated in the form of expectancies they tend to interact and/or consolidate with one another. And I would also assert that "thinking" as we know it in human beings, is in essence no more than an activated interplay among expectancies resulting from such previously acquired readinesses which result in new expectancies and resultant new means-end readinesses.

Tolman conceded the weakness of this formulation in terms of specific empirical measures. He recognized the difficulty of implementing such constructs operationally but at the same time repeatedly pointed to what he saw as a comparable weakness in the Hull-Spence $r_g - s_g$ construct (see Chapter 10).

Although the concept of cognition, however phrased, is the key one in Tolman's system, he has considered other types of concepts and other kinds of learning. In his (1949b) effort to cover the major types of learning processes, he pointed to the following six "types of connections": *cathexes,* which represent the affective properties acquired by objects (similar to Lewin's "valence"); *equivalence beliefs,* which are the cognitive representations of subgoals or secondary reinforcers; *field expectancies,* which are the presumed central variables that underlie the animal's dispositions to one object as a signal for another (called "sign-gestalt-expectations" in the earlier versions of the system); *field-cognition modes,* which are the higher-order functions that produce field expectancies through perceptual, memorial, or inferential processes; *drive discriminations,* which are the demonstrated abilities of animals to behave differentially under different deprivation conditions; and *motor patterns,* which are the responses and combinations of responses (skills) themselves.

Only the sketchiest effort was made by Tolman to indicate the kinds of laws, or empirical relationships among variables, that might relate to these various kinds of learning. No laws were seriously suggested, for example, for the important field-cognition modes or for drive discriminations. A simple contiguity principle, following Guthrie, was accepted for motor patterns. Hullian need-reduction was considered to be at least partially responsible for cathexes and equivalence beliefs. And no definitive interpretations were offered for the key concept of field expectancies, although the reinforcement principle here was specifically denied more than an incidental role.

Tolman's (1951b) model contained three major constructs: the *need system,* closely related to orthodox drive notions; the *behavior space,* closely related to Lewin's life space, described earlier in this chapter; and the *belief-value matrix,* which consists of hierarchies of learned expectations concerning environmental objects and their roles in relation to behavior.

These briefly outlined formulations by Tolman should indicate the essentially preliminary nature of his system. Few would deny that he has pointed up problems of critical importance and often in a new and insightful manner. But lawful relationships or even suggested logical relationships among the variables have not been offered.

The above observation is somewhat surprising in view of Tolman's early concern with at least a prototype of experimental design intended to make possible the functional interrelationships of independent, intervening, and dependent variables. In his early works (1936, 1938) he specified in some detail the particular variables which he felt were significant ones in behavior and indicated the kind of "standard" experimental situation in which their values might be determined by means of a large number of permutations and combinations of such variables. In this connection it is interesting to note that Tolman very recently (1959, p. 110) has suggested a similar kind of experimental procedure, while the editor of the same publication (Koch, 1959) has emphasized in his commentary how this particular notion has been generally discarded. In spite of his espousal of this kind of methodology, nothing like it was actually attempted by Tolman in his own research.

Tolman's experimentation

The kind of experimental research performed by Tolman is well illustrated by an early study on insight learning in the rat (Tolman & Honzik, 1930). An elevated maze with three alternative paths to the goal box was used, as shown in Figure 7. The three paths varied in length. In preliminary training path 1, the shortest, was blocked, and the animals then learned to use the next shortest, path 2. It will be noted that paths 1 and 2 share the final part of the direct runway to the goal box. During training trials the block had been placed close to the starting place, well before the common segment of paths 1 and 2. For the test trials the block was moved to position B, toward the end of the common segment and close to the goal box. According to the insight prediction the animal would now return to path 1, rather than previously preferred path 2, since this was also blocked. A non-insight type of simple S-R view would presumably predict the mechanical running off of the next strongest response in the hierarchy established in training, that of running down path 2. Most of the animals tested in the study chose path 3, thus supporting Tolman's cognitive or expectancy position.

This experiment has been followed by several replications and modifications, not all of which have given clearly confirmatory results (cf. Hilgard, 1956, p. 195). It nevertheless stands as an important early research which not only supported Tolman's general cognitive theory but also served to stimulate further, more analytic researches. In these respects it is representative of much of Tolman's experimentation.

Even more characteristic of Tolman's research is the latent-learning experiment, originated by Blodgett (1929) in the California laboratory. The fundamental problem here is whether reward (or reinforcement) is essential for learning to occur. As a cognitive theorist, defining learning in terms of perceptual rather than response factors, Tolman insisted that learning will occur in the absence of reward but simply will not be demonstrated until the appropriate motivational conditions obtain.

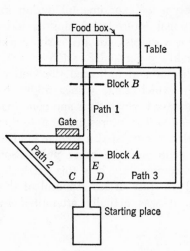

FIGURE 7. Maze used to test insight in rats. The paths become established as a hierarchy according to length, path 1 preferred to path 2, path 2 to path 3. If path 1 is closed by block A, the rats run by path 2. If path 1 is closed by block B, the rats run by path 3 if they have insight that the barrier closes path 2 as well as path 1. (*From Tolman & Honzik*, 1930, *p.* 223.)

In a typical latent-learning experiment, designed to test Tolman's cognitive position, a hungry animal is permitted access to a learning device, such as a maze, without being rewarded by food in the goal box. After a certain number of such trials, on which numerous errors are made and limited overt learning evidenced, the animal finds food in the goal box for the first time. The subsequent test trials generally show a remarkably improved performance, indicating that the animal had been learning something about the maze on the earlier trials but had not been motivated to perform appropriately (i.e., to take the true path to the goal box and avoid the blind alleys). When reward is introduced, the performance of such experimental animals quickly approximates that of controls which have had the same number of trials, all reinforced by food.

Although there is still some controversy on this issue, especially about the various subtle sources of reinforcement now suspected to operate (e.g., removal of the animal from the maze), the majority of the results seem to support Tolman's original position. (See Thwistlewaite, 1951; MacCorquodale & Meehl, 1951; and Kimble, 1961, for reviews of the pertinent literature.)

criticisms of Tolman

The most persistent criticism of Tolman's work has already been indicated: his failure to develop anything like a logically integrated theory. In this respect certain of his own comments may be instructive. For example, in refusing to comment on a requested distinction between his of immediate data language and construct language, Tolman noted that "I myself can neither get very interested in nor completely understand such more refined logical distinctions" (1959, p. 149). Apparently his lack of interest in problems of logical relationships at least partly accounts for the programmaticity of his systematizing.

One particular and important criticism which Tolman has shared with Lewin is that he has paid insufficient attention to the problem of relating overt behavior to cognition and similar central states. Guthrie, for instance, has commented that Tolman leaves the rat "buried in thought" (1935, p. 172). This weakness in Tolman's system may be seen as part of the over-all inadequacy of specification, discussed above.

Finally, as a representative of a kind of common-sense approach to behavior, Tolman has come in for a variety of criticisms from the more tough-minded type of psychologist. An obvious point of attack has involved his alleged mentalism, largely as a result of the kind of language Tolman has used and the centralist nature of his constructs. In answer to such attacks, he has stoutly and persistently defended his basic behaviorism. Even the more sympathetic of Tolman's critics, however, have entertained some doubt on this score. Thus Mac-Corquodale and Meehl have noted "a certain affinity for the dualistic" even while not meaning "even to suggest that he is anything else [than a behaviorist] consciously or unconsciously" (1954, p. 185). In considering this criticism Tolman had at least a partial explanation, if not justification, to offer in terms of his inital exposure to objectivism. He has stated that "although I was sold on objectivism and behaviorism as *the* method in psychology, the only categorizing rubrics which I had at hand were mentalistic ones. So when I began to try to develop a behavioristic system of my own, what I really was doing was trying to rewrite a commonsense mentalistic psychology . . . in operational behavioristic terms" (1959, p. 94).

Tolman's contributions

In spite of the undeniable programmaticity of his systematizing, Tolman has had a great influence upon the course of psychology over the past four decades. We shall describe several general forms of this influence and then mention some more specific contributions.

Tolman's role in leavening the behavioristic loaf, in its early formative period, was a most significant one. Although his emphasis on a molar point of view and an acceptance of purposiveness was never quite accepted by some behaviorists, nevertheless this kind of interpretation served to make the system more readily understandable and acceptable to many others.

The influence of his cognitive learning system has also been very great. For two decades Tolman's cognitive position offered the major alternative to the Hullian need-reduction theory. As a matter of fact, much of the learning experimentation and literature was directly concerned with one attempt or another to pit cognitive theory against reinforcement theory. Thus in reviewing the learning literature for the first issue of the *Annual Review of Psychology*, Melton could say that "these past twenty years of experimental-theoretical development have been increasingly under the influence of the opposed theoretical systems of Tolman and Hull" (1950, p. 9).

A different kind of general influence may be noted in Tolman's long-standing support of the rat as a laboratory animal and appropriate subject for even the field-theoretical and centralist thinking which he espoused. Such use of this favored laboratory animal by Tolman was undoubtedly responsible for a large amount of the acceptance generally accorded "rat psychology" in spite of the strong opposition of many psychologists. His position on this issue was very clearly and forcefully stated in his delightful (1945) essay. Here Tolman, always humorous and self-effacing, is at his best. The concluding sentences are especially noteworthy (1945, p. 166):

> What, by way of summary, can we now say as to the contributions of us rodent psychologists to human behavior? What is it that we rat runners still have to contribute to the understanding of the deeds and the misdeeds, the absurdities and the tragedies of our friend, and our enemy—*homo sapiens?* The answer is that, whereas man's successes, persistences, and socially unacceptable divagations—that is, his intelligences, his motivations, and his instabilities—are all ultimately shaped and materialized by specific cultures, it is still true that most of the formal underlying laws of intelligence, motivation, and instability can still be studied in rats as well as, and more easily than, in men.
>
> And, as a final peroration, let it be noted that rats live in cages; they do not go on binges the night before one has planned an experiment; they do not kill each other off in wars; they do not invent engines of destruction, and, if they did, they would not be so inept about controlling such engines; they do not go in for either class conflicts or race conflicts; they avoid politics, economics, and papers on psychology. They are marvelous, pure, and delightful. And, as soon as I possibly can, I am going to climb back again out on that good old phylogenetic limb and sit there, this time right side up and unashamed, wiggling my whiskers at all the silly, yet at the same time far too complicated, specimens of *homo sapiens,*

whom I shall see strutting and fighting and messing things up, down there on the ground below me.

Of many particular contributions that Tolman made, two early ones need to be mentioned. One is his invention (1936) of the intervening-variable paradigm, later adopted and much more thoroughly implemented by Hull (see Chapter 10). An intervening variable is an intraorganismic function (e.g., hunger) that is postulated to account for a particular kind of behavior (e.g., eating) in a certain stimulus situation (e.g., presentation of food object after one day of food deprivation). Although Tolman apparently intended a purely abstractive usage of the intervening variable, he eventually renounced such a usage for the less operationally valid "hypothetical construct" (cf. Marx, 1963, Chap. 1, 5). He has recently stated (1959, p. 97): "My intervening variables are generally speaking mere temporarily believed-in, inductive, more or less qualitative generalizations which categorize and sum up for me various empirically found relationships." He further observed that they are not "primarily neurophysiological . . . but are derived rather from intuition, common experience, a little sophomoric neurology, and my own phenomenology" (1959, pp. 98 ff.).

Tolman is generally credited with having made the first effective distinction in the psychological literature between learning and performance. He early pointed out that learning alone is not sufficient to produce the learned behavior, that the motivational conditions must also be appropriate. The distinction between learning and performance has been a most important one in the development of learning theory and research. Tolman credited Blodgett, who performed the first latent-learning experiment, for having forced this distinction on him and also noted (1959, p. 149) that Lashley had anticipated him.

Finally, Tolman must be credited with having played a major role in the opening up of many significant areas of research. Of these, the most important are probably the latent-learning problem, which deals with the necessity of the reinforcement principle in learning; the transposition problem, which concerns the dependence of learning upon relative as contrasted with absolute cues; and the continuity-noncontinuity issue, which involves the question whether each single reinforcement or nonreinforcement has an effect in learning (the continuity position). Each of these problem areas relates directly to the theoretical opposition between Hull and Tolman. While the large-scale systematic issues posed by these two views are no longer of prime concern to learning theorists, many of the particular problem areas developed in the theoretical controversy have not only produced much valuable research but are still themselves of first importance in learning research. In this way Tolman, like Hull, has had a great and continuing influence on experimental-theoretical psychology.

FIELD THEORY OF ACHIEVEMENT: BRUNSWIK'S PROBABILISTIC FUNCTIONALISM

The probabilistic functionalism developed and propounded by Egon Brunswik (1903–1955) is difficult to categorize within the simplified theoretical framework which we have utilized for expository purposes in the present volume. Certainly Brunswik was not an S-R theorist, although under the influence of Tolman and others he very definitely moved in the direction of behaviorism after he came to this country. It is equally certain that he was in no obvious way a field theorist of the sort that Lewin represented. Although his research on the perceptual constancies is often related to orthodox gestalt psychology, Brunswik himself (1949, p. 57) has explicitly denied any such historical or conceptual relationship.

We have categorized Brunswik as a field theorist primarily because he has so persistently and successfully considered the totality of interacting factors in his attempt to establish a meaningful systematic framework within which to evaluate psychological systems and behavioral problems. In this respect he has outdone even Lewin, especially with his explicit emphasis upon distal, as compared with proximal, antecedent and consequent conditions. Furthermore, his insistence upon a representative, rather than merely a systematic, design for experimentation likewise indicates a deep concern for all the interacting factors involved in the determination of behavior. These statements should be clearer after the reader has grasped some of the basic points that Brunswik attempted to make and to implement in his own research.

Brunswik's career

Egon Brunswik was born in Hungary, where he received an unusually varied education. After being trained in engineering and passing the first state examination, he shifted to the study of psychology at the University of Vienna. There he was much influenced by contacts with the logical positivists, in the Vienna Circle. He studied psychology under Karl Bühler, taking his doctorate in 1927. In the meantime he passed the state examination for teaching mathematics and physics.

Following several years of various academic appointments, a critical turning point in Brunswik's career occurred during the 1933–1934 academic year. E. C. Tolman, visiting in Vienna, met and was quite impressed with Brunswik. Two years later Brunswik received a Rockefeller Fellowship and largely at Tolman's instigation was invited to serve as visiting lecturer and research fellow in psychology at the Berkeley campus of the University of California. In 1937, he returned to Berkeley as assistant professor. He spent the remainder of his career there.

Brunswik's research

Brunswik is best known in psychology for the breadth and intensity of his research on visual constancy factors, usually referred to as *thing constancy*. This research program was well begun in Europe and was a major factor in attracting Tolman to Brunswik. The heart of Brunswik's thing-constancy research is the dichotomy between the physical nature of an object and its sensory representation. The extent to which the perceptual effect tends to approximate the more remote physical (distal) or the more immediate sensory (proximal) value is the fundamental problem of this kind of research. For example, consider a wooden table. As a distal object, the table has a certain determinate physical length; as a proximate object, in perception, it also has a certain length, equivalent to the physical distance delimited on the appropriate receptor surface of the subject. It is the physical, or distal, dimension that remains relatively stable while a wide variety of other conditions, such as distance or angle of view, directly affect the proximal dimension.

The major finding of Brunswik's thing-constancy research was that there is almost inevitably a compromise in experience, or—more operationally—in the subject's reported judgment, between the distal and the proximal dimensions. Normally the subject tends to approximate more closely the distal, or real, characteristics of the object in spite of the various distorting conditions: thus the term thing constancy. Appropriate instructions, however, can markedly reduce the influence of the distal factor so that the proximal dimension is more closely approximated. The index of this influence (Thouless's "regression to the real") is called the Brunswik ratio. This ratio is unity when constancy is perfect—that is, when perceived factors such as size, shape, and brightness are independent of distance, angle of tilt, luminous flux, etc. When the proximal (retinal) stimulus completely determines visual perception, the Brunswik ratio is zero. Thus the ratio indicates, on a scale ranging from zero to unity, the degree to which the constant aspects of the stimulus situation determine perception.

In subsequent research Brunswik extended this basic methodology to new problems of a somewhat wider interest. First, within the area of perception, he brought into his experiments such variables as monetary value. For example, in one experiment (Brunswik, 1934, pp. 147–150; see also Brunswik, 1956, p. 78) the experimenter asked subjects to make comparisons between cards containing varying numbers of coins of varying sizes and monetary value. In accordance with the basic principle repeatedly demonstrated in the simpler research, judgments of equality between stimuli were compromised to some extent by each of the three variables. Later, under the influence of Tolman and American neobehaviorism, Brunswik came to concern himself with instrumental behavior as well as perception (cf. the early collaborative paper, Tolman & Brunswik, 1935). In one important study (Brunswik, 1939b), he attacked the problem of what is now called partial or intermittent reinforcement. The all-or-none reward situation almost invariably used in American learning experimentation up to that time Brunswik felt to be quite unrepresentative of normal situations. Accordingly he varied the proportion of reward to total trials in the two ends of a standard T maze. The rat subjects cooperated and expressed preferences that were roughly correlated with degree of probability of reward in the two ends. This research is related, conceptually, to the earlier work in perception in that the primary concern is again with the degree to which the subject normally achieves a kind of constancy relationship.

Brunswik's system

The probabilistic functionalism which Brunswik came to feel most adequately systematizes psychological problems was a fairly direct and logical outgrowth of the research program outlined above. Brunswik's system is *probabilistic* since it holds that the perceptual and behavioral goals in the natural environment are related usually in an equivocal and rarely in a univocal manner to cues and responses. The system is a *functionalism* since it is primarily concerned with the degree of success, or achievement, in perception and instrumental behavior.

An illustration of Brunswik's systematic thinking is his conceptual framework (1939a) in which a succession of temporally and spatially ordered "levels" or "layers" of variables is envisioned. These range from the temporally most remote (those farthest back in the past of the individual) through manipulable physical objects (distal stimuli) to the outer physical areas of the organism (proximal stimuli) and thence to intraorganismic functions and states; on the response side, a comparable array is conceptualized, from proximal reactions through distal effects (achievements in regard to environmental objects) to long-range successes and ultimate products of the individual's life span. These relations are represented in Figure 8.

Brunswik's lens model (1952), shown in Figure 9, illustrates the way in which a great variety of different but interacting processes can be initiated from a single focal factor (such as an object in the stimulus situation in perception research, or as some aspect of a learning problem in instrumental behavior research) and also the way in which a similarly differentiated array of response processes mediated within the organism may focalize into a single perceptual or instrumental achievement. For an illustrative commonplace application of the lens model, consider the behavior of a baseball player

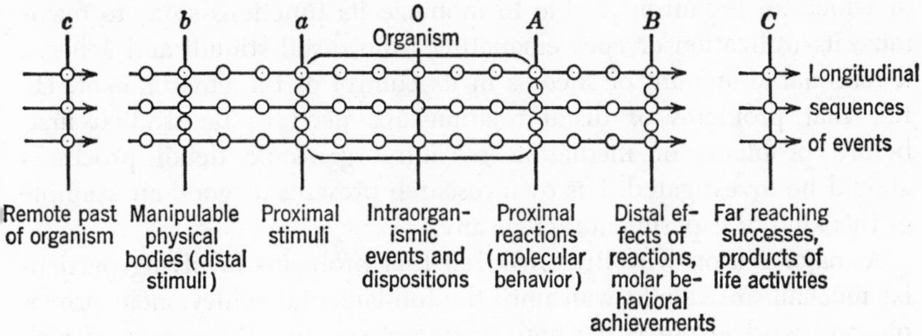

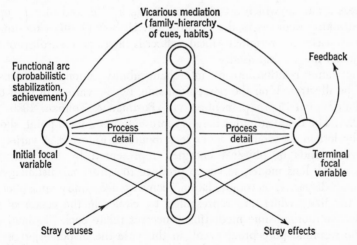

FIGURE 8. Scheme of the organism in its surroundings. (*From Brunswik, 1939a, p. 37.*)

FIGURE 9. The lens model: Composite picture of the functional unit of behavior. (*From Brunswik, 1952, p. 20.*)

who is attempting to catch a high fly ball (the "initial focal variable"). A number of different perceptual cues emanate from the ball in flight—its speed, height, etc.—and must be quickly taken into account by the fielder as he estimates its trajectory and ultimate destination. Such "stray causes" as the direction and force of the wind and position of the sun may also need to be taken into account. On the response side, the fielder needs to mobilize his energies so as to time his movement toward the ball properly without interference from other stray causes such as teammates, fences, and the like. "Stray effects" would then be exemplified by collisions with other fielders, bumping into fences, etc. An ultimate instrumental achievement such as catching a difficult fly ball (the "terminal focal variable") is thus seen as dependent upon the successful coordination of a variety of "process details" on both the perceptual and the response sides.

Brunswik felt that the double-convex model represents the manner in which an organism is able to mobilize its functions so as to maximize its utilization of cues emanating from distal stimuli and achieve a reasonable amount of success in its control of the environment. He felt that problems of distal relationships need to be studied first, before problems of mediation by intraorganismic detail processes should be investigated. His own research presents as good an example of this kind of experimentation as any.

A major reason why Brunswik felt that problems involving particular mechanisms should wait until the fundamental achievement principles are worked out is the high degree of substitutability among such mechanisms. On the instrumental side, this may be simply illustrated by the variety of particular responses (habits) which a rat can use to depress a bar, or which a cat can use to tip a pole, and thereby open a restraining door, as in the Guthrie and Horton (1946) experiment. In these cases the terminal—focal—effect is the same regardless of the particular mechanism used.

The same relationship of interchangeability among mechanisms may be illustrated, on the perceptual side, by the variety of cues that mediate visual depth perception (cf. Postman & Tolman, 1959, pp. 511 ff.). The distal stimulus here is represented as a focal point, shown on the left in the double-convex lens model of Figure 9. A variety of different kinds of physical energies, represented by the diverging lines of the lens model, serves to produce the proximal distance cues (retinal disparity, accommodation, convergence, linear perspective, and the like) which are represented by circles in the center of the model. Intraorganismic mediating processes relate each proximal cue to the terminal perceptual event, in this case the distance judgment.

A number of interesting points are suggested by this kind of analysis. The *ecological validity* of cues (or habits) is defined as the degree of correlation between each such proximal condition and the value of the distal stimulus. For example, the ecological validity of retinal disparity is generally higher than that of accommodation or convergence as a cue to distance. This means simply that retinal disparity is a more effective cue, correlating more highly with physical distance. But it is not essential; other cues can substitute for it and mediate depth perception. In its normal adjustment to the flux of events in the environment the organism needs to have considerable flexibility with regard to which cues (or habits) are most often given the greatest weight. The necessarily probabilistic nature of the terminal focal events (perceptual and instrumental) is clearly indicated by this analysis. As Brunswik has put it (1955a, p. 207):

> The general pattern of the mediational strategy of the organism is predicated upon the limited ecological validity or trustworthiness of cues. . . . This forces a probabilistic strategy upon the organism. To improve its bet, it must accumulate and combine cues. . . . No matter how much the attainment is improved, however, distal function remains inherently probabilistic.

Brunswik's emphasis on representative design

Perhaps the most far-reaching aspect of Brunswik's conceptual formulation was his increasing emphasis on the necessity for psychology to use what he called representative, rather than systematic, design in its experimentation (Brunswik, 1956). This emphasis follows directly out of the probabilistic functionalism which he developed. As long as rigorous control of variables is practiced, in the orthodox systematic design used by most psychologists, there will be serious limitations about how representative experimental results are of the natural behavior of the subject. In order to permit a more adequate analysis of the organism's achievements in relation to the environment—seen by Brunswik from his functionalistic position as the primary problem for psychology—a wider sampling of effective variables must be utilized, even if this means less rigorous control in the usual sense.

As a corollary of this position, the highly general laws aimed at in orthodox systematic research would need to be replaced by statistical statements in which only probabilistic values can be expressed. Such statistical expressions concern the probabilities with which the various conditions sampled are found to correlate with the achievements of the organism in dealing with the environment. In representative designs correlational techniques thus replace the statistical tests of differences that are usual in systematic designs.

Although the positive side of these methodological proposals seems reasonably clear, since they follow directly from Brunswik's own research program, his criticisms of the orthodox type of systematic design may require further specification. Brunswik felt that any experiment which deals with only one variable at a time, in the classic manner, is hopelessly inadequate to present a realistic picture of the organism's behavior. Although the recent trend toward multivariate design was considered to be a step in the right direction, it has been nonetheless a small and seriously limited one. Furthermore, the variables ordinarily manipulated are proximal rather than distal ones, in the conceptual framework described above; from Brunswik's point of view, this places the emphasis on the wrong kind of investigation.

Distal variables require a wider sampling of situations because behavior with regard to them is influenced by a wider variety of variables (cf. the lens model described above).

Brunswik was also highly critical of the way in which variables are
artificially "tied" and "untied," as well as "interlocked," in orthodox
systematic design. Although a detailed specification of these problems
is beyond the scope of the present book, the general point here is that
a truly representative design should permit a freer kind of covaria-
tion among factors (see Postman & Tolman, 1959, pp. 516 ff., for an
especially clear presentation of this argument). This point may be
illustrated by a relatively simple example which Brunswik (1955a,
pp. 194 ff.) developed on the basis of a problem earlier suggested by
Holt (1915). Imagine a flock of
birds flying (1) over a green field
(dotted line) and (2) southward
(solid line). As shown in Figure 10,
these two variables are confounded,
or tied. Merely returning the birds
to point 0 does not resolve the confounding, nor does adding new subjects from the same population. The
typical technique used to untie these
two variables in systematically designed experimentation is called
"diacritical" by Brunswik. It is indicated in Figure 10 by the movement
of the birds to a new position, so
that the two alternative interpreta-
tions may be clearly separated, that is, have different consequences
(birds either fly to green fields and not directly south, or fly south
and thereby miss the green fields). But, Brunswik pointed out
(1955a, p. 195):

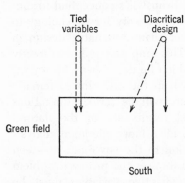

Tied
variables

Diacritical
design

Green field

South

Figure 10. Systematic design in the
study of behavior constancy. For
explanation, see text. (*From Brunswik, 1955a, p. 194.*)

> We soon discover that southwardness is still tied to such factors as the
> general area of start, temperature and other climatic conditions, topo-
> graphic landmarks, magnetic cues, and so forth; and so is the greenness
> of the field to its squareness or size. What we have accomplished in
> diacritical design is to separate or "split" an original encompassing clus-
> ter into two subclusters of tied variables; but we have not really "iso-
> lated" our variable as it may have seemed at first glance, and therefore
> are not yet entitled to speak of its attainment as a constant function.

For Brunswik the only satisfactory solution to this kind of problem
would be a truly representative design in which a more adequate
sampling of situational variables is possible. A partial solution would
not be enough. A simple example of the inadequacy of such artificial

untying of variables, in systematic design, has been provided by Brunswik (1956, p. 27). In an experiment on judgment of personality traits, subjects are placed in identical bodily positions and given identical clothes to wear. While this experimental procedure controls for the influence of these two variables, it also makes impossible the assay of any normal interaction between the personality traits estimated and such factors as body tone and dressing habits. This typical experiment is thus incompletely designed, according to Brunswik. For completeness, one would need to include a much wider range of important variables in the behavior sampling (e.g., have subjects take different positions, wear different clothes, etc.).

Brunswik's contribution to psychology

Brunswik's logical analysis of design problems is almost certain to have more influence upon the future course of psychological science than is typical of such logical endeavors. Already there is evidence that his position is being implemented far outside the experimental study of perception in which it started. An outstanding example of this is Hammond's (1954, 1955) demonstration of the importance of considering representative design in clinical psychology. Research on the diagnostic use of test scores is criticized for not sampling adequately the personality characteristics of the examiners themselves and the situational variables involved in the test administration. As a matter of fact, frequently the range of examiners is severely limited, such as to a single person, for the express purpose of eliminating variability in results. Such application of the typical systematic design does not prevent investigators from generalizing their results, at least implicitly, to a presumably wide range of examiners and situations as well as to a population of tested individuals (the representativeness of whose selection in sampling is generally explicitly considered). Some extension of the principles of more fully representative design to other experimental and clinical situations would seem to be indicated, regardless of the extent to which one accepts Brunswik's strictures of orthodox systematic design.

Most of the criticisms of Brunswik's methodological points have centered around his apparent opposition to research on mediational mechanisms and his apparent assumption of a basic nonuniformity or nonuniversality in behavioral laws (cf. Postman, 1955; Hilgard, 1955). On the former point, Postman and Tolman (1959, p. 558) have attempted a clarification. They say that Brunswik was not so much opposed to the experimental analysis of mediational mechanisms as he was opposed to their being given priority over research on distal correlations involving perceptual and instrumental achievements. He is, of course, entitled to his opinion on this point, but, as we have pointed out before, it is difficult to say in advance which of several alternative procedures will be most effective; the safest position is simply to let each researcher follow his own inclinations on this issue. On the second point, Brunswik has taken pains to say that he does not think that behavioral laws are fundamentally probabilistic but only that their establishment is necessarily limited to statistical or probabilistic expression because of the limitations imposed by the great variety of interacting factors in behavior. As he has put it (1955b, p. 236): "The crucial point is that while God may not gamble, animals and humans do, and that they cannot help but to gamble in an ecology that is of essence only partly accessible to their foresight."

Apart from the ultimate significance of his methodological position, Brunswik has contributed substantially to the advancement of our understanding of the perceptual constancies. Secondarily, he has helped to free research on instrumental learning from certain of its early limitations, as described above. These achievements, added to his insightful analyses of design problems, are more than sufficient to ensure a prominent place for him in the history of systematic psychology.

MISCELLANEOUS FIELD THEORIES

Lashley's neuropsychology

Karl S. Lashley (1890–1958) cannot be easily assigned to any single simple category. We have already met him in Chapter 7, since he was one of the most enthusiastic of the early behaviorists. He belongs also in this chapter, however, since as his career developed he moved more and more in the direction of a kind of field theory and could be found increasingly on the gestalt or field-theory side of particular theoretical issues.

Lashley did his graduate work at the University of Pittsburgh and Johns Hopkins University, receiving the Ph.D. in psychology in 1914 at the latter school. His major teaching appointments were at the Universities of Minnesota and Chicago and at Harvard. He then became director, in 1942, of the Yerkes Laboratory of Primate Biology, the world-renowned chimpanzee-research station at Orange Park, Florida. In this capacity he retained his professorship at Harvard because the two institutions were then administratively related.

Lashley's earliest research was performed in collaboration with the bioligist H. S. Jennings and the behaviorist John B. Watson at Johns Hopkins. His research interests ranged quite widely, from problems concerning the inheritance of size in paramecia to cerebral factors in migraine headaches in humans (see Beach et al., 1960 for these and many of his other papers). However, the problem of brain function related to behavior was his most important and most persistent interest and the one for which he is best known.

Lashley's interest in brain function was formed early in his training, but it was only in 1917, when he became associated with the eminent neurophysiologist Franz, that he embarked upon the line of research utilizing ablation of the rat brain as a technique to determine localization of function. Here we can but summarize certain of the most important of the principles that he produced. The principle of *mass action* states that for certain general intellectual functions, such as maze learning, it is the total amount of cerebral cortex left intact that is the major determiner of learning efficiency; and the correlated principle of *equipotentiality*, more directly relevant to the localization problem, states that within limits one area of the cerebral cortex is as important as another in helping to determine general intellectual efficiency. The research underlying these conclusions is summarized in Lashley's monograph, *Brain mechanisms and intelligence* (1929).

The extent to which Lashley was recognized by the physiologist as well as the psychologist is suggested by the tribute paid him by the neurologist Stanley Cobb, who said that in the early days at Hopkins, Lashley "fascinated us by the breadth of his interest and by his flair for ingenious and adventurous experimentation" (Beach et al., 1960, p. xvii). Cobb added (p. xviii): "During the next forty years, Lashley was to be the psychologist most frequently chosen by neurologists and psychiatrists to come to their meetings to give a paper or to discuss the papers of others." He concluded by saying (p. xx): "And so, in paying Karl Lashley our homage, we claim at least a tithe of his work for neurology!"

But it is, of course, not only for his neurological contributions that Lashley is honored in psychology. In a twin introduction to the memorial volume of Lashley's selected papers (Beach et al., 1960), E. G. Boring reviewed his systematic contributions to psychological theory. The field-theoretical flavor of Lashley's interpretations is illustrated in certain quotations selected by Boring. For example, Lashley wrote that "it is the pattern and not the localization of energy on the sense organ that determines the functional effect" (Beach et al., 1960, p. 492); and referring to brain action, that "all of the cells of the brain are constantly active and are participating, by a sort of algebraic summation, in every activity" (Beach et al., 1960, p. 500).

Lashley's field-theoretical orientation is illustrated also by his position in support of a pattern, or relational, interpretation of transposition learning rather than the S-R, or connectionistic, position. In his presidential address to the American Psychological Association in 1930, he attacked the simple connectionistic view. He later presented a novel alternative to the orthodox S-R interpretation of generalization and discrimination learning. The Lashley-Wade hypothesis is that differential training on several values of a stimulus dimension is necessary for generalization to occur, denying the fundamental S-R assumption that reinforcement of a single stimulus value produces a generalization gradient whereby similar values of the stimulus automatically gain similar but reduced potency to elicit the conditioned response. Whatever the ultimate fate of this position (see Kimble, 1961, pp. 369 ff., for a recent review of the issue), it has had a stimulating effect on research and, like many of the more orthodox gestalt and field-theoretical propositions, has offered a refreshing rethinking of some assumptions not otherwise challenged.

Apart from his systematic influence per se, Lashley made other significant contributions of an experimental and methodological sort. For the former, his long series of researches on visual discrimination and the analysis of the visual cortex (see Beach et al., 1960) are perhaps the best examples; for the latter, his invention of the jumping stand, which forces an animal such as a rat to step or leap from a platform to one of two discriminable doors, is probably the most important contribution. This new experimental device enormously facilitated discrimination learning in the rat, presumably by forcing the animal to attend more directly to the relevant visual cues. Among the many subsequent users of the device, Norman R. F. Maier should be mentioned in the present context. Not only was he responsible for the most controversial utilization of the jumping stand (1938, 1949; and see Chapter 1), he also has been a strong supporter of the field-theoretical position (e.g., Maier & Schneirla, 1935).

In conclusion, it is fitting to quote Boring's final tribute to Lashley's scientific perspicacity (Beach et al., 1960, p. xvi): "The impressive thing about the papers in this volume is the way in which discovery leads speculation, not speculation discovery." Would that this commentary could be applied to more of us!

Kantor's interbehaviorism

Jacob Robert Kantor (1888–   ) was born in Pennsylvania and educated at the University of Chicago, receiving his Ph.D. in 1917. He was an instructor in philosophy and psychology for two years at the University of Minnesota and then for three years at the University of Chicago following his obtaining the doctoral degree. In 1920, he went to teach at Indiana University and served as professor of psychology there from 1923 until his recent retirement.

Kantor has been first and foremost a logical analyst and critic of the general scientific scene, with special reference to psychology. His major concern for well over one-third of a century has been, as he put it, "smoothing the path of psychology toward its goal of natural science" (1958, p. 223). Two favorite targets have been: (1) "mental fictions" of various sorts, as represented in theoretical constructions within psychology, and (2) major tenets of physiological psychology. These and related "errors" he attributed to the widespread acceptance in our culture of the dualistic heritage and the resultant failure of many scientists to look closely at their data. He has felt that the problems produced by the dualistic heritage are especially aggravated in psychology.

On the positive side, Kantor has contributed little in the way of substantive theory. In his most recent effort (Kantor, 1958) he has offered what he calls "a formal logical system" (1958, p. ix). This effort is strictly a logical one; it was prepared, as he has noted, in order to present his ideas more efficiently and to avoid an excess of duplication from earlier works.

It is difficult to classify Kantor's system. He does not have one in the sense that Hull, or even Tolman or Lewin, had. Kantor has been above all else a metatheoretician, emphasizing a broad philosophical approach to behavior problems rather than specific solutions to such problems. He is included in the present chapter because of his stress on the psychological field and its constantly changing interactions.

The heart of Kantor's logical system is the notion of the interbehavioral field, which is an interaction between the "response functions" of the organism and the "stimulus functions" of the environment. These two basic factors must always be considered together, in Kantor's view. The properties of the interaction between organism and stimulus are largely built up in the history of the interbehavioral relation. Both biological and cultural factors need to be considered.

Except perhaps for a lessened enthusiasm for S-R psychology, Kantor's critical views have changed little throughout the course of his long career, beginning with the publication of his *Principles of psychology* in 1924. His major attention has been directed towards physiological psychology (1947), language (1952), and logic (1945–1950, 1953). Many less extensive papers by him, and by sympathetic students on whom he has had a remarkably strong and lasting influence, will be found also in the journal, *Psychological Record*. Kantor's most recent summarizing work, *Interbehavioral psychology* (1958), should be consulted by interested readers as probably the most comprehensive single source of his ideas.

Wheeler's organismic system

Raymond Holder Wheeler (1892–1961) was born in Massachusetts and educated at Clark University (Ph.D., 1915). He then taught at the University of Oregon (1915–1925). The important part of his academic career was spent at the University of Kansas (1925–1947), which under his influence became a kind of gestalt oasis in the otherwise generally behavioristic or at least functionalistic climate of the Middle West. This influence has persisted long past Wheeler's own departure from Kansas.

Wheeler developed a kind of Americanized gestalt system. His formalization, on a programmatic level at least, of basic gestalt principles was of a much greater scope than the comparable efforts made by the major German proponents, whose work tended to stay closer to the original visual perceptual demonstrations (cf. Chapter 8). Köhler had related gestalt psychological principles to physics; Wheeler attempted to relate them to biology. His particular reference was to the rapidly developing discipline of experimental embryology, where field principles found their greatest biological utility. (See Hilgard, 1948, Chap. 9, for a simplified review of these relationships as well as a thorough description of Wheeler's system and its applicability to learning and education especially.)

The dynamic laws that Wheeler laid down for his organismic or holistic system were largely centered around the basic concept of the whole. They were most simply presented in his early version (Wheeler & Perkins, 1932) and were only slightly modified later (e.g., Wheeler, 1940). These principles dealt directly with the functions of wholes and may be summarized as follows. Wholes are more than the sum of their parts; wholes determine the properties and activities of their parts; wholes evolve and function (adjusting to disturbances and responding to energy transactions) as wholes; and parts emerge from wholes rather than vice versa. One additional principle involves the law of least action: minimal energy will be expended when alternative behaviors are available to the organism.

An interesting side line in Wheeler's career was his research and speculation concerning the manifold ways in which climate affects behavior. In a literal sense, this application of a field approach to behavioral problems may be regarded as of the broadest possible scope. As a consequence of his historical research on the topic, Wheeler concluded that "a culture pattern representing all important phases of human activity was fluctuating back and forth in rhythmic fashion as a vast, complex, but integrated whole or gestalt, each detail of which was related logically with the others in so intimate and clear a manner that, knowing one of them, the others could be predicted" (1946, p. 81). In addition to his exhaustive historical and climatological research on the problem, Wheeler supervised laboratory investigations on the behavior of white-rat colonies maintained under hot, cold, and normal temperature conditions. The data from these studies are interpreted as supporting his general position (Wheeler, 1946, pp. 84–85).

Although Wheeler's organismic formulations were influential for a time, that influence has within the past decade greatly declined. A major reason for this decline is probably the strongly polemic character of their presentation and the failure of effective empirical research to follow from them. Like Tolman, Wheeler presented a large number of provocative and suggestive notions without definitive theoretical statements of the sort Hull attempted; but unlike Tolman, he was not successful in translating these into equally provocative experimental designs and empirical demonstrations.

SUMMARY AND CONCLUSIONS

Three contemporary field-theoretical views have been surveyed in this chapter. These theories generally emphasize patterns of organization at the expense of discrete connections. The differences between S-R and field theories have diminished within recent years, but the two types are still at least grossly distinguishable.

Historically, field theories are related most closely to *Gestalttheorie,* of the classic systems which we have reviewed. In terms of content they tend to be concerned with perception and cognition rather than with action. This is both a strength, in that they deal with important problems and variables often ignored by peripheralistic theorists, and a weakness, in that they are often too loosely tied to behavioral variables and too little concerned with relating perception and cognition to responses.

The first of the three field theories considered was that presented by Kurt Lewin. Lewin's contributions have included a brilliant series of experimental attacks upon motivation and personality factors and the initiation of the group-dynamics movement; theoretically, however, he is best known for his conceptionalization of life space. The second field theory considered was that of E. C. Tolman, who early espoused a molar, purposive behaviorism. His experimental and conceptual innovations leavened the behavioristic doctrine and gave cognitive psychology an experimental basis; for a time Tolman offered what seemed to be a clear contrast to Hullian, S-R doctrines. The third theory was Egon Brunswik's probabilistic functionalism, which offered alternatives to many otherwise unquestioned methodological assumptions in perception and learning.

Briefer consideration was given to Lashley's neurophysiological theory, Kantor's interbehaviorism, and Wheeler's organismic theory.

The major strength of field theory comes from the fact that it has unhesitatingly concerned itself with some critical problems which orthodox S-R theory has tended to avoid. These are in general problems concerning central functions (cf. Hebb, 1949; Miller et al., 1960) rather than peripheralistic ones, the latter having been the typical concern of the S-R theorist.

At the present time, the kind of approach to behavior problems represented by the field theorist is being increasingly supplemented by newer conceptual (e.g., the computer model of thinking) as well as experimental techniques, so that the distinction between it and other approaches is becoming more blurred. The major need in this kind of approach is to spell out more adequately the empirical referents for the central functions posited. To take one example from the present chapter, the concept of purpose, as conceived by Lewin and Tolman, is an obviously significant one in behavior; but little seems to have been done to develop anything like an adequate *experimental* attack upon it. Unfortunately, the stimulating lead initiated by Lewin, particularly in his tension-system research and conceptualization, has not as yet been fruitfully followed. When this kind of research is thoroughly developed, perhaps as a result of the amalgamation of field-theoretical and other more empirically oriented approaches, the promise implicit in the earlier field theories may well be fulfilled.

further readings

Recent volumes intended to illuminate cognitive, or field-theoretical, methodology are Kuenzli's *The phenomological problem* (1959) and Bruner et al., *Contemporary approaches to cognition* (1957).

The best introduction to Lewin is provided by his four slender books published in English. *A dynamic theory of personality* (1935) and *Principles of topological psychology* (1936) summarize the earlier, European, phase of his career. *Resolving social conflicts* (1948) and *Field theory in social science* (1951) are concerned with his later work in this country. His monograph, *The conceptual representation and measurement of psychological forces* (1938), is a more elaborate but difficult exposition of his metatheoretical position. An early critique by Leeper (1943), Estes' very critical evaluation (1954b), and two more sympathetic reviews by Deutsch (1954) and by Cartwright (1959) are among the more useful of the secondary sources on Lewin and his psychology. Tolman is well represented by his early book, *Purposive behavior in animals and men* (1932); his collected works, *Collected papers in psychology* (1951a); and his final systematic statement (1959). In addition, MacCorquodale and Meehl (1954) have provided an interesting and helpful formalization of Tolman's system. Although there is no easy road to Brunswik's thinking, the reader may be referred to his much-cited paper, "The conceptual focus of some psychological systems" (1939a); his more difficult methodological monograph, *Perception and the representative design of psychological experiments* (1956); and his two papers (1955a, b) in the symposium on probability theory. The latter, in the May 1955 issue of *Psychological Review*, contains several other important papers on the topic and should be consulted by any interested student. Brunswik's system is also intensively treated by Postman and Tolman (1959). Lashley's work is well summarized in the volume of his selected papers, *The neuropsychology of Lashley*, edited by F. A. Beach et al. (1960). Kantor's *Interbehavorial psychology* (1958) is the best introduction to his systematic thinking. Wheeler's *The science of psychology* (1940) is probably the most useful single source for his work.

varieties of personality theory 12

Personality theory is behavior theory. We have already considered two of the most important theories of personality: psychoanalytic theory and Lewinian theory. However, classic personality theory does have some general characteristics that set it apart as a subvariety of behavior theory.

Theories of personality are distinguished primarily by an attempt at completeness. Theorists in other areas of psychology may safely limit themselves, at present, to partial or full explanations of learning or motivation or perception or auditory threshold effects. In contrast, the personality theorist is faced with the task of explaining the complex behavior of the total human organism. He can ill afford to ignore any concept which seems to be functionally significant in the behavior of human beings.

Closely related to its characteristic comprehensiveness are the other marks of distinction. First, the functional nature of personality theory should be noted. Theories of personality focus upon an understanding of the development, survival, and general adjustment of the organism. Second, an emphasis on motivational ("dynamic") processes is characteristic of such theories. Third, the object of study is the whole person in his natural habitat. On this point, the study of personality clearly separates itself from the experimental tradition in psychology, which has typically advocated the study of more limited aspects of behavior. Fourth, personality theories are characteristically integrative, whereas much of psychology has moved in the direction of more specialized explanatory attempts. Fifth, personality theories frequently have rebelled against the prevailing psychological thought of the times. Certainly Freud's psychoanalytic theory offered dissenting explanatory principles at the time of its inception. More recently, Gordon Allport has persisted in advocating the basic principles he felt necessary for an adequate theory of personality even when he seemed to stand alone. The fact that much of personality theory has developed outside the main stream of academic psychology—frequently as a result of clinical observation—may account, in part, for its taking the highroad while the rest of psychology proceeded along the low road.

Thus we find in personality theories concern with variables typically left out of more limited theories. Psychoanalysis opened up the study of the unconscious determinants of behavior and offered a model of the structure of personality; Chapter 9 contains a more complete discussion of the empirical areas whose study was initiated by psychoanalysis. This and other personality theories have pointed to the need for detailed study of dynamic (motivational) variables, of individual differences, heredity, biological factors, child and developmental psychology, abnormal and social psychology, and all the interrelationships between these and other fields. Every one of this formidable array of fields plays an important role in any attempt at a complete theory of personality.

Implied in the preceding discussion of the characteristics of personality theory are both its weaknesses and its strengths. The personality theorist is faced with a dilemma composed of, on the one hand, mounting needs to predict and control human behavior and, on the other hand, a distressing scarcity of knowledge about the basic laws needed for the task. Consequently, the structure of personality theory tends to be loosely cemented for lack of sufficient cohesive material in the form of empirical observables. The major weakness of such theory, and the shortcoming at which criticism is continually leveled, is its disproportion of explanatory principles in relation to the limited amount of empirical data at hand. Similarly, personality theories frequently fail to distinguish clearly between that which they assume and that which is empirically testable. Consequently, the derivation of predictions and empirical hypotheses from these theories is severely hampered.

Personality theory may also be criticized on the basis of its self-stated criterion—completeness—when it is noted that few theories, to date, have attempted explanation of all the areas considered essential to a comprehensive theory. Table 9, adapted from Hall and Lindzey (1957, p. 548), indicates these authors' evaluation of the degree of attention paid to various factors by the theorists they review in their book. All but two theorists (Murphy and Sullivan) have shown little concern for some of the factors deemed necessary for an all-encompassing theory. Thus it may be concluded that efforts toward a *complete* description of personality have been rare.

As to other limitations, we might save a great deal of time by saying that Freud's psychoanalytic theory is in many ways the most influential theory of personality and that most of the criticisms leveled against the form of and evidence for his theory also hold for the other theories

Table 9 Dimensional comparison of theories of personality*

	Purpose	Unconscious determinants	Reward	Contiguity	Learning process	Personality structure	Heredity	Early develop-mental experience	Continuity of development	Organismic emphasis	Field emphasis	Uniqueness	Psychological environment	Self concept	Group membership determinants	Interdisciplinary emphasis Biology	Interdisciplinary emphasis Social science	Multiplicity of motives
Freud	H	H	H	M	L	H	H	H	H	M	L	M	H	M	L	H	M	L
Jung	H	H	M	L	L	H	H	M	L	H	L	M	M	M	L	H	L	M
Adler	H	M	L	L	L	M	H	H	H	M	H	H	M	H	H	M	H	L
Horney	H	H	M	L	M	M	L	M	M	M	M	M	M	H	H	L	H	L
Fromm	H	M	M	H	M	M	M	M	M	M	H	M	H	M	H	L	H	L
Sullivan	H	M	M	L	M	M	M	L	H	L	M	H	H	M	H	M	M	M
Lewin	H	L	L	M	M	H	M	L	L	H	L	L	H	M	L	L	L	H
Allport	H	L	L	L	L	H	H	L	L	H	H	M	M	M	L	H	L	H
Murray	H	H	M	L	L	H	H	L	H	L	L	L	L	L	M	H	H	H
Sheldon	L	M	M	L	L	H	H	L	M	M	L	M	L	L	L	H	L	L
Eysenck	L	L	H	L	H	L	L	M	L	H	L	L	L	L	L	M	L	H
Cattell	M	M	L	M	M	L	M	L	H	H	L	L	L	L	M	M	L	M
Miller & Dollard	L	M	L	L	M	M	H	M	M	L	M	L	H	L	L	H	H	L
Angyal	H	M	L	L	M	L	M	H	H	H	M	M	H	H	M	M	H	L
Goldstein	H	M	L	L	M	M	M	L	H	H	M	L	H	H	L	M	L	L
Rogers	H	M	L	L	M	L	L	M	M	H	M	L	H	H	M	H	L	L
Murphy	H	M	H	H	H	H	H	H	H	H	H	M	M	M	H	H	H	H

Key: H, high (emphasized); M, moderate; L, low (deemphasized).
* From Hall & Lindzey (1957, p. 548).

of personality. However, this judgment will be modified somewhat as the individual theories are discussed.

And what of the positive functions of personality theory? Curiously, its strengths often derive from the same characteristics which harbor its weaknesses. Through its rebelliousness and its attempts at integration and completeness, it has drawn attention to previously neglected problem areas. Motivation, which only recently has received widespread attention from psychologists, has long been heralded by personality theorists as basic to the understanding of behavior. In addition, personality theories have generated empirical investigation both directly and indirectly: directly, by providing a framework for research and parameters and dimensions suitable to the investigation of questions raised by theory; indirectly, by engendering either curiosity or conviction in those who encounter the personality theorists' efforts to describe the complex nature of human behavior.

S-R THEORIES

We begin our examination of personality theories with the one which is closest to a traditional behavior theory. S-R theory tries to develop a personality theory with a minimum of concepts added to its basic principles of learning and behaving.

Dollard and Miller's S-R theory. John Dollard (1900–   ) and Neal Miller (1909–   ) began their collaboration at Yale's newly formed Institute of Human Relations in the 1930s. The institute—an innovation in cooperation among the behavior sciences of psychology, psychiatry, sociology, and anthropology—provided an environment both receptive to psychoanalytic investigation and strongly influenced by Hull. Here Dollard and Miller conducted research and, with others at the institute, published *Frustration and aggression* (1939) in an attempt to apply S-R concepts to the problem of frustration. Shortly thereafter Miller and Dollard (1941) published a volume on social learning, where they provided a basic S-R framework in which complex behavior problems could be conceptualized. They subsequently explicated their joint theorizing further in *Personality and psychotherapy* (1950). Both have remained at Yale.

Aside from their joint theoretical effort, Dollard and Miller have contributed to different areas of psychology. Both received laboratory and clinical training. However, Dollard has generally shown an interest in a wider range of problems than Miller, whose work has been centered on experimental problems. Dollard received his Ph.D. in sociology at the University of Chicago and has taught both anthropology and sociology at Yale. Further training at the Berlin Psychoanalytic Institute crystallized his interest in psychoanalysis. Dollard has consistently dedicated himself to the unification of the social sciences and has published in the areas of anthropology and sociology (e.g., 1937). During World War II he conducted a psychological analysis of military behavior, published as *Fear in battle* (1943).

Miller took his Ph.D. at Yale and, shortly thereafter, became a Social Science Research Council traveling fellow. During his stay in Europe, he underwent training analysis at the Vienna Institute of Psychoanalysis. Miller directed psychological research for the Army Air Force during the war years and then returned to Yale. He is characteristically a careful experimentalist and theorist, having conducted numerous studies on drive acquisition, reinforcement, conflict, and, most recently, on the effects of drugs and physiological variables on behavior.

In their collaborative work Dollard and Miller have come closer to a complete theory of personality than have any other S-R theorists, though Guthrie (1938) and Skinner (1953a) have generalized their findings freely to the human case. Mowrer (1950) has also been interested in personality as well as in learning; however, none of these men have developed an integrated S-R personality theory as thoroughly as have Dollard and Miller.

Dollard and Miller (1950; Miller, 1959) have not found the Hullian system, upon which their personality theory is ultimately based, adequate to the task without considerable interpretation. Both authors are interested in psychoanalytic theory as well as in S-R theory, and their interpretation takes the line of a reduction of many psychoanalytic concepts to S-R terms (e.g., Miller, 1948). Their aim is to combine the assets of the two systems; they need the scope of psychoanalytic theory in order to have anything like the desired coverage of dependent and independent variables. Where in Hull does one find a discussion of neurotic guilt or anxiety? At the same time, they prefer the greater precision of statement and degree of empirical confirmation found within the confines of Hullian theory. The drawing of precise parallels between theories as different as psychoanalysis and Hullian theory is always difficult, perhaps sometimes impossible. Yet Dollard and Miller have made an attempt at integration that is stimulating and worth while, though in their system it is possible to see the outlines of two distinct subsystems.

There are systematic similarities between psychoanalysis and Hullian theory which make a partial amalgamation easier than might at first appear. A version of the law of effect is found in both. Freud speaks of maintaining a fixed tension level or reducing the tension level as a goal of the organism. Hull speaks of drive-reduction, or a reduction in the intensity of a drive stimulus, as a condition which strengthens behavior. Both formulations seem essentially the same on this point. There are also similarities in the attitude toward learning. Hull's basic learning construct, $_sH_R$, is conceived of as building up through repeated practice and staying at a high level; once $_sH_R$ builds up, it is not destroyed. If the behavior which reflected $_sH_R$ stops, it is because of opposition to it by inhibitory factors or because there is no motivation left for the behavior. This account of learning, with its assumption of the permanence of the effects of experience, is in this way much like Freud's; he also seemed to believe that early experiences left ineradicable effects, though the effects might not be easily seen because of repression, a concept which here plays the same role as Hullian inhibition.

The heart of the Dollard-Miller account is learning, or habit formation. They point out four significant features of the learning process: drive, cue, response, and reward. They give as an example a child looking for concealed candy in a room containing bookshelves. The initial *drive* is the hunger for candy; the *cues* are the instructions for playing the game plus the stimuli from the room; varied *responses* are made until the candy is found behind a book; and the response of moving the appropriate book is reinforced by finding and eating the candy *reward*. If the game continues with the candy in the same place each time, the drive gradually decreases, the significant, discriminative cues become only those helpful in making the correct response, and the response is now made more quickly and strongly. In this way *habits* are reinforced and become the basic and enduring elements of personality.

Dollard and Miller have not borrowed only the simplest concepts from Hull's (1943) theory; they have found a use for the hierarchy of responses, secondary reinforcement, the generalization gradient, and other more complex theoretical notions. They have also shown great ingenuity in relating complex concepts to simpler ones, thereby "explaining" what is involved. Their attempt to handle the problems of symbolic behavior is particularly valuable.

One of the contributions which Dollard and Miller have made, then, is the integration of two originally separate—if not opposed—theories in such a way that it becomes reasonable to apply the results of laboratory investigations with animals to practical human problems. Though Hull intended his theory to have such applications, he never personally took time to show how they could be made. Two such human problems which Dollard and Miller have treated are fear and conflict.

Fear in the neurotic human being may seem an irrational thing. Dollard and Miller, however, believe that this irrationality is a matter of appearance only; we as observers of irrational human behavior arrive upon the scene too late to observe the development of the fear, and we often do not know enough of the laws that determine the learning and spread of fear. Consider, in an analogous situation, a rat placed in a white box and shocked. If he is allowed to escape through a door to a black box, he will quickly learn to fear the white one. Furthermore, he will continue to respond in order to escape the white box even when there is no longer any shock present. The fear may even spread (generalize) to similar boxes. If we had not observed the learning process but only the fearful animal in a harmless white box, we should consider his fear irrational. Similarly, if we did not understand the process of generalization, we should consider fear of a *light gray* box irrational even if we had observed the process.

Dollard and Miller have given an equally stimulating account of the nature of conflict. Their analytic approach involves at least five assumptions derived from theory or from empirical observations. They assume that: (1) the tendency to approach a goal increases as the distance to the goal decreases; (2) the tendency to avoid a negative stimulus (punishment) increases as the distance to it decreases; (3) the gradient for negative stimuli is steeper than the gradient for positive stimuli; (4) changes in drive increase or decrease the *level* (not the slope) of the appropriate gradients; (5) if two responses (say, approach and avoidance) compete at any point, the one associated with the stronger tendency will occur. Empirical studies of this model have typically involved white rats, shock, food, and a spatial scale, but the model has been freely applied to quite different situations, such as bachelors contemplating marriage. Summaries of experimental research on this problem have been provided by Miller (1944, 1959).

This short sketch should be enough to indicate that the original contribution of Dollard and Miller shares the strengths and weaknesses of S-R theory more than of psychoanalytic theory. Their approach tends more toward analysis and the application of laboratory principles to human behavior. They take Hullian theory as the methodological model; psychoanalytic theory is used because it is based on the content, the observations, they wish to explain. Dollard and Miller seem to be molding psychoanalytic *content* into S-R *form*. In doing so, it may be argued, they incorporate the elementaristic weakness of S-R theory. Their "personalities" become bundles of habits without the consistency and purposefulness which most other personality theorists see as guiding human behavior. In choosing a theory which treats learning much more thoroughly than other determinants of behavior, Dollard and Miller take a more environmentalistic position than many theorists think is justifiable.

In spite of these criticisms, the Dollard-Miller theory may well turn out to be of great importance in the history of the development of personality theory. If personality theory is to be a complete theory of human behavior as opposed to the partial theories found in other branches of psychology, it follows that the ultimate task of the personality theorist is to tie together all part theories into the one grand theory of personality. Psychoanalysis, despite its patent weaknesses, is perhaps the grandest extant theory; S-R reinforcement learning theory is one of the tightest subtheories, and Dollard and Miller have tried to combine it with psychoanalytic theory. Though none can expect that psychoanalytic theory will determine the shape of personality theory as it will exist in a hundred years or that Hullian theory will do this for learning theory, Dollard and Miller have indicated the nature of the synthesizing task.

TRAIT AND FACTOR THEORIES

In addition to comprehensiveness, personality theories have another characteristic which generally sets them apart from other theories of behavior: nearly all personality theories have within them a concept which serves to explain and emphasize the *consistency* of behavior per se. Nonpersonality theories typically predict such consistency only in so far as there is consistency of circumstances; that is, the same response should be observed only if the external stimuli are the same, or are equivalent because experiences with each were the same, or are related closely enough via generalization to produce the same response. Obviously the "ors" in the preceding sentence give the S-R theorist enough latitude to predict some consistency of behavior; but most personality theorists have not been content with this.

Two general classes of personality theory, not ordinarily categorized together, are alike in that they both give primary attention to the problem of consistency in behavior, albeit in markedly different ways. These are the trait theories, best exemplified by the views of G. W. Allport, and the factor theories, shown by the work of Eysenck and Cattell.

The trait theorist believes that the job of the personality theorist is to isolate and describe certain properties of the individual which underlie and determine overt behavior, thereby giving the individual's behavior a consistent, integrated direction. These properties are called traits, and the traits may be very general, influencing all or nearly all the individual's behavior, or very specific, in which case only behavior in certain kinds of situations is influenced by the trait.

The factor theorist derives concepts (factors) from a statistical analysis of consistency observed in test performance. Like traits, factors may be general or specific, though the nature of their derivation makes them usually less all-encompassing than a general trait.

Allport's trait theory. Gordon Willard Allport (1897–   ) was educated in a variety of fields and has continued his interest in many of them. He received his A.B. at Harvard in economics, taught sociology and English in Istanbul, returned to Harvard for his Ph.D., and subsequently studied at three European universities—Berlin, Hamburg, and Cambridge. While in Europe Allport developed his persisting interest in international affairs. As a by-product of his stay abroad, he became one of the major interpreters of German psychology in the United States.

Allport has taught in the department of social ethics at Harvard, at Dartmouth, and presently is at Harvard in the department of social relations, which he helped to form.

In the area of test construction, Allport collaborated with his brother, Floyd, in the development of the *A-S reaction study* (1928) and with Vernon to produce *A study of values* (1931).

Allport's publications reflect his diversity of interests and his recognition of the complexity and uniqueness of human behavior. A former editor of the *Journal of Abnormal and Social Psychology*, Allport has written on subjects ranging from *The individual and his religion* (1950a) to *The psychology of radio* (Allport & Cantril, 1935). His major works in the area of personality theory are *Personality: A psychological interpretation* (1937), *The nature of personality* (1950b), *Becoming* (1955), and *Personality and social encounter* (1960).

Allport recognizes that there are many factors which determine behavior. These form a hierarchy from most specific to most general, as follows: conditioned reflex, habit, attitude, trait, self, and personality. Allport believes that the level most profitable for the personality theorist to study is probably the trait, whose best-known definition was given by Allport (1937, p. 295): "a generalized and focalized neuropsychic system (peculiar to the individual), with the capacity to render many stimuli functionally equivalent, and to initiate and guide consistent (equivalent) forms of adaptive and expressive behavior."

This comprehensive definition points out clearly the role of the trait as a determiner of consistency in behavior and reveals Allport's emphasis on individuality as well as his interest in adaptive and expressive behavior. His studies of expressive behavior (Allport & Vernon, 1933) have afforded evidence for consistency; they also indicate his interest in idiographic rather than nomothetic investigation. Idiographic studies lead to intensive study of individuals. Nomothetic investigation is concerned with lawful regularities in the "typical" individual, and Allport believes that such studies tend to overlook significant features of behavior. Expressive behavior is that aspect of behavior which is related to an individual's own style of behaving rather than to the function of the behavior in adaptation; for example, two individuals writing or saying the same words in response to a question may do so in quite different ways, their individual ways expressing their own personalities.

Allport and Vernon studied the expressive aspects of several types of behavior, obtaining thirty-eight measures. They determined that there was satisfactory reliability for the measures when the behavior was repeated and when the same behavior was measured from different muscle groups. Then they examined the intercorrelations of their thirty-eight measures to see if a few general traits or factors might account for the observed intercorrelations. They concluded that three general factors were indicated by the data: one was a kind of motor expansiveness indicated chiefly by the extensiveness of responses such as writing; a second was called the "centrifugal group factor," related to distance from the individual's center and having to do with outward tendency and extroversion; the third had to do with emphasis, as indicated by gestures while speaking, writing pressure, and so on.

Typically, Allport did not rest content with the group aspect of the study. He and Vernon then proceeded to an intensive study of four individuals and concluded that the expressive measures were quite congruent with the subjective estimates of personality study. This part of the study is typical of both the strength and the weakness of Allport's approach; the results are suggestive and provocative yet somewhat unconvincing because of their subjectivity and the lack of specific predictions.

There are several aspects of Allport's psychology which deserve comment, aside from his definition and study of traits. Allport has emphasized the complexity and individuality of behavior, together with the multiplicity of its determinants. Accordingly, he has not been attracted by the aseptic laboratory studies which some others have used in the construction of their theories of personality. For one thing, the apparently pure laws so derived are based on nomothetic studies indicating only group trends (see Beck, 1953; Eysenck, 1954; and Falk, 1956, for a discussion of the idiographic-nomothetic issue). Allport does not believe that we can ever understand individual behavior via the application of laws which do not in themselves accurately describe the behavior of any individual. Furthermore, the complex interrelations between behavioral determinants are not reflected in laboratory experimentation.

Psychoanalytic theory made it fashionable to emphasize past experiences and unconscious influences in the determination of behavior. Allport provided a needed antidote by pointing out the necessity for determination of present behavior by present influences and by insisting that, in normal people at least, conscious influences on behavior are far more powerful than unconscious ones. It follows that the verbal report of an individual on the reasons for his behavior is likely to be the best single source of information about those reasons. In addition, the conscious *intentions* of an individual provide a better indication of how he will behave than any searching into the past (see especially Allport, 1955).

Allport's ideas on the functional *autonomy* of motives (Allport, 1937) have inspired more criticism than any other single one of his ideas. Behavior, according to this view, may persist independently of the motive originally responsible for its occurrence. No other biological or primary motive need replace the original one; the behavior, once it has become functionally autonomous, may be engaged in for its own sake only. The old track star who in college ran for adulation or for pay may continue to run years afterward when there is no motive, external to the behavior itself, for continuing.

It is easy to see that such a concept invites critical attack. Allport cannot be saying that all behavior becomes functionally autonomous, or extinction could never be observed. He should then give an account of why some behaviors or motives become autonomous and some do not. He has never spelled out the details of this account to the satisfaction of his critics, who tend to explain the behavior Allport calls autonomous by recourse to concepts like prolonged resistance to extinction, generalization, or substitutability of motives. At the very least, however, Allport has drawn attention to the necessity for giving a contemporary account of the dynamics of any given behavior; one cannot rely on an account of the motives active when the behavior was originally acquired.

We have pointed out ways in which Allport sometimes opposed prevailing opinion. Yet in many ways Allport's theory is a prototype of most personality theory. He emphasizes structure and hierarchic arrangement of personality. He stresses the complexity and individuality of personality and the multiple determination of behavior. He opposes laboratory methods and nomothetic studies, preferring some looseness of conceptualization to oversimplification. For the tough-minded, these are serious defects; for the more tender-minded, the same attitudes are sources of inspiration and wisdom.

Factor theories. Factor theories are conceptually related to Allport's trait theory though historically more closely related to a statistical technique called factor analysis (Spearman, 1931). The search of the factor analyst leads to something which accounts for an observed consistency of behavior, that is, a something much like Allport's traits. The rigor of the method of search, however, tends to set factor theory apart from trait theory and give it a kinship in spirit with S-R theories, though the two proceed toward the goal of precision via very different paths (Cattell, 1959).

Factor theories are more closely related to a particular method of study than are other personality theories. To understand them we must know something of the reasoning behind factor analysis as a statistical technique. In order to make the discussion concrete, we shall relate factor analysis to the study of intelligence, the context in which factor analysis actually developed.

We may look at the problem in this way. Say we have observed, in a gross way, that some people consistently stand higher than others on some loosely defined dimension which we shall call intelligence. We understand little about either the dimension or the reasons for individual variations in amount of intelligence. Assume now that we are able to agree on a large number of measures of behavior which are related to this gross intelligence dimension. We can now obtain measures from each of a large number of people and correlate every measure with every other measure. If all tests are positively related to some degree, it is clear that some general factor must play some role in determining all the test scores. If groups of the tests have a positive relationship which is larger than the one attributable to the general factor alone, there is a group factor present which underlies performance on these groups of related tests. The remaining variation in test scores is attributable to factors specific to the individual or to the circumstances surrounding the administration of the test. Burt (1941) has given a full description of these various types of factors.

There are generally several ways in which the tests can be associated so that mathematically reasonable factors can be isolated. In selecting a single one from the several available factor accounts of the observed correlations, a decision must be based upon some variety of psychological acumen.

Once the factors have been determined, the measures, or tests, can be looked at again. For an individual measure, we can ask how much its value has been determined by the general factor, how much by each of the group factors involved, and how much by specific and error factors. The pattern of determination for the measure is called the factor loading, or saturation, of the measure.

Finally, we can reexamine the gross concept, intelligence, and answer questions about its composition, its nature, and its usefulness as a concept. The outcome of the factor analysis will have suggested new ways to test intelligence and to conceive of intelligence; it may at this stage appear that intelligence is not what we thought it was or that our measures were not good measures of that which we wish to continue to call intelligence.

Although our discussion has been concerned with the more or less orthodox type of factor analysis, in which scores from many individuals are analyzed, there is also a somewhat different type of factor analysis which stresses the responses of a single individual and subjects them to an intensive analysis. Stephenson (1953, 1961) has pioneered in the use of this technique, called the Q sort, which he feels gives proper emphasis to the study of the self, or the unique attitudinal organization of an individual person. The subject is required to make judgments concerning himself and others in a wide variety of situations to provide data for the factor analysis.

At this point it should be clear that factor analysis is a complex, sophisticated, and fascinating method for the study of multiple variables. As such, it is clearly applicable to the study of personality. But it, like any other method in any science, is no substitute for ingenuity and insight. It will not produce hypotheses or interpretations. Furthermore, it is important to remember that the results of a factor analysis can be no better than the data that are fed into it (see Anastasi, 1958, pp. 335 ff., for a simple, well-reasoned discussion of this problem).

Eysenck's factor theory. Hans Jurgen Eysenck (1916–　), a German by birth, left his homeland during the rise of Nazis and has spent most of his life in England. After taking his Ph.D. at the University of London, Eysenck served as a hospital psychologist during World War II. He then returned to the University of London and became director of the psychological department at the Institute of Psychiatry, where he conducted research in institute hospitals. Eysenck is presently associated with the University of London and serves as senior psychologist at two hospitals. During visits to the United States, he has taught briefly at the universities of Pennsylvania and California.

Eysenck's contributions to personality theory are exemplified by *Dimensions of personality* (1947), *The scientific study of personality* (1952), *The structure of human personality* (1953a), *The dynamics of anxiety and hysteria* (1957), and his editorship of the recent comprehensive *Handbook of abnormal psychology* (1961). In addition to research in the areas of clinical psychology and personality, he has studied aesthetics, attitudes, and humor. Eysenck's publications, too, have strayed from his major field of interest into *The psychology of politics* (1954) and the *Uses and abuses of psychology* (1953b).

As an outstanding contemporary factor theorist, Eysenck tends to be tough-minded and operational in approach. He puts little credence in the dimensions of personality which have been initiated from outside the framework of quantitative method. At the same time, he recognizes the usefulness of the clinical approach at the present primitive stage of personality theorizing, when we do not yet know exactly what we should be measuring.

The basic structure of Eysenck's theory is not unlike that of Allport's. He too recognizes a hierarchic arrangement of consistencies from least to most: the specific response, the habitual response, the trait, and the type. The trait is an observed consistency of action-tendencies, while the type is a constellation of traits. Most of Eysenck's interest is directed to the types, though much of his research is necessarily concerned with traits; one cannot constellate regularities in behavior without first discovering them. Eysenck, with his operational orientation, does not accept traits unless they have been operationally validated.

In Eysenck's early research on 700 neurotic soldiers (Eysenck, 1947) he uncovered two fundamental underlying variables, or typal polarities: introversion-extraversion and neuroticism. The first of these is recognized by Eysenck as almost exactly the introversion-extraversion earlier proposed by Jung as a basic personality dimension. It is different chiefly because it was extracted by Eysenck from the intercorrelations of a large number of ratings and classifications available on a large number of people. A major result of this study was that the neurotic type was found to be inferior in nearly every respect: intellectually, physically, emotionally, and especially with respect to the ability to sustain motivation.

Personality for Eysenck is divided, in the classic British tradition, into areas or sectors: the cognitive or intellectual, the conative, the affective, and the somatic. For the first three of these areas Eysenck is willing to suggest underlying general factors. For the first, of course, it is intelligence. Neuroticism is, in a sense, a conative or character defect, since it represents an inability to persist in the face of obstacles. Intraversion-extraversion is a general factor in the affective area.

More recently (1952) in a study of normal subjects and hospitalized mental patients. Eysenck discovered a third type, psychoticism. Somehow this does not seem surprising. Psychotics, like neurotics, tended to do more poorly than normals, though by no means on all tests. They were distinguished from normals and neurotics by a number of specific behavioral deficiencies.

Eysenck has made a methodological contribution which promises to be important. It is called the method of criterion analysis (1950). The method is simply a stipulation that the factor analyst should begin with two groups which are known to differ on some hypothesized underlying factor. Eysenck's normal and psychotic subjects would provide an example. When the measures are obtained from the two groups, only those which discriminate between the groups can justifiably be assumed to relate to the hypothesized factor. If Eysenck's criterion analysis is used, it ensures that the investigator must plan the investigation carefully in advance; he cannot simply administer a haphazard truckload of tests to a randomly selected flock of subjects and let the factors fall where they may.

Eysenck has been an extremely controversial figure. Serious questions have been raised concerning both the empirical and the theoretical aspects of his research. It has been frequently noted that the evidence for his assertions is typically meager; he has also been criticized for overlooking alternative interpretations of his data in the absence of adequate controls to eliminate such factors (e.g., cf. Jensen, 1958, p. 300).

Nevertheless, Eysenck's influence on personality theory has been substantial, and his research looks very promising. He has tended to toughen thinking without eliminating valuable methods of observation. He has applied quantitative methods to the data of the clinic; this has been one of the crying needs of personality research. He has been quite as willing to eliminate a concept as to accept it; yet he is not at all antitheoretical. If these techniques succeed in further integration of the relatively fragmentary factors thus far isolated and tested, they will have made a most significant contribution to personality theory.

Cattell's factor theory. Raymond Bernard Cattell (1905–   ) was born, educated, and recognized as a leader in the field of personality research in England before coming to the United States. Cattell took his Ph.D. at the University of London and held both academic and clinical positions at that institution in close succession. His later career has been characterized by broad interests, encompassing both of these areas of psychology.

In the United States, Cattell has taught at Columbia Teachers College, Clark University, Harvard, and the University of Illinois, where he is now a research professor. His major work is *Personality and motivation structure and measurement* (1957). It contains a variety of objective measures of motivation and interest, the use of which in factor analysis supplements the older questionnaire materials. In addition to his work in personality theory, Cattell has published in the areas of measurement (1936) and experimental and social psychology (1952). Cattell has also authored three widely used tests: *The culture free test of intelligence* (1944), *The O-A personality test battery* (1954), and *The 16 personality factor questionnaire* (1950).

Like Eysenck, Cattell is intellectually indebted to the factor analysts. His general personality theory shows similarities to McDougall's, whereas his developmental theory is markedly Freudian. *Description and measurement of personality* (1946) and *Personality* (1950) contain the major tenets of Cattell's personality theory.

Cattell combines the qualities of tough-minded factor theorists like Eysenck with the qualities of more traditional personality theorists who stress comprehensiveness. His theory is therefore at once extensive and, in part, quantitative in emphasis and content. Eysenck has a far stronger tendency to limit himself to concepts derived from factor studies; Cattell sometimes allows himself more range in order to make his theory inclusive and to avoid ignoring data from other sources.

Cattell has defined personality as "that which permits a prediction of what a person will do in a given situation" (1950, p. 2). This definition is consistent with our contention that a theory of personality is really identical with a general theory of behavior, for Cattell's definition would fit theories of behavior.

Traits are Cattell's basic elements of personality. He explicitly recognizes that traits are concepts used to explain observed consistencies of behavior and agrees with Allport and Eysenck that there are many levels of generality of traits, some applying only to particular individuals or circumstances, others applying to very large groups. He has been mostly concerned, however, with the intraindividual organization of traits.

The chief distinction made by Cattell is between *surface traits* and *source traits*. The former are simply based on observed behaviors that occur together, while the latter underlie the surface traits, determining observed behavior consistencies through particular combinations. There is a rough correspondence between Eysenck's trait and Cattell's surface trait, and Eysenck's type and Cattell's source trait. The latter pair is in both cases more stable and more general, and both investigators have concentrated their interest more intensively upon such general factors.

Cattell also recognizes two kinds of traits according to their origins: constitutional and environmental-mold traits. He has performed some ingenious research in an attempt to discover to what extent traits are determined via these two influences. For example, in one study (Cattell et al., 1955) a personality test was administered to identical twins, to fraternal twins, to siblings reared together and apart, and to unrelated subjects. The test measured traits established as significant personality factors in earlier factor studies. Study of the results from subjects who thus differed to varying degrees in both hereditary and environmental similarity allowed the investigators partially to evaluate the relative contributions of heredity and environment to the factors studied. Such research is noteworthy within the personality area for its logical consistency and coordination with earlier research as well as for its ingenuity.

Cattell differentiates between source traits on the basis of their origins. The *erg* is a dynamic source trait with a constitutional origin; the *metaerg* is identical except for its environmental origin. Both determine patterns of behavior because they consist of motivational predispositions toward environmental objects. Metaergs are further subdivided into attitudes, interests, and sentiments. Sentiments are the most stable class.

The most powerful sentiment of all is the self sentiment. Cattell, like other personality theorists, introduces the self to explain the consistency that seems to suffuse all the behavior of an individual. Thus the self sentiment acts on all other sentiments and may strengthen or inhibit the tendency to action aroused by other sentiments. There are two selves, the real and the ideal. These have their obvious meaning, the former being the most realistic estimate an individual could make of himself, and the latter the individual as he would ideally like to be.

The development of personality depends upon the evolution of ergs and metaergs and the organization of the self through the process of learning. Cattell accepts both contiguity and reinforcement as principles of learning. Learning is conceived of as occurring via a series of stages, each involving alternative outcomes called *crossroads* by Cattell.

The framework within which personality development takes place is the social context. Cattell has turned his talents to the description of this context as well as to the description of personality. The dimensions of social institutions combine to form an analog to individual personality, the *syntality* of the institution. In several studies (e.g., Cattell & Wispe, 1948; Cattell, 1949) he has found factors which he believes are useful for the description of families and nations. The use of a variety of measures to derive social factors is still another example of Cattell's originality and enterprise.

Allport, Eysenck, and Cattell have developed theories which have considerable logical similarity. All three men are alike in their vigor and iconoclastic tendencies—traits which psychology presently needs, especially in personality theory. Allport is very different from the other two in attitude and in method of study, having little sympathy for factor analysis or for the massive experiment. Eysenck and Cattell have shown unusual aptitude for originating experimental designs that wed quantitative methods to the study of personality. Their theories promise a long and happy marriage.

ORGANISMIC THEORIES

Many personality theorists start from a point of view systematically close to that of the gestalt psychologists. Murphy, Rogers, Goldstein, Angyal, Maslow, Lecky, Murray, and Sheldon are members of this class. Any or all of these men might be included as organismic theorists. The decision must be based on the extent to which a holistic, gestalt orientation toward the individual is a *central* feature of their personality theories. Quite arbitrarily, we are choosing Goldstein and Sheldon as organismic theorists and omitting the rest or treating them in a separate section. The choice of Goldstein needs no justification; Sheldon would often be put in another class because the really central feature of his theory is his preoccupation with constitutional influences on personality; he does, however, espouse a general organismic point of view, and his interest in organic effects qualifies him as an organismic theorist in the popular meaning of the word.

Goldstein's holistic theory. Kurt Goldstein (1878–   ) established his reputation as a neuropsychiatrist in Europe before coming to this country in 1935. Having received his medical degree from the

University of Breslau, he associated himself with the Psychiatric Hospital at Königsberg. At an early age, Goldstein became a professor of neurology and psychiatry and director of the Neurological Institute at the University of Frankfurt. He later held a similar position at the University of Berlin.

During World War I, Goldstein conducted the fundamental studies of brain-injured soldiers which laid the groundwork for his organismic theory (1942) and his most significant publication, *The organism* (1939).

In the United States, Goldstein has held academic and clinical positions in a variety of institutions in addition to maintaining a private neuropsychiatry and psychotherapy practice in New York City for many years. He delivered the William James Lectures at Harvard, discussing human nature in the light of psychopathology (1940), and has been associated with the New York Psychiatric Institute, Tufts Medical School in Boston, Columbia University, Brandeis University, City College of New York, and the New School for Social Research.

Aside from his theoretical and clinical work, Goldstein has published works on language disturbances (1948) and, with Gelb (1920), on the gestalt problem of figure-ground relationships (although Goldstein has disclaimed any ties with gestalt psychology).

To Goldstein, a primary feature of organisms is their organization. In behavior as in perception, processes are organized into figure and ground. The figure is the principal and outstanding feature of the ongoing activity, just as a perceptual figure stands out from its ground (cf. Chapter 8). In an organism's behavior, those features which are related to the strongest drives stand out.

The normal organism is structured but flexible, capable of tailoring its behavior to fit the needs of the ongoing stimulus situation. Its behavior can be understood only as part of an organic unity; the significance of its behavior can be assessed only as a contribution to the ongoing goal of the organism.

For Goldstein, the goal of the organism is unitary. It is self-actualization. Self-actualization sums up all the needs of the organism. A sexually driven organism actualizes itself in coitus, a hungry one in eating; but the self-actualization of the complex human adult is expressed in many less organically driven acts.

Goldstein believes that the strongly organized organism is capable of choosing a favorable environment or manipulating an unfavorable one to some extent. It is thus not the victim of blind forces or the pawn of fortuitous stimulus situations. But no organism is insulated from environmental effects; it must thus come to terms with its environment. Only through accepting those terms of the environment which cannot be avoided or changed can the organism continue in its attempt to actualize itself.

Organismic theorists tend to avoid analysis; Goldstein is no exception. If it is necessary to study every behavioral event within the context of the whole organism, it is tempting to stay on the level of generality without coming to terms with the problem of specificity of
prediction. In this Goldstein is again no exception. His central concept, self-actualization, leaves one uncertain of the defining characteristics of such behavior and wondering if there is much behavior
which is not in some sense self-actualizing. Does this concept say
very much more than that an organism will do what it will do, and
that, if it does it, we assume that it needed to do it in order to actualize itself?

It is interesting that brain-injured patients and their symptoms led
Goldstein to his holistic point of view. He found that the behavior
manifested by a patient with a brain injury could be understood only
by an examination of the whole matrix of the patient's behavior. What
at first appeared to be a direct result of injury might, upon closer examination, turn out to be a quite indirect reaction stemming from an
attempt to fit the results of injury into the mosaic of life. The same
physical injury might lead to a variety of behavior syndromes, depending upon the patient's circumstances and personality structure.
In general, a specific deterioration in some ability would lead a patient to be generally more sensitive, less self-confident, and more with-
drawing; if one did not know this, he might uncritically attribute
various performance decrements to direct results of injury rather than
to these indirect manifestations.

With his background of clinical experience, it is natural that Goldstein should prefer the intensive study of the individual to the group
approach. Through this approach, Goldstein made his best-known
discovery: the most characteristic difference between patients with
extensive brain injury and normal individuals is that the former have
lost the abstract attitude. Their ability to do concrete things and to
react to concrete situations may be relatively unimpaired, but their
ability to abstract is likely to be extremely limited. For example, the
brain-injured patient may be unable to make statements that are obviously contrary to fact, such as "the moon is green." He cannot abstract common properties of dissimilar objects, such as a radio and a
newspaper. This lack of abstract ability permeates his behavior. Goldstein and Scheerer (1941, 1953) have developed tests to determine
the extent to which abstract behavior is impaired; these tests therefore help to diagnose brain damage.

Goldstein is an example of an organismic theorist at his observational, clinical best. He is self-consciously antiexperimental, sharing
the organismic belief that by thus restricting conditions and controlling behavior we lose the significance which the activity might have in
its natural context. But Goldstein has been shrewd and industrious in

taking advantage of the wealth of material which paraded before him in his psychiatric practice. Methodologically, he has added few innovations to the organismic view, which has said in essence: "Take gestalt principles from the study of perception and apply them to the study of the whole individual."

Sheldon's typology.   William H. Sheldon (1899–   ) is a trained physician, as his theoretical efforts to relate behavioral and body components might indicate. After receiving both his Ph.D. and M.D. from the University of Chicago, he interned at a children's hospital. Sheldon taught at the University of Chicago, Northwestern University, and the University of Wisconsin before continuing his studies with two years of psychiatric training abroad. His visits with Jung, Freud, and Kretschmer contributed directly to his later theorizing, which owes most to constitutional theorists such as Kretschmer and Viola but also shows resemblances to Freudian, and particularly Jungian, theory.

At Harvard, Sheldon entered into a collaborative relationship with experimentalist S. S. Stevens, who brought to Sheldon's work a new sophistication in procedure and measurement. Together they published the basic works in constitutional psychology: *The varieties of temperament* (1942) and *The varieties of human physique* (1940).

Sheldon's writing has been characterized by concern for the identification of and relationships between structural and temperamental factors, particularly as applied to the problem of delinquency (1949). He has recently written a somatotyping guide, *Atlas of men* (1954), and is working on similar volumes for women and children. Always the taxonomist, Sheldon ventured away from personality theory temporarily, only to produce *Early American cents* (1949)—a classification of coins!

Sheldon's road has not been an easy one. American psychology generally has been unfriendly to the idea that constitutional factors are important influences on behavior. Our democratic ideals and, more specifically, the extreme environmentalism of John B. Watson, have made us unwilling to believe that innate predispositions really have a directive influence on our personality.

Despite this resistance, it has remained obvious to the man in the street that there are associations between constitutional factors and personality. To him, the fat man appears jolly; the skinny kid with glasses remains a withdrawn bookworm. It is not surprising, then, that the man who reinforced these long-held popular beliefs is one of the better-known theorists.

Sheldon is also well known to the beginning psychology student, perhaps because he stands out among the personality theorists as a man who has said something comprehensible to the beginning student. Regrettably, Sheldon has sometimes been presented as having made ludicrous or incautious statements. He may have advocated something unpopular or capable of misinterpretation, but not something ludicrous.

Sheldon's system is a modern version of statements running back at least as far as Hippocrates, who believed that there were associations between body fluids and temperaments and that there were two basic types of physique, short and fat or long and thin. Ernst Kretschmer, many years later, added a third body type—the muscular—between the two extremes and designated them as follows: pyknic—short and squatty; athletic—broad and muscular; and asthenic—tall and thin. He studied then the relationship between these three types and the varieties of psychoses.

Sheldon's contributions have been primarily an elaboration and tightening of Kretchmer's basic physical types and further empirical work in relating these types to behavioral variables. An important difference exists between his work and earlier theorizing, such as Kretschmer's. Sheldon has recognized that any given individual is marked by some degree of each type and thus is in this sense always a blend of types rather than a pure type.

Sheldon's attempt to establish a constitutional interrelationship between behavior and body build is anchored in the belief that the outward physical appearance (phenotype) is determined and guided by a hypothetical biological process (morphogenotype). Measurement of the physique is utilized by Sheldon in an attempt to evaluate indirectly the function of the morphogenotype. The obtained data fall into three categories of body types: endomorphy, mesomorphy, and ectomorphy.

This trichotomy was determined by evaluating 4,000 standardized photographs taken from three angles—front, back, and side. These were sectioned into seventeen parts (Sheldon, 1940, p. 55) from which anthropometric measurements could be obtained. Sheldon is thus unique among personality theorists in being able to work with variables that can be, and have been, measured with a ruler. After analyzing the data, Sheldon concluded that all the physical characteristics could be grouped into three components according to the presumed embryonic origin of most of the individual's tissue in the outer (ectomorphic), middle (mesomorphic), or inner (endomorphic) layer.

The endomorph tends to be soft, fleshy, and round; the mesomorph is square, tough, muscular, dense, and athletic; the ectomorph is tall, thin, fragile, and small boned. The endomorph is massive in relation to his surface area; the mesomorph, intermediate; and the ectomorph, more exposed to the world because of his high proportion of surface area to mass.

Besides the primary components of body type there are several which are classified as secondary. These are dysplasia (disharmony between the body parts), gynandromorphy (bisexuality denoted by the physique), and texture (as of hairiness of the body) (1940, p. 7).

Three components of temperament correspond, according to Sheldon, to the three components of the physique: visceratonia, somatotonia, and cerebrotonia. The visceratonic individual loves comfort, food, and affection, and is good natured. The somatotonic person is active, vigorous, and aggressive. The cerebrotonic individual is a bookish, sensitive, shy individual who withdraws from social contacts.

If we assume that there are such identifiable components of constitution and of personality, are the two related or not? Sheldon (1942, p. 400) found a remarkably high correlation between the components that one would expect to find associated: endomorphy-visceratonia; mesomorphy-somatotonia; and ectomorphy-cerebrotonia. These correlations are all about .80! Personality theorists seldom find their expectations so gratifyingly corroborated.

It is easy to be dubious about Sheldon's components of personality, since they seem so close to the layman's stereotypes, until one discovers that the clusters of traits were derived from careful correlational studies using a large number of original traits rather than from the depths of the armchair (Sheldon, 1944, pp. 526–549). Sheldon's components of personality are each defined by twenty related traits (Sheldon, 1942, p. 26).

Sheldon seems to be on safe ground when he maintains that, descriptively, the postulated correlations exist. However, other experimental findings have tended to substantiate the fact that positive correlations do exist but at a significantly lower level (Child, 1950; Sanford, 1953; Seltzer et al., 1948). The seemingly spurious correlations between temperament and physique could be attributed to a "halo effect" since both sets of ratings were done by the same person; that is, there was no attempt at blind analysis. Although in *The varieties of temperament* (1942, pp. 411–425) Sheldon made an effort to justify his position, his attempt in no way negates the possibility that a subjective bias may have contaminated the results. The procedure, despite the possibility of subjectivism, remained unaltered.

An additional criticism has been made by Lubin (1950), who discovered that some of the coefficients found in the tables of intercorrelation among the temperamental traits (Sheldon, 1942, pp. 506–511) are not mathematically possible.

Sheldon has also been attacked on the grounds that he assumes that genetic, strictly biological factors account for the observed correlations. If Sheldon really maintained that these direct biological influences were *the* reason for the correlations, he would be open to attack. He does not; he recognizes, as do his detractors, that different cultural expectations or differential rewards related to different body builds might account for the observed personality differences. For example, a boy who is muscular by nature probably finds more reward in athletics than an endomorphic type. The rewards of sport would then increase both active competitive behavior and the accumulation of muscle tissue. Sheldon admits that, although the morphogenotype is invariant, the phenotype (from which measurements are taken) does fluctuate because of cultural and other influences. This admission forces him to relinquish partially his grasp on his basic theoretical relationship between the constitution and temperament. He says that the crucial relationship is between the morphogenotype and the temperament. The phenotype is only an attempt to measure the morphogenotype; this measurement is the best we have to date despite its inexactness. It seems to the present authors that operational criteria are highly applicable to this issue. Operationally, the morphogenotype has no meaning not exhausted by the measures of phenotype. The notion of morphogenotype may be lent *credibility* by analogy with other genetic characteristics, but no genetic observations directly justify the theoretical use of the morphogenotype. Therefore, we suggest, on grounds of parsimony, that the stated relationships be restricted to those holding between observed properties.

Sheldon is less willing to recognize the possibility that exclusively environmental factors, such as diet, might explain the observed relationship. However, Anastasi has pointed out that "habitual overeating does lead to the accumulation of fat tissue. It is interesting to note in this connection that recent literature in abnormal psychology as well as in psychosomatic medicine contains many references to 'psychological overeating' resulting from frustration and other emotional problems" (1958, p. 182).

Anastasi has also stated that "the original identification of the three temperamental components . . . can likewise be questioned because of inadequacy of data" (1958, p. 177). That is, in the original study there were only thirty-three male college subjects, and although further attempts were made to revise the original twenty-two traits, the procedure for doing so was clearly dependent upon the original study and its results.

A major asset of Sheldon's theory is that it has kept public the fact that there is some type of relationship between physique and temperament; at the present time, however, we cannot ascertain its direction. Does the physique direct the temperament, or does the temperament determine the physique, or, more logically, is it a two-way process whose exact interrelations have not yet been ferreted out?

NEOANALYTIC PERSONALITY THEORIES

There are several closely related theories of personality that owe a great deal to psychoanalytic theory. Though they are by no means identical, their similarity of background and emphasis justifies their treatment under a single heading. The term neoanalytic is used to reflect their basic psychoanalytic framework as well as their modification of such principles in one way or another.

Karen Horney, Erich Fromm, Harry Stack Sullivan, and Henry Murray all developed their own personality theories as improvisations on the primary Freudian, Adlerian, and Jungian themes (see Chapter 9). In these newer theories social factors are emphasized, this emphasis concurring especially with Adler's. In playing up social factors, there has been a concomitant tendency to deemphasize biological factors. It is the relative neglect of the instinctive that sets these theories apart from Freudian analytic theory and that keeps at least the first three from having any basic commonality with Jungian theory.

All four of these theorists, and Sullivan especially, have contributed to the theory of ego functioning. This emphasis on ego functioning has been regarded as a strong point by sympathizers with the same point of view; on the other hand, some Freudians have regarded it as evidence that the theories represent an elaboration of Freudian theory rather than any really original contribution. Regardless of basic originality, each of these theorists has said unique things about the relationship of the individual to his society.

Horney's social theory. The training and contributions of Karen Horney (1885–1952) were entirely within the field of psychoanalysis, although she represented an important outbranching from orthodox psychoanalytic theory. German by birth, Horney studied medicine at the University of Berlin and received her psychoanalytic training at the Berlin Psychoanalytic Institute, where she was analyzed by Karl Abraham and Hans Sachs.

In the United States, Horney served as associate director of the Chicago Psychoanalytic Institute, taught at the New York Psychoanalytic Institute, and conducted a private practice in psychotherapy. Her efforts to break away from orthodox psychoanalysis led to the formation of the Association for the Advancement of Psychoanalysis and the American Institute of Psychoanalysis, of which she was dean.

Horney's theoretical emphasis is reflected in the titles of three of her works on personality theory: *Neurotic personality of our times* (1937), *Our inner conflicts* (1945), and *Neurosis and human growth* (1950). Her theory is further explicated in *New ways in psychoanalysis* (1939) and *Self-analysis* (1942).

Horney's social theory flies the banner of *basic anxiety*. This essential factor in personality development is "the feeling a child has of being isolated and helpless in a potentially hostile world" (Horney, 1937, p. 79). Horney's concept of helplessness as experienced by the infant does not have the universal flavor that Adler assigned to it. It provides a predisposition for the future development of pathological conditions; it does not lead to a striving for superiority but merely accentuates a predilection for security.

The home environment and the social structure within the family receive by far the most emphasis in Horney's theory. In this structure and the child's reaction to it Horney believed she had the key to the development of an individual's personality structure. The predominant reason that basic anxiety develops from parent-child relationships is the absence of genuine love and affection, and this can almost invariably be traced to neurotic parents. It should be noted, however, that Horney defines neurosis as any deviation from normal, efficient behavior; the term is not used in a pathological context unless so indicated.

The child responds to his basic anxiety by developing some strategy of behavior, *neurotic trends,* in an attempt to overcome it. It is this character structure arising from the reaction to basic anxiety which accounts for neurotic symptoms; it is *not,* as Freud said, a frustration of the sexual instinct. Horney maintained that sexual difficulty is the result and not the cause of conflicts. Furthermore, it is not a compulsion to repeat experiences based on unchanged, repressed childhood experiences (Horney, 1939, p. 9): "There is no such thing as an isolated repetition of isolated experiences; but the entirety of infantile experiences combines to form a certain character structure, and it is this structure from which later difficulties emanate."

The child also develops an idealized self-concept by internalizing the aspirational levels and ethics of others in his culture. This concept develops without regard for his own potentialities or limitations. Consequently, when he attempts to realize these ideational concepts he is curtailed both by his own limitations and by those which are imposed upon him by the existing culture. In other words, a person's basic conflict is between self-realization and self-idealization. The idealized self becomes a crutch for the neurotic person. He comes to believe that he *is* his idealized picture. This solution brings a temporary reduction of anxiety but in the long run increases it. The attempts of the neurotic to live up to his idealized, unrealistic picture of himself result in new conflicts and consequently greater tension. The only real conflict which Horney recognized is that of the present situation and the demands it makes upon the individual.

The devices the individual uses to face his conflicts (neurotic trends) are generally unrealistic and lead to some degree of neurotic behavior. These may be classified into two categories: (1) those which have their roots in the early developmental period of the child and which demonstrate a discernible etiology and (2) those which are a reaction to some situational stress and are usually transitory (Munroe, 1955). A vicious circle develops once these neurotic trends are initiated. Anxiety causes the original neurotic behavior which in turn, because of its inadequacy, leads to further anxiety that initiates another cycle.

In a person's attempt to find security he utilizes three types of behavioral patterns. He may move toward people, against them, or away from them (Horney, 1945). Fundamental to these three types of behavior are the need for affection, the need for self-sufficiency, and the need to exploit people. In respect to the type of behavior he selects there are corresponding personality types: compliant, aggressive, and detached. Again one must be cautioned not to assume that an individual utilizes only a single type. As the person vacillates from one situation to another, he utilizes the one most efficient for the specific situation. However, if one pattern is used exclusively, regardless of the situation, that is an index of neurosis.

The compliant individual relies upon other people; is ostensibly loving, kind, and loyal; and finds personal criticism devastating. Cynicism, a philosophy of the survival of the fittest, and extreme independence characterize the aggressive personality. The detached individual is perfectionistic, uncreative, and has a paucity of interpersonal relationships.

Horney emphasized only two of the many unconscious defense mechanisms: rationalization and externalization. Rationalization is used in the Freudian sense except that it is explained in the context of the social theory of Horney; that is, it is concerned with the whole organism and is not related to Freud's instinctual personality components. Externalization is merely a more general term for projection. The whole organism participates in an attempt to explain *every* motive and action externally, not just the undesirable ones.

Horney was optimistic about the possibility of avoiding neurotic reactions, as one tends to be when he believes that social factors are of preponderant importance. A secure and loving home would be insurance against the development of a neurotic character structure. Those, like Freud, who emphasize biological factors find it harder to be optimistic; if conflict is based on hereditary factors, change can come but slowly. Horney's more hopeful views have been welcomed by many as a relief from the oppressive pessimism of the orthodox Freudian assumptions.

Fromm's escape-from-freedom theory. Erich Fromm (1900–   ) was born and trained in Germany before emigrating to the United States. He studied sociology and psychology at the universities of Munich, Frankfurt, and Heidelberg, where he took his Ph.D. His psychoanalytic training was conducted mainly at the Berlin Psychoanalytic Institute.

Fromm cannot be clearly identified by his affiliation with any one institution, although he has lectured at the Chicago Psychoanalytic Institute and has taught at numerous universities and institutes in this country. For several years he directed his major efforts toward his private practice in New York City. At present, Fromm is a fellow of the William Alanson White Institute and a professor of psychoanalysis at the National University of Mexico.

Escape from freedom (1941), *Man for himself* (1947), and *The sane society* (1955)—Fromm's major contributions to personality theory—probably have drawn more cross-scientific and public attention than the works of any other neo-Freudian.

Fromm's primary interests lie in the larger segments of society as they affect the individual (Fromm, 1955, 1961). He believes that our political organizations no longer provide the firm direction and secure framework which they did when the units of political organization were smaller and man had less freedom to determine his own fate. Today, man suffers from a feeling of insecure aloneness engendered by his lack of a framework; that is, man desires to actualize his self-potential and develop a feeling of belongingness.

Fromm's basic premise that an individual attempts to escape from freedom and return to a more secure existence first gained public notice through his *Escape from freedom*. A child's physical condition at birth and shortly thereafter makes his survival dependent upon his environment in general and upon his mother in particular. The child is soon weaned from his early postnatal surroundings and gradually achieves more and more independence. However, the accompanying amount of strength necessary to augment his independence and to cope with the elements of society is conspicuously lacking. Moreover, man alone has the power to reason and imagine, and with the acquisition of this power he has lost the animal's ability to react instinctively, intimately, and directly to nature. Thus man finds himself in a unique position of being separated from his fellow man by political conditions and from the rest of nature by being a man. His first reaction to this situation is to try to recapture his earlier form of security. Upon finding this physically impossible and socially inefficient, he attempts other means. The two most common solutions are *authoritarianism* and *humanism*.

Broadly defined, authoritarianism is that which externally imposes a set of principles on society. It may be exemplified by a totalitarian state, dictatorship, or belief in a supreme being. This solution is inadequate because it does not permit the individual an opportunity to realize his potentialities. Frustration and hostility against the imposed conditions are then mobilized.

Fromm believes that humanism is a better solution. All the actualities of human life have a chance to develop through love of fellow man and mutual cooperation. In a humanistic society, each man would be a brother to every man, and no man would be alone.

Fromm identifies four ways of escaping isolation and insecurity prevalent in modern society. He refers to them as types of orientation, or relatedness. They are receptive, exploitative, hoarding, and marketing. No person exhibits a pure orientation. However, it is possible to manifest one type so that it subordinates all others.

The receptive orientation "is often to be found in societies in which the right of one group to exploit another is firmly established" (Fromm, 1947, p. 79). Individuals with this type of orientation sacrifice everything in order to maintain their identification with the group or the leader. They expect to receive something gratis, and when adversity occurs they are extremely rebellious and aggressive, exhibiting behavior not unlike that of a spoiled child.

The philosophy of "might makes right" characterizes exploitative individuals. The value which they place upon an object is directly proportional to the value which others place on the object. They would feel no compunction in taking some object for no other reason than that it is highly prized by another.

The hoarding orientation is what one might expect it to be: frugal, impecunious, and miserly. Security is evaluated in terms of tangible physical wealth.

The last orientation, marketing, is relatively new and is associated with the advent of modern capitalism. Here the emphasis is centered upon such superficial objectives as keeping up with the Joneses and social climbing.

As society now stands, it is absolutely necessary to warp the individual to fit the needs of society. Though man will always have to fit into human society, Fromm sees hope in a society which would give each man a chance to develop into a fully human creature.

Murray's need-press theory. Henry Murray (1893–   ) was a rigorously trained, productive biological scientist before turning to psychology. His academic degrees include an A.B. from Harvard in history, an M.D. from Columbia's College of Physicians and Surgeons, and an M.S. in biology from Columbia. Murray subsequently completed a surgical internship at Columbia's Presbyterian Hospital, taught physiology at Harvard, conducted embryological research at the Rockefeller Institute for Medical Research, and then journeyed to England to take his Ph.D. in biochemistry at Cambridge University.

While in Europe, a visit with Jung dramatically shifted Murray's interest to depth psychology. Shortly thereafter he took a position in academic psychology at Harvard and directed the psychological clinic there. Murray is presently associated with Harvard's Psychological Clinic Annex, which he established as a site for personality research. Murray took his psychoanalytic training under the direction of Franz Alexander and Hans Sachs, is a charter member of the Boston Psychoanalytic Society, and has stimulated widespread psychoanalytic research among his students.

The Thematic Apperception Test (1943), which Murray developed, has become one of the most widely used empirical tools of clinicians and personality theorists. His major theoretical work is *Explorations in personality* (1938). However, his *Assessment of men* (1948), written as a result of his work in the Office of Strategic Services during World War II, is also considered a significant contribution to the area of personality assessment. As an intellectual side line, Murray has engaged in a twenty-five-year study of author Herman Melville and has published an analysis (1951) of the psychological meaning of the novel *Moby Dick*.

One cannot read Murray (e.g., 1959) without receiving the impression that he is deeply preoccupied with the notions of process and field. Yet Murray is too well rounded to deny the importance of a controlled and reductive approach to psychology. The reductive approach is certainly foreign to Murray's own nature, for he sees too vividly the interactions that occur among all the processes that constitute a system. The system, to Murray as to the gestaltist, is the unit to be studied. Only systems maintain their boundaries and provide the hope for that stability which is so rare in nature but so necessary to scientific study. Murray sees science as operating, not primarily with stable structures, but with processes which may, with some probability, be predictable.

Murray has said of himself (1959, p. 13): "But at no time, to the annoyance of my friends, was I a good Jungian, a good Freudian, a good Adlerian, or a good schoolman of any breed." Despite this independence of thought, Murray is close to Freud in many basic attitudes as well as in some of the details of his theory. Two of these attitudes are a belief in the great importance of the early history of the organism and an emphasis on the physiological processes accompanying the behavioral events in which the psychologist is interested. Murray allows for more changes of the personality by later events than Freud did. However, Murray still recognizes the possibility that the effects of infantile experiences may be so great that they lead to various complexes in adulthood. On the physiological issue, Murray is one with Freud in recognizing the independence of the science of psychology from that of physiology, while at the same time pointing out that there is a necessary relationship of dependence between the two types of events: without physiological processes, there can be no psychological processes. Some particular dominant configuration of processes in the brain always accompanies a particular conscious process.

Another theme in Murray's theorizing is his recurrent clear statement that the concepts of his theory are constructions, hypothetical entities, not reality. Murray is not the kind of man who believes that nailing a name onto the flow of process can make it hold still or behave as a convenient structure that the scientist can then deal with complacently. Murray is more like a man who builds a transparent map with rough lines and shadings, through which he can view reality more conveniently; he builds and rebuilds systems of classification, analyzes and reanalyzes processes as his understanding is enriched. His theory could be called a tool as much as a description.

Murray has presented one of the most elaborate taxonomies of needs (1938). He does not attempt to talk about needs as things isolated from the context of behavior. Although needs are related to internal states, they are also related to the presence of valued external stimuli which impel to action (presses). The need directs behavior to objects which can lead to a desired state; though this state may often involve the reduction of tension, it may sometimes involve an increase in tension. Murray does not believe that the normal person always seeks the numbness of no tension. Most needs have as accompaniments certain emotions and feelings.

Murray has redefined Freud's term, *cathexis*, to describe need-related objects; an object may have a positive or negative cathexis according to its ability to press the individual into responses of approach or avoidance. The individual's feeling for the object is called a *sentiment*. Cathexis and sentiment therefore refer to the same relationship between person and object; one is applicable when we are concerned with the properties of the object, the other when we are concerned with the properties of the person. Thus Murray has subdivided Freud's concept of cathexis into two parts.

Needs are interrelated as well as embedded in ongoing processes. Some needs are subsidiary to more global superordinate needs, and the satisfaction of the subsidiary need is not for itself but only as it represents a step toward the greater satisfaction. Different needs may occur in the individual at the same time, in which case a conflict is engendered; one of the needs will be or become the strongest, in which case it is called prepotent, and will demand satisfaction before the concurrent needs can be attended to.

Closely related to Murray's acceptance of possible needs for tension increase is his description of two types of needs which do not involve a Thorndikian type of effect. He adds to the Thorndikian type of need *process needs* and *modal needs*. Process needs are needs to do, as the adult may need to exercise or the infant to babble. Modal needs are needs to perfect some behavior and differ from process needs only in that the need to improve is involved.

Murray's thoroughness in his treatment of needs is also reflected in his full discussion of significant units of behavior. He has relatively little use for a formulation as molecular as S-R. His most analytic unit is the *proceeding*, which is an interaction involving a person and an object or a person and a person; the interaction must be long enough to be of dynamic significance. The proceeding need not be overt; it may be a daydream or plan.

Proceedings may follow each other in a coherent fashion, in which case they may constitute another unit, a *serial*. The serial involves planning and organization, and its nature imposes direction upon the proceedings which comprise it. A marriage is an example of a serial. Proceedings, and therefore serials, may overlap and intertwine; all of us are involved in many endeavors in a single day or even hour.

A *thema* is another of Murray's behavioral units. It lays more emphasis upon the press and need which determine the behavior in question and therefore is a more analytic and theoretical unit than is the more descriptive proceeding. The thema, like the proceeding, may be serially organized. The thema is less fixed in scope than the proceeding and may persist over a longer period of time.

A serial program may also be considered a unit of behavior, but it lays emphasis upon the plans of the individual. He may plan a life goal, for example, college graduation, which involves a very large number of subgoals before it can be accomplished. A subgoal might be passing a course or completing a major.

We can see that Murray puts realism before precision, creativity before compulsion, in his theory of personality. Though many of his ideas are basically psychoanalytic, there can be no doubt whatever that he is a thinker who is not afraid to modify or innovate whenever he feels that the evidence is in his favor. He has also devised new methods for getting evidence, as we know from his Thematic Apperception Test (TAT) (1943) and from the ingenuity of his wartime work in assessing men for special assignments (Office of Strategic Services, 1948).

Murray is like many personality theorists; he has no desire to weigh heavily in the scales of parsimony or traditional scientific methodology, but he would and does weigh heavily in the scales of original endeavor and the creation of significant problems.

Sullivan's interpersonal theory. Harry Stack Sullivan (1892–1949) was first and foremost a psychiatrist, although his contribution to psychology through his personality theory is undeniable and he also was influential as a scientific statesman and educator. After receiving his M.D. from the Chicago College of Medicine and Surgery, Sullivan became a medical officer for the Federal Board for Vocational Education. He was later affiliated with the U.S. Public Health Service; with Saint Elizabeth's Hospital in Washington, D.C.; and with the University of Maryland medical school, where he conducted investigations of schizophrenia.

As a scientific statesman, Sullivan served as consultant for the Selective Service System and the UNESCO Tensions Project. He helped plan the International Congress of Mental Health. He also edited

Psychiatry, a journal whose publication was stimulated mainly by the need to publicize Sullivan's theory.

Neuropsychiatrist William Alanson White exerted a permanent influence upon Sullivan, who later was president of the William Alanson White Foundation and founded and directed its training institution, the Washington School of Psychiatry. The psychoanalytic influences of Sigmund Freud and Adolph Meyer are also discernible in Sullivan's theory. Sullivan published only one book in the area of personality theory, *Conceptions of modern psychiatry* (1947). However, a collection of his theoretical papers has been published posthumously (1953).

The interpersonal theory of Sullivan is less exclusively analytic than that of Horney or Fromm. Although Sullivan acknowledged intellectual indebtedness to Freud, his theory bears a closer resemblance to Adler's. Much of Sullivan's thinking is related to men who have a nonanalytic approach, for example, William Alanson White, Adolph Meyer, and George Herbert Mead. Moreover, Sullivan's closer relationship to psychiatry and to academicians (particularly social scientists) has resulted in a greater acceptance of his theory and may have something to do with its fuller statement (Sullivan, 1953); these features of his theory have, in turn, led to its generating more clinical research.

Personality as defined by Sullivan is "the relatively enduring pattern of recurrent interpersonal situations which characterize human life" (1953, p. 111). That is, it is regarded as an intervening variable inferred from an individual's behavior in relation to other people and objects. Personality exists only in interpersonal relationships. It follows that personality cannot be studied unless more than one person is interacting, although one of the persons need not be physically present; a person's interactions may be with an image, dream, fictional character, and the like. Sullivan has not entirely rejected the influences of heredity and biological factors; in fact, he has acknowledged their importance during infancy and at puberty. He proposed a hierarchy of physiological needs from which tension arises, which must be dissipated by satisfying the needs. However, he held that man's distinctively human characteristics are interpersonally developed and may directly affect the physiological needs.

In the development of the personality Sullivan stated that three processes are evidenced: dynamism, personifications, and cognitive processes. A dynamism is a prolonged behavior pattern which is revealed in characteristic interpersonal relationships. Dynamisms may also be described as classes of habits or personality traits which characterize an individual; toward certain people an individual may display a dynamism of hostility or of friendliness, depending upon his habitual behavior toward them. The self dynamism is the individual's picture of himself as he perceives it through his social interactions.

Personifications are images that an individual holds of other people or of himself. They are often products of his infancy. If they remain intact so that they influence his future opinion toward people, they are called *eidetic personifications*. An example of this might be a child's attitude toward a domineering father; this personification could influence responses toward other authority figures. However, when an image occurs solely in connection with a particular situation, only the word personification is used. A stereotype is any personification which is held by a group of people. It is interesting to note that these are in some ways a socialized and conscious version of Jung's archetypes.

Cognitive processes are subdivided into three classes: *prototaxic, parataxic,* and *syntaxic*. In the prototaxic mode, the individual simply experiences directly, without connecting the raw feelings or attaching meaning to them. It is not unlike what has been called a stream of consciousness: all the thoughts, visions, ideas, sensations, and perceptions occurring at any given moment. This is followed by the parataxic mode, in which the individual connects his experiences as they occur and regardless of their logical relations: casual relationships between nonrelated events and experiences. Logical connections are accomplished in the syntaxic mode by the use of *consensually validated* symbols. Consensual validation is a Sullivanian concept which refers to any symbol to which a particular meaning has become attached and agreed upon by a number of people. It is used chiefly for communication, and the most common are words.

Sullivan proposed six stages in the development of the individual. These are roughly delineated into age groups corresponding to maturational levels. However, the importance of maturation is limited in the degree to which it enables the individual to achieve a new and higher level of interpersonal relationships.

Sullivan noted that in the development of the individual it is often apparent that certain entities are outside his realm of awareness. Three major reasons may be posited for this: selective inattention, disassociation, and parataxic distortion. Selective inattention is merely the unwillingness on the part of the individual to perceive in the immediate environment that which contradicts his beliefs. Disassociation is approximately what the Freudians refer to as repression. Parataxic distortion occurs when an individual's personal and autistic meanings, rather than the socially validated meanings, accrue to a symbol and influence his thinking.

In sum, Sullivan held that the individual functions because he needs to secure satisfaction; his basic needs are not instinctual or biological, as Freud would have us believe, but are based on interactions with people.

SELF THEORIES

Habits, traits and factors of varying degrees of generality, the organism, social interactions—we have already run quite a gamut of concepts that are used either to explain or to describe the consistency of an individual's behavior. The last organizer is the self. There are nearly as many definitions of self as there are self psychologists, and the definitions often seem to lack operational meaning; however, the common element in all definitions of self is the character of self as an organizer that imposes a consistency of some order on behavior.

There are three general ways in which self has been postulated to operate in achieving a harmony of diverse activities. The time-honored way was to use self as though it were a little man-inside-the-man who ordered all activities so that they pretty well suited his imperial self-ship. Such a self, having his own sources of energy and will, is inaccessible to scientific investigation and is discredited in all scientific psychologies, including modern self theories.

A second way in which the self might organize behavior is as a kind of template or picture into which all ongoing behavior must fit. If the self is an objective, existing set of representations of an individual's past behaviors and experiences, these representations may somehow resist changes that would result from the impact of divergent new experiences on the old structure called self. We may think of this self as though it were a picture against which a contemplated new behavior is projected; if the discrepancy between the picture as it presently exists and the picture as it would have to be modified to accommodate the new behavior is too great, the behavior does not occur.

The third view of self is as a summary name for a set of psychological processes. The exact processes that are subsumed vary from theorist to theorist but generally include evaluative and attitudinal functions. These processes, acting upon the materials that govern behavior, can thus themselves play a role in directing behavior.

A danger in constructing self theories is that a regression from meanings two and three to meaning one may occur. Certainly no theorist will intend such a regression and will, when defining self for theoretical purposes, carefully exclude meaning one. The danger lies in less-cautious uses of the term when dealing with specific cases. The self theorist shares this possible pitfall with all those theorists who are adventurous enough to postulate structures of personality, and all personality theorists have been daring to that extent.

Rogers's self theory. The career of Carl Ransom Rogers (1902–) has been marked by an interest in divergent fields, the first of which was scientific agriculture, which he encountered during his boyhood days on a farm. Rogers subsequently attended the University of Wisconsin and Union Theological Seminary before terminating his education at Columbia Teachers College, where he took his Ph.D. and fell under the philosophical influence of John Dewey. Columbia also provided Rogers's first introduction to clinical psychology; he grew better acquainted with the field during his internship at the psychoanalytically oriented Institute for Child Guidance. While there he felt a definite conflict between psychoanalytic theory and the Thorndikian statistical influence which had prevailed at Columbia.

Rogers served as director of the Rochester Guidance Clinic, finding stimulation in the eclectic staff there. Their constant search for effective treatment was a problem Rogers turned to in *The clinical treatment of the problem child* (1939). He then shifted to academic psychology, teaching at Ohio State University, the University of Chicago, and now at the University of Wisconsin, but remained active in clinical activities. Rogers received the American Psychological Association's Distinguished Contribution Award in 1956.

The major stimulus for Rogers's personality theory came from his clinical therapeutic work, although he was strongly influenced by psychoanalyst Otto Rank. Rogers first advanced his views on personality in *Counseling and psychotherapy* (1942). That book was followed by his major theoretical work, *Client-centered therapy* (1951). His views provoked a great amount of research on psychotherapy, and he has made significant methodological contributions (e.g., tape recording of interviews) as well as substantive contributions.

The central concept of Rogers's theory is the self. The therapy which Rogers developed over a period of time is consistent with the belief that the patient has a self structure which he himself must change if improvement is to occur. Rogers believes that his observations demand both this kind of therapy and a concept of self like the one he evolved.

To Rogers, the self is a structure compounded out of the experiences which the individual is able to attribute to his own body or to the results of his own behavior; the self, then, is a self-picture, or self-awareness. The experiences come with value tags attached; that is, some aspects of the self-picture are positive, while others are negative. The self regulates behavior, for behavior that is not consistent with the self-picture either does not occur or is not fitted into the self-picture.

Though Rogers was at times subjected to psychoanalytic influences, he tends to reject the analytic emphasis on unconscious processes. He does recognize the possibility that self-inconsistent behaviors will occur as a result of unconscious influences, but he still feels that understanding of an individual can occur most easily if the therapist can enter the phenomenal field that appears to the patient. For Rogers, the consciousness of the individual contains most of what is needed for understanding his personality.

The self-picture is not supposed to be a static thing; although its structure has some stability, it can at times assimilate new experiences in such a way that the structure changes and the particular type of experience is subsequently experienced more easily. The threatened self is rigid and rejecting, but the secure self is fluid and tolerant. This single statement is the conceptual basis for Rogers's nondirective therapy.

Nondirective therapy sets a situation in which the patient can accept experiences into the self structure because the self is at no time threatened and reports of experiences are at no time rejected or devalued by the therapist. Studies have shown that, in therapeutic circumstances, the patient's conceptions of themselves and their ideal selves came into closer agreement (Butler & Haigh, 1954; Rudikoff, 1954, pp. 85–98). Whether the change occurs in the self-picture as such or in the ideal self, the observed changes in therapy should be helpful. The individual's experiences would be more easily assimilated so long as the real self was accepted as a satisfactory structure in relation to the ideal. The self would be less threatened and more subject to adjustment as necessitated by life experiences.

Rogers, like Goldstein, believes that the organism has a single goal. It strives to actualize, enhance, and maintain itself. The possible lines of actualization are laid down by heredity, and the organism has, as a part of its native equipment, a creative urge. Human beings, however, cannot actualize themselves effectively unless they can symbolize their experiences and choose the path that leads to self-enhancement.

It is the failure to symbolize all of experience which makes Rogers's distinction between the objective world and the world as perceived by the individual so important. The individual responds to his perceived world rather than directly to the objective world; thus it is essential for his adjustment that the two worlds be as similar as possible.

Carl Rogers is a clinician's clinician. He has spent much of his professional life in his role as therapist, and his theory could hardly be other than closely related to his therapy. We should not expect the theory to be simple, static, dogmatic, or complete. It is the opposite of all these. His theory is, and will be, inductive.

A surprising and often-criticized aspect of Rogers's theory is its strong emphasis upon conscious processes; one might expect that he would follow more behavioristic or psychoanalytic lines, since he studied both at Columbia, where Thorndikian views were strong, and with Otto Rank. Though Thorndike was not a behaviorist, anyone familiar with his writing knows that he believed in the unconscious automaticity of the operation of the law of effect. Nevertheless, Rogers has preferred an attitude like that of Snygg and Combs (1949) and holds that the experienced world as available to the consciousness of the individual plays the preponderant role in the determination of his behavior. Rogers thus stands with Allport and many others in stemming the psychoanalytic tide, which seems today to run less strongly toward the depths of the unconscious.

Murphy's personality synthesis. Gardner Murphy (1895–) has brought to psychology a wide range of interests and has made professional contributions in each of his seemingly divergent fields of endeavor. Educated at Yale, Harvard, and Columbia, Murphy turned first to academic psychology. While teaching at Columbia, he collaborated with Likert to publish *Public opinion and the individual* (1938) on the subject of polling and attitude measurement. Murphy later became department chairman at City College of New York and presently is research director at the Menninger Foundation.

Long interested in parapsychology, Murphy has served as president of the London Society for Psychical Research and has been a strong and persistent exponent of the need for expansion of such research.

In the area of world peace and international relations, Murphy has studied social tensions in India as a UNESCO consultant and published *Human nature and enduring peace* (1945). He is also the author of two introductory psychology texts (1933, 1951) and has written on the history of psychology (1929; rev. 1949), social psychology (Murphy & Murphy, 1931), perception (Solley & Murphy, 1960), and the effect of scientific choices today upon the world's tomorrows (1958). Murphy made his major contribution to personality theory in *Personality: A biosocial approach to origins and structure* (1947).

It would seem that Murphy's personality theory could be treated under any heading. Murphy includes concepts from all important predecessors in his theory. His scholarship and literacy are highly esteemed. He exemplifies the fact that in personality theory the eclectic needs to deal with the whole of psychology. It has been our contention that the final form of personality theory will be just a synthesis of all of psychology; Murphy has come closer to this goal of selective synthesis than any other personality theorist. He has also introduced a number of key concepts which have been of wide influence.

Thumbnailing Murphy, then, is like thumbnailing a large part of the psychology of personality and does Murphy an even greater injustice than most other personality theorists. Murphy calls his approach biosocial, and one can say that he emphasizes everything: the biological organism, the individual personality, the society, the physical environment, the field nature of events wherein interchanges between organism and environment take place, the stages of personality development —all are treated by Murphy.

Murphy displays more critical selectivity than unique originality. His strength lies in synthesis. Still, there are striking aspects of Murphy's theory; for example, his definition of self is unexcelled for brevity and simplicity: "The individual as known to the individual" (1947). This definition stands as an island in an otherwise turgid sea.

One of Murphy's best-known concepts is called *canalization*. There is some similarity between canalization and Allport's functional autonomy. Murphy's word refers to the tendency individuals may develop to satisfy their drives in quite particular ways; for example, the hunger drive may always be satisfied by eating German food, or a particular kind of German food, when any food would satisfy the biological need as well. Murphy's canalization does not require that the activity be engaged in for its own sake, but it is as if something like Allport's functional autonomy tipped the motivational scales in favor of the preferred mode of need-reduction.

Murphy's research cuts across the boundaries of psychology. It is often used by him to demonstrate the unity of the individual, whose functioning can be understood only by viewing his part processes as they are embedded in the whole. One of Murphy's best-known studies (Levine, Chein, & Murphy, 1942) has been widely cited as demonstrating that the tendency for hungry subjects to report more food objects in ambiguous pictures is a function of food deprivation. This, according to Murphy, demonstrates the general point that no aspect of behavior (such as perception) can be considered apart from other aspects (such as needs). Postman and Murphy (1943) similarly demonstrated that the degree to which pairs to be associated in memory fit into a subject's attitudinal framework has an important effect on his ability to learn and remember the associated pairs.

There are numerous pitfalls in trying to be all things to all people, as Murphy in a sense has done. In his case, there are many benefits too. His theory, more than any other, tries to deal with all the facts in all their stubbornness, preferring to treat and relate all the features of personality theory rather than ignore factors which might not fit into any preconceived theory. A look at Table 9 shows Murphy with no columns that contain an "L." Perhaps such trivial tributes are all that can be given any personality theorist today, and Murphy would probably be content with such faint praise (Murphy, 1947, p. 927):

Despite all these lessons of the past we write and speak today as if the full concept and stature of man were known. But like our predecessors, we shall rectify mistakes not primarily by the minor readjustment of the lines of the argument but by the recognition of the fundamental limitations of the whole present system of conceptions. It is preparation for this destruction and rebirth of knowledge to which serious research should be directed.

This, we believe, would constitute a good credo for all psychological theorists.

SUMMARY AND CONCLUSIONS

The present chapter has attempted a broad overview of the major theoretical approaches to personality. We have classified these theories into five major categories: S-R (Dollard and Miller); *trait and factor* (Allport, Eysenck, Cattell); *organismic* (Goldstein, Sheldon); *neo-analytic* (Horney, Fromm, Murray, Sullivan); and *self* (Rogers, Murphy). Salient characteristics of each of these types of theory have been examined.

Some final comment is in order concerning the contemporary status and future prospects of the type of theory generally labeled "personality." Such theories have, in general, been disappointingly unproductive of well-controlled empirical research. If research stimulation is accepted as a primary criterion of the value of a theory of personality, most have failed to meet the major objective of theorizing. An important exception to this conclusion is the factor theory. In general, however, even the most exciting and potentially valuable concepts have lain dormant as far as empirical research is concerned. Good examples here are Allport's functional autonomy and Murphy's canalization. The fact that experimental research on such concepts is difficult, especially with human subjects, cannot be allowed to stand as an adequate excuse. There simply has not been sufficient motivation to perform well-controlled and systematic research on the key concepts in the major personality theories.

The harshness of this stricture must be tempered by the admission that personality theories, unlike most other theories we have considered, may be reasonably judged from certain viewpoints other than the strictly scientific. For example, they have a unique relation to clinical practice. Such other functions—the provision of a systematic framework for various practitioners, to mention one such function commonly assumed—can certainly be accepted as legitimate, although of limited importance from our present point of view.

On the positive side, we may point to the growing emergence of new kinds of theorizing, relatively independent of the classic forms. These new theories are proving to be much more productive of experimental research. Such theorizing tends to differ from the classic theories considered in certain important ways. First, it is much more specifically related to particular problems and tends to avoid the grand scale and the comprehensive coverage of the older theories. Second, it is not as easy to classify in terms of the classic objectives (e.g., McClelland's theorizing on achievement, 1953; Festinger's consonance-dissonance theory, 1957). Although it remains for historians to determine whether such kinds of personality theorizing are ultimately more fruitful, it would be very surprising indeed if this strong tide of more circumscribed theory and experiment did not produce a marked improvement in the scientific interpretation of personality. Perhaps some common meeting ground can be achieved, with the more recent theories building up from below to make contact with modifications of the older theories largely constructed at a far different level of discourse and conceptualization. Such *rapprochement* would mark the real maturing of a scientific theory of personality.

further readings

The best single introductory source is Hall and Lindzey's *Theories of personality* (1957). It provides a good, critical, and balanced overview. David and von Bracken's *Perspectives in personality theory* (1957) and David and Brengelmann's *Perspectives in personality research* (1960) are sources for contemporary trends. They are particularly valuable in that European contributions are thoroughly covered. The format of Chapter 12 is such that the student can easily find there the sources most likely to be of interest for each of the individual authors. However, the following list indicates the one source for each author which we believe is of most general and contemporary interest: Dollard and Miller (1950), Allport (1961), Cattell (1959), Eysenck (1953a), Goldstein (1939), Sheldon (1942), Horney (1939), Fromm (1955), Murray (1938), Sullivan (1953), Rogers 1951), and Murphy (1947).

engineering and mathematical 13
influences on psychology

Psychology has undergone many revolutions. Revolution in a science becomes more difficult as the body of established knowledge increases, and psychology is approaching a position from which it can more coolly survey new developments without suffering the extreme revisions that revolution necessitates. Nevertheless, it seems that today psychology is undergoing an overhaul in its point of view because of a technical explosion in the field of engineering.

For the last few years, engineering has been increasingly concerned with the handling of information. In the more distant past, engineers had been most interested in the production of devices whose chief output was work or heat or material. Today the engineers have turned their attention to devices that carry on humanlike activities, devices for data processing. Such devices are not entirely new, having developed over centuries from abacus to adding machine, but the scope of successes is now of a different order of magnitude. We must recognize that today is the age of automation, while yesterday was not. The names of computers become household words, but by the time they do, the Eniac has been overshadowed by the Illiac and it in turn by the Univac.

What has this to do with psychology? Perhaps the implications of automation for psychology can be summed up by saying that the replacement of human function encourages the study of human function. If we wish to have a computer recognize speech, we are likely to begin by finding out how humans recognize speech. If a device is to detect signals, it may very well ape the human being in its detection. In deciding whether a given device is needed or useful, we compare its cost and performance with human cost and performance. A common quip in computer circles is that the human being is still the only general-purpose computer weighing in the neighborhood of 150 pounds which is mass produced free. The comparative psychology of man and device is developing across the disciplinary line that divides psychology and engineering, much as the comparative psychology of man and animal developed out of biology and psychology about a century ago.

This new comparative psychology is related to the use of mathematical models, but it is more than that. It is a very far cry from the hodological space of Lewin (see Chapter 11) to the computer program which recognizes digits as they are spoken to a sensing device. The really serious and practical consideration of how a human function can be performed mechanically lends interest, urgency, and precision to the task of describing the process. The engineer who wants to automate a function forces the psychologist to recognize that he does not really know how the function is carried out. The actual testing of theory in devices gives an immediate knowledge of results which discourages fuzzy thinking.

The emphasis on devices should not lead one to the conclusion that it is the devices per se which are important for psychology. Rather, the important things are the conceptual sharpening which is likely to attend the development of the devices and their application to human functions, and also the impetus which the development lends to psychology. This impetus comes partly from engineers, whose primary intention is practical rather than scientific, and partly from psychologists who see in the computer and its program an unparalleled device for theory construction.

Although the devices themselves are not the most important theoretical end result of the new trend, it is worth while to review briefly some general properties of the two main types of computers in order to see why these properties can be useful in the construction of psychological theory.

THE ROLE OF THE COMPUTER

The analog computer accepts continuous inputs and gives continuous outputs. Data are presented to the input of the computer in the form of continuously variable voltages or dial settings. The answers to problems are also given in the form of voltages or dial settings, so long as one is talking about only the analog portion of the computer. The correct solution is obtained because the gears or electrical circuitry provide a physical analog for the equations being solved. If the analog computer is to be changed from solving one type of problem to solving another, its physical structure must be altered; that is, interconnections of gears or wires must be changed. The analog computer is therefore likely to be less flexible, though often more economical for a particular application, than the digital computer.

The human being may be likened to an analog computer with respect to certain functions, in the sense that responses or perceptions seem to depend directly on the structure of the organism rather than on the momentary state of the organism or on some sequence of logical steps which might be traversed in reaching a decision. For example, color is perceived directly as a function of the stimulus situation, and no conscious, verbal, or logical intervening steps need occur. The same might be said for the perception of movement, and other instances of analogy between human and analog computer may occur to the reader.

The digital computer is so named because its inputs and outputs can take on only digital values, with no fractional values between numbers. We can therefore specify exactly the range of numbers that can be represented in a register of a particular digital computer. A representative register might hold ten decimal digits. An overwhelming majority of digital computers are electronic. The electronic digital computer can be quickly adapted to new problems without gross physical changes; the programs, or sequences of instructions to be performed, are changed. The presence of a program of operation distinguishes computers from calculators. The human operator "instructs" a simple calculating machine, one instruction at a time, by hitting keys. The operator instructs a computer, many instructions at a time, by writing down a sequence of operations which the computer is to carry out. Then, once the computer starts, it proceeds through the whole programmed task without outside intervention. It is this independence from the human operator which allows the computer to be so fast, for example, to add 20,000 numbers per second. Any figures that are given on speeds achieved by computers quickly become too conservative; engineers are already talking in terms of basic computer operations that occur in billionths of a second. It is no wonder that machines which perform such computational miracles capture the imagination.

It is not their speed, however, which makes computers of unique importance to psychology. Their speed makes them wonderful labor-saving devices and helps the psychologist as it helps every other scientist. Data-reduction problems that would have taken years without a computer may take minutes with a computer, though writing the program may now take years. Problems that could not previously have been attacked can now be studied. However, this in itself would have no more theoretical significance than would the invention of an automatic cage-cleaning machine that made it possible to do more animal research. The fact that man has created the computer in his own image makes the computer uniquely fascinating to the psychologist. A computer is manlike, of course, in a functional rather than a structural sense. We do not care whether the computer operates in a way which physically apes man, as long as the answers are "correct," that is, the same answers that a man would give to the same question. This requires that the computer be the same as man in some logical sense.

The logical similarity between man and computer holds even for the basic elements of their information-processing systems. Both von Neumann (1958) and Wiener (1948) have been led to compare human neurons to computer elements. Physically, the latter are larger, faster, fewer, and simpler; but both neurons and the basic elements of computers seem to follow a two-valued logic. The human neuron is either responding or not responding, just as the computer element is either in one state or in another.

Over a hundred years ago, George Boole (1854) developed an algebra which has turned out to be very useful in computer design. It is a two-valued logic, based on the notion that elements are either in or out of a set. This computer logic was developed by Boole as an expression of the laws of *human* thought; he had no intention of writing logic which would apply to *mechanized* thinking. Future developments may make it possible to reapply Boole's algebra to the problem for which he intended it.

Digital computers use a two-valued number system which is compatible with Boolean algebra and with the two-valued character of computer elements. This so-called binary (two-valued) number system is worth looking at because of its almost universal use in digital computers and because an understanding of binary numbers is necessary for understanding information measures. The binary equivalents for the decimal numbers are: $0 = 0$, $1 = 1$, $10 = 2$, $11 = 3$, $100 = 4$, $101 = 5$, $110 = 6$, $111 = 7$, $1000 = 8$, and $1001 = 9$. It is clear that only two things can occur in a particular binary column, 0 or 1. In the decimal number system, ten alternatives can occur in a given column, so we can designate ten events by different symbols in a single column. Numbers for each of 10 times 10 events can be written in two decimal columns, 10 times 10 times 10 (10^3) events in three columns, etc. Correspondingly, two events can be symbolized in a binary column, 2^2 in two, 2^3 in three, 2^4 in four, etc. For example, numbers for 1024 events clearly take four decimal columns (we could go up to 9999 in the same space); writing the binary equivalent for 1024 decimal numbers would take ten columns. Binary numbers use much more space on paper, but they can be represented physically with simpler, more reliable, cheaper elements. Nature seems to have used logically similar binary elements in its animal brains.

Binary addition is easy to specify: $0 + 0 = 0, 0 + 1 = 1, 1 + 0 = 1$, and $1 + 1 = 10$. For example:

$$\begin{array}{rcl} 11110110 &=& 246 \\ 11101100 &=& 236 \\ \hline 111100010 &=& 482 \end{array} \qquad \begin{array}{rcl} 111 &=& 7 \\ 111 &=& 7 \\ \hline 1110 &=& 14 \end{array}$$

The multiplication table is equally simple: $0 \times 0 = 0, 0 \times 1 = 0$, $1 \times 0 = 0, 1 \times 1 = 1$. For example:

$$\begin{array}{rcl} 11010 &=& 26 \\ 1011 &=& 11 \\ \hline 11010 \\ 11010 \\ 00000 \\ 11010 \\ \hline 100011110 &=& 286 \end{array}$$

The digital computer operates internally on binary numbers, and even the simple operations of binary addition and multiplication depend upon several operations at the Boolean-algebra level; each summation carried out in an adder is the result of a number of "AND" and "OR" operations. For example, the computer puts a 0 in the first column after summing if the two components of the sum were both 0 *or* were both 1; the second column has a 1 if one component in the second column had a 1 *and* both components in the first column had 1, *or* if one component in the second column had a 1 *and* both components in the first column had 0. The curious student can extend the translation of sums into the logical language of "ORS" and "ANDS" as an exercise.

The digital computer can do complex things because it is able to combine literally millions of elementary operations. The logical "ORS" and "ANDS" combine to make arithmetical operations possible. Numbers can therefore be combined, and the computer can compare these numbers one with another and perform different operations depending on the outcomes of such comparisons. Since alternative courses of action can be numbered, computers can, say, trigger a gun if its computations based on several sources of information indicate that some preset level of threat has been exceeded. The junior author vividly recalls an eerie experience he had putting a program into a computer (which had previously contained another program). The date of the program was supposed to be entered at the same time. The computer blinked its lights for a tiny fraction of a second and then, seemingly almost wearily, typed out on its automatic typewriter the simple query, "Date?" Then, when the date had been entered and the run button pushed, the computer, following the directions of its earlier program, examined the program which had last been fed to it and started typing out a stream of human errors, "Undefined routine jumped to from Cell 27624. . . ." Several pages later, the typewriter stopped, and, one may imagine, the computer waited patiently for a more intelligent programmer to give it a more reasonable program to compile.

Such apparently intelligent behavior makes it easy for the incautious to forget that the sequence of computer operations is completely fixed by a set of operations prepared by a human computer programmer. Some have suggested (e.g., Newell et al., 1958; Newell & Simon, 1961) that these programs can constitute a theory of intelligent *human* behavior. However, there is great danger in jumping to the conclusion that, because a computer program operates in some particular way, so does the human. The computer program is like the more traditional mathematical model in this sense; each may allow the correct prediction to be made, but neither is likely to describe how the human being accomplishes what he does.

Without its program, the computer "knows" nothing. The human worker who is given inadequate or incomplete instructions may manage to muddle through somehow or may even fall back on previous knowledge or experience and do perfectly well. It is quite likely that neither worker nor instructor will be able to say precisely and completely how the job was done. It is because of this that the complete moronic stupidity of a computer may sometimes be an advantage. If a computer is required to do a task with a program which is *in any way* incomplete, it simply cannot proceed. Imagine that some learning theorist is programming a computer to produce "behavior" that would be predicted from his theory. He may discover that some of his thinking is not sufficiently explicit for him to write the program, although until that time his theory had seemed perfectly clear. He may find that, when the program runs, the results do not conform with empirical findings in several unusual cases which he had previously not bothered to examine. In short, the stupidity of the unprogrammed computer demands complete foresight on the part of any person who wants the computer to do anything; no human taskmaster would be likely to exact such explicitness of statement. Yet the computer, once programmed, is so fast that it can afford to examine untoward conditions and so rigid and thorough that it "forgets" to overlook them.

The simulation of human functions is likely to lead the psychologist or engineer to take a particular series of steps. In any particular case, the series of steps is likely to be disjointed, unrelated, and undirected. It may be recognized only later, or perhaps never, that any simulation of human function was accomplished. However, if the process is self-conscious, the steps may occur as follows. A function needs to be carried out—for example, the detection of a target on a radar display. Man and device are regarded as substitutable for each other. The man is observed as he performs the task. His behavior is described mathematically. This behavior is compared with the behavior of existing or realizable devices that will do the same job. A new device is or is not made. If made, its behavior may be compared with human behavior.

Each of the several steps in this process is likely to be very interesting and instructive for the science of psychology. The mathematical description, however, is perhaps most likely to be useful. Its range of interest may turn out to extend considerably beyond the situation in which it was developed; we shall later see two excellent illustrations of this.

An increasing range of human functions can be performed by inanimate devices. Machines can detect signals, sort events into classes, recognize patterns presented visually, recognize a limited range of sounds, and play checkers or chess. They may work out geometric theorems or develop a desired algebraic formula, working until the proof (with the stated correct properties) is found by "chance." These complex functions are not yet carried out well, but more mundane behavior has been automated with great success. It is impossible to see how far the present trend will go. A small-scale computer of today can do things no computer could do fifteen years ago.

We can now turn to two specific influences which have straddled the boundary between engineering and psychology: information theory (cf. Attneave, 1959) and detection theory (cf. Licklider, 1959). The present chapter is not the place for a detailed substantive examination of either theory, but it is appropriate to look at each of them in broad perspective.

Both these theories grew in intimate association with engineering problems. Shannon (1951) did his work on information theory at Bell Telephone Laboratories, and no doubt much of the impetus for his work came from the desire of Bell Telephone to develop better devices for the transmission of information. Detection theory has emanated in large part from the Electronic Defense Group at the University of Michigan, and devices for detection are certainly desired products of this group. To date, a human being is likely to be a part of such a detection device.

INFORMATION THEORY

Information measures. According to Norbert Wiener, no one man can be credited with the development of a measure of information (1948, p. 18): "This idea occurred at about the same time to several writers, among them the statistician R. A. Fisher, Dr. Shannon of the Bell Telephone Laboratories, and the author." However, Shannon has worked most persistently on the theoretical development of information theory and has most widely disseminated information theory through his publication of both theory and data (e.g., Shannon, 1951; Shannon & Weaver, 1949). We may therefore give Shannon the primary credit.

The argument that underlies the definition of an information measure can be presented rather simply as long as we remain content with an approximate and intuitive treatment. Shannon was, as we have said, concerned with actual communication systems, containing at least a transmitter, communication channel, and receiver. What was desired was a measure of the capacity of channels to carry information. Shannon described one such measure.

First, assume that only a limited number of alternatives can be communicated via any communication system. For example, if an English-speaking radio announcer is transmitting, his set of messages is limited to the words of the English language. What he does in speaking is to choose from all the possible words a single word to transmit. Until he speaks, a person at the receiver is uncertain what word will be spoken. He does know that one of the set of English words will be chosen. The process of information transmission can be regarded as a process of reducing uncertainty. If there is no uncertainty remaining after a message is sent and received, then the amount of information transmitted is the same as the amount of uncertainty that existed initially. It seems reasonable to make the amount of uncertainty proportional to the number of possible messages that might conceivably be sent; the more alternatives there are, the harder it would be to guess which would be sent.

Shannon noted that it would be possible to number all the alternatives using the binary number system, as we pointed out in our discussion of binary numbers. If there were 64 alternatives, we would number them from 0 through 111111 (which corresponds to a decimal 63). This requires a six-place binary number to complete the numbering.

We saw earlier that if we have some number, N, of columns of binary numbers, we can designate 2^N different alternatives. In the present case, $2^6 = 2 \times 2 \times 2 \times 2 \times 2 \times 2 = 64$. Shannon lets the number of columns of binary digits required to number the alternative messages equal the number of units of information. These units of information are called *bits*, an abbreviation for *binary digits*. If you are told which of 64 possible alternatives is true, you have received 6 bits of information. The logarithm of some number, X, is defined as the power to which some base number must be raised in order to obtain X; that is, base$^{\log x} = X$. For example, if 2 is used as the base, $2^{\log 64} = 64$. We just noted that $2^6 = 64$; therefore, log 64 to the base 2 equals 6. This is usually written $\log_2 64 = 6$. This suggests that we can find the number of bits involved in selecting one of a set of N alternatives by taking $\log_2 N$, and this is in fact the way the bit is defined, as $\log_2 N$. The student should remember that $\log_2 N$ equals the number of columns required to number a set of alternatives with binary digits.

A concrete example at this point may be useful. Consider a game in which a person has to discover which book from a shelf containing 16 books has been marked with a $10 bill inserted between the pages. His problem is to locate the book by asking the minimum number of indirect questions. (Of course, he can not tell which book has been marked from the external appearance, and he cannot ask a direct question, such as "Which book is it?" The only questions permitted are ones that can be answered by "yes" or "no.") The proper procedure, from the point of view of minimizing the number of questions, is to ask first: "Is the book to the right (or left) of center?" After this question is answered, there will remain 8 rather than 16 possibilities. The same question, halving the possibilities each time, should then be asked until the marked book has been isolated. Four questions of this kind are required to make this determination, as one can easily verify by an empirical test. This number is exactly the number of columns of binary units required to designate 16 alternatives; also, $\log_2 16 = 4$, the number of bits of information transmitted. In this case, the information was transmitted, 1 bit at a time, by the four answers. Even if the statement, "It's the thirteenth book from the left," were directly made, 4 bits would still have been transmitted.

The use of the simple definition of the number of bits, $H = \log_2 N$, is justified only if every message in the set of alternative messages is equally likely to occur. It seems intuitively obvious that the occurrence of unlikely events is more informative than the occurrence of very probable events. Thus, man bites dog is newsworthy, while dog bites man is not. The difference in information content as a function of the probability of occurrence of a particular alternative is considered in the more general formula, $H = \log_2 1/P$, where P is the probability that the message would have occurred. If an honest die comes up 4, the occurrence of this event transmits $\log_2 1/\frac{1}{6}$ bits $= \log_2 6$ bits $= 2.58$ bits. If the die is heavily loaded, the occurrence of a 4 may transmit almost no information. A die that always comes up 4 transmits $\log_2 1/1 = 0$ bits of information when it turns up 4.

Often the occurrence of a sequence of messages may present problems very similar to a gradual transition from a situation like throwing a fair die to one like throwing a loaded die; that is, the occurrence of a particular message in the first position may change the probabilities in the next position and so on through the whole series of messages. Language is an excellent example of this kind of relationship between the messages in a sequence. In English, the letter "T" is very likely to be followed by an "H" and not at all likely to be followed by an "L." The effect of 100 letters on the 101st is so great that the 101st carries somewhere between .6 and 1.3 bits of independent information (it is not practical to make exact determinations). If every letter were equally probable, the occurrence of a letter or space at position 101 would carry $\log_2 27 = 4.76$ bits. It is clear, then, that a given amount of information transmitted via the English language is shared among many symbols. To put it another way, each symbol really carries *less* than the maximum information which it would be capable of carrying.

Systems of this kind are called redundant, and English would seem to be about three-fourths redundant. Redundancy is not all bad; if the information transmitted is shared among words, the information may be available even though part of the message is missed. For example, the blank in psychol gy can easily be filled in with an "o," for the remaining letters give us sufficient information and, in effect, we still have the whole message. If we reflect on the frequency with which children respond with "Huh?" to an attempt at communication, we shall no doubt be grateful for all the redundancy English contains. Probably the child's query is more often produced by an inferior ability to reconstruct missed parts of the message than by inferior hearing.

Empirical studies.   With this brief background, we can look at the psychological application of information measures and of the point of view afforded by information theory. We can ask how great man's channel capacity is, and some answers have been given. Pierce and Karlin (1957) have reported one of the highest rates of continuous transmission. They had subjects read words aloud as rapidly as possible from a fixed vocabulary. The sequences of words were random, so that it was easy to calculate the amount of information involved in reading words and so that information was not lost to the usual sequential effects. About 45 bits per second were transmitted. Husbands have long known that information is presented fastest verbally, but it is comforting to have quantitative evidence that this is the fastest medium.

For a time it seemed that the rate of information transmission of the human channel might be almost independent of the nature of the transmission task, but it now appears that this is far from true. In reading words the information rate equals information per word times words per unit of time. Since information per word equals $\log_2$ (vocabulary size), larger vocabularies would have to be read more slowly than small vocabularies if the information-transmission rate were to remain constant. However, Pierce and Karlin, and earlier, Sumby and Pollack (1954), found that reading speed does not decrease markedly with increases in the size of the vocabulary. For a fixed number of syllables per word, the transmission rate increases almost linearly as vocabulary size increases.

In the reading task, subjects transmitted information continuously. It is also possible to have subjects observe a single brief presentation of a stimulus and then have them respond at leisure to what was observed. Here the measure is a measure of a kind of "absorption" rate rather than of what we would intuitively feel should be called a transmission rate. It may be considered a measure of the channel capacity of the sensory channel involved. Miller (1956) has reviewed the evidence from a number of studies of human abilities to discriminate between stimuli varying along some single dimension. Judgments of pitch, loudness, pointer position, and square size are examples of the tasks involved. Surprisingly, the number of values of stimuli which can be discriminated accurately is small, Miller's "seven plus or minus two"! This number is much smaller than the number of just-noticeable differences along these scales. The subject's task is very different in the situation Miller is discussing and in the situation where just-noticeable differences are being determined. In the latter case, a reference is presented so that the subject need only discern a difference. In studying information transmission, the subject is required to state which of several alternatives was presented; he has no reference present and must make an "absolute" discrimination. Very surprisingly, the number of absolutely discriminable values is insensitive to the spacing along the scale of the chosen values, at least to a considerable extent (Attneave, 1959, pp. 67 ff.). Recent work (Garner, 1960) has indicated that a larger number of values may be useful on rating scales; the total information transmitted increases with the number of scale values up to twenty.

Several experiments (Klemmer & Frick, 1953; Pollack & Klemmer, 1954; Pollack & Ficks, 1953) indicate that increasing the number of stimulus dimensions increases the number of bits that can be assimilated at a single observation. Klemmer and Frick, for example, got a transmission value for eight-dimensional stimuli of 7.8 bits, as compared with a value for single-dimensional stimuli of about 3 bits. Quastler, Osborne, and Tweedell (1955) investigated the best combination of number of scales and number of divisions and found that five or six scales each divided into five or six scale positions could be arranged to transmit 12 bits per look. Using three symbols in conjunction with a dial increased transmission to 17.6 bits. Other studies (Augerstine, 1958) indicate that most of the information uptake occurs in the first 40 milliseconds, with little additional information assimilated in the next 200 milliseconds.

MacKay (1952) made a distinction between two kinds of information content of stimuli which is useful in talking about this set of results. He called the information carried by the different values along a single scale the *metron content* and the information carried by the different dimensions the *logon content*. It appears that the useful metron content, then, is limited to about eight values, and additional information can best be carried by increasing the logon content.

Information measures are useful in the study of memory as well as in the study of human information transmission. For example, Pollack (1954) found that immediate memory span was approximately constant at about seven units whether the units were binary numbers containing only 1 bit of information per digit, decimal numbers containing $\log_2 10 = 3.32$ bits, or letters of the alphabet containing 4.76 bits. It occurred to Smith and Miller (1952) that the information span might be increased for the smaller units if they were coded into units containing more information; then the larger units would be remembered and decoded back into the smaller units as they were reproduced. Binary digits could easily be coded three at a time as follows: $000 = 0$, $001 = 1$, $010 = 2$, $011 = 3$, $100 = 4$, $101 = 5$, $110 = 6$, and $111 = 7$. The code would then be remembered and finally reconverted into binary digits upon demand. For example, the stimulus digits 111011100010001 would be converted to 73421, which would be remembered easily. If the conversion-reconversion process were perfectly efficient, the memory span for binary digits would be increased threefold. Empirically, the improvement is not quite that marked.

Information measures have found further application in the description of the perceptual process. Attneave (1954) and Hochberg and McAlister (1953) pointed out the applicability of information measures to gestalt concepts. For example, they noted that good figures contain less information. It is easier to predict the continuation of a line from a knowledge of previous portions of the line in a good figure than in a poor one. One can fill in a circle from a knowledge of any short arc, or a triangle from a knowledge of its three corners. Such figures are highly organized, redundant, and good. Similar informational descriptions can be given for many other gestalt principles of organization. Information measures are more precise as measures of organization and accordingly should help to bring the heretofore qualitative gestalt principles more fully into the province of quantitative psychology.

The foregoing has been a summary review of completed work utilizing information measures or concepts. We have ignored such important problems as the determination of transmitted information when the transmitter and receiver are not in agreement, that is, when behaviors are less-than-perfectly correlated. Attneave (1959), Quastler (1955), Garner and Hake (1951), and McGill (1954) have given methods for calculating transmitted information from a knowledge of the inputs, outputs, and their relationships. We cannot deal with these more technical problems here, but we hope that the diversity of areas in which information theory plays a part has been indicated. The future of information theory will probably include experiments which compare human transmission rates on many additional tasks; the existence of a rationale for comparing diverse tasks stimulates the researcher to greater activity in measuring what the human being can do.

The strength of information theory is that its measure does not specify in any way whatever the nature of the message. It can be applied to things as different as binary digits, musical notes, and hormone flow from one part of the body to another. The generality is based on the simple but ingenious insight that any finite set of alternatives can be coded by numbering the alternatives. This same possibility is the basis for the variety of abilities which a digital computer can display.

Although information theory has had a useful past and has a promising future, it is appropriate to conclude our brief look at it with the cautionary paragraph with which Attneave ends his book (Attneave, 1959, p. 88):

> Although the techniques of information theory are useful in the study of the organism's information-handling processes, other techniques may often be more useful and more appropriate. That aspect of information measures which gives them so wide a range of application also limits their usefulness in any specific area. . . . The value of the concepts of information theory in leading us into new areas of investigation is not lessened, however, if in the pursuit of these investigations we find it possible to abandon information measures in favor of others more informative.

DETECTION THEORY

During World War II, engineers developed a theory of detection which would apply to the detection of targets by radar receivers. Tanner and Swets (1953, 1954) and Smith and Wilson (1953) took over the mathematical treatment and applied it to human detection. These men and many others have since extended the theory.

Signal-detection theory is a special case of statistical decision theory. A detection involves a decision based on statistical considerations rather than a simple statement of the form, "Yes, I heard the signal," or "No, I did not hear the signal." Detection theory regards the experiment which attempts to determine a sensory threshold as a game between subject and experimenter. According to this view, the subject would always say he heard the signal, whether he heard it or not, if he knew in advance that it would be presented. This does not mean that subjects should simply be regarded as dishonest; it means that

there is no sharp division between detecting and not detecting a signal. The subject is always making a decision based on probabilistic
rather than certain information.

Since the decisions are based on probabilistic information, the decision may be determined by the relative values and costs of making
various decisions. These values and costs determine a *payoff matrix*
like the one in Table 10. According to this matrix, the subject gains

Table 10   Payoff matrix for detection experiment

	subject's decision	
signal presented?	*yes*	*no*
Yes	10	−5
No	−1	1

10 units (say 10 cents) if he says the signal was presented when it
was but loses 5 units (5 cents) if he says it was not when it was. If he
makes an incorrect decision when a signal was not presented, he loses
1 cent, and he gains 1 cent if he makes the correct decision. It is intuitively clear that, given this payoff matrix, cases where the probability that a signal was presented is about equal to the probability
that no signal was presented should be resolved in favor of signal.
More will be gained if this turns out to be right than will be lost if it
is wrong; putting it another way, more can be gained by saying "yes"
correctly than by saying "no" correctly.

Another factor combines with the payoff matrix in biasing decisions.
This is the advance, or a priori, probability that a signal will be presented. Again our intuition tells us that if we know in advance that
signals will be presented in nine intervals out of ten, we should say
"signal presented" in uncertain cases. The a priori probability, in conjunction with the payoff matrix, determines how probable it must be
that a signal was presented before a mathematically perfect (ideal)
observer would say "signal presented." The probability that a signal
was presented is determined by examining the characteristics of the
sensory input during the interval in question. If the probability obtained from the sensory input exceeds the criterion probability obtained from mathematical calculations, the ideal observer says "signal"; if it does not, the ideal observer says "no signal."

The criterion value chosen is usually such that some function is
maximized; that is, we assume that the ideal observer is trying to

make decisions so that the most money will be obtained or the most correct responses made. Peterson, Birdsall, and Fox (1954) have discussed possible criteria and developed the formula which appropriately combines the a priori probabilities and payoff matrix to determine a maximum payoff criterion.

In order not to digress from the main outlines of the theory, the preceding paragraphs have proceeded on the assumption that one could operate with a simple probability that a signal had occurred. This is not true; one must compute two probabilities, and neither is of the kind suggested. Detection theory computes (1) the probability that *if* a signal had been presented, the observed sensory input would have occurred, and (2) the probability that *if* no signal had been presented, the observed sensory input would have occurred. These two probabilities are then used to form a ratio called the *likelihood ratio*. These likelihood ratios are compared to a likelihood-ratio criterion in reaching a decision, as outlined above. It can be shown that the likelihood ratio gives the observer all the information needed for making optimal decisions. Computationally, it turns out to be much easier to use a transformation of likelihood ratio as the actual decision axis, but none of the consequences change.

The reader may be wondering at this point what sense it can possibly make to consider the probability that a sensory input would occur if no signal were presented. Such a probability becomes reasonable on the assumption that there is always random stimulation, or noise, present in any sensory system. The name generally given to a sensory system within detection theory is *receiver*. So far as a receiver is concerned, there are two kinds of noise. One comes from the outside world, the other from the receiver's own workings. In case the receiver is a human observer, the internal noise is usually called neural noise. Such internal noises can never completely be eliminated, even if it were possible to eliminate completely noise at the receiver input. The origin of the noise, as far as the performance of the detector is concerned, is irrelevant. Any noise will degrade the performance of the system. Hence there will always be some likelihood, however small, that the observed sensory input could have occurred even though no signal was presented.

The determination of the necessary probabilities for the computations of likelihood ratio is not a trivial accomplishment. It is really this determination which distinguishes detection theory from decision theory, or the testing of statistical hypotheses, in general. The basic difficulty in characterizing the likelihood ratio associated with a given sensory input is that the input is initially given as a continuous waveform, while statistical decision theory is intended to work with discrete numerical measurements. If the waveform has certain properties, it can be characterized, without loss of information, by a limited number of measurements. The number of measurements required depends on the highest frequency present in the waveform (W) and the length of time (T) over which the waveform is to be measured; the number of measurements required is exactly $2WT$. Still other difficulties have to be overcome before the signal and noise can meaningfully be compared; the reader who is interested in the details of this treatment should consult Licklider (1959). Here we will simply say that, given the necessary assumptions, the detection-theory model can generate the necessary likelihood ratios.

Figure 11 is a general block diagram of the ideal observer as visualized in detection theory. Let us now examine an experimental situation in conjunction with this block diagram in order to get a clearer idea of how detection theorists think about signal detection.

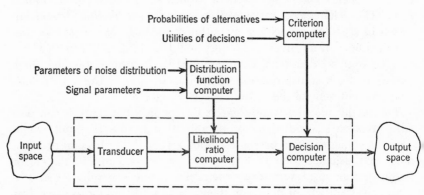

FIGURE 11. Block diagram of ideal observer in detection theory. (*Source: Figure 5, from Tanner, W. P., Jr., Physiological implications of psychophysical data. Ann. N.Y. Acad. Sci., vol. 89, art. 5, pp. 752–765, January 1961.*)

Two general types of situations may be presented to the observer. Either he must say whether or not a signal was presented within a single fixed time interval or he must say which of several specified intervals contained a signal, knowing that one of them did. It is simpler to talk about the former situation, although it is easier to relate the theory to the latter. In the multiple-interval case, the subjects readily choose intervals containing the event with the largest likelihood ratio when they understand that the payoffs and a priori probabilities are equal. In a case involving only a single interval, it may be difficult to specify what a subject thinks about the a priori probabilities, what he is using for a payoff matrix, and whether he is using a maximum payoff criterion. The subject's instructions are usually intended to specify these parameters exactly, but may fail to do so perfectly.

We shall consider the block diagram as it relates to the single-interval case. In the simplest case, the distribution-function computer could be given the signal-plus-noise and the noise-alone distributions within the signal space. Then these distributions would not need to be computed progressively from experience, although the ideal observer would be perfectly capable of doing this if necessary. In either case, the distributions are needed so that probabilities which determine the likelihood ratio for the particular observation can be computed.

The a priori probabilities that signal plus noise, or noise alone, will be presented on a particular trial are needed by the criterion computer. The payoff matrix would also be necessary to its computation of the criterion.

With the distributions and the criterion in hand, the ideal observer is ready to begin its observations. An input is presented within an interval. The observer takes the sample through its transducer, which performs the necessary operations in order to obtain the $2WT$ measurements. The output of the transducer is fed into the likelihood computer along with the distribution functions for the two distributions. This information is sufficient for the likelihood-ratio computer to compute its output. The decision computer needs only to compare the likelihood ratio with the criterion computed by the criterion computer in order to make its decision.

How well can an ideal observer do in discriminating between signal plus noise and noise alone? Detection theory shows that the optimal performance possible depends on the relationship between the energy of the signal (E) and the power per unit bandwidth of the noise (N). To be more specific, the distance in standard deviation units between the means of the distribution of likelihood ratios for signal plus noise and noise alone, on a logarithmic scale, is the square root of $2E/N$. This distance between the distributions is called d'. The value of d' determines what performance can be achieved by the observer. A perfect performance would be defined by the observation that the subject always said "signal" when a signal was in fact presented (called a *hit*) and never said "signal" when noise alone was presented (called a *false alarm*). Most performances are less than perfect, but their excellence must always be described as a certain relationship between the probability of a hit, $P_s(S)$, and the probability of a false alarm, $P_s(N)$. Since $P_s(S)$ and $P_s(N)$ can be determined from the value of d', the reverse computation, plus certain assumptions, will give d' if one knows $P_s(S)$ and $P_s(N)$. This is indeed fortunate when d' is to be computed for the human observer, for in this case it is not possible to measure the noise distribution which is presented to the distribution-function computer or, for that matter, the signal-plus-noise distribution. The neural noise cannot be directly measured. Therefore it is impossible to compute d' from a knowledge of E and N as they come through the human transducer. Instead, the experimenter computes what d' would have to be in order that the ideal observer duplicate the observed values of $P_s(S)$ and $P_s(N)$. The required d' can then be compared with the d' computed from the physical measures of signal energy (E) and power per unit bandwidth (N). These physical measures, as we have seen, determine what d' would be for the ideal observer. Actual observers can never perform as well as the ideal observer; the latter, being a mathematical abstraction, is unbeatable.

The d' values so far obtained for human observers have shown good consistency for a given individual over a considerable range of values of a priori probability and payoff matrix. It is this consistency which represents perhaps the greatest victory of detection theory, for this consistency cannot be achieved by the traditional theory based on thresholds. The threshold has been found to vary with conditions. Corrections for guessing cannot eliminate inconsistencies in threshold. Psychophysicists were coming to regard thresholds as significant only under the specified conditions in which the threshold had been determined. The d' measure with its greater generality escapes this limitation. If d' has been determined for a particular pair of values $P_s(S)$ and $P_s(N)$, then the pairing of other values of $P_s(S)$ and $P_s(N)$ can be given with greater generality (for a particular subject, as values in the payoff matrix and a priori probabilities are changed).

The ability to do this is given by the fact that d' determines a receiver operating curve, or ROC. Figure 12 shows a set of such curves. The diagonal line represents chance performance; we note that if the observer gives no false alarms he cannot ever correctly call out "signal." However, if he is willing to call "signal" each time, he will always be correct if the signal is presented and always incorrect if the noise is presented. The diagonal line is the only possible ROC if d' equals 0; as d' increases, the ROC moves further from the diagonal line. There is never any sudden shift to a new level of responding as the signal and noise are made more discriminable, as a naïve view of the threshold concept might suggest. Swets (1961) has recently reviewed several versions of threshold theory and showed that the modifications required to bring threshold theory in line with empirical results may make it look quite similar to detection theory.

The ROC has been a useful device for predicting results in both vision and audition (Carterette & Cole, 1962); this could indeed be said for the whole of detection theory. The foregoing brief summary cannot be expected to give an adequate picture of the theory, especially of the details of mathematical treatment of different cases. The theory is not like information theory in the sense that neither theory nor experiment lends itself so easily to the simplified and piecemeal treatment which can be used to sample the results of information theory.

We can, however, review what has been presented and note the relationship of the general point of view to some systematic considerations. First, we note that signal-detection theory takes as its primary datum a *decision* made by the observing organism or equipment. The observer is playing a game (in the mathematical sense) which he tries to win, rather than describing a sensory experience. If the organism has information that the a priori probability that a tiger is present is equal to 1.00, the organism does not even listen to present stimuli; it does not introspect, it runs. The observer in the psychophysical experiment is regarded as a similar expression of a tendency for an adjustive organism to use whatever information *should* be related to a

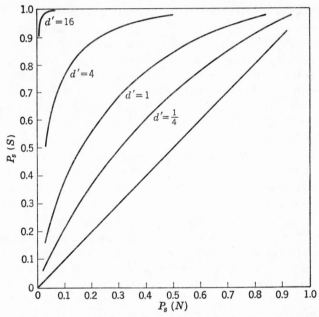

FIGURE 12. Receiver operating curves for varying values of d'. (*Source: Figure 2, from Peterson, W. W., Birdsall, T. G., & Fox, W. C., The theory of signal detectability, Transactions of Professional Group on Information Theory, Institute of Radio Engineers, PGIT-4, pp. 171–212, 1954.*)

decision, with no prejudice that all relevant information is given on a sensory channel on a particular trial. This point of view resembles the functionalist point of view in its emphasis on adaptation, and it is behavioristic in its acceptance of the overt decision as the significant experimental datum. It is modern in its use of a mathematical system as a model; it shows the impact of another modern influence of mathematics on psychology in its relationship to game theory (see Birdsall, 1953). Its realm of relevance is limited and its specificity often very high, yet the theory has sufficient generality so that experimental results which had seemed to disagree can be related in a consistent and meaningful way. Despite the fact that the theory is specific and hence sensitive to experimental results, it is not so rigid that it must fall whenever any deviation of experiment from theory occurs; it can be modified to accommodate, to some extent, new and unexpected results.

Both detection theory and information theory represent what may be considered a new middle of the road for psychological theory. They strike a balance between specificity and generality, and between sensitivity and flexibility. The information measure lends itself easily to use in predictive formulas, and detection theory often provides such predictive formulas, given certain preliminary measures in the case of the human observer. Both bodies of theory are quite rigorous compared with the theory and systems of yesteryear, and neither takes all psychological knowledge for its province. Both theories have runners that cross into other gardens; or, to be more accurate, their roots are actually in engineering gardens and their runners in psychology. Finally, they are not isolated from each other or from other theories in terms of the people interested in them, the disciplines involved, or the problems treated. On one level of generality, they have much in common. Both theories deal with signals in a mathematical way, both originated in the study of equipment, and both apply in a most satisfying manner to the study of man. Both are heavy in considerations of probabilities of messages or signals, respectively. Neither is divorced from the study of cybernetics (here one could note again Wiener's discussion of information measures in his book called *Cybernetics*). As we saw earlier, computers play a role in the thinking of the men interested in all these areas. As a matter of fact, there is a cohesiveness within the group of scientists interested in the problems outlined in this section which gives them as much reason to be called a school of psychology as, for example, the functionalists, who were quite a loose group. The contemporary engineering psychologist, like the contemporary learning psychologist, has a sense of identity and community of interest which is not altogether unlike that of the earlier schools of psychology, which have largely disappeared within the last decade.

MATHEMATICAL MODELS IN LEARNING THEORY

The usefulness of mathematics. Mathematics has always been a tool of the scientist. It has been said that mathematics lends to science rigor, precision, richness, logic, and other highly valued properties. It is not surprising that psychology, which has been a sort of scientific second cousin, should turn increasingly to mathematics as a gateway to respectability. However, mathematics cannot be guaranteed to be such a gateway; let us consider briefly what mathematics can and cannot be expected to do.

Logic and mathematics are very closely related. We can say, at the very least, that any mathematical system has formal postulates at its foundations. These postulates are such that further statements (theorems) can be derived from them via rules for logical deduction.

Mathematical theorems are thus derived from the postulates for the particular mathematical system.

Consider a mathematical system that can be used as a model for a physical system. New statements that are valid within the mathematical system can be generated. If these new statements turn out to be true of the physical system, the mathematical model is at that point a successful model. If the mathematically valid statement does not fit the physical system, the model fails. The possibility of checking statements in this way is the basis of the hypothetico-deductive approach and underlies the effort to construct mathematical models.

There are two extreme ways in which a theorist might proceed to relate a mathematical system to a physical system. He might select empirical relationships to which existing mathematics apply without modification. In one sense, this is not an unusual procedure; detection theory, for example, took a mathematical framework and specialized it to apply to an extant area of psychological investigation. Some degree of specialization is nearly always necessary, even though no real mathematical innovation is needed. The mathematical system would be complete, with postulates and most theorems worked out, in this case.

At the other extreme, the theorist might decide to take a defined empirical area and construct whatever model was necessary to fit that area. Hull and his collaborators (Hull et al., 1940) seem to have made an attempt of this kind. The postulational structure that was necessary to encompass the area of rote learning was so formidable that the model has aroused more amazement than interest on the part of psychologists. The model was too complex and unwieldy to be of much use, even if it had provided significant predictive advances over those possible from simpler empirical generalizations.

Rashevsky (e.g., 1948) provides a second example of mathematical brilliance that has been largely wasted as far as psychological interest is concerned. His model is not a single special model as Hull's was, and there is no detailed attempt to apply any one part of the model to all the data within a prescribed empirical area. However, the weakness of Rashevsky's work is similar to the weakness of Hull's rote-learning model in that there was insufficient interaction between model and experiment in the construction of the model. Such interaction seems necessary in order that a model provide the necessary fit to an empirical area and so that the components of the model at each stage survive limited tests made in earlier stages.

Mathematics is useful to science because it provides convenient and conventional deductive apparatus for prediction and generalization. There are many general types of mathematics as well as many possible models within a given type. One does not need to ask whether it is appropriate to use mathematics, because the ability to predict and generalize is useful, and mathematics, conceived of very broadly, is just a tool for accomplishing these functions. Whether some new tools need to be invented for psychology's use remains to be seen.

Mathematics and measurement. Some people confuse mathematics and measurement, but the two are to a considerable extent independent. Measurement, as far as we are concerned, is a process that establishes a correspondence between mathematical systems and empirical systems. Manipulations within the abstract system of mathematics are possible whether any correspondence exists or not. Traditional measurement established a correspondence between some number system (usually the real numbers) and some property of an empirical system (like the deflection of a needle on an appropriate meter applied to a point in a physical system). Measurement requires showing that the rules postulated to hold for the abstract elements in fact hold for the empirical property in question.

It is clear that the problem of measurement is inextricably intertwined with the problem of constructing mathematical models, though measurement is not necessarily part of mathematics per se. As we shall see later in studying Estes' model, it is not true that all the abstract elements are measured directly, but measurement in the sense of establishment of correspondences between model and empirical data is nevertheless an absolutely essential part of the process.

Properties of mathematical models. There is no single criterion defining what a mathematical model is. A single functional relationship between two variables can be considered a mathematical model, since it provides a method of deducing values of one variable from values of another. This function may hold only for a highly restrictive situation, as for rote learning of digits presented at a fixed rate under rigidly specified conditions, and only given several parameters of the equation.

At the other extreme, we might consider all of Newtonian mechanics as another mathematical model. Here the model is of enormous scope and is far more complex.

One dimension of models, then, is their scope. In psychology we see at one extreme Ebbinghaus's empirical learning curve (see Hilgard, 1956) and at the other Hull's theory of mammalian behavior (e.g., Hull, 1952). A related dimension is complexity. Though simplicity is desirable, it is not legitimate to criticize a model because of complexity, for it may be that even a complex model is the simplest one possible.

Another dimension of models has to do with their origins; the most common question asked is whether a portion of the model was derived empirically or rationally. Further questions then concern the adequacy of whatever grounds are produced. These are all legitimate questions, but they cannot have any bearing on the adequacy of the model. If the model had been, like commandments, simply handed to the theorist, there would be no formal grounds for criticism. The critic might justifiably be skeptical, but the final verdict must in every case await empirical observations of the adequacy of the model.

Another broad category of dimensions is the mathematical and logical adequacy of the model. The model should meet the usual criteria, such as independence and consistency of assumptions, and the necessary correspondence between model and data must be established in order that mathematical operations be justified.

The dimension that is the final arbiter has already been emphasized; it is the degree of empirical verification of predictions made with the use of the model. Values of this dimension are by no means easy to establish. Most models can make particular predictions only with a particular probability, and competing models may make the same prediction with a greater or lesser probability. It is not a simple matter to relate hypotheses to empirical outcomes; some excellent papers have been devoted to this problem (e.g., Watanabe, 1960). It will suffice for our purposes to say that a successful model must have predicted all outcomes to which it applies with some probability greater than zero and that in general the model is better the higher the probability and the greater the number of outcomes predicted.

A final property of mathematical models is the type of mathematical or logical system used. Lewin's work, discussed earlier in Chapter 11, is one illustration that the usual kind of mathematics taught in algebra and calculus courses is not the only type which has been tried in application to psychology. There is no a priori reason to prefer one type of mathematics to another. The type of mathematics to be preferred in psychology will be determined on other than a priori, logical grounds. It is clear that a model cannot be successful without diligent and prolonged effort. There is no ready panacea either in new and esoteric or in old and established mathematics.

A representative model. W. K. Estes has been a highly successful pioneer among contemporary psychologists who have attempted to develop mathematical models for learning (see also Chapter 10). His first statement of the preliminary version of his statistical association model was published in 1950. The scope of the effort that has gone into the development of his model is reflected in his comprehensive article of 1959b. The present chapter can consider only some of the orienting attitudes involved, the basic assumptions underlying the model, and a sample of the techniques involved.

Estes is one of an increasing number of psychologists who is willing to pledge allegiance to the basic methods of the older sciences, especially physics. His orientation is quantitative, operational, physical-istic—generally hardheaded. This orientation seems typical of those who are or have been in the business of constructing mathematical models.

Estes is frankly behavioristic. His general orientation toward learning theory is similar to Guthrie's. His is an S-R theory which considers a stimulus as decomposable into elements and which considers the termination of a situation a reinforcing event; it is a contiguity theory.

In this last respect, Estes' recent position is less clear than his initial position. He has said (1959b, p. 405): "In brief, our answer to the question 'reinforcement or contiguity?' is simply, 'both.' Whether we can have our cake and eat it and still not grow fat is a much more difficult question." In spite of this apparent hedging, Estes leaned toward contiguity assumptions. He recently (1959a, 1960; Estes et al., 1960) has made a radical shift in the basic assumptions underlying his statistical association learning theory. The newest theory, backed by experimental results from human paired-associate learning, regards learning as an all-or-none process. The stimulus pattern to be learned either is or is not associated with the correct response on a particular trial. There is a certain probability of correct association on a single trial and a similar but much lower probability that the association will be forgotten, so that a correct response on one test will be followed by an incorrect response on a subsequent test. (As yet, it is not certain whether the correct-incorrect series should be attributed mostly to forgetting or to change in the stimulus pattern.) If the correct association is not learned on a particular trial, there seems to be no increase over the chance probability that a correct response will be made at a subsequent test.

Despite the drastic revision in basic assumptions that has recently occurred, we have elected to present Estes' more classic version of statistical association theory. More data have been collected in tests of the original theory, and the classic theory may still turn out to be more appropriate in the analysis of the free-response situation.

In the original version (Estes, 1950) learning is regarded as a basically statistical process which occurs in discrete jumps. The stimulus is conceived of as a set of stimulus elements. Not all elements are available on any given trial; that is, on any given trial, the organism samples some proportion of the total set of elements. If an element is sampled on a trial, and some response terminates the trial, that element will be conditioned (connected) to that response as a result of that single pairing. Any stimulus element can be connected to only one response at a time. Extinction occurs, then, whenever the stimulus elements become connected to some other response than the previously reinforced one.

The response measure used is probability of response. Such a measure is simple enough to obtain when some fixed interval is given in which an organism can respond or not, or in which the organism must choose one response from a set before a trial terminates. Some difficulties are encountered when the situation is a free-response situation, and multiple responses occur within a single experimental session.

Estes overcomes this difficulty by assuming some minimum time required to execute a response; let this be expressed in minutes by h. Then $1/h$ responses can occur per minute. For example, if the animal requires $\frac{1}{60}$ minute to complete a response, the maximum rate of responding is 60 per minute. If the maximum rate is 60 responses per minute, but the probability that a response will occur in any one interval is only .25, then the rate will be only .25 $\times$ 60 = 15 responses per minute. At this point, the theoretical output, a probability, has made contact with an empirical measure, rate.

Other empirical relationships follow almost immediately from the initial computation. This situation contrasts markedly with Hull's method of handling response measures (see Chapter 10), in which each new response measure had to be linked to the reaction potential by means of a new postulated function. Let us look at how simple it is to relate probability to latency.

In any time interval, T, there will be T/h intervals, or T/h possible responses. In our hypothetical case there would be 60 $\times$ 10 = 600 intervals or possible responses in a 10-minute period. Since the probability of responding in an interval is only P rather than 1.00, PT/h responses would be expected to occur. In our case, 150 responses would occur. Each response required h minutes, in our case $\frac{1}{60}$ minute. These responses will require a total of $PT/h \times h = PT$ minutes (in our case 2.5 minutes), leaving $T - PT$ minutes (7.5 minutes) for intervals of no responding. The mean time between responses will then be $T - PT$ divided by PT/h, that is, just the time for no responding divided by the number of responses. In our case, this would be 7.5 minutes divided by 150 responses, or .05 minute. Carrying out the division, we obtain $(h/P) - h$ as the mean time preceding a response. If latency is measured as the time from completion of the prior response to completion of the next, we add h and obtain latency = h/P. In our example, the mean latency can be obtained directly by dividing $\frac{1}{60}$ by .25 to get $\frac{1}{15}$, or by adding $\frac{1}{60}$ to our previous answer, .05, to get $\frac{1}{15}$. No special assumptions were necessary, and we found that the number of responses equaled PT/h automatically in the process of deriving latency. As Estes has said (1959b, p. 395):

> We have no guarantee that our approach will lead to anything passable as a learning theory, but we can have some confidence that if we do arrive at a theory, it will not be found floating idly in mid-air while the constructors try belatedly to drop a few ad hoc mooring lines down to the plane of observables.

In the language of our earlier discussion, we might say that Estes took care of the problem of response measurement early in the process of theory construction.

Let us now return to the stimulus side of the model and see how almost equally simple assumptions and derivations lead to some predictions about the form of learning curves.

A critical question that must be answered is what proportion of stimulus elements is sampled by the organism on a particular trial. Let us ignore for a moment the problem of how this proportion is determined and assume that we know it. We shall call this proportion theta (θ). The question then is, "What effect will a single trial have on the probability of making a specified response?"

At any moment, we can divide the total number of stimulus elements, S, into two classes: those conditioned to the response in question and those conditioned to other responses. Let X be the number of elements conditioned to the response in question. If S is the total number, then there will be $S - X$ elements conditioned to some other response. Consider what this implies for a situation in which the response in question always occurs last and terminates a trial, that is, a situation in which the response is always reinforced.

In the first place, we should expect $\theta(S - X)$ unconditioned elements to be sampled on any given trial. For example, if there were 100 elements, 80 of which were not conditioned, and if the organism samples 50 elements on each trial, θ would equal 50/100, or .5, and we should expect 40 of the unconditioned elements to be sampled [.5 $(100 - 20) = 40$]. Every one of these elements will be connected to the response at the end of the trial. The expected *change* in the number of elements conditioned (ΔX) as the result of a single trial therefore equals $\theta(S - X)$.

The probability of response is taken to be X/S, the number of conditioned elements divided by the total number of elements: $P = X/S$. The change in probability is then just the change in X divided by S: $\Delta X/S$. To convert the equation $\Delta X = \theta(S - X)$ to an equation for ΔP, we can divide both sides by S and obtain $\Delta X/S = \theta(S - X)/S$ or $\Delta X/S = \theta(S/S - X/S)$. Since $\Delta X/S = \Delta P$ and $X/S = P$, we can rewrite this $\Delta P = \theta(1 - P)$. With this equation in hand, we can always say what, on the average, the probability of response should be if we know the probability of response on the previous trial. We have an equation that will give us the *difference* between the two probabilities. If P_n is the probability of response on the nth trial, and P_{n+1} is the probability of response on the next trial, then $P_{n+1} = P_n + \theta(1 - P_n)$. This is Estes' basic learning equation. It can be solved to yield a general equation for probability of response on any trial, given the probability on the first; this general equation is $P_n = 1 - (1 - P)(1 - \theta)^{n-1}$. This equation has provided a good fit to acquisition data obtained from rats in runways, T mazes, and bar-pressing experiments.

This concludes our brief look at the early version of Estes' theory, but there are a few points that should be cleared up before we consider some additions to the theory. First, there is the question of determining θ, the proportion of elements sampled. The determination cannot be made directly by any sort of observation of a sampling process; for one thing, there is no correspondence established between the theoretical stimulus elements and elements of any experimentally defined stimulus. Even if such a correspondence existed, it is hard to visualize how one could determine what proportion of elements an organism sampled on a given trial. The determination of θ must, then, be indirect. That value of θ is chosen which provides the best fit of the theoretical curve to acquisition data. At this stage, the model becomes, for the moment, superfluous; that is, if success in fitting a curve to data were *all* the model provided, the theorist would be no better off than if he had started out directly in quest of a curve. However, if the value of θ obtained from a part of a set of data yields a good fit to the remainder, that is a gain over what might be expected from extrapolation of a curve. If values of θ obtained in one situation apply to others, that is a substantial gain. We saw in the earlier part of this chapter that the measure of separation d', used in the theory of signal detectability, provides this kind of predictability from situation to situation, whereas the threshold as a measure did not. It is too early to say what extent of generality can be expected of θ as a parameter, but the results to date are promising.

One of the most important modifications to Estes' theory has been the addition of a "barrier" which divides the total set of stimulus elements into two subsets. One subset is composed of those elements which are available for sampling. Over a period of time, elements move from one subset into the other. Since each subset is in turn divided further into two subsets on the basis of conditioning to a particular response, there are really four subsets altogether. It is clear that movement of unconditioned elements into the available subset may decrease probability of response, while movement of conditioned elements into the available subset will increase this probability. The over-all set of stimulus elements has the property that the proportion of conditioned and unconditioned elements in the available and unavailable subsets tends to become equal over a period of time. The reader can verify that this complication of the model makes it possible to handle such phenomena as effects of interpolated learning, spacing of trials, spontaneous recovery, and forgetting. Estes has suggested (1958, 1961) that the effects of drive may also be amenable to this treatment.

SUMMARY AND CONCLUSIONS

A coherent group of ideas emanating from engineering and mathematics forms a nucleus which is serving to organize a new school in psychology. The organizing concepts are information transmission, decision and detection theory, feedback, and the computer's simulation of human function. In the present chapter, the basic concepts of information theory and detection theory have been presented. An indication of the relationships between computer technology and these theoretical developments has been given.

Finally, Estes' statistical learning theory has been examined in its earlier form. The mathematical development presented by Estes is a distant relative of detection theory and information theory; only the extensive use of statistical models relates them. This relationship, however, sets these statistical theories sufficiently apart from more traditional pychology so that they can be treated together. Estes' recent changes in his model have been discussed last.

It is appropriate that our survey of systematic and theoretical psychology has ended with the reader immersed in the modification of a miniature system and a specific question about the generality of a sampling parameter. It began with very general philosophic issues that seem to us to lie at the foundations of the science of psychology. This is the same progression that has occurred in systematic psychology. The traditional systems have disappeared in a host of specific issues, and the systematist in the old sense is today a rarity. His loss will be psychology's gain, as our young science turns to the collection of more enduring facts that bear on more resolvable issues.

further readings

It is difficult to suggest readings that give an adequate background on the computer revolution. However, Miller, Galanter, and Pribram's *Plans and the structure of behavior* (1960) gives a good picture of the attitude toward human behavior which is fostered by computer technology. For acquiring a genuine familiarity with the technology per se, some direct contact with it is almost a necessity. Attneave's little book, *Applications of information theory to psychology* (1959), should be read by every psychology major. The student can go on from the references there if he wishes. Swets's article in *Science* (1961) is perhaps the best initial bridge to detection theory. Licklider's article, "Three auditory theories," in Koch's Volume I of *Psychology: A study of a science* (1959), is devoted to detection theory in part. Licklider is a clear and selective summarizer. From there, the logical step would be back to Tanner and Swets's early article (1954). Two recent articles, by Swets, Green, and Tanner (1962) and by Carterette and Cole (1962), show recent directions of research; the latter article is good also because it leads back to the important work done by Egan and others at Indiana. To learn about Estes, the obvious suggestion is to read Estes; an economical sequence would be the publications in 1950, 1959a, and 1960.

epilogue

Having surveyed the major systematic and theoretical developments within the recent history of American psychology, we pause now to review some of the most important themes and to take a brief look forward. Separate consideration will be given to systems and theories, as these have been distinguished throughout the present work, followed by some comments on what seem to us to be certain of the most persistent and pernicious obstacles in the way of scientific advance in psychology.

THE FUTURE OF SYSTEMS

What are the prospects for the development of relatively new and different systems? Several sources of such systems may be considered. First, new systems may occur as the result of the accretion and organization of salient theories. Such development would be the most natural consequence of the normal growth of low-order empirical propositions into high-order theoretical principles. Organization of theories into systems would then follow no set pattern but would occur as a consequence of the integration or amalgamation of a given methodology and point of view with the resulting substantive contributions. Systematic formulations would not be forced but would wait upon the full maturation of the foundation theories. It should be pointed out, however, that such a system would be considerably different from the systems that we have treated and that there might be some question about whether it should even be called a system.

A related but somewhat different and more typical form of systematic development would follow the appearance of radically new ideas and methodologies (such as psychoanalysis) or of strong protests against old orthodoxies (such as *gestalttheorie*). Here the system would appear more or less full-blown, in advance of any extensive substantive theoretical contributions. Any feeling of completeness concerning current coverage of the field should not mislead us into the belief that such new systems cannot occur.

A more probable source of new systems would be through the more or less gradual transformation of all or part of extant systems. Here the recent history of psychology offers examples in the form of such trends as neoanalysis and neobehaviorism. The extent of modification would of course determine whether the resulting system would be considered merely a revision of the old or something sufficiently different to justify recognition as a completely *new* system.

Transformation of only a part of an older system offers an interesting form of this phenomenon. The contemporary emergence of Skinnerian psychology from some of the basic Watsonian notions into a tight-knit system affords an illuminating illustration of the possibilities of this process.

Finally, we need to consider the extreme alternative of the gradual elimination of all systems, a prospect that fails to daunt many contemporary psychologists and critics of psychology. Probably no other discipline has seen so much system making and so much dependence on systems by investigators and theorists. The early systems may have had some role in helping to establish psychology as an active scientific discipline, mainly in that they set the stage for initial investigations of behavior problems and maintained enthusiasm among the investigators. Today, however, they tend to hamper rather than facilitate research by emphasizing outdated issues and hindering fresh looks at problems. While we take no stand on whether *all* systems are doomed in psychology, we think it safe to say that most of the present systems will disappear, at least so far as any effective impact upon behavior science is concerned.

THE FUTURE OF THEORIES

At the present time theories of the mathematical type appear to offer great promise for future theoretical advance in psychology. Whether or not such promise is ultimately realized is one of the most intriguing questions to be answered within the next few decades. Our guess is that it will be, but not necessarily in the manner envisioned in contemporary models. Mathematical techniques, applied to behavior theory as elsewhere, are essentially tools, and to be maximally useful they will need to be guided and governed by imaginative and inventive thinkers and experimenters.

A somewhat different kind of development is the growth of so-called miniature systems (see Chapter 3). As commonly defined, these consist of a cluster of interrelated hypotheses in a highly circumscribed problem area (e.g., Harlow, 1959; Logan, 1960; Festinger, 1957). Such theories, as they are perhaps more appropriately labeled, certainly do not need to be mathematical in nature. Whatever their character, there is definitely a strong trend toward such relatively restricted but tightly organized theoretical productions, in personality theory (cf. Chapter 12) as well as other areas. Miniature systems thus appear to offer a valuable model for future theory construction.

A third kind of theoretical development that offers much in future promise is the interrelationship of behavior theory with other fields of investigation. Here two especially fertile unions may be cited. First, and most impressive, is the area of brain physiology. After long years of relatively little progress, a remarkable series of researches has recently appeared and has interacted most fruitfully with techniques for studying behavior. Unfortunately, we have had no opportunity in this work to review these studies and can here do little more than point to two or three especially striking breakthroughs. New techniques of permanent implantation of electrodes in the brain have resulted in a great variety of investigations involving self-stimulation by the animal and the consequent mapping of functional areas (cf. Zeigler, 1957; Miller, 1958; Olds, 1959). The combination of such physiological techniques (including also the implantation of minute packets of chemicals) with Skinnerian operant-conditioning procedures has thus opened up new research areas with emphasis upon neurophysiology as well as behavior. Also, the rapidly mushrooming research on the reticular arousal system (RAS) of the brain, with critical relationships to sensory systems as well as behavioral indices such as those involving attention and curiosity and the like, has also opened up new research problems and theoretical vistas (cf. Berlyne, 1960; White, 1959; Malmo, 1959). All in all, this kind of research is a far cry from the gross ablation and extirpation experiments which marked the early phases of brain-behavior investigation in psychology. The great ferment now evident in this area of research gives promise of continuing productivity—and perhaps even ultimately some kind of general unifying principles for behavior science.

The area of social psychology, viewed as a junction of psychology and sociology, is another most promising field for interdisciplinary research (although it may of course be viewed, alternatively, as a field of investigation in its own right—which is customary for such ventures when sufficiently successful). While this area has also been omitted from direct consideration in the present work, it obviously has much to offer for future scientific advance. Extension of such interdisciplinary efforts to other social-scientific fields, notably economics, is an interesting prospect (e.g., Katona, 1960).

A fourth development in theoretical psychology is the recent prominence of *models*, as we have contrasted these with more orthodox kinds of theories (Chapter 3). The as-if type of thinking characteristic of modelizing, and the resultant lack of any need to commit oneself to particular substantive propositions, has attracted many psychologists and promises to play an even greater role in future theory making.

Finally, we need to consider the extreme antitheoretical, or at least atheoretical, position adopted by a number, perhaps an increasingly large number, of positivistic psychologists. At an even more basic level there is the related disinclination of many such persons to use the raw tools of theories—constructs—and preference for dealing only with directly observable variables. Since psychology is so obviously replete with all sorts of such constructs (e.g., emotions, motives, feelings, and the like) which have proved of questionable scientific utility, the temptation is strong to accept the radical excision of such terms along with the theories they are used to construct. It is our opinion that this position will flourish and will contribute much in the way of empirical propositions and interesting and important experimental techniques, although it will not by itself prove sufficient to produce a well-rounded scientific psychology. But it has had, and should continue to have, a most salutary effect on theorizing in that it should help to eliminate much of the older, less-rigorous kind of speculation presented in the guise of theory. What remains should provide a sounder basis for behavior science.

SPECIAL PROBLEMS

Here we are concerned with a résumé of some of the major obstacles that stand in the way of scientific growth of psychology, particularly with regard to theoretical structures.

Applied pressures. The tremendous growth of applied forms of psychology during and after World War II has accentuated the differences between the purely scientific aspects of the field and the applied aspects, particularly clinical and counseling practices. Although there is certainly no essential reason why science and practice cannot live together peaceably, the fact nonetheless is that their relations within psychology have been considerably strained.

There are two related facets of the applied pressures that affect scientific work in psychology. These may be briefly characterized as the pressure for (1) quick results to be applied to urgent problems and (2) real-life models and theories rather than highly abstracted ones.

On the whole, these pressures are seriously detrimental to sound scientific progress. The pressure for quick results is likely to lead to prematurely committed direction of research as well as hastily constructed experiments and theories. Obsession with real-life models likewise presents a major handicap to theory development, especially perhaps in the area of personality theory. Real-life considerations are important ones, but primarily they are springboards from which scientific problems develop. Real life with its multiplicity of variables may present interactions not readily observed in simpler laboratory experiments; thus real-life investigation may be helpful before definitive statements of relationships among variables are made. Nevertheless, the ultimate scientific test of theoretical principles is an experimental one, and real-life models should serve as guides rather than criteria or objectives.

Resistance to differentiation. An interesting and important by-product of continued scientific advance in psychology is certain to be the differentiation (if not the dismemberment; cf. Klüver, 1949) of the discipline into a number of related but distinct areas of research and theory. It is perhaps possible that the appearance of some great unifying principle, comparable to evolutionary theory in biology, will tend to mitigate this development—but hardly to stay it completely. And, of course, there is as yet no clearly discernible sign of any such great principle; the Freudian unconscious, the Pavlovian conditioned reflex, and the like seem not quite to have qualified, although they might have been candidates.

The general resistance to the division of psychology is somewhat difficult to explain logically, but it could become a serious obstacle to effective theory construction. That is, the compulsion to maintain psychology as a single unified discipline might have ramifications for the kind of theory constructed and encouraged and for theory criticism. On the other hand, the normal and expected development of divergent lines of theory, even with questionable coordinations, as well as the continued divergence of various subject-matter areas, should all be encouraged as an evidence of scientific maturity, it seems to us, rather than discouraged, lamented, and deprecated.

Premature theorizing. The problem here has been mainly that the relative failure of certain grand-style efforts at comprehensive theorizing has served to disenchant so many psychologists with theory in general. Here the instructive examples are many: to mention two, consider Titchener with his monolithic structuralism and Hull with his equally monolithic but essentially flexible behavior system. Also, the global efforts of the typical personality theorist may be cited.

The alternative to this kind of theorizing is the development of many probing points of research and theory on diverse fronts. While the monstrous blinders necessarily worn by any comprehensive theorist may have some virtue—mainly perhaps in that they permit undeviating adherence to a given direction of research—they also inevitably conceal huge areas of ignorance. When such ignorance is covered up by imposing arrays of words alone, in the absence of empirical supports, the progress of scientific psychology is seriously hindered.

Extreme positivism. This position, discussed briefly above, represents the other side of the picture. Here we wish merely to emphasize that all kinds of scientific effort are permissible, and we decry attempts by either faction of this issue to depreciate the alternative techniques, theoretical or empirical.

From a larger point of view, the ultimate objective of all science may be seen to be testable generalizations. Theories typically provide such general statements directly applicable over the range of the theory. The extreme empiricist, reasoning intuitively, discriminates situations more carefully perhaps, but must also finally arrive at similar general statements (inductions); otherwise, his data would be for the most part scientifically worthless. Thus the manner or style of approach to generalization appears to be the major distinguishing characteristic of these two methodologies, and other broader distinctions need not be drawn.

glossary

abacus. A manual computational device using beads that slide on rods; though of ancient origin, an abacus may be used for some operations by an expert at a speed as great as that of a desk calculator.

abreaction. Process of emotional release that occurs with the reliving of past experiences (psychoanalytic); the basic mechanism in catharsis ("talking-out cure").

act psychology. A school of psychology that stressed mental processes rather than the contents of consciousness (Brentano).

adaptive act. Carr's primary unit of behavior, which involves three phases: (1) a motivating stimulus, (2) a sensory situation, and (3) a response that alters the situation to satisfy the motivating conditions.

adder. A device for adding numbers; the adders in electronic digital computers are almost without exception designed to add binary numbers because the adding equipment is much simpler to build for base-two arithmetic.

afferent stimulus interaction. Hull's postulate that stimuli interact in such a manner that the resulting behavior is more than a mere summation of the behavioral effects of the stimuli taken separately.

afterimage. The lingering sensation following the removal of stimulation; usually noted in connection with visual stimulation.

anal stage. The period in an individual's development which is marked by interest in the anal region and which has certain concomitant effects on personality that may be characteristic of the adult individual if fixation at this stage occurs (Freud).

analysis. Separation into constituent parts; conceptually, as in science, as well as physically.

and. A commonly used connective in Boolean algebra; $C = A \cdot B$ may be read "C is true if and only if A and B are both true."

anecdotal method. The utilization of casually observed events as scientific data.

anima. A well-developed archetype representing the feminine characteristics in man (Jung).

animus.   A well-developed archetype representing the masculine charac-teristics in woman (Jung).

anthropomorphism.   The attributing of human characteristics or capaci-ties to other things, especially infrahuman species.

anthroponomy.   Term advocated by Hunter as a name for the "science of human behavior."

antimosaic hypothesis.   Theoretical view opposed to structuralist bundle hypothesis.

apperception.   Clear and vivid perception.

approach-approach conflict.   A conflict which occurs when an individual desires to achieve two goals only one of which can be obtained (Lewin).

approach-avoidance conflict.   A conflict which is characterized by one anticipated goal which is both desired and not desired (Lewin).

archetypes.   Inherited predispositions to perceive or act in a certain way (Jung).

associationism.   The view that learned behavior is the result of the connections between the elements of experience, or between responses.

asthenic.   Body type identified by Kretschmer as tall and thin.

attensity.   Clearness of a sensation which varies with attention rather than with the objective characteristics of the stimulus (Titchener).

avoidance-avoidance conflict.   A conflict which is present when two anticipated consequences are both undesirable (Lewin).

axiom.   A self-evident truth, a proposition not susceptible to proof or disproof.

bandwidth.   The range of frequencies in a signal containing more than some threshold level of power; for example, a particular filter may have a bandwidth of 100 cycles per second.

basic anxiety.   The feeling a child has of being isolated and helpless in a potentially hostile world (Horney).

behaviorism.   Generally, the systematic position that all psychological functions can be explained in terms of muscular reactions and glandular secretions, and *nothing more;* therefore, the objective study of the stimulus and response aspects of behavior (Watson). Specifically, 1. *methodological* (empirical) behaviorism: the view that behavior is all that scientists can study and that strictly objective techniques are therefore required, as in all other natural science; 2. *metaphysical* (radical) behaviorism: the philosophical position that there is no mind; a kind of physical monism.

belief-value matrix.   Hierarchies of learned expectations concerning environmental objects and their roles in relation to behavior (Tolman).

belongingness, principle of.   The proposition that items are more easily associated if they are related in a recognizable way.

binary number.   A number to the base two; in any place the value of the coefficient can be only one of two values, 0 or 1.

birth trauma.   The emotional experience of the infant ending its pre-natal life (emphasized by Rank as having subsequent personality effects).

bonds.   Connections of stimulus and response; hypothetical linkage used to account for the formation of associations.

Boolean algebra.   The algebra of sets, developed by George Boole.

bundle hypothesis. Assumption that complex perceptions are a group of simple perceptions.

canalization. The development of a single preferred means of satisfying a need (Murphy).

catharsis. The psychoanalytic principle of releasing tension and anxiety by emotionally reliving experiences; originally described as the "talking-out cure" (Breuer and Freud).

cathexis. The investing of psychic energy in some object, person, or thing (Freud).

centralism. A viewpoint which stresses brain functions in the explanation of psychological phenomena.

centrifugal group factor. The tendency to make gestures away from the body; an expressive factor in Allport's theory of personality.

cerebrotonia. A component of temperament referring to a bookish, shy, and sensitive individual (Sheldon).

circular conditioned response. A conditioned response sequence in which each successive response serves as a stimulus for the ensuing response.

clinical validation. The demonstration of a theoretical principle through successive confirmations within the same clinical setting from which it was derived.

coded. Transformed into other than the original form; for example, the letters of the alphabet might be coded by transforming each into a unique decimal number, which in turn might be coded into binary numbers, which finally might be coded as holes in a punched card.

cognitive. Pertaining to the mental process involved in achieving awareness or knowledge of an object.

cohesive forces. Tendency of excitations in the cortex to attract each other (gestalt).

collective unconscious. That part of a persons's unconscious which is inherited phylogenetically and is common to all members of the species (Jung).

compensation. Development in those areas in which an individual feels inferior, and the attempt to overcome this inferiority.

compile. To translate a program written in a problem language into the language of machine instructions; the problem language is designed to be more natural for the programmer to use than the machine language.

computer. A device, usually electronic, which carries out a sequence of operations under the control of a stored program of operation.

condensation. A single object serving several needs.

conditioning, classical. Relatively simple associative learning in which the reinforcement occurs contiguously with the learned response but independently of its performance.

conditioning, instrumental. Relatively simple associative learning in which certain consummatory behavior (e.g., eating, sexual activity) is made contingent upon the performance of the learned response.

conditioning, operant. Instrumental conditioning in which the subject "emits" the learned response in the absence of any particular eliciting stimulus (Skinner); the *free operant* is a response whose emission leaves the subject in a position to make further such responses (e.g., pressing a bar in a box as contrasted with running down a runway).

conditioning, respondent. Classical conditioning, in which there is an eliciting stimulus and in which reinforcement occurs independently of the performance of the response.

confirming reaction. A cerebral function hypothesized by Thorndike as the physiological basis of reinforcement through reward.

conflict. The simultaneous operation of two or more contradictory tendencies; the condition resulting therefrom.

connectionism. The school of psychology which considers a stimulus-response connection or bond as the basis of all or most behavior.

consensual validation. Validation of a symbol or word by agreement on its meaning by a number of people (Sullivan).

conservation of energy, principle of. The proposition that energy is neither created nor destroyed in physical systems; it is only transferred into other forms.

construct. A concept that represents relationships between objects or events.

contemporaneity, principle of. The proposition that only present factors influence present behavior; the past influences behavior only as it is represented in the present (Lewin).

context theory of meaning. View that the meaning of anything results from the context in which it occurs in consciousness (Titchener).

contiguity. Nearness in time and/or space.

continuum. A continuation of a variable along a dimension possessing different degrees of that variable.

control. 1. The method by which extraneous variation is eliminated in science, permitting a less ambiguous assignment of cause-effect relationships. 2. The exerting of influence over some variable(s).

controlled variable. A condition whose influence on the dependent variable in an experiment is eliminated, usually either by eliminating the condition entirely (e.g., sex differences can be eliminated as a variable by using only one sex) or distributing it evenly over experimental treatments (e.g., putting equal numbers of men and women in each treatment group).

corollary. A proposition derived from a postulate which is indirectly testable through further deduction; the link between the postulate and the theorem.

correlation. A relationship between two or more variables so that a change in one occurs with a change in the other; the degree to which two or more variables are so related.

creative synthesis. The proposition that new characteristics emerge from the combination of elements into wholes (Wundt).

criterion analysis, method of. A method of factor analysis in which two groups known to differ in some hypothesized underlying factor are selected; test batteries are then administered and only those tests which differentiate between the groups are submitted to factor analysis (Eysenck).

data processing. The manipulation of data, usually for the purpose of making them more comprehensible; most frequently used when the data are to be handled by a computer.

decoded. Converted back into a form which had been coded into some other form; for example, if letters of the alphabet were *coded* into numbers, the numbers would be *decoded* into letters of the alphabet.

deduction. A mode of logic which proceeds from general premises to more specific statements.

delayed response. A response whose performance is permitted only after some set duration of time following the original presentation of the relevant stimuli

dependent variable. The condition which is measured in an experiment; in psychology, usually some kind of behavior.

determining tendency. A predisposition to behave in a particular manner.

determinism. An assumption that all phenomena can be explained by natural law in a cause-effect manner; the view that all events are therefore explicable entirely in terms of relevant antecedent events.

diacritical design. The division of intertwined variables into subclasses in an attempt to separate the variables (Brunswik).

dimensional analysis. The structuring of a total situation into specific continua which are measurable.

discrimination. Process of differentiating between objects or actions; the ability to point to a difference.

displacement. The temporary substitution of a secondary goal for a primary one (psychoanalytic).

distal effects. The achievements resulting from an organism's activity in relation to more or less remote environmental objects (Brunswik).

distal stimuli. The remote object from which the stimuli originate (Brunswik).

double-alternation task. An experimental design in which the responses must be AABB.

double-aspect view. Metaphysical position in which both mind and body are assumed to be a function of one underlying reality.

dramatization. Children's play activities which emulate adult behavior (Sullivan).

drive (D). A construct used by Hull to indicate a condition of the organism resulting from a deprivation which increases the organism's activity toward a particular class of stimuli.

drive discriminations. The demonstrated ability of organisms to behave differentially under different deprivation conditions.

dualism. Metaphysical position in which both mind and body are assumed to exist.

dynamism. A habitual way of responding toward others (Sullivan).

dysplasia. Disharmony or disproportioning between body parts (Sheldon).

eclecticism. The selection of what seems best from various systems, theories, or procedures.

ecological validity. The extent to which cues aid an organism's accomplishing a successful interaction with the environment (Brunswik).

ecology, psychological. The attempt to determine the effect of the physical world upon the life space of an individual (Lewin).

ectomorphy. A body type characterized as tall, thin, and small boned (Sheldon).

effect, law of. The proposition that strengthening of stimulus-response connections, as measured by the increased probability of the occurrence of a response in a particular stimulus situation, results from the action of reward following a response (satisfying aftereffects, as formulated by Thorndike); the original corollary proposition that punishing aftereffects produce a weakening of responses was subsequently discarded by Thorndike.

effect, spread of. Proposition that reinforcement by reward tends to strengthen erroneous responses in close temporal and/or spatial contiguity (Thorndike).

ego. 1. The self. 2. That part of mental activity which is conscious and in close contact with reality (psychoanalytic).

ego-defense mechanism. Any unconscious process which protects the individual from unpleasant reality; irrational manner of dealing with anxiety (psychoanalytic).

element. The irreducible unit into which all conscious states can be broken down (Titchener).

elementarism. The methodological bias that mental and behavioral states and processes should be analyzed as far as possible into their constituent components; strongly attacked by gestalt psychology (structuralism).

empathy. The sympathetic awareness of an emotional state in another person.

empirical. Relating to facts and sensory experience; denotes reliance on observation.

empiricism. 1. The school of philosophical thought that believes all knowledge originates in experience. 2. A methodology that emphasizes data and minimizes theoretical inference.

endomorphy. A body type characterized as soft, fleshy, and round (Sheldon).

entropy. In physics, the energy of a physical system which is unavailable for work; in information theory, the average information content of a symbol emitted by a source.

epiphenomenalism. Metaphysical position in which mind is assumed to be a noncausal by-product of body.

epistemology. A branch of philosophy concerned with the acquisition and the validity of knowledge.

equipotentiality, principle of. The principle which states that within cerebral areas performing the same function, all parts are equally capable of carrying on that function (Lashley).

equivalence belief. A hypothesized state of an organism as a result of which it behaves as though a subgoal were the goal (Tolman).

erg. An underlying motivational trait having a hereditary origin (Cattell).

erogenous zones. Different zones or regions of the body which are especially sensitive to manipulation (psychoanalytic).

exercise, law of. The proposition that performance of a response improves subsequent performance through practice alone.

existential psychology. 1. Name often given to structuralism because it treated the elements of consciousness as existent. 2. The school of personality theorists who stress the individual's understanding of himself.

exploitative orientation. A means of escaping insecurity by obtaining objects valued by others (Fromm).

expressive behavior. That aspect of behavior which is related to an individual's own style of behaving rather than to the behavior's adaptive function (Allport).

exteroceptor. A sense organ or receptor directly stimulated by energy sources outside the body (e.g., eye).

extrasensory perception (psi phenomenon). Responsivity to external events that are not mediated by any known sense modality.

extraversion. Mode of responding to the world in which the person's attention is directed toward the external world (Jung).

fact. A verbal statement accepted by a certain group at a particular time.

factor analysis. A statistical technique utilizing sets of correlations; used for evaluating scores from a variety of different sources.

factor theory. Personality theory which emphasizes the isolation of factors by the statistical analysis of test performances.

feedback. In an energy system, the part of the output energy that is returned to the system to regulate further output.

fictional future. A person's plans and aspirations for the future which are presently believed in (Adler).

field-cognition modes. A combination of thinking, perceiving, and remembering on the part of the organism which gives rise to a specific way of knowing some characteristic of the environment (Tolman).

field expectations. A set of the organism that a particular response to a certain cue or stimulus will produce a particular situation or consequence (Tolman).

field theory. Any psychological theory which attempts to utilize fields of force analogous to those in physics as an explanation for psychological data.

figure-ground. A general property of perception; the figure is that which stands out and is attended to, while the ground is that which surrounds the figure and is secondary to it.

film color. A transparent color which is not substantial and lacks definite localization.

fixation. 1. Perseveration of a particular response. 2. The persistence of immature behavior or thought processes accompanied by a lack of normal development (psychoanalytic).

fractional antedating goal response. A stimulus-trace concept utilized in the explanation of the acquisition of a response chain; an implicit goal response which occurs progressively earlier in the response chain, thus providing stimuli which may become conditioned to ensuing responses (Hull, Spence).

free association. An unrestrained sequence of ideas or thoughts; the technique of having a subject respond with unrestricted verbalizations for clinical purposes (psychoanalytic).

free operant. See conditioning, operant.

frequency, law of. The proposition that the rate of learning is a function of the frequency of occurrence of a response.

functional autonomy. The performance of a task for its own sake; the drive state is thus independent of the need which gave rise to it (Allport).

functionalism. The psychological system that stresses the function or utility of behavior in adapting to the environment (Angell, Carr, Woodworth).

genital stage. The final psychosexual stage in the individual's development, in which one desires normal sexual relations with members of the opposite sex (Freud).

gestalt. A figure or configuration which is a whole greater than the sum of its parts and which, if analyzed into its parts, is destroyed.

gestalt psychology. The psychological system that stresses the phenomenological study of molar stimulus and response units, with emphasis placed on the primacy of wholes and on the existence of brain fields and configurations (Wertheimer, Koffka, Köhler).

Gestaltqualität. Patterns of time and space that are presumed to inhere in the mind and so are independent of physical elements; emphasis thereon is often considered as the immediate precursor of gestalt psychology (von Ehrenfels).

goal gradient. The progressive increment in response strength that occurs as a function of closeness to the goal (Hull).

gynandromorphy. Refers to bisexuality as denoted by the physique (Sheldon).

hab. A unit of learning invented to quantify habit strength $(_sH_R)$; equal to 1 per cent of the physiological maximum (Hull).

habit family hierarchy. The ordering into a hierarchy of strength of the total set of habits which may occur in a given stimulus situation (Hull).

habit strength $(_sH_R)$. An intervening variable representing learning; a function of (1) number of reinforcements, (2) amount of reinforcement, (3) time between stimulus and response, and (4) time between response and reinforcement (Hull, 1943); in the final Hullian system (1951, 1952) only (1) was retained as a determiner.

hallucination. A false perception for which appropriate external stimuli are absent.

hedonism. Philosophic belief that behavior is directed at the attainment of pleasure and the avoidance of pain.

Heisenberg principle. A mathematical proof that exact simultaneous measurement of the position and the momentum of a single electron is impossible.

hodological space. A qualitative geometry of spatial relations invented by Lewin to utilize vectors to represent dynamic psychological factors.

holistic. Referring to the theoretical position stressing that an organism must be studied as a whole since the whole is greater than its constituent parts.

hypochondria. A neurosis which is characterized by excessive concern for one's health.

hypothesis. 1. A proposition concerning the relationship among variables. 2. A tentative explanation.

hypothetical construct. An intraorganismic construct whose meaning goes beyond the relationship between the antecedent (stimulus) and consequent (response) conditions which it represents.

hypothetico-deductive method. A method of theory construction which starts with a few general postulates from which testable theorems and corollaries are derived by rigorous deduction.

hysteria. The manifestation of such bodily symptoms as anesthesia and paralysis as the result of psychic trauma or conflict.

id. A psychic structure or process which is the original reservoir of psychic energy and operates according to the pleasure principle (Freud).

ideal observer. An abstract mathematical ideal within detection theory; the behavior of this ideal defines the ideally achievable behavior within specified situations amenable to the necessary mathematical treatment.

ideomotor action. Term expressing belief that an idea, unless inhibited by other ideas, will lead directly to motor action (James).

idiographic. Referring to an individual case or event and to that methodology which stresses intensive rather than extensive investigation of an individual.

image. The relatively faint reproduction in consciousness of a previous sensation (Titchener).

imageless thought. Mental processes or functions which elude introspective analysis into elements.

independent variable. The factor whose influence (on the dependent variable) is determined in an experiment.

induction. A mode of logic which proceeds from specific statements to general conclusions.

inferiority complex. The feeling an individual has as the result of real or imagined deficiencies (Adler).

information. Whatever reduces uncertainty (information theory); the receipt of an information-bearing message reduces uncertainty or ignorance by reducing the number of alternative possible messages or by biasing their probabilities so that the remaining uncertainty is reduced.

inhibition, conditioned. The hypothesized acquisition of inhibitory properties to a stimulus through its repeated association with reactive inhibition.

inhibition, reactive. Hypothesized explanation for the decrement of a learned response owing to the effortfulness of the activity (Hull).

insight. 1. A sudden understanding of a previously insoluble problem. 2. A sudden reorganization of the perceptual field (gestalt).

instinct. 1. Innate, complex, stereotyped mode of behaving. 2. Need (Freud).

instinct, death. The wish of an organism to return to an inorganic state (Freud).

instinct, life. The desire of the organism to maintain a balance between the anabolistic and catabolistic forces of the body—to maintain life (Freud).

instructions. Specifications of computer operations to be performed; the typical computer has approximately sixty basic instructions to which it can respond, and all the more complex functions carried out by the computer are synthesized from these basic instructions.

interactionism. Metaphysical position in which mind and body are assumed to be two separate but interrelated entities.

interbehaviorism. Field theory with emphasis on the interaction between stimulus and response functions (Kantor).

interoceptor. A sense organ or receptor within the organism sensitive to stimuli within the body.

intervening variable. An intraorganismic construct which abstracts the relationship between antecedent (stimulus) and consequent (response) conditions, with no meaning beyond this relationship.

introspection. A generic term for any method which relies upon the subjective report of the subject.

introversion. Mode of responding to the world in which the person's attention is directed toward himself (Jung).

irradiation. The phenomenon of generalization, with the implication of excitatory brain functions (Pavlov).

isomorphism. The 1:1 relationship assumed to hold between brain fields and experience (gestalt).

J curve. Graphic description of the distribution of responses when some social institution influences behavior in a particular direction so that scores pile up markedly at one end of the scale (F. Allport).

kinesthetic. Pertaining to the sense of body movement or position.

kymograph. A revolving drum which makes graphic records of temporal variations; often used in recording respiration and other metabolic processes.

Lamarckian evolution. The doctrine of the evolution of acquired characteristics: the use or disuse of organic structures results in changes which are passed on to the organism's offspring.

latent learning. Learning in the absence of reinforcement (Tolman).

law. 1. A statement of regular and predictable relationship among empirical variables. 2. A well-accepted theoretical proposition.

lens model. Conceptualization of the interaction of the functional variables affecting behavior (Brunswik).

level of aspiration. The performance level which an individual expects to reach in a given situation and by which he judges his performance as a success or failure (Lewin).

libido. Energy in the service of the life instincts (Freud).

life space. The totality of effective psychological factors for a given person at a particular moment in time (Lewin).

life style. The particular manner which an individual develops in order to deal with reality (Adler).

likelihood ratio. The ratio of the probability that an observed event would occur given one hypothesis to the probability that the observation would occur given some second hypothesis; within detection theory, the hypotheses are most commonly that "a signal was presented," and that "noise alone was presented."

linear graph. A graph representing an equation of the first degree between two variables.

linear perspective. A monocular depth cue in which parallel lines tend to converge.

Lloyd Morgan's canon. Law of parsimony applied to comparative psychology: "In no case may we interpret an action as the outcome of the exercise of a higher psychical faculty, if it can be interpreted as the outcome of the exercise of one which stands lower on the psychological scale."

logical positivism. A philosophical movement headed by Schlick to rid philosophy of metaphysics and to establish a science of science.

mandala. The magic circle found in many religious cults which Jung believed to be symbolic of man's striving for unity.

manic-depressive insanity. A psychotic disorder characterized by marked emotional cycles from extreme elation to marked depression.

marketing orientation. A means of escaping insecurity by emulating the social stratum in which one lives (Fromm).

masculine protest. The desire of both males and females to overcome femininity (Adler).

mass action, principle of. The principle which states that brain tissues function as a whole in higher mental processes (Lashley).

materialism. Metaphysical position in which a single underlying physical reality is assumed.

means-end readiness. State of selective readiness which endures independently of the present motivational state of the organism and which leads to the acquisition of certain expectancies more readily than others (Tolman).

mechanism. A purposive response or set of responses (Woodworth).

mental activity. Generic term for adaptive behavior according to Carr.

mental chemistry. The doctrine that simple ideas coalesce to form new, more complex ideas and lose their individual identity (John Stuart Mill).

mental mechanics. The doctrine which states that a complex idea is no more than the simple ideas from which it is formed and which maintain their individual identity (James Mill).

mesomorphy. A body type characterized as tough, muscular, and athletic (Sheldon).

metaerg. An underlying motivational trait acquired through environmental influence (Cattell).

metaphysics. A branch of philosophy concerned with the identification and understanding of ultimate reality.

metatheory. A set of general rules governing the construction of a theory; a theory about a theory.

method, scientific. The fundamental process by which all science proceeds, which is characterized by analysis and control.

modal need. Need to perfect some type of behavior (Murray).

model. A particular subclass of theory; a conceptual analog which functions in the direction of empirical research; it differs from a theory in that the postulates of a model are not to be tested empirically; an *as if* statement.

model, deterministic. Any theoretical position which stresses the complete predictability of a response when the antecedent conditions are known.

model, mathematical learning. Any learning theory which utilizes a probabilistic statistical approach.

model, stochastic. Any model in which response probabilities are the theoretical dependent variable.

molar.   Referring to large units of study.

molecular.   Referring to small units of study.

monad.   Element of all being, which is indestructible, uncreatable, immutable, and active (Leibniz).

monism.   A metaphysical position in which only one basic reality is assumed, either mind or body.

morphogenotype.   A hypothetical unchanging biological state of the organism which determines both body type and temperament (Sheldon).

morphology.   The study of biological forms and structures.

motor patterns.   Responses and combinations of responses.

movement-produced stimuli (mps).   Stimuli originating in the movements of the organism (Guthrie).

nativism.   The doctrine which emphasizes hereditary factors in the development of an organism rather than environmental ones.

neurosis.   A class of personality disorders which are characterized by extreme anxiety and which are not usually severe enough to require hospitalization.

neurotic trends.   The particular environmental approach an individual utilizes in an attempt to avoid conflict and find security (Horney).

noise.   Anything (e.g., meaningless sounds) which interferes with the signal being transmitted.

nomothetic.   Referring to the use of group data in an attempt to discover laws that apply to groups.

non-Euclidian geometry.   A geometry that rejects one or more of the central axioms of traditional Euclidian geometry, especially the postulate concerning parallel lines.

nonsense syllable.   A term composed of two consonants separated by a vowel; invented to reduce variation in prior experience in materials for experimentation on human verbal learning and memory (Ebbinghaus).

Occam's razor.   See parsimony, principle of.

Oedipal conflict.   The feeling of hostility of the child toward the parent of the same sex and love for the parent of the opposite sex (Freud).

operant behavior.   Behavior which is characterized by its effect on the environment and for which there is usually no known or manipulated eliciting stimulus (Skinner).

operationism.   A movement intended to clarify the language of science; an operational definition is any definition in which the term is synonymous with the corresponding set of operations (Bridgman).

or.   A connective used in writing Boolean algebraic equations; typically the inclusive *or* is used, and $C = A + B$ would then mean "C is true if A is true or if B is true or if both A and B are true."

oral stage.   The first period in an individual's psychosexual development; marked by interest in the oral region (Freud).

organ inferiority.   See inferiority complex.

organismic.   Pertaining to any point of view which stresses studying the behavior of the whole organism rather than of its particular parts.

parameter.   1. A constant which is a mathematical expression of the change in a curve caused by varying experimental procedure. 2. Less technically, a systematically manipulated variable in an experiment.

parapsychology. A branch of psychology which studies extrasensory phenomena, those that do not fall within the range of known sensory modalities (e.g., clairvoyance, telepathy).

parataxic. Referring to a cognitive process in which continuous events are considered as causal relationships irrespective of their true relationship (Sullivan).

parsimony, principle of. The scientific principle that the simplest of two hypotheses should be accepted, all else equal. It does not negate the acceptance of complex explanations if the data require such. (Also called William of Occam's razor and, in comparative psychology, Lloyd Morgan's canon.)

penis envy. The repressed female desire to possess a penis; the female form of castration anxiety (Freud).

peripheralism. Explanation of psychological phenomena emphasizing muscular action and other distal events rather than the functioning of the central nervous system.

permutations. All the possible arrangements of a certain number of different items; each arrangement is called a permutation.

persona. A well-developed archetype which represents man's social self (Jung).

personal unconscious. The part of a person's unconscious containing material originating in personal experience (Jung).

personification. Images one holds toward other persons or oneself (Sullivan).

personification, eidetic. A personification which persists and influences a person's opinion of others (Sullivan).

phallic stage. The period in an individual's development when the Oedipus complex develops; marked by interest in the penis (Freud).

phenomenalism. Metaphysical position in which neither mind nor body is considered as real; only ideas resulting from sensory impressions exist.

phenomenology. Method of observation in which experimental data are accepted in a more or less naïve manner, without any attempt at analysis.

phenotype. 1. A bodily characteristic, as contrasted with the underlying hereditary factor (genotype). 2. The physique of an individual (Sullivan).

phi phenomenon. The name given by Wertheimer to the perception of apparent motion generated by stationary stimuli.

phrenology. The belief that mental characteristics can be determined by examining the contours of the skull (Gall).

physicalism. The philosophical position that all scientific propositions are ultimately reducible to the language of physical science.

physiologizing. Advancing physiological explanations and conjectures in the absence of definite physiological knowledge.

pleasure principle. The immediate satisfaction of instinctual desires; governs the development of the id (Freud).

positivism. A metatheoretical and general scientific position that emphasizes parsimony and operationism in data language and eschews theorizing and inferential commitment.

postremity, postulate of. The proposition that the last response made in a particular stimulus situation is the one most likely to occur on the next occasion of that stimulus situation; a primary postulate in one formalization of Guthrie's contiguity theory of learning (Voeks).

postulate. 1. A fundamental assumption not meant to be tested. 2. A theoretical proposition used within a given logical framework and tested indirectly by means of its empirical implications (theorems).

practitioner. One trained in a scientific or similar discipline; one who is engaged in some service function in a profession in which he has been more or less intensively trained to practice at a relatively high level of responsibility.

pragmatism. Validation of a principle through its utility; the philosophical position that that which is useful is true.

Prägnanz, law of. Gestalt principle that a figure will be perceived in its best possible form.

preconscious. That part of mental activity which consists of materials not presently conscious but readily recallable (psychoanalytic).

press. The environmental forces acting upon the individual (Murray).

primary memory image. A lingering memory trace postulated to maintain a sensation for a relatively short duration of time, permitting an accurate introspective report (Titchener).

primary process. Direct and immediate instinctual satisfaction, mediated by the id (psychoanalytic).

primary qualities. Those qualities which are alleged to inhere within the object and to be independent of the perceiver, such as size and shape (Locke).

primitive term. A term which is not defined by any more basic term within a theory.

probabilistic functionalism. The systematic position which emphasizes the probability of success in perceptual and behavioral events (Brunswik).

proceeding. A person's interaction with an object or another person, of sufficient duration to have dynamic significance (Murray).

process need. A need for activity per se (Murray).

program. A sequence of instructions that can be carried out by a computer.

programmatic. Lacking in systematic specificity.

projection. A defense mechanism in which the individual attempts to externalize his own values, faults, and ideas (psychoanalytic).

proprioceptor. A sense organ or receptor sensitive to the position and the movement of the body (e.g., vestibular canal).

protensity. Temporal duration of a sensation or an image (Titchener).

prototaxic. Referring to a cognitive process in which the individual experiences directly without attaching meaning to his sensations; similar to stream of consciousness (Sullivan).

proximal reactions. The peripheral motor responses of the organism, without regard for the consequences on the environment (Brunswik).

proximal stimuli. Stimuli as they are when they impinge upon the organism (Brunswik).

psychical satiation. A reduction in performance of an activity as a function of the continued repetition of the activity.

psychoanalysis. 1. A school of psychology developed by Sigmund Freud which places a great deal of emphasis upon unconscious motivation, conflict, and symbolism. 2. A type of psychiatry stressing the free-association technique and long-term, deep psychotherapy.

psychogenesis. The origin and development of mind or behavior.

psychometrist. A person skilled in the administration and scoring of mental tests.

psychopathology. The scientific discipline which studies abnormal behavior.

psychophysical parallelism. The metaphysical position in which mind and body are independent yet perfectly correlated entities.

psychophysics. The scientific study of the relationship between stimuli and sensations.

psychosis. A class of severe behavior disorders which are characterized by the patient's general lack of contact with reality and which usually require hospitalization.

purposivism. The doctrine that behavior is more than purely mechanical and that it is directed toward some goal.

puzzle box. An enclosure which prevents an organism from reaching a goal until a particular device is manipulated (Thorndike).

pyknic. Short and squatty body type (Kretschmer).

Q sort. A personality inventory, utilizing factor analysis, in which the subject evaluates his own personality by sorting into different piles statements which apply to him (Stephenson).

qualitative. That which can be distinguished or identified as different in kind.

quantification. The process of establishing relationships between empirical objects of study and the mathematics of real numbers.

quantitative. That which can be distinguished or identified as different in number or amount.

rationalism. The philosophical position which maintains that truth can only be found through pure reason.

rationalization. A form of projection in which the individual attempts to find a justifiable cause for his actions (psychoanalytic).

reaction potential $(_sE_R)$. An intervening variable that indicates the degree of strength of a particular response (Hull).

reaction time, motor. Latency of response made with attention to the response rather than to the stimulus onset.

reaction time, sensory. Latency of response made with attention to the stimulus onset rather than to the response.

readiness, law of. Principle which states that when a conduction unit is ready to conduct, conduction by it is satisfying, providing nothing is done to alter its action (Thorndike).

reality principle. The ego's realization of the demands of the environment leading to the eventual satisfaction of these demands in such a way that the organism continues to exist (Freud).

receiver operating curve. A curve relating the probability of a "hit" (correct detection) to the probability of a "false alarm" (incorrect report of detection).

recency, law of. Principle stating that all else equal, that which is best remembered is that which is most recently learned.

receptive orientation. A means of escaping insecurity by strong identification with a group or its leader (Fromm).

reduction screen. An opaque screen with two small holes, used to view stimuli without the subject's knowledge of the surrounding illumination.

reductionism. The attempt to understand complex phenomena by analyzing them into their elementary components.

redundant. Repetitious of information; redundant transmission systems are systems carrying information which is less than the system could potentially carry.

reflex. An unlearned, involuntary, stereotyped response of a body part to a stimulus.

reflex arc. Simplest functional unit in the nervous system, composed of a receptor, synapse, and effector.

reflexology. The school of psychology which holds that reflexes and combinations of reflexes are the basis of all behavior (Bekhterev).

regression. The tendency to return to a former state or condition.

reinforcement. Any process by which a response is strengthened; generally assumed to involve more than mere contiguity of stimulus and response elements.

repetition compulsion. An irrepressible desire to repeat some act over and over (Freud).

representative design. Experimental approach allowing a large sample of variables to change together in a random fashion (Brunswik).

repression. The unconscious removal of unpleasant thoughts or events from consciousness (Freud).

resistance. The inability of a subject to recall past events because of some unconscious repression (psychoanalytic).

respondent behavior. Behavior which is characterized by its identification with a specific eliciting stimulus.

restraining forces. Brain excitations preventing attraction of cohesive forces; usually the result of present stimulation (gestalt).

retinal disparity. Visual depth cue resulting from the slight difference between the two retinal images in binocular vision.

retroactive inhibition. The interference of a second task with the retention of a previously learned task.

retrospection. Introspection on a past event.

reward. An object or activity that satisfies some motivating condition; often assumed to be necessary for learning (as in Thorndike's law of effect or Hull's S-R behavior system).

routine. A computer program or part of a program, generally named because it is designed to carry out a specific function (for example, finding square roots); the word "routine" is generally used if the portion of the program is on the main line of the program, whereas the word "subroutine" is used for units which are called upon periodically from the main program.

scaling. The construction of any type of ordered measuring device used to represent any type of continuum.

schedule, fixed interval (FI). A program of reinforcement in which the first response made after some fixed period of time is reinforced.

schedule, fixed ratio (FR). A program of reinforcement in which the first response made after some fixed number of responses is reinforced.

schedule, reinforcement. A program indicating how a reinforcing stimulus is arranged.

schedule, variable interval (VI). A program of reinforcement in which the first response made after some variable period of time is reinforced.

schedule, variable ratio (VR). A program of reinforcement in which the first response made after some variable number of responses is reinforced.

schizophrenia. A psychotic disorder characterized by disturbances of the thought processes and lack of contact with reality.

school. A collection of adherents to a particular systematic position, with varying degrees of temporal and spatial contiguity.

science. The enterprise by which men obtain ordered knowledge about natural phenomena, working with a particular methodology (controlled observation and analysis) and set of attitudes (skepticism, objectivity, etc.).

science, applied. The discipline concerned with the investigation of variables believed to have practical application and with the immediate utility of their findings.

science, pure. The discipline concerned with the discovery of new facts and the development of theories without regard for the immediate utility of such knowledge.

secondary process. Conscious activity in the preconscious or ego (psychoanalytic).

secondary qualities. Those qualities alleged to inhere not within the object but within the perceiver, such as color (Locke).

secondary reinforcement. The reinforcement of behavior by a previously neutral stimulus which has acquired its reinforcing properties through association with a primary reinforcer.

self. 1. An existing picture of an individual's past behavior and experiences as perceived by him. 2. A summary name for a set of psychological processes, usually including evaluative and attitudinal functions, involving an individual and his relationship to the world.

sensation. A conscious experience which cannot be further analyzed (Titchener).

separation anxiety. Anxiety resulting from birth trauma and basic to neurotic symptoms (Rank).

serial. A group of proceedings which follow each other in a coherent fashion, involving planning on the part of the organism and providing direction and meaning (Murray).

set. A predisposing disposition or determining tendency.

shadow. A well-developed archetype inherited from man's prehuman ancestors; the animal instincts (Jung).

shaping. A technique used to produce a desired behavioral pattern by selectively reinforcing responses that approximate or are a part of it.

sibling rivalry. A feeling of competition among offspring (Adler).

sign learning. Learning of the relationships among signs—what leads to what (Tolman).

sign significate (sign gestalt). An object which gives rise to the expectation that a particular response will lead to a goal (Tolman).

Skinner box. An operant-conditioning chamber provided with a device which the organism can manipulate to produce some type of reinforcement.

solipsism. The philosophical view that one can be certain of nothing but one's own experience.

solution learning. Overt instrumental learning or problem solving (Mowrer).

somatotonia. A component of temperament referring to an active, vigorous, and aggressive individual (Sheldon).

somatotype. A ratio of body measurements which represents an individual's body type (Sheldon).

state variable. A hypothesized, unanalyzed, enduring condition of the organism which is the result of a past interaction of the organism and the environment.

stereotypy. A condition in which the organism persistently manifests certain invariable responses.

stimulus error. The paying of attention to the properties of the stimulus rather than to the characteristics of the sensation (Titchener).

stimulus field. The totality of stimuli that act on the organism at any given moment (gestalt).

stimulus-intensity dynamism. The principle that reaction potential or response amplitude increases monotonically with the size of the stimulus (Hull).

stimulus pool. The total population of stimuli from which different samples may be drawn (Estes).

stimulus trace. A presumed continuation of activity in the nervous system after brief stimulation has ceased (Hull).

structuralism. The system that stresses the analysis of consciousness into elements through the method of introspection (Wundt, Titchener).

subjective idealism. Metaphysical position in which a single underlying mental or spiritual reality is assumed.

subjectivism. The tendency to be biased in perception and thinking by preconceived ideas.

sublimation. The permanent substitution of a secondary goal for a primary one (Freud).

superego. A psychic structure or process which develops out of the ego; the internal representation of external values (Freud).

surface color. Reflected color.

symbol. Anything that pertains to or is used as a substitute for something else.

synchronicity. The occurrence of events at the same time but without causal relation (Jung).

syntality. The dimensions or traits of a social institution, analogous to the traits of an individual (Cattell).

syntaxic. Referring to a cognitive process in which thoughts and ideas become connected in a logical fashion (Sullivan).

system. An organization and interpretation of the data and theories of a subject matter, with special assumptions (postulates), definitions, and methodological biases.

systematic design. Classic experimental methodology utilizing rigorous control of variables.

tabula rasa. Blank tablet; usually refers to the doctrine that the mind at birth is blank and is developed through sensory experience.

technician. One trained to provide technical services for the practitioner or scientist.

teleology. The explanation of behavior in terms of its ultimate utilities, in the absence of evidence that these are actually determining factors.

tension system. A motivational factor in which some particular act or set of acts acquires directive influence in behavior until dissipated (Lewin).

terminal focal event. The response of the organism which may be either perceptual or instrumental (Brunswik).

thema. A unit describing behavior in terms of the press and need which are involved (Murray).

theorem. Statement derived from postulates through the rules of deduction; to be directly tested empirically.

theory. 1. A group of laws deductively connected. 2. Generalizations beyond the data which are used to bridge gaps in knowledge and to generate research.

thing constancy. The tendency of an organism to view an object as having a stable size and shape irrespective of variations in the retinal image (Brunswik).

topology. A nonmetric and nondirectional geometry of spatial relationships in which boundaries are the critical factors and a variety of transformations may be achieved; utilized by Lewin as a model for representation of behavior functions (see also hodological space).

trait. A generalized and focalized neuropyschic system (peculiar to the individual) with the capacity to render many stimuli functionally equivalent and to initiate and guide consistent (equivalent) forms of adaptive and expressive behavior (Allport).

trait theory. Personality theory which emphasizes the isolation of factors accounting for consistency and integration of behavior.

traits, constitutional. Traits having an innate origin (Cattell).

traits, environmental-mold. Consistencies in behavior which are acquired through environmental influences, especially social institutions (Cattell).

traits, source. Underlying general predispositions which account for observed consistencies in behavior (Cattell).

traits, surface. Observed consistencies in behavior (Cattell).

transducer. A device that changes energy from one form to another; a radio receiver is a transducer that changes electromagnetic energy into acoustic energy; the human retina transduces light energy into the electrochemical energy of the nerve impulse.

transference. The shifting of emotion from an object or person to the psychoanalyst during therapy (Freud).

transposition experiment. An experimental design in which the subject learns to respond to relationships among stimuli rather than to particular stimuli.

tropism. A forced movement of the whole organism which is a direct function of stimulation.

two-factor learning theory. Any theoretical position in which two separate learning processes are considered essential in the acquisition of behavior.

typology. A systematic personality classification according to types or kinds.

uncertainty. That property of a set of alternatives which determines its information content; the amount of uncertainty in a set of messages or alternatives is the same as the amount of information transmitted in reducing that uncertainty to zero (see information).

unconscious. Collective term for mental activities of which the person is not aware (psychoanalytic).

variable. A class of objects or events, or their properties; a factor or condition conceptualized for scientific investigation (see also controlled variable, dependent variable, independent variable, intervening variable).

visceratonia. A component of temperament referring to a love for comfort, food, and affection (Sheldon).

vitalism. The philosophical position that life cannot be explained entirely in physicochemical principles.

volumic color. The extensiveness of a color.

Weber-Fechner law. A psychophysical law which states that a geometric change in the stimulus intensity will produce an arithmetic change in the intensity of the sensation.

Weber's law. A psychophysical law which states that a noticeable change in a stimulus intensity is always a constant proportional part of the original stimulus.

Zeigarnik effect. The phenomenon that tasks which are not completed are better remembered than tasks which are completed (Lewin).

references

Ach, N. *Über den Willensakt und das Temperament: Ein experimentelle Untersuchung.* Leipzig: Quelle & Meyer, 1910.

Allport, F. H. *Social psychology.* Boston: Houghton Mifflin, 1924.

Allport, F. H. *Theories of perception and the concept of structure.* New York: Wiley, 1955.

Allport, G. W. *Personality: A psychological interpretation.* New York: Holt, 1937.

Allport, G. W. *The individual and his religion.* New York: Macmillan, 1950a.

Allport, G. W. *The nature of personality: Selected papers.* Reading, Mass.: Addison-Wesley, 1950b.

Allport, G. W. *Becoming: Basic considerations for a psychology of personality.* New Haven: Yale, 1955.

Allport, G. W. *Personality and social encounter: Selected essays.* Boston: Beacon Press, 1960.

Allport, G. W. *Pattern and growth in personality.* New York: Holt, 1961.

Allport, G. W., & Allport, F. H. *A-S reaction study.* Boston: Houghton Mifflin, 1928.

Allport, G. W., & Cantril, H. *The psychology of radio.* New York: Harper, 1935.

Allport, G. W., & Vernon, P. E. *A study of values.* Boston: Houghton Mifflin, 1931. Rev. ed. with P. E. Vernon & G. Lindzey, 1951.

Allport, G. W., & Vernon, P. E. *Studies in expressive movement.* New York: Macmillan, 1933.

Alper, Thelma G. Memory for completed and incompleted tasks as a function of personality: Correlation between experimental and personality data. *J. Pers.,* 1948, **17,** 104–137.

Anastasi, Anne. *Differential psychology.* (3rd ed.) New York: Macmillan, 1958.

Angell, J. R. The relations of structural and functional psychology to philosophy. *Phil. Rev.,* 1903, **12,** 243–271.

Angell, J. R. *Psychology: An introductory study of the structure and function of human consciousness.* New York: Holt, 1904.

399

Angell, J. R. The province of functional psychology. Psychol. Rev., 1907, 14, 61–91.

Angell, J. R. Behavior as a category of psychology. Psychol. Rev. 1913, 20, 255–270.

Attneave, F. Some informational aspects of visual perception. Psychol. Rev., 1954, 61, 183–193.

Attneave, F. Applications of information theory to psychology: A summary of basic concepts, methods, and results. New York: Holt, 1959.

Augenstine, L. G. Human performance in information transmission. Part VI. Evidence of periodicity in information processing. Control Systems Laboratory, Univer. of Illinois, Report R-75, 1958.

Bain, A. The senses and the intellect. 1855. Reprinted, 1886.

Bain, A. The emotions and the will. 1859.

Bakan, D. Sigmund Freud and the Jewish mystical tradition. Princeton, N.J.: Van Nostrand, 1958.

Beach, F. A., Hebb, D. O., Morgan, C. T., & Nissen, H. W. (Eds.) The neuropsychology of Lashley. New York: McGraw-Hill, 1960.

Beck, S. J. The science of personality: Nomothetic or idiographic? Psychol. Rev., 1953, 60, 353–359.

Becker, R. J. Outstanding contributors to psychology. Amer. Psychol., 1959, 14, 297–298.

Bekhterev, V. M. Objektive Psychologie: Oder Psychoreflexologie, die Lehre von den Assoziationsreflexen. Leipzig: B. G. Teubner, 1913. Translated from original 1910 Russian ed. London: Jarrolds Publishers, 1933.

Benjamin, A. C. Operationism. Springfield, Ill.: Charles C Thomas, 1955.

Bergmann, G. The contribution of John B. Watson. Psychol. Rev., 1956, 63, 265–276.

Bergmann, G. Philosophy of science. Madison: Univer. of Wisconsin Press, 1957.

Bergmann, G., & Spence, K. W. The logic of psychophysical measurement. Psychol. Rev., 1944, 51, 1–24. Reprinted in M. H. Marx (Ed.), Psychological theory: Contemporary readings. New York: Macmillian, 1951. Pp. 256–276.

Berkeley, G. New theory of vision. 1709.

Berkeley, G. Principles of human knowledge. 1710.

Berkeley, G. Theory of vision vindicated. Reprinted in A. A. Luce & T. E. Jessop (Eds.), Works. Vol. 1. New York: Nelson, 1948. Pp. 251–279.

Berlyne, D. E. Conflict, arousal, and curiosity. New York: McGraw-Hill, 1960.

Birdsall, T. An application of game theory to signal detectability. Electronic Defense Group, Univer. of Michigan, Technical Report 20, 1953.

Blodgett, H. C. The effect of the introduction of reward upon the maze performance of rats. Univer. Calif. Publ. Psychol., 1929, 4, 113–134.

Boring, E. G. The physical dimensions of consciousness. New York: Appleton-Century-Crofts, 1933.

Boring, E. G. A psychological function is the relation of successive differentiations of events in the organism. Psychol. Rev. 1937, 44, 445–461.

Boring, E. G. *A history of experimental psychology.* (2nd ed.) New York: Appleton-Century-Crofts, 1950.

Boring, E. G. A history of introspection. *Psychol. Bull.*, 1953, **50**, 169–187.

Boring, E. G. When is human behavior predetermined? *Scientific Mon.*, 1957, **84**, 189–196.

Boring, E. G. Lashley and cortical integration. In F. A. Beach et al. (Eds.), *The neuropsychology of Lashley.* New York: McGraw-Hill, 1960.

Boring, E. G., et al. (Eds.) *A history of psychology in autobiography.* Vol. IV. Worcester, Mass.: Clark Univer. Press, 1952.

Braithwaite, R. B. *Scientific explanation.* London: Cambridge, 1955.

Breland, K., & Breland, Marion. A field of applied animal psychology. *Amer. Psychol.*, 1951, **6**, 202–204.

Breland, K., & Breland, Marion. The misbehavior of organisms. *Amer. Psychol.*, 1961, **16**, 681–684.

Brentano, F. *Psychologie von empirischen Standpunkte.* Leipzig, 1874.

Breuer, J., & Freud, S. *Studien über Hysterie.* Vienna: Franz Deuticke, 1895.

Bridges, Katherine M. B. Emotional development in early infancy. *Child Develpm.*, 1932, **3**, 324–341.

Bridgman, P. W. *The logic of modern physics.* New York: Macmillan, 1927.

Bridgman, P. W. *The nature of some of our physical concepts.* New York: Philosophical Library, 1952.

Bronk, D. W. The role of scientists in the furtherance of science. *Science,* 1954, **119**, 223–227.

Brown, J. F. On the use of mathematics in psychological theory. *Psychometrika*, 1936, **1**, 7–15; 77–90. Also in M. H. Marx (Ed.), *Psychological theory: Contemporary readings.* New York: Macmillan, 1951. Pp. 233–256.

Brown, J. F., & Voth, A. C. The path of seen movement as a function of the vector-field. *Amer. J. Psychol.*, 1937, **49**, 543–563.

Brozek, J. Current status of psychology in the U.S.S.R. *Annu. Rev. Psychol.*, 1962, **13**, 515–566.

Bruner, J. S., et al. *Contemporary approaches to cognition: A symposium held at the University of Colorado.* Cambridge, Mass.: Harvard, 1957.

Brunswik, E. *Wahrnehmung und Gegenstandswelt.* Vienna: Franz Deuticke, 1934.

Brunswik, E. The conceptual focus of some psychological systems. *J. unif. Sci.*, 1939a, **8**, 36–49. Reprinted in M. H. Marx (Ed.), *Psychological theory: Contemporary readings.* New York: Macmillan, 1951. Pp. 131–143.

Brunswik, E. Probability as a determiner of rat behavior. *J. exp. Psychol.*, 1939b, **25**, 175–197.

Brunswik, E. Organismic achievement and environmental probability. *Psychol. Rev.*, 1943, **50**, 255–272.

Brunswik, E. Discussion: Remarks on functionalism in perception. *J. Pers.*, 1949, **18**, 56–65.

Brunswik, E. The conceptual framework of psychology. *Int. Encycl. unif. Sci.*, 1952, **1**, No. 10.

Brunswik, E. Representative design and probabilistic theory in a functional psychology. *Psychol. Rev.*, 1955a, **62**, 193–217.

Brunswik, E. In defense of probabilistic functionalism: A reply. *Psychol. Rev.*, 1955b, **62**, 236–242.

Brunswik, E. *Perception and the representative design of psychological experiments.* Berkeley: Univer. of California Press, 1956.

Brunswik, E., & Kamiya, J. Ecological cue-validity of "proximity" and of other gestalt factors. *Amer. J. Psychol.*, 1953, **66**, 20–32.

Burt, C. L. *The factors of the mind.* New York: Macmillan, 1941.

Bush, R. R., & Mosteller, F. A mathematical model for simple learning. *Psychol. Rev.*, 1951a, **58**, 313–323.

Bush, R. R., & Mosteller, F. A model for stimulus generalization and discrimination. *Psychol. Rev.*, 1951b, **58**, 413–423.

Bush, R. R., & Mosteller, F. *Stochastic models for learning.* New York: Wiley, 1955.

Butler, J. M., & Haigh, G. V. Changes in the relation between self-concepts and ideal concepts consequent upon client-centered counseling. In C. R. Rogers & Rosalind F. Dymond (Eds.), *Psychotherapy and personality change: Coordinated studies in the client-centered approach.* Chicago: Univer. of Chicago Press, 1954. Pp. 55–76.

Butterfield, H. *The origins of modern science: 1300-1800.* (Rev. ed.) New York: Macmillan, 1957.

Cabanis, P. J. G. *Rapports du physique et du moral de l'homme.* Paris, 1802.

Carr, H. A. *Psychology: A study of mental activity.* New York: Longmans, 1925.

Carr, H. A. Teaching and learning. *J. genet. Psychol.*, 1930, **37**, 189–219.

Carr, H. A. The quest for constants. *Psychol. Rev.*, 1933, **40**, 514–532.

Carterette, E. C., & Cole, M. *Repetition and confirmation of messages received by ear and by eye.* Psychology Department, U.C.L. A., Technical Report No. 3, 1959.

Carterette, E. C., & Cole, M. Comparison of the receiver-operating characteristics for messages received by ear and by eye. *J, acoust. Soc. Amer.*, 1962, **34**, 172–178.

Cartwright, D. Lewinian theory as a contemporary systematic framework. In S. Koch (Ed.), *Psychology: A study of a science.* Vol. 2. *General systematic formulations, learning and special processes.* New York: McGraw-Hill, 1959. Pp. 7–91.

Cattell, R. B. *A guide to mental testing.* London: University of London Press, 1936. Rev. ed., 1948.

Cattell, R. B. *The culture free test of intelligence.* Champaign, Ill.: Inst. Pers. and Abil. Test, 1944.

Cattell, R. B. *Description and measurement of personality.* New York: Harcourt, Brace & World, 1946.

Cattell, R. B. The dimensions of culture patterns by factorization of national character. *J. abnorm. soc. Psychol.*, 1949, **44**, 443–469.

Cattell, R. B. *Personality: A systematic theoretical and factual study.* New York: McGraw-Hill, 1950.

Cattell, R. B. *Factor analysis: An introduction and manual for psychologist and social scientist.* New York: Harper & Row, 1952.

Cattell, R. B. *The O-A personality test battery.* Champaign, Ill.: Inst. Pers. and Abil. Test, 1954.

Cattell, R. B. *Personality and motivation structure and measurement.* New York: Harcourt, Brace & World, 1957.

Cattell, R. B. Personality theory growing from multivariate quantitative research. In S. Koch (Ed.), *Psychology: A study of a science.* Vol. 3. *Formulations of the person and the social context.* New York: McGraw-Hill, 1959.

Cattell, R. B., & Wispe, L. G. The dimension of syntality in small groups. *J. soc. Psychol.*, 1948, **28**, 57–78.

Cattell, R. B., Saunders D. R., & Stice, G. F. *The 16 personality factor questionnaire.* Champaign, Ill.: Inst. Pers. and Abil. Test, 1950.

Cattell, R. B., Blewett, D. B., & Beloff, J. R. The inheritance of personality. *Amer. J. Hum. Genet.*, 1955, **7**, 122–146.

Child, I. L. The relation of somatotype to self-ratings on Sheldon's temperament traits. *J. Pers.*, 1950, **18**, 440–453.

Cobb, S. A salute from neurologists. In F. A. Beach et al. (Eds.), *The neuropsychology of Lashley.* New York: McGraw-Hill, 1960.

Cohen, M. R., & Nagel, E. *Introduction to logic and scientific method.* New York: Harcourt, Brace, 1934.

Comte, A. *Politique positive.* 1824.

Comte, A. *The positive philosophy.* Translated by H. Martineau. London: G. Bell, 1896.

Conant, J. B. *On understanding science: A historical approach.* New Haven: Yale, 1947.

Conant, J. B. *Harvard case histories in experimental science.* Cambridge, Mass.: Harvard, 1957.

Cotton, J. W. On making predictions from Hull's theory. *Psychol. Rev.*, 1955, **62**, 303–314.

Dallenbach, K. M. Phrenology versus psychoanalysis. *Amer. J. Psychol.*, 1955, **68**(4), 511–525.

Danto, A., & Morgenbesser, S. (Eds.) *Philosophy of science: A reader.* New York: Meridian Books, 1960.

Darwin, C. *Expression of emotions in man and animals.* (2nd ed.) London: J. Murray, 1872.

Darwin, C. *Origin of species.* (2nd ed.) London: Collier, 1909.

David, H. P., & von Bracken, H. (Eds.) *Perspectives in personality theory.* New York: Basic Books, 1957.

David, H. P., & Brengelmann, J. C. (Eds.) *Perspectives in personality research.* New York: Springer, 1960.

Davis, R. C. Physical psychology. *Psychol. Rev.*, 1953, **60**, 7–14.

Dennis, W. (Ed.) *Readings in the history of psychology.* New York: Appleton-Century-Crofts, 1948.

Deutsch, M. Field theory in social psychology. In G. Lindzey (Ed.), *Handbook of social psychology.* Reading, Mass.: Addison-Wesley, 1954. Pp. 181–222.

Dewey, J. *Psychology.* New York: Harper, 1886.

Dewey, J. The reflex arc concept in psychology. *Psychol. Rev.,* 1896, **3,** 357–370.

Dewey, J. Psychology and social practice. *Psychol. Rev.,* 1900, **2,** 105–124.

Dewey, J. *How we think.* Boston: Heath, 1910.

Diserens, C. M. Psychological objectivism. *Psychol. Rev.,* 1925, **32,** 121–152.

Dollard, J. *Caste and class in a southern town.* New Haven: Yale, 1937.

Dollard, J. *Fear in battle.* New Haven: Yale, 1943.

Dollard, J., Doob, L. W., Miller, N. E., Mowrer, O. H., & Sears, R. R. *Frustration and aggression.* New Haven: Yale, 1939.

Dollard, J., & Miller, N. E. *Personality and psychotherapy.* New York: McGraw-Hill, 1950.

Driesch, H. A. *The problem of individuality.* (A course of four lectures delivered before the University of London in 1913 by Hans Driesch.) London: Macmillan, 1914.

Duncker, K. On problem solving. Translated by L. S. Lews from the 1935 original. *Psychol. Monogr.,* 1945, **58,** No. 270.

Ebbinghaus, H. *Über das Gedächtnis.* 1885. Reprinted as *Memory.* Translated by H. A. Ruger & Clara E. Bussenius. New York: Teachers College, 1913.

Ellenberger, H. Fechner and Freud. *Bull. Menninger Clin.,* 1956, **20,** 201–214.

Ellis, W. D. *A source book of gestalt psychology.* New York: Harcourt, Brace & World, 1938.

Escalona, S. K. The influence of topological and vector psychology upon current research in child development: An addendum. In L. Carmichael (Ed.), *Manual of child psychology.* (2nd ed.) New York: Wiley, 1954. Pp. 971–983.

Estes, W. K. Toward a statistical theory of learning. *Psychol. Rev.,* 1950, **57,** 94–107.

Estes, W. K. Models for learning theory. *Symposium on psychology of learning basic to military training problems.* Washington, D.C.: Committee on Human Resources, Research and Development Board, 1953. Pp. 21–38.

Estes, W. K. Individual behavior in uncertain situations: An interpretation in terms of statistical association theory. In R. M. Thrall, C. H. Coombs, & R. L. Davis (Eds.), *Decision processes.* New York: Wiley, 1954a. Pp. 127–137.

Estes, W. K. Kurt Lewin. In W. K. Estes et al., *Modern learning theory.* New York: Appleton-Century-Crofts, 1954b. Pp. 317–344.

Estes, W. K. Stimulus-response theory of drive. In M. R. Jones (Ed.), *Nebraska symposium on motivation, 1958.* Lincoln: Univer. of Nebraska Press, 1958.

Estes, W. K. Component and pattern models with Markovian interpretations. In R. R. Bush & W. K. Estes (Eds.), *Studies in mathematical learning theory.* Stanford, Calif.: Stanford, 1959a. Pp. 9–52.

Estes, W. K. The statistical approach to learning theory. In S. Koch (Ed.), *Psychology: A study of a science.* Vol. 2. *General systematic formula-*

tions, learning and special processes. New York: McGraw-Hill, 1959b. Pp. 380–486.

Estes, W. K. Learning theory and the new "mental chemistry." *Psychol. Rev.,* 1960, **67**, 207–223.

Estes, W. K. Growth and function of mathematical models for learning. In R. A. Patton (Ed.), *Current trends in psychological theory.* Pittsburgh: Univer. of Pittsburgh Press, 1961. Pp. 134–151. Reprinted in Marx, M. H. (Ed.), *Psychological theory: Contemporary readings.* (2nd ed.) New York: Macmillan, 1963.

Estes, W. K., & Burke, C. J. A theory of stimulus variability in learning. *Psychol. Rev.,* 1953, **60**, 276–286.

Estes, W. K., Hopkins, B. L., & Crothers, E. J. All-or-none and conservation effects in the learning and retention of paired associates. *Psychol. Rev.,* 1960, **60**, 329–339.

Estes, W. K., Koch, S., MacCorquodale, K., Meehl, P. E., Mueller, C. G., Jr., Schoenfeld, W. N., & Verplanck, W. S. *Modern learning theory.* New York: Appleton-Century-Crofts, 1954.

Eysenck, H. J. *Dimensions of personality.* London: Routledge, 1947.

Eysenck, H. J. Criterion analysis: An application of the hypothetico-deductive method to factor analysis. *Psychol. Rev.,* 1950, **57**, 38–53.

Eysenck, H. J. *The scientific study of personality.* London: Routledge, 1952.

Eysenck, H. J. *The structure of human personality.* New York: Wiley, 1953a.

Eysenck, H. J. *Uses and abuses of psychology.* Baltimore: Penguin, 1953b.

Eysenck, H. J. *The psychology of politics.* London: Routledge, 1954.

Eysenck, H. J. *The dynamics of anxiety and hysteria: An experimental application of modern learning theory to psychiatry.* New York: Frederick A. Praeger, 1957.

Eysenck, H. J. (Ed.) *Handbook of abnormal psychology.* New York: Basic Books, 1961.

Ezriel, H. The scientific testing of psychoanalytic findings and theory. *Brit. J. med. Psychol.,* 1951, **24**, 26–29.

Fairbairn, W. R. P. Theoretical and experimental aspects of psychoanalysis. *Brit. J. med. Psychol.,* 1952, **25**, 122–127.

Falk, J. L. Issues distinguishing idiographic from nomothetic approaches to personality theory. *Psychol. Rev.,* 1956, **63**, 53–62.

Farrell, B. A. The scientific testing of psychoanalytic findings and theory. *Brit. J. med. Psychol.,* 1951, **24**, 35–41.

Fechner, G. T. *Elemente der Psychophyisk.* 1860.

Feigl, H., & Brodbeck, M. (Eds.) *Readings in the philosophy of science.* New York: Appleton-Century-Crofts, 1953.

Feigl, H., & Maxwell, G. (Eds.) *Current issues in the philosophy of science.* (Proceedings, Section L, American Association for the Advancement of Science, 1959.) New York: Holt, 1961.

Feigl, H., & Scriven, M. (Eds.) *Minnesota studies in the philosophy of science.* Vol. I. Minneapolis: Univer. of Minnesota Press, 1956.

Feigl, H., Scriven, M., & Maxwell, G. (Eds.) *Minnesota studies in the philosophy of science.* Vol. II. Minneapolis: Univer. of Minnesota Press, 1958.

Feigl, H., & Sellars, W. (Eds.) Readings in philosophical analysis. New York: Appleton-Century-Crofts, 1949.

Felsinger, J. M., Gladstone, A. I., Yamaguchi, H. C., & Hull, C. L. Reaction latency (st$_R$) as a function of the number of reinforcements (N). J. exp. Psychol., 1947, 37, 214–228.

Fenichel, O. The psychoanalytic theory of neurosis. New York: Norton, 1945.

Ferenczi, S., & Rank, O. The development of psychoanalysis. Trans. by Caroline Newton. New York: Nervous and Mental Disease Publishing, 1925.

Ferster, C. B., & Skinner, B. F. Schedules of reinforcement. New York: Appleton-Century-Crofts, 1957.

Festinger, L. A theory of cognitive dissonance. New York: Harper & Row, 1957.

Frank, J. D. Some psychological determinants of the level of aspiration. Amer. J. Psychol., 1935, 47, 285–293.

Frank, P. Modern science and its philosophy. Cambridge, Mass.: Harvard, 1949.

Frenkel-Brunswik, Else. Meaning of psychoanalytic concepts and confirmation of psychoanalytic theories. Scientific Mon., 1954, 79, 293–300.

Freud, S. The history of the psychoanalytic movement. In A. A. Brill (Ed. & Trans.), The basic writings of Sigmund Freud. New York: Random House, 1938. Pp. 933–977.

Freud, S. A general introduction to psychoanalysis. Translated by J. Riviere. Garden City, N.Y.: Doubleday, 1943.

Freud, S. Beyond the pleasure principle. In J. Strachey (Ed. & Trans.), The complete psychological works of Sigmund Freud. Vol. 18. London: Hogarth, 1955.

Fromm, E. Escape from freedom. New York: Holt, 1941.

Fromm, E. Man for himself. New York: Holt, 1947.

Fromm, E. The sane society. New York: Holt, 1955.

Fromm, E. May man prevail? An inquiry into the facts and fictions of foreign policy. Garden City, N.Y.: Doubleday, 1961.

Garner, W. R., Hunt, H. F., & Taylor, D. W. Education for research in psychology. Amer. Psychol., 1959, 14, 167–179.

Garner, W. R. Rating scales, discriminability, and information transmission. Psychol. Rev., 1960, 67, 343–352.

Garner, W. R., & Hake, H. W. The amount of information in absolute judgments. Psychol. Rev., 1951, 58, 446–459.

Garner, W. R., Hake, H. W., & Eriksen, C. W. Operationism and the concept of perception. Psychol. Rev., 1956, 63, 149–159.

Gates, A. I. Connectionism: Present concepts and interpretations. Yearb. natl. Soc. Stud. Educ., 1942, 41, Part II.

Geissler, L. R. The measurement of attention. Amer. J. Psychol., 1909, 20, 473–529.

Gelb, A., & Goldstein, K. Psychologische Analysen hirnpathologischer Faelle. Leipzig: Barth, 1920.

Goldiamond, I. Indicators of perception I. Subliminal perception, subception, unconscious perception. Psychol. Bull., 1958, 55, 373–411.

Goldstein, K. The organism. New York: American Book, 1939.

Goldstein, K. *Human nature in the light of psychopathology.* Cambridge, Mass.: Harvard, 1940.

Goldstein, K. *After-effects of brain injuries in war.* New York: Grune & Stratton, 1942.

Goldstein, K. *Language and language disturbances.* New York: Grune & Stratton, 1948.

Goldstein, K., & Scheerer, M. Abstract and concrete behavior: An experimental study with special tests. *Psychol. Monogr.,* 1941, **53,** No. 2.

Goldstein, K., & Scheerer, M. Tests of abstract and concrete thinking. A. Tests of abstract and concrete behavior. In A. Weider (Ed.), *Contributions toward medical psychology.* New York: Ronald, 1953.

Graham, C. H. Visual perception. In S. S. Stevens (Ed.), *Handbook of experimental psychology.* New York: Wiley, 1951.

Graham, C. H. Sensation and perception in an objective psychology. *Psychol. Rev.,* 1958, **65,** 65–76.

Guthrie, E. R. *The psychology of learning.* New York: Harper & Row, 1935. Rev. ed., 1952.

Guthrie, E. R. *The psychology of human conflict.* New York: Harper & Row, 1938.

Guthrie, E. R. Conditioning: A theory of learning in terms of stimulus, response, and association. *Yearb. natl. Soc. Stud. Educ.,* 1942, **41,** Part II, 17–60.

Guthrie, E. R. Psychological facts and psychological theory. *Psychol. Bull.,* 1946, **43,** 1–20.

Guthrie, E. R. Association by contiguity. In S. Koch (Ed.), *Psychology: A study of a science.* Vol. 2. *General systematic formulations, learning and special processes.* New York: McGraw-Hill, 1959. Pp. 158–195.

Guthrie, E. R., & Horton, G. P. *Cats in a puzzle box.* New York: Holt, 1946.

Hall, C. S. *A primer of Freudian psychology.* Cleveland: World Publishing, 1954.

Hall, C. S. & Lindzey, G. *Theories of personality.* New York: Wiley, 1957.

Hall, G. S. *Adolescence.* New York: Appleton, 1904.

Hall, G. S. *Jesus, the Christ, in the light of psychology.* Garden City, N.Y.: Doubleday, 1917.

Hall, G. S. *Senescence.* New York: Appleton, 1922.

Hammond, K. R. Representative vs. systematic design in clinical psychology. *Psychol. Bull.,* 1954, **51,** 150–159.

Hammond, K. R. Probabilistic functioning and the clinical method. *Psychol. Rev.,* 1955, **62,** 255–262.

Hammond, W. A. *Aristotle's psychology.* London: Swan Sonnenschein, 1902.

Harlow, H. F. Primate learning. In C. P. Stone (Ed.), *Comparative psychology.* Englewood Cliffs, N.J.: Prentice-Hall, 1951.

Harlow, H. F. Learning set and error factor theory. In S. Koch (Ed.), *Psychology: A study of a science.* Vol. 2. New York: McGraw-Hill, 1959. Pp. 492–537.

Harlow, H. F., Davis, R. T., Settlage, P. H., & Meyer, D. R. Analysis of frontal and posterior association syndromes in brain damaged monkeys. *J. comp. physiol. Psychol.,* 1952, **45,** 419–429.

Harrower, M. R. Organization in higher mental processes. *Psychol. Forsch.*, 1932, **17**, 56–120.

Hartley, D. *Observations on man, his duty, and his expectations.* London: W. Eyres, 1749.

Hartmann, G. W. *Gestalt psychology.* New York: Ronald, 1935.

Hartmann, H. Comments on the psychoanalytic theory of instinctual drives. *Psychoanal. Quart.*, 1948, **17**, 368–388.

Hebb, D. O. *The organization of behavior.* New York: Wiley, 1949.

Heidbreder, E. *Seven psychologies.* New York: Appleton-Century-Crofts, 1933.

Heisenberg, W. *The physicist's conception of nature.* Translated by A. J. Pomerans. New York: Harcourt, Brace & World, 1958.

Helson, H. The fundamental propositions of gestalt psychology.*Psychol. Rev.*, 1933, **40**, 13–32.

Henle, Mary. Some problems of eclecticism. *Psychol. Rev.*, 1957, **64**, 296–305.

Henle, Mary (Ed.) *Documents of gestalt psychology.* Berkeley: Univer. of California Press, 1961.

Hilgard, E. R. *Theories of learning.* New York: Appleton-Century-Crofts, 1948. Rev. ed., 1956.

Hilgard, E. R. Experimental approaches to psychoanalysis. In E. Pumpian-Mindlin (Ed.), *Psychoanalysis as science.* Stanford, Calif.: Stanford, 1952. Pp. 3–45.

Hilgard, E. R. Discussion of probabilistic functionalism. *Psychol. Rev.*, 1955, **62**, 226–228.

Hobbes, T. *Leviathan.* London: Oxford, 1651.

Hochberg, J. E. Effects of the gestalt revolution: The Cornell symposium on perception. *Psychol. Rev.*, 1957, **64**, 73–84.

Hochberg, J., & McAlister, E. A quantitative approach to figural "goodness." *J. exp. Psychol.*, 1953, **46**, 361–364.

Holt, E. B. *The Freudian wish and its place in ethics.* New York: Holt, 1915.

Holt, E. B. *Animal drive and the learning process.* New York: Holt, 1931.

Holton, G. (Ed.) Science and the modern world view. *Daedalus*, 1958, **87**. Reprinted as G. Holton (Ed.), *Science and the modern mind.* Boston: Beacon Press, 1958.

Holton, G. Science and technology in contemporary society. *Daedalus*, 1962, **91**.

Holton, G. Scientific research and scholarship. *Daedalus*, 1962, **91**, 362–399.

Hoppe, F. Erfolg und Misserfolg. *Psychol. Forsch.*, 1930, **14**, 1–62.

Horney, Karen. *Neurotic personality of our times.* New York: Norton, 1937.

Horney, Karen. *New ways in psychoanalysis.* New York: Norton, 1939.

Horney, Karen. *Self-analysis.* New York: Norton, 1942.

Horney, Karen. *Our inner conflicts.* New York: Norton, 1945.

Horney, Karen. *Neurosis and human growth.* New York: Norton, 1950.

Hull, C. L. Quantitative aspects of the evolution of concepts. *Psychol. Monogr.*, 1920, **28**, No. 123.

Hull, C. L. The influence of tobacco smoking on mental and motor efficiency. *Psychol. Monogr.*, 1924, No. 150.

Hull, C. L. *Aptitude testing*. New York: World, 1928.

Hull, C. L. The goal gradient hypothesis and maze learning. *Psychol. Rev.*, 1932, **39**, 25–43.

Hull, C. L. *Hypnosis and suggestibility: An experimental approach*. New York: Appleton-Century, 1933.

Hull, C. L. Mind, mechanism, and adaptive behavior. *Psychol. Rev.*, 1937, **44**, 1–32.

Hull, C. L. *Principles of behavior*. New York: Appleton-Century-Crofts, 1943.

Hull, C. L. *Essentials of behavior*. New Haven: Yale, 1951.

Hull, C. L. *A behavior system*. New Haven: Yale, 1952.

Hull, C. L., Felsinger, J. M., Gladstone, A. D., & Yamaguchi, H. C. A proposed quantification of habit strength. *Psychol. Rev.*, 1947, **54**, 237–254.

Hull, C. L., Hovland, C. I., Ross, R. T., Hall, M., Perkins, D. T., & Fitch, F. G. *Mathematico-deductive theory of rote learning*. New Haven: Yale, 1940.

Hume, D. *A treatise on human nature*. London: Longmans, 1886.

Hunt, W. A. Clinical psychology: Science or superstition. *Amer. Psychol.*, 1951, **6**, 683–687.

Hunter, W. S. Problem of consciousness. *Psychol. Rev.*, 1924, **21**, 1–31.

Hunter, W. S. Psychology and anthroponomy. In C. Murchison (Ed.), *Psychologies of 1925*. Worcester, Mass.: Clark Univer. Press, 1926. Chap. IV.

James, W. *The principles of psychology*. New York: Holt, 1890.

James, W. *A pluralistic universe*. New York: Longmans, 1909.

Jensen, A. R. Personality. *Annu. Rev. Psychol.*, 1958, **9**, 295–322.

Johansson, G. *Configurations in event perception*. Uppsala: Almquist & Wiksell, 1950.

Johnson, H. K. Psychoanalysis: A critique. *Psychiat. Quart.*, 1948, **22**, 321–338.

Jones, E. *The life and work of Sigmund Freud*. New York: Basic Books. Vol. 1, 1953; Vol. 2, 1955; Vol. 3, 1957.

Jung, C. G. *Symbols of transformation*. New York: Random House, 1956.

Jung, C. G., & Pauli, W. *The interpretation of nature and the people*. New York: Random House, 1955.

Kallen, H. M. (Ed.) *The philosophy of William James*. New York: Modern Library, 1925.

Kantor, J. R. *Psychology and logic*. Bloomington: Principia Press. Vol. I, 1945; Vol. II, 1950.

Kantor, J. R. *Problems of physiological psychology*. Bloomington: Principia Press, 1947.

Kantor, J. R. *An objective psychology of grammar*. Bloomington: Principia Press, 1952.

Kantor, J. R. *The logic of modern science*. Bloomington: Principia Press, 1953.

Kantor, J. R. *Interbehavioral psychology*. Bloomington: Principia Press, 1958.

Kardiner, A. *The individual and his society*. New York: Columbia, 1939.

Karsten, A. Psychische Sättigung. *Psychol. Forsch.*, 1928, **10**, 142–154.

Katona, G. *The powerful consumer: Psychological studies of the American economy.* New York: McGraw-Hill, 1960.

Katz, D. Die Erscheinungsweisen der Farben. *Z. Psychol.*, 1911, **7**, 1–3.

Keller, F. S., & Schoenfeld, W. N. *Principles of psychology.* New York: Appleton-Century-Crofts, 1950.

Kimble, G. A. *Hilgard and Marquis' conditioning and learning.* (2nd ed.) New York: Appleton-Century-Crofts, 1961.

Klemmer, E. T., & Frick, F. C. Assimilation of information from dot and matrix patterns. *J. exp. Psychol.*, 1953, **45**, 15–19.

Klüver, H. Psychology at the beginning of World War II: Meditations on the impending dismemberment of psychology written in 1942. *J. Psychol.*, 1949, **28**, 383–410.

Koch, S. Review of Hull's principles of behavior. *Psychol. Bull.*, 1944, **41**, 269–286.

Koch, S. Clark L. Hull. In W. K. Estes et al., *Modern learning theory.* New York: Appleton-Century-Crofts, 1954. Pp. 1–176.

Koch, S. Epilogue. In S. Koch (Ed.), *Psychology: A study of a science.* Vol. 3. New York: McGraw-Hill, 1959. Pp. 729–788.

Koffka, K. *Principles of gestalt psychology.* New York: Harcourt, Brace, 1935.

Kohler, I. Über Aufbau und Wandlugen der Wahrnehmungswelt. *Oesterr. Akad. Wiss. Philos.-Histor. Kl.; Sitz.-Ber.*, 1951, **227**, 1–118.

Köhler, W. *Die physischen Gestalten in Ruhe und im stationaren Zustand.* Erlangen: Weltkreisverlag, 1920.

Köhler, W. Gestaltprobleme und Anfange einer Gestalttheorie. *Jahresbericht u. d. ges. Physiol.*, 1925, **3**, 512–539.

Köhler, W. *The mentality of apes.* New York: Harcourt, Brace, 1925.

Köhler, W. Kurt Koffka. *Psychol. Rev.*, 1942, **49**, 97–101.

Köhler, W. Max Wertheimer, 1880–1943. *Psychol. Rev.*, 1944, **51**, 143–146.

Köhler, W. *Gestalt psychology: An introduction to the new concepts in modern psychology.* New York: Liveright, 1947.

Krechevsky, I. "Hypotheses" in rats. *Psychol. Rev.*, 1932, **39**, 516–532.

Kris, E. The nature of psychoanalytic propositions and their validation. In S. Hook and M. R. Konwitz (Eds.), *Freedom and experience: Essays presented to Horace Allen.* Ithaca, N.Y.: Cornell, 1947. Reprinted in M. H. Marx (Ed.), *Psychological theory: Contemporary readings.* New York: Macmillan, 1951.

Kubie, L. S. Problems and techniques of psychoanalytic validation and progress. In E. Pumpian-Mindlin (Ed.), *Psychoanalysis as science.* Stanford, Calif.: Stanford, 1952. Pp. 46–124.

Kuenzli, A. E. *The phenomenological problem.* New York: Harper & Row, 1959.

Külpe, O. *Outlines of psychology, based upon results of experimental investigation.* Trans. by E. B. Titchener. New York: Macmillan, 1895.

Kuo, Z. Y. The nature of unsuccessful acts and their order of elimination. *J. comp. Psychol.*, 1922, **2**, 1–27.

Kuo, Z. Y. A psychology without heredity. *Psychol. Rev.*, 1924, **31**, 427–448.

Kuo, Z. Y. The genesis of the cat's response to the rat. *J. comp. Psychol.*, 1930, **11**, 1–35.

Kuo, Z. Y. Ontogeny of embryonic behavior in Aves. I. The chronology and general nature of the behavior of the chick embryo. *J. exp. Zool.*, 1932a, **61**, 395–430.

Kuo, Z. Y. Ontogeny of embryonic behavior in Aves. II. The mechanical factors in the various stages leading to hatching. *J. exp. Zool.*, 1932b, **62**, 453–489.

Kuo, Z. Y. Ontogeny of embryonic behavior in Aves. III. The structure and environmental factors in embryonic behavior. *J. comp. Psychol.*, 1932c, **13**, 245–272.

Kuo, Z. Y. Ontogeny of embryonic behavior in Aves. IV. The influence of embryonic movements upon the behavior after hatching. *J. comp. Psychol.*, 1932d, **14**, 109–122.

Kuo, Z. Y. Ontogeny of embryonic behavior in Aves. V. The reflex concept in the light of embryonic behavior in birds. *Psychol. Rev.*, 1932e, **39**, 499–515.

Kuo, Z. Y. Further study of the behavior of the cat toward the rat. *J. comp. Psychol.*, 1938, **25**, 1–8.

Lamarck, J. B. *Zoological philosophy: An exposition with regard to the natural history of animals.* Translated by High Elliot. London: Macmillan, 1914.

La Mettrie, J. O. de *L'homme machine.* Leyden, 1748. Republished as *Man a machine.* La Salle, Ill.: Open Court, 1912.

Land, E. H. Experiments in color vision. *Scientific Amer.*, 1959, **200**, 84–99.

Lashley, K. S. The behavioristic interpretation of consciousness. *Psychol. Rev.*, 1923, **30**, 329–353.

Lashley, K. S. *Brain mechanisms and intelligence.* Chicago: Univer. of Chicago Press, 1929.

Lashley, K. S. Cerebral control versus reflexology: A reply to Professor Hunter. *J. gen. Psychol.*, 1931, **5**, 3–20.

Lawson, R., & Marx, M. H. Frustration: Theory and experiment. *Genet. Psychol. Monogr.*, 1958, **57**, 393–464.

Leeper, R. W. *Lewin's topological and vector psychology.* Eugene: Univer. of Oregon Press, 1943.

Leeper, R. W. Cognitive processes. In S. S. Stevens (Ed.), *Handbook of experimental psychology.* New York: Wiley, 1951.

Levine, R., Chein, I., & Murphy, G. The relation of the intensity of a need to the amount of perceptual distortion: A preliminary report. *J. Psychol.*, 1942, **13**, 283–293.

Lewes, G. H. *Study of psychology.* 1879.

Lewin, K. Die psychische Tatigkeit bei der Hemmung von Willensvorgängen und das Grundgesetz der Assoziation. *Z. Psychol.*, 1917, **77**, 212–247.

Lewin, K. *A dynamic theory of personality.* Translated by K. E. Zener & D. K. Adams. New York: McGraw-Hill, 1935.

Lewin, K. *Principles of topological psychology.* Translated by F. Heider & Grace Heider. New York: McGraw-Hill, 1936.

Lewin, K. *The conceptual representation and measurement of psychological forces.* Durham, N.C.: Duke, 1938.

Lewin, K. Field theory and experiment in social psychology: Concepts and methods. *Amer. J. Sociol.*, 1939, **44**, 868–896.

Lewin, K. Formalization and progress in psychology. *Univer. Iowa Stud. Child Welf.*, 1940, 16, 9–42.

Lewin, K. Defining the "field at a given time." *Psychol. Rev.*, 1943a, 50, 292–310. Reprinted in Marx, M. H. (Ed.), *Psychological theory: Contemporary readings.* New York: Macmillan, 1951. Pp. 299–315.

Lewin, K. Forces behind food habits and methods of change. *Bull. Natl. Res. Council*, 1943b, 108, 35–65.

Lewin, K. Constructs in psychology and psychological ecology. *Univer. Iowa Stud. Child Welf.*, 1944, 20, 1–29.

Lewin, K. *Resolving social conflicts.* New York: Harper & Row, 1948.

Lewin, K. *Field theory in social science.* New York: Harper & Row, 1951.

Licklider, J. C. R. Three auditory theories. In S. Koch (Ed.), *Psychology: A study of a science.* Vol. 1. *Sensory, perceptual, and physiological formulations.* New York: McGraw-Hill, 1959. Pp. 41–144.

Lippitt, R. An experimental study of authoritarian and democratic group atmospheres. *Univer. Iowa Stud. Child Welf.*, 1940, 16, 43–195.

Lippitt, R., & White, R. K. The "social climate" of children's groups. In R. G. Barker, J. S. Kounin, & H. F. Wright (Eds.), *Child behavior and development.* New York: McGraw-Hill, 1943. Pp. 485–508.

Lissner, K. Die Entspannung von Bedürfnissen durch Ersatzhandlungen. *Psychol. Forsch.*, 1933, 18, 218–250.

Locke, J. *An essay concerning human understanding.* Vol. 2. Boston: David Carlisle, 1803. Reprinted from 20th London ed.

Logan, F. A. A micromolar approach to behavior theory. *Psychol. Rev.*, 1956, 63, 73–80.

Logan, F. A. The Hullian approach. In S. Koch (Ed.), *Psychology: A study of a science.* Vol. 2. *General systematic formulations, learning and special processes.* New York: McGraw-Hill, 1959. Pp. 293–348.

Logan, F. A. *Incentive.* New Haven: Yale, 1960.

London, I. D. Psychologists' misuse of the auxiliary concepts of physics and mathematics. *Psychol. Rev.*, 1944, 51, 266–291.

Lorge, I. D. (Comp.) Edward L. Thorndike's publications from 1940 to 1949. *Teach. Coll. Rec.*, 1949, 51, 42–45.

Lubin, A. A note on Sheldon's table of correlations between temperamental traits. *Brit. J. Psychol., statist.*, 1950, 3, 186–189.

Luce, R. D. (Ed.) *Developments in mathematical psychology.* New York: Free Press, 1960.

Ludwig, E. *Doctor Freud.* New York: Hellman, Williams, 1947.

MacCorquodale, K., & Meehl, P. E. On the elimination of cul entries without obvious reinforcement. *J. comp. physiol. Psychol.*, 1951, 44, 367–371.

MacCorquodale, K., & Meehl, P. E. Edward C. Tolman. In W. K. Estes et al., *Modern learning theory.* New York: Appleton-Century-Crofts, 1954. Pp. 177–266.

MacKay, E. M. The nomenclature of information theory. In H. von Foerster (Ed.), *Transactions of the eighth conference on cybernetics: Circular causal and feedback mechanisms in biological and social systems.* New York: Josiah Macy, Jr., Foundation, 1952.

MacLeish, A. Why do we teach poetry? *Atlantic Mon.*, 1956, 197(3), 49–51.

MacLeod, R. B. Review of *Cumulative record* by B. F. Skinner. *Science,* 1959, **130,** 34–35.

Mahler, V. Ersatzhandlungen verschiedenen Realitätsgrades. *Psychol. Forsch.,* 1933, **18,** 26–89.

Maier, N. R. F. Experimentally produced neurotic behavior in the rat. Paper read at annual meeting of the American Association for the Advancement of Science, Richmond, 1938.

Maier, N. R. F. *Frustration: The study of behavior without a goal.* New York: McGraw-Hill, 1949.

Maier, N. R. F., & Schneirla, T. C. *Principles of animal psychology.* New York: McGraw-Hill, 1935.

Malinowski, B. *Argonauts of the western Pacific.* New York: Dutton, 1950.

Malmo, R. B. Activation: A neuropsychological dimension. *Psychol. Rev.,* 1959, **66,** 367–386.

Mandler, G., & Kessen, W. *The language of psychology.* New York: Wiley, 1959.

Marx, M. H. Spread of effect: A critical review. *Genet. Psychol. Monogr.,* 1956, **53,** 119–186.

Marx, M. H. Gradients of error-reinforcement in a serial perceptual-motor task. *Psychol. Monogr.,* 1957a, **71,** 1–20.

Marx, M. H. Gradients of error-reinforcement in normal multiple-choice learning situations. *J. exp. Psychol.,* 1957b, **54,** 225–228.

Marx, M. H. (Ed.) *Theories in contemporary psychology.* (2nd ed.) New York: Macmillan, 1963.

Maudsley, H. *Physiology of mind.* New York: Appleton, 1899.

McClelland, D. C., et al. *The achievement motive.* New York: Appleton-Century-Crofts, 1953.

McDougall, W. *Physiological psychology.* London: Dent, 1905.

McDougall, W. *Psychology, the study of behavior.* London: Williams & Norgate, 1912.

McGeoch, J. A. The formal criteria of a systematic psychology. *Psychol. Rev.,* 1933, **40,** 1–12.

McGeoch, J. A. *The psychology of human learning.* New York: Longmans, 1942.

McGeoch, J. A., & Irion, A. L. *The psychology of human learning.* (2nd ed.) New York: Longmans, 1952.

McGill, W. J. Multivariate information transmission. *Psychometrika,* 1954, **19,** 97–116.

Mead, Margaret. *Coming of age in Samoa.* New York: Morrow, 1928. Garden City, N.Y.: Doubleday, 1950.

Mednick, S. A., & Freedman, J. L. Stimulus generalization. *Psychol. Bull.,* 1960, **57,** 169–200.

Meehl, P. E. On the circularity of the law of effect. *Psychol. Bull.,* 1950, **47,** 52–75.

Melton, A. W. Learning. In C. P. Stone (Ed.), *Annual review of psychology.* Vol. I. Stanford, Calif.: Annual Reviews, 1950. Pp. 9–30.

Meyer, M. *The fundamental laws of human behavior.* Boston: R. G. Badger, 1911.

Meyer, M. *The psychology of the other one.* Columbia: Missouri Book Store, 1921.

Mill, J. Analysis of the phenomena of the human mind. Vol. I. London: Longmans, 1829.

Mill, J. S. A system of logic. London: Longmans, 1843. Republished, 1956.

Miller, G. A. The magical number seven, plus or minus two: Some limits on our capacity for processing information. Psychol. Rev., 1956, 63, 81–87.

Miller, G. A., Galanter, E., & Pribram, K. H. Plans and the structure of behavior. New York: Holt, 1960.

Miller, N. E. Experimental studies of conflict. In J. McV. Hunt (Ed.), Personality and the behavior disorders. Vol. I. New York: Ronald, 1944. Pp. 431–465.

Miller, N. E. Theory and experiment relating psychoanalytic displacement to stimulus-response generalization. J. abnorm. soc. Psychol., 1948, 43, 155–178.

Miller, N. E. Comments on multiple-process conceptions of learning. Psychol. Rev., 1951, 58, 375–381.

Miller, N. E. Central stimulation and other new approaches to motivation and reward. Amer. Psychol., 1958, 13, 100–108.

Miller, N. E. Liberalization of basic S-R concepts: Extensions to conflict behavior, motivation, and social learning. In S. Koch (Ed.), Psychology: A study of a science. Vol. 2. New York: McGraw-Hill, 1959. Pp. 196–292.

Miller, N. E., & Dollard, J. Social learning and imitation. New Haven: Yale, 1941.

Mintz, A. Recent developments in psychology in the U.S.S.R. Annu. Rev. Psychol., 1958, 9, 453–504.

Mintz, A. Further developments in psychology in the U.S.S.R. Annu. Rev. Psychol., 1959, 10, 455–487.

Morgan, C. L. Introduction to comparative psychology. London: W. Scott, 1891. 2nd ed., 1899.

Morgan, C. L. Animal behavior. London: E. Arnold, 1900.

Morgan, C. T., & Morgan, J. D. Auditory induction of an abnormal pattern of behavior in rats. J. comp. Psychol., 1939, 27, 505–508.

Mowrer, O. H. On the dual nature of learning: A re-interpretation of "conditioning" and "problem solving." Harvard educ. Rev., 1947, 17, 102–148.

Mowrer, O. H. Learning theory and personality dynamics. New York: Ronald, 1950.

Mowrer, O. H. Two-factor learning theory: Summary and comment. Psychol. Rev., 1951, 58, 350–354.

Mowrer, O. H. Learning theory: Historical review and re-interpretation. Harvard educ. Rev., 1954, 24, 37–58.

Mowrer, O. H. Two-factor learning theory reconsidered, with special reference to secondary reinforcement and the concept of habit. Psychol. Rev. 1956, 63, 114–128.

Mowrer, O. H. Review of Dynamics of behavior by R. S. Woodworth. Contemp. Psychol., 1959, 4, 129–133.

Mowrer, O. H. Learning theory and behavior. New York: Wiley, 1960a.

Mowrer, O. H. Learning theory and the symbolic behavior. New York: Wiley, 1960b.

Mueller, C. G. Jr., & Schoenfeld, W. N. Edwin R. Guthrie. In W. K. Estes et al., *Modern learning theory*. New York: Appleton-Century-Crofts, 1954. Pp. 345–379.

Müller, G. E. Komplextheorie und Gestalttheorie: Ein Beitrag zur Wahrenehmungspsychologie. Göttinger, 1923.

Mullahy, P. *Oedipus: Myth and complex.* New York: Hermitage House, 1948.

Munroe, Ruth. *Schools of psychoanalytic thought.* New York: Holt, 1955.

Murchison, C. (Ed.) *A history of psychology in autobiography.* Vols. I–III. Worcester, Mass.: Clark Univer. Press, 1930–1936.

Murphy, G. *General psychology.* New York: Harper, 1933.

Murphy, G. (Ed.) *Human nature and enduring peace.* Boston: Houghton Mifflin, 1945.

Murphy, G. *Personality: A biosocial approach to origins and structure.* New York: Harper & Row, 1947.

Murphy, G. *Historical introduction to modern psychology.* New York: Harcourt, Brace & World, 1949.

Murphy, G. *Introduction to psychology.* New York: Harper & Row, 1951.

Murphy, G. *Human potentialities.* New York: Basic Books, 1958.

Murphy, G., & Likert, R. *Public opinion and the individual.* New York: Harper & Row, 1938.

Murphy, G., & Murphy, Lois B. *Experimental social psychology.* New York: Harper, 1931. Rev. ed. with T. M. Newcomb, 1937.

Murray, Elsie. Peripheral and central factors in memory: Images of visual form and color. *Amer. J. Psychol.*, 1906, **17**, 225–247.

Murray, H. A., and collaborators. *Explorations in personality.* New York: Oxford, 1938.

Murray, H. A. *Manual of thematic apperception test.* Cambridge, Mass.: Harvard, 1943.

Murray, H. A. In nomine diaboli. *New England Quart.*, 1951, **24**, 435–452. Reprinted in *Princeton Univer. Library Chronicle*, 1952, **13**, 47–62.

Murray, H. A. Preparations for the scaffold of a comprehensive system. In S. Koch (Ed.), *Psychology: A study of a science.* Vol. 3. *Formulations of the person and the social context.* New York: McGraw-Hill, 1959.

Nafe, J. P. The psychology of felt experience. *Amer. J. Psychol.*, 1927, **39**, 367–389.

Newbury, E. Current interpretation and significance of Lloyd Morgan's canon. *Psychol. Bull.*, 1954, **51**, 70–74.

Newell, A., Shaw, J. C., & Simon, H. A. Elements of a theory of human problem solving. *Psychol. Rev.*, 1958, **65**, 151–166.

Newell, A., & Simon, H. A. The simulation of human thought. In W. Dennis et al., *Current trends in psychological theory: 1961.* Pittsburgh: Univer. of Pittsburgh Press, 1961.

Newman, E. B. Public relations—for what? *Amer. Psychol.*, 1957, **12**, 509–514.

Office of Strategic Services Assessment Staff. *Assessment of men.* New York: Holt, 1948.

Olds, J. Physiological mechanisms of reward. In M. R. Jones (Ed.),

Nebraska symposium on motivation. Lincoln: Univer. of Nebraska Press, 1955.

Olds, J. High functions of the nervous system. *Annu. Rev. Physiol.*, 1959, **21**, 381–402.

Oppenheimer, R. Analogy in science. *Amer. Psychol.*, 1956, **11**, 127–135.

Orbison, W. O. Shape as a function of the vector field. *Amer. J. Psychol.*, 1939, **52**, 31–45.

Ovsiankina, Maria. Die Wiederaufnahme von unterbrochenen Handlungen. *Psychol. Forsch.*, 1928, **11**, 302–379.

Pavlov, I. P. *Conditioned reflexes.* London: Oxford, 1927.

Pavlov, I. P. *Lectures on conditioned reflexes.* New York: Liveright, 1928.

Pavlov, I. P. The reply of a physiologist to psychologists. *Psychol. Rev.*, 1932, **39**, 91–127.

Pavlov, I. P. *Lectures on conditioned reflexes.* Vol. II. *Conditioned reflexes and psychiatry.* Translated and edited by W. H. Gantt. New York: International Publishers, 1941.

Pavlov, I. P. *Selected works.* Translated by S. Belsky; edited by J. Gibbons, under supervision of Kh. S. Koshtoyants. Moscow: Foreign Languages Publishing House, 1955.

Perky, C. W. An experimental study of imagination. *Amer. J. Psychol.*, 1910, **21**, 422–452.

Peterson, W. W., Birdsall, T. G., & Fox, W. C. *The theory of signal detectability.* Transactions of Professional Group on Information Theory, Institute of Radio Engineers, PGIT-4, 1954, 171–212.

Pierce, J. R., & Karlin, J. E. Reading rates and the information rate of a human channel. *Bell Syst. tech. J.*, 1957, **36**, 497–516.

Pollack, I. *The assimilation of sequentially-encoded information.* HFORL Memo Report, TR-54-5, 1954.

Pollack, I., & Ficks, L. Information on multidimensional auditory displays, *J. acoust. Soc. Amer.*, 1953, **25**, 765–769.

Pollack, I., & Klemmer, E. T. The assimilation of visual information from linear dot patterns. *Air Force Cambridge Research Center, Technical Report*, 1954, **54**, 16.

Popper, K. *The logic of scientific discovery.* New York: Basic Books, 1959.

Postman, L. The probability approach and nomothetic theory. *Psychol. Rev.*, 1955, **62**, 218–225.

Postman, L. Spread of effect as a function of time and intraserial similarity. *Amer. J. Psychol.*, 1961, **74**, 493–505.

Postman, L., & Murphy, G. The factor of attitude in associative memory. *J. exp. Psychol.*, 1943, **33**, 228–238.

Postman, L., & Tolman, E. C. Brunswik's probabilistic functionalism. In S. Koch (Ed.), *Psychology: A study of a science.* Vol. 1. *Sensory, perceptual, and physiological formulations.* New York: McGraw-Hill, 1959. Pp. 502–564.

Pratt, C. C. *The logic of modern psychology.* New York: Macmillan, 1939.

Prentice, W. C. H. The systematic psychology of Wolfgang Köhler. In S. Koch (Ed.), *Psychology: A study of a science.* Vol. 1. *Sensory, perceptual, and physiological formulations.* New York: McGraw-Hill, 1959. Pp. 427–455.

Pumpian-Mindlin, E. (Ed.) *Psychoanalysis as science.* Stanford, Calif.: Stanford, 1952.

Pumpian-Mindlin, E. The position of psychoanalysis in relation to the biological and social sciences. In E. Pumpian-Mindlin (Ed.), *Psychoanalysis as science.* Stanford, Calif.: Stanford, 1952. Pp. 125–158.

Quastler, H. (Ed.) *Information theory in psychology: Problems and methods.* New York: Free Press, 1955.

Quastler, H., Osborne, J. W., & Tweedell, K. *Human performance in information transmission.* Part III. Control Systems Laboratory, Univer. of Illinois, Report R-68, 1955.

Rank, O. *The trauma of birth.* New York: Harcourt, Brace, 1929.

Rashevsky, N. *Mathematical biophysics.* Chicago: Univer. of Chicago Press, 1938. Rev. ed. 1948; rev. ed. 1961, in 2 vols.

Razran, G. Stimulus generalization of conditioned responses. *Psychol. Bull.,* 1949, **46**, 337–365.

Razran, G. The observable unconscious and the inferable conscious in current Soviet psychophysiology: Interoceptive conditioning, semantic conditioning and the orienting reflex. *Psychol. Rev.,* 1961, **68**, 81–147.

Reese, T. W. The application of the theory of physical measurements to the measurement of psychological magnitudes, with three experimental examples. *Psychol. Monogr.,* 1943, **55**, 1–88.

Roback, A. A. *A history of American psychology.* New York: Library Publishers, 1952.

Rogers, C. R. *The clinical treatment of the problem child.* Boston: Houghton Mifflin, 1939.

Rogers, C. R. *Counseling and psychotherapy: Newer concepts in practice.* Boston: Houghton Mifflin, 1942.

Rogers, C. R. *Client-centered therapy: Its current practice, implications, and theory.* Boston: Houghton Mifflin, 1951.

Romanes, G. J. *Animal intelligence.* London: Kegan Paul, Trench, Trubner, 1886.

Romanes, G. J. *Mental evolution in animals.* New York: Appleton, 1898.

Romanes, G. J. *Mental evolution in man.* New York: Appleton, 1902.

Rubin, E. *Syncopleoede figurer.* 1915.

Ruckmick, C. A. The use of the term function in English textbooks of psychology. *Amer. J. Psychol.,* 1913, **14**, 99–123.

Rudikoff, Esselyn C. A comparative study of the changes in the concepts of the self, the ordinary person, and the ideal in eight cases. In C. R. Rogers & Rosalind F. Dymond (Eds.), *Psychotherapy and personality change: Coordinated studies in the client-centered approach.* Chicago: Univer. of Chicago Press, 1954. Pp. 85–98.

Russell, B. *A history of western philosophy.* New York: Simon & Schuster, 1945.

Sanford, R. N. Physical and physiological correlates of personality structure. In C. Kluckhohn, H. A. Murray, & D. Scheider (Eds.), *Personality in nature, society, and culture.* (2nd ed.) New York: Knopf, 1953.

Sarton, G. *A guide to the history of science.* Waltham, Mass.: Chronica Botanica, 1952.

Schlosberg, H. The relationship between success and the laws of conditioning. *Psychol. Rev.,* 1937, **44**, 379–394.

Sears, R. R. *Survey of objective studies of psychoanalytic concepts.* New York: Social Science Research Council, 1943.

Seltzer, C. C., Wells, F. L., & McTernan, E. B. A relationship between Sheldonian somatotype and psychotype. *J. Pers.*, 1948, **16**, 431–436.

Seward, J. P. An experimental study of Guthrie's theory of reinforcement. *J. exp. Psychol.*, 1942, **30**, 247–256.

Seward, J. P., Dill, J. B., & Holland, M. A. Guthrie's theory of learning: A second experiment. *J. exp. Psychol.*, 1944, **34**, 227–238.

Shannon, C. E. Prediction and entropy of printed English. *Bell Syst. tech. J.*, 1951, **30**, 50–64.

Shannon, C. E., & Weaver, W. *The mathematical theory of communication.* Urbana: Univer. of Illinois Press, 1949.

Sheffield, F. D. Avoidance training and the contiguity principle. *J. comp. physiol. Psychol.*, 1948, **41**, 165–167.

Sheffield, F. D. "Spread of effect" without reward or learning. *J. exp. Psychol.*, 1949, **39**, 575–579.

Sheffield, F. D., & Roby, T. B. Reward value of a non-nutritive sweet taste. *J. comp. physiol. Psychol.*, 1950, **43**, 471–481.

Sheffield, F. D., Wulff, J. J., & Backer, R. Reward value of copulation without sex drive reduction. *J. comp. physiol. Psychol.*, 1951, **44**, 3–8.

Sheldon, W. H., with the collaboration of S. S. Stevens & W. B. Tucker. *The varieties of human physique: An introduction to constitutional psychology.* New York: Harper & Row, 1940.

Sheldon, W. H., with the collaboration of S. S. Stevens. *The varieties of temperament: A psychology of constitutional differences.* New York: Harper & Row, 1942.

Sheldon, W. H. Constitutional factors in personality. In J. McV. Hunt (Ed.), *Personality and the behavior disorders.* New York: Ronald, 1944. Pp. 526–549.

Sheldon, W. H. *Early American cents, 1793–1814.* New York: Harper & Row, 1949.

Sheldon, W. H., with the collaboration of E. M. Harth & E. McDermott. *Varieties of delinquent youth: An introduction to constitutional psychiatry.* New York: Harper & Row, 1949.

Sheldon, W. H., with the collaboration of C. W. Dupertuis & E. McDermott. *Atlas of men: A guide for somatotyping the adult male at all ages.* New York: Harper & Row, 1954.

Sherrington, C. S. *The integrative action of the nervous system.* London: Constable, 1906. Republished, with a new foreword and a bibliography of Sherrington's publications, by Yale Univer. Press, 1947.

Sidman, M. *Tactics of scientific research.* New York: Basic Books, 1960.

Skinner, B. F. *The behavior of organisms: An experimental analysis.* New York: Appleton-Century-Crofts, 1938.

Skinner, B. F. "Superstition" in the pigeon. *J. exp. Psychol.*, 1948a, **38**.

Skinner, B. F. *Walden two.* New York: Macmillan, 1948b.

Skinner, B. F. Are theories of learning necessary? *Psychol. Rev.*, 1950, **57**, 193–216.

Skinner, B. F. *Science and human behavior.* New York: Macmillan, 1953a.

Skinner, B. F. Some contributions of an experimental analysis of behavior to psychology as a whole. *Amer. Psychol.*, 1953b, **8**, 69–78.

Skinner, B. F. Critique of psychoanalytic concepts and theories. *Scientific Mon.*, 1954a, **79**, 300–305.
Skinner, B. F. The science of learning and the art of teaching. *Harvard educ. Rev.*, 1954b, **24**, 86–97.
Skinner, B. F. A case history in scientific method. *Amer. Psychol.*, 1956, **11**, 221–233.
Skinner, B. F. The experimental analysis of behavior. *Amer. Scientist*, 1957a, **45**, 343–371.
Skinner, B. F. *Verbal behavior.* New York: Appleton-Century-Crofts, 1957b.
Skinner, B. F. Teaching machines. *Science*, 1958, **128**, 969–977.
Skinner, B. F. *Cumulative record.* New York: Appleton-Century-Crofts, 1959.
Skinner, B. F. Pigeons in a pelican. *Amer. Psychol.*, 1960, **15**, 28–37.
Skinner, B. F., & Ferster, C. B. *Schedules of reinforcement.* New York: Appleton-Century-Crofts, 1957.
Smith, M., & Wilson, E. A model of the auditory threshold and its application to the problem of the multiple observer. *Psychol. Monogr.*, 1953, **67**.
Smith, S., & Guthrie, E. R. *General psychology in terms of behavior.* New York: Appleton, 1921.
Smith, S. L., & Miller, G. A. *The effects of coding procedures on learning and memory.* Quarterly progress report of Research Laboratory of Electronics, M.I.T. to Air Force Human Resources Research Laboratories, 1952.
Snygg, D., & Combs, A. W. *Individual behavior.* New York: Harper & Row, 1949.
Solley, C. M., & Murphy, G. *Development of the perceptual world.* New York: Basic Books, 1960.
Spearman, C. E. *Creative mind.* New York: Appleton, 1931.
Spence, K. W. The nature of discrimination learning in animals. *Psychol. Rev.*, 1936, **43**, 327–449.
Spence, K. W. Analysis of the formation of visual discrimination habits in chimpanzees. *J. comp. Psychol.*, 1937a, **23**, 77–100.
Spence, K. W. The differential response in animals to stimuli varying within a single dimension. *Psychol. Rev.*, 1937b, **44**, 430–444.
Spence, K. W. Continuous vs. non-continuous interpretations of discrimination learning. *Psychol. Rev.*, 1940, **47**, 271–288.
Spence, K. W. The methods and postulates of behaviorism. *Psychol. Rev.*, 1948, **55**, 67–78.
Spence, K. W. Theoretical interpretations of learning. In C. P. Stone (Ed.), *Comparative psychology*, (3rd ed.) New York: Prentice-Hall, 1951a. Pp. 239–291.
Spence, K. W. Theoretical interpretations of learning. In S. S. Stevens (Ed.), *Handbook of experimental psychology.* New York: Wiley, 1951b. Pp. 690–729.
Spence, K. W. *Behavior theory and conditioning.* New Haven: Yale, 1956.
Spence, K. W. *Behavior theory and learning.* Englewood Cliffs, N.J., Prentice-Hall, 1960.
Spencer, H. *The principles of psychology.* New York: Appleton, 1855.

Stengel, E. The scientific testing of psychoanalytic findings and theory. *Brit. J. med. Psychol.*, 1951, 24, 26–29.

Stephenson, W. *The study of behavior: Q-technique and its methodology.* Chicago: Univer. of Chicago Press, 1953.

Stephenson, W. Scientific creed—1961: Philosophical credo, abductory principles, the centrality of self. *Psychol. Rec.*, 1961, 11, 1–18.

Stevens, S. S. Psychology and the science of science. *Psychol. Bull.*, 1939, 36, 221–263. Reprinted in M. H. Marx (Ed.), *Psychological theory: Contemporary readings.* New York: Macmillan, 1951. Pp. 21–54.

Stevens, S. S. (Ed.) *Handbook of experimental psychology.* New York: Wiley, 1951.

Stout, G. F. *Analytic psychology.* New York: Macmillan, 1902.

Sullivan, H. S. *Conceptions of modern psychiatry.* Washington, D.C.: William Alanson White Psychiatric Foundation, 1947.

Sullivan, H. S. *The interpersonal theory of psychiatry.* New York: Norton, 1953.

Sumby, W. H., & Pollack, I. *Short-time processing of information.* HFORL Report, TR-54-6, 1954.

Swets, J. A. Is there a sensory threshold? *Science*, 1961, 134, 168–177.

Swets, J. A., Green, D. M., & Tanner, W. P. On the width of critical bands. *J. acoust. Soc. Amer.*, 1962, 34, 108–113.

Tanner, W., & Swets, J. *A new theory of visual detection.* Electronic Defense Group, Univer. of Michigan, Technical Report 18, 1953.

Tanner, W. P. & Swets, J. A. A decision-making theory of visual detection. *Psychol. Rev.*, 1954, 61, 401–409.

Thistlethwaite, D. A critical review of latent learning and related experiments. *Psychol. Bull.*, 1951, 48, 97–129.

Thorndike, E. L. *Animal intelligence.* New York: Macmillan, 1882.

Thorndike, E. L. *The elements of psychology.* New York: A. G. Seiler, 1905.

Thorndike, E. L. *Educational psychology.* Vol. II. *The psychology of learning.* New York: Teachers College, 1913.

Thorndike, E. L. *Human learning.* New York: Century, 1931.

Thorndike, E. L. *The fundamentals of learning.* New York: Teachers College, 1932.

Thorndike, E. L. An experimental study of rewards. *Teach. Coll. Contr. Educ.*, 1933a, No. 580.

Thorndike, E. L. A theory of the action of the after-effects of a connection upon it. *Psychol. Rev.*, 1933b, 40, 434–439.

Thorndike, E. L. *The psychology of wants, interests, and attitudes.* New York: Appleton, 1935.

Thorndike, E. L. *Selected writings from a connectionist's psychology.* New York: Appleton-Century-Crofts, 1949.

Thorndike, E. L., & Woodworth, R. S. The influence of improvement in one mental function upon the efficiency of other functions. *Psychol. Rev.*, 1901, 8, 247–261; 384–395; 553–564.

Titchener, E. B. The postulates of a structural psychology. *Phil. Rev.*, 1898, 7, 449–465. As reported by W. Dennis (Ed.), *Readings in the history of psychology.* New York: Appleton-Century-Crofts, 1948, Pp. 366–376.

Titchener, E. B. *An outline of psychology.* New York: Macmillan, 1899.

Titchener, E. B. *Text-book of psychology.* New York: Macmillan, 1910.

Titchener, E. B. Prolegomena to a study of introspection. *Amer. J. Psychol.,* 1912a, **23,** 427–448.

Titchener, E. B. The schema of introspection. *Amer. J. Psychol.,* 1912b, **23,** 485–508.

Titchener, E. B. Psychology as the behaviorist views it. *Proc. Amer. phil. Soc.,* 1914, **53,** 1–17.

Titchener, E. B. *Systematic psychology: Prolegomena.* New York: Macmillan, 1929.

Tolman, E. C. A behaviorist's definition of consciousness. *Psychol. Rev.,* 1927, **34,** 433–439.

Tolman, E. C. *Purposive behavior in animals and man.* New York: Appleton, 1932.

Tolman, E. C. Operational behaviorism and current trends in psychology. *Proceedings Twenty-fifth Anniversary Celebrating Inaug. Grad. Stud.* Los Angeles: Univer. of Southern California Press, 1936. Reprinted in M. H. Marx (Ed.), *Psychological theory: Contemporary readings.* New York: Macmillan, 1951. Pp. 87–102.

Tolman, E. C. The determiners of behavior at a choice point. *Psychol. Rev.,* 1938, **45,** 1–41.

Tolman, E. C. A stimulus-expectancy need-cathexis psychology. *Science,* 1945, **101,** 16–166.

Tolman, E. C. The psychology of social learning. *J. soc. Issues, Suppl. Ser.,* 1949a, **3,** 5–18.

Tolman, E. C. There is more than one kind of learning. *Psychol. Rev.,* 1949b, **56,** 144–155.

Tolman, E. C. *Collected papers in psychology.* Berkeley: Univer. of California Press, 1951a.

Tolman, E. C. A psychological model. In T. Parsons and E. A. Shils (Eds.), *Toward a general theory of action.* Cambridge, Mass.: Harvard, 1951b, Pp. 279–361.

Tolman, E. C. Principles of purposive behavior. In S. Koch (Ed.), *Psychology: A study of a science.* Vol. 2. *General systematic formulations, learning and special processes.* New York: McGraw-Hill, 1959. Pp. 92–157.

Tolman, E. C., & Brunswik, E. The organism and the causal texture of the environment. *Psychol. Rev.,* 1935, **42,** 43–77.

Tolman, E. C., & Honzik, C. H. "Insight" in rats. *Univer. Calif. Publ. Psychol.,* 1930, **4,** 215–232.

Toulmin, S. The logical status of psychoanalysis. *Analysis,* 1948, 9, 23–29.

Underwood, B. J. *Experimental psychology.* New York: Appleton-Century-Crofts, 1949.

Underwood, B. J. *Psychological research.* New York: Appleton-Century-Crofts, 1957.

Underwood, B. J., Keppel, G., & Schulz, R. W. Studies of distributed practice: XXII. Some conditions which enhance retention. *J. exp. Psychol.,* 1962, **64,** 355–363.

Valentine, W. L., & Wickens, D. D. *Experimental foundations of general psychology.* (3rd ed.) New York: Holt, 1949.

Verplanck, W. S. Burrhus F. Skinner. In Estes et al., *Modern learning theory*. New York: Appleton-Century-Crofts, 1954. Pp. 267–316.

Voeks, Virginia W. Postremity, recency, and frequency as bases for prediction in the maze situation. *J. exp. Psychol.*, 1948, **38**, 495–510.

Voeks, Virginia W. Formalization and clarification of a theory of learning. *J. Psychol.*, 1950, **30**, 341–362.

Voeks, Virginia W. Acquistion of S-R connections: A test of Hull's and Guthrie's theories. *J. exp. Psychol.*, 1954, **47**, 137–147.

von Neumann, J. *The computer and the brain.* New Haven: Yale, 1958.

von Neumann, J., & Morgenstern, O. *Theory of games and economic behavior.* Princeton, N.J.: Princeton, 1953.

Walker, N. Science and the Freudian unconsciousness. In T. Reik (Ed.), *Psychoanalysis and the future.* New York: National Psychological Association for Psychoanalysis, 1957. Pp. 117–124.

Walls G. L. "Land! Land!" *Psychol. Bull.*, 1960, **57**, 29–48.

Warren, H. C. (Ed.) *Dictionary of psychology.* Boston: Houghton Mifflin, 1934.

Washburn, Margaret Floy. *The animal mind.* New York: Macmillan, 1908.

Watanabe, S. Information—theoretic aspects of inductive and deductive inference. *IBM J. Res. & Developm.*, 1960, **4**, 208–231.

Watson, J. B. Image and affection in behavior. *J. Philos.*, 1913a, **10**, 421–428.

Watson, J. B. Psychology as the behaviorist views it. *Psychol. Rev.*, 1913b, **20**, 158–177.

Watson, J. B. *Behavior: An introduction to comparative psychology.* New York: Holt, 1914.

Watson, J. B. Experimental studies on the growth of the emotions. In C. Murchison (Ed.), *Psychologies of 1925.* Worcester, Mass.: Clark Univer. Press, 1926a. Pp. 52–53.

Watson, J. B. Recent experiments on how we lose and change our emotional equipment. In C. Murchison (Ed.), *Psychologies of 1925.* Worcester, Mass.: Clark Univer. Press, 1926b. P. 66.

Watson, J. B. What the nursery has to say about instincts. In C. Murchison (Ed.), *Psychologies of 1925.* Worcester, Mass.: Clark Univer. Press, 1926c. P. 13.

Watson, J. B. *Psychology from the standpoint of a behaviorist.* Philadelphia: Lippincott, 1919. 3rd ed., 1929.

Watson, J. B. *Behaviorism.* New York: Norton, 1925. Rev. ed., 1930.

Watson, J. B. John B. Watson. In C. Murchison (Ed.), *History of psychology in autobiography.* Vol. 3. Worcester, Mass.: Clark Univer. Press, 1936. Pp. 271–281.

Watson, J. B., & McDougall, W. *The battle of behaviorism.* New York: Norton, 1929.

Weiss, A. P. Relation between structural and behavior psychology. *Psychol. Rev.*, 1917, **34**, 301–317.

Weiss, A. P. *A theoretical basis of human behavior.* Columbus, Ohio: Adams, 1925.

Weitzenhoffer, A. M. Mathematical structures and psychological measurements. *Psychometrika*, 1951, **16**, 398–496.

Wertheimer, M. Experimentelle Studien über das Sehen von Bewegunen. *Zool. Psychol.*, 1912, **61**, 121–165.

Wertheimer, M. Untersuchungen zur Lehre von der Gestalt. II. *Psychol. Forsch.*, 1923, **4**, 301–350.

Wertheimer, M. The general theoretical situation. In W. D. Ellis (Ed.), *A source book of gestalt psychology.* New York: Harcourt, Brace & World, 1938.

Wertheimer, M. *Productive thinking.* New York: Harper & Row, 1945.

Wheeler, R. H. *The science of psychology.* (2nd ed.) New York: Crowell, 1940.

Wheeler, R. H. Climate and human behavior. In P. L. Harriman (Ed.), *Encyclopedia of psychology.* New York: Philosophical Library, 1946.

Wheeler, R. H., & Perkins, F. T. *Principles of mental development.* New York: Crowell, 1932.

White, R. W. Motivation reconsidered: The concept of competence. *Psychol. Rev.*, 1959, **66**, 297–333.

Wiener, N. *Cybernetics, or control and communication in the animal and the machine.* New York: Wiley, 1948. 2nd ed., 1961.

Wiener, P. P. (Ed.) *Readings in philosophy of science.* New York: Scribner, 1953.

Wirth, W. Die Klarheitsgrade der Gegionen des Schfeldes bei verschiedenen Verteilungen der Aufmerksamkeit. *Psychol. Studien*, 1906, 30 ff. As reported by E. B. Titchener, *Lectures on elementary psychology of feeling and attention.* New York: Macmillan, 1908. P. 239.

Woodworth, R. S. *Dynamic psychology.* New York: Columbia, 1918.

Woodworth, R. S. Four varieties of behavior. *Psychol. Rev.*, 1924, **31**, 257–264.

Woodworth, R. S. *Experimental psychology.* New York: Holt, 1938.

Woodworth, R. S. Reënforcement of perception. *Amer. J. Psychol.*, 1947, **60**, 119–124.

Woodworth, R. S. *Contemporary schools of psychology.* New York: Ronald, 1948.

Woodworth, R. S. *Dynamics of behavior.* New York: Holt, 1958.

Woodworth, R. S., & Schlosberg, H. *Experimental psychology.* New York: Holt, 1954.

Wundt, W. *Human and animal psychology.* New York: Macmillan, 1894.

Wundt, W. *Principles of physiological psychology.* Vols. 1–10. New York: Macmillan, 1904.

Wundt, W. *Völkerpsychologie.* Leipzig: Engelmann, 1900–1920.

Yamaguchi, H. G., Hull, C. L., Felsinger, J. M., & Gladstone, A. I. Characteristics of dispersions based on the pooled momentary reaction potentials (sE_R) of a group. *Psychol. Rev.*, 1948, **55**, 216–238.

Yerkes, R. M. *Chimpanzees: A laboratory colony.* New Haven: Yale, 1943.

Zeigarnik, Bluma. Über das Behalten von erledigten und unerledigten Handlungen, *Psychol. Forsch.*, 1927, **9**, 1–85.

Zeigler, H. G. Electrical stimulation of the brain and psychophysiology of learning and motivation. *Psychol. Bull.*, 1957, **54**, 363–382.

James Drever
University of Edinburgh
Edinburgh, Scotland

appendix A EUROPEAN PSYCHOLOGY

It is impossible in a short survey of this kind to do justice to the variety of psychological research going on in any one European country, let alone in Europe as a whole. Nor would it be particularly helpful, even if it were possible, to produce an annotated bibliography which had any claim to completeness. Instead, what has been done is to pick out a few key figures. The theoretical position of each of them is briefly indicated, and in a number of cases an example is given of the kind of data upon which the position rests. It may be felt that the result is to some extent a list of Grand Old Men. Whatever truth there may be in this derives from the nature of the material surveyed for the chapter. In European psychology today, although there is much activity in many fields, the key figures are still to a large extent men who made their most significant contribution to psychology before World War II. It has been said that we have no giants under the age of sixty. There is perhaps a lesson to be learned here. We might ask, and not only for Europe, how many great psychologists were primarily trained as psychologists? It is too early to give a fair answer to this question, but it is one that the contemporary situation forces us to ask. It may be that the best way into psychology is through biology or physics or even philosophy. Certainly of all scientists the psychologist is the last who should limit his range of studies too early.

In describing European psychology it is convenient to use linguistic rather than national boundaries. A common tongue means a common research literature, and other kinds of affinity soon develop. For our purposes German, French, and English are the most important languages. Psychologists belonging to the smaller linguistic groups, such as Scandinavia or the Low Countries, try to publish in one or another of the three major languages. For example, the new *Scandinavian Journal of Psychology* (1960) is published in English. The most notable exception is the Italian research literature, which is considerable.

425

GERMANY

Psychological work published in German may be given first place, if only on historical grounds. World War II had a particularly crippling effect on research in Germany and Austria. This was because of the great losses suffered through exile in the previous decade. Partly, too, it was because German psychologists had for so long been accustomed to influence others, and the outside world was thought of as a sort of academic colony. Under these circumstances isolation is not felt to be a hardship, however serious its effects may be. In this case its first effect was to intensify certain rather characteristic kinds of German psychology—in particular, verbal, descriptive studies of personality— that nowadays seem to belong to literature rather than science. In its earlier manifestations this approach was important, and it continues to have an influence, especially in its typological forms. Spranger's *Types of men* (1928) led to *The study of values* (1951) by Allport and Vernon. Jung's *Psychological types* (1924) gave our language *extrovert* and *introvert*. Kretschmer's *Physique and character* (1925) is the early formulation of a classification which has influenced, among others, Eysenck. Finally, the typological elements in Rorschach's *Psycho-diagnosis* (1942), though much less prominent, are sufficiently definite to make it clear that he too belongs to this important German-speaking movement. His work has given rise to a whole research literature of its own.

It is easy to see how arbitrary and intuitive typologies could become under unfavorable circumstances, such as those provided by National Socialism. Some good work continued, however, and since the later 1940s it has steadily become more empirical. A useful survey of the whole area, with comparisons between the German and other approaches, is to be found in *Perspectives in personality theory* edited by David and von Bracken (1957).

Another field in which German psychology has held a distinctive position is perception. The gestalt psychologists, first in Frankfurt-am-Main and then in Berlin, exercised a far-reaching influence from 1920 until 1934. The senior members of the group, Wertheimer, Köhler, Koffka, and Lewin, went into exile, but one or two good experimentalists among the younger generation stayed on. Of these Metzger has been the most productive. His book *Gesetze des Sehens* appeared in a second edition in 1953 with much new data. In general, Metzger's work resembles most closely that of Koffka (1936) but increases the degree of stimulus complexity. In particular, there are some very interesting data on the kinds of perceptual organization which occur when we are presented with visual stimuli in motion.

More original, and at present more influential in the field of perception, has been the work going on at Innsbruck. Ivo Kohler has made a number of visits to the United States, and some of his experiments are well known, though for the most part they are only to be found in the German literature at present. What Kohler does, as he puts it, is to place his laboratory on the bridge of his subject's nose—that is, use prisms and filters in a spectacle frame, which allows an experiment to run for several weeks.

In such a frame, 10-degree prisms may be inserted with the same orientation, so as to produce a horizontal displacement of visual objects. The prisms are not corrected spherically or chromatically. At first the subject bumps into obstacles, sees vertical straight lines as curved, and finds that the world has become curiously elastic when he moves his head. In addition, all sharp vertical gradients of illumination show a marked fringe of blue or orange. Over a period of three days of continuous wear, these effects largely disappear. Some of the changes had already been described by Gibson (1933). The chromatic adaptation is unusual, however, since complementary aftersensations are obtained when the prisms are removed. These are not retinal but remain anchored to the vertical gradients of illumination although the eyes may move. The theory which Kohler puts forward to account for these, and many other phenomena like them, which he has demonstrated, is not unlike Helson's adaptation level (1958, pp. 565–621). The organism establishes over time a null point for any constant feature of the stimulus milieu.

The third and, during the postwar decades best known, German research has been in the field of animal behavior. While American psychologists were coming more and more to depend upon the maze and the Skinner box, German biologists, protected against methodological insecurity by a great tradition, went on observing animals in their natural surroundings. Their observations were systematic, and nowadays a good deal of controlled experimentation goes on, but always the emphasis has been upon the reactions of a particular species to the various characteristics of its natural environment.

The literature is a big one, and one or two striking studies must represent it. Von Frisch, whose work on bees had long been famous, made some observations during World War II that aroused a good deal of skepticism. He claimed that workers returning to the hive after discovering a new source of honey can indicate both the direction and the distance to their fellows. They do this by dancing. There are two dances—the "round" dance and the "waggle" dance. Round dances consistently indicate food 50 meters or less from the hive, and waggle dances are used for longer distances, though there is a range between 50 and 100 meters when either may occur. Over 100 meters, increasing distance is coded into changes of pace and emphasis. The direction of the food is indicated simply by the direction of the straight part of the waggle dance if the bee is on a horizontal surface; if the bee is on a vertical surface it indicates direction by quite a complicated code, using the position of the sun. If the waggle part of the dance moves upward the food is toward the sun, if downward away from the sun. A dance to the right means that the food is to the right of the sun and at the angle by which the dance deviates from the vertical. The same holds good for all other directions. These remarkable observations have since been confirmed. A description of the dances and the table of observations may be found translated in the *Bulletin of Animal Behavior* (1947).

For psychology, the most important of the German students of animal behavior is probably Lorenz. In particular, his work on the stimuli required to "release" certain characteristic behavior patterns has given rise to a new kind of psychophysics. One of Lorenz' many contributions is the concept of "imprinting," the process by which the young of a species become attached normally to their mothers. At first this was described as sudden and irreversible. Perhaps it is not quite so dramatic as all that, but it still happens quite quickly, and the species on which any individual imprints tends to determine its choice of a mate at sexual maturity. Exploration of the stimulus parameters involved in imprinting shows that these vary from species to species. Ducklings will attach themselves to a box on wheels with a buzzer in it. Graylag goslings will convince themselves that they are human if a human being is the first large moving object they see, and so on. The journal literature contains an increasing number of well-controlled experiments in this field.

Lorenz himself is perhaps at his best in English in the delightful and popular *King Solomon's ring* (1956). A more technical account of this kind of work is to be found in *A study of instinct* (1951) by Lorenz' disciple Tinbergen. Thorpe's *Learning and instinct in animals* (1956) makes an attempt to relate this biological field to studies of animal learning.

One last development in German psychology is worthy of note. During the past twelve years there has been a great deal of psychological traffic in both directions across the Atlantic. As a result a new generation of German psychologists is beginning to make its presence felt. Its work shows the rigor and methodological sophistication which were so lacking in the years immediately before World War II, allied to a breadth and solidity which derive from the German academic tradition. Some idea of the growing community of interests between Anglo-Saxon and German psychology may be gained by looking at the volume *Psychologie* (1957) edited by Hofstätter in the Fischer Lexikon series. This book incidentally is quite the best text for a student of psychology who wishes to improve his German. It is clear and well illustrated with enough familiar material to serve as a guide through linguistic novelties.

FRANCE

For many years the French psychological scene has been dominated by three individuals: Piéron, Michotte, and Piaget. Each has been influential in his own distinctive way. It is interesting, but probably not significant, that only Piéron is a Frenchman; Michotte is Belgian, and Piaget is Swiss. Some work by each has been, or is shortly to be, published in English; Piaget is particularly accessible in this respect.

Of the three, Piéron is least easy to identify through his theoretical affiliation; above all he is an empiricist and an experimentalist. He himself would perhaps be prepared to trace his descent from Helmholtz. They share an interest in sensory processes and a conviction that psychology and philosophy should not be allowed to drift too far apart. Some impression of Piéron's enormous contribution to psychology may be gained from the pages of *L'année psychologique* 1898–   ) over the last forty years. As editor, research worker, and reviewer, he has played a unique part. A comparison between *L'année psychologique* and *Annual Review of Psychology* (1949–   ) shows that the amount of material from the experimental, and especially the physiological, fields is greater in the French publication, though the difference has not been quite so marked in the last few years. It is still true that the stereotype which represents European psychology as verbal and philosophical finds no support at the Sorbonne. *L'année psychologique* is of course not merely a review of the research publications in any given year, it is itself an important source of new material.

Piéron is rather inadequately represented in English; his *Thought and the brain* (1927) has been overtaken by events. *The sensations* (1952) is perhaps a better sample of his work, but someone who reads no French or who fails to realize the dominating position of the Sorbonne in the academic life of France cannot hope to appreciate the extent of Piéron's influence.

Michotte by contrast seems to belong to quite a different tradition. He is a phenomenalist, interested in the characteristics of immediate experience. At the same time he illustrates the important fact that one can be a phenomenalist and an experimentalist of the first rank as well. Probably Wertheimer is the psychologist with whom Michotte has most in common, and so one can think of him as having worked out along highly original lines certain ideas put forward by the gestalt psychologists. *La perception de la causalité* (1946) is likely to remain a classic and exemplifies admirably Michotte's approach. It is currently being translated into English.

What Michotte does here is to study the conditions under which the apparent movements of two visual objects seem to be causally related to one another. The impression of causal relationship is stated to be immediate and not dependent upon inference or previous experience. Though he later used a pair of synchronized projectors, his first apparatus was very simple and ingenious. Two strips of different colors are drawn on a disk so that they approach and recede from one another. When this disk is rotated at various speeds behind a slit equal in width to either strip, two square objects appear to move toward one another and away again. The spatiotemporal characteristics of this movement determine whether it be seen as involving a causal relationship or not. If it is so seen, the causal relationship may be of one of two kinds. *L'effet lancement*, or the launching effect, occurs when one square appears to push or propel the other in much the same way as a billiard ball might do when it strikes a second during the course of a game. *L'effet entrainement*, or the carrying effect, is quite easily distinguished. Here one square seems to drag or bear the other along with it. All the physical conditions for these two phenomena have been very carefully worked out, and quite confident predictions can now be made.

More recently Michotte has been working on the phenomenal characteristics which seem to distinguish mechanical causality from purposiveness or intentionality. His findings have much in common with those reported by Heider and Simmel (1944).

It is possible to think of Piéron and Michotte as elder statesmen now that they have retired, but Piaget is still very active, and his influence is spreading not merely across the Atlantic but across that much more formidable barrier, the English Channel. So original a thinker is hard to place in any historical sequence. Claparède provided the opportunity by founding the J. J. Rousseau Institute at Geneva, Binet made an important early attempt to solve problems relating to the intellectual development of young children, but Piaget's mixture of logic and biology is his own and may well turn out to be the most important contemporary contribution to psychology in Europe. There are those who feel that his disregard for the nicer points of methodology makes his results suspect. Perhaps he does generalize too readily. It is important, however, to realize just what Piaget is doing. He is no hypothetico-deductive formalist trying to convince himself and his colleagues that he can operate in the manner of the more advanced physical sciences. Rather he is a natural historian in the descriptive, data-collecting phase, and small errors of timing and identification are of little consequence when weighed against the wealth of insights and observations he has produced. A classificatory framework is not like a deductive theory which can be invalidated by one wrong prediction. Its value depends on the simplifications it enables us to make and the controlled experiments it stimulates us to perform.

Piaget's own work shows something of the developmental characteristics which it expounds. The ideas in such early works as *The language and thought of the child* (1926) and *Judgment and reasoning in the child* (1928) have been elaborated and specified by such later studies as *The child's conception of number* (1952) and *The child's conception of space* (1956). This last, by Piaget and Inhelder, is of particular interest because of its relevance to the psychology of perception. Using such material as drawings and simple performance tests, the development of spatial thinking is traced from its early beginning in notions like proximity, separation, and enclosure to fully developed geometrical operations. Piaget's treatment of linear and circular order may be used to illustrate his methods. Colored wooden beads or pieces of paper are arranged in order along a piece of string which to begin with is held straight and horizontal. The child is given a second piece of string and is asked to reproduce the order of colors on the first. Before the age of three and one-half years, on the average, children, though they may enumerate all the required colors, seem to have no ability to arrange these in order. By four years most children begin to cope with the notion of an ordered sequence, as long as they are allowed to lay their test string alongside the model and check the items one by one against each other. It is clear from the types of errors made that the second stage is reached because the child has become able to maintain a constant order of progression. At first, however, it is very easy to disrupt the ordered sequence by moving the model to one side or by having the child reproduce a vertical order on a horizontal string. The perceptual pattern is necessary to maintain the constant direction.

Between five and six years new possibilities begin to emerge. The child can maintain the sequence and even reverse it without a point-to-point comparison. He is then given the model with the items arranged in a circle and asked to produce the order on a straight line. Here he must work at a more abstract level, and the perceptual separation of the two ends of the line causes trouble. It is not until he is six or seven years old that the child is able to handle spatial order as such and reproduce or reverse models presented to him vertically, circularly, or even twisted into a figure-of-eight.

One can see how this patient, rather informal exploration could be used as the basis for test construction or a more rigorous experimental design, but Piaget's own interests seem to be moving in the direction of a theoretical analysis of thinking as such. *The growth of logical thinking from childhood to adolescence* (1958) gives some indication of his current activities. It would be wrong to think of the work at Geneva as in any way isolated from French psychology as a whole. There are many links with Michotte through studies of causality, movement, and speed as understood by children, while Fraisse at the Sorbonne in *Les structures rhythmiques* (1957) shares with Piaget an interest in the development of our perception of time.

GREAT BRITAIN

British psychology tends to look across the Atlantic just now but still retains a few distinctive features. Oddly enough in the country of the "English" empiricists and associationists, one of these is a lack of interest in associationism. This is probably the result of historical accidents. Empirical psychology as formulated at the beginning of the present century by the philosophers Ward (1918) and Stout (1913) had been transformed by post-Kantian German thought. Bartlett, who more than anyone else determined the present nature of British psychology, was a pupil of Ward. This did not make him a philosopher —he has always been impatient of armchair theorizing—but it did make him suspicious of a simple S-R approach. It is important that psychologists in the United States, or in Russia for that matter, should realize that the rather general European indifference to associationism springs from the fact that it is an "old-fashioned" point of view and can be found quite fully developed in the eighteenth century. While the Kantian re-formation of Hume's position did not deal with associationism as such, it did imply the existence of cognitive structures other than those based upon contiguity and frequency. Since that time all variants of the simple S-R theme have appeared too easy. This prejudice is held to have been justified by events, and there is a strong suspicion that the amount of information generated per rat-mile has not been great.

Bartlett's *Remembering* is a study of perception and thinking as well as memory, and his more recent *Thinking* does no more than develop some of the themes in the earlier work. But Bartlett has been much more influential through his teaching than through his writings. The Cambridge laboratory was for many years a leading nursery for experimental psychologists. More than two-thirds of the chairs in Great Britain are held by Bartlett's pupils. They may not all have been docile, but most of them show identifiable characteristics. Prominent among these are a preference for human rather than animal subjects and a tendency to use cognitive types of explanation. The latter are more often stated nowadays in neurological or electronic than in logical terms.

A key figure in the development of British psychology in the field of perception and thinking was Craik, who died, still a young man, as the result of a road accident in 1943. He was a philosopher by training, an experimentalist by inclination, and a genius at inventing apparatus. Some of the basic ideas of cybernetics owe their origin to him, and a short statement of his theoretical position is to be found in *The nature of explanation* (1943). Broadbent in *Perception and communication* (1943) has described important experimental work which follows up some of Craik's ideas. According to Broadbent, two of the basic problems in perception as related to skilled performance are channel capacity and selectivity. How much information can the human operator handle and how can it protect itself against overloading or from unwanted signals? In vision many of the necessary adjustments are carried out peripherally, but in hearing they must be done centrally. Thus Broadbent uses auditory stimuli in experiments where the subject has to listen selectively to one of two simultaneous messages or to a message accompanied by irrelevant noise; the filtering process which takes place is central rather than sensory. It depends upon the amount of information, as one might expect, but it also depends to a marked extent upon the sequential probability values within the two messages. It is this that makes the word stimulus about as specific and psychologically useful as the word thing. The theoretical position which emerges from Broadbent's work resembles that advocated by Bruner (1957) and others in the United States.

A second strand in British psychology can be traced back to Galton through Spearman, Thomson, and Burt. It was to the study of individual differences and the development of appropriate statistical techniques that Britain made its most distinctive psychological contribution during the first quarter of the present century. Spearman stated his hierarchic theory of intelligence in *The nature of "intelligence" and principles of cognition* in 1923, followed by *The abilities of man* in 1927. Thomson waited until 1939 to publish *The factorial analysis of human ability*, but the two had long been engaged in a lively academic duel. Thomson's attitude toward Spearman, and later toward Thurstone, was on the whole one of skepticism. In particular he doubted Spearman's claim that factor analysis could be used to prove the necessity of one particular solution. Burt is still active in statistical psychology, and his book, *The factors of the mind* (1940), is an objective summing up of the earlier controversies and a statement of the still-distinctive British position in the factor-analysis field.

The application of mental testing in British education has been surprisingly wide for a country with such a reputation for conservatism. Nearly every child in the state school system is given the so-called "eleven" examination, which is an intelligence and achievement test. What happens educationally thereafter is determined, perhaps too much, by the results. As a consequence much present-day British research in this area has a marked practical and educational bias, and theoretical issues are no longer being raised. Of the younger workers, that is, workers whose main contribution belongs to the period since World War II, P. E. Vernon has been most influential. He is a pupil of Bartlett, who belongs to the school of Burt. In *The structure of human abilities* (1950) he shows an empirical and cautious approach with the marked practical bias that has just been mentioned.

The British view of the nature of intelligence differs from the American in being hierarchic. Thorndike (1914) thought of intelligence as a multitude of specific skills. Thurstone (1938) later worked with a relatively large democratically ordered collection of abilities. British workers in the field, though differing among themselves, have moved toward an analysis of intelligence which starts with a general factor. Once the general factor has been removed from the matrix of test intercorrelation, it is found that two large group factors tend to show up, one of them verbal-numerical-educational in nature, the other spatial-practical-mechanical. Below these again are smaller group factors corresponding roughly to the primary mental abilities of Thurstone, with specific factors deriving from particular skills and circumstances at the bottom. The differences between the British and American views are not basic but depend to some extent upon method. For example, Thurstone has a second-order general factor which in some respects resembles Spearman's original "g" factor.

To the outside observer, Eysenck might seem to belong here too, but the impression is misleading. It is true that his early work was based on the factor analysis of personality tests, and at one stage he was influenced by Burt, but his statistical procedures are only part of a wider strategy. More recently Hullian learning theory has been utilized in the same way. As has been suggested, Eysenck has much in common with the German typologists, though his methods are much more rigorous than theirs tend to be. Even so there are those who feel that he sometimes uses his data in a forensic rather than a scientific way. At all events his output is much greater than that of any other British psychologist just now and ranges all the way from highly technical to popular works. Perhaps *The scientific study of personality* (1952) gives the best general statement of his theoretical position. He is concerned, on the basis of objective test data, to rate his subjects on a number of dimensions of which introvert-extrovert and normal-neurotic are the most important. Having done this he hopes to identify the underlying neurological variables for these dimensions. Much of his work has been done in a clinical setting, and he has recently edited a *Handbook of abnormal psychology* (1960) in which most of the contributors are present or former colleagues.

It is unnecessary to do more than note in passing that the naturalistic study of animal behavior, which was a feature of British biology at the end of the nineteenth century, is again becoming more prevalent as a result of influences from the Continent. Reference has already been made to works by Tinbergen, now at Oxford, and by Thorpe of Cambridge. This kind of approach seems more congenial to British psychologists than the use of mazes and Skinner boxes, but a good deal of animal research on quantitative lines is going on as well.

SCANDINAVIA

Scandinavia is unexpected in that its appearance of geographical remoteness is so often associated with scientific and cultural developments of an advanced kind. Psychology as a profession has obtained more official recognition here than elsewhere in Europe, and, in Norway particularly, an admirable scheme of training and certification has been worked out. On the research side there is widespread activity without any distinctive trend. Perception has always tended to be more important than learning. Katz, though he came late to Stockholm, was very influential. The phenomenological point of view, which he shared with Rubin, is well stated by Von Fieandt of Helsinki in a paper in the *Psychological Review* (1958). Johansson at Uppsala is more of an experimentalist than a theoretician. His work (1958) shows affinities with that of Gibson at Cornell. The *Scandinavian Journal of Psychology* started publication in 1960 and gives a good impression of Scandinavian research. It is quantitative and methodologically advanced by European standards. Perhaps the number of psychophysical papers in the first volume is an accident due to the Fechner centenary.

HOLLAND

Holland has much in common with Scandinavia. Applied psychology is quite advanced, particularly in the industrial and cultural fields, but there is no distinctive theoretical position that would make separate treatment necessary.

ITALY

Italian psychology retained its philosophical characteristics longer than did more northerly European countries. A notable early development of experimental work was at the Catholic University of Milan. Here Gemelli rivaled Piéron in the extent of his output and excelled him in diversity. Of recent years there have been many signs of a direct American influence on Italian psychology, but earlier Gemelli played a twofold role. Not only was he a productive research worker and policy maker, he also maintained a closer contact with the psychological world as a whole than did any of his colleagues.

CONCLUSION

Stepping back to look at European psychology as a whole, it is possible to make a few impressionistic comments. The younger research workers seem to be in the process of discovering a common language. Here, as in the United States, the mathematicians and communications engineers are influential. The possibilities of information theory are being freely exploited on both sides of the Iron Curtain. Cherry (1957) gives a salutary reminder of the limitations of this kind of thinking, but it clearly offers possibilities not otherwise available at this stage in the development of psychological theories. Other cognitive systems are being used in other contexts. Piaget's analysis of children's thinking is logical as well as descriptive. Decision theory is becoming important, especially in France. What has been conspicuously absent, as was mentioned earlier, is systematic learning theory of the Hullian type. This was largely an American phenomenon, just as a rigid conditioned-reflex theory had to be characteristic of Russia. With the American move toward mediation types of formulation and the growing Russian interest in symbolic processes as shown, for example, by Luria (1959), there seems every chance that psychology will soon lose its geographical peculiarities, as most other sciences have already done.

references

Allport, G. W., & Vernon, P. E. *The study of values: A scale for measuring the dominant interests in personality.* (Rev. ed.) Boston: Houghton Mifflin, 1951.

Annual review of psychology. Stanford, Calif.: Annual Reviews, 1949– .

Broadbent, D. E. *Perception and communication.* London: Pergamon Press, 1943.

Bruner, J. S. On perceptual readiness. *Psychol. Rev.*, 1957, 64, 123–152.

Burt, C. *The factors of the mind.* London: Univer. of London Press, 1940.

Cherry, E. C. On the validity of applying communication theory to experimental psychology. *Brit. J. Psychol.*, 1957, 48, 136–188.

Craik, K. J. W. *The nature of explanation.* London: Cambridge, 1943.

David, H. P., & von Bracken, H. *Perspectives in personality theory.* London: Tavistock Publications, 1957.

Eysenck, H. J. *The scientific study of personality.* London: Routledge, 1952.

Eysenck, H. J. (Ed.) *Handbook of abnormal psychology.* London: Pitman, 1960.

Fraisse, P. *Les structures rhythmiques.* Paris: Presses Universitaires, 1957.

Gibson, J. J. Adaptation, after-effect, and contrast in the perception of curved lines. *J. exp. Psychol.*, 1933, 16, 1–31.

Heider, F., & Simmel, M. An experimental study of apparent behavior. *Amer. J. Psychol.*, 1944, 57, 243.

Helson, H. Adaptation-level theory. In S. Koch (Ed.), *Psychology: A study of a science.* Vol. 1. *Sensory, perceptual, and physiological formulations.* New York: McGraw-Hill, 1959. Pp. 565–621.

Hofstätter, P. R. (Ed.) *Psychologie.* Frankfurt-am-Main: Fischer, 1957.

Johansson, G. Rigidity, stability, and motion in perceptual space. *Acta psychol.*, 1958, **14**, 359–370.

Jung, C. G. *Psychological types*. London: Routledge, 1924.

Koffka, K. *Principles of gestalt psychology*. London: Kegan Paul, Trench, Trubner, 1936.

Kretschmer, E. *Physique and character*. London: Kegan Paul, Trench, Trubner, 1925.

Lorenz, K. Z. *King Solomon's ring*. London: Methuen, 1956.

Luria, A. R., & Vinogradova. An objective investigation of the dynamics of semantic systems. *Brit. J. Psychol.*, 1959, **50**, 89–105.

Metzger, W. *Gesetze des Sehens*. Frankfurt: Waldemar Kramer, 1953.

Michotte, A. *La perception de la causalité*. Belgium: Ouvrage publié avec la Fondation Universitaire de Belgique, 1946.

Piaget, J. *The language and thought of the child*. London: Routledge, 1926.

Piaget, J. *Judgment and reasoning in the child*. London: Routledge, 1928.

Piaget, J. *The child's conception of number*. London: Routledge, 1952.

Piaget, J., & Inhelder, B. *The child's conception of space*. London: Routledge, 1956.

Piaget, J. *The growth of logical thinking from childhood to adolescence*. London: Routledge, 1958.

Piéron, H. (Ed.) *L'année psychologique*. Paris: Presses Universitaires de France, 1898– .

Piéron, H. *Thought and the brain*. New York: Harcourt, Brace, 1927.

Piéron, H. *The sensations*. New Haven: Yale, 1952.

Rorschach, H. *Psycho-diagnosis*. New York: Grune & Stratton, 1942.

Scandinavian Journal of Psychology. Stockholm: Almquist & Wiksell, 1960.

Spearman, C. *The nature of "intelligence" and the principles of cognition*. London: Macmillan, 1923.

Spearman, C. *The abilities of man: Their nature and measurement*. London: Macmillan, 1927.

Spranger, E. *Types of men*. Halle: Niemeyer, 1928.

Stout, J. F. *Manual of psychology*. London: University Tutorial Press, 1913.

Thomson, G. H. *The factorial analysis of human ability*. London: Univer. of London Press, 1939.

Thorndike, E. L. *Educational psychology*. Vol. III. New York: Teachers College, 1914.

Thorpe, W. H. *Learning and instinct in animals*. London: Methuen, 1956.

Thurstone, L. L. Primary mental abilities. *Psychosometric Monogr.* 1938, **1**.

Tinbergen, N. *A study of instinct*. Oxford: Clarendon, 1951.

Vernon, P. E. *The structure of human abilities*. London: Methuen, 1950.

Von Fieandt, K. Towards a unitary theory of perception. *Psychol. Rev.*, 1958, **65**, 315–320.

Von Frisch, K. The dances of the honey bee. *Bull. animal Behav.*, 1947, **5**, 1–22.

Ward, J. *Psychological principles*. London: Cambridge, 1918.

Josef Brozek
Lehigh University
Bethlehem, Pennsylvania

appendix B SOVIET PSYCHOLOGY[1]

Since 1955 there has been a remarkable spurt in the growth and development of psychology in the Soviet Union. Razran (1960) has estimated that the volume of Russian nonperiodical publications in psychology issued in 1957 and 1958 was at least double the total output of the preceding seven years (Razran, 1957). This upward trend still continues (Brozek, 1962). Razran noted that there was not only an increase in quantity but also a rise in quality, including broader conceptualization, better experimental control, and improved technical skill. One of the external signs of the rebirth of psychology as a (relatively) independent science was the reestablishment in 1955, after a lapse of about two decades, of a psychological journal, *Voprosy Psikhologii* (*Problems of Psychology*), and the formation of the Society of Psychologists two years later. Beginning with the 1960 volume, the journal is also being published in English.

Soviet psychologists and their sympathetic interpreters (Tomaszewski, 1949, p. 1) do not regard the Soviet approach as another "school" of psychology, as "a psychology among psychologies," parallel to behaviorism, depth psychology, or gestalt psychology. There is, in fact, no single new psychological concept or methodological innovation which would give it a similar, well-defined place and status in systematic psychology. Nevertheless, there are certain features which, considered jointly, make it meaningful to speak of "Soviet psychology" in a more comprehensive sense than simply psychology in the U.S.S.R. Among these we may note (1) insistence on the definition of human psychology as the study of consciousness; (2) unquestioning acceptance of the philosophical foundations of psychology provided by the

[1] The acquisition of publications on which this presentation is based was facilitated by a grant from the Institute of Research, Lehigh University.

The preparation of the chapter was supported by National Science Foundation Grant 19469.

438

official philosophy of Marxism-Leninism and the impact of political decisions and maneuvers on psychological practice and theory; and (3) "Pavlovization" of psychology, by resolution.

Other general characteristics could be added. Thus in methodology distinct emphasis is placed on "natural experiments," an approach which represents an intermediary stage between the observation of ongoing, uncontrolled psychological processes and the rigorous laboratory experimentation in which the phenomena to be observed are elicited purposefully by the experimenter, frequently with the use of special apparatus. The best example of natural experiments are the educational action studies, which examine the effect of different teaching methods on the students' achievement and the effect of lectures, discussions, or movies on the formation of various aspects of personality, such as students' interests. Interviews of the unstandardized variety are used. The questions are prepared by the investigator beforehand, are answered by the subject verbally, and can be altered if this is called for by the course of the interview or by the individual characteristics of the subject. Questionnaires seem to be taboo. The typical qualifying adjective for questionnaires seems to be "nonsensical" (Ivanov, 1959, p. 65).

In general, Soviet psychology is very weak in regard to quantitative analysis of the results. Some textbooks do make reference to statistical methods. For example, Rudik (1958, pp. 44–46) notes that psychological investigations cannot be confined to isolated single observations no matter how interesting these might be in themselves; only on the basis of observations of an adequate number of individuals is it possible to make conclusions concerning the real, not accidental, features of the phenomena that are being studied. The fact remains that Rudik's account of statistical treatment of data is hopelessly outdated, with the statistical operations restricted to the construction of a distribution curve and the computations of arithmetical means and standard deviations. He does not differentiate clearly between the use of standard deviation as a measure of the variability of measurements in a sample of subjects (extent of interindividual differences) and as indicator of intraindividual variability. It is totally misleading to state, without further qualifications, that "the smaller the standard deviation, the more trustworthy are the results obtained."

psyche and consciousness

Typically, the Soviet textbooks (e.g., Zaporozhets, 1959, p. 3) begin by defining psychology etymologically: psyche plus logos. There is not much of a problem, in this context at any rate, with "*logos*" and "-logy," the study or science of this or that. *Psyche* is a good deal more troublesome.

While they reject psyche in its original metaphysical meaning of soul as a legitimate subject matter of (scientific) psychology, the Soviets retain the untranslatable term *psikhika* ("psychics," psyche). It refers to psychological processes (sensations, perceptions, remembering, thinking) and to psychological ("psychic," *psikhicheskii*) characteristics (abilities, needs, interests, temperament, character). Plants have no psyche. Simpler forms of psyche are encountered in animals. Man, in the course of social interaction, develops the highest form of psyche—the consciousness (*soznanie*).

There is the usual tirade against "idealists," who are said to insist that psyche (not matter) is primary and that it develops independently of matter and exerts a determining influence on material processes. Next in line for a thorough drubbing is the "vulgar" (gross) materialism of some bourgeois scholars who negate the existence of distinct psychological (psychic) phenomena and who try to reduce psychological processes to material, mechanical phenomena. They ignore man's consciousness and wish to limit education to the elaboration of mechanical habits. This is held to be a false theory, fundamentally incompatible with the Communist aims in education.

The genuinely scientific, consistently materialistic answer to the question regarding the nature of psychological phenomena was given, according to the Soviet textbook writers, by the founders of dialectical materialism—Marx, Engels, and Lenin. According to them, the psyche is a specific property of highly organized matter (Zaporozhets, 1959, p. 5).

The specific features of man's psyche, including speech, are the resultant of the history of human society, in which work and the social interaction it involves have played a dominant role. Words constitute the second uniquely human system for the signalization of reality. They are the symbolic signals of concrete signals, of perceptions mediated by the special senses which constitute the first signal system. The development of the second (verbal) signal system has brought a totally new principle into man's higher nervous activity, making him capable of abstract thought and of communication with his fellow men. Consciousness (*soznanie*) is the outcome of social interaction and reflects man's social existence.

politics and psychology

The decree of the Central Committee of the Communist Party of the Soviet Union, dated July 4, 1936, and entitled "On the pedological perversions in the system of the People's Commissariats for Education," still remains one of the most far-reaching documents in the history of psychology in the Soviet Union. The full text is available in

English as an appendix to Wortis's *Soviet psychiatry* (1950, pp. 242–245), but Ivanov's reinterpretation (1959, p. 65) has added some contemporary flavor. Two points in the decree are of special relevance for scientific psychology: (1) the interpretation of factors accounting for an individual's psychological development (development of consciousness) and (2) the use of psychological tests and questionnaires.

Ivanov asked: "What affects man's mental development?" Before attempting to answer the question positively, he insisted that it is necessary to reject resolutely the antiscientific, reactionary theory, widespread in bourgeois psychology and education, according to which man's psychological development is determined by two factors —the biological factor (i.e., heredity) and the social environment. Heredity, Ivanov went on, is regarded by the proponents of this view as something unchangeable, transmitted from generation to generation; the social environment is also conceived of as something stable for all time. Here Ivanov was close to his 1936 bible, which speaks of "some sort of unchanging environment." Such a reactionary theory, Ivanov continued, is being advocated with the aim of convincing people that man remains unchanged from generation to generation and that the existing Capitalist order must retain its *status quo*.

The second point has had a good deal more serious consequences since it has affected, indirectly but profoundly, all quantitative studies of individual differences and their manifold applications and discredited fact-finding social psychology. It dealt with crucial problems of methodology. We are informed by the decree (Wortis, 1950, p. 242):

> Pedological practice was founded on pseudo-scientific experiments and on an endless number of senseless and harmful research questionnaires and tests conducted among pupils and their parents. These tests have long been condemned by the Party. . . . This elaborate system of investigations of mental development and student abilities was uncritically transplanted to Soviet soil from bourgeois class pedology, and is a complete affront to the student. It stands in complete contradiction to both the aims of Soviet schools and to common sense.

The resolution specified, among other recommendations, that the connection of pedologists with the schools be ended, the teaching of pedology in teachers colleges be abolished, and all pedological textbooks be removed.

While pedology was conceived of as a comprehensive human biology of the child, the Soviet practice apparently emphasized the psychological and psychometric aspects. It has been the applied psychology and basic quantitative study of behavior, with roots in individual and group differences, that have suffered heavily in the

U.S.S.R. Bauer (1952, p. 127) included the virtual abolition of industrial psychology among the practical implications of the decree.

Pavlov, Pavlovism, and Soviet psychology

One of the features of contemporary Soviet psychology is its "Pavlovism." The loud and vigorous battle cry of "Back to Pavlov" was sounded at the 1950 Scientific Session of the Academy of Sciences and the Academy of Medical Sciences of the U.S.S.R. on the Physiological Teachings of the Academician I. P. Pavlov. The cardinal sin was spelled out as follows (Kline, 1960, pp. 217–222):

> Certain scientists in a number of the leading institutions that were entrusted with the task of promoting Pavlov's teachings, far from heading the struggle against pseudoscientific, anti-Pavlov trends have themselves departed from Pavlov's ideas on a number of basic problems, and have endeavored to revise many of his cardinal theses.

Psychology was noted specifically among the areas of science and technology brought to task for "the inadequate penetration of Pavlov's ideas," explained by the fact that "Pavlov's teachings have not held the leading place in university curricula and textbooks." Within two years the psychologists had a Pavlovian session of their own.

In the course of the conference, held from June 20 to July 5, 1952, under the sponsorship of the Academy of Pedagogical Sciences and attended by over 400 Soviet psychologists, a proclamation was formulated calling for the rebuilding of psychology on the basis of the philosophy of dialectical and historical materialism and Pavlov's teachings concerning the higher nervous activity.

Is, then, the current Soviet psychology Pavlovian? Our answer would be that it is beginning to be more and more so, at least in places (cf. Sokolov, 1958, 1959). Razran (1957, p. 93) answered both "Yes" and "No" to the above query: "Yes," in the sense of Soviet psychology's conforming to what Pavlov said or to what is interpreted as the intent of what he said; "No," in the sense of not being based on what Pavlov did and stimulated others to do (i.e., upon a broad critical evaluation of experimental research on classic conditioning). Razran (1957, p. 96) noted that the categories around which Russian textbooks are built are old-fashioned and mentalistic, having no basis in Pavlov's principles and concepts, and he asked: "Why retain in full bloom the traditional categories in a Pavlovian psychology when Pavlov himself was so manifestly concerned with scrapping, not only the (mentalistic) categories, but the whole of psychology as well?"

Seen from the outside, twelve years after the call to arms was sounded (1950), much of the Soviet psychology still apparently *remains* to be reconstructed on the basis of Pavlov's teachings.

SOME SPECIFIC AREAS OF RESEARCH

experimental bases of psychosomatics

In the review (Brozek, 1959) of Bykov's book *The cerebral cortex and the internal organs* (1957) we have noted that for almost a hundred years—from I. M. Sechenov (1963) through I. P. Pavlov to his coworkers and followers—Russian physiologists have participated with fervor in the task of analyzing and interpreting "psychic activity" and "mind-body" interaction, using the concepts of the physiology of the nervous system.

In his "Reply of a physiologist to a psychologist," originally (1932) published in the *Psychological Review*, Pavlov (1941, p. 117) expressed unequivocally his conviction that the interpretation of psychological activities in terms of physiological processes constitutes one of the most important tasks of contemporary science. The action of the mind on the body is part and parcel of psychophysiological experimentation and theory.

In the course of the study of "experimental neuroses," Russian neurophysiologists noted disturbances in the function of organs traditionally considered to be under the control of the autonomic nervous system. These functional alterations, which were present together with general changes in the behavior of the experimental animals, were sometimes relatively slight (increase or decline in unconditioned salivary excretion, altered respiration), sometimes profound (ulceration, eczema). The detailed information about these changes, obtained in the course of extensive experimental work begun in Pavlov's lifetime and greatly expanded during the subsequent two decades, has remained largely inaccessible to those scientists who were unable to follow the Russian literature in the original.

A brief summary of the Russian work on the "Vegetative disturbances connected with experimental neuroses" was presented by Ivanov-Smolensky in his *Essays* (1954, pp. 124–128). However, it is Bykov's *opus magnum* (1957), made available in English by W. Horsley Gantt, that one has to consult for a systematic exposition of the physiological principles and the relevant experimental data.

It may be noted that there is available, in Russian, an up-to-date presentation by Bulygin (1959) of information concerning the function of the receptors of internal organs and the significance of interoceptive reflexes in the functioning of the organism as a whole and in its interaction with the environment. But let us return to his master, with whom he worked for some six years in Leningrad.

Bykov began his explorations of visceral conditioned reflexes in the early 1920s by observations on the secretion of urine, which is profoundly influenced by appropriate conditioned stimuli. The secretory activity of the kidney proved to be a criterion no less effective than the activity of the salivary gland—the classic object of study in Pavlov's school—for studying the details of "cortical dynamics." In time, this work was greatly expanded in terms both of the number of coworkers and of the problems and functions that were studied. These included the conditioned-reflex activity of the liver, the heart and the blood vessels, the respiratory apparatus, the digestive tract, general metabolism (oxygen consumption), thermoregulation, and the periodicity of physiological functions.

It was shown that interoceptors not only can participate in the formation of "temporary connections" (conditioned reflexes) but also differentiate between stimuli fairly closely resembling each other. Consequently, using Pavlov's terminology, these receptors were classed as "analyzers," with representation in the cerebral cortex. This kind of receptor was intensively studied by Bykov and his coworkers (see especially pp. 242–325).

The cerebral cortex, then, "reflects" not only the outer world but also the inner world of the organism. The mechanism regulating the work of the viscera represents a many-storied function, and Bykov has neither minimized the role of the centers located in the brain stem nor disregarded the fact that, functionally, the cerebral cortex is connected with the viscera through the subcortical ganglia. Nevertheless, acording to him, the cortex deals with the most mobile parts of the mechanism and directs the continuous regulation of bodily economy in accordance with the ever-changing conditions outside and inside the organism.

In comparison with the conditioned reflexes elaborated to exteroceptive stimuli, the formation of temporary connections to at least some interoceptive stimuli proceeds at a slower rate, the responses tend to be more diffuse, and the reflex responses are to a considerable extent predetermined by the nature of the stimulus and the properties of the receptor stimulated. Nevertheless, interoceptive stimulation—especially when combined with exteroceptive stimuli—may also induce complex behavior in the organism. On the other hand, the cerebral cortex, by the very same mechanism of temporary connections, is able to change the activity and the state of the viscera. Both nervous and neurohumoral efferent pathways are involved in such transmission of cortical stimulation.

Why should these facts concern psychologists? There are several, very good reasons:

(1) First, and most importantly, we have here not an atomized physiology of individual organs but physiology that aims to study integrated reactions of the organism in interaction with its environment. While differences in emphasis (behavior versus the complex of physio-

logical functions) remain, the *rapprochement* between physiology so conceived and physiologically oriented psychology becomes striking.

(2) Experimental study, by the method of conditioned reflexes, of the role of the central nervous system in the coordination and regulation of the processes taking place in the viscera opens new vistas for a rigorous study of problems in the field of psychosomatic medicine.

(3) Last, but not least, refined study of cortical-pituitary-visceral interaction, together with the study of metabolic activities and humoral factors, should shed important light on such traditional psychological problems as fluctuation of awareness, feeling of well-being, mood, drive, emotion—yes, even that queen in the hierarchy of psychological concepts, man's personality.

Unquestionably, the Soviet studies on interoceptive conditioning have important implications for scientific psychology, and Razran's endeavor (1962) to bring together the recent literature on the subject is fully justified. [See also London's early (1951) but brief discussion of Bykov's work.]

perception à la Pavlov

Systematic investigations on the role of conditioned reflexes in perception have been carried on for some time by E. N. Sokolov and his coworkers. A progress report, concerned especially with orienting and adaptive reflexes, was published in 1958. The term perception is used in a broader sense (reception) than is customary for American psychologists. It is defined by Sokolov as the activity of analyzers (which includes specific peripheral receptors, afferent pathways, and cortical areas) registering—the Russians, sticking to Lenin's vocabulary, say "reflecting"—external events and influences. In accordance with the general Pavlovian concept of reflex mechanisms, receptive processes are interpreted as reflex activity of the analyzers.

Sokolov believes that the concept of perception as a reflex adjustive act opens the way to the investigation of sensory processes along lines which differ importantly from the classic psychophysiology of special senses. Thus he has pointed out that the perception of a stimulus is dependent, in part, on its meaning for the organism (significance of the stimulus as a signal). In man, the perceptual processes can be affected profoundly by verbal instructions.

In studying perception, the Soviet authors have paid close attention to ongoing processes in the organism. A conditioned response, both in regard to its receptor and effector components, is viewed as consisting of a series of partial reflex acts. These form a single system which has an adaptive significance for the organism as a whole. This approach, which would be called molecular in American parlance, has been contrasted by Sokolov with the molar approach, limited to the study of integral behavior. Sokolov has cited specifically C. L. Hull (*Principles of behavior*, 1943; *A behavior system*, 1952) as the protagonist of molar behavioral theories. Sokolov has not actually used the term molecular in reference to the contrasting Soviet approach.

In regard to the peripheral components, Sokolov has insisted that perception (reception) can no longer be reduced to the registration of sensory stimuli by the receptors and the conduction of the nervous impulses through the centripetal pathways to cortical terminations. This position is in line with the differentiation between the specific and the nonspecific systems for the transmission of excitation via the traditional afferent pathways and the recently discovered reticular system. The reticular system does not transmit specific sensory information but is concerned with the regulation of the excitability of the cortical cells (cf. Magoun, 1958).

Sokolov has been concerned only with perception (reception). In his formulation, the impact of sensory stimuli on the organism is represented as a complex process, involving a whole series of interacting reflex responses. Special emphasis is placed on the orienting reflex and the delicate adjustments made by the organism in order to obtain adequate information about its external environment.

While the terminology is different, we have here a parallel to the idea, formulated and experimentally amply documented by the Western scientists, that receptor activities are under efferent control from the central nervous system. The literature has recently been summarized and interpreted by Pribram (1960, p. 3), who suggested that, in view of the experimental evidence indicating that the afferent activity originating in the receptors can be directly modified by CNS excitation, it is difficult to maintain an uncomplicated view of behavior based on simple stimulus-response reflex arcs. The "new look" consists of a shift "from the notion that an organism is a relatively passive protoplasmic mass whose responses are controlled by the arrangement of environmental stimuli to a conception of an organism that has considerable control over what will constitute stimulation. This control is exercised both through regulation by central processes and through a double feedback to receptors from response through environment and through the nervous system" (Pribram, 1960, p. 4).

The work on the orienting reflex, a form of attention, along the lines explored by Sokolov is clearly considered by the Soviet psychologists as pay dirt. In 1959 an extensive collection of studies was published, edited by Sokolov, in which various facets of the phenomenon were examined. In the early studies attention was devoted to the motor aspects of the orienting reflex (such as the movement of the head and of the eyes). The present investigations, designed to explore the phenomenon from other angles, are based on the observation that the orienting reflex is associated with changes in the functional status of the brain cortex and in various autonomic functions. The physiological criteria employed in these studies include electrodermal responses, pulse volume (plethysmography), brain potentials (electroencephalography), muscle potentials (electromyography), and pupillary reactions.

The endeavors of Sokolov and his coworkers have been centered on the clarification of the role of the orienting reflex—classified as an unconditioned reflex—in the activity of the analyzers and in the complex forms of conditioning. The disturbances of the orienting reflex and their effects have been studied in the presence both of cortical pathology and of peripheral (sensory) handicaps such as blindness.

Consideration has been given also to sensory thresholds in relation to the orienting reflex and to the related topic of intersensory stimulation (e.g., effect of sound stimuli on light sensitivity, evaluated by means of a monochromatic adaptometer), which has intrigued Soviet investigators ever since Lazarev published his first paper on this subject in 1918 (cf. London, 1954). There has been a substantial amount of controversy regarding both the facts and their interpretation. In regard to the latter, Lazarev proposed the hypothesis that in the region of corpora quadrigemina excitation is transmitted from the auditory nervous pathways to the visual pathways. Kravkov, some thirty years later (in 1947), postulated that the interaction takes place at the higher levels of the central nervous system, specifically in the cortex, and is mediated by association fibers. In the same year, Kekcheev, in tune with Orbeli's theories, interpreted the intersensory stimulation as the effect of a diffuse autonomic reflex involving adaptive-trophic change in tissues mediated by the autonomic nervous system. R. P. Steklova (Sokolov, 1959, pp. 304–311) regarded the effect as a manifestation and as a component of the orienting reflex, a point of view first expressed, ten years earlier, by Snyakin.

Thus there is no lack of theories. But how about facts? Steklova observed, in individual experimental subjects and under different experimental conditions, all three possible effects of acoustic stimuli: increased light sensitivity, decreased light sensitivity, and no effect.

Are these facts? In experimental sciences facts are *verified* sequences of events, *dependable* relationships. When there are too many raw facts, theories are apt to proliferate. We are not sure whether this is not exactly the case when Steklova, in view of the positive, negative, and no effects of acoustic stimulation on visual thresholds concluded that "the differences in response presuppose, it appears, different underlying mechanisms" (Sokolov, 1959, p. 311).

mental development

Mention will be made of the work of Soviet scientists concerned with the problems of ontogenetic and/or phylogenetic development of behavior from the point of view of general experimental psychology (Leont'ev), animal psychology (Ladygina-Kots), and classic Pavlovian study of the higher nervous activity of the child (Krasnogorskii).

Leont'ev. "Mental development is one of the central problems of Soviet psychology." With these words Leont'ev (1959) began the Foreword to his monograph. He underscored the appeal of developmental studies; they provide the foundations for the solution of important theoretical problems of the science of mental life and have far-reaching consequences for education.

Leont'ev differentiated between simple irritability and sensitivity. Plants react only to biotic environmental factors, such as light or nutrients, which are involved directly in the processes of metabolism. By contrast, animal organisms react to stimuli which in themselves are neutral, that is, which do not participate directly in the exchange of substances between the organism and its environment but which signalize external events, such as the presence of food or danger. The reactivity to stimuli which are in themselves indifferent but which under certain conditions may assume the function of signals is taken by Leont'ev as the objective criterion of sensitivity. Leont'ev did not stop with theoretical considerations but attempted to develop a model of the process of the genesis of sensations so that it could be studied experimentally in man.

Leont'ev differentiated three stages of psychological development: sensory, perceptive, and socially (historically) conditioned. Language plays a crucial role in the last stage. Having designated objects by verbal symbols, man can explore and appraise his environment by the manipulation of these symbols. Language enables man to store knowledge and to acquire the experience gained by the preceding generations.

Leont'ev has been concerned in particular with the psychological aspects of one phase of man's ontogenesis, his childhood, and, more specifically, with the development of memory. One of the methods utilized by Leont'ev involves experiments on "mediated remembering." The child is given the task of learning a list of words, the list being longer than the child can retain under the conditions of the experiment. He is given memory aids in the form of pictures, which may or may not bear meaningful relations to the listed words, and is encouraged to use effectively the memory aids. It was found that the pictures do not facilitate recall and, in fact, through the formation of collateral associations, may impair the recall.

At the second stage, corresponding to the early school age, the situation fundamentally changes: external aids markedly increase the effectiveness of remembering. The child is able to remember a substantially greater number of words than he could without the "props." At the third stage, labeled by Leont'ev as the stage of "internal mediation," the child begins to organize the material in terms of internal connections, of meaningful relationships between the words.

These changes involve not only a quantitative increase in efficiency but also, and to Leont'ev much more importantly, qualitative changes in the psychological structure of the process of remembering. The pattern seen in the development of memory is regarded as characteristic for the development of all the higher mental functions—purposeful perception, creative imagination, and abstract thought. At the earlier stages psychological functions have the character of external operations. In the process of development they take on more and more the form of internal mental activities characteristic of the fully developed mind of the adolescent and the adult.

In addition to Leont'ev's work in developmental psychology, reference will be made to the approach and accomplishments of a neurophysiologist, Krasnogorskii, one of Pavlov's early students concerned with human development, and of a student of animal behavior, Ladygina-Kots.

Ladygina-Kots. Associated with the Zoopsychological Laboratory of the State Darwin Museum in Moscow, Ladygina-Kots has assured herself a place in the history of Soviet comparative study of behavior by her work on the young of man and of the chimpanzee (1935), published a dozen years following her monograph on cognitive abilities of the chimpanzee (1923) and only two years after the 1933 monograph by W. N. Kellogg and L. A. Kellogg, *The ape and the child,* had appeared in print.

On the basis of many years of research experience and wide reading, which included earlier American studies on animal behavior, Ladygina-Kots published a systematic summary of the field (1958). The amount of space devoted to invertebrates, subprimate vertebrates, and primates differs only slightly, with some increase from one category to the next. On account of her extensive firsthand experience with primates, the last section is a specially valuable summary of the Soviet work in this sector of comparative psychology.

Investigations on the behavior of primates are considered to be of special interest in connection with the problems of anthropogenesis. In the process of organic evolution, behavior represents an adaptive function of organisms and determines their survival in the struggle for existence.

The study of organisms lined up in respect to the phylogenetic scale reveals progressive increase in the precision with which the environment is analyzed (perceived) and in the complexity with which the environmental stimuli are synthesized (integrated). This brings about an increased plasticity in attaining equilibrium with the external environment. Consciousness, the highest form of reflection of the external milieu, develops only in man and is the culmination of a long process of the evolution of highly organized matter.

Krasnogorskii. Krasnogorskii's (1958) account of half a century of investigations on conditioned reflexes, first reported in 1907 and carried out in the best Pavlovian tradition of research on higher nervous activity, is a remarkable testimony to one man's lifelong dedication to the study of the normal and disturbed brain function of the child.

In his work on the functions of the cerebral cortex, Pavlov utilized the salivary secretion in dogs as the conditioned response. Krasnogorskii's work was stimulated by the question, raised in many quarters, about whether Pavlov's methodological principles and the laws derived from the study of the higher nervous activity in animals are applicable to man and, more specifically, to the child. The goal was to replace gradually the subjective psychological approach in pediatrics by objective physiological procedures and concepts—in the clinic and at the bedside—in matters of prevention and treatment of neuropsychiatric disorders.

Krasnogorskii and his coworkers carried out intensive studies on higher nervous activity in a variety of clinical conditions (oligophrenia, hypothyreosis, epidemic encephalitis, children's hysteria, and neurosis). More relevant, perhaps, are the development of new, original investigative methods and adaptation of procedures applied in animal research and the factual data obtained by these methods.

In the early phase of the work Krasnogorskii studied sucking, swallowing, and reflex opening of the mouth. Subsequently, Pavlov's favorite technique of the quantitative study of salivary conditioned reflexes was adapted for work with young children. A special suction pump was constructed which made it possible to measure the secretion of saliva by the parotid and the submaxillary glands. Motor reflexes were also registered, including such responses as opening of the mouth, mastication, and depression of a telegraphic key. The apparatus for the registration of the responses, dating from 1952, consisted of a nine-channel kymograph, with six electromagnetic and three pneumographic markers. The drops of excreted saliva were registered graphically and automatically, separately for the unconditioned and the conditioned secretion. The manipulative controls for the presentation of food reinforcements and of conditioned stimuli (acoustical, light, dermal, verbal) were perfected.

Subsequent modifications of the apparatus by V. V. Alyarinskii have made it possible to time directly the duration of the latent periods of the secretory and motor reflexes, to register not only the timing but also the magnitude of motor reflexes and the intensity of a mechanical dermal stimulus. The verbal and acoustic stimuli are recorded on a tape for the purposes of rigorous standardization. Most American physiological psychologists would probably be pleased with this equipment. The registration apparatus and controls are placed in the experimenter's room, separated from the subject's room. The laboratory is located directly in a children's home, which makes it possible to carry out well-controlled, long-term studies.

In view of the complexity of man's higher nervous functions introduced by the use of speech, I. P. Pavlov encouraged Krasnogorskii to start his investigations on man with young children. This work provided a solid basis for subsequent studies of cortical functions in the course of ontogenetic development. It was only natural that substantial attention was devoted to the formation of speech—the second signal system of Pavlov—and its interaction with the first (sensory) signal system. The following arrangement may serve as example of the approach to the study of the thought processes by the method of conditioned responses. The word "ten" (*deysat'*) is reinforced by food; the presentation of the word "eight" (*vosem'*) is never followed by food. In time the word "ten" alone comes to elicit a salivary conditioned reflex; the word "eight," never reinforced by food, remains without a positive effect on salivary secretion. When a child is given the task of adding in his head five plus five (or six plus four) and arrives at the correct answer, saliva begins to flow copiously. When he subtracts four from twelve, with the result of "eight," the secretion is inhibited. The sensory stimulus constituted by the bit of food introduced into the mouth belongs to the first signal system; the verbal stimuli "ten" and "eight" belong to the second signal system. The process of conditioning involves the formation of temporary (conditioned) connection between the two signal systems. The technique was used in investigations on the processes of abstraction and generalization under normal and pathological conditions.

Krasnogorskii felt strongly that research on cortical functions in the speaking and thinking man requires careful attention to the development of additional methods. In his laboratory N. N. Krasnogorskii (Jr.) extended the work to a variety of autonomic functions, including electrodermal responses, infrared radiation, and sweating. I. S. Kanaev developed an apparatus for the application of tactile stimuli to the palm of one or both hands; the child reproduces the stimulus pattern by depressing a telegraphic key. This method was used to study the "mobility" of nervous processes (i.e., ability to reproduce precisely stimuli increasing in rapidity) and more complex processes of sensorimotor differentiation between acoustic and dermal stimuli. V. V. Alyakrinskii designed equipment for the analysis of speech reactions in terms of their temporal and dynamic characteristics.

Krasnogorskii (1958, p. 210) differentiates among three categories of conditioned connections:

(*1*) Conditioned connections involving the first (sensory) signal system and reinforced by unconditioned stimuli; these are the ordinary conditioned reflexes.

(*2*) Conditioned connections between sensory stimuli on the one hand and verbal stimuli on the other hand (i.e., connections between the first and second signal systems); these connections involve the cortical terminations of various analyzers (tactile, olfactory, visual, etc.) and the speech division of the acoustic and the kinesthetic analyzer and are referred to as "connections of abstraction."

(*3*) Conditioned connections between words ("speech stimuli"); their formation is facilitated by the meaning of individual words.

in conclusion: six principles of Soviet materialist psychology

The principles of the Soviet psychology have been stated succinctly by Rudik (1958, pp. 22–23):

(*1*) *The principle of materialist monism.* Mental phenomena (the psyche) are a property of the brain. The psychological processes are regarded as superimposed upon the physiological processes. Consequently, psychologists must be thoroughly familiar with the physiology of higher nervous activity.

(*2*) *The principle of determinism.* Mental phenomena are the results of interaction between the processes of higher nervous activity and the external environment.

(*3*) *The principle of reflection.* Consciousness (mind, psyche) is a subjective reflection of an objective reality. Mental processes are not regulated by special, immanent laws, but have their roots in objective existence.

(*4*) *The principle of the unity of consciousness and activity.* Man's mind is not only manifested in activity but it is *formed* in the process of activity. As a corollary, mental processes can not be studied abstractly but only in connection with concrete forms of activity.

(*5*) *The principle of historism.* Mind (psyche, consciousness) develops in the process of the historical development of man. Consequently psychologists must study mental phenomena in reference to their genesis and bring out the social roots of different aspects of man's consciousness and personality.

(6) *The principle of the unity of theory and practice.* Through their research, psychologists must take an active part in the solution of practical problems met in the building of socialism, such as development of more effective methods for the training and education of the coming generation, improvement of work conditions and the process of production, and the protection of (mental) health.

references

Anan'ev, G. B. et al. (Eds.) *Psikhologicheskia nauka v S.S.R. (Psychological sciences in the U.S.S.R.)*. Moscow: Acad. of Pedagogical Sci., 1959.

Bauer, R. A. *The new man in Soviet psychology.* Cambridge, Mass.: Harvard, 1952.

Brozek, J. Review of *The cerebral cortex and the internal organs* by K. M. Bykov. *Contemp. Psychol.*, 1959, 4, 86–88.

Brozek, J. Current status of psychology in the U.S.S.R. *Annu. Rev. Psychol.*, 1962, 13, 515–566.

Bulygin, I. A. *Issledovanie zakonomernostei i mekhanizmov interotseptivnykh refleksov (Investigations on the laws and mechanisms of interoceptive reflexes).* Minsk: Acad. of Sci. of the Byelorussian S.S.R., 1959.

Bykov, K. M. *The cerebral cortex and the internal organs.* Translated and edited by W. H. Gantt. New York: Chemical Publishing, 1957.

Hull, C. L. *Principles of behavior.* New York: Appleton-Century-Crofts, 1943.

Hull, C. L. *A behavior system.* New Haven: Yale, 1952.

Ivanov, P. I. *Psikhologiya (Psychology).* Moscow: Gosuchpedizdat, 1959.

Ivanov-Smolensky, A. G. *Essays on the pathophysiology of the higher nervous activity according to Pavlov and his school.* Moscow: Foreign Language Publishing House, 1954.

Kellogg, W. N., & Kellogg, L. A. *The ape and the child.* New York: McGraw-Hill, 1933.

Kline, N. S. The organization of psychiatric care and psychiatric research in the U.S.S.R. *Ann. N.Y. Acad. Sci.*, 1960, 84, Art. 4, 147–224.

Krasnogorskii, N. I. *Vysshaya nervnaya deyatel'nost' rebenka (Higher nervous activity of the child).* Leningrad: Medgiz, 1958.

Ladygina-Kots, N. N. *Issledovanie poznavatel'nykh sposobnostei shimpanze (Investigations on the cognitive abilities of the chimpanzee).* Moscow: State Publishing House, 1923.

Ladygina-Kots, N. N. *Ditya shimpanze i ditya cheloveka v ikh instinktakh, emotskykh, igrakh, privychkakh i vryazitel'nykh dvizheniyakh (Instincts, emotions, games, habits and expressive motions of a baby chimpanzee and a human child).* Moscow: Darwin Museum, 1935.

Ladygina-Kots, N. N. *Razvitie psihiki v processe evolutsii organizmov (The development of the mind in the process of evolution of organisms).* Moscow: Sovietskaya Nauka, 1959.

Leont'ev, A. N. *Problemy razvitiya psikhiki* (*Problems of mental development*). Moscow: Academy of Pedagogical Sciences, 1959.

London, I. D. A historical survey of psychology in the Soviet Union. *Psychol. Bull.*, 1949, 46, 241–277.

London, I. D. Psychology in the U.S.S.R. *Amer. J. Psychol.*, 1951, 64, 422–428.

London, I. D. Research on sensory interaction in the Soviet Union. *Psychol. Bull.*, 1954, 51, 531–568.

Magoun, H. W. *The waking brain.* Springfield, Ill.: Charles C Thomas, 1958.

Pavlov, I. P. *Lectures on conditioned reflexes and psychiatry.* Translated and edited by W. H. Gantt. New York: International Publishers, 1941.

Pribram, K. H. Theory in physiological psychology. *Annu. Rev. Psychol.*, 1960, 11, 1–40.

Razran, G. Recent Russian psychology: 1950–56. *Contemp. Psychol.*, 1957, 2, 93–101.

Razran, G. 1957 and 1958 Russian books in psychology, psychophysiology, and related areas in psychiatry. *Amer. Psychol.*, 1960, 15, 205–207.

Razran, G. *Interoceptive conditioning: A review of Russian experiments and applications,* in preparation, 1962.

Rudik, P. A. *Psikhologiya* (*Psychology*). Moscow: Fizkul'tura i Sport, 1958.

Sokolov, E. N. *Vospriyatie i uslovnyi refleks* (*Perception and conditioned reflexes*). Moscow: Moscow Univer., 1958.

Sokolov, E. N. *Orientirovochnyi refleks i voprosy vysshei nervnoi deyatel'nosti v norme i patologii* (*Orienting reflex and problems of the higher nervous activity in normal and abnormal children*). Moscow: Academy of Pedagogical Sciences, 1959.

Tomaszewski, T. *Zasady psychologii w Z.S.S.R.* (*Principles of psychology in the U.S.S.R.*). Warsaw: Cxytelnik, 1949.

Wortis, J. *Soviet psychiatry.* Baltimore: Williams & Wilkins, 1950.

Zaporozhets, A. V. *Psikhologiya* (*Psychology*). Moscow: Uchpedizdat, 1959.

further readings

Anan'ev, B. G., et al. (Eds.) *Psikhologicheskaya nauka v S.S.R.,* (*Psychological sciences in the U.S.S.R.*). Washington, D.C.: U.S. Joint Publication Research Service. Vol. 1, 1961; Vol. 2, 1962.

Bauer, R. A. (Ed.) *Some views on Soviet psychology.* Washington, D.C.: American Psychological Association, 1962.

Brozek, J. *Soviet studies on nutrition and higher nervous activity.* New York Academy of Sciences Monograph No. 24. 1961.

Brozek, J. Current status of psychology in the U.S.S.R. *Annu. Rev. Psychol.* 1962, 13, 515–556.

Brozek, J. Soviet studies on nutrition and higher nervous activity. *Ann. N.Y. Acad. Sci.*, 1962, 93, 665–714.

Dmitriev, A. S., & Kochigina, A. M. The importance of time as stimulus for conditioned reflex activity. *Psychol. Bull.*, 1959, 56, 106–132.

Luria, A. R. *The nature of human conflicts.* Translated and edited by W. H. Gantt. New York: Grove Press, 1960. Reprint of the 1932 ed. by Liveright.

Mintz, A. Recent developments in psychology in the U.S.S.R. *Annu. Rev. Psychol.,* 1958, 9, 453–504.

O'Connor, N. (Ed.) *Recent Soviet psychology.* New York: Liveright, 1961.

Mintz, A. Further developments in psychology in the U.S.S.R. *Annu. Rev. Psychol.,* 1959, 10, 455–487.

Platonov, K. I. *The word as a physiological and therapeutic factor: The theory and practice of psychotherapy according to I. P. Pavlov.* Translated by A. Myshne. Moscow: Foreign Languages Publishing House, 1959.

Razran, G. Soviet psychology and psychophysiology. *Science,* 1958, 128, 1187–1194.

Razran, G. The observable unconscious and the inferable conscious in current Soviet psychophysiology: Interoceptive conditioning, semantic conditioning, and the orienting reflex. *Psychol. Rev.,* 1961, 68, 81–147.

Russian Scientific Translation Program, National Institutes of Health. *The central nervous system and behavior: Translations from the Russian medical literature.* Bethesda: U.S. Dept. of Health, Education and Welfare, Public Health Service, 1959, 1960.

Simon, B. *Psychology in the Soviet Union.* Stanford, Calif.: Stanford, 1957.

Winn, Ralph B., & six contributors. *Soviet psychology: A symposium.* New York: Philosophical Library, 1961.

Shinkuro Iwahara
Nara Women's College
Nara, Japan

appendix C ORIENTAL PSYCHOLOGY[1]

Psychology in the Orient has been little known to the West partly because of its relatively small number of significant contributions and largely because of the language barrier. However, the language problem is one-sided: the Oriental scientist is likely to know English, German, and French, but the scientist in the West is very unlikely to be familiar with Japanese and Chinese. India is an exception, since her scientific output is written mostly in English.

According to the *International directory of psychologists* (1958), only 20 per cent of all the psychologists in the world exclusive of the United States belong to the Orient. In addition, the distribution is very skewed: 63 per cent of the Oriental psychologists listed in the *Directory* are Japanese, 17 per cent are Indian, and 9 per cent Chinese. The remaining 11 per cent are scattered among the other Oriental countries.

CLASSIC ORIENTAL PSYCHOLOGY

Psychological studies in a very broad sense are very ancient in the East, especially in India and China. Most of the systematic approaches to human experience can be found in the ancient Hindu and Buddhist literature. According to one of the Hindu works, four stages of the mental process are differentiated: sleeping, dreaming, awakened states, and the superconscious (Akhilananda, 1953). The first two stages, which belong to the subconscious, are considered by Hindu leaders as important aspects of human experience. This is in contrast with some of the classic Western psychological systems such as English associationism, Wundtian structuralism, and Brentano's act psychology. Although these systems are considerably different from one

---

[1] The author is greatly indebted to Dr. Koji Sato of Kyoto University, Japan, for his valuable criticisms and suggestions.

456

another, they all deal with the intellectual aspect of consciousness or experience as the subject matter of psychology.

The Hindu psychologist, like the psychoanalyst, places special importance upon the subconscious (*samskara* in Sanskrit) because it is believed to be an integration of past experiences, impressions, and tendencies of the individual. However, unlike psychoanalysis, Hindu psychology does not assume sex and death urges as the basic human instincts; the basic urge is, according to the Hindu theory, directed to eternal happiness or complete freedom from bondage. Notice its similarity to the Rogerian theory which postulates a drive toward growth, health, and adjustment of the individual.

The superconsciousness (*samadhi* in Sanskrit) has no exact correlate in the Western culture. It is an experience of spiritual enlightenment in which the individual is neither conscious nor subconscious. It is quite different from hallucination or pathological states since, in such states, spiritual insight cannot be attained. It is a mystic experience only in the sense that it is not an intellectual experience but a whole mind-body experience or a holistic integration of the self and the world. The study of the superconscious is not unscientific because the normal individual can experience it. It does not matter whether he is Hindu, Buddhist, or Christian.

The Hindu and Buddhist thinkers have not only performed a detailed analysis of our inner life but have also shown a number of methods for attaining spiritual insight, or *samadhi*. Two of these methods are now well known: *yoga* (a Sanskrit word which means "union"), and *Zen* (a Japanese word, derived from *dhyāna*, a Sanskrit word, indicating "meditation"). Yoga and Zen appear quite different, but their principles are not very different. Zen is often said to be a blending of Indian rationalism, Chinese realism, and Japanese sentiments.

In ancient China, the universe was believed to consist of Heaven, the Earth, and Man. Heaven and the earth obeyed the natural law, while the law of man was morality. According to Confucius (551–479 B.C.), morality was baséd on the three faculties of wisdom, benevolence, and valor. Later, Mencius (ca. 372–289 B.C.) divided morality into five elements: benevolence, righteousness, propriety, wisdom, and sincerity.

Like Aristotle, the ancient Chinese believed that mind (*hsin* in Chinese) lies in the center (heart) of the body. Besides mind and body, Mencius assumed *ch'i*, which roughly corresponds to spiritual energy or pneuma in classic Western psychology. Body is filled with *ch'i*, which is controlled by mind. Later scholars mentioned that *li* and *ch'i* make personality. *Li* is innate and identical in all human beings, while *ch'i* can be modified by learning and environment and thus is the main source of individual differences and temperament.

Personality traits were systematically studied by Liu-shao in about A.D. 220. His theory was based on the then-current doctrine of the five elements of the universe (wood, fire, earth, metal, and water). It assumed that body, temperament, duty, and morality each has five different characteristics corresponding to the five elements. When all these are mixed in proper proportions, an ideal personality is attained (Kuroda, 1948). The Chinese typology bears a remarkable resemblance to the Hippocratic theory of temperament.

ZEN BUDDHISM AND PSYCHOLOGY

Among the various Oriental philosophical positions, Zen Buddhism is probably one of the best known in the West. It was first introduced to the West by Dr. Y. Motora of Tokyo University. He presented a paper entitled "The concept of self in the Oriental philosophy" at the Seventh International Congress of Psychology at Rome in 1905. There he criticized the English associationists' view of mind as mechanical and devoid of an active self. The essential nature of mind, according to him, is a dynamic psychic potentiality into which the subject-object dichotomy is melted, or simply *tathata* (Sanskrit) in Zen theory (Motora, 1905).

Kuroda (1931; Otsuka, 1960) defined psychology as a science of consciousness and comprehension (*kaku* in Japanese). It is our usual experience that volitional acts are eventually automatized with practice and become unconscious or half-conscious unless special attention is paid to them. This mental state is an example of comprehension. Another illustration of it is the knack, hunch, or *kan* (in Japanese) which refers to the occasional experience which we know but cannot make clear. Although comprehension is a naïve, preanalytic mental state, it evidently directs our behavior and plays an important role in our life. The purest form of comprehension, according to Kuroda, is the Zen enlightenment. A number of experimental works have been done by Kuroda on the exact nature of comprehension. Similar positions have been taken by T. Chiba (1960) and K. Sakuma.

Morita therapy, developed by the Japanese psychiatrist, S. Morita, is a unique psychotherapy in the Zen mode of thought even though Morita was not aware of Zen theory (Kora & Sato, 1958). According to Morita theory, neurasthenia, or *nervosis* in its own terminology, is attributed to a hypochondriac disposition and a mechanism of psychic interaction. The hypochondriac individual is overconscious of himself and feels that he is unusual or maladjusted. Consequently he concentrates attention upon his physical condition, especially upon his sensations, and thus his sensations become keener and in turn attract his attention. The interaction between sensation and attention exaggerates the hypochondriac tendency and consumes a great deal of mental energy, with consequent behavior disorders.

In order to break up this vicious circle, the patient must accept the sufferings and worries as they are and must become carefree. Morita therapy starts with an absolute bed-rest period during which the patient is prohibited from reading, writing, and even talking with others and is instructed to leave himself to the dynamics of his present situation. Through a light-work period to a hard-work period, the patient is gradually guided to lead a realistic daily life. Unlike psychoanalysis, there is no free association or interpretation (Kawai & Kondo, 1960). Another characteristic point of the Oriental therapy is the absence of labeling during treatment. Thus, Morita therapy is closely related to Zen in that both emphasize the present situation, "letting-be," and spontaneity rather than etiology, interpretation, and direct guidance (Kora & Sato, 1958).

In spite of all these works, Zen has only recently been introduced to the West through English publications by D. T. Suzuki and Sato. According to Suzuki, Zen is "the art of seeing into the nature of one's being and it points the way from bondage to freedom . . . (and it) liberates all the energies properly and naturally stored in each of us, which are in ordinary circumstances cramped and distorted so that they find no channel for activity" (1956, p. 3). The final aim of Zen is the experience of spiritual enlightenment or *satori* (Japanese). *Satori* is a trance which has a kind of direct contact with reality. Sato has written a number of introductory papers on Zen for Western readers in an international journal in the Orient, *Psychologia*, edited by himself. One of his articles refers to a brief description of *Zazen*, or seated Zen, which is one of the commonest practices to attain *satori*. In *Zazen*, the individual sits squarely on his seat with half-opened eyes and breathes quietly with his whole body; sometimes he adjusts respiration by counting it. He applies a strain to the abdomen and starts with a calm cry and gradually increases the voice, ending with a vigorous shout which results in high muscular tension in face, shoulders, and arms. Thus, he is able to meditate deeply into himself without diverting his attention. Meditation is characterized by a condition of "no mind" or nothingness or "being one with the world." In course of time, if the practice is successful, *satori* occurs rather suddenly with the released tension. One of Sato's students described his own Zen experience as follows (Sato, 1959, p. 112): "The mind became clear and serene, and a kind of joy was felt, with a force coming up from the bottom of the belly."

One of the recent psychophysiological studies has utilized electroencephalographic (EEG) measures. During *Zazen*, alpha waves are dominant and continuous; they are not easily blocked as in the normal waking state. The pulse is normal or slightly faster; perception is normal (Kasamatsu, 1957).

The Japanese Zen literature has appealed to some Western scientists including psychoanalysts, existential psychotherapists, and general semanticists. Erich Fromm, for example, has enumerated several similarities between Zen and psychoanalysis. According to him, the "description of Zen's aim could be applied without change as a description of what psychoanalysis aspires to achieve" (1959, p. 86), and "Zen can have a most fertile and clarifying influence on the theory and technique of psychoanalysis" (p. 98), even though the two methods are quite different.

A close kinship is discussed by Hora (1959) among Taoism, Zen, and existential psychotherapy in their common emphasis on non-teleological, nonintellectual, and existential aspects as well as on openness and "letting-be." Charles Morris (1951) has stated that Zen therapy, although it may appear mystic, can be legitimately accepted by current general semantics, and Holmes (1957) has pointed out the transactional aspect of Zen. The French psychotherapist, Hubert Benoit has emphasized the thoroughgoing naturalism and realism of Zen in contrast with the idealistic position of Christianity.

Recently, some criticisms have been raised against Zen theory from foreign countries, as well as from Japan. First of all, Zen and its practice have not been fully delineated in terms of objective and scientific language, and thus direct evaluation of it is not possible. Secondly, Zen is criticized for lack of social concern, although this is not the true spirit of Zen Buddhism. Certainly, some early Zen masters lived in seclusion and were unwilling to work among the din and bustle of the world. The evasive, noncommittal characteristics of Zen, if any, are well indicated by these seclusive Zen students. Thirdly, it is claimed that although Zen appears to be closely related to psychoanalysis, their historical origins are entirely different (Becker, 1960). Japanese Zen was grown in her feudal age; its aim was then to create a good *samurai* (warrior) who was taught to fight for his lord at the risk of his life. Man's service to the highest authority with the annihilation of self was once believed to be the final goal of Zen. Thus, "it seems erroneous to consider only the reported endings in the early accounts from the literature as a basis on which to conclude that Zen represents a resolution of ambivalence toward authority in the sense of full, complete individuation and freedom" (Becker, 1960, p. 104).

INTRODUCTION OF WESTERN SCIENTIFIC PSYCHOLOGY AND CURRENT PSYCHOLOGICAL TRENDS IN THE EAST

Scientific psychology was introduced to the East from the West around the end of the last century. However, there are some national differences. Indian psychology was early influenced by British psychology, since most of the Indian pioneers in psychology went to England for graduate training. They devoted themselves to theories of intelligence and mental testing. Psychoanalytic interest was also great in India, fostered through literature as well as direct introduction by those who had studied in Europe. As has already been mentioned, psychoanalysis has a number of affinities with the traditional Hindu thought. The Indian Psychoanalytic Association was founded in 1922, three years earlier than the establishment of the Indian Psychological Association (Sastry, 1932). Since World War II, the psychological scene in India has been oriented toward America, as in other Asian countries except the Chinese mainland.

Psychological knowledge is now largely applied in India in order to solve some industrial, social, and cultural problems. A center for research in the social implications of industrialization and technological problems has been recently established by UNESCO at Calcutta. Change of research interest during the last three decades is suggested in Table 11.

Indian concern with depth psychology and mental hygiene has not waned. A biosynthetic approach to personality was proposed by Gopalaswani in the study of values (Ramadevi & Rao, 1957). Very recently, Nand (1959, 1960) described what he called "total psychoanalysis," which puts special emphasis on self-analysis. In addition to the usual psychoanalytic methods, total psychoanalysis requires the patient to carry three cards in his pockets and to write down reminiscences about himself, any significant events, and all the theories and hypotheses he discovers about his philosophical and self-analytic problems. Indra Sen (1959) has criticized psychoanalysis as not being interested in the problem of emotional life as a whole. Emotion is defined in the West as simply impulsive effusions or sudden boiling of feelings. Sen has argued that if this is so, a harmonious and integral personality is impossible. On the other hand, the real essence of emotion is the self-existent joy, or *atma* (Sanskrit), the most potent unifying force in personality. As all problems of psychic disorders are based on mental disharmony, disintegration, and dissociation, their cure must depend upon the realization of *atma*. The integral yoga of Scri Aurobindo, according to him, is one of the most efficient techniques to attain *atma*.

In the field of intelligence, Paknikar (1958) has presented a theory of three elements of intelligence. These elements are comprehension, memory, and constructive ability, in accordance with one of the traditional Hindu schools. Ramachandra Rao (1958) has pointed out an affinity of gestalt theory with the Sphata school which was proposed by Indian grammarians over 2,600 years ago.

India is probably the only country in the East which attaches a special importance to the classic thought characteristic of the country.

Table 11   Major areas of research interest, based on content analysis of titles of articles in one leading journal in each of the three major countries in the East

Research area	India		China	Japan		
	Ind. J. Psychol.		*Acta psychol. sinica*	*Jap. J. Psychol.*		
	1931 (4 nos.)	1958 (4 nos.)	1959 (4 nos.)	1931 (6 nos.)	1940 (6 nos.)	1959 (6 nos.)
General	4	3	28	1	0	1
Physiological	0	1	2	0	0	2
Perceptual	2	1	1	8	11	9
Learning	2	2	0	3	6	8
Personality and clinical	1	10	3	13*	2	2
Educational and developmental	4	2	2	3	6	9
Social	0	4	1	2	1	2
Industrial	1	6	6	0	2	2
Criminal	0	1	0	1	0	2
Other	0	1	4	0	3	5†
Total	14	31	47	31	31	42

* This number is especially large since one of the issues in 1931 is a special edition on personality measurement.
† On information theory.
Note: There are a number of other psychology journals in India and Japan (see Table 12). Thus the present table does not give a complete picture of current trends in the two countries.

Adequate acquaintance with the traditional Indian psychological systems is recommended at the graduate level in Indian universities, together with sufficient knowledge of Western psychology (Sen, 1958).

The most drastic change in psychological thought occurred on the Chinese mainland soon after the last war. Chinese psychologists before the war had been greatly indebted to American functionalism, partly because of the Chinese realistic characteristics. The Chinese Association of Psychological Testing was established in 1930, and the Chinese Psychological Association was founded in 1937. Their functional disposition can still be found in Taiwan.

Table 12   *Current psychological periodicals in the East*

CHINA (MAINLAND)

1. Acta Psychologica Sinica (in Chinese with Russian and English abstracts; 1956–)
2. Translation Journal of Psychology (in Chinese; 1956–1958)

CHINA (TAIWAN)

1. Acta Psychologica Taiwanica (in Chinese with English abstracts; 1958–)
2. Psychological Testing (in Chinese; ?–1957)

INDIA

1. Education and Psychology (in English; 1954–)
2. Indian Journal of Psychology (in English; 1926–)
3. Journal of All-India Institute of Mental Health (in English; 1958–)
4. Journal of Education and Psychology (?)
5. Samiksa (Journal of Indian Psychoanalytic Society) (in English; 1947–)

JAPAN

1. Annual of Animal Psychology (in Japanese with English abstracts; 1943–)
2. Japanese Annals of Social Psychology (in Japanese; 1960–)
3. Japanese Journal of Educational Psychology (in Japanese with English abstracts; 1952–)
4. Japanese Journal of Educational and Social Psychology (in Japanese with English abstracts; 1960–)
5. Japanese Journal of Psychology (in Japanese with English abstracts; 1926–)
6. Japanese Psychological Research (in English; 1954–)
7. Japanese Psychological Review (in Japanese; 1957–)
8. Psychologia (An International Journal of Psychology in the Orient) (in English; 1957–)
9. Tohoku Psychologica Folia (in English or German; 1933–)
10. Tohoku Journal of Experimental Psychology (in Japanese; 1954–)

KOREA

1. Studies in Psychology (Ewha Womans University) (in English; 1954–)

TURKEY

1. Instanbul Studies in Experimental Psychology (University of Istanbul (in Turkish, English, German, or French; 1940, 1952, 1956–)

On the Chinese mainland, American functional psychology has been shaken off as an idealistic psychology of the Capitalist countries. The mainland psychologists have attempted to reconstruct a scientific psychology based on Pavlovian conditioning theory and Marxist principles (Shuh, 1958, 1959). To attain this objective, they published the *Translation Journal of Psychology* in 1956 (discontinued in 1958) which contained articles selected from the Russian journal, *Voprosy Psikhologii* (*Problems of Psychology*) (1955–   ).

The Chinese Psychological Association (reorganized in 1955) has another journal called *Acta psychologica sinica* (1956–   ). About half the total articles in the 1956–1959 issues of the journal were either theoretical, political, or philosophical, such as C. S. Chu's (1956) "Problems on the object of psychology" and D. J. Chen's (1959) "How psychology can be of service to the socialistic reconstruction." According to the new Chinese view, psychology is a science whose aim is to explore the material basis of psyche and the fundamental laws governing the activities of the brain as well as the physiological mechanisms underlying them (Shuh, 1959).

Watson's behaviorism, as well as gestalt theory, has been criticized from the Communist viewpoint. According to C. F. Ni (1957), behaviorism is a product of American capitalism. In order to secure greater profits, the Capitalist class, then flourishing in America, attempted to make the laborer like a machine or a man without consciousness. Thus behaviorism is fundamentally reactionary. What is worse, the behaviorist pretended to be a scientist by borrowing Pavlov's conditioning theory to his system and so deceived people. Z. Y. Kuo, a widely known animal psychologist who introduced behaviorism to China, is blamed as one of the most reactionary propagandists of behaviorism.

Both behaviorism and Communist psychology are based on a kind of materialism, but they are otherwise entirely different. First, behaviorism is mechanistic, while Communist theory is dialectic. Second, the behaviorist erroneously limits the subject matter of psychology to stimulus and response, neglecting the important functions of the higher nervous systems, which are the basis of psychic activities. Consciousness is denied by Watson, but it is accepted by the Communist psychologist as a reflection of the objective world. Third, Watson confuses human psychology with animal psychology. According to the Chinese psychologist, man and animal are different in quality rather than in quantity; human behavior is developed with a social and historical background which is lacking in animals. Fourth, thinking, in behavioristic terms, is nothing but inner speech or muscular activity. On the contrary, the Communist theory maintains that thinking cannot be reduced to language or to muscular activity. Language, according to Stalin, is an instrument of thinking.

A critical evaluation of gestalt theory was attempted by H. L. Chu (1958). According to him, gestalt theory was born when capitalism had turned to imperialism and subjective idealism had been dominant over the objective world view in Europe. First, although gestalt theory emphasizes totality or wholeness and the risk of analysis, it fails to recognize the fact that the brain has both analyzing and synthesizing functions as was proved by Pavlov. The Pavlovian theory is nothing but dialectic materialism. However, psychological systems colored by Capitalistic idealism cannot understand it. On the one hand, associationistic psychology puts too much emphasis on analysis and thus is deviated from our daily life, while gestalt theory concerns itself only with synthesis and consequently regresses to transcendental idealism. This is illustrated by Köhler's statement that field structure is a primitive sensory fact and is not dependent upon experience.

Secondly, isomorphism, proposed by Köhler, has no relationship to Pavlovian theory. It is merely a mystic speculation based on misunderstood neurophysiology. Thirdly, the gestalt concept of insight in chimpanzees is criticized as anthropomorphism. Animal mentality must be differentiated from human mentality because only the latter develops the second signal system, making dialectic thinking possible. Lastly, such terms as behavioral environment (Koffka) and psychological environment (Lewin) are blamed as typical examples of subjective idealism. Incidentally, it is interesting to note that the same gestalt theory is still supported by East German psychologists (K. Gottschaldt, for example) who are related by blood to the advocators of gestalt theory (Razran, 1958; Lun, 1958; Woo, 1958).

Nor does psychological structuralism escape Chinese criticisms. In his article, "Theoretical foundations of structuralism in Wundt's and Titchener's works," Cheng has given a critical evaluation of structuralism (Cheng, 1959). First, structuralism is historically an amalgam of subjective idealism (of the Capitalist class) and natural science. For the structuralist, there is nothing but experience, which is the subject matter both for psychology and for physics. This is an agnostic view. According to this Chinese author, psychic phenomena or consciousness are reflections of the objective physical world, which is primary, with the psychic phenomena secondary.

Wundt believed that the task of psychology was to analyze consciousness into simple elements, but the Chinese view is that psychic elements are only reflections of attributes of the objective world. There is no such thing as a psychic element; it is merely an abstraction. Thus Wundtian theory is isolated from concrete human life. Lastly, the mind-body parallelism of structuralism is misleading, since it fails to recognize the Pavlovian view of consciousness, according to which consciousness is the material attribute of the highest nervous system.

Another kinship of the new China to the Soviet Union in the field of psychology is her exclusion of mental testing and psychoanalysis. Besides these theoretical, political articles, *Acta psychologica sinica* includes papers on Pavlovian physiological, industrial, medical, perceptual, and educational problems (see Table 11).

As has already been noted, the psychological scene on the Chinese mainland is definitely oriented to the Soviet Union. However, quite recently some Chinese workers have become interested in the classic Chinese psychology in the field of psychotherapy. K. C. Liu (1957), for example, has proposed a therapeutic method similar to the Japanese seated Zen. The Chinese practice aims to cure chronic diseases such as psychoneurosis, tuberculosis, and hyperpiesis.

Probably Japan has the oldest history of experimental psychology in the Orient. Dr. Y. Morota (Ph.D. at Johns Hopkins) and Dr. M. Matsumoto (trained in the United States and Germany) are well-known pioneers in this field. The first number of the all-Japan psychological journal, called the *Japanese Journal of Psychology*, appeared in 1926. Before 1926, two journals had been published, one in Kyoto, and the other in Tokyo. In 1927, the Japanese Psychological Association was established, and sixty-one papers were read at the first annual meeting.

In contrast with Indian and Chinese psychologists, Japanese workers have been devoted to experimental studies in perception and memory, particularly after the introduction of gestalt theory. This is perhaps due partly to the affinity of gestalt with the Oriental holistic thought. The Japanese contribution in the field of perception has reached a fairly high level by international standards. Numerous experimental works have been reported on perceptual constancy, geometric-optic illusion, figural aftereffect, apparent movement, and related fields.

But unfortunately, most of these works have been buried, unknown to the Western scientist. For example, the converse of the tau effect was discovered by S. Abe as early as 1935, but the same fact was reported by Cohen et al. (1953) almost two decades later as a new phenomenon. In his recent review of Japanese experimental psychology, the American psychologist Hake (1958) stated that it is a tragedy that some review articles in visual perception which appeared in recent issues of the *Psychological Bulletin* contain no Japanese references, although Japanese psychologists have much to offer.

As for theoretical aspects, Obonai has been criticizing gestalt theory as philosophical romanticism and devoid of sound empirical basis. Scientific psychology, according to him, should be studied analytically and elementalistically like physics and physiology. On the basis of his voluminous and energetic work on visual perception, Obonai has proposed a theory called *psychophysiological induction*. Its basic idea is that the stimulation of a receptor will induce both excitation and inhibition around the stimulated area, and the resulting effect is an algebraic summation of these antagonistic functions which leads to actual perception. The induction occurs temporally as well as spatially. Obonai claims that some perceptual phenomena which are separately treated can be integrated by this theory.

One such evidence has been shown recently. The simultaneous contrast-confluence illusion and the figural aftereffect were found to be different aspects of the same phenomenon (Ikeda & Obonai, 1955). Obonai believes that induction theory can be applied to explain various psychological facts not only in perception but also in other areas (Obonai, 1957).

The Japanese physiologist, K. Motokawa, and his students, including a number of psychologists, have investigated many aspects of visual perception. They have used his ingenious techniques based on his own finding that the electric excitability of the retina changes as a function of time after cessation of illumination and that the time function is characteristic of the wave length of the light used for illumination. According to Motokawa (1953, p. 369): "As . . . the retina is ontogenetically a part of the brain, and its structure resembles that of central nervous system . . . it is not surprising that psychological phenomena such as optical illusions should be interpreted in terms of retinal processes." His theory and method are now known to American scientists.

Z. Yokose has attacked visual perception based on a theoretical model on the assumption that visual perception and electrophysiological processes in the brain are functionally correlated (Yokose, 1957). Akishige (1960) has compiled a lengthy article on Japanese studies on perceptual constancy, with 203 Japanese references, including a series of experimental studies of his own on the possibility of application of theories of perceptual constancy to architecture.

The second most popular research area in experimental psychology in Japan has been learning and memory. One of the original works on memory is concerned with the functions of stimulus and response words. Kuraishi (1937) established the relative difficulty of recalling a foreign word from the corresponding word in one's own language compared with the recall in the reverse order and explained it in terms of gestalt theory. More recently, Umemoto (1959) has attempted a systematic study of this phenomenon and has concluded that the effect of response items on recall is greater than that of stimulus items. This has been confirmed by Morikawa, who stated that the stimulus item is learned as a cue to the response item, while the response item is acquired as the goal to be responded to, and thus backward recall is inferior to forward recall (Morikawa, 1959). Recently similar studies have appeared in the United States (e.g., Feldman & Underwood, 1957).

Another important contribution has been made by Ishihara and his coworkers. A significant positive transfer was found in paired-associate learning between two response items whether they were opposite or similar in meaning. This is contrary to Underwood's theory of reciprocal inhibition (Underwood, 1953). In addition, Ishihara's group has proposed a different kind of association value, defined in terms of frequency of appearance as associated items in a given free-association situation. A series of experimental works has been done on the functions of the new association value in contrast with the ordinary association values (Ishihara, 1960).

A large-scale research project has been undertaken under the leadership of Professor Imanishi on the social behavior of Japanese monkeys, and Imanishi and his colleagues are attempting to establish a sociology of monkeys based on their findings. A number of new terms were coined in order to describe animal behavior in its native environment. Imanishi has shown special interest in the "personality" of monkeys, to which he has given psychoanalytic interpretations (Imanishi, 1957).

Japanese works which appear to be original, to the West, are few in social, clinical, personality, and industrial fields. We have already mentioned Morita therapy, which is highly related to Zen doctrine. An interesting study was reported on the hypnotic image by Naruse (1959). When a stimulus is presented in the waking state after it has been associated with another stimulus under a deep hypnotic trance, a mental image corresponding to the associated stimulus appears, with amnesia for the associating situation. A similar result is also found under the hypnotic trance. These findings suggest that both posthypnotic and hypnotic images lie between the memory image and the actual percept, but that the hypnotic image is closer to the percept than the posthypnotic image. The image in its common usage is essentially a conditioned sensation. The image is generally weak and obscure because the occurrence of the conditioned sensation or image is inhibited by the higher cerebral cortex. However, the image is clear in the posthypnotic or hypnotic state because of the diminution of the cortical inhibition (Naruse & Obonai, 1952). An application of the hypnotic method to personality studies is now in progress. K. Sato has attempted to establish a personality theory based on not only Western but also Oriental systems and has discussed the *Bodhi-sattva* as one of the ideal personality types (Sato, 1951).

The psychological scene in Oriental countries other than India, China, and Japan does not seem to be very active. A general overview indicates that it is oriented to America and that psychologists in these countries are interested in applied psychology rather than in experimental and systematic psychology. *Psychologia*, the international journal, gives detailed accounts of activities in psychology in some of these Oriental countries.

CONCLUSION

Although the Oriental contribution to the current psychological systems is not very significant, still it cannot be neglected for the advancement of scientific psychology. First, Oriental thought has its own characteristics, which are distinct from the Western thought. As psychology is a science of organic behavior and science is a human achievement, it will surely make for more rapid progress if Eastern and Western thoughts are integrated harmoniously. Second, we have seen a number of overlapping studies between the Eastern and Western workers, and it is a certain fact that the Eastern scientific output is often unknown to the Western scientist. However, science should not be restricted to any one country or countries, and consequently an international cooperation both in research and practice is urgently needed.

references

The author tried to restrict the references to those written in English. Unavoidably, however, some references are in other languages, which are indicated immediately after the titles.

Akhilananda, S. *Hindu psychology.* London: Routledge, 1953.

Akishige, Y. Studies on constancy problem in Japan. *Psychologia*, 1958, 1, 143–157.

Akishige, Y. Studies on perceptual constancy in Japan (in Japanese). *Annu. Rep. Phil. Kyushu Univer.*, 1960, No. 22, 1–264.

Becker, E. Psychotherapeutic observations on Zen discipline: One point of view. *Psychologia*, 1960, 3, 100–112.

Chen, D. J. How psychology can be of service to the socialistic reconstruction (in Chinese). *Acta psychol. sinica*, 1959, 3, 142–145.

Cheng, N. I. On Ching Chi-cheng's "Theoretical foundations of structuralism in Wundt's and Titchener's works" (in Chinese). *Acta psychol. sinica*, 1959, 3, 57–58.

Chiba, T. On the proper consciousness (Koyū-ishiki). *Psychologia*, 1960, 3, 65–72.

Chu, C. S. Problems on the object of psychology (in Chinese). *Acta psychol. sinica*, 1956, 1, 11–19.

Chu, H. L. Critical comments on gestalt psychology (in Chinese). *Acta psychol. sinica*, 1958, 2, 85–98.

Cohen, J., Hansel, C. E. M., & Sylvester, J. D. A new phenomenon in time judgment. *Nature*, 1953, No. 172, 901.

Feldman, S. M., & Underwood, B. J. Stimulus recall following paired-association verbal learning. *J. exp. Psychol.*, 1957, **53**, 11–15.

Fromm, E. Psychoanalysis and Zen Buddhism. *Psychologia*, 1959, **2**, 79–99.

Hake, H. W. Japanese experimental psychology viewed from America. *Psychologia*, 1958, **1**, 184–186.

Holmes, S. W. Zen Buddhism and transactional psychology. *Etc.*, 1957, **14**, 243–249.

Hora, T. Tao, Zen, and existential psychotherapy. *Psychologia*, 1959, **2**, 236–242.

Ikeda, H., & Obonai, T. Studies in figural after-effects. IV. The contrast-confluence illusion of concentric circles and the figural after-effect. *Jap. psychol. Res.*, 1955, No. 2, 17–23.

Imanishi, K. Social behavior in Japanese monkeys, *Macaca fuscata*. *Psychologia*, 1957, **1**, 47–54.

Ishihara, I. *Psychology of verbal behavior* (in Japanese). Tokyo: Kobunkan, 1960.

Jacobson, E. H. (Ed.) *International directory of psychologists exclusive of the U.S.A.* Assen, Netherlands: Royal van Gorcum, 1958.

Kasamatsu, A. Brain wave and Oriental meditation: An experiment on Zen and yoga (in Japanese). In Y. Sugi et al. (Ed.), *Lectures on psychosomatic medicine.* Vol. IV., 1957. Pp. 73–88.

Kawai, H., & Kondo, K. Discussion on Morita therapy. *Psychologia*, 1960, **3**, 92–99.

Kora, T., & Sato, K. Morita therapy: A psychotherapy in the way of Zen. *Psychologia*, 1958, **1**, 219–225.

Kuraishi, S. On the reproduction of simple thought-configuration by using the method of paired comparison (in Japanese). *Jap. J. Psychol.*, 1937, **12**, 578–602.

Kuroda, R. Stereopsychology: Its scope and method. *Acta psychol. Keijo*, 1931, **1**, 69–82.

Kuroda, R. *A history of Chinese psychological thought* (in Japanese). Tokyo: Koyama-shoten, 1948.

Liu, K. C. *Practice on the breathing therapy* (in Chinese). China: Hopei People's Press, 1957.

Lun, S. H. Researches in perception in Democratic Germany (in Chinese). *Acta psychol. sinica*, 1958, **2**, 45–52.

Morikawa, Y. Functions of stimulus and response in paired-associate verbal learning. *Psychologia*, 1959, **2**, 41–56.

Morris, C. W. Comments on mysticism and its language. *Etc.*, 1951, **9**, 3–8.

Motokawa, K. Retinal traces and visual perception of movement. *J. exp. Psychol.*, 1953, **45**, 369–377.

Motora, Y. *An essay on Eastern philosophy.* Leipzig: Voigtländer, 1905.

Nand, D. S. The methods of total psychoanalysis. *J. all-India Inst. ment. Hlth*, 1959, **2**, 5–7.

Nand, D. S. The study of religion and culture through the total psychoanalysis of the individuals. *Psychologia*, 1960, **3**, 119–130.

Naruse, G. Recent development of experimental hypnosis in Japan. *Psychologia*, 1959, **2**, 20–26.

Naruse, G., & Obonai, T. Decomposition and fusion of mental images in a drowsy and post-hyponotic hallucinatory state (in Japanese). *Jap. J. Psychol.*, 1952, 22, 175–188.

Ni, C. F. A preliminary criticism on the behaviorism of J. B. Watson (in Chinese). *Acta psychol. sinica*, 1957, 1, 194–200.

Obonai, T. The concept of psycho-physiological induction: A review of experimental works. *Psychologia*, 1957, 1, 3–9.

Otsuka, N. Stereopsychology and studies on *k'an* by Ryo Kuroda. *Psychologia*, 1960, 3, 73–79.

Paknikar, K. K. Can we determine the elements of intelligence objectively? *Ind. J. Psychol.*, 1958, 33, 108–111.

Ramadevi, S. T., & Rao, S. K. R. Personality investigations in India. *Psychologia*, 1957, 1, 86–91.

Rao, S. K. R. *Studies in Indian psychology.* All-India Institute for Mental Health. Research Bulletin No. 2, 1958.

Razran, G. Psychology in Communist countries other than the U.S.S.R. *Amer. Psychol.*, 1958, 13, 177–178.

Sastry, N. S. N. Growth of psychology in India. *Ind. J. Psychol.*, 1932, 7, 1–40.

Sato, K. *Psychology of personality.* Tokyo: Sogensha, 1951.

Sato, K. How to get Zen enlightment: On Master Ishiguro's five-days' intensive course for its attainment. *Psychologia*, 1959a, 2, 107–113.

Sato, K. Zen and psychology (in Japanese). *Jap. J. Psychol.*, 1959b, 30, 286–295.

Sen, I. Teaching of psychology in Indian Universities. *Ind. J. Psychol.*, 1958, 33, 129–133.

Sen, I. The objectless or self-existent joy in Indian psychology. *J. all-India Inst. ment. Hlth*, 1959, 2, 5–7.

Shuh, P. A general review of psychology in China (in Chinese). *Acta psychol. sinica*, 1958, 2, 3–9.

Shuh, P. China's recent research work in psychology. *Psychologia*, 1959, 2, 193–202.

Suzuki, D. T. *Zen Buddhism.* Garden City, N.Y.: Anchor Books, 1956.

Umemoto, T. Japanese studies in verbal learning and memory. *Psychologia*, 1959, 2, 1–19.

Underwood, C. E. *Method and theory in experimental psychology.* New York: Oxford, 1953.

Woo, C. L. Research work on psychology of personality in the German Democratic Republic (in Chinese). *Acta psychol. sinica*, 1958, 2, 36–45.

Yokose, Z. Theoretical formula of vector-field and its experimental proof. *Psychologia*, 1957, 1, 17–21.

further readings

The following articles (all in English) will give a general overview of the current psychological activities in Oriental countries.

Ceylon: Jayasuriya, J. E. Psychology in Ceylon. *Psychologia*, 1957, 1, 127–128.

China (Mainland): Shuh, P. China's recent work in psychology. *Psychologia,* 1959, 2, 193–201.

China (Taiwan): Su, H. Y. Psychological activities in Taiwan. *Psychologia,* 1959, 2, 202–205.

India: Mitra, S. C. Progress of psychology in India. *Ind. J. Psychol.,* 1955, 30, 1–21.

Mitra, S. C., & Mukhopadhyay, P. K. Development of psychological studies in India from 1916–1950. *Psychologia,* 1958, 1, 191–202.

Pareek, U. Psychology in India. *Psychologia,* 1957, 1, 55–59.

Japan: McGinnies, E. Psychology in Japan: 1960. *Amer. Psychol.,* 1960, 15, 556–562.

Sato, K., & Graham, C. H. Psychology in Japan. *Psychol. Bull.,* 1954, 51, 443–464.

Korea: Koh, S. D. (Ed.) *Studies in psychology.* Seoul, Korea: Ewha Woman's Univer., 1954, No. 1.

Pakistan: Zaidi, S. M. H. Psychology in Pakistan. *Psychologia,* 1958, 1, 187–190.

Zaidi, S. M. H. Pakistan psychology. *Amer. Psychol.,* 1959, 14, 532–536.

Thailand: Saradatta, L., & Miyake, K. Psychology in Thailand. *Psychologia,* 1959, 2, 120–123.

Turkey: Birand, B. Psychology in Turkey. *Istanbul Stud. exper. Psychol.,* 1956, 3–5.

index

Page numbers in **boldface** type indicate bibliography references; *gl.* indicates glossary definitions. Glossary items not otherwise indexed are not included. Personal proper names appear in italics.